BATH

THE

ENIGMA

A History of Bath Rugby Club

1865 – 2015

By
Harry W. Barstow

Paperback ISBN 978-1-78092-860-9
ePub ISBN 978-1-78092-861-6
PDF ISBN 978-1-78092-862-3

Published in the UK by MX Publishing
335 Princess Park Manor, Royal Drive, London, N11 3GX
www.mx-publishing.co.uk [UK]
www.mxpublishing.com [USA]

Cover Artwork compiled by www.staunch.com
featuring Bath players Stuart Hooper (L) Peter Stringer, and George Ford with ball (R)

This book is dedicated to my family

For their wonderful support and patience over the last twelve years, during which time I researched and wrote this book, namely:

Kathryn (my wife) for her computer skills that put me to utter shame, her creative ideas and her artistic input, and our two sons, Adam and his photography input and computer skills and Thomas for his computer advice and back-up proof reading.

ACKNOWLEDGEMENTS:

My sincere thanks to the following, without whose help and advice this book could not have been written:

Anne Buchanan: Bath Library, the Podium;

Bath Chronicle (and sister papers): archives in Bath Library;

Ben Hartley: Bath Combination;

Bob Ascott: Photography; and assistant Alan Grebby; (www.rugbyrec.co.uk)

Derek Carter: Photography;

Geoff Frankcom: Proof reader;

Geoff Pillinger: Head of Bath Past Players' research team;

Kathryn, Adam and Thomas Barstow;

Kevin Lawrence: Chairman, Bath Rugby Supporters' club; (www.allez-bath.co.uk)

Mark Hoskins: (Hon) historian, Bristol RFC.;

Mike Short;

Patrick Casey: Rugby historian, and author of 'For College, Club and Country,' (Clifton RFC).;

(the late) **Reg Monk**: photography;

'World Rugby Museum, Twickenham': www.rfu.com/museum (Tel: 020 8892 8877)

SCHOOLS:

Cheltenham College: (Christine Leighton, archives);

Clifton College, (archives)

Edinburgh Academy (archives);

Kingswood School, Bath, (David Brown, archives);

Marlborough College, (Terry Rogers, archives);

Monkton Combe School, Bath, (archives);

Forward

I feel truly honoured to be asked by Harry Barstow to write the Foreword for his latest book. He has spent many, many hours of research and the result is a marvellous piece of informative writing.

When I joined Bath from my junior club, Frome, in 1970, it was with trepidation. But it was not long before I realised that I had joined a Club that was so welcoming and friendly. I have Bath to thank for giving me my nickname 'The Mayor of Frome'

The character of the Club was such that it welcomed everyone, this included visiting teams. The supporters appreciated good rugby and applauded the home or away side.

My career of nearly 200 games throughout the 70's was not spectacular but very fulfilling. The majority of the team were very local and they are still friends to this day.

When I finished playing in 1981, I took on the role of Chairman of Selectors, a highlight was winning the John Player Cup in 1984 when we beat Bristol 10pts to 9. What followed was a long period of winning teams and international recognition of our players.

These were halcyon days which are etched in the minds of the Bath folk who took the annual trip to Twickenham to see their team sweep all before them.

Being involved with The Bath Past Players was also a very special time for me. The camaraderie of keeping in touch with people of the same ilk makes this organisation very special. At different times, I was Asst. Secretary, Secretary, and a short time Chairman. But in 2010 I was invited to be President which made me feel very humble, thinking of all the famous past players who have gone before me.

We owe a lot to Andrew Brownsword and Bruce Craig who in the professional era have kept us up there with the best. We are enjoying watching some flamboyant rugby in the true Bath fashion.

Good luck Harry, and well done for producing such an interesting and illuminating book.

Radley Wheeler

Contents

Chapter 1. 'THE BEGINNING.'

It seems a virtual certainty that playing around with a football reaches far back into distant millennia; though until recently there were no widespread sets of rules or established governing bodies for participants to follow. Organised sport after all was somewhat limited in ancient times, albeit not forgetting the athletic events among our Greek forebears, chariot racing (the Romans' answer to Formula One), and the medieval jousting that would never in a million years have gained a licence from today's Health & Safety inspectorate. But cricket enthusiasm was already evident in 18th century England; and come the 19th century sport really 'took off,' not least thanks to developments at Cambridge University and Rugby School respectively regarding the foundations of modern football, without doubt the world's number one sporting activity.

Initially these two academic institutions attempted to consolidate football under one guiding set of rules. However, by the end of the 1830's (if not before) undergraduates at Cambridge realised that consolidation might be impossible to achieve. For while Old Rugbeians argued that handling was legitimate, others (Old Etonians for example) begged to differ, and the end result of this impasse was a divide, each side now embarking upon their own chosen course and culminating in 1863 with the publication by Cambridge University of the codified Association Football rules. The football world (literally the world) was now to adopt these very same rules globally, and as a result football separated into two distinct forms, namely football (soccer) and football (rugby). The Rugby School version however had yet to be consolidated into anything other than a somewhat vague format of guidelines, as would remain the case until the rules (laws) were standardized in 1871. Even then, as Bath themselves could testify, a variation of rules would continue for some years yet.

But although we know, thanks to the Cambridge codification, the origins of modern football (soccer), do we know with any accuracy the origins of modern football (rugby)? The answer, possibly, is *"yes,"* not least because it is a far younger game than soccer for the purposes of research. Even so, one should treat the scarce available evidence with some caution because 'hard' (corroborated) proof is lacking. Nonetheless Matthew Bloxham, a former Rugby pupil from 1813-20, submitted an article to The Meteor (the Rugby School magazine) in October 1876, stating that he had learned from an unnamed source that the change from a kicking game to a handling game had *"....originated with a town boy and a foundationer of the name of Ellis, William Webb Ellis. "*

He would further add: "that [in 1823] one William Webb Ellis, whilst playing football, *"caught the ball in his arms. This being so, according to the then rules, he ought to have retired back as far as he pleased, without parting with the ball, for the combatants on the opposite side could only advance to the spot where he had caught the ball, and were unable to rush forward till he had either punted it or had placed it for someone else to kick, for it was by means of these placed kicks that most of the goals were in those days kicked, but the moment the ball touched the ground, the opposite side might rush on.*"

Matthew Bloxham then continues: "*Ellis for the first time, disregarded this rule, and on catching the ball, instead of retiring backwards, rushed forwards with ball in his hands towards the opposite goal, with what result as to the game I know not, neither do I know how this infringement of a well-known rule was followed up, or when it became, as it is now, a standing rule.*" This is a somewhat vague evaluation, since Matthew Bloxham neither knows 'how the infringement was followed up or when it became a standing rule.' Yet interestingly, it was (is) a common misunderstanding to assume that it was forbidden to 'handle' the ball at Rugby School during this era. Instead it was forbidden 'to run forwards with the ball in hand,' not the same thing. Equally it is a misunderstanding to assume that Rugby School immediately prepared a set of rules and duly announced to a startled world their discovery of a new form of football to be known as rugby football; because the Webb Ellis story is merely a report of a pupil who (true or otherwise) reportedly broke the rules as then practiced on the football fields at Rugby. Nor should it be forgotten that Rugby School itself did not codify its own version of football until 1845.

William Webb Ellis Photograph courtesy of *Thomas J. Barstow*

Today alongside the school one can see the imposing statue of William Webb Ellis that commemorates this very event with the now iconic words: "*This stone commemorates the exploit of Will Webb Ellis who with a fine disregard for the rules of football as played in his time first took the ball in his arms and ran with it thus originating the distinctive feature of the rugby game A.D. 1823.*"

Yet not everyone accepts the above exploits as valid. After all, Matthew Bloxham had actually left Rugby School three years prior to this particular game that has passed into folklore. But his brother John was a contemporary of Webb Ellis, and furthermore one is entitled to ask: "*why would Matthew Bloxham anyway wish to write a fiction?*" Yes, it appears that his account was not substantiated by other sources. But if inaccurate, then Bloxham himself would have risked almost certain ridicule. None came it seems. Indeed, if his comments had raised doubts then one would have expected that his contemporaries (surely the best jury in this matter) would have stated them openly. But it appears that they didn't. Nor, perhaps significantly, has anyone else submitted a different tale as to how and why the rugby game actually originated at Rugby School. Moreover Webb Ellis was not a name plucked from an obscure archive at Rugby.

On the contrary, records tell us that he was in fact a bright young pupil destined to gain a scholarship to Oxford. He was furthermore a capable sportsman and certainly a very good cricketer, good enough in fact to play for Oxford against Cambridge in the 1827 Varsity match. So it is at least a possibility that 1823 might just be 'that year' when handling the ball and running simultaneously at the opposition laid the foundations of the game we know today.

If so, then it was well timed, an era no less when Britain and Europe would witness the dawning of a new age from that epic moment in 1815 when Waterloo had concluded some 20 years of European conflict. Thus the Industrial Revolution would now move into over-drive, and sport was set to be one of the countless beneficiaries of the advances being made. Furthermore, exactly twenty years since Master Webb Ellis reportedly ran illegally with the ball a rugby football club was founded in London, namely Guys Hospital in 1843. Initially playing high up on the green, open spaces of Blackheath that rise above Greenwich and the Thames, it was their early endeavours upon this vast south-east London arena that may well have inspired some of those who would later establish another club, one which took its name from that same venue.......Blackheath.

Now it is often claimed that Blackheath were the first 'open' club in the history of rugby football. Indeed, they became affectionately known as 'The Club' precisely because in contrast to the likes of Guys, Blackheath were a club that was indeed open to all-comers. Yet the Liverpool club would dispute this, and correctly so, arguing that their formation on the 19th December 1857 got them across the 'start-line' ahead of Blackheath (founded in 1858). Meanwhile seven years later Bath were formed in 1865, thought to be the first 'open' club in the South West.

The Rugby Football Union itself was formed six years later, the twenty one founder members attending their inaugural meeting at London's Pall Mall Restaurant, Regents Street in *1871*; and included among those members would be the Harlequins, Richmond, Blackheath and Guys Hospital, all of them rugby families destined to adorn the pages of an illustrious rugby history. Others however, for instance Queens House (Greenwich) and the once famed Marlborough Nomads would pass into the pages of that same history, but alas names now long forgotten. Meanwhile it was in 1871 that the first standardised set of laws for Rugby football were finalised; and at Raeburn

Place, Edinburgh, the first rugby international was played (between Scotland versus England), the hosts winning by one goal and one try against England's single try.

Then, a further one year onwards in 1872 at Menton in the south of France, the days of one William Webb Ellis would end, the former Rugbeian who on leaving Oxford had devoted his life to service with the Church. Yet it seems that we will never know if he ever played in any official game of rugby football. Nor can we confirm if he ever expressed an interest in the significance of those early years of football at Rugby School, a perplexing fact for those seeking to establish the accuracy or otherwise of that oft-quoted report of a one-time pupil who *"first took the ball in his arms and ran with it."* But......someone it seems claimed to have witnessed such a game, and noted too the part played by a certain player. That player (according to M.H. Bloxham) was William Webb Ellis.....and who are we from this distant point in history to dismiss outright such a report of a possibly pressed-ganged participant, maybe clueless as to what on earth he was supposed to do, and who ran with the ball (at that time in the wrong direction).

Rightly or otherwise we revere this young schoolboy. The rugby World Cup is named in his honour as the Webb Ellis Cup. And Master Webb Ellis will surely live on in the annals of rugby history….for ever!

Chapter 2.   WITHIN THE RUGBY TRIANGLE.
(The 1840''s onwards)

Bath Football Club, founded in 1865, is thought to be the first open club in the West Country. But the reasons for the club's formation are not exactly clear, unlike the Clifton club for example (founded 1872) who were inspired by the nearby Clifton College. However, this begs the question: did a nearby rugby playing school lead to the founding of the Bath club too? The answer is 'no,' since Kingswood school, high up on the Lansdown hillside and with Turneresque views across the city did not introduce a form of rugby football until 1868-69 (see: *History of Kingswood School, p. 265).* But perhaps the founding fathers of Bath Football Club were acquainted with, or followed the progress of two other West Country rugby schools, namely the aforementioned Clifton College in Bristol or Marlborough, situated amid the green Wiltshire landscape. Again there is no certainty here; but it is history's lasting benefit that details of the early years of the rugby game are recorded in the archives of such pioneer rugby academies.

Marlborough College (twenty five miles east of Bath) founded in 1843 would rank among the greatest influences in rugby's early development, and it was thanks to the arrival *"of [Mr] Cotton as Master in 1852, bringing with him the traditions of the Rugby Bigside ....*that rugby would, step by step, gain a foothold at the College. The early format would doubtless have been something of a sporting culture-shock to the uninitiated (see: *A History of Marlborough College, 1843-93, Ch. XXV),* not least the sight of that curious rugby-shaped ball, of which one had already been displayed at the Great Exhibition (Crystal Palace) in 1851. Meanwhile rugby posts were now erected; the art of drop-kicking encouraged and each team could comprise of forty or even fifty players. But those same players, alas, were allowed no rights under the Geneva Convention, and *"when a player was collared he was supposed to be bound to have the ball down, but not infrequently he had to be 'scragged' into submission...."* And if that wasn't bad enough, there was the infamous 'grovel,' and the name says it all, whereby the ball could be held up over the line to secure (or not secure as the case may be) a touchdown.

Not surprisingly it would have been a rarity to see anything approaching a swift passing movement in those early days, and the rules were, to put it mildly.....liberal. Admittedly 'hacking' over a player (hooking the instep of an opponent's leg) was frowned upon at Marlborough, though not at some schools. But good old scragging was allowed, so too tripping a running player, an action which in 21st century rugby can mean the sin-bin or even worse; but not at Marlborough it didn't. So initially this was a sort of hybrid game, part soccer and part rugby.

But did Marlborough's law-abiding majority really enjoy this form of 'recreation?

Probably for the bigger and/or stronger players the answer was *"you bet we do."* Less certain is how those smaller guys felt about this 'heathen' form of recreation. After all, initially *"anybody who cared to put in an appearance was welcome to play, but it was seldom that more than thirty or forty out of the whole School availed themselves* (ie: volunteered) *of the doubtful privilege."* In house-matches some teams could be sixty strong and one tactic was to grab the smaller players whose hapless fate was *"being bodily thrown on to the top of the 'squash' to bring it down."* Nonetheless, the decision of Mr Tomkinson (the Bursar) and rugby enthusiast to allow beer for capped players would likely have provided a rocket-booster to rugby recruitment, because Marlborough College were destined to be at the very forefront of the development of the rugby game.

There was much to develop moreover, with considerable confusion in the process, and not least in methods of scoring. In the formative years for instance, the chief aim in rugby football was to kick goals, and under Marlborough rules these could be gained by a place kick or a drop goal. In fact until 1869, Marlborough allowed a goal to be scored from a punt. The scrums, known then as scrimmages, consisted of players standing upright, while tries initially counted for nothing at Marlborough, nor it seems, anywhere else.

The Marlborough XX 1867.
Acknowledgements to Marlborough College

XX. June 18

6

Although the first ever recorded inter-school (rugby) match had already been held in Scotland on 13th February 1858 between Merchiston Castle versus the High School, it is thought that the Marlborough v Clifton College game (20th November 1864: Mr T. Rogers, Marlborough archivist) was both Marlborough's inaugural inter-school's match and generally regarded as the first inter-school rugby game in England. Such a delay in commencing inter-school competition is hardly surprising however, for there were no cars or coaches available. Furthermore at an isolated Marlborough College there were no other established clubs or rugby playing schools in the neighbourhood either. But now the railway was beginning to connect the Nation ('thank you' Mr Brunel), and though there seems to be an absence of records, it seems likely that it was the train that enabled Clifton to reach Marlborough via the Swindon junction, while horse-carriages would then have brought the team to the College; and if it was cold on that winter's journey across the Wiltshire Downs, then no matter, because on the rugby field the temperature was about to get decidedly hot.

Having been founded barely two years previously in 1862, Clifton College nonetheless embraced rugby football almost as soon as the school opened its elegant front door to their first intake of pupils. But of course they were still a team with barely two years rugby experience, and there was another difficulty common to rugby football throughout this era, concerning different interpretations of the rules. Marlborough had always permitted both tripping and scragging. Clifton went one better. They permitted tripping, scragging and.......hacking!

The two teams that day were twenty strong and Marlborough were captained by J.A. Boyle, described by his contemporaries as a 'fast runner and a sure place-kicker.' He was further described as a brilliant "drop" (ie: a drop goal specialist). He needed to be, because the match soon got somewhat heated, not least as Clifton, having agreed beforehand to refrain from their own practice of hacking, nonetheless found it increasingly hard to resist the temptation to do so. Marlborough's reaction was predictable. They too began hacking. Things then deteriorated further and skipper Boyle was then heard to shout a request to a member of staff (Dr Bradley): *"I think we'd better stop the game, sir, hadn't we?"* Dr Bradley's response was loud and clear: *"No, no! They'll think we're afraid of them. Win the game first, and then talk about stopping if you like!"*

Well J.A. Boyle did just that, as with time fast running out, he dropped a clincher 'plumb and fair between the Clifton goal-posts.' Marlborough pride was thus preserved. But, the friendliest of occasions this was not. Indeed, Marlborough's own post-match report included the observation that *"....the harmony of the game was rather spoilt by differences as to rules and the rather eccentric notions on hacking that the Cliftonians seemed to have."* As always however, there are two sides to a rugby tale, and not surprisingly Clifton's C.B.L. Tylecote (see: a History of Clifton College, pp. 272-3) saw things somewhat differently: *"I was one of the Clifton football team that went to play against Marlborough. What a match it was! You could hardly call it football!! I was playing full-back, and being pretty quick on my feet in those days, got off pretty cheaply."* He was obviously one of the lucky ones, because by all accounts others were somewhat less fortunate. Furthermore such was the angst aroused by the events that day that these two great rugby schools would not resume fixtures until 1891, almost three decades later.

But if the tactics that day in 1864 were somewhat basic, rugby kit in this formative era was somewhat basic too, with trousers (casuals) simply tucked into socks. Shorts (and initially they would be knee-length shorts) were not common until the 1890's. Boots would be stud-less, with bars (usually two) instead of studs; and while changing-rooms would often be arranged by clubs with a local pub or inn, the schools would utilise their own facilities. In fact in these early years it was sometimes the schools who were the teachers and the clubs their pupils. Indeed, when in 1872 the Clifton club was founded, they announced that their football would be played *"as at Clifton College,"* although the new club did stipulate that it would not follow the practice of tripping or hacking!

But until the late 1870's at least the backs were primarily a defence line, and very little else. They were positioned behind the forwards, often only four in number, and consisting of two half-backs (ie: half-way back behind the forwards) and two other backs who were positioned well back in defence (ie: full-backs). It was during the 1860's however that Marlborough, and very probably other teams, were already experimenting with another back player who was positioned between the half-backs and the full-backs; in other words he was positioned three-quarters behind the forwards and hence the origin of the 'three-quarter' terminology. Even so, for some years this lone threequarter back was simply an extra tackler. Indeed not until the 1870's and the perception of those such as Sydney Morse of Marlborough (later Marlborough Nomads & England) did this attitude change. Morse did realise that a threequarter back could fulfil an attack role, but these were still early days. And 'early days' they would remain at Marlborough until the captaincy of the legendary England international Harry Vassall in the late 1870's. Vassall's days at Marlborough were then followed by his inspirational leadership at Oxford University in the early 1880's; a leadership that would help transform rugby football from the negative to the positive and from defence to attack, not least due *"to the plan of systematic combination among the forwards which he evolved."*

As for the all-important question of scoring, confusion reigned well beyond 1871 when the RFU had established the official laws of rugby football, and this partly explains why games were not infrequently recorded with two quite different results that depended entirely upon whose scoring method one was utilising. Indeed Marlborough were but one school/club who during the 1860's had devised their own scoring system, their rules reading as follows: *"3 Rogues (touchdown by defence behind their own goal line) = 1 touchdown. 4 touchdowns = 1 goal. 3 goals = a game was won.* " Nor was it unknown for the method of scoring to depend upon negotiation between the two captains prior to the game. It was not uncommon therefore to see a result given not in points actually scored, but rather by the way scores were made.

Hence the first Scotland v England international in 1871 (Edinburgh) was scored as follows: *"Scotland won by 1 goal, 1 try as against 1 try by England."* It is nonetheless significant that by the time of this first international the 'try' had now been accepted into the scoring system. Meanwhile it was in 1873 that the Anglo-Scottish momentum continued with the first game between Carlisle and Scottish Border club Langholm, an encounter that both clubs claim (with some justification) as the first ever international club fixture.

Down in the West County meanwhile and situated in the shadows of the Cotswolds some forty miles north of Bath lay the emerging rugby academy of Cheltenham College, who alongside Marlborough and Clifton now completed a West Country triangle of three inspirational centres of rugby football. Founded in 1841, Cheltenham College had adopted the rugby game as early as 1844 thanks partly to the influence of Charles Acton (later Ball-Acton) from Rugby school. However, as was invariably the case during this period, the rugby actually played in Cheltenham's early days had little resemblance to the game the college would later help to inspire. Indeed, one chastened pupil described it thus: *"….as merely a rush in which someone is sure to go down and perhaps get well kicked before he gets up again;"* good training for one Francis D'Aguilla on later serving as a major (Royal Engineers) in the Afghan War of 1878-80, but not before gaining the distinction as Bath's first international when capped for a victorious England in their second encounter against Scotland at the Kennington Oval in February 1872. Moreover the D'Aguila name lived on, because his brother J.D'Aguila was another impressive player who captained both Bath and Somerset from the late 1870's to the mid-1880's, while J.B.S. D'Aguila (a son) would later play for both Bath and Somerset in the 1890's.

The Cheltenham College name would live on too, and it was noticeable that when Francis D'Aguila ran out with England at the Oval, so too did fellow Cheltonians William Pinching (England) and likewise Renny Tailyour and W. Brown for Scotland. Capable therefore of producing no less than four internationals in a single international match, it is hardly surprising that the College's sphere of influence would extend far beyond the Cotswolds. In fact it would extend as far as Cardiff who, on their formation in 1872, chose initially to adopt the Cheltenham College rules. For a Cardiff club that one day would become legend, this was no mean compliment. Furthermore, this link then continued for a number of years and it was in season 1883-4 that Cardiff, on a visit to the College, reportedly first fielded the four three-quarter system into their back division.

As for the Cheltenham College rules, there were in addition those originating at Clifton and Marlborough, and probably one will never know just how many variations did exist until the official RFU laws were finally accepted as uniform throughout the game. In fact at Cheltenham there was at least one player who claimed that he had played under seven (yes, seven!) different sets of rules during his playing career. Wiveliscombe in West Somerset (once a formidable side) were another club who had produced their own version in 1872, albeit the RFU had already issued their formalized laws of rugby in 1871. But in an era when communications were not exactly 21st century, it would take at least a decade before the official laws had fully percolated down to the far corners of the game itself. Indeed it was not until 1880 that Cheltenham College itself had fully adopted those same RFU laws initially formulated in 1871.

Rule variations notwithstanding, the rugby trio of Clifton, Cheltenham and Marlborough would prove worthy disciples of Rugby School. Clifton can lay claim to producing three England captains in E.K. Scott (1948), P.D. Young (1955) and D.G. Perry (1965); a stream of internationals (for England, Wales, Ireland and Scotland) have flowed from the ranks of Cheltenham College, while Marlborough's influence reached not only westwards, but equally to London by way of the formation of their remarkable Old Boys club, namely the Marlborough Nomads (London based and among the original members of the RFU), who from their formation in 1868 to their sad disbandment in 1911 competed at the very highest levels of the game. As for internationals, Old Marlburians seemed to run off a conveyor belt, with some twenty nine England players produced even before the 1914-18 War.

It is no mere coincidence therefore, that within the influence of this 'Rugby Triangle' a group of formidable club sides would emerge, namely Bath, Bristol, Gloucester (and not forgetting the Cheltenham club), and whose collective genesis in all probability was partly influenced by a trio of famous rugby schools, namely Marlborough, Clifton and Cheltenham.

Chapter 3. A GEORGIAN TO A RUGBY CITY. (The mid to later 19th century)

When from 1836 to 1841 the great engineer Isambard Brunel was constructing a two mile railway tunnel under North Wiltshire's towering Box Hill, the great man could never have guessed who one of the beneficiaries might be. But once Brunel had completed the Railway link from London's Paddington terminal to the far corners of the West Country, it was to prove a veritable Godsend to a whole string of rugby clubs, perhaps none more so than the city (and club) situated bang in the middle of this link......Bath.

The Bath rugby club (see: Bath Football Club, Centenary book, 1865-1965, p.17) *"was formed by a few enthusiastic men of the city,"* among whom were Mr T.Gandy (later a chairman of the club), Mr Walter Sants and Mr Martin Wood. It should not be forgotten either that Major-General C. Fitzroy Mundy was the club's first President. These and other gentlemen had thus founded a club generally recognised as the first rugby football club in the South West, and as was general practice in the 19th century they numbered among many rugby clubs describing themselves as 'football clubs.' It seems quite likely moreover that these gentlemen were aware of the rugby developments within the Marlborough-Clifton-Cheltenham Triangle; while the Centenary book (p. 17) suggests that *"there is no doubt that [the game] originally came to Bath through the colleges in the city."* But regrettably no dates are given; a number of local rugby schools folded prior to or during the Great War and their relevant records are scarce at best or no longer exist; although it is certain that the Bath College fielded a full XV by 1878 (see: Bath College Register, 1878-1908, p.123, at Bath Records Office, the Guildhall, Bath).

But we do know from the Kingswood School archives (History of Kingswood School, p.265) that in the late 1860's when former pupil Frederick Robert Wilton (now a Cambridge graduate) returned, he *"introduced a new code of football rules, drawn up by the masters for the use of the school. This would be 1868 or 1869. The rules were quite impracticable, and were soon withdrawn; then we fell into a kind of spurious Rugby, which served its purpose fairly well;"* an apt description no doubt of rugby as played everywhere at this time. So now we have an actual year when the game was definitely introduced at a Bath School. Nonetheless Kingswood played a Bath XV on the Rec on 26th October 1977 (Bath winning 30-7) to commemorate the school's rugby centenary, neither contestant aware that the school had first played the game near ten years previously and thus probably the first rugby playing school in the city.

But Bath, founded in 1865, thus commenced the game at least three seasons prior to Kingswood, and it seems near certain therefore that 'they' founded the game in the city. Indeed among the possible clues for their establishment was the availability during the winter months of the broad expanses at North Parade, and the Centenary Book (p.18) refers to an 1871 report in Keene's Bath Journal of *"an interesting [rugby] match that was played on the North Parade Ground"* between Bath and Bedminster, and those witness to the game might have noted the name of the opposition captain who kicked the game's one and only goal. It was a certain W.G. Grace, the same 'WG' who one day would pass into cricketing legend.

But Bath did not stay for ever at North Parade. In fact, they proceeded to make almost a grand tour of the city with venues including the Lambridge Meadows, Claverton Down, the Kensington Meadows, next a possible short stay at the Taylor's Field along the Warminster Road, followed by arrival at the delightful Henrietta Park. And interestingly a letter (Bath & Wilts Chronicle & Herald, 6th September 1930) from club enthusiast Frank Melluish refers to most of these venues when describing his first visits some *"48 years ago"* with his brother to watch Bath, a club which he says *"played first at Lambridge, then Kensington Meadows, then in Henrietta Park, later on the Rec [far side of the ground] and now on the present side by the river."* Mr Melluish makes no mention of the use of North Parade as reported in Keene's Bath Journal, though this is perhaps explained by the fact that he was first acquainted with the rugby club some 48 years prior to his above letter (circa 1882) and thus approximately 17 years after Bath were founded. Nonetheless no doubts concern Bath's move to Henrietta Park, and it was then that fortune smiled upon the club with the sudden availability of the Pulteney Meadows.

Now Pulteney Meadows was, to coin a phrase, the Big One! But no little water had meanwhile passed under the bridge before the club reached those green spacious acres. Indeed the club's enthusiasm led to a willingness to 'try-out' some new ideas, bizarre or otherwise, ideas that included adding something extra to the club name, apparently a fashionable practice at this time. Hence for a period Bath were known as the Bath Zoaves (famed French-trained Algerian troops). However this name didn't really 'catch on.' So they had another try, calling themselves the Bath Rovers. This too hit the proverbial buffers soon afterwards. The last attempt, namely the Bath Wanderers, also failed to survive for long. So they went back to basics, settled for Bath once again, and so it has remained, save for the addition of 'Bath Rugby' come the professional era. As for matches, these would have included 'friendlies' within the club; and as for rules, these would typically have caused some uncertainty since none officially existed until the formation of the RFU in 1871, and even then took some years to be fully standardized throughout the game.

Furthermore there was the task of building up a fixture list, the stronger the better. But wishful thinking alone has never created such a list, nor have good players simply appeared from nowhere. But that being said, a programme of some twenty or more matches a season had been established by the early 1880's, while the following Bath fixture list for season 1880-81 and arguably the first compete list on the club records tells us who the club were now playing (see: Centenary book, p. 19):

1880

October	30th	Great Western FC at Bath.
November	3rd ...	Wells FC at Bath.
"	6th ...	Devizes FC at Bath.
"	13th...	Rockleaze FC at Bath.
"	17th.... ..Competitive College – College Ground.
"	20th.....	Bath College – College Ground.
"	24th.... .Weston super Mare at Bath.
"	27th...	Competitive College – College Ground.
December	4th...	Swindon Rangers FC at Bath.
"	11th...	Bristol Grammar School at Bath.
"	15th...	Wells FC at Wells.
"	18th...	Westbury Park FC at Bath.

1881.

January	1st	.. Rockleaze FC at Bristol.
"	8th	... Clifton FC at Bath.
"	15th	...Devizes FC at Devizes.
"	22nd	Clifton FC at Redland.
"	26th	...Bristol Medical School at Bath.
"	29th	...Swindon Rangers at Swindon.
February	12th	....Great Western FC at Swindon.
"	26th	....Weston super Mare at Weston super Mare.
March	5th	.....Westbury Park FC at Clifton.

Admittedly this was not even approaching first-class rugby from a later perspective; but at this stage there simply was no fully recognised club hierarchy. Later of course, acknowledged senior clubs would become established. But in the 19th century it was virtually guess-work as to who might gain that coveted status. In the fullness of time, Weston-super-Mare, Clifton and especially Gloucester (among Bath's fixtures of the 1880's) would indeed join the higher ranks of the game. But few if any rugby sages in that era would have been certain of that. Nonetheless, there were already hints that Bath might one day reach the senior level of the game when, within two years since Francis D'Aguila's debut cap for England in 1872, the club was taking a serious interest in a young forward by the name of Herbert Fuller. He possessed both weight and speed and he showed considerable promise. Albeit a mere nineteen years of age, Bath liked the look of him and despite his still tender years, awarded him the club captaincy. It proved to be a wise choice, for Fuller (he played for the Clifton club too) was not only a gifted player, he was a born leader and Bath's faith in him was to be fully justified. He proceeded to win six Blues at Cambridge (leading the university to limit Blues to a maximum of four) and then between1882-84 he gained six caps for England. True, other clubs, Blackheath for example, would yield many more internationals in these early years of rugby. But Bath had proved, not least to themselves, that they too could produce players of international class.

The England XX that beat Scotland at the Kennington Oval (5 Feb 1872) One player and his signature is absent from the Photograph. D'Aguila (circled) was Bath's first International player.
Photograph by kind permission of the World Museum of Rugby, Twickenham.

Simultaneously there was a growing momentum for rugby among the local schools in the city, one of which was Monkton Combe who switched from soccer to rugby in 1878 (see: A goodly heritage, A History of Monkton School, 1868-1967, p. 34). In addition the wider rugby parish now included the Competitive College, Grosvenor School, the Hermitage School, and Bath College, each a privately run school; although as mentioned none survived beyond the Great War. Meanwhile Bath Grammar School (later King Edward's) were competing against the likes of Kingswood by 1882, and not surprisingly the Bath club wanted a slice of the local action against the schools sides, not least for a potentially invaluable source of future players. Indeed Monkton Combe had barely got the rugby posts up before Bath were only too happy to field a team against the newcomers and winning (rather embarrassing if they had lost) by 2 goals and 1 try to nil.

It was now simply a matter of time before local rugby would extend further afield, and the 1888-9 fixtures of Kingswood reflected this expansion (see: History of Kingswood School, p.221):

Hermitage:	Won 2 goals 2 tries to nil;
Bristol G.S.:	Won 2 tries to nil;
Monkton Combe:	Won 1 goal to nil;
Old Boys:	Won 2 tries to 1 try;
Hermitage:	Lost to 1 goal 4 tries;
Monkton Combe:	Lost to 2 goals;
Wycliffe College:	Lost 1 goal to 4 goals 2 tries;
Bristol G.S.:	Draw 2 tries each;
Wycliffe College:	Lost to 3 goals 1 try.

Prior Park College and Beechen Cliff would be among other schools adding their names to this growing 'football' dynasty, and it was almost inevitable therefore that the rugby DNA of this Georgian city was to be further enhanced as a result of this expansion, producing

as a result (among many others) the Timmins brothers of Bath College, of whom forward T.B. Timmins would later captain Bath from 1903-1906, while England Trialist centre James Timmins would step into the Bath team in the late 1890's to play for the club and Somerset with huge distinction for more than a decade (see: Bath College Register, 1878-1908, Bath Records Office, Guildhall, Bath). Then there was winger Vincent Coates (Monkton Combe and later Haileybury & ISC) who would one day accompany Timmins in the same Bath team, and who was set to achieve great things.

'But what of a club-house,' one asks, the 'home from home' where rivalry on the pitch is (fingers crossed) transformed into friendship off it.' And the answer is that for many a long year the club did not have one. So they improvised, and included among their 1890's favourites was the Christopher Hotel, and the Angel Hotel in Westgate Street; while from 1914 onwards the Red House was utilised until the opening of the Club House on the Rec in 1954.

Even so, for Bath to fully evolve into a rugby city there remained one not immediately obvious piece of the jig-saw to be put in place; and by the early 1880's put in place it emphatically was with the arrival on the rugby scene of Walcot, or to be more precise.....the Victoria club. Not for the first time, few if any in Bath would have foreseen the significance when in 1882 a newly formed club-side appeared along the Upper Bristol road at Victoria Park; and since Victoria Park was the venue for home matches, Victoria was the name the club adopted. It was not the only such club in and around the city formed during this era. But Victoria, later re-named Walcot Victoria in 1893 and finally to Walcot in 1895 were to be the first of a remarkable family of 'Junior'clubs destined to underpin rugby football in the city, and who would form themselves into the Bath Combination in season 1902-3.

ith this Combination the rugby foundations were effectively complete; and by the early 1890's there were numerous schools playing rugby, while new clubs would be emerging around a Bath club that, with Soane's first cap for England in 1893, now boasted three internationals to its credit. So the basics were in place for this Georgian city to become in addition a Rugby city. And none too soon either. For during this same era the wider game was undergoing far-reaching changes. Hence a further question now required an answer: 'could Bath show that they had the capability to successfully adapt amid the ever growing competition now set to confront them?'

Chapter 4. BATH, BRISTOL AND SOMERSET–A SPECIAL RELATIONSHIP, (latter 19th century).

As Bath stepped into the 1880's, they were now one club among many, as throughout the previous decade the rugby family had rapidly extended its borders. It had undergone change too. Hence by the late 1870's the game had discarded 20-a-side rugby and reverted to the 15-a-side game; the Home Internationals now included Ireland and Wales, joining in 1875 and 1881 respectively; and at the club level Blackheath had risen to the forefront of the game, and one distant day a 'son' of this same London club would set Bath on the road to greatness.

But during the rugby evolution of the 19th century it was men such as Harry Vassall who shone (see Ch. 2), the Old Marlburian hailing from Yeovil, whose captaincy of Oxford University in the early 1880's helped to transform the forward tactics of the game. Meanwhile his native county of Somerset (for whom he played) leads one to another phenomenon of the 1880's, namely the emerging popularity and prestige of county rugby. Then....in 1888 another outstanding West Country club was founded, namely Bristol, resulting in a rivalry with near neighbours Bath that would prove to be perhaps unique in English rugby.

Bristol in fact, could hardly have timed their arrival on the rugby scene better, as this same 1880's era had witnessed (inter alia) the development of the four-man three-quarter line, consisting of two centre backs and two wing backs. This story officially begins with the legend that is Cardiff. But it is possible that it began with a lesser known rugby family tucked away among the approaches to the Brendon Hills in West Somerset. Its name was, and is, Wiveliscombe, barely a town in fact, yet among its 19th century inhabitants lived the sports-worshipping Hancock family. By trade they were brewers; a family of ten sons (two thirds of a rugby team in fact) of whom no less than seven would progress to play for Somerset. And of these, Froude Hancock (a giant of his day) would play for England; while Frank (moving to the family's business branch in Cardiff) would later grace the Welsh team as a back, or to be absolutely precise, as a three-quarter back.

It is here that one is indebted to former Vice Presidents of Wiveliscombe R.F.C., namely Mr & Mrs Ted and Margaret Baker; and moreover to Mr D.E. Davies (author of 'Cardiff Rugby Club, history & statistics 1876-1975') who, writing of the 1883-4 season, refers to 'the Cardiff club when short of a three-quarter to go to Cheltenham College.....secured the services of F.E. Hancock, recently arrived from Wiveliscombe. Two tries were scored that day, both by Hancock, and Cardiff realised immediately that here was a special talent in their midst. However, this now presented the club selectors with a headache for Cardiff's next (and more demanding) encounter at formidable Gloucester. The Welsh club were reluctant to drop the talented Hancock but, with their three regular three-quarters available again, and with a surplus of riches at their disposal, Cardiff opted for the unorthodox. Thus the team-sheet was duly produced, and there was something unusual about the line-up, because instead of nine forwards, there were eight. Instead of six backs, there were seven. And, instead of three names in the three-quarter backs, there were four, namely: W. B. Norton, Tom Williams, A.J. Stuart …..and F. Hancock.' Thus did Cardiff meet the hard men of Gloucester on 23rd February 1884, and although no scores were reported on that day, doubtless many present (and others) would have realised soon enough that the potential for running back play could now advance to a new level as a result of the four-strong three-quarter line, positioned as it was between two half-backs and a full-back, and playing in a back division increased to seven; in fact virtually half the team now operating in open play outside the scrum.

The fact that a club such as Cardiff had adopted this formation would partly explain why this new concept soon caught the attention of others; why nothing would be quite the same again, and why back-division play would be transformed as a result. In season 1888-9 Wales too adopted the formation, likewise Somerset in season 1890/1 and by each of the Home Unions by the mid-1890's. And Bath? Well (see: match programme, Sat. 29th February 1936, Bath v Bristol 100th match anniversary game) the club first played with four three-quarters in 1888, ironically in their first ever game against Bristol, and no more appropriate occasion could ever have been chosen. For the tale that is Bath and Bristol is itself a history in its own right and one in which coincidence was set to play a sometimes mysterious role in the decades that followed.

This inaugural game between the two clubs (according to the 100th match anniversary programme, see above) commenced on Bath's Kensington Meadows on 27th October 1888, and Bristol, although a newly formed club, were nonetheless not new to rugby football. On the contrary! They were in fact an amalgamation, one led by the Carlton club, who had convinced rivals Redland Park that combining forces was essential if they were ever to rival the then formidable Clifton club on equal terms. Westbury Park too were invited to join, but declined. However, the newly adopted name of Bristol was to exert a strong pull on local players, indeed so strong that Westbury Park would fold as a direct result of their own players switching to the Bristol club. And talk about jumping in at the deep end, because Cardiff were among the Bristolians' first opponents and not surprisingly the newcomers lost heavily. Nonetheless their first game against Bath appears to have concluded on a more encouraging note, because according to the afore-mentioned programme the match finished with a draw at three minors each.

Ah, but if only the accounts of early rugby history were that simple. Because, as Bristol RFC archivist Mark Hoskins has revealed, details are complicated somewhat by Bristol records indicating that the inaugural game of 27th October 1888 was played at Bristol's County ground, with a 3-5 win for Bath; while the records further report that a return match was played on 2nd February 1889 at Bath's Kensington Meadows, the Bathonians winning again by way of five points to nil. This inconsistency is of course unfortunate. Nonetheless there are possible explanations for such discrepancies. First, in the formative years of rugby it was still far from unusual for different clubs to play by marginally different rules, and/or to apply marginally different methods of scoring. Secondly, during these same early years, contemporaneous notes of rugby matches were not always produced, press reporting (assuming there was any) was often somewhat vague, and thus much depended on memory, and memory alone is not always a reliable source of evidence.

Yet perhaps the most significant outcome to emerge from the commencement of Bath v Bristol encounters was the forging of a Special Relationship between the two rivals. This friendship would remain genuine despite the intense rivalry, and because of the impressively high standards soon to be set by Bristol, Bath would now be tested to the very limits of their resources and capabilities. Indeed, the sheer scale of the challenge that Bath now faced would be shown clearly enough some forty-eight years later on the eve of their 100th official game,

for Bristol had already won no less than 71 victories. By contrast Bath could only comfort themselves with a tally of a mere 17 wins, with eleven matches drawn (see again: 100th match, anniversary programme). This then was the sheer scale of Bristolian domination that seemed at one stage might last forever! Yet, it was to Bath's credit that, save for one known exception that would be unexpectedly revealed on the occasion of that same 100th game (see Ch.18), they never allowed themselves to become resentful of Bristol's undoubted achievements. Instead they would draw inspiration from them, and it was precisely this attitude that many decades later would yield the richest of dividends.

Meanwhile prior to the formation of Bristol, there was already the aforementioned Clifton club to think about, who in their first full season played Bath twice and comfortably beat them twice. Now Clifton (founded in 1973) shared many similarities with Bath, first by way of the characteristics of the two clubs themselves, and secondly by the similarities of their respective localities set amid the charms of Georgian splendour. Yet one crucial difference did separate these two rugby families, because while Bath were sufficiently close to Bristol to be a rival club, they were far enough away not to be in contention for resources. This contrasted dramatically with the situation for Clifton. They were most certainly close enough to be rivals, but anything but far enough away to avoid competition for that most essential of commodities......players! Hence Clifton, who in their first season had already produced a full England international in James Bush and would produce another by the late 1880's in Hiatt Cowles Baker, would find themselves in direct competition with Bristol. Bath, to their immense good fortune, were to be spared this serious drawback.

It was thanks again to good fortune during the 1880's that Bath were to make their acquaintance with a young man by the name of Mr Frank Soane. Perhaps we should say 'Master Soane,' for when first introduced to the club he was a mere fifteen years of age. At Clifton House School, Eastbourne, he was playing association football. Fortunately he was also playing rugby football and Bath, a player short on one occasion, learned that young Soane was available and willing to play. And play he could!

Soane was a forward who grew strong and powerful. They called him 'Buster' for the simple reason that he tackled so hard, and by season 1888-9 he was good enough (along with Bath three-quarter C.J.B Moneypenny) to gain selection for Somerset to play at Wellington against the first ever touring side from the Dominions, The New Zealand Maoris. Somerset went down by 4-17 (old scoring format). But this was hardly a disgrace against such formidable opponents. Then, by season 1892-3, Soane was judged good enough for England with his debut against Scotland and with three further caps to follow. He was now Bath's third international. Much liked, Soane was a warrior on the rugby field, yet a gentleman off it. Indeed, he and his brother ran a music business in Old Bond Street. He was elected Bath captain from 1890-1898, 'walked' effortlessly into the Somerset side on numerous occasions and led the county from 1896-9. He was without doubt one of Bath's greatest and most popular players of the 19th century.

So how good were Bath during this same 19th century? Or to put it differently, how did Bath face the challenges of a rugby transformation that occurred during the last twenty years of that extraordinary Victorian age? After all, the likes of Bristol, Gloucester and Cardiff were surging ahead; so too Blackheath, Richmond, Harlequins and others in the South East; nor forgetting the likes of Northampton and Leicester in the Midlands. Meanwhile up North dramatic developments were set to happen. But for Bath arguably the best guide to their abilities was provided by the level of recognition from their parent county, namely Somerset, not least because county rugby expanded so rapidly in the latter years of the 19th century and because county selectors generally provided an independent opinion.

Somerset in fact fielded county teams from as early as season 1875/6 and played their first ever match at Taunton against Devon, the Devonians winning narrowly (see: Seventy Years of Somerset Rugby, 1875-1945, p.4); with the rugby game generally described as *"a very different affair to the one we now know. The teams usually changed at a pub, under crude conditions and walked to the ground. The maul in goal was still in being, the referee carried a flag, and was assisted by two Umpires - the fore-runners of the modern touch judge - heeling back was almost unknown, and the main idea was for the forwards to carry the ball on by sheer weight and strength, leaving the outsides to snap a scoring chance, generally from a pass by the half-backs."* But remember, this was still mid-1870's rugby. It would soon change.

At the administration level too, Somerset affairs would remain somewhat 'ad hoc,' until, that is the 6th September 1882 when a meeting was held at the Clarence Hotel in Bridgwater and the Somerset Rugby Union was officially formed. So a new chapter had begun. The previous colours of yellow and black were cast aside. In their place the newly formed Union adopted the colours of the Somerset Cricket club, namely

Herbert Fuller

crimson, white and black. The results too were encouragingly good in that same 1882/3 season, Somerset winning all their inter-county games, victory against Devon (by a goal to nil) being the first. The peerless Vassall played in the Devon game, likewise Bath's 2nd England international Herbert Fuller, and for the newly formed Somerset Rugby Union this first season had generally been a good start. Moreover, although the official County Championship was not launched until 1890, the county game was already arousing considerable enthusiasm, not least in the West Country, a phenomenon typified by a reported 'five thousand crowd at a drawn Gloucestershire v Somerset encounter played on the spa at Gloucester' (Bath Chronicle, 28th December 1882).

Somerset furthermore enjoyed the good fortune of possessing a considerable number of established clubs from whom to select the county teams, and whose collective ability was shown by the performances on their first ever Northern tour to face both Lancashire and Yorkshire in season 1886/7. With Yorkshire soon to prove themselves the best county side in England and Lancashire not far behind, it was the latter who would provide the first hurdle to face the following Somerset line-up:

S.*M.J. Woods (Bridgwater) at full-back; B.W. L. Ashford, H.V.Merry (Wellington), S.C.Smith, captain (Weston super Mare) threequarters; F.H. Fox (Wellington) and F.C.Duckworth (Weston super Mare) half-backs; P.F. Hancock, E. Hancock, A.A.Glass (Wiveliscombe), W.H. Manfield (Yeovil), R.M.P. Parsons (Crewkerne), A.A.Hammil (Bridgwater), J.R. Walter (Wellington), H.Paterson, H.T. Gilmore (Weston super. Mare) forwards.*

Few if any of those witnessing this game in Manchester would ever have seen Somerset in action. But by the end of day they would have learned that the Cider Men knew a thing or two about rugby. They not only held the Lancastrians, they beat them by a dropped goal and two tries to the Northerners' three tries; and assisting Somerset were no less than three England internationals in their line-up, namely fullback S.M.J. Woods, F.H.Fox at half-back and the immensely strong forward Froude Hancock. Yorkshire at Wakefield was to prove just too much however, the result going to the hosts by way of three tries to one. But then during this period that was to be the norm with virtually all opponents entering white rose country, such was their domination. But even here Somerset had shown that they were no push-overs; and if any gap existed between county rugby in the West Country and the North, then it was a narrow gap.

It was a likely disappointment for Bath that not one of their players had been selected for that Northern tour of 1886/7. But at this period it was the likes of Weston super Mare and Wellington who ranked among the strongest clubs in the county. Wiveliscombe too, thanks not least to the remarkable Hancock rugby family, proved to be another valuable source of playing talent. Nonetheless a glance at the successful Somerset season of 1896/7, a decade after that first northern tour, would show just how far Bath had progressed up the learning curve. This county team (now fielding seven backs) had a distinctive Bath look about it, with no less than five playing for the county in a 25-3 win, especially convincing as they played against a fast-improving Devon team:

Somerset: *H.T.Gamlin (Wellington) fullback; R. Forrest (Taunton), W.F. Long (Bath), J.McTier (Bath), C.J.Sealey (Bridgwater Albion), three quarters; J.Merry (Wellington), C.G.Vincent (Bath) half-backs; F.Soane (Bath), E.T.Gilmore, T.P Gilmore (Weston super Mare), P.J.Ebdon (Wellington), G.Bradshaw (Bridgwater), H.B.Mole (Castle Cary), L.C.Powys (Yeovil), J.B.S D'Aguila (Bath), forwards.*

So by the mid-1890's Bath had both survived and adapted to a number of challenges and changes confronting all clubs during this pioneering era, as was imperative if they were to achieve status as a first-class club. But the signs at least were promising, and although Bath were not leading the pack, they arguably ranked among the pack that was doing the leading. Already three Bath players had won caps for England, while Somerset selectors were taking far more interest too, and not least in the county performances of T.N. Parham, whose rugby career extended from the 1880's into the 1890's and who was rated by many of his contemporaries as the best Bath half-back of the 19th century. Significantly the fact that Parham was a half-back now posed an important question: could Bath now produce the quality of backs that would be absolutely essential to any club with ambitions of first-class status in the post 1900's rugby game?

Chapter 5. NO ALTERNATIVE – SEPARATE WAYS.

As the rugby game advanced into the 1890's there were many enthusiasts who would have been perfectly justified to believe that 'all was well' throughout the far flung corners of the rugby world. The game was bigger, the game was better, and sometimes the game was attracting increasingly large and enthusiastic support. Yet it was this same undeniable success that was producing a new and perhaps unexpected problem for the Game's governing body. Just one single detail that dropped onto a certain club treasurer's table in the late 19th century is quite sufficient to explain the situation. The occasion was an encounter between rivals Leeds and Halifax. The venue was Headingley. The attendance (Peter Jackson, Daily Mail, 1st September, 2001) was.... *"27,654"*

 For an inter-club game to attract such crowds would even now raise eye-brows among the faithful. But in northern parts during those latter years of the 19th century, such crowds raised some fundamental questions too. Indeed, amid the smoke-filled chimneys and down the deep, dark mines, where money was scarce and work was hard, northern rugby followers were speaking ever more frequently of one particular topic, namely *'Broken Time.'* Or as one would describe it nowadays, 'part-time professionalism,' an arrangement that would allow for reimbursement to players for wages lost owing to their rugby commitments.

It was a forceful argument, not least because its timing coincided with the same question being discussed in soccer circles and, as it happens, cricket; two fast-growing sports whose moves to accommodate professionalism seemed effortlessly simple by comparison. But the RFU viewed matters differently, very differently in fact; and regarding an issue that at this period appears to have dominated much of the rugby agenda, the game's governing body made their decision, one moreover with profound ramifications for the foreseeable future of rugby football. It was nothing less than a determination to ensure the continuation of a totally amateur game, notwithstanding that the issue of broken time payments was to reach *"boiling point at the RFU's AGM [1893],"* where Hornby (in fact a true amateur) exposed an element of hypocrisy in this debate and reportedly argued for broken time payments because *"the so-called amateur sides ask for large guarantees, publish no balance sheets and distribute expenses far larger than paid to a professional player."* Yorkshire representatives further complained that 'although there are more clubs in the North of England than in the South, more Southerners than Northerners people the RFU committee;' (see: Rugby Chronology, Museum of Rugby, Twickenham; now World Rugby Museum).

As for a compromise....there would be no compromise! Indeed the 'Great Schism.' as it became known *"was now to take on its own unstoppable momentum."* Initially

(Museum of Rugby) 'twenty clubs from Lancashire, Yorkshire and Cheshire met at the George Hotel, Huddersfield and decided to turn professional, forming their own governing body in 1895, namely the Northern Union (later known as Rugby League from 1922).' It was a bold decision, and the 'Divide' when it came was as sad as it was courageous. Yet it meant that the rugby family was now no longer one single family. Indeed two different paths would now be trod, and the siblings would not meet again for a long, long time. Yet each code (Union and League) would now have the freedom to decide its own destiny, and do so furthermore without internal divisions regarding payments or otherwise forever disrupting their chosen, albeit separate, journeys.

This separation into two rugby codes inevitably depleted the ranks within the rugby union game, and particularly so in the North. Yorkshire, the first ever winners of the County Championship in 1889, would triumph a further six times until relinquishing the title to Kent in 1897. But by then the inroads of professionalism had taken their toll, and not for another thirty years would the Tykes, in 1926, triumph again in County rugby.

Unlike Wales, who in the late 1890's would already experience the loss (among others) of the brilliant James brothers to the professional game, the South West had by contrast remained less affected by the dramatic events that had taken place in the North. Nonetheless, in the following decade, Bath were to discover that they too were not entirely out of range of those northern scouts, who on occasions would take more than just a passing interest in what their West Country counterparts had to offer; and while Salford failed to tempt Bath's powerful forward Billy Thomas into professional ranks with a signing-on fee of £500 (big money then) plus bonuses for wins and further bonuses for tries scored, Oldham during this same period did succeed in tempting Bath's Tom White to 'go north' in 1909. A very versatile player, he was furthermore good enough to win international honours in his newly adopted code.

Bert Comm .... The fullback went North with Woodward and Haines in the 1920's

Acknowledgements: Bath Chronicle

Soon afterwards Bath utility back Vickie Alcott signed professional with Hull Kingston Rovers; likewise promising young forward Riley West (no relation to Tom West who had earlier joined Rochdale Hornets), and it was regrettable that J. Robinson went North too. Commenting on this movement into professional ranks the Bath Daily Chronicle (Football Talk, 14th April 1910) wrote of 'a Bath and Somerset flavour in the Oldham v Rochdale Hornets game of 2nd April, where Tom West ran home 2 tries for

Hornets and Tom White scored another for Oldham.' It was therefore fortunate that Bath's recovery at this time from an earlier slump in the 1900's was not adversely affected by this loss of talent. Nor, again surprisingly, was Bath's surge during the 1920's seemingly affected by the loss to professional ranks of Albert Woodward, Bert Comm and Ted Haines. In fact notwithstanding the huge inducements offered from Leeds to legendary centre Ron Gerrard in the 1930's (an offer he declined) no further player left the Rec to head North until centre Peter Fearis in the 1950's.

But in the early days of 1895 when the professional Northern Rugby Union was formed, it would be a hundred years before the Rugby Football Union in 1995 finally relented, bowing at last to the growing pressure to permit some form of professionalism into its own hallowed ranks. And when at the climax of season 1995-6 the hatchet was finally buried, two great teams were chosen from each code to meet at Twickenham in a game of friendship and conciliation. One team were Rugby League giants Wigan. The other was a once humble club from the West Country….Bath, of whom a century previously it would have been fanciful to even have dreamed of such an extraordinary possibility.

Chapter 6. NEW HOME. NEW CHALLENGE. (1890's onwards)

The Great Schism of the mid-1890's, albeit a decisive and dramatic event, was only one aspect of this crucial, final decade of the 19th century. Yes, the departure from the amateur fold of those twenty two clubs most certainly affected the rugby game in the North. But it did not stop the momentum that was taking place elsewhere in the amateur sphere, and contrary to common perception, rugby (not least in the West Country) was far from exclusive to the Public Schools and Oxbridge alone. Moreover at the higher level it was now a crowd-puller, particularly at the county level, with Devon's 3-0 win v Somerset drawing 10,000 (Chronicle, Football Talk, 12th December, 1895); while Cornwall's 17-3 County final triumph against Durham in 1908 drew a crowd of 17,000 at Redruth (D. Mail, 31st March 1989).

Meanwhile a hierarchy of elite club-sides was evolving, though as yet this did not include Bath. Admittedly they possessed a number of talented individuals, yet their main strength and tactics had for some years depended (although not entirely) upon their forwards, a pack usually good enough to 'hold their heads above water' in a rugby game that was becoming both better and faster. To their credit they had already produced three internationals ....D'Aguilar, Fuller and Soane; and they were known (and sometimes feared) for their much favoured tactic of the combined forward 'foot-rush.' Indeed the chant of *"Feet Bath, feet"* as a rush got moving was a chant commonly heard echoing from the Bath terraces during the 1890's and beyond.

15-man rugby it was not! Furthermore clubs relying on a limited forward strategy would discover soon enough that such tactics were no longer sufficient to win the 'big' games against the leading clubs of England and Wales. Bath knew this only too well. Indeed they could hardly 'not' have known, located as they were near their increasingly powerful neighbours Bristol and those often inspirational Welsh sides now joining the Bath fixture list. Ah yes....Wales! Admiration for the back play among those sides from the valleys was increasingly recognised throughout the rugby game. Indeed by the turn of the century neighbours Bristol had already adopted the Welsh tactic, whereby once the ball had reached one attacking wing, it would be re-passed along the backs to the other wing, so sustaining the crucial momentum of a sweeping attack from one flank to the other. This added another dimension to the 'running' game. But it had yet to be developed at Bath. Nor could one fail to notice the prowess of those leading London clubs such as Blackheath, the London Scottish and Richmond. For rugby union really was developing into a national game, with many top clubs (thanks now to an established rail network) able to travel the length of the Country to play fixtures. So Blackheath, for example, did not merely face fellow Home Counties teams. On the contrary, their fixtures extended to Wales (Cardiff and Newport for instance) and beyond.

Another reason for Bath's sometimes pedestrian progress however had nothing to do with a lack of an effective back division, but instead the lack of satisfactory and permanent playing facilities. Good fortune was about to intervene nonetheless when in 1892 there came the opportunity to move to Henrietta Park; and talking of the 'Park' it was a rarity in the annals of Bath rugby to see a team-sheet from this era of pre-1900's rugby. But thanks to an original post-card submitted to the Bath Chronicle by Mr Bob Tarrant, formerly Hon.Sec of St. Stephen's RFC (and later printed on 6th April 1932) the names of a team captained by Frank Soane when the club played at Henrietta Park (between 1892-4) was indeed revealed. It was as follows: *A.E. Pinch, W. Pattinson, B. Vincent, P. Dykes, B. Helps, T. N. Parham, and G.Vincent, F. Soane (capt.), Roberts, L.J. Fry, W. Coles, A. Timmins, R. Dykes, A.E. Clarke and Milsom.*

But while the Park was not without its virtues, a yet better venue lay barely a stone's throw away, namely the wide expanse that is the Pulteney Meadows, all seventeen lush green acres of it. Situated literally in the centre of the city, instinct alone told the Bath committee that the Meadows reflected the very soul of the city. Could there possibly be a better home than this? The simple answer was 'no.' Could Bath obtain the rights to play their rugby here? The answer would be 'yes.' Because fortuitously Captain Foster, owner of Henrietta Park, now wished to convert his land for other uses; moreover Bath (Sydney) College, who during this period had been playing on the Pulteney Meadows, now departed. As a result the 'Bath Recreation Ground Company Ltd' was duly formed so as to purchase the land, and Bath successfully negotiated with the company for long term usage from September 1894 onwards. Hopefully the club's nomadic days were over.

With the acquisition of the Pulteney Meadows, soon to be termed 'the Recreation Ground' and then equally soon to be dubbed 'the Rec' by all Bathonians, the club now possessed a rugby venue of unusual quality. Alongside the Avon river and overlooked by the timeless beauty of Bath Abbey, some commentators have described the Rec as 'the most beautiful rugby ground in the world,' (reportedly the 1912/13 Touring South Africans among them). Furthermore during this same era there developed the association of the club with an off-field rugby servant of great loyalty, namely the much respected John Townsend Piper. Quiet and thoughtful, he was appointed Hon. Secretary in 1890, and once the use of the Pulteney Meadows was assured, he held an extra card when seeking to strengthen the Bath fixture list. In fact among the first visiting club sides to face Bath on the Rec (possibly 'the' first) were Exeter. They were not new opponents, but they were certainly strong ones and their visit on 6th October 1894 proved to be (for Bath at least) an ideal result for an ideal occasion. The home side were inspired, perhaps by the influence of their new surroundings, defeating their visitors 22 points to nil; and during that era the Bath encounters against formidable Exeter did not always conclude as successfully as that.

So with the Rec at their disposal, and hence able to attract bigger 'fish' to the city, no less a touring side than the Barbarians played Bath on Christmas Eve, 1894, their following side 'stepping out' as follows: **Barbarians**: Gwynne, C.B.Fry, Baker (all Oxford), Tandy (Blackheath), Toller (Cardiff and possibly Blackheath), Biggs (Cardiff), Dyas (Sandhurst), Maud, Finlinson (both Blackheath), Dixon, Falcon, Tucker (all Cambridge), Todd, Carey (both Oxford), Gould (Liverpool). While facing the far from simple task of holding out against so strong a team, the following **Bath** side was fielded to face them: Barrett, J.Long, T. Fry, J.MacTier, F. Rowlett, Seers, G.Vincent, F.Soane, D'Aguila, B.Belsom, E.Taylor, L. Fry, W.Coles, J.Ruddock, W.England.

FRANK SOANE 1893

With the founding of the Barbarians in 1890, Frank Soane was claimed as the first Bath player to wear the coveted touring side's shirt in 1891; and their 1894 team sent to the city was packed with internationals, Oxbridge Blues and leading club players; so their 14-0 win was hardly surprising. But the result was far from a humiliation and in truth the margin mattered little. Because in an age of no radio and certainly no television, there was really only one way to learn about the best in rugby, and that was to play the best in rugby. This did matter, and the words of at least one admiring reporter for the Chronicle said it all: "…*how it opens our eyes and makes us realise what first class football is. The Barbarians are Par Excellence.*"

A repeat of this Par Excellence was seen again on 2nd April 1896 (13 points apiece) and later on 15th April 1897 with the visitors winning 3-8. In the following 1897-8 season the aforementioned half-back G. Vincent was duly honoured as another Bath Barbarian, to be followed by centre James Timmins in 1905-6. But Bath could not afford to rest on their laurels. After all, their spacious new home required some 'extras.' Hence within a season of their arrival on the Rec the club completed a seated stand alongside the West side of the ground, and though initially bemoaning the annual rent of 20% of gate receipts to their landlords the Recreation Ground Company (Chronicle, 8th January 1896), this did not prevent the Bath committee from applying a little touch of chivalry when permitting members to bring two ladies to watch the games on match-days…free of charge. And such would be the sense of belonging to this unique ground that it was destined to be nothing less than Bath's spiritual home.

Sadly it was during this same era that Bath would bid farewell to an outstanding former player and England international, namely Herbert George Fuller (1856-1896). Very much a Bathonian, Fuller had received part of his education at Christ's College, Finchley, and both at Finchley College and later at Cambridge University he was to make a deep impression upon all those who knew him. An outstanding forward for Bath (later Clifton RFC), Somerset and England during the 1880's, his qualities both as sportsman and a natural born role model would impress all those who knew him. An academic, he would later become a proctor at Cambridge, and this in addition to his outstanding sporting prowess. In his last days, which were spent at the home of an elder brother in Streatham, Herbert finally lost his fight against a cerebral tumour on 2nd January 1896. Buried in Bath (Lansdown) his loss was 'felt' by many. Later in July of 1896, the club mourned another of their former internationals, namely Major Frank D'Aguila (and likewise the passing away of one of his two sons, namely J.B.S. D'Aguila in 1901, himself a much liked Bath and Somerset player).

There was little doubt that Frank D'Aguila, Fuller and Soane had helped to enhance Bath's reputation at forward. But for some three decades since their formation finding good backs had often proved less fruitful. And yet......at long last there were signs that this situation might be about to change. In fact from the mid-1890's onwards certain individuals among the Bath back division showed signs of potential, strengthened not least by the welcome arrival of co-centres Dan MacTier and former Welsh international 'Tich' Fry (a real 'jinking' little maestro), while the long career of Bath and Somerset winger W. F. (Joe) Long had commenced on one wing, and that of his brother Jim Long on the other. Individually good, it was they who helped Bath bring home a rare (and much cherished) 0-3 triumph at Bristol in the spring of 1897, potentially a very promising sign for the future. Moreover, when a certain ex-Bath (Sydney) College schoolboy by the name of J.T. Timmins first slipped a club shirt over his shoulders in season 1896-7, Bath might just possibly have seen enough to already predict an outstanding future for this exciting young player. Because here was a newcomer whose presence in the team at centre-threequarter would one day inspire the one asset that Bath now most needed and most wanted........the complete all-round back division to lift them up a class.

Norman Biggs

That being said, one should not dismiss outright the abilities of certain backs of earlier years, among them the Hills brothers, two notable players of the Lambridge era (circa, mid-1880's). Long-time supporter Frank Melluish (letters, The Chronicle, 6th September 1930) recalled one brother sending over a 'drop-kick from just inside the touch-line from half-way.' He recalled too the famous Biggs brothers, also of Cardiff and Wales (Bath & W. Chronicle & Herald, 4th September 1930), and who graced the Bath backs in the Soane days (the 1890's era). While centre M. Baker, added an admiring Frank Melluish, "would cut out some fine openings for Norman Biggs who, with his long stride making for the corner flag was a treat never to be

Selwyn Biggs

forgotten." But among the major tasks now would be first to strengthen the fixture list, and secondly to produce results good enough to maintain it. Because make no mistake (as any fixture secretary has long known): 'there were and are other ambitious clubs always willing to take one's place.'

So when in the spring of 1898 the Hartlepool Rovers came southwards to play both Llanelli and Bristol, Bath negotiated a match with their north-east compatriots Percy Park to visit the Rec on the latter's own Easter tour. The Newcastle team were a class side, sufficiently strong in fact to provide no less than seven players for the then current Northumberland team, who just happened to be that season's County Champions. Yet Bath, with that young man J.T. Timmins in their back- division, were entitled to feel encouraged with a performance that led to their 8-3 victory. Hopefully, such results were a sign of better things to come following an 1890's era when the club continually struggled, usually fruitlessly, against the likes of Bristol and Gloucester.

But doubt not that life was often fun and hectic; just such being the case towards the end of season 1898-9 when the team found themselves ('thanks' to train delays) in a race against the clock to reach opponents Exeter (Chronicle, Football Talk, 14th April, 1899). Their timetable was thus: the train would not depart from Bath until 1.35pm, so the team would be unlikely to reach the Exeter ground much before 4pm. Then there was a match to play, albeit on a reduced time-scale. There was a further 'slight' problem as the return train departed from Exeter soon after 5.30pm. That meant Bath dare not depart from their opponent's ground for the homeward journey later than 5.15pm. This made for a 'pretty tight' schedule. So as to save time the team donned their kit while still aboard the train (reportedly changing in the saloon of all places), and somehow they reached the ground for a 4.05 pm kick-off. It was quite dramatic. Elsewhere there was further drama, far away in fact 'up North,' where Northumberland (winners in the previous season) were facing their challengers in the 1899 County Championship final. And the challengers on this occasion of the last full season of the century were Devon. It would be symbolic if they could capture the crown.

Well, if it would be a good omen for a leading Devon club to win on that day, then Exeter were playing their own part to perfection, clinching as they did an 11-0 victory. Meanwhile come the final whistle the Bath team had barely fifteen minutes to reach the station for their return journey; another journey that like the first was to prove positively hectic! For important news had been signalled from Newcastle. It was that 'oh so special' County Championship final. Devon?…Devon had won! The news of the victory (by a goal) led to crowds thronging the streets, those same streets in which a Somerset club were now struggling valiantly to make headway towards St David's station. There was joy. There was celebration. Exeter, it was recorded, *"was mad with delight."* Indeed, amid the carnival atmosphere of it all, few could have doubted the profound effect of the County game in the West Country. Moreover, perhaps no one would even have dared to predict the West Country 'enlightenment' that Devon's triumph would help to inspire. For inspire it did! Indeed, the Western Counties were now poised to dominate the County Championship for near a quarter of a century, on occasions almost putting a stranglehold on it. And Devon were the first, on that glorious April day. Oh....and Bath did catch that train!

Chapter 7.   A NEW CENTURY BECKONS. (The early 1900's)

As dawn broke over Bath on 1ˢᵗ January 1900, the optimism of this era could not have been better demonstrated than the manner of the celebrations three years previously for the Diamond Jubilee of Queen Victoria (as later reported in the Chronicle, 8ᵗʰ September, 2005, p.13). Bunting and flags had adorned the streets of Bath on that glorious day of 22nd June 1897; a hot air balloon was launched from a packed Victoria Park; medals (seven thousand in number) were gifted to the children of the Georgian city by direct order of the mayor, Mr George Woodiwiss; and Henrietta Park, where the Bath club had once played, was formerly opened as parkland to a grateful city. Oh the changes during her Majesty's life-time! Wooden warships of Nelsonian fame had been superseded by iron-clad giants of the sea; horse and carriage had been overtaken by railroad and train. Cars too were now seen on the roads, and soon the Wright Brothers would, quite literally, reach for the skies. Such a transformation, and all witnessed within barely seventy five years since young William Webb Ellis reportedly picked up a football at Rugby School and ran with it (in the wrong direction).

Indeed regarding rugby, an observer would doubtless have realised that the game (likewise the world itself) had 'come a long way' in rather a short time. The Chronicle (and its sister papers) was rapidly expanding its rugby coverage, usually under the pen-name of 'Football Talk' or 'Play Up,' superseded by 'the Mascot' in the 1920's. Meanwhile cricket, Association football, and Rugby were each carving out a niche for themselves in the everyday lives of an increasingly sporting nation. Here there were heroes to admire, among them W.G. Grace (Gloucestershire and England), a colossus of the cricketing world; C.B. Fry who gained triple Blues at Oxford, selection for the Barbarians, and then triple selection for England at athletics, soccer and cricket; while rugby union too would produce a new generation of legends, among them Adrian Stoop (Oxford, Harlequins and England) whose brilliance and ideas would help transform half-back play in the English game. As for the 'wannabe' sporting stars of the future there was the must-have bible of the Boys Own album. Describing the early days of the rugby game, the 1907-8 edition wrote thus: *"....the credit of its origins and development for many years was entirely due to Rugby School, until Marlborough College came on the scene and gallantly seconded the efforts of its notable rival....."* Understandably, admiration was expressed too for the Marlborough Nomads, the first fully established Old Boys team.

By the 1900's, as the pages further revealed, others had caught up. For instance there was Bedford School who, as the Boys Own enthused, were by this time *far and away the greatest of English schools to-day."* There were Fettes and Loretto in Edinburgh (who as the pages tell us) were so dominant in the rugby ranks of Oxford and Cambridge (and of course Scotland) as to be *"the subject of universal comment."* In

Scotland in fact there had been occasions when schoolboys had actually gained full caps for their national team. In England too J.G. Milton (Bedford School), a young forward full of promise, was to achieve this same remarkable distinction. He was selected for England against the iron men of Wales in January 1904 at a mere 18 years of age. It was the ultimate baptism of fire. In addition, details of University rugby were described, informing readers that 'such was this prevalence of Old Rugbians and Marlburians at Oxford in the 1870's that they alone had been required to pay the university club subscriptions, all other students being regarded as honorary members of the rugby club and thus excused entirely the requirement to contribute towards membership funds.'

But what then did the future hold for Bath? This usually contented rugby family, now settled at long last with its own rugby home on the Rec, was suddenly faced with a totally unexpected event within the first few months of this new and seemingly bright 20th century. The precise date was the 16th April 1900. The actual occasion was a visit by the Portsmouth rugby club, visiting Bath to play a near-end of season game which, according to a post-match report from Portsmouth captain (Edmonds) was *"more free from rough or unfair play than any game he had ever played."* Playing too that day was Portsmouth vice-captain George Llewellyn Trerise. A sail-maker, he was employed in the Government dockyards at the naval port. A Falmouth man from Cornwall by origin, Trerise played in the visitors' pack.

It was late in the game however that he was to suffer a head injury (Chronicle, 19th April, 1900). Nonetheless, he was able to walk off the field at the final whistle without arousing serious concern. Indeed, he remained with his colleagues until reaching the Angel Hotel in Westgate Street, where the Portsmouth team had 'changed' for the match. Then suddenly concerns did begin. Trerise fell unconscious, his colleagues now realising that all was far from well. He was taken to the Royal United Hospital, for unknown to anyone during the match, he had suffered a fractured skull during that encounter on the Rec. Moreover, as both clubs were soon to realise, things were far more serious than anyone had previously realised. Even so, nobody was fully prepared for the news that would follow that same evening. For George Llewellyn Trerise, twenty four years of age, single and vice-captain of Portsmouth, had died. The shock for both Bath and Portsmouth was numbing, two thoroughly decent clubs suddenly finding themselves having to come to terms with events so shattering and so totally unforeseen. This then was their unexpected introduction to the 20th century.

After this tragedy all else in purely human terms was mundane that season. Nonetheless there were other matters to occupy the mind, the respective strengths of Bristol and Gloucester among them. These two clubs were getting better and better, while Bath by contrast were struggling to maintain equilibrium at the higher level to which they aspired, and if they should fall too far behind the leading clubs of the day, then sooner or later the stronger clubs would abandon them. Indeed, the contrast between the Bath results of the moderately successful season of 1900-1 (17 wins) and the mere eight wins in season 1901-2 was early warning of the uncertain days that lay ahead. Another reality was the growing dominance of Wales, whose hardened steelworkers and miners were proving themselves natural born rugby players, both at forward or in the backs. True, English clubs including Bath did on occasions win against their Welsh brethren. But if so, that was generally on English territory. In Wales it was usually a different story. There was furthermore the question of tactics, because this aspect is to no small degree dependent on the respective abilities of players available. Therefore should (or even could) Bath attempt to emulate the adventurous style of Bristol? Or should they apply the rather different tactics of the likes of Lydney, for example? Because this small yet passionate rugby stronghold on the edge of the Forest of Dean (regular Bath opponents in the 1900's) might not have played the most attractive of rugby. But by heck, mustard keen, fit and hard, their destructive forward style (Chronicle, 12th November, 1903, p.5) albeit *"with no brilliant men in their midst to inspire football ideas [could] by sheer determination and consistent preparation [bring] themselves into such proficiency that they made teams with considerable reputations lick the dust."* Two years previously, after a reverse at Lydney, Bath had decided that enough was enough, and commenced training twice weekly as a result.

Meanwhile 'tough' play can on occasions descend into 'rough' play (or worse). Even so a perhaps somewhat surprising feature of this era concerned not only excessive play on the field, but even rowdiness among spectators off it (Chronicle, 14th September 1899, p.2). True, Victorian and Edwardian England may indeed have been noted for its finesse and genteel behaviour in the Lords members' lounge and the Henley regatta, but such behaviour did not always extend to the rugby arena.....not by a 'long shot!' So alarmed in fact were Somerset County that in season 1899-1900 the committee had issued a circular to every member club, warning all concerned that adverse behaviour would be dealt with accordingly. Furthermore, posters were ordered to be displayed at every Somerset ground, duly warning clubs and followers as to how seriously the Committee regarded the worsening situation. So it would hardly have pleased these same good gentlemen when in the following season the Bath encounter at Taunton became so unmanageable that the game was abandoned, with one player from each side having received their marching orders for 'unacceptable' behaviour; or to put it more bluntly....thuggery.

But.... the simple fact was that rugby football was as now a contact sport. Moreover, it was developing into an increasingly popular contact sport. Indeed, by the turn of the century the membership alone of the Gloucester club totalled near twelve hundred enthusiasts, and the six thousand strong attendance at the drawn encounter at Exeter between Devon and Gloucestershire in season 1902/3 was nothing unusual in West Country county games. But these pleasing figures did not only make good reading for the respective club treasurers, they gave a clear and simple message to the Game's governing bodies. And the message was this: that rugby football attracted followers not in spite of, but precisely because of the fact that it was a tough, physical sport. It was therefore not always a simple task to distinguish between tough play that was acceptable and tough play that was not. Nor will it ever be. Paradoxically this same confrontational game on the field of play possessed (usually) an almost unique spirit off it, and the Somerset committee were doubtless aware of that fine line that exists between hard play and actual dirty play. If nothing else the circular would hopefully warn both clubs and players to pause and think carefully about this same fine line, and therefore to respond accordingly.

So this was part of the rugby landscape surrounding Bath in the 1900's, a club doubtless aware that its place in the hierarchy of the game would likely be judged by comparison with Gloucester and especially Bristol. True, Bath were generally strong at forward where a charismatic Frank Cashnella had now joined the ranks. Yet even here there was no certainty that sufficient quality-newcomers would be found to replace the old guard. This situation furthermore applied to the backs, as that reliable quartet of J. Long and W. Long and centres Dan Mactier and 'Tich' Fry were no longer available as a unit. The outstanding James Timmins would not always be on-call either, based as he was in the capital and playing on occasions for the ever improving London Welsh.

Yet behind the scenes the wider Bath rugby family were laying foundations that would at least help secure the long-term future of the parent club through thick and thin. First, the Bath and District Combination was formed in the season of 1902-3. Then barely one season later a group of local schoolteachers established the Bath and District Schools Rugby Union. Admittedly the potential or otherwise of these two fledgling organisations could only be guessed at initially. But as the seasons passed the club would have reason to realise that the launching of the Combination and the Schools Union would prove to be inspired decisions. Moreover, despite somewhat ordinary

James Timmins

performances down on The Rec and elsewhere, Bath were still producing certain individual players of real class. Somerset had noted this fact too. Theirs was an outstanding county side in season 1902-3 that included Wellington's (and England's) fearsome tackling full-back Herbert Gamlin and the tenacious forward Robert Dibble of Bridgwater Albion, who would soon join England ranks himself. Furthermore, this was a Somerset team (Bath's Cashnella and James Timmins playing) good enough to reach that season's County semi-final against Kent (losing 0-12), with Durham then winning the Championship final.

Nonetheless in season 1905-6 there was to be a totally unexpected reason for not only Somerset, but for the entire rugby fraternity to sit up and take notice when British rugby awaited the first ever visit by our cousins from far away......the New

Zealanders! Little was known about the tourists on their arrival; after all, what did they know about rugby in New Zealand? But this knowledge-deficit was about to receive a somewhat rude awakening. It was in fact the West Country who would have the honour (for want of a better word) of hosting the tourists, as their first game was an encounter against Devon (destined ironically to be that season's County Champions) and where any queries concerning the tourists' ability would shortly be answered. And....the stunning 4-55 result to the New Zealanders was that answer!

The reaction in the Bath Chronicle and in rugby circles everywhere to this first and totally unexpected result was naturally one of amazement. But the reality was that rugby football had already captured the imagination in Countries far removed from those playing-fields of Rugby School and Marlborough College. Moreover, our New Zealand cousins came with their own ideas and tactics that were both exciting and challenging. After that first encounter against Devon the excitement aroused by the tourists was reported to be at 'fever pitch,' and the third game on their itinerary was against Somerset at Taunton. Here, watched by a reported crowd of nine thousand the 'Cidermen,' fielding Bath backs R. Meister and J. Timmins (captain) limited the now fearsome tourists to a 0-23 defeat, an outcome that in the circumstances was deemed a far from unworthy result.

Nonetheless the tourists continued on their seemingly unstoppable way against clubs, counties and Countries. Scotland (7-12), Ireland (0-15), England watched by 45,000 at Crystal Palace (0-15) and France (8-38) would all fall. Indeed only Wales would check the advance thanks to a try by Dr Teddie Morgan in a passionate 3-0 encounter at Cardiff Arms Park in front of 47,000 fervent spectators. This one upset, notable too for the disallowed Bob Deans try that New Zealand always insisted was genuine, did not however disguise perhaps the most significant message of their eventful visit. Because although few, if any, at the time could have realised the long term impact of this first New Zealand tour, hindsight gives one a different perspective from which to make judgement. For the fact was this: that a mere five years into a new century, rugby football had taken its first real steps towards becoming global!

Chapter 8. IN THE MIDST OF WINTER. (The 1900's continued)

Reviewing the sports pages of The Bath Daily Chronicle on Saturday 21st April, 1906 would have been a deeply depressing task for a Bath rugby enthusiast. For if the meagre return back in 1901-2 of a mere 8 wins from 30 matches had seemed as poor a season as it could possibly get, then the results of 1905-06 would prove that they could even worse. Because of the 33 games played, a mere seven were won, two were drawn and no less than 24 were lost. Things simply could not carry on like this. Morale was falling and dark clouds were descending over the Rec. Meanwhile, with Bristol and Gloucester now establishing themselves firmly amongst the elite of the game, Bath could be facing the prospect of a second class rugby existence at best. It was not a pleasing thought. Furthermore, as if the results were not bad enough, those same sports pages concluded that the main problem in the side was a *"lack of a sufficiently strong forward rank and a lack of a permanently allied pair of halves."*

"A lack of a sufficiently strong forward rank!" Surely not? After all, was not the strength in the pack the one asset that could always be relied upon? Well, with the exception of the likes of Cashnella the club found itself unable to rely even on this once reliable resource. This to put it mildly was both a psychological blow and a drawback with serious long term implications, because in rugby as played in the West Country and Wales no team could possibly succeed without a strong set of forwards. Furthermore, Bath could not continue losing this number of games without some reaction from their stronger opponents, and sooner or later if this situation continued the better clubs would drop Bath from their own fixture lists and bid 'farewell.'

Arnold Ridley ....a varied Career

Acknowledgements: Bath Chronicle

Confusing matters further was that in the previous season Bath had returned an encouraging total of twenty one wins from 39 matches. Yet this did not signal any revival, and during an otherwise seven year struggle from 1901-1908, there was a period when crowds barely reached a hundred. So with results now failing and finances now falling the situation on the Rec was so precarious that in the words of Arnold Ridley (actor, playwright and later club President): 'Bath came close to being disbanded;' (Bath Centenary book, p.14). So it was that the season of 1905-06 was the mid-winter of Bath's misfortunes, the ultimate low point in fact since their formation forty years previously.

Yet if there was one saving grace it was the fact that although Bath were defeated far too often, it was only on rare occasions that they were defeated badly. In fact at times they could get close to success against the best of their opponents; and winning against the likes of the then highly rated Penarth (9-4), ironically in this most dire of seasons. But in such encounters it was Bath who usually 'came off worse.' Revival therefore depended partly on that vital ingredient of self-belief, and notwithstanding the slightly better season of 1906-7, Bath would field no less than 56 players for 1st XV duty, hardly an ideal situation for team stability.

However season 1906-07 at least gave some cause for slight relief, not only because a lowly twelve victories was in fact an improvement, but because this total included unexpectedly good wins over Neath and Pontypridd (by 5-3 and 3-0 respectively). There were narrow upsets too, including the close 3-6 fall against Bristol at their former home on the County Ground at Ashley Hill. But one could not lightly shrug off the 15 defeats that included the 31-0 mauling at Pontypool, and the harsh reality was that during the 1900's Bath remained well outside the boundaries of the first class rugby scene. Indeed perhaps the one notable aspect of this season was the adoption of an all white shirt to replace the dark blue and black hooped shirts of previous seasons.

It can take years, sometimes even decades, to change one's perception of the prowess of, for example, a rugby club. Yet in the 'clouds' that hung over the Rec during this era it was not all gloom. For hidden behind the scenes so to speak there were a few (albeit only a 'few') signs for optimism. The pack was slowly responding to the inspiration of Cashnella, although there remained, for the time being at least, a lack of weight. Utility player Fred Russell and the ever reliable Alby Hatherill were bonding at half-back, while R. Meister, H. Lewis and Tom West were adding genuine pace into the three-quarters. The task therefore was to mould such individual abilities into a winning team. Tom West for instance, whose career-change required a move to the Gloucester club, was soon a 1st teamer with the Cherry and Whites. As for the ever reliable Meister, he gained selection for the Somerset backs against the 1906-7 visiting South Africans at a packed Taunton, playing his part in a brave rear-guard 0-14 defeat at the hands of these superb tourists. But such encouraging signs were admittedly no more than 'straws in the wind' for an often struggling club, and no one was suggesting that a sudden transformation had occurred, because it hadn't. At best, it was merely a tentative step in the right direction and, make no mistake, there remained the steepest of mountains to climb.

There was nonetheless one further event of season 1906-07 that would be long remembered, and this concerned "*the notorious county cup final against Bridgwater Albion*" (Bath Daily Chronicle, 20th April, 1907). This competition, namely the recently inaugurated Somerset Cup, had been launched for the very best of motives, not least to channel the huge enthusiasm in the County into a club knock-out contest; and initially there was considerable interest shown, not least at Bath. However, when at four minutes past seven on the evening of Saturday 23rd March the Bridgwater Albion team had secured victory by 5-0 against fellow finalists Bath, notice had already been given that all might not run smoothly with this fledgling event. It had been barely ten minutes into this oft-interrupted match when Bath's T.B. Timmins (brother of James) was reportedly 'tackled with great violence' by Albion's England International forward Bob Dibble. The referee 'blew up,' but in the resulting uproar Bath's Loo Hatherill apparently 'did not hear it.' Albion's Parr then picked up the ball and was subsequently tackled by Hatherill. As a result and to the great indignation of his team-mates, the Bathonian was given his marching orders.

Now hard tackling is part of rugby culture, so whether or not Dibble's tackle on Timmins was actually illegal or otherwise (high perhaps) was never fully clarified. But Bath were angered by their man's dismissal, and it was this dismissal rather than Bob Dibble's tackle that particularly upset them. Indeed their ire was directed, not at Albion, but rather at the refereeing. True, these were early days in this recently launched Somerset Cup and there was no immediate reason to doubt its long-term potential. But as the seasons passed (and with Bath set to be embroiled in yet further fracas in the following year) the County Cup did not evolve into the success story as intended. Instead teams usually adopted the dour strategy of 'win at all costs' and open, handling rugby was a rarity. It was of little surprise therefore that by 1914 this particular competition would be discontinued, and few would mourn its passing.

Perhaps an optimist would be hoping that the following season of 1907-8 would yield a few promising signs. The fixtures were an interesting mix and two impending encounters in particular caught the eye. First there would be the first ever match against the Harlequins. Secondly, there would be the first ever visit of a French side, and a particularly exciting French side too.....Racing Club de France. There would in addition be a game against arch rivals Weston super Mare in the First Round of that season's Somerset Cup, and it would transpire that all three fixtures would be long remembered; not for entirely disconnected reasons either.

Of these encounters the first was against the Harlequins in London on the 19th October. This remarkable club, founded one year after Bath in 1866 and originally known as Hampstead Football Club until 1870, was by the late 1900's a glamorous name in rugby football. Soon to depart from their Wandsworth ground to Twickenham, they possessed numerous outstanding players, and one man especially aroused both apprehension and awe in opposition ranks. That man was half-back Adrian Stoop, a name that would pass into England legend, and for Bath this inaugural game was to be a salutary experience. They lost. In fact it was far worse than that. Bath were white-washed, and this by a 49-8 total. Could the West Countrymen possibly recover from so shattering a result knowing full well that this superb Harlequins team would later visit the Rec in March of that same season? It seemed unlikely.

The season passed into the New Year and the lone bright spot for Bath had been a commendable 0-0 draw at neighbours Bristol. Yet this one encouraging result apart, there was precious little to suggest that the Harlequins (Quins) could then be tamed on their impending visit to the Rec on the 21st March. Furthermore, Bath's preparations for the Quins game were now to be affected by the ramifications of an earlier encounter, namely the 'small' matter of the Somerset Cup First Round game of 15th February. This had brought Bath head to head with rivals Weston super Mare, and in the length and breadth of Somerset there were perhaps no fiercer rivals than these two clubs. Added to this rivalry were two sets of supporters known for their partisan feelings towards each other, and then as now, this heady mix can ignite the unwholesome events that took place in this particular encounter.

One report estimated that some three thousand spectators attended this cup tie, and what is absolutely certain is that whoever did watch this match saw a game that they would probably never forget, and for all the wrong reasons. The match was as tense as it was close (the visitors narrowly winning), and the trouble that erupted on the field then actually spread to the terraces. To make matters even worse, the referee was mobbed at the game's conclusion, necessitating an actual escort to assist his safe passage to the dressing room. Indeed, so serious were these events that a full meeting of the Somerset Rugby Union (S.R.U.) was later summoned, and this body duly met on Tuesday, 3rd March at the Royal Station Hotel in Bath. The Union's highly respected president, namely Mr W.S. Donne was in the chair, and in the words of the Bath Weekly Argus (7th March, 1908, p.12) the " *report of the referee (Mr H. Smith, of Bridgwater) in the Bath and Weston super Mare Cup Tie on the Recreation Ground on February 15th was considered. He alleged that the spectators after the game mobbed and threatened him.*"

It was further reported that *"the referee, in his report, expressed his thanks to members of the Bath committee who came to his protection, and the Committee exonerated the officials from all blame in connection with the incident.*" But the committee were not in the mood to let matters rest there. Players A. Fear (W.s.M) and W. Watts (Bath) were duly suspended for the rest of the season for fighting, while C. Perkins (W.s.M) was suspended until March 27th for the same offence. But perhaps most threatening for Bath was the real possibility that rugby on the Rec itself could be suspended, this at a time when the club were preparing for the vital return match against the Harlequins later that same month.

Indeed the S.R.U. did place a ban on the Rec!! But perhaps mindful that Bath were due to host the Harlequins on 21st March, the ban was set only until the 20th March. So to the club's enormous relief, they were free to now play the visiting Harlequins in one of the most prestigious club matches yet played in the city. It was fortunate too that Bath were able to put the recent disturbing events to the back of their minds. The superb Harlequins came, but this time they did not conquer. Bath ran home three tries; the Quins ran home two with one converted; hence a home victory by 9-8! A narrow win only, but no less sweet for that,

Harlequins however would not be the only new opponents to the Rec during yet another uncertain season, as some four months previously (1st November 1907) Bath had hosted the Racing Club de France. It was just Bath's 'luck' however that on the morning of the match itself they had found themselves short of a wing-threequarter due to the sudden illness of their first- choice wingman. There were of course the reserve backs in the 2nd string, but Bath 'A' had already departed for an away game. So in desperation (literally desperation) Bath contacted Monkton Combe asking if they might have a player, be it schoolboy or master, who would be willing to accept the daunting task of facing a positively scintillating French club side.

Well the nearby school did suggest a player, one Alfred Kitching, an Oxford graduate (and not forgetting an ordained Minister) who had recently joined the school staff. Although there was no certainty that he could play at this level of rugby, he was nonetheless a winger when playing as a freshman at Oxford. Hence this slightly built and kindly schoolmaster, whom no one at the club had ever heard of, would now put on a Bath shirt for the first time. It would not be the last! Encouraging too for Bath was the result of that first visit by an overseas club. For the 6-6 draw against Racing Club in front of a large and appreciative crowd could be described as The Entente Cordial at its very best. Equally pleasing was the performance of that same polite schoolmaster from Monkton Combe. He was quite simply the fastest winger Bath had ever seen and whose pace generated a similar excitement to that of young David Trick's arrival on the Rec seven decades later.

Yet 'The Season Review' of the Bath Weekly Argus (2nd May 1908) made no reference to Kitching, and the relief expressed at the home win against Harlequins was tempered by misgivings: *"There have been seasons,"* the report stated, *"when the Bath team has done worse than in 1907-8, but the record of the campaign just closed is one of the most unfavourable in the annals of the club. Altogether 33 matches were played; of these 10 were won, 3 drawn, and 20 lost."* Yes, a mere ten games were won (club records quote 9), and among them a late season 14-0 success against the Old Millhillians, a side now ranked highly among the leading Old Boys clubs in England. But yes, twenty games were lost!

Nonetheless, could Alfred Kitching prove to be a crucial missing link; a player whose speed could turn the excellent work of centres Meister and James Timmins into much needed tries, and thereby transform some of those narrow defeats into narrow wins? As this sometimes fraught season of 1907-08 came to a close, one could only say that time alone would tell.

Chapter. 9. WINTER TURNS TO SPRING. (1908-14)

Those sometimes bleak rugby years that had over-shadowed Bath since that dawn of a new century were nonetheless not entirely fruitless. For although come the new season of 1908-09 the club was now facing the potential danger of failing (and by some distance) to secure a place in the ranks of first-class rugby, Bath did not lose the will or lack the necessary people to give them that precious thing called hope. Moreover adversity is an experience that can strengthen as well as weaken, and despite the many disappointments, the club never quite lost belief in itself. Behind the scenes and on the field meanwhile there were those club 'servants' whose greatest gift was dedication. The aforementioned John Townsend Piper for instance, who served as secretary and later joint- secretary from 1890 until 1944. Included too were excellent centres J. Timmins and R. Meister. There was furthermore the utility player to beat all utility players, namely Fred Russell, who over the years played in virtually every position on the field. And there was Frank Cashnella!

Frank Cashnella

Ah, that man Cashnella! Now, when the going gets tough, it is sometimes said that the tough get going. Well 'Cash' was tough! From a youngish age he was to enter into folklore not only in Bath, but wherever Bath plied their rugby trade (Centenary book, 'from Arnold Ridley,' pp. 13-14). He was barely 5ft. 11in and weighed slightly under 13 stone, but he was as strong as he was tenacious. Arnold Ridley would speak in awe of the 'Cash' he once knew: *"ashen faced, black-haired and heavily moustached, Cash was always in the fore-front of battle and in that era of the Somerset Cup the word 'battle' can be taken pretty literally."* Then years later while Arnold Ridley and a former West Country England forward were deep in discussion concerning former playing days, the latter commented that *"Old Cash was the only man who had ever put the wind up him. Cash - he was ruthless – absolutely ruthless"* was the international's authoritative verdict.

Yet as is sometimes the case with such charismatic men, 'Cash' was hugely popular with friend and foe alike. Born in 1879, he switched at fifteen years of age from soccer in the mid-1890's to the former Widcombe Institute rugby club. This change from round to oval ball was, to quote his very own words, because Association Football *"was too rough,"* a reason that would soon enough arouse incredulity to anyone watching Cashnella perform on the rugby field. He first put a Bath shirt over his broad shoulders in 1899 and from that first moment he was set to make an immediate impact as a forward of intense determination and zeal. Two seasons later in 1901 he was to commence his County career with Somerset and his fearsome reputation would now advance to wherever club and county played. 'Is Cashnella here?' was the question always asked wherever Bath travelled. Twenty years after his Rec' debut the same question was again asked when Bath played at Leicester in their first major game since the 1914-18 conflict and Cashnella, now some forty years of age, played his irrepressible part in a 3-16 triumph. If this was not enough to achieve in anyone's rugby life-time, Arnold Ridley adds that Cashnella *made his last appearance for the 'A' team [later United] at the age of 51.*"

Of course Frank Cashnella was a mere 'youngster' of barely thirty years when Bath prepared for season 1908-09, and any thoughts of beating the likes of Leicester (and away from home too) were then but a forlorn dream. Time was now running out and it was imperative for the club's long-term future that results improved and improved very soon. If not, then the day was approaching when major clubs might decide to drop Bath from their fixture lists (once and for all). So, when the likeable Arthur Ford was appointed captain for season 1908-09, this powerful forward now shouldered arguably the heaviest responsibility of any captain in the club's previous history.

The first hopeful sign of his captaincy was the sudden improvement in results, for Bath doubled the number of wins from the previous season's nine to an encouraging total of eighteen. Further satisfaction resulted from the selection of not only James Timmins for Somerset against the 1908-09 touring Australians, but the selection on the wing of Bath's Richard Ascott, a highly versatile back who was equally good at outside-half or centre. The match itself did not disappoint either, proving to be yet another encounter that demonstrated the prowess of the county game in the West Country. Indeed, led by England and Bridgwater Albion's Robert Dibble at forward, the quality of Somerset's performance was emphasised by the narrowness of their 0-8 defeat; only marginally less than the England's losing total of 3-9.

The following season was significant too, not so much for the fifteen wins and the unusually high total of nine draws, but more so for the twelve games lost from thirty-six played. At first glance this might seem a rather poor 'return.' But for Bath it was a much improved win-lose ratio, and in addition there was a noticeable drop in the number of heavy defeats. There was cause therefore for at least some optimism, and while the likes of powerful Pontypool were still able to show who was boss in Wales, Welsh sides did not always have things their own way on the Rec, as revealed by Bath home wins that included Abertillery (5-3), Penarth (16-0), exiles London Welsh (11-6) and Pontypool (6-0). Furthermore, Alfred Kitching was proving to be an outstanding asset on the Bath wing. *"This brilliant player"* was how The Bath Herald spoke of him in its introduction to the 1909-10 season, though the ever modest Kitching always insisted that much of his success was due to James Timmins at centre. *"I could wish no wing better good fortune than to have such a centre as I had in Timmins,"* remarked the ever modest Kitching.

Alfred Kitching ....first demonstrated his searing speed against Racing Club de France

Acknowledgements: Bath Chronicle

In addition to a strengthening back division, Bath were now to reap the benefit of a new and quite outstanding Penarth recruit to their forwards, namely W.H.Thomas (Billy), now based with the railway industry at Swindon. He too was poised to carve out a big reputation in England, and he was soon enough recommended to the Somerset selectors. His county debut on a chilly January day in 1910 could hardly have been a more demanding baptism, with a scintillating Gloucestershire side as opponents and the foreboding Kingsholm as a venue. Moreover, added to the difficulties for Thomas and his colleagues was Somerset's loss of their Bridgwater forward Walter 'rattler' Roman who had recently switched to the Northern Union. Both in psychological and physical terms this was a serious blow. The remedy however was to select W.H. Thomas as replacement. The Welshman did not disappoint.

In fact there were to be no fewer than six Bath players wearing Somerset colours on that January day, namely E.C. Hartell, A. Kitching, James Timmins and Alby Hatherill (backs), with E. Cambridge and W. H. Thomas playing at forward. Their mission furthermore was about as tough as it gets. Somehow Somerset had to overcome a Gloucestershire side literally hell-bent on reaching that season's County semi-final and then the final itself, and watching the action that day was the rugby journalist of the Morning Leader, whose comments were printed in the Bath Chronicle, 22nd January 1910. There was much that impressed him about West Country rugby: *"well trained, the Somerset and Gloucestershire eights went all the way with an abandon that one does not always see in the London district......the Somerset men, great big-boned fellows, were simply splendid for two-thirds of the match. One of them, Thomas, was irresistible.....just the sort of man who would be useful for England to play against Ireland."*

Regrettably for Bath followers, Welshman Billy Thomas did not play for England against Ireland. But he was selected for the 1910 British Isles touring-party to South Africa, alas an honour which owing to work commitments he was reluctantly compelled to decline. But, such tours at this period lasted for some four months duration, and for Billy Thomas this was four months too long. There was disappointment too for his Somerset colleagues in the outcome of that clash at Kingsholm. Gloucestershire clinched a 16-8 victory in front of an estimated five thousand crowd, and strode onwards to a semi-final win against Kent, prior to their capture of the coveted crown itself with an emphatic 23-0 triumph against Yorkshire. It was Gloucestershire's first County Championship title.....but by no means would it be their last! Bath too had reason to smile if only because their form, once so erratic and unpredictable, now appeared to stabilize. Furthermore their representation at county level (always a good indicator of form) now jumped to an impressive eleven Somerset players called-up for duty during the season; while a further indicator was the interest (sometimes successful) shown by certain professional Northern Union clubs as regards individual talent in the Bath ranks (see Chapter 5); albeit an interest that depleted Bath ranks somewhat.

Another feature of the season was the decision to adopt the colours with which they have long been associated. Originally the club had worn shirts of blue. However by season 1892-93 this had evolved into colours of dark blue and black hoops. Then there was yet another change in season 1906-07 when Bath adopted an all-white shirt. But once more these colours had failed to satisfy everybody. So it seems possible (indeed probable) that someone had a brain-wave and suggested that the club could combine all three previous colours, so resulting with a shirt which was duly described at the time as *"blue, white and black hoops."* This strip (with hoops more narrow than in the 1920's onwards) met with much approval. Indeed the favourable reaction was best expressed in the pages of The Bath Herald, (4th September, 1909) who positively drooled at the transformation: *"the new jerseys.....look wonderfully handsome,"* and no one, but no one, has ever questioned the club colours again.

By season 1911-12 the admirable James Timmins would soon be ready to hang up his boots from senior rugby football. But among those who would be donning those 'wonderfully handsome' jerseys were two newcomers whose prowess would soon enough be widely recognised too. Their names were Norman and Vincent Coates, brothers with previous experience at the Bridgwater club (merging with Bridgwater Albion in 1922) and who had arrived with their parents in the previous year to take up residence in Bath. Their impact on the Rec was immediate, and with the likes of

Vincent (Left) and Norman Coates

Kitching and Vincent Coates on the wings, Norman Coates at centre, and half-backs Alby Hatherill and F. Hill, Bath had never possessed such an abundance of quality 'outsides.' Indeed the luxury of a truly first-class back division at their disposal was the realisation of a dream for a club who so often in the past had struggled behind the scrum.

Furthermore this acquisition now opened up entirely new possibilities, and no one understood this more than Eddie Simpkins, a former student teacher at St. Luke's College, Exeter, who owing to injury had turned his considerable energies towards the administration side of the game. Now a master at Oldfield Boys School, Eddie Simpkins was imbued with a longing to see his beloved club both attain and then hold on to first-class rugby status; and his service to Bath that continued until 1957 would never falter from that time in 1911 when his secretarial partnership with John Townsend-Piper commenced. Many were their tasks, for the influence of the Rugby game was widening and the competition for places at the 'top table' was intensifying. It was little wonder therefore that among their priorities was the need to develop the strongest possible fixture-list. But did Bath even now have a team able to attract top opponents to join such a list? Well happily they did, even though barely five seasons previously their future had seemed so bleak. For a transformation was taking place, and with better results being achieved and more expansive rugby being played, Bath began to realistically look like a first-class club; or at the very least potentially first class. A long winter was turning into spring.

In the four seasons from 1910 to the conclusion of season 1913-14 the number of wins increased from 16, 20, 21 and then 22 victories respectively. Contrast these results with the seven wins of 1905-06 and the difference is striking, not least as the fixtures were now growing progressively stronger. Indeed the likes of Leicester, Llanelli, Coventry and Northampton were among those added to the Bath programme during this same 1910-14 period. The importance of captaincy too could not be over-stated and there would be three popular players holding this responsibility during these years of increasing improvement.

The church (and the match) on time.

First there was that excellent half-back Alby Hatherill (1910-11), followed by Norman Coates (1911-13) and finally Philip Hope, each stamping his authority and indeed his personality upon the club.

Acknowledgements: Bath Chronicle

Naturally rugby being rugby, affairs of the heart sometimes intervened, as indeed they did in the midst of Hatherill's captaincy when the 'small' matter of his marriage to Miss Sutton clashed with Bath's home game with Abertillery. A tricky problem this one; but not too tricky for Alby. His wedding at St. Paul's church took place in the morning. Come the afternoon he then made a dash to the Rec for the game. And no doubt receiving a rousing cheer from his troops who would surely have wondered if the skipper really would make it to the ground (hopefully sober), he proudly led his men onto the field against Abertillery. Just one slight problem skipper! Abertillery took home a two try win into Wales (Ouch!).

However, if it were not enough for a club to attain an ever improving fixture list and with it steadily improving results, the Somerset RFU now chose Bath as the venue for their encounter against the 1912-13 South African tourists, a decision surpassing any honour yet bestowed upon the club. This encounter against the tourists on Thursday, 3rd October 1912 was in fact the first match of the South African tour, the visitors due at Southampton (28th September) the previous weekend and then travelling by train direct to Bath. There (Chronicle, September 1912) they would meet a club determined to make the tourists feel 'at home.' A concert was arranged at the Roman Baths on the evening of their arrival; so too another evening at the Theatre Royal. The Rec was made available for the tourists' training programme; so too a visit to Longleat, the incomparably beautiful estate of the Marquis of Bath. A motor-car tour of the city was planned (cars even then something of a novelty); so too a further informal concert-party in the Georgian splendour of the Assembly Rooms; *"entertainments which were much appreciated by [the County] guests"* (70 years of Somerset Rugby, 1875-1945, p.28).

Four Bath men played for Somerset on that Autumn day of 3rd October, namely brothers Norman and Vincent Coates (backs), F. Hill (half-back) and W. F. Warde in the forwards, and although the Cidermen never lacked for endeavour, the visitors (winning 3-24) were yet another team to demonstrate the huge strides made by the Southern Hemisphere rugby nations, first emphasised by the 1905-6 New Zealanders. Bath much enjoyed hosting their esteemed guests however, and the tourists reciprocated by expressing their much felt appreciation of the welcome shown throughout their stay. Interestingly prior to their departure, the South Africans are reliably reported to have described the Rec as *"the most beautiful rugby ground in the world."* It was fascinating therefore that a rugby follower (Mr Vic Rosenburg) not only vividly remembered the occasion of the South Africans' visit in 1912, but six decades later (Bath chronicle, 26th October 1973) recounted his memories as follows: *"Sportsmen in Bath were delighted when Somerset's game with the Springboks was allotted to the Recreation Ground in October 1912. Before the 1914 War, only about a dozen counties competed for the county rugby championship and therefore each of them was given a fixture with rugby tourists from overseas. The Bath club had a powerful and versatile line of threequarters at this time consisting of the brothers Vincent and Norman Coates, J.T. Timmins and A.J. Kitching.*

Vincent Coates was a Cambridge Blue, a strong runner with a fearsome "hand-off." His brother Norman was a well-built centre with a safe pair of hands. Timmins, a local solicitor, was also a well-equipped and strong player. A.J. Kitching, a master at Monkton Combe School, was probably the most elusive runner to have played for Bath. He was a slim man of medium height, probably weighing ten stone plus. But what a runner! He was once likened to a hare as he weaved his way through an opposing XV. His defence was very good and he rarely failed to get his man.

It was generally expected that Somerset would choose the entire Bath threequarter-line for this Springbok game, but to the surprise and disappointment of every local supporter, Kitching was left out. The County selectors chose a wing named R.V. Knight (later killed in the 1914-18 War) who was then at the Wells Theological College, and who had played in the previous season for the East Midlands in the county championship. Knight was tall and well built with a mop of fair hair. It was thought his physique would enable him to deal more effectively with the powerful Springboks than the lighter Kitching, who, 61 years later is quietly living in retirement.

Fortunately the weather was dry and kind on the day. In those days the two teams changed in the cricket pavilion and then walked across the Rec to the rugby area. There was a wooden stand on a brick foundation and about 50 yards long running alongside the river bank, but otherwise there was no cover for spectators. The ticket enclosure for spectators began at the Johnston Street end and along the north bank and then parallel to the river. Temporary stands were erected along the north bank and down the popular side. And the crowds gathered six to eight deep around the ground. The Press were accommodated in the stand and everyone, Press and spectators, sat on long, hard wooden forms.

The Springboks, a mixture of British South Africans and Dutch South Africans, looked a physically strong and powerful XV, wearing green jerseys bearing a badge showing a golden "Springbok." They included three players named Morkel. G. Morkel played at full-back and could kick goals from any angle. The two Springbok wingers were J. Stegmann and E. McHardy, and Millar was the captain. The game produced many shining moments and as expected, the Springboks won. But reputations were made that day. Stegmann was reputed to be a "flier" but that day he met his master in Vincent Coates. Whenever Stegmann got the ball, he was floored by Coates. Whenever Coates had the ball he tore down the wing and usually handing off Stegmann as though the Springbok was a bag of flour.

The crowd roared and the English selectors then present selected Vincent Coates for all the international games played that season. The Somerset forwards, led by Dibble, a Bridgwater Albion player and current English international, harried the Springboks, but were finally worn down by the superior physique of the visitors. It was a great occasion. Bathonians were proud of their county that day."

As Vic Rosenburg related, Vincent Coates was a formidable winger, one who had risen fast in rugby ranks since his early schooling at Monkton Combe, then onwards to Haileybury and ISC, and later winning his Blue at Cambridge prior to completing his medical studies at Bristol University. It was thus hardly surprising that he subsequently played for England against South Africa (the tourists winning 3-9) and again in all four Home internationals. In fact his six tries in the Home Championship set a new record which ironically was bettered in only the following season by fellow England winger C.N. Lowe of Blackheath. A tale is told, and one that is quite possibly true, concerning the performance of Vincent Coates in England's win over Wales in Cardiff that season. The Bath wingman had got home with a typical Coates try of forceful power, causing the Welsh skipper to shout at his full-back: *"why didn't you stop him?" "Stop him!"* the full-back replied, *"why, it took me all the time to get out of his way."* Many a chastened opponent attempting to stop V.H.M. in full flight would have sympathised with the Welsh defender.

Barely three years later the qualities of Dr Vincent Coates would be displayed in another theatre of a rather different kind. But for now his surging runs on the wing, and the abilities too of his club colleagues, were reasons enough to bring a smile to Bath rugby. Indeed 1913-14, the season of twenty two wins (from 35 played) was arguably the most impressive in the club's history so far, and this in terms of both the quality of opposition that was faced and the over-all success that was achieved. Neither was a Bath defeat any longer a cause for a loss of confidence (as had happened in former years), but rather a cause to make amends the 'next-time.' So, Bath's first ever encounter with awesome Coventry (season 1912-13) was a salutary lesson, Bath losing away from home by 23-0. Their first ever encounter against Leicester (13th September 1913) was a further set-back with the Tigers' 19-5 victory at Welford Road. However, come the last quarter of the 1913-14 season and the home 9-0 win over Bristol, further confirmation of Bath's increasing prowess was revealed in their spring programme. At home strong Welsh opposition from Pontypool (5-0) and Penarth (9-8) had already been overcome, and now as Easter approached, the Bath Chronicle headlines beckoned the faithful to witness *"the opportunity of seeing on The Rec three of the finest teams in England,"* namely Coventry, Leicester and Gloucester. It could hardly get stronger than that!

It was Coventry who were encountered first during this Easter weekend of 'three of the finest teams in England,' that same Coventry who had convincingly defeated Bath in their first ever meeting in the previous season, and had furthermore defeated Bath again in February of the current season by 14-3; and where (Bath & Wilts Chronicle, 2nd March, 1914, p.4) matters had got somewhat out of hand either side of half-time: *"language was lurid, tackling hard, and throws into touch forcible. Then after Harry*

Vowles, Bath's young and highly talented scrum-half, was downed with altogether unnecessary violence, matters deteriorated yet further. There was a succession of loose scrums just after, fists were flying, boots swinging, and had the referee ordered off every man who struck a blow there would have been not many left to continue the match." Fortunately in terms of sportsmanship the Midlanders' visit to The Rec in April turned out to be different. There was good Easter cheer, an estimated crowd of 4,500 spectators (Bath & Wilts Chronicle, 14th April, 1914, p.4) and an impressively good outcome. Bath defeated Coventry by 41-10. Next it was Leicester on The Rec. and another inspiring result. Bath ran home four tries (one converted) to win 14-3. Then last, but by no means least, there was the visit of Gloucester.

Oh dear….it just 'had' to be Gloucester, whose Kingsholm fortress had already earned the notable accolade as 'the graveyard of Welsh reputations' (and not only Welsh reputations) could be just as lethal away from home. And yes, not for the first time the Cherry and Whites arrived with their own script. Bath played well. Gloucester played better, and they departed from Bath in jovial mood. With a 3-10 win under their belts they had reason to be. But there was one significant difference from years gone by. Because as Gloucester returned homewards they doubtless knew that now it was no small achievement to beat Bath, especially on the Rec. That was the difference, and it was a big one. For at long last the 'Big Guns' were taking Bath seriously.

As Bath's final game of their 1913-14 rugby campaign was an away encounter at Penarth (the Welshmen 'ungraciously' winning by 16-0) it was reported that the club would celebrate their season by way of an after-match dinner in Cardiff. There, in the congenial atmosphere around the dining table the conversation no doubt flowed as delightfully as did the food, ale and wine. The upset that day against old friends Penarth, who had lost 9-8 to Bath in February, would hardly have dampened Bathonian spirits however. For this was a season of some big, big wins among the twenty two victories, and that included a 5-0 success on the Rec in late March against Llanelli, who, taking no chances fielded a full strength side that included Welsh internationals the Rev. Alban Davies, Isaac Davies and W. Watts in their line-up.

So at long last there was reason to believe that Bath had climbed the proverbial steep and challenging slope since stepping into a new century some fourteen years previously. During this era the club had often experienced life in that fabled school of hard knocks. Yes, they had known deep and sometimes very deep, disappointment. But the experiences had taught them never, ever, to give up on their mission to build a first-class rugby team. And as Bath reportedly dined happily on that April evening in Cardiff to celebrate a sometimes inspiring season, they were a club whose long and sometimes hazardous 'rugby winter' had indeed turned into a rugby spring.

Chapter 10. THE SUMMER THAT NEVER CAME. (1914)

It was the 1st August 1914 and there, featured among the pages of Keene's Bath Journal was the forthcoming Bath fixture list for season 1914-15. It made for good reading, and local rugby followers would surely have been enthused by the prospects that lay ahead, thanks to a list that was arguably the most exciting and demanding that Bath had yet faced. The opening game was at Leicester, a team already rated among the finest in the Land, and yet such was the transformation at Bath over recent years that even this daunting encounter looked possibly winnable. Winnable at Leicester!! A few seasons previously such a suggestion would have seemed fantasy. But how times had changed for Bath in a few short years, and how times were about to change once again.

Because (as a direct result of the earlier assassination of Archduke Francis Ferdinand, heir to the Austria-Hungary throne, and his wife, on 28 June 1914), those same pages featured news of a rather different kind, both in tone and content: *German and Russian mobilization....Extraordinary Precautions,"* proclaimed one headline. Other ominous reports followed: *"Great precautions are being taken to protect Home defences and no vulnerable point is to be left exposed."* It was further stated that at *"the request of the government the Great Western Railway are specially guarding their bridges and telegraphs;"* moreover that *"there are over a dozen men employed in patrolling Box Tunnel,"* adding that *"in the vicinity of Bath men were yesterday to be seen on duty protecting the bridges."* Meanwhile the First Fleet (at anchorage off the Dorset coast during the summer days of 1914) was believed to have already set sail from Portland under the command of Admiral Sir G. Callaghan with sealed orders.

On Saturday the 8th August further ominous news filled the pages of Keene's Bath Journal (Britain having already declared war with Germany on the 4th August). The British cruiser HMS Amphion, striking a mine, was reported sunk on 7th August with the loss of 131 lives. Bath seaman W.C. Comley (gunner) was one of the survivors. Sadly, C.D.Gedge, the nephew of the Mayor of Bath, was not. He was the lone officer fatality in the crew. Meanwhile perhaps the one report most directly affecting Bath (and every sports club in the Country) was the statement reporting that on 6th August the sum of one hundred million pounds (an astronomical sum at that period) had already been granted by parliament, and with it the sanction of plans to increase the army by 500,000 men.

On 1st September the Bath committee, aware that duty would require the services of every sportsman in the Land to serve King and Country, met at the Red house. The mood was sombre. It was decided to cancel all fixtures until further notice. A telegram was dispatched to Leicester, stating that Bath (with deep reluctance) would not be fulfilling their away fixture on 5th September. It was furthermore decided that all club property would be stored at the Red House for the duration of the emergency. The committee, furthermore realising that the younger generation would now have a vital role to play in reviving the game at some future date, prepared accordingly. It was announced that the club would now unite with the Bath Schools Rugby Union so as to *"do everything in their power to train the lads at rugby."* Meanwhile the North Somerset Yeomanry were granted the use of The Rec for military purposes.

Each and every rugby club in the Land, at the bequest of the Rugby Union (Museum of Rugby, Twickenham) was acting in similar mode with members requested to 'join up' with the Forces, likewise the Football Association and the Football League. Soon enough the harsh realities of the events now unfolding on the Continent would strike at the very heart of these same sporting families, though their French cousins would feel the consequences first.

In early September it was learned that Sub-Lieutenant de Castelnau, among the best known rugby footballers in France and now serving under the command of his father, General de Castelnau, had been killed. And for Bath, one bleak day in November 1914, there was also news. It concerned former 1st team player Alfred Cleall, who had volunteered for service with the North Somerset Yeomanry. At Vlamertinghe on a Flanders Field, he had been killed in action. He was the club's first recorded fatality of the Great War. He would not be the last.

Alas, there would be no encounter at Leicester, indeed no rugby for four long dark years; and the summer for the hitherto most promising team in Bath's history would not arrive after all.

.

Chapter 11. A TIME FOR QUIET REFLECTION. (1914-18)

As the 'lights went out all over Europe' in the autumn of 1914 and Bath's season of such potential was so abruptly halted, a harsh reality had to be faced. Britain was now preparing for a conflict without parallel in its history, and no one could possibly predict when or how this conflict would end. Hence sport, not least Rugby Football, ceased completely at any official level, although not entirely at the unofficial level. For example, schools-rugby did continue; and with Dominion servicemen now stationed in the UK throughout much of the conflict, there were occasions when teams, not least those schools sides, did engage those hardened men from Australia and New Zealand.

But there was no normal club rugby activity, nor international rugby (Rugby Chronology, World Museum of Rugby, Twickenham). Hence, for those who followed Bath, be they at home or on 'The Front,' these were to be days for perhaps a quiet reflection upon the successes that might have been achieved, and doubtless upon those players now elsewhere who hopefully would return some distant day. Nonetheless for reasons that reached back to the early 1900's, there was at least some consolation thanks to certain developments instigated by a dedicated group of rugby followers, whose benefits in the fullness of time would prove invaluable to Bath's long term future.

Among such developments was a meeting of rugby enthusiasts (reportedly held on 24th November 1901), and attended by representatives from the junior clubs that included Walcot, Combe Down, Batheaston (now Avonvale), Oldfield Park and quite probably Fairfield Rovers respectively (see too Ch. 3). These were men with a mission, namely to form a rugby alliance of local clubs both in and around the city, and as a direct result of this meeting the Bath & District Rugby Combination would be launched. Bath as it happens were not the only city where such an idea had been discussed. In fact the concept had already caught on, or was catching on, elsewhere, and great rivals Bristol were forming just such a Combination during this same period.

Such a concept not only galvanised junior rugby activity, it furthermore yielded mutual advantages between the junior clubs and their senior partners. So in the case of the Bath Combination it was accepted that the senior club (namely Bath) could in normal circumstances acquire the use of a Combination player on condition that sufficient prior notification was given. How London clubs would surely have relished such an agreement, although the Chronicle & Herald (2nd January 1934) later reported that Richmond had established a somewhat similar arrangement with North London club Barnet RFC. But there was little doubt that there was a 'return' for the provider, because it was a virtual certainty that a Combination player on his return to his junior club would now be a better player for the experience gained at the senior level.

Bath as it happened were not exactly new to such arrangements, as Walcot would have testified. In the 1890's for example, Walcot had embarked on negotiations with Bath for partial use of the Kensington Meadows; and initially Bath had held out for an annual rent of £5 (small change now, but not in fact then), and in addition a right to claim up to five Walcot players (yes five!) each week. Happily commonsense and a friendship between the two clubs intervened, and as a result Walcot's request was subsequently reduced to £3 per annum, and Bath were limited to a far more 'civilised' Friday night deadline for two (not five) Walcot players.

However, as these not untypical negotiations with Walcot indicated, Bath's chief priority at this stage was not one of financial gain, but instead the need to widen their pool of players. Indeed in the 1900's recruitment was critical for any club hoping to establish itself among the top rank, as was only too evident when considering that during the next two decades the leading London clubs such as Richmond could reportedly utilise a sizeable 'pool' of some 200-250 players at any one time. On the other hand a sizeable player-pool could be attained if clubs formed an alliance, and a Combination was precisely such an alliance. It was significant furthermore that some players on receiving the call-up to the Rec (Robbie Lye in the 1970's-80's for example) would subsequently remain in Bath colours for the remainder of their rugby careers, so perfectly did they adapt to senior rugby. It should be added though that in the goodness of time the Combination members grew into fully constituted clubs in their own right, with healthy fixture-lists, their own sometimes impressive facilities and club-houses. Not surprisingly they did not wish to be regarded solely as a rugby-nursery for the Bath club. Indeed theirs was a thriving rugby culture in its own right,

Early records are not always precise, nor always clearly referenced. But written reports exist and it is hoped will be archived accordingly, perhaps with the Bath Past Players records. What is certain however is that in the early 1900's Oldfield Park (not to be confused with Oldfield Old Boys) won no fewer than three from four League Championships, with Walcot winning another. Furthermore an historically valuable photo of the Oldfield Park club, *"1901-2 Bath Rugby Champions,"* remains, indicating that the Combination itself and its League Championship competition commenced from the 1901-2 season. A perfect example of the sheer passion of the Combination competition was witnessed decades later in season 1983-4. Appropriately staged on The Rec on a balmy spring evening and watched by some 3,000 followers, Glyn Broom of Old Culverhaysians would get the clincher with a massive late penalty to beat Combe Down by 3 points to nil in a quite pulsating encounter.

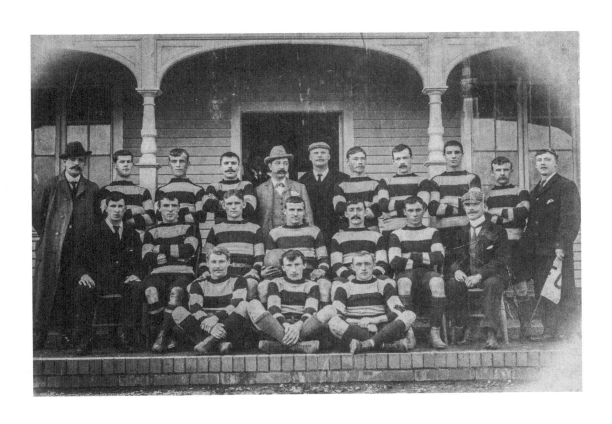

OLDFIELD PARK RUGBY FOOTBALL CLUB
1901-2 Bath Rugby Champions

Acknowledgements to Ben Hartley (former Bath RFC player)

Such events form just one part of the legacy of those pioneers who founded this vibrant hotbed of local rugby activity. For this alliance developed into a rugby family destined to flourish, a family of sometimes 18 plus clubs among its membership and capable of reportedly attracting crowds of three thousand plus to watch the likes of Walcot confronting their great rivals Combe Down during the 1920's and 1930's. It was (is) 'some' family too, that has in addition included 'Avonvale, Bath Civil Service, Bath Harlequins, Bradford on Avon, Corsham, Frome, Keynsham, Melksham, Midsomer Norton, O Culverhaysians, O Edwardians, Oldfield Park, Oldfield Old Boys, O Sulians and Stothert & Pitt's.'

Meanwhile a century onwards from that inaugural November meeting of 1901 upon which the Combination was founded, their successors would gather for the Centenary in the splendour of the Guildhall on 30th November 2001. That great servant of Bath rugby, namely Gerry Moore (Walcot), would be among those attending, and likewise Bath mayor Cllr Marian McNeir. Present too was no less a guest than the President of the RFU himself, Roy Manock, who spoke of the Combination (and indeed of junior rugby in general) as a part of *"the foundation on which the game stands."* True words indeed, for the Combination, despite many difficulties encounted by its members, not least financial, has always remained a bed-rock for local rugby and the Bath club itself, usually willing (sometimes at a moment's notice) to release players; aware moreover that a player called-up for senior duty might never return to his respective Combination club; yet always delighted to welcome home such a player if and when he finally returns.

However three years onwards from the launch of the Combination another foundation stone was laid, on this occasion the inspiration of a group of local Bathonian (many of them Welsh) schoolmasters. They gathered at Northgate Chambers on 16th February 1904, agreeing forthwith to found the Bath Schools Rugby Union (launched in season 1905-6) so as *"to foster the playing of the game among the schoolboys of the city."* Almost immediately this innovative body was endorsed by the Bath Football Club, who anxious to encourage a strategy of long term rugby development in the city, chose to underwrite the initial costs of this fledgling Union. Enthusiasm abounded from the outset, and would include among its members Oldfield Council, Widcombe, St Pauls, Weymouth House, Bath Forum, St Stephens, Batheaston and Walcot School.

Almost immediately a Schools League Cup competition was established, and with it a trophy duly donated by the supportive Egbert Lewis, a local JP and the Bath Schools Rugby Union's first president.

One school however would initially shine above them all, namely the East Twerton Council School, which in the 1900's would soon enough earn a formidable reputation. Playing in colours of black and red hoops and coached by the dedicated Mr R. R. Stephenson, they won every game of the League Cup competition launched in season 1905-6 without conceding so much as a single point. They played fourteen matches and they won fourteen matches. They scored 441 points and they did not conceded a single one. They topped the League with maximum points, and so became the first-ever winners of that much coveted Cup trophy. Furthermore within the first three years of the Bath Schools RFU the East Twerton School (which almost a century later in 1999 would become the Oldfield Park Infants School) had produced two schools internationals in forward C. Parsons and half-back Harry Vowles; while in the Schools Trial at Coventry of 1906-7 there were no less than four East Twerton Council School pupils playing, namely Hingston, Brice, Love, and that youngster Harry Vowles, of whom much more would later be heard.

Nonetheless Bath were not alone in their enthusiasm for the development of schoolboy rugby football. The Leicester & District Schools Union for example was formed during this same period, and it was to be their own enlightened Hon.Secretary (J.C.Cooper) who was prominent among other supportive clubs (which included Bath, Bristol, Gloucester and Exeter) to establish The Schools Rugby Union, itself a national body with the aim of advancing schools rugby football throughout the whole Country.

Yet as Bath realised, further work remained, because for many pupils (the standard State School leaving-age being fourteen years until the 1940's) their rugby progress halted abruptly when their schooldays ended. Moreover, in an era whereby few (if any) clubs had yet formed a Colts or Youth team, this could entail a long wait before a young player was able to join a club such as Bath. Of course in those bleak years of 1914-18 no one could envisage if or when this drawback might be overcome. But two decades onwards, thanks partly to the dedication of club stalwart Harry Slade, the Bath Ex-schools XV would be established in 1934, a team partly influenced by Cardiff's already established system of post-schools rugby development. There remained however the crucial sixteen to eighteen years group, and fully aware of the need to rectify this omission, Bath promptly formed the Colts team in the season following the establishment of the Ex Schools side.

So the 'bridge building' was complete. There was now a direct route from schoolboy rugby to senior rugby, and the framework for this system originated from the efforts of that small and enlightened group of local school-teachers, whose foresight back in 1904 ensured that no barriers would prevent even the youngest of players from one day reaching the Rec. But…..a decade onwards from that launch in 1904, the epic conflict of 1914-18 had intervened, and during those often desperate days one could merely reflect upon the possibility of a future for the Bath Schools RFU, the Bath Combination, and indeed the entire Bath rugby family.

Chapter 12. THE GREATEST DAY IN HISTORY. (11th Nov 1918)

On Saturday, 16th November, 1918, the front page headline of the Bath Weekly Chronicle spoke in effect a million words: *"The Greatest Day in History."* On the same front page was a photograph of the Abbey churchyard now thronged with joyous people. Beneath were the following words:

"Monday, when the news arrived that the Armistice had been signed and that the "ceasefire" had sounded along the whole of our far-flung battle-line, has been described as the "greatest day in history." It was celebrated in Bath with an unprecedented outburst of rejoicing, and the inhabitants thronged to the Abbey to render thanksgiving to the Great Disposer of Events for the happy news the day had brought. So general was the desire to participate in such a memorable service that the Abbey was filled a few minutes after the doors were opened, and the Abbey Churchyard, as our photograph shows, was crowded with people unable to gain admission. The Mayor and Corporation attended in State."

So it was that Bath, and countless other towns, villages and cities around the Country, stepped back into the 'daylight.' As for rugby football however (and the sporting world generally), their playing ranks were now sadly depleted. Hence it remained to be seen exactly when any form of official rugby might be restored. Yet no doubt to the surprise of many, Bath had tentatively launched their own initial post-war rugby game (a trial match) as early as Saturday, 15th February 1919. The venue appropriately was The Rec, Bath's spiritual rugby home, a ground that during the conflict had been requisitioned for use by the Armed Forces and vacated by the RAF (prior to April 1918 known as the Royal Flying Corps) only in the previous week. But be it that this would be an occasion for fresh hopes and a new beginning, there were recent memories that had yet to heal.

Such sentiments moreover found expression in the sporting columns of the Bath Chronicle reporting on the trial game, and few stones were left unturned: *"included in the teams turning out for the Bath Football 'trial' were many who have suffered torturing wounds, and others who have tasted the cruelties of Hun internment camps, while the committeemen looking on to select the wherewithal for "reconstruction" mourn two gallant colleagues blown to atoms or buried by German shells, for their fate had never been actually known."*

In fact there were to be rather more than 'two' gallant colleagues who would alas not be returning from the Front, among them Bath's Alf Cleall, Loo Hatherill, Tom West (Rifle Corps), Douglas West (Manchester Regiment), lieutenant-Colonel Gustavus Perreau (Indian Army) and not forgetting sub-Lieutenant Frederick Hill who as a half-back won schoolboy international honours in 1905-6. Furthermore there were the twelve fatalities suffered by the former Widcombe Juniors, who partly as a result of their terrible loss would never recover and from whose ranks many a Bath player had previously come (Bath & Wilts Chronicle, 5th September, 1919). Mercifully there were those former players (thankfully reasonably unscathed) yet to return from war-time action, but whose availability nonetheless remained uncertain. Captain Vincent Coates for example (decorated with the Military Cross for gallantry in France, later posted to the Balkan Forces for research as a bacteriologist and then transferred to the Croydon Military Hospital) and who would not arrive home until the Autumn of 1919, but who if fit could add inspiration both on (and off) the field. Fortunately others (and not forgetting new arrivals) were available to step onto a rugby field once again, there to feel after four long years the sheer elation and calm of freedom.

At this same period the Bath Chronicle (15th February 1919) reported that among the guests residing at Bath's Empire Hotel (later the Admiralty building) that overlooked the Rec and perhaps casting a watchful eye, was no less an icon than Rudyard Kipling; and as befits an author of the exploits (inter alia) of British soldiery, he doubtless would have understood the poignancy of this particular encounter....Bath v Bristol, two rivals, but two rivals sharing a unique bond, not least in the aftermath of the shattering events of the previous four years.

For the Bristolians too had suffered grievously in the recent conflict. Indeed it is recorded that they had lost no less than fourteen players killed in action. In fact so severe was this depletion that the club did not play as Bristol for fully another season, and instead played as Bristol United (their reserve team's title). Nonetheless in Bath's first inter-club game since World War 1, played on the Rec on 22nd February 1919, there could be no more worthy opponents. The result (Bath won 8-3) was really of secondary importance. What did matter was the fact that one's thoughts were no longer of deep and muddied trenches in places far away, but instead of a regained liberty to play rugby on the playing fields of England. Other fixtures duly followed, including Bath versus a New Zealand Services side (lost 3-13), a further upset in front of a large Rec crowd against Abertillery (lost 0-14), and an end-of-season home victory against old adversaries Pontypool (8-4), again attracting a large and enthusiastic attendance.

There was one further victory for followers of rugby to cherish, namely the fact that within barely three months since the Armistice the rugby game was active, in some form at least, across much of the British Isles. While in Bath's concluding match against the hard men of Pontypool, the club were to witness the first appearance of a young outside-half by the name of S.G.U. Considine. In his late teens and still at Blundell's School, reports of his rugby prowess had nonetheless reached the Rec. He looked a smart little player of exciting promise did this young S.G.U., and around his later partnership with scrum-half Harry Vowles (now returned from four years military service in France) a 'special' team was to be forged; and notwithstanding that few if any would have been advised to raise their expectations too soon, halcyon days now beckoned.

Chapter 13. THE RESTORATION. (1919-1920)

On the evening of Tuesday, 26th August, 1919, members of the Bath Football Club gathered at the Red House, there to attend the 'after-the-war-dinner.' Originally planned to celebrate Bath's Golden Jubilee in season 1914-15, this was an occasion long delayed. Now however it was time perhaps to smile again and the mayor, who submitted the toast at this emotional gathering, commented to the assembled party that *"they little thought that this time twelve months ago they would see such a revival of sport this year."* But a revival there was, and on this occasion there was opportunity for speeches, for music and of course song. Mr W.E. Angell was at the piano and the delightful presence too of Miss Appennea Roberts and Miss Lily Morgan added singing and charm to the happy occasion; while among those present was a certain Mr T.J. Gandy, no less than one of the original founder members of the club (Bath Centenary Book, pp. 25-26).

Maybe the conversation amongst the gathering included reference to the brothers James and Christian Pitman of Bath (grandsons of the late Sir Isaac Pitman). Still at Eton, their prowess was now attracting serious comment among sporting journalists and athletic journals. Both outstanding middle distance runners, hurdlers and sprinters, James Pitman had won the 880 yards event at the 1918 Public Schools Championships. But rather less was known about his rugby potential. Small wonder, because Eton was a soccer school, although soon enough any doubts as to whether young James might have a future in rugby football were cast aside.....and in some style too (Bath Chronicle, 5th April 1919, p.1).

Almost certainly news of another Bathonian, one Arnold Ridley, was discussed. The one-time school teacher and graduate of the Bristol University Dramatic Society was earning commendable reviews that year with the Birmingham Repertory Theatre, and like so many of his generation he too had a tale to tell. Serving with the 6th Somersets, he was reportedly engaged in a deadly hand-to-hand encounter with a German soldier near Delville Wood during the Somme offensive of 1916. It was here that a resulting bayonet wound would cause a long term handicap to his left arm, and a wound moreover that would require much skilful make-up whenever Arnold 'trod the stage.' But the kindly actor was already laying the foundations for a notable theatrical career that would span five decades and include the stage success of his own creation 'The Ghost Train' (he wrote over 30 other plays) and not forgetting his appointment as club president of Bath (1950-52), nor later the national acclaim for his role in 'Dad's Army,' the much loved World War Two television comedy series, and furthermore his award of an OBE in 1982 two years before he passed away at 88 years of age (see too: review of *Godfrey's Ghost; From Father to Son, by Nicholas Ridley*), Bath Chronicle, 24th September 2009.

Undoubtedly discussions would have included the all-important topic of the future of the club, and the crucial question as to whether or not the momentum of that fine pre-war team could be continued despite the four years curtailment of rugby football. Because it was by no means forgotten that Bath had once experienced the deeply worrying lean years of the early 1900's, a time still so vividly instilled into memory that as late as the 1960's the likes of Arnold Ridley recalled that the club came close to folding completely. So now only those hastily arranged matches in the spring of 1919 provided any clues as to Bath's future prospects. While lying in wait for them in their opening game of season 1919-20 was one of the greatest names in rugby.....Leicester!

Happily, there were no worries regarding the use of the Rec. A further ten year lease had been agreed with the Recreation Ground Company, partly because Bath had been 'good paying tenants ever since the Company was formed.' Finances too had been helped if only marginally by those matches played in the previous spring, though to the club's regret it was financially imperative to increase season tickets from six shillings annually to twelve shillings (men), and five shillings for ladies. Today such prices appear a virtual give-away, but such was not the case in those post-war straightened times. Fixtures too required a revamp, as not every club had yet recovered from the effects of the War. Hence to fulfil Bath's season of 1919-20 no fewer than four games with Bristol were arranged and a number of less-known opponents were added, including Paignton and Burnham.

Stability too was a priority, and hence the decision to offer the captaincy (and his subsequent acceptance) to winger Philip Hope. Meanwhile new faces in the backs appeared, among them centre Harry Richardson, the athletic utility back Clarence Whittaker, and young wingman Tom Fry, nephew of 'Tich' Fry who had so delighted Bath crowds in the 1890's. In addition there was the potential brilliance of half-backs Harry Vowles and Blundell's schoolboy S.G.U. Considine. They looked another promising 'bunch' did this lot! But the question was: could they blend into an effective back-division? As yet any answer was guesswork only. Meanwhile at forward it was decided that W.H.Royal (an Old Monktonian) would lead the pack, and finally there was the one man whom Philip Hope (and others) still felt was indispensable. That man was Frank Cashnella, now forty years of age, yet often worth points on the score-board just by 'being there.' After all Bath, notwithstanding possessing some players of proven experience (including forward Fred Russell) were pinning their hopes on a number of untried newcomers.

So to Leicester on the 6th September 1919, and striding out at Welford Road not only to the accompaniment from a local band playing 'Should auld acquaintance be forgot,' but furthermore the applause of a reported ten thousand crowd, the following Bath team (no less then eleven Bath born) braced itself for one of the truly iconic encounters in the club's entire history: *C. Whittaker, P.P. Hope (Capt.), A. Hope, H. Richardson, T.*

61

Fry, S.G.U.Considine, H. Vowles, W.H. Royal, W. Worger, E. Hodges, F. Russell, W. Harding, J. Pope, L. Richardson, F.J. Cashnella.

Of course only an exceptional performance would ever win against the Tigers on their home territory. But Bath did not just win, they triumphed 3-16 thanks to four tries (two converted) against Leicester's one. Skipper Philip Hope clinched two touchdowns, his second an absolute gem launched from his interception inside Bath's 25 yard line to scream off for a scorcher that no defender could stop. New boy Tom Fry then caught a cross kick to jink over for another, before Cashnella (who else?) crashed through some three opponents to bludgeon over the line, dropping the ball but enabling Harding to touch down for Bath.

Subsequently described by the Bath & Wilts Chronicle (6th September 1919) as *"a finer result than ever before recorded in the Club's long history,"* this was no ordinary success. Moreover, the fact that two weeks later Leicester would defeat Coventry 39-3 simply confirmed the sheer scale of the Bath achievement. It assured for the club a self-belief in their abilities, and it is no exaggeration to say that its long-term effect would help inspire the finest Bath team yet seen.

It was hardly surprising therefore that the train journey home from the East Midlands was quite an occasion for a jubilant Bath team, whose spirits were not to be dampened either by an unexpected three hour delay at Didcot. Now Didcot has never claimed to be anyone's answer to Paris. Nonetheless, by a happy coincidence a travelling fair just happened to be encamped nearby, and to that same fair the Bath team not surprisingly now made tracks. With commendable understatement the Chronicle (13th September 1919) commented upon this same opportune visit: *"there was more fun at that fair than its proprietors could ever have contemplated."* Boy, it makes one absolutely green with envy not to have been there.

Yet in all seriousness something almost spiritual was happening that day (and night). The War was over. Leicester had been beaten at Welford Road. The Bath team were bonding again, and each and everyone was soaking up the atmosphere that only a sense of a renewed post-war freedom could bring. So it was that amid the carnival atmosphere of a travelling fair at Didcot a somewhat tired yet truly joyous rugby team were experiencing one of the most enchanting days in Bath rugby history.

But there remained as yet other bridges to cross, and any accurate assessment of the future could not be made until the club had completed a full season at the very least. Meanwhile, although the outstanding Norman Coates would be joining Leicester, the November return of his brother Dr Vincent Coates to establish a practice at number 10, The Circus, had aroused hopes that he might resume his career on the Rec. He did, but initially infrequently. Autumn then passed into winter, and Bath with narrow upsets at Llanelli (6-3) and then Abertillery (3-0) showed yet again that they could on occasions get close to winning in Wales, but still not get close enough. But in the run-up to

Christmas, Hope's team completed the first half of the season with a 9-0 home victory against Cheltenham prior to hosting a thoroughly enjoyable six-try Boxing Day romp with a 15-5 win against Glasgow University. So it was that the second half of the season appeared to hold further promise.

To no small degree it did, but not before another tragedy had struck! Once again, memories of a grievous injury would haunt the Rec, where twenty seasons previously

Clifford Walwin
'Tragedy on the Rec.'
Acknowledgment : Bath Past Players

Bath and the Portsmouth club were confronted with the numbing experience of the fatal injury to the visitor's vice-captain George Trerise. Now, with the visit of Welsh side Cross-Keys on 27th December 1919, those same memories would return with a vengeance, when midway through the second half of this Christmas holiday game George Greenslade of Cross Keys tackled Bath utility back Clifford Walwin. A violent collision resulted and both men fell unconscious. Walwin, after initial attention from the St. John's Ambulance Brigade, returned by taxi to his Lambridge home accompanied by his wife who had been watching the game. But soon enough (Chronicle, 3rd January 1920) it was learned that Clifford Walwin had suffered a serious injury.

On the following Monday fuller details would be described at the inquest requested by the Bath City Coroner. It was stated (inter alia) that the injured Clifford Walwin, shortly after arriving at his home was then attended professionally by Dr James Lindsay. He instructed that the injured player be taken immediately to a nearby nursing home, whereupon Mr Forbes Fraser (in consultation with Dr Lindsay) decided that an operation was now necessary. By 9pm, with surgery now completed, witnesses were able to speak to Clifford, and it was stated that they were hopeful of a recovery. But as the inquest would later learn: *"About five minutes to mid-night he simply collapsed."* Then, five minutes after mid-night, Clifford Walwin, 29 years of age, died suddenly. To many, it must have seemed that 'only yesterday' a similar incident had cast its shadow over the Rec with the fatal injury to George Trerise. But, numbing tragedy had struck once again.

The feeling of sadness throughout the club was palpable. Born in Gloucester and educated at the Crypt School, he had played with distinction for Bath as early as season 1911-12 under the captaincy of Norman Coates, who ironically (as a guest player) was co-centre with Walwin in the fateful game with Cross Keys. Walwin (a trained pharmacist with a Bath practice) was a player good enough in fact to have represented Somerset against Devon and Middlesex respectively in 1914. The War then followed (in which Clifford lost a younger brother) and he joined the Somerset 35 Red Cross Voluntary Aid detachment. He had married Hilda Blake, a well-known Bath soprano, on 4th October 1914 at the Walcot Wesleyan church, and they would later have a daughter, who was two and half years old at the time of the tragedy. An indication of the deepest affection he attracted was shown by the packed church on the day of his funeral, held on the Wednesday after the accident; it was shown by the words of the Rev. A. G. Tuck (the officiating minister at that service) who spoke of his grief when he heard of the tragedy; it was revealed again by *"a great crowd"* who assembled outside that same church to show its respects; and not least by the words of The Bath Chronicle in describing Clifford Walwin thus: *"……….there was no man who has ever donned the Bath jersey who was more generally beloved."*

It is absolutely essential to add that the Coroner jury were unanimous in finding that this had been a case of accidental death and that the Cross Keys player was exonerated from all blame. Indeed, Bath regarded Cross Keys as the cleanest side in Wales, and the referee (schoolmaster George Hancock from Bristol) stated to the inquest that *"the game was peculiarly free from anything like rough play."* Just such sentiments were readily supported by Bath official Mr W.F. Long; while Mr William Edwards (secretary, Cross Keys F.C.) spoke of the deep sympathies of the Welsh club for both Bath and the bereaved relatives. Nor should it be forgotten that George Greenslade too had been seriously injured in the collision and it was later reported that he himself did not recover for at least another two seasons. Hence there was no animosity whatsoever between the two clubs, and it was former Gloucester and England half-back D.R. Gent, who as a correspondent for the Sunday Times (and reported in the Chronicle, 5th January 1920) would express just how widespread was the resulting sense of loss with the following eulogy: *"I knew Walwin (an old Gloucester boy by the way) well, both as a player and a man. A more genuine sportsman never played for Bath or any other club. He was not quite a first-class player but he was a first-class sportsman, a man the club could always rely upon to turn out, even at the last minute, and every minute of the game he was heart and soul for his side. What admirable fellows these are: always at their club's disposal, consistently good in their play, and ever clean in their tactics. They are to be found in every club – its backbone, really. They do not get the plaudits of the crowd or Press, like the "stars," but their worth is appreciated by players, officials, and all who understand the stuff of which the torch-bearers of the traditions of Rugby are made. Of such was Walwin."* Come the following Saturday and the Rec was silent, the club withdrawing from all rugby activity. Bath hockey players did likewise and a sorrow hung over the sporting heart of the city.

But….the next encounter following the tragedy was at Gloucester, among the key games of this and every other season for Bath. That Bath lost heavily by 24-0 was in the circumstances understandable, a situation not entirely helped by the fact that the team were weakened through call-ups for Somerset on the same day. Yet Bath 'would' recover, as their performances would soon enough show, while reliable reports that scouts from Leeds (Northern Union) were watching certain Bath players with more than a passing interest was evidence of the talent down on the Rec.

Certain results however of the 1919-20 season revealed some of the puzzling traits that characterised the club for years to come. For example, Bath encountered Bristol on four occasions, winning but once, albeit a notable away success by 9-19. Interestingly this 3:1 ratio in Bristol's favour would remain a reasonably reliable guide to Bath-Bristol games for the foreseeable future. Meanwhile the magnificent victory at Leicester would reveal another Bath trait, namely their ability to reach the heights, only then to rest on their laurels and let 'smaller fish slip through the net.' For instance, although Bath gained a narrow late-season away victory at un-fancied Paignton, the Devonians had earlier narrowly beaten Bath (victors at Leicester) with a shock win on the Rec. And, it was inconsistency such as this that made it unusually difficult to decide exactly where the club stood in the first-class hierarchy of English rugby, a level Bath arguably attained from season 1911-12 onwards, and posing a question moreover that would remain unanswered for literally decades.

Yet the fact is that the over-all performance of the 1919-20 side, one with huge expectations thrust upon its shoulders, was sufficient to indicate that the club was again capable of survival at the first-class level. Admittedly 15 games were lost and 4 drawn. Yet there were 21 victories from 40 played (the Centenary Book quotes 20 wins from 39 played), and the successes included London Irish (37-8), Leicester again (8-16) and finally London Welsh (18-0). Thus this crucial season upon which so much would depend could hardly have started better, nor have ended better. Indeed Bath it seemed had accomplished their mission, namely to put together the broken pieces resulting from the Great War and so re-build a firm foundation for a future in first-class rugby. That they would soon field the most exciting and mature team yet seen in Bath colours was in no small measure a result of Hope's 1919-20 side.

Thus....the Restoration had begun!

Chapter 14. 1922-3....WHEN BATH CAME OF AGE.

Looking back through the previous decades of rugby it was the season of 1922-3 under captain Harry Vowles (and thanks not least to the legacy of his predecessor Philip Hope) that could be described as that year when 'Bath came of age.' Claims such as these are of course subjective, and the Philip Hope teams either side of the Great War must also come very much into the reckoning. So, how come that it was the succeeding Vowles side that arguably raised it to so high a status? The short answer is 'glamour.' But the full answer is rather longer to explain.

First, the team was built around the outstanding (and sometimes brilliant) half-back partnership of scrum-half Harry Vowles and S.G.U. Considine. Secondly, talented players were in abundance, not least the brothers Joe Richardson (forwards) and Harry Richardson (backs). Third, the club itself no longer felt itself a stranger amid the first-class ranks of the game; it had grown in self-belief (spread its wings so to speak); while the 11-3 victory (admittedly at home) over Stade Bordelais in April of the previous season would have provided another confidence boost. And what a previous season that had been, with 25 wins to its credit! That was the best yet. Now the challenge was to beat it.

In actual fact Bath's introduction to the 1922-3 season included away defeats at Leicester (16-8) and Gloucester (17-5) respectively. But later in the month (Bath Herald, 23rd September, 1922) *"W.J.A, Davies, England's premier rugby exponent, brought his famous side of United Services [Portsmouth] to Bath,"* a club that for decades would rank high among first-class rugby circles. They produced legions of county players and not a few internationals that during this era included the acclaimed England half-back partnership of scrum-half C. A. Kershaw and W.J. A. Davies, although Kershaw's late withdrawal that day was doubtless a deep disappointment to a reported four thousand plus crowd. Meanwhile, a small group of gentlemen was present among that same crowd, men particularly interested in this Bath team and with a mission to find a Somerset side capable at long last of capturing the then Holy Grail of English rugby......the County Championship.

Their presence was therefore hardly surprising, as Bath by now were possibly the strongest team in the West Country apart from Bristol and Gloucester (and near their equals too), and so possessed a number of potential candidates for the county team, not least their backs. These included wingers James Pitman (also a Harlequin, Oxford Blue and by now England) and W.J. Gibbs (already a Warwickshire county back), L.V. Burt, G.Woodward, Bert Morgan and Harry Richardson; likewise the ever-improving Bert Comm (later signing professional) at full-back and the brilliant half-backs of Vowles and Considine. Another factor of significance was that during this era Bath had adopted the 'five-eighth game,' originally a New Zealand formation that had found favour with certain clubs in the British Isles in the early 1920's and involved playing a seven man pack (rather than eight) and a back-division of eight rather than seven. This extra back played as an additional outside-half, and is a tactic not entirely unknown even in the 21st century (for brief periods of a game admittedly) when an attacking team close to their opponent's try line calculates that seven forwards are sufficiently strong to feed their backs now strengthened with an extra player.

The Vowles Team was always a team of excitement, win or lose

L to R Back Row (standing): W.T. Davis (Touch Judge), F.J. Cashnella (Committee), L.J. Richardson, L.W. Bisgrove, W.H. Sheppard, J. Dobson, C.C. Wills (Vice-Chairman), R.S. Chaddock, J.T. Piper (Hon. Sec.), C.E. Carruthers, C.Mannings, E.F. Simpkins (Hon. Sec), A. Hatherill (Trainer). Middle Row (Sitting): H.J. Comm, H. Richardson, G. Woodward, H. Vowles (Captain), Dr. F.A. Meine, W.J. Gibbs, G.A. Roberts (Hon. Treas.). In front: L.V. Burt and S.G.U. Considine.

For the Somerset selectors Bath's 5-8th experience in the 1920's could prove useful, even crucial, should the county find itself facing opposition applying this same tactic. And crucial it would later prove to be. Meanwhile the 9-4 win against US Portsmouth was to be Bath's first major win of a memorable season that included victories against 'big guns' such as Aberavon (18-3) in October, a match that witnessed an 80 yard dash by England wing James Pitman for a try so spectacular that it raised a roar from the Rec that was reportedly heard on the Odd Down golf links two miles away (Herald, 14th October, 1922). This outstanding athlete would likely have scored many more but for the curse of a leg fracture that would shortly halt Pitman's rugby for the remainder of the season. But, injuries are an accepted occupational risk in rugby, and Bath, likewise other clubs in similar situations, must simply 'get on with it.' They did and marched onwards and for the most part upwards. Further high profile victories duly followed, including home wins over London Welsh (20-0), Cross-Keys (4-3), while in December the notable 9-6 victory over Gloucester was the latter's first defeat by English opponents that season.

Acknowledgements to Bath Chronicle
April 1925 (Football Herald) Bath 18 vs U.S Portsmouth 10.
C. Mannings scores. Note original seated West Stand.

Arousing equal excitement was the red hot form produced by Somerset in the County Championship, a competition won by Gloucestershire for the past three years, and a Gloucestershire side determined to increase that total to four years; a team moreover primarily selected around the formidable Bristol and Gloucester duo, though not forgetting the talent to be found in the ranks at Cheltenham, Clifton and to a lesser extent Lydney. Somerset sides by contrast were chosen from a rugby parish stretching from Bath in the East to Wellington and Wiveliscombe in the West, while mid-way between the two were Weston-super-Mare, Bridgwater and Taunton. Just occasionally Bristol and Clifton players qualified too, and not surprisingly it was as a result of this more scattered rugby community that Somerset selection tended to be less straightforward than that of their Gloucestershire neighbours.

But it was Bath's ever increasing experience at the first-class level that was partly to prove so valuable, a fact confirmed by an unprecedented ten Bath players representing the county during that season. Meanwhile the combined effect of typically strong Somerset forwards and the class that existed outside the pack was evident from the outset as Somerset blazed a trail through the South West division with wins over Cornwall (21-7) at Bridgwater, Gloucestershire (10-8) at Bridgwater again, and a 0-14 victory over Devon at Torquay watched by a reported seven thousand crowd. All then

68

was set in mid-February for a semi-final dual against Kent, former County Champions themselves and equally blessed with ability outside the scrum. Thus Taunton (17th February) was the venue for a game so packed with a reported nine thousand crowd that not surprisingly many had serious difficulty in viewing events on the field of play. Kent ran home a Jacob try converted by McLennan. Somerset replied with three tries (Reg Quick, J. Reed and F. Spriggs) and added a penalty by W. Gaisford, sufficient for a 12-5 victory that opened the gates to the County Championship final. The Cidermen now stood one step away from a previously unattained dream. But it would be the hardest step of all.

Bath meanwhile continued to enhance their reputation with a string of high profile victories that included home successes over Plymouth Albion, Pontypool and Blackheath, all then formidable opposition; and likewise a narrow 5-4 win over Devonport Services who provided no less than four players in that season's final England Trial, of whom both fullback F.G.Gilbert and forward William Luddington would be selected for England. Among this list of eye-catching victories there was to be a deeply satisfying away success against Oxford University (28th February, 1923), and it was realised from the outset that if the Dark Blues were to be beaten then it was absolutely essential that their international outside-half Harold Kittermaster must be kept 'in check.' So a ploy was planned whereby this danger-man was to be tempted to turn inwards through a seemingly unopposed corridor whenever receiving ball from his forwards. It was a trap and Oxford took the bait! For lying in wait at the far end of the corridor was the highly effective Bath back-row of Carruthers, Dobson and Humphries. And the ploy worked; the Oxford attack was blunted; and Bath duly ran home three tries (none converted) by Considine, Joe Richardson and F.A.Meine to gain a prestigious win (0-9) where Bath in the words of the Chronicle were *"full value for their victory in a game very brilliant in patches."*

Sometimes (ironically) it is not only prestigious victories that are long remembered, but so too valiant defeats, and especially so if the results are close and inflicted by two of the best sides in British rugby, as indeed was the case with Bath's agonisingly narrow 9-10 upset at Llanelli in November; while on 10th February 1923 fellow Welsh side Newport arrived in the city. Hailed by the Chronicle as *"perhaps the most famous side in the world"* the visitors drew an estimated 7,000 spectators to the Rec, an attendance that included some hundreds arriving on chartered trains from Wales. And, with not a weakness anywhere, much depended on whether Newport could be held at forward. The watching 'South Wales Argus' reporter provided an answer: *"Bath have a fine pack of forwards. They made good at the line out, quick to get away with footwork, clever in supporting each other in combined rushes. They were often dangerous."* Of the outsides The Argus further noted that *".....the backs of both sides did their utmost to attack by running and passing, and both put in movements which were excellent..."*

Newport however came unbeaten, and thanks to a lone drop goal ensuring an 0-4 away victory they departed unbeaten.

But as at Llanelli, Bath had again made their mark. They were proving that they could live among the elite, though not as yet qualifying for a place among those clubs (Bristol and Gloucester for instance) that occupied the top half of this elite. To achieve this status however it was not sufficient to fall to narrow 'valiant' defeats against teams the calibre of Llanelli and Newport, but to defeat them! And that was the real test.

On Saturday, 14th April 1923 at Bridgwater it was to be Somerset who would face another awesome test, namely the task of adding their name to the County Championship's roll of honour. Confronting them would be Leicestershire, a team ominously selected entirely from the Leicester club with the exception of Nottingham's C.J. Burton in the backs. Somerset meanwhile were drawn from a wider field, and there was some seriously good competition throughout the county for places in their own back division. It was therefore unwise (and that is putting it mildly) for county skipper R.G.B. Quick to have risked an appearance for Bristol in their 3-0 mid-week home victory over Bath just three days prior to the final. A shoulder injury resulted, just about the last thing the county selectors needed and this to a player then rated (see; Seventy Years of Somerset rugby, p.34) as "*among the finest wings we have ever had.*" Clifton's E.H.Esbester was then hurriedly chosen to fill the vacancy on the wing, and the captaincy switched to Bridgwater half-back J. Jarvis.

Yet another late quandary for the Somerset selectors concerned the use of the five-eighth formation successfully adopted by the Leicester club, and during this same season equally successfully utilised by the Leicestershire county side. The question therefore was whether Somerset could afford 'not' to play with the same all-attack formation. One view held that it was now too late to switch to such unorthodox tactics; while the other view held that it was a risk that simply 'must' be taken, and a factor that almost certainly influenced the final decision was Bath's own 5-8th experience. Furthermore with half-back Considine and the entire county (and Bath) back-row of Sheppard, Bisgrove and Mannings all experienced in these tactics Somerset were a team equipped to deal with a Leicestershire side certain to apply them at Bridgwater. So the selectors gambled on risk and opted for a 5-8th formation with Considine and Jarvis.

Certainly Somerset's back division looked impressively strong. Centres E. Hammett and A.E. Thomson had previously played for England and Scotland respectively, and Vowles and Considine ranked among the best halves in English rugby. Meine too was a proven wingman, so late replacement E.S. Esbester could be assured that he was surrounded by considerable experience; and not forgetting the possible psychological 'lift' provided by Bath's recent 17-3 home win over the Leicester club, **Somerset team** took the field as follows:

W. Gaisford (Clifton), F.Meine (Bath), E.Hammett (Blackheath), A.E. Thomson (Wellington), E. Esbester (Clifton), J.Jarvis (Bridgwater, capt.), S.G.U. Considine (Bath), H. Vowles (Bath), *backs*. A. Spriggs, F. Spriggs, P. Lewis and J. Reed (all Bridgwater), W. Sheppard, L.Bisgrove and C. Mannings (all Bath), *forwards.*

Facing them for **Leicestershire** (with former Bath favourite Norman Coates of the Leicester club in their ranks) were: L.C.Sambrook, E. Haselmere, P.Laurie, N. Coates, A.M.Smallwood, C.J. Burton, G.J. German, T.F.Taylor, G.Ward, J.C. Davis, C.Cross, H. Grierson, D.J. Norman, M.T.Thornloe, H. Sharratt (all Leicester except back C.J. Burton of Nottingham). *Referee:* Mr T. Vile, Newport.

An estimated ten thousand crowd filled the Bridgwater ground to witness the most important encounter so far in Somerset's rugby history, one that according to county records (Seventy Years of Somerset rugby, p.34) was *"an intensely thrilling match,"* with home captain J. Jarvis scoring the opening try within seven minutes (W. Gaisford converting superbly from wide out) to set pulses racing. Winger F. A. Meine (Bath) then sent them racing yet further when running home a second try, although an 8-0 lead in rugby was easily catchable as Leicestershire soon showed. Having absorbed the earlier Somerset pressure and not forgetting either the passionate home crowd, the visitors then settled into their own stride and replied with a Smallwood try and then another by Burton far out, while sheer relief rose from the Somerset crowd as Thornloe's attempt at conversion missed its target.....just! With the Cidermens' lead literally now hanging on a thread, the closing phase featured ever more determined Leicestershire attacks that drove Somerset backwards into desperate defence, while two further Thornloe penalty attempts again fell just short. It would prove however to be the Midlanders' last throw of the dice. Somerset held on to their 8-6 lead and with it captured the coveted County Championship. It was to be their finest day, one that they would never again equal.

Bath, with six players in that county side were very much a part of this epic day, and albeit that many argued that the October win at Blundells School (0-17) should not have been included as a 1st XV fixture, Bath achieved their highest total yet with 26 victories. But it was not only the number of wins, but furthermore the quality of rugby played that made things so special. True, three games were drawn, sixteen were lost and if discounting London Welsh then fortress Wales remained unconquered territory. True also that Bristol (beaten 6-3 on the Rec in the last game of the previous season) could not be beaten either. But this resulted partly from Bath's Somerset commitments that affected two of their three derby encounters. Nonetheless, some of the strongest sides in England and Wales (including Leicester at home) were defeated on the Rec, and the home and away double was achieved against both London Welsh and Moseley. *"Better rugby has never been seen in Bath,"* wrote The Mascot, adding that *"the splendid crowds which have witnessed the home games are evidence of the popularity of the game in Bath."*

The further news that the forthcoming 1923-4 season would commence *"with the fixture list strengthened"* would have resonated too with those who remembered the days when many had feared if there would be a rugby future at all for Bath, doubts that would be swept aside however by the standards reached by the early 1920's. Admittedly Bath were not yet a great side, but a genuinely good first-class side nonetheless; and following in the footsteps of Philip Hope, the Harry Vowles team of 1922-3 signalled that Bath had 'come of age!'

Chapter15. TEMPORARY MID-TWENTIES CRISIS?

Following the two year leadership of Harry Vowles (1922-24), the captaincy baton passed to S.G. U. Considine, and Bath's momentum would continue for another season with a healthy total of wins under their belts. Some of these were especially impressive, not only for Bath's first ever triumph over Bristol at the Memorial ground (7-11) in early December, but their role in striking a later blow in March for West Country prestige, when over the same weekend Bristol gained their first ever win at Pontypool, Gloucester defeated Llanelli, and Bath defeated Newport 6-3 on the Rec watched by a reported 7,000 spectators (Bath Football Herald, 14th March, 1925).

The return from injury of James Pitman was an added bonus, not as a wing (his England position), but this time as a centre, two quite different roles to which some wingers can never fully adjust. But Pitman did, so well in fact that Bath would rate him no less than in the same company as the likes of James Timmins and Norman Coates. Meanwhile another late season recruit to make an unexpected appearance in the backs was outside-half J.R. Wheeler. A practicing doctor with four Irish caps to his credit in the 1920's, his parent club (the London Hospital side) had already concluded their own rugby programme, so allowing Wheeler to guest for another club for the remainder of the season if so choosing. His choice was the Rec. He was excellent. As for a genuine utility player (such useful people to have around) they did not come much better than Combe Down product Harry Slade, whose great value was his ability to play literally anywhere in the backs, and it was as a result of this versatility that he would develop into one of the great Bath stalwarts of his era.

S.G.U Considine ....outhalf artistry.

Acknowledgements: Bath Chronicle

1924-5 was the season too of the second New Zealand tour to these islands, where the 'Invincibles' remained unbeaten, yet where at Weston super Mare (20th September) Somerset, with Bath's Considine and forward L.W. Bisgrove in their ranks, threw everything they knew into so formidable a challenge, only falling narrowly to a 0-6 defeat, no disgrace for any side that faced a team of such power as the All Blacks.

For Bath meanwhile the call-up of Considine for England against France (13th April 1925) was an honour to savour, although his selection on the wing, not at outside half, would have surprised many. He would learn of his selection (Chronicle, 11th April 1925) by way of a telegram from the English Rugby Union, and his reaction was typical of this supremely talented yet modest player. He simply placed the telegram in his pocket and departed for a game of golf. Born in Darjeeling, India, on 11th August 1901, Stanley George Ulick Considine had completed his schooling at Blundell's (Tiverton) after his junior schooldays at St. Christopher's, Bath. An outstanding sporting talent, he played for Bath when still at Blundell's, while his Irish background had allowed him to play in the Irish Trial of 1920. Arnold Ridley later spoke of the *"audacity of Considine's play, the instantaneous nature of his reactions,"* adding that some colleagues claimed that *"with Consi' it was as difficult to play with him as against him."* Excelling furthermore at cricket, Considine had played for Somerset since 1919 as a 'splendid bat,' and proved to be a fielder of such quality that at cover-point he was acknowledged by some commentators as *"the finest in the Country since the days of Gloucestershire and England legend, Gilbert Jessop."*

It was at the Colombes stadium however where Considine would reach both the pinnacle and yet the demise of his otherwise supreme sporting career. England would triumph 11-13. But the victory came at a cost, not only for England but for Bath too as a result of a first-half injury to Considine. In an age when substitutes were prohibited (and not permitted until the late 1960's) he courageously (and typically) refused to leave the field. But the entire second-half would be an ordeal. The injury appeared severe, as indeed it was, and with the advances in surgery in later decades he may have fully recovered. But this was the 1920's and the treatment of injuries (sporting or otherwise) was not yet a sufficiently advanced science. Thus one of the finest backs ever to wear Bath colours would subsequently never play a serious game of rugby again.

For his host of admirers at Bath the disappointment was tangible, and the effects of his injury would extend into the following season, as many would no doubt have realised. Nonetheless, those who had witnessed his performances would have memories to treasure of his unique qualities, qualities perhaps never better expressed than in the words of his centre colleague on that fateful day in Paris, namely Bristol's L.J. Corbett. Writing four decades later (Bath Football Club Centenary book, pp. 8-9) and by now rugby correspondent for the Sunday Times, he wrote thus: *"on his day "Consi" was surely the most brilliant player behind the scrum ever to wear the Bath jersey..........whose genius in attack was quite outstanding."* No words therefore need be added to such unstinting praise.

The loss of Considine was the one serious set-back in an otherwise successful season, and then as now it is normally a case that a team with ability both at forward and in the backs should, on paper at least, perform well. Nor was Bath's 1924-5 season an exception to this general rule. Despite 13 defeats and 2 draws, there could be no complaints about the 22 victories gained at this level of rugby; wins moreover that included three notable away victories at London Welsh, Bristol and Richmond. Furthermore, the late season 5-3 home win over a Llanelli side fielding no less than nine internationals was further convincing proof that by this stage, Bath when at their best (and if at home) were a 'match' for any side in the Country.

But, after ten seasons riding the crest of a wave, Bath would now experience a severe jolt to their confidence in season 1925-6. This just happened to be the 20th anniversary of season 1905-6 when it seemed that Bath (with a total of seven wins only) had teetered on the edge of possible oblivion, a nightmare that the club hoped they would never re-live again. Yet with an identical seven wins once again in 1925-6, share it they did, hardly an ideal start for W.J. (Bill) Gibbs's two years of captaincy. Yet depressing (even alarming) though these figures were, the statistics when viewed out of context were deceptive. The situation was not identical to those worrying days of the early 1900's, and although the severity of the loss of form was unexpected, its main cause was identifiable, not least the departure of full-back Bert Comm into professional ranks at Oldham and the fact that some of the stalwarts were 'moving on.' There was another factor: the loss of the near irreplaceable Considine! Meanwhile during the Bath Spring that had commenced from 1910 onwards (if not before) the off-field administration of the club had improved in tandem with its on-field progress. Hence it was that sudden setbacks could now be better contained, better cushioned from shocks, and a recovery more speedily launched. Exactly this was to happen but one season onwards.

Yet there was no denying that the 1925-6 campaign was an uncomfortable ride. There were after all a demoralising 27 defeats; and not only upsets away at tougher opposition such as London Welsh, but that Bath were bettered by the likes of the Old Blues (normally a guaranteed victory) that added to the disquiet.

But it was not all gloom. First, Bath celebrated their Diamond Jubilee (15th October) with a game against the combined Western Counties, albeit losing 3-19. While later, again on the Rec, Bath hosted the England Trial of 19th December with their new North stand now open for business. Not surprisingly in a season in which the club was, to put it mildly, far from its best, no Bath player was included. Yet the Centenary Book (p.28) records that 8000 spectators did attend, there to witness the Probables led by England's W.W. Wakefield unexpectedly lose 14-22 to the Possibles. While if there was a hint of a possible recovery, then it was the first ever visit by Cardiff to the Rec on 16th January that provided one, although the inaugural game between the clubs commenced in Cardiff one season previously (24[the] December 1924), with the Welshmen winning 22-6. Among the best teams in the British Isles, the visitors were nonetheless held to a 13-13 draw, and not kept in check by defensive tactics alone. On the contrary….both sides ran home three tries apiece, with two conversions apiece, and Bath were entitled to take genuine satisfaction from arguably their best performance that season on the field; nor forgetting Cardiff's diplomacy off it, their committee expressing thus in their post-visit letter to the club: *"The genial hospitality only proves what a wonderful club of sportsmen you have. Gatherings of the sort that took place on Saturday last only tend to bring us closer together;"* (Football Herald & Chronicle, 23rd January 1926).

The January 14-6 home win over Cross-Keys (then a powerful club) fielding three Welsh internationals and the later 3-0 home victory over Gloucester most certainly made one sit up and take notice, yet simultaneously invited an important question: because if Bath could win victories such as these, then how come so bleak a season as 1925-6? At the time it was difficult to provide an explanation. But with the much improved results that would shortly follow, the nearest one could get to the answer (and not forgetting the departure of certain players, S.G.U. Considine and Bert Comm for instance) was that Bath experienced something similar to a 'rogue' opinion poll that leads to panic, instead of an acceptance that a similar loss of form occurs to most (perhaps all) clubs at some stage in their history.

Sure enough the crisis was not as serious as feared, and especially encouraging was that in support of Bill Gibbs (again skipper), the recovery that followed in the following 1926-7 season was partly a result of a new generation of players that included H. Burgess, W. Hancock, Norman Matthews, A.F.Lace, R.S.Chaddock, E.Chard, W.Banyard, D. James, R. Collett, A.Milsom, E. Dunscombe, G. Nudds, and not forgetting the powerful running three-quarter J.B. Hannah. Within a year the decline was reversed, Bath clinching a number of sometimes impressively good results that included victories over Plymouth Albion (home and away), Moseley, the Royal Air Force, Leicester, Blackheath, U.S. Portsmouth, London Welsh, London Irish and Newport. Calm returned.

Yet ironically it was not the victories, but the defeats, that raised further questions, though that is to overlook the quality sometimes present among the London Old Boys clubs during this era. Corinthian in outlook, teams such as Old Merchant Taylors, Old Millhillians and Old Blues (Christ Hospital School) played much of their rugby in the Home Counties, but willingly travelled westwards, especially so during the Christmas and Easter holiday periods. Cavalier almost to a fault, such teams were justifiably ranked as senior clubs, and remained so regarded until the late 1960's. A glance at the Taylors' team-sheet on their Easter tour match at Bath in mid-April 1927 would confirm this fact, with a line-up that included full-back R.Melluish (Cambridge Blue and England Trials), centre W. Cheeseman (Oxford Blue & England), F. Collier and D. Hodgson (Middlesex half-backs), and county forwards G. Bryant (Kent), H. Fagrari (Middlesex) and G.H. Earle (Surrey). If this was not impressive enough, they were led by forward R. Cove-Smith, one of the England greats of the 1920's.

Meanwhile Bath, who prior to the Old Merchant Taylors' arrival had put all their efforts into notching four straight wins over U.S.Portsmouth, Bridgwater, London Irish and London Welsh, rested certain players from their own line-up. This was asking for trouble, as Bath probably realised, having made a similar error when losing to the Old Blues during the Christmas break. But now it would be an opportunity for the O.M.T.'s to shine. And shine they did, with an 8-18 win to prove it too.

Yet the over-all results of season 1926-7 were clear confirmation of a swift turn-around in club fortunes, with 21 wins, one draw and 13 defeats, a positive record at the first-class level of the game; while a number of previously less known individuals would now stamp their own authority upon the Rec. G. Nudds proved to be a real find at scrum-half, while R. Collett and W.B. Wake at forward joined Bath centre H. Partridge in the Somerset line-up during the season, all four called-up for the county against the touring Maoris at Weston-super-Mare, albeit losing 8-21 to the tourists. L.H. Scott, when available, proved to be a genuine speed-merchant in the backs, while skipper 'Bill' Gibbs again demonstrated his qualities of leadership during a time of transition and topping Bath's try list with 16 scores that season, this despite missing 12 matches.

Another aspect of the season was the emerging role of club coaches, in Bath's case Alby Hatherill and Jack Cutting, as the Bath Chronicle duly confirmed in their fulsome end-of-season review. Admittedly coaching was not fully recognised as an integral part of club rugby until the 1960's. But coaches were nothing new, as records clearly show, including fortuitously the following letter previously sent to the Bath Herald on 5th February 1910. The writer, having returned from India to whence he had journeyed in the 1880's, now exclaimed, with no little disapproval, that the changes he found were not to his liking. He was now witness to *"huge stands, huge attendances, players found in everything, not wearing anything they have paid for, with trainers to look after them as though they were prize fighters or gladiators."* Well, if those were his feelings in February 1910, it is just as well he was oblivious to the changes that would occur by February 2010!

Finally, this season that had introduced a largely new generation of players to the Rec would take a step back into its past with a concluding match against Wellington. Not seen in the city since October 1906, their presence stirred memories of their 19th century pre-eminence, their string of county players, and their iron-tackling England full-back Herbert Gamlin. For years past the West Somerset club had expressed a wish to play Bath again, and now that wish was granted. So it was that two rugby families who now occupied two quite different strata of the game celebrated a common friendship; and that mattered, not the fact that Bath (in a carnival atmosphere) won 16-8.

Chapter 16.   THE 1920'S – A LANDMARK DECADE?

At the culmination of the 1920's the overall results achieved (notwithstanding the disappointments of season 1925-6) exceeded those of any previous decade in the club's history, this in both quantity of victories and quality of opponents now willing to add Bath to their fixture lists. Furthermore, the speedy return to normality that followed the mid-20's 'dip' was an indication of a stability at the Rec, with returns of 21, 22, 17 and 19 victories respectively from seasons 1926 to 1929.

It was perhaps significant that during this decade Bath (apart from a few exceptions) were rarely a team of nationally known stars, though not infrequently they were a star team, as some of their best results proved. Their family atmosphere and their team spirit was another asset, although on occasions their supporters could be (as in Somerset Cup days) partisan, not least in the less than happy season of 1925-6. True, the second half of the decade was perhaps not quite the equal of the first, yet the 1927-8 team captained by England winger James Pitman was arguably as good as most during the 1920's.

Bath lost fourteen, drew another three, but importantly won twenty-two victories, and this included a highly prestigious 9-5 triumph over Cardiff, where of the four tries ran home that day Bath scored three. Indeed this and many victories throughout the 1920's were top-notch, and it was noticeable too that Pitman's side clinched the double against the likes of Moseley and London Welsh; while Bath were fully aware that to beat the best demanded that they must prepare accordingly. Hence rotation of players (by no means a later practice in rugby) was not uncommon at the club during the Twenties, and Bath did rest key players in supposedly less demanding fixtures (sometimes losing as a result) so as to enable the club to field full-strength and hopefully fully fit sides to face opponents at home such as Leicester and Gloucester (Pitman's team winning both).

James Pitman ....a soccer background at Eton, a Blue at Oxford, a cap for England.

Acknowledgements: Bath Chronicle

However for Pitman (likewise previous Bath captains) it too often remained a different story on 'foreign fields,' and his side experienced some painful lessons (not least psychological) from upsets that included defeats at Leicester (0-33) and an inexplicable and humiliating home defeat to Bristol (0-32) against whom Bath had only narrowly lost (6-3) away in that same season.

Such sobering defeats notwithstanding, the overall results of the 1920's indicated that Bath were a good, solid first-class club, who in some seasons were a very good first-class club, though it was 'just their luck' that by stint of both geography and history Bath could not escape the shackles of a comparison with nearby rivals Bristol. And what rivals....nothing less in fact than one of the best and most consistent sides in the Country! By contrast Bath were sometimes excellent at home, too often vulnerable away, and no doubt 'in the eyes' of their supporters annoyingly inconsistent.

Significantly, Bath did not forget their own humble origins, part reason for their willingness to arrange fixtures from a 'broad church.' The result of this policy was that alongside the Big Guns of Leicester, Cardiff (et al) the less glamorous teams featured in the typical Bath season too. During 1927-8 for example Bath met Old Alleynians (Dulwich), Old Paulines (St. Pauls), Old Blues (Christ's Hospital), Old Dunstonians and Old Merchant Taylors; while Edgware (little known nowadays) were then an ambitious club who were mustard keen to strengthen their own fixture list. Furthermore in this same season and despite earning a pittance 'from their own home gates,' (Football Herald, 28th February, 1925) this North London rugby family, subject to at least one heavy earlier upset against Bath, were more than willing to pay for their long journey out of their own pockets. They could cause one or two surprises moreover, only narrowly losing 6-5 down on the Rec in October 1927. In addition to the Old Boys there was the visit of St. Thomas's Hospital. Only marginally less successful than Guys (a major first-class team in the 1920's), St. Thomas's too had played a notable part in forging a hugely respected Hospitals rugby tradition, who along with Guys had produced a legion of internationals that any club in England would have been proud of.

So, as a result of living in the wider rugby family and playing clubs ranked at both the higher and the less prestigious levels of the game, Bath had developed a distinctive character that by now was both West Country and yet worldly in outlook. James Pitman (Centenary Book, 1965, pp. 9-10)) expressed such a point so simply yet so well when commenting on his days at the club: *"Happy times! Those luncheon baskets at Bath station. Solo! Cashnella; Eddie Simpkins. The smell of embrocation in the changing room; the band. The hot bath afterwards. Our home ground was the most beautiful by far....What a glorious setting!"*

Yet and yet again, Bristol remained the yardstick by which others judged Bath, and Bath in fact judged themselves. Indeed it was a constant frustration, though accepted with humour, that albeit Bristol rarely won 'big' against Bath, they usually did win! However, at the Memorial Ground (28th November 1929) they didn't. It was a typical derby clash, in other words an absolute nail-biter with the score finely balanced at 3-3. It was then that the ball reached the eager hands of Bath's young nineteen year old winger Bill Hancock. Suddenly ball in hand, this former England schools Trialist hit the pace button and sped clear. Clear that is save for Bristol full-back Jim Watts. It was now man against boy and it looked odds-on that the boy would probably come off worse (a lot worse). Sure enough the menacing Watts closed in for the 'kill' and……Hancock had other ideas. He literally leaped over the off-balanced Bristolian to notch a gem of a try, one so unusual that it reportedly startled a full-house Memorial Ground and was still recalled decades later in Bath (if not Bristol) rugby folklore. More importantly still, it clinched that rarity for Bath, an away win at Bristol by 3-6 and the first part of a cherished two-timer for that season. Furthermore, as if one high-profile double was not enough for season 1929-30, another was achieved with the club's pair against Northampton.

However, in this hugely significant 1920's era for Bath there had been one small event in the Autumn of 1927 that had initially passed by barely noticed. It concerned nothing more startling that the arrival of a polite fifteen year old schoolboy at Taunton School. The youngest of five children (two girls and three boys) he had journeyed with his recently widowed mother from distant Hong Kong where his late Scottish father had risen to the position of Assistant Superintendent of Police. The boy was new to England, new to Taunton school and furthermore new to rugby football. But soon, and for the first time in his life, a rugby ball was put into his hands. Almost immediately he displayed a natural-born talent for sports and within two months of his first autumn term he was fast-tracked as a three-quarter into the senior colts XV. Come the Spring term and he went one better, this time gaining selection for the Taunton school 1st XV side.

It was hardly surprising that few if anyone beyond the confines of Taunton School knew much about this promising young player, that is until season 1929-30 when Somerset, owing to a late withdrawal, suddenly found themselves short of a centre to play against Gloucestershire. However someone, possibly a schools-referee (see 'Men of a Stout Countenance,' p.29) notified the County selectors about a promising centre at Taunton school. His name was R.A. Gerrard. What is positively recorded nonetheless is that Gerrard *"was spotted by the [Somerset] County selectors as a player of the greatest promise"* (Seventy Years of Somerset Rugby, p.36) and was thus rushed into the County side at short notice, so stepping out into the 'take-no-prisoners' cauldron that is Kingsholm. And although Gloucestershire won a narrow, grimly fought victory, the fearless Taunton schoolboy never shirked a tackle, nor wilted under the intense pressure so unexpectedly placed upon his young shoulders. Now a wider audience did know at least something about this young protégé. They would soon learn much, much more. Happily it was Bath that was to be both his chosen home and his chosen club, and as the rugby world moved on from the 1920's the young man from Hong Kong was destined to take a step into rugby legend.

Likewise Bath would now take a step into the next decade, a club that had answered a crucial question when previously setting out into daylight from the aftermath of the Great War. For that rugby Spring from season 1909-10 onwards until 'the lights went out all over Europe' had not been a false dawn. Bath had indeed maintained their momentum (bar one brief season) throughout the 1920's, had held their position within first-class rugby, and instilled (as confirmed by 5,000 plus crowds on some days) a passion for the game in the city.

This could justly be claimed as no small achievement, and undeniably an important one. Indeed, this was an age of splendid victories (usually at home). But on the downside there were in all honesty too many heavy defeats (usually away from home). So could the 1920's be described as a 'landmark decade?' Not Quite!

Chapter 17.   A COUNTRY WITHIN A COUNTRY.   (1930-35).

On Monday 7th April 1930 the Bath & Wilts Chronicle & Herald (Chronicle & Herald) reported the events of the club's annual dinner held on the previous Saturday at the Fortts Restaurant, Milsom street, where numbered among the eminent guests were former Bristol outside-half Mr W. Pearce (by now president of the RFU) and Mr Frank Cowlin (President of the Bristol club). Various toasts were duly made, and it was the RFU President who would then refer to certain characteristics of the rugby game, among them the sacrosanct principle of that era, namely that rugby football was "*for the amateur and the amateur only.*" But it is doubtful that few if any of the President's two hundred plus listeners that evening would have envisaged how half a century later this same principle would so torment this same rugby union game.

Mr Frank Cowlin spoke too, arousing laughter when stating that "*Bath had done the dirty on Bristol that season by winning the double over their great rivals,*" adding that rugby "*is one of the cleanest, if not 'the' cleanest of sports.*" Well…..yes and no! For the truth is that rugby history (including Bath's) is not without its own rogues gallery, and ironically the 1930's were to witness at least two occasions when Bath (and not for the first time either) would find themselves embroiled in fracas both on, and off the field! That being said, as the glasses clinked amid the rugby-banter during that early Spring evening, Bath with both youth and experience on their side had reason for justified optimism as they stepped into a new decade.
Indeed having achieved a moderately successful 1929-30 season with nineteen wins under their belts, the club would now enjoy five seasons of good to very good success that on occasions would compare with anything the club had experienced before. And how the local schools were proving to be a nursery for talent, an invaluable production-line producing backs the likes of Billy Hancock, Albert Merrett (Weymouth House) and all-rounder Ralph Banks (St. Saviours).

By the conclusion of the 1930's meanwhile there would be much about the organisation and structure of the game that would change little until the advent of professionalism in the mid- 1990's. There was an established hierarchy of first-class clubs in England and Wales, and a thriving County championship would remain a major attraction until the late 1980's. As early as January 1927 the England v Wales encounter at Twickenham had been the first international to be broadcast live on radio; while the England v Scotland encounter of 19th March 1938 (again at Twickenham) would be the first to be screened live on television. Another feature of the first-class rugby game throughout the 1930's was the continued influence of the Services clubs, namely U.S. Portsmouth, Devonport Services (no strangers to the Rec) and the Aldershot Services who were less familiar faces. All three competed at the senior level of rugby, and the inclusion of

Services players (likewise the Hospital and the London Old Boys sides) in the Home International teams was the norm, rather than the exception.

Bath too would continue to attract the attention of international selectors, and they did their own reputation no harm with their 3-3 away draw at Leicester to kick off their 1930-31 season. Not quite a perfect result, yet one that hinted at the success that would shortly follow. Scrum-half and Cambridge Blue E.Benson had now arrived on the Rec, his half-back combination with Charles Gough looking highly promising. In the backs Herbert Buse (a full Somerset County cricketer like Considine previously and Gerrard later), Louis St. V. Powell, Albert Merrett and Billy Hancock could cause problems to most opponents; and come the 11th October 1930 the young R. A. Gerrard would make his debut for Bath at Plymouth Albion. Albeit that his new club lost 6-5, he looked every bit a player for the future, and England selectors would soon be taking a far closer interest in this youthful nineteen year old centre.

Equally satisfying for prop forward Ian Spence (captain from 1929-1931) and the club was the performance of the pack, usually (though not always) a Bath strength, and to be strengthened furthermore by D. Crichton Miller (previously Gloucester and Scotland) and G.G. Gregory (previously Bristol and England). They would now team-up with England Trialist Mervyn Shaw and local hero Norman Matthews. Furthermore in E.G. Haydon (strong and very fast) one saw the personification of the modern day wing-forward. A player of perpetual motion, he created club history in season 1930-1 when running home a remarkable 29 tries, a record that would not be surpassed for some half a century when finally wing Barry Trevaskis (1982-3) touched down for 32 tries. During this same era

Ian Spence

newcomers Crichton-Miller and Gregory would make their own contribution to Bath rugby history. For the club had yet to field two players in the same international and certainly not each player representing opposing sides. But at Murrayfield (21st Mar.1931) in a Scottish 28-19 victory, Crichton-Miller packed down for Scotland and G.G.Gregory for England. For some observers however it is puzzling that Bath have never claimed either player as Bathonian internationals, and the reason for this exclusion appears to be one of protocol; because since both players had arrived on the Rec as fully fledged internationals, it seems highly probably that Bath considered that their former clubs alone should be accorded the recognition for their international status, and although not written down anywhere in the club rules, this same protocol has normally remained unchanged.

One player who 'did,' but then did 'not' receive international recognition was Bath's lion-hearted all-round forward Norman Matthews, who, impressive in recent England

Trials, duly accompanied the England team as travelling reserve for the 18th January 1930 encounter against Wales. Suddenly it was realised that forward Harry Rew (Army) would not be fully match fit and as a result Matthews was therefore put on

Norman Matthews ....minutes from England's cap at Cardiff.

Acknowledgements: Bath Chronicle

stand-by. However, efforts were made to contact experienced Bristol and England hooker Sam Tucker. It was now that fate intervened. For literally at that moment that England (including Matthews) had changed and were now preparing to step on to the Arms Park, Sam Tucker arrived in the dressing room, having been flown from Bristol to Cardiff. Matthews never did represent England that day when Wales were overcome 3-11, nor on any other day; and at Bath, and perhaps elsewhere, there was both deep sympathy and puzzlement. If a travelling reserve is selected for a specific purpose, why one asks did Matthews not play at Cardiff? Some at Bath found it 'hard to take.' But if one was to condemn Sam Tucker then one was aiming at the wrong target, because if anyone had questions to answer it was the England officials, not the Bristolian.

As for the 1930-31 campaign, *"one of the best-if not the best [seasons] in the long history of the club"* (Bath & Herald, 14th April 1931), one eye-catching result was the 27-0 home win against Moseley; although the later February 19-9 home success against Leicester, with Ian Spence inspirational, was perhaps the result that really did show just how formidable Bath could be on home territory. Even on away soil, Bath overcame the likes of then formidable Devonport Services (6-10). But on the minus side they fell 8-0 at Llanelli, next 14-3 at Neath and later 18-0 at Pontypool. So, despite a collection of 22 wins and three draws from thirty seven encounters, the same questions remained: 'where exactly did Bath stand in the rankings of the English first-class game, and how did they compare with their formidable foes at Bristol and Gloucester? This was a tricky question, partly because the Bath - Bristol - Gloucester triangle was a Country within a Country, an island separate from the rest. Thus whatever Bath achieved outside this island mattered less than what Bath achieved within it. This age-old perception moreover could only change by domination over their massive rivals, a task lest it be forgotten that was as difficult as any in English rugby.

Yet nothing could diminish the fact that Bath were among the happiest of rugby families, as Crichton Miller once articulated (Centenary Book, (1865-65, p.12). Bath (he wrote) played *"neither with the humourless intensity that is met further west, nor in the irritating happy-go-lucky style that characterised some of the London clubs......it was serious rugger, but jolly."* Nicely put; and there would be no doubting that Bath at their best (and usually, though not always on home territory) could indeed beat some of the best in England and Wales in seasons 1931-2 and 1932-3, with results that would have placed them in a comfortable position in any official National league table of first-class clubs. Of significance too was the effect of their inspiring new captain, Mervyn Shaw. Now, Shaw had arrived as an England Trialist in 1929 from Bristol, a club whom he had captained with distinction. Yet he arrived on the Rec as an exile, and in those days this was highly unusual. For few players who joined Bristol ever wished to leave this most splendid of clubs. Indeed, he was the popular choice of both players and committee to remain as Bristol captain. But a faction within the membership begged to differ; and this faction got their way. Thus Shaw, now chastened by this rebuff but nonetheless the nicest of men, felt it only diplomatic to depart. His destination would be Bath, where he would prove himself both a magnificent player and an admired general during his two year captaincy.

However despite the fact that on the Rec his adopted club could overcome some of the best opposition in England and Wales, Shaw would soon enough discover that London rugby rated Bath in a somewhat different 'light' compared to its regard for the Bristol club he had only recently left. Reviewing the begrudging reports on Bath wins in the capital (assuming they did win) the Chronicle & Herald (21st October 1931) asked: *"Why are Bath's wins always lucky?"* Why indeed, for surely a win is a win?! But London rugby (and elsewhere) remained undecided as where exactly to place Bath in 'the order of things.' Rightly or wrongly it would take literally years for this perception to change.

Bath nonetheless made a far quicker perception-change regarding a recent arrival who played in the home pack for the Boxing Day (1931) visit of the Old Blues. Typically a Christmas holiday game, Bath winning 15-11, the visitors reiterated their view that they *"always look upon [their] game at Bath as the most enjoyable of the season."* A Rec crowd of 6,000 plus (yes, 'six' thousand plus) most likely agreed, witnessing a game described as a 'thrill a minute' holiday clash and notable (inter alia) for the outstanding performance of the recent arrival. His name was H. Minte who had joined Bath without ceremony on a temporary basis only (he was serving with the Army) and was content to play in the 'A' XV, now effectively the 3rd team since the recently launched United side. But after several performances and then his eye-catching play against the Old Blues, further enquiries were made as to the modest Minte's rugby background. It was discovered that the unassuming Scot was in fact a fully-fledged Scottish international Trialist, and not surprisingly his promotion to 1st XV rugby was rapid.

The young 19 years old centre Gerrard too had already played at the international Trial level, and one week prior to the Old Blues match he was to receive a telegram: *"Heartiest congratulations……from your club-mates, friends and admirers in Bath"* it began. Then there followed the England team to play South Africa in the forthcoming international at Twickenham on 2nd January 1932: **backs:** *"R.Barr (Leicester), C. Aarvold (Blackheath, capt),* **R.A. Gerrard (Bath),** *J. Tallent (Cambridge Univ), C.Tanner (Gloucester),* **half-backs:** *R.Spong (Old Millhillians), W. Sobey (Old Millhillians),* **forwards:** *D. Norman (Leicester), G.Gregory (Bristol), A. Carpenter (Gloucester), R.G. Hobbs (Richmond & Army), C. Webb (Devonport Services & R. Navy), L. Saxby (Gloucester), A.Rowley (Coventry), J. McD. Hodgson (Northern)."*

So began the international career of Ronald "Gerry" Gerrard, who again at a young and tender age would be thrown into the 'deep end,' on this occasion to face the might of South Africa at Twickenham. Could England triumph? Well, not quite, as the tourists (whose defeat by the Midland Counties would be the sole setback of their tour) commenced their clean sweep of the Home countries with a 0-7 triumph over England. But defeat notwithstanding, the National press as reported in the Chronicle & Herald (4th January 1932) spoke thus: *"Gerrard proved the big success of the line ....."* (Daily Mail); *"Gerrard in attack was the best of our threequarters"* (Sunday Express); *"R.A. Gerrard made a splendid first appearance, a couple of dashes of his in the second half being wonderfully good"*(Sunday Times). Thus spoke the press, unanimous in their collective praise for a young protégé whose mature reading of the game, his almost frightening strength of tackling and a hand-off to be avoided if at all possible would lead to no fewer than fourteen caps for England.

For Gerrard's parent club too the 1931-2 season would arguably equal the prowess of the Vowles team of 1922-3! For among thirty eight matches played there would be twenty five victories (and one draw), and importantly five of these wins would be 'away' successes at Bristol (8,000 attendance) that secured the double, US Portsmouth, Northampton, Devonport Services, and an emphatic 7-21 win at the London Welsh that was highlighted by the try hat-trick of Bath wing-forward Leslie Moore. In addition Pontypool, Llanelli and Leicester were among those teams defeated on the Rec, as was an eye-catching 28-0 victory over London Irish. Even the recently founded United side was attracting crowds of 2,000 (Chronicle & Herald, 4th November 1931). Then, in the perfect finale to any Bath campaign, the club gained an 8-3 home win against Gloucester. Added to these achievements were the individual honours of Gerrard's selection for England, the selection of forwards Norman Matthews and Derek Wilson for the England Trials and the call-up of seven Bath players for Somerset.

Indeed, only the sad news on 2nd April 1932 that former Bath international Frank 'Buster' Soane had lost his brief battle against a sudden illness would dampen the spirits; while a post-card printed in the Chronicle & Herald (6th April 1932) listed a team that played under his captaincy 40 years previously: *A.E. Pinch, W. Pattinson, B. Vincent, P. Dykes, B. Helps, T.N. Parham, G. Vincent, F. Soane (capt.), Roberts, L.J. Fry, W. Coles, A. Timmins, R.Dykes, A.E. Clarke and Milsom.*

The following 1932-3 campaign would mirror closely the previous season and illustrate again the inspiring leadership of Mervyn Shaw. It was appropriate too that the 'Friendly' arranged between Bath and Bristol to celebrate the opening of the Rec's new West stand (6th September) would witness a Shaw led Bath gain a 6-3 win against his former club; and any ill-feeling at the Memorial Ground that had led to his departure to Bath now largely forgotten, it was Shaw and the then current Bristol and England centre Don Burland whose efforts were largely responsible in arranging this encounter. The match was a celebration therefore not only of the new stand, but of that unique bond that these two clubs shared.

Another celebration involved Bath's October tour of 1932; and when one reads of journeys to the likes of Marazion, Gweek, Manman's Smith, Elford Passage, Swan Pool and Port Leven one soon realises that much of this tour was in Cornwall country, though the first stop was a close run 6-7 win over the Devonport Services. It would be the farmers and miners of Redruth next, a team fielding England Trialist centre Roy Jennings and eight Cornish caps, and despite the fearsome roar of a reported 3,000 Cornish crowd, Bath won a hard earned 8-10 victory with Rec favourite Albert Merrett scoring an absolute gem on the wing. Then followed Penzance (merging as Penzance & Newlyn in 1945) where Bath *"throwing the ball about in brilliant style"* ran home 5-24 winners. So three wins on the trot and for some players in those pre-motorway days their first and quite possibly their only opportunity to cross the Tamar and into King Arthur's kingdom, there to see that bleak yet awesome Bodmin Moor, Saint Michael's Mount and not forgetting Jamaica Inn. Ah….those tours were magical times.

Back to the Rec once again and Bath, usually on home territory, continued to record some spectacular wins. But if only the team could export such form, then people really would sit up and take notice. Travelling to Richmond for instance in January 1933 they pushed and shoved their way to a narrow 5-8 win. But Bath had overcome formidable Coventry 11-9 at home one week previously, and it was understandable that London rugby was expecting to see something a little special. But something special is not what they saw; and the Chronicle & Herald (9th January 1933) could only lament thus: *"How strange it is that [Bath] so seldom do well in town, just where for the good name of the club, everyone is always hoping for them to do so."* Sadly, a club who on rare occasions away from home could really 'cut loose' (their 9-17 win at Moseley that season for example, despite seven short on Somerset duty) would too often hit a psychological barrier when travelling. And, this drawback understandably blocked their path to a higher reputation among the first-class rugby hierarchy.

But nothing could dampen the enthusiasm of the Bath Rugby Supporters in their work for club and rugby in general. This included the admirable efforts to enrol every club in the Combination to insure their players for full benefits against injury (Chronicle & Herald, 3rd January 1933) *"by each club getting the supporters 12 new members, thereby having the whole of their insurance premiums paid for them."* Injury payments of £3 per week (maximum) for married players and £2 weekly for single players appear almost trivial when viewed from later decades; but not insignificant in the 1930's, and such assistance was certainly a world away from previous days when rugby injuries could sometimes subject a player to serious consequences. For instance former player J. Humphreys had been rendered near helpless when playing for the Widcombe Institute club in the early 1900's.

The Supporters Club efforts extended further to that season's trip to Twickenham for England's clash with Wales, commencing 21st January when some one hundred members departed from the Bath Spa station, travelling in 'reserved' saloons (but of course) and arriving at Paddington at 11.45 where awaiting buses duly transported the merry band to the Regent Palace Hotel for luncheon. From thence to Twickenham; the buses wedged amongst the infamous 'crawl' for the last three miles to the ground, but fortunately reaching their destination by 2pm, so allowing the party to pack itself into a 60,000 crowd for kick-off! 'England's day?' Not a good question to ask, with Wales (fielding schoolboy centre Wilfred Wooller) winning 3-7 and Bath's Gerrard receiving a potentially serious eye injury. But upsets apart, it was into those buses again, dinner at the Regent Palace Hotel and then an evening spent among the bright lights of the big city, though perhaps best not to ask too many questions about that. At midnight the party assembled at Paddington for the homewards journey, and as luck would have it for England fans the train was packed with (you guessed it) joyous Welsh supporters in full voice. But win or lose, rugby folk live for such times as these, and on arrival at the Spa station the ad hoc choristers of the Supporters Club reportedly interrupted a by now peaceful Bath city with their own somewhat inferior rendition of a traditional Welsh choir.

There were other reasons for celebration in season 1932-3, among them Gerrard's performances for England, forward Peter Clothier's selection for England Trials and the perfect climax to any season with a 15-8 home win over Leicester. Twenty four Bath victories and one draw were gained from thirty eight played, and among the many top-class wins was the 9-17 win over Moseley (away!) where *"Hancock's try after a brilliant break by Charlie Gough was the best outside move of the whole game...."* This success was yet more impressive since backs R.A. Gerrard, Louis St V. Powell and Albert Merrett, plus forwards Peter Clothier, Derek Wilson and Norman Matthews were representing Somerset that same day.

GREAT GOUGH! ....Bath's outstanding utility back takes two Llanelli players over the line for a try against 'the Scarlets'.   Bath 21-Llanelli 3 (8th Sept 1934).

Acknowledgements: Bath Chronicle

But of the Bath 1932-3 home victories there were at least three candidates for the 'Win of the Season Awards.' The late successes over Newport and Leicester were of course impressive. Indeed in the case of the Welshmen, Bath had triumphed only twice in the ten previous years, but now would gain a notable 12-5 win by four tries as against a goal by Newport. Meanwhile the 11-9 success in January over powerful Coventry had clearly demonstrated the strength of the Bath pack. Indeed if such results as this continued, then it seemed possible that it might be only a matter of time before Bath could be spoken of in the same breath as their prestigious rivals at Bristol and Gloucester.

Two further satisfactory seasons of twenty wins apiece in 1933-4 and 1934-5 would follow under the respective captaincy of B.C.Barber and Gerrard; and it was the name of Gerrard in particular with whom Bath were by now most commonly identified. He was now a national rugby figure whose abilities not surprisingly had been noted by the Rugby League, with offers that included one 'approach' of a four-figure signing-on fee that in the 1930's amounted to seriously 'big' money. Bristol's talented squad attracted Northern interest too, not least their England backs Don Burland and Thomas Brown. Burland too declined all overtures. But Brown, to his later regret, accepted an offer from Broughton Rangers.

But Rugby League ambitions south of Yorkshire and Lancashire did not stop at the recruitment of players. It now extended to the establishment of a short-lived club base in the South East, and there was nothing 'amateurish' about the preparations. Indeed on 13th September 1933 at the White City stadium (and under floodlights) an exhibition League match was played between the first and reserve sides of the recently launched London Highfield RL club; and taking more than just a passing interest in the matter, the Chronicle & Herald referred to a 'number of prominent Union players taking part at the White City, among them former Plymouth Albion and England scrum-half Eddie Richards who had already signed for London Highfield.' The Chronicle & Herald further enquired if *"those Union players in the White City game would henceforth be classed as professional?"* adding that *"in the North anyone over 17 years playing Rugby League would be professionalised, whether or not receiving payment."* The answer to this query would later come loud and clear when Thomas Brown's request for reinstatement to the Union code was firmly rejected.

Of course it was easy to understand the concerns that such inroads might cause to the strictly amateur RFU. But even playing League as an amateur was banned; and this sheer intransigence would leave the RFU little room for manoeuvre when facing challenges to its authority from within the Union game itself some fifty years later, challenges moreover that the governing body would find increasingly difficult to defy.

League matters apart, the recently formed United XV continued their promise both on the field and fulfilling another role, namely providing on-going back-up for the First XV. They would meet some interesting opponents in their travels, among them the Trojans club from Eastleigh near Southampton, who although not a fully recognised senior club nonetheless possessed a forward in season 1933-4 who so impressed selectors that he was chosen for the Possibles XV in that season's first England Trial. His name was D.T. Kemp, a talented player who later headed for the capital and joined Blackheath, winning an England cap and destined to be president of the RFU in 1969-70. Another opportunity to see possible internationals of the future was provided in February 1934 when Bath hosted an international Schools Trial between England and the Rest, resulting with a 7-12 win for the Rest XV. Here local boy Tommy Hicks was playing on the wing for the Rest XV, a promising back who by the late Thirties would be a Bath first teamer and who would form an unshakeable friendship with a yet unknown half-back by the name of Norman Halse, both remaining Bath rugby stalwarts into the following century.

Season 1933-34 under new skipper B.C. Barber could not 'but' look full of promise with an opening morale-booster of a 5-3 victory over Swansea, a win partly inspired by out-half discovery Lance Wardle. But just one month later Bath fell 8-10 to Guys Hospital on their first visit to the Rec, and although Bath were five players short on county duty it was an upset that suggested that another typically unpredictable season was underway. It certainly was! Gloucester, 23-8 winners at Kingsholm, were avenged 13-8 on the Rec. Bristol, 0-3 losers at the Memorial Ground, avenged Bath 0-12 on the Rec. Bath triumphed 0-7 at Coventry. Coventry recovered to win 3-13 on the Rec. Bath won 8-7 against Llanelli at home, then fell 20-3 at Neath. So the inconsistencies continued and would do so into the following 1934-5 campaign under the leadership of Ron Gerrard, clearly demonstrated in the opening fortnight of the season. Bath fell 14-3 at Llanelli. One week later and with recently joined wingers J.S. Bartlett and G. Wynne-Jones showing scorching pace, Bath triumphed 21-3 with a four try blitz against Llanelli on the Rec! Indeed, the Scarlets and Wales scrumhalf Dai John commented later that he had *"never seen Llanelli more completely outclassed."* Outclassed! Few clubs ever outclassed Llanelli.

Another Bath characteristic, noticeable since their early days, was mentioned almost as an afterthought in the Chronicle's post-match report of the Bath v Aldershot Services match in Autumn 1934; where the visitors contributed much to the enjoyment of the game: *"Apart from the Harlequins, Aldershot Services were the best side Bath have met this season....behind a pack of huge fellows......their backs threw the ball about in a way that often changed the point of attack with breathless rapidity from one flank to another. If the exceedingly mobile back division were not brought down on some part of Bath's line, giant forwards came smashing through."* And yet despite all the undoubted qualities of the Services, it was Bath who won (11-3), with the Chronicle concluding thus: *"That Bath were so well fortified against these battering attempts to score was due to the yeoman way all took part in the robust business of defence......"* Ah yes: the 'yeoman way!' Of this more later.

Harlequins meanwhile were mentioned too as 'class' opposition, and senior London clubs would hardly have failed to note the potential (Chronicle & Herald, 5th January 1935) that *"on condition that they appear in the first team, the Barnet club have agreed to allow members of their side to play for Richmond in a number of matches."* This was not identical to the established Combination systems to be found elsewhere, not least in the West Country; but it was similar, and potentially a valuable source of players, especially in cases of injuries or representative call-ups.

Later that month it was indeed fortunate for a group of young friends frolicking by the Avon that a strong swimmer was nearby. Because one eleven year old (a non-swimmer) suddenly lost his balance and fell into the icy, deep waters at Batheaston. Nearby there happened to be a small party from the city's engineering staff to whom a companion of the stricken youngster called out: *"Quick, he can't swim."* Aware now of the danger, a member of the group plunged into the river fully clothed (save for his coat) and brought the young schoolboy safely back to the bank. The rescuer just happened to be R.A.Gerrard (Chronicle & Herald, 17th January 1935), who politely dismissing all attempts to publicise his potential life-saving action, joined his colleagues two days later when Leicester were in town. The result….. a four try Bath victory without reply. One week onwards this form was repeated with a 3-14 win at Moseley whose match programme notes generously acclaimed their visitor's win over Leicester as *"the outstanding result of last Saturday's games."*

Less generous it must be said was the reaction of certain Bath supporters on the popular side when Norman Matthews seemingly crossed the line to score for Bath against Blackheath on 16th March 1935. But the referee saw things differently, disallowing the try and ruling that Matthews had first knocked over the corner flag. The popular side did not agree, believing (almost certainly correctly) that the corner flag had indeed been knocked down, but by a Blackheath player, and voiced their disapproval in no uncertain terms at the decision. Nor was the volatile situation helped by the fact that Blackheath won the encounter by 8-13. In fact so angered were a section of the home crowd that come the final whistle they held a demonstration of protest outside the entrance to the North stand changing rooms. This was hardly the reaction expected of a city where the likes of Jane Austen (domiciled at Sydney Place) once trod. But the fact is that it did happen and…lest it be forgotten, had previously happened (on 15th February 1908 to be precise) against then arch-rivals Weston super Mare in a Somerset Cup encounter. Furthermore the club would have been only too aware that since the Somerset RFU could ban rugby on the Rec in 1908, then they could ban it again in 1935. Yes, Bath 'had' to tread very carefully to avoid such incidents occurring again.

Ironically only one week previous to the best-forgotten Blackheath game the Rec had hosted a great rugby occasion, nothing less in fact than the County Championship final. A record crowd estimated at 12,000 packed the Rec, where Somerset would now face a formidable and highly rated Lancashire side. Four Bath men were lined up for Somerset that day, namely Gerrard (centre), H. Davies and J.H. Bailey (scrumhalf & out-half respectively) and J.S. Wood (forward); and though the Cidermen had previously overcome Eastern Counties by 11-6 in their semi-final at Bridgwater, they held no illusions about the challenge facing them. The Lancastrians were strong, not least with international centres Leyland and Heaton in their line-up. Yet it would not be until the final stages of a tenaciously fought game that Lancashire's domination in attack would break down Somerset's defence. Then suddenly it happened! Lancashire struck with a devastating final burst, adding eleven points in ten minutes to win 14 points to nil. Thus it was their day, their triumph, and their time to raise aloft the County Championship trophy.

This disappointment at the county level apart, Bath marched onwards to achieve some impressive club results during the 1934-5 season, not least the aforementioned 3-14 away success at Moseley and home wins over the likes of Bridgend, Leicester and Gloucester. But while twenty games were won (with one drawn), nineteen were lost, and of these one in particular was a shocker, and in more ways than one. This was a late season visit to Llanelli, where Bath's reputation would have soared after their superb 21-3 early season extravaganza against the Scarlets on the Rec. Indeed with Bath's return to this proud Welsh rugby stronghold, countless rugby devotees would have wanted to see the Bath team that previously had so impressed Llanelli's genius of a scrumhalf, Dai John. Yet the reason for Bath's agreement to play three games against the Scarlets (two away from home) was anyone's guess. Needless to say they did agree. It was moreover asking for trouble and the always knowledgeable Llanelli crowd was to witness a shadow of a Bath side, one consisting of reserves and a sprinkling of first-teamers who, putting it bluntly, got trounced. The end result was that the club's hard earned reputation suffered an equally hard knock by way of a humiliating 42-0 drubbing. It was (according to club Hon. Secretary Eddie Simpkins) the biggest defeat so far in the club's rugby history.

It was such setbacks as this and a lack of consistency (despite some outstanding performances for some twenty years from 1910 onwards at least) that explain the reason why Bath could not shake off the tag as the junior partner of the West Country Triangle. But then few clubs could equal, let alone surpass, such formidable rivals as Bristol and Gloucester. For this was a Country within a Country and the only way to escape the shadow cast by these two giants was to better them; a challenge so demanding as to seem virtually impossible.

The 1934-5 season of highs and lows would experience one further event that would deeply affect both the club and the city, occurring as it did on the night of 13/14th of November 1934 (Chronicle & Herald, 14th, 15th, 16th November 1934). It was now half-past midnight as the night train steamed out from Paddington to the West, and among the passengers was a Bath doctor who by now was described as *"among the foremost young physicians of his day."* He was an assistant physician at Bath's Royal United Hospital, a Fellow of the Royal Society of Medicine and furthermore the Medical Society of London; and since 1921 he was a physician at Bath's Royal Mineral Hospital where he had founded a post-graduate course for the study of rheumatic complaints. His name was Vincent Coates (son of a Bathonian but born in Edinburgh) who had three brothers, among them former Bath captain Norman Coates, and a sister. Previously an acclaimed Bath and England winger, he had married the former Miss Ethel Bertha Longuet Layton of Essequebo, British Guiana (now Guyana) on July 1915 at Charlcombe Church. They were now resident at No.10 the Circus (Bath). When qualifying as a doctor in October 1915 he had joined the Army the next day. In October 1916 he then won the Military Cross for bravery while tending the wounded during action on the Western Front.

However on the evening of November 1934 in London Dr Coates (now forty five years of age) had been invited by an 'influential and grateful patient' to a banquet at the Mercers' Hall, one reportedly attended among others by the Lord Mayor himself. As on previous late night return journeys from London, Dr Coates had asked the train guard if he would kindly call him at Bath, for it was not uncommon (then as now) for late night passengers to sleep while travelling. But as the midnight express *"was passing Maidenhead East signal box the signalman noticed that a carriage door was open. He stopped the train at Twford, a search of the line was made,"* and Dr Coates was subsequently found lying injured *"at the side of the line."* First aid was rendered by ambulance men, Dr Coates was taken to hospital, but alas he had not long to live. The news when reaching Bath was received with shock.

The inquest was held at Maidenhead on 15th November by the Coroner (Mr W.Owen Stuchbery) and a jury of eight. They were mindful of evidence that barely a month previous to the tragedy a guard who had been requested to call Dr Coates at Bath had forgotten, and the doctor *"had to get out as the train was leaving Bath."* And the jury verdict was indeed *"accidental death,"* the Coroner concluding that the doctor *"might suddenly have seen the light from the signal box (and) ..... drowsy from sleep, he could have suddenly decided that he was at Bath station and that it was time to get out."*

Dr Vincent Coates, a rugby great whose skills in medicine would later attract to his clinics numerous patients from South Africa, Canada, USA, Holland and France; whose kindness ensured that others unable to afford treatment nonetheless *"had the best for nothing;"* these were among a legion of people now mourning this much admired physician. A throng packed Bath Abbey on the morning of 19th November 1934 at the service performed by the Archdeacon of Bath (the Ven. S.A. Boyd) and the Vicar of St. Stephen's, Lansdown, (Rev. G.L.Fitzmaurice). Outside in the Abbey churchyard another crowd watched silently as Dr Vincent Coates was then driven to his resting place high upon the hill above the city at the Lansdown cemetery. Thus not only a rugby club, but a city he had served so well, were now united in their sense of loss.

Chapter 18. A SEEMINGLY IMPOSSIBLE CHALLENGE. (1935-39).

Following the Great War there would be (see too Ch.16) fifteen seasons of near uninterrupted success. Admittedly Bath did not break into the highest level of first-class rugby, yet they did anchor themselves solidly into the then unofficial mid-table rankings. But, with the departure in the mid-Thirties of a number of established players, results took a turn for the worst.

Ron Gerrard : Classic Bath and England centre.
Acknowledgements: Bath Past Players

Surprisingly the pack, usually a strong point in any Bath team, suffered the most from this exit, albeit that the invaluable Norman Matthews and Peter Moon remained to mentor a new intake of players into the mores of the senior game. In the backs it was a somewhat different story, because Gerrard remained outside the exciting potential of out-half Roy Harris; while the scintillating J.S. (Jack) Bartlett of the RAF and B.V. Robinson would make their noticeable mark on the scene. Backs however feed on good ball and they weren't getting enough of it; a drawback compounded by the fact that the team included perhaps too many young rugby apprentices, whose vulnerability was exposed soon enough in the opening exchanges of season 1935-6. In fact not a single win was recorded until 28th October when Bath defeated Clifton 28-5 at home, so ending a trail of defeats that had included a home 0-34 September horror show at the hands of Llanelli. Thus a confidence built on long seasons of success now gave way to uncertainty; while rumblings of discontent among followers (perhaps not surprising in the circumstances) were once again reported in the Chronicle pages; and forcefully expressed in the letter of 'F.S.' (Chronicle & Herald, 30th September 1935) when asking *"What's wrong with Bath rugby"* and warning that if the reluctance of some players to travel into, for example, the Welsh heartlands, then top fixtures could be lost. Too true they could!

Yet not for the first time, and most certainly not the last, Bath sprung one of their surprises out of the hat. Boxing Day was as good a moment to start as any, and following their Christmas holiday 8-5 win against the Old Blues, a team suddenly inspired proceeded to defeat Bridgend (3-0), Richmond (9-8), Northampton (11-0), Leicester (14-0) and Bedford (8-3), six straight victories, admittedly at home, but all against quality opposition and followed moreover by home drawn games against Gloucester and Bristol

It was during this run of success that a delighted Chronicle & Herald (20th January 1936) emphasised the *"growing striking power of the young players,"* not least the success of recent scrum-half arrival Dai Davies and utility back 'Bud' West. Others too were showing promise, among them the Rev. John Downward (lock) who rather interestingly *"was always in the thick of the fight,"* and front-row men Les Phillips and A. Ash, soon joined by prop Harry Oak, flanker Bill Gay and lock Kenneth Foss. But aside of the potential of the new arrivals and this welcome return to winning form, the harsh reality was that this was partly a new generation of players and time would be needed to mould them into a successful side. Indeed the post-Christmas uplift was short-lived and one swallow does not necessarily make a summer, a fact that became clear with the final season total of a meagre 13 wins (not one success way from home), 3 draws and a worrying 18 defeats.

That being said, there would be no shortage of events (and incidents) awaiting Bath, and England's 13-0 triumph over the New Zealand All Blacks (4th January 1936) ranked among them, beginning with the English line-up: *(backs): H.G.Owen-Smith (St Mary's Hospital), A.Oberlensky (Oxford University), P. Cranmer (Richmond),* **R.A. Gerrard (Bath)**, *H. Sever (Sale), P. Candler (St Bart's. Hospital), B.C. Gadney (Leicester, capt). (Forwards): D.Kendrew and E. Nicholson (both Leicester), R.Longland (Northampton), C.Webb (Devonport Services), A. Clark (Coventry), E. Hamilton-Hill and P. Dunkley (both Harlequins), W. Weston (Northampton).*

For his countless admirers in the city it was deeply satisfying that Gerrard, as reported in the Chronicle & Herald (6th January 1936), received unreserved plaudits in a game famous (inter alia) for the startling two try performance of England winger Alex Oberlensky. *"Nicely fed in the first instance by a suddenly swift burst of passing by Candler, Cranmer and Gerrard, Oberlensky went galloping ahead....he flashed past Gilbert for his touchdown"* (News Chronicle). Then there was the impregnable defence of the England backs: *"New Zealand would concentrate on mid-field attack. Very well, Hamilton-Hill, Candler, Cranmer and Gerrard would be there to stop them, and stop them they did, with a vengeance"* (D. Telegraph). *"For this [victory] no praise can be too high for Candler, Gerrard and Cranmer"* (D. Mail). *"But New Zealand failed badly outside. Praise here for the English defence, Cranmer, Candler and Gerrard, deadly tacklers, every man"* (Daily Express).

Yet on a day for England to savour, it is doubtful that many knew of the origin of that famed New Zealand trademark.....the 'All Blacks!' Nonetheless, just one month prior to England's encounter against the Tourists the Chronicle & Herald, 'Sports Gossip' (6th December 1935) reported the following communication from Reuters: *"The man mainly responsible for the nickname "All Blacks" has just died at Christchurch, New Zealand......he was* **Mr E.E. Booth***, a member of the New Zealand side which toured*

*England in 1905, and was out training one day by himself and wearing black elastic knee bands and anklets in addition to a black vest and shorts. Asked the reason, he made the jocular reply, "**Oh, just to be all black.**"* Significantly this report was circulated by no less an authority than Reuters, and though it appears that other conflicting tales exist as to the origins of the 'All Blacks' title, the fact is that Reuters on this occasion had specified an individual's name from Rugby's past. For that alone the archivist can be grateful.

This same season was memorable too for the 100th official match between Bath and Bristol (29th February 1936) and a rivalry where, to put it mildly, Bristol had enjoyed something of a monopoly. Suffice to say that in 99 previous outings, Bristol had won 71 games to Bath's 17 (with 11 outings drawn). The 100th encounter (on the Rec) was another draw. In fact the 3-3 result, thanks to tries from Bristol's P.J. Haskins and Bath winger Les Matthews, would mirror to perfection the same 3-3 result of that first derby game in 1888, when according to Bath records, a draw resulted from three minors each.

This particular statistic of the 1888 encounter was quoted in the match programme notes for the 100th encounter. So too was another matter, concerning the brother of Bath try scorer Les Matthews, and one that hinted at a painful Bath memory that seemingly was not as yet fully exorcised. These notes gave praiseworthy reference to Bristol internationals L.J. Corbett and Sam Tucker. But… a further reference to Sam Tucker was included: *"Much as we admire "Sam" here in Bath, we can never forgive him for flying to Cardiff and robbing us of another international player, Norman Matthews."* Now, six years had passed under the proverbial bridge since that day when Matthews was stood down minutes before running out with England; six years in which to air this grievance. Yet now on this historic 100th occasion between two uncommonly fierce yet friendly rivals the 'Cardiff incident' was briefly, yet noticeably, highlighted.

If this reference was intended in jest (as it may have been) then it did not quite read that way. Indeed it appeared that Bath (who had never born a grudge against Bristol) could not as yet entirely forget or forgive. Yet Sam Tucker was not the villain of the peace, far from it in fact. The Bristolian had merely answered the bugle call for King and Country as instructed to do so by the England hierarchy at Cardiff. And arguably they, not Sam Tucker, bore the responsibility for Matthew's last minute withdrawal at Cardiff (see too: Ch.17. pp. 2-3).

Meanwhile one further plus on the playing side in this eventful though not particularly successful Bath season was that Neath, already victors over Swansea, Bristol and Llanelli, were defeated 11-6 on the Rec, whereupon the Chronicle & Herald (7th April 1936) spoke of Bath's *"wonderful forwards…and a rock-like resistance under the severest pressure;"* while adding that this victory *"proved what a tremendously difficult side [Bath] are to subdue on their own ground."* This was no ordinary praise from the Chronicle and no ordinary victory. Hopefully it raised hopes too for a much needed recovery come the following season, hopes doubtless shared by Eddie Simpkins (he of the 'unruffled temperament') who had now completed twenty five years as club secretary, and of whom the Bath Chronicle wondered *"if anyone has done so much for the club as he has."*

The eighteen wins (six away) of the following 1936-7 campaign that included home victories over Harlequins (6-5) and Northampton (15-0), plus three away draws at U.S. Portsmouth, Richmond and Moseley did suggest that Bath might now be 'over the worst.' The pack responded positively to the captaincy of the great all-round forward that was Norman Matthews, and consistency was much improved from the previous season. While among the backs those stalwarts Billy Hancock and Les Matthews were still good enough (and fast enough) to get around defences. Les Matthews (*"once he is off, there is not much stopping of the winger")* gave a two try contribution in Bath's January 15-0 home win over Northampton; and the Chronicle further noted the influence of Roy Harris, the new out-half discovery who *"took the ball at speed, and his masterly cuts through, with pace, dummy and swerve, were a treat to watch."*

Yet doubts persisted. For although away performances showed an improvement, indeed Bath came close at Cardiff in a nail-biting 3-0 defeat, far bigger upsets were experienced during the season at Llanelli (27-0), and later a 29-3 loss at Bridgend; setbacks that were hardly the best advertisement for the club. Yet that alas was the unavoidable impression given to opponents and their supporters, especially in Wales, when Bath visited 'their' home territories. After all, they judged on what they saw! Small wonder then there were doubts as where to now place Bath in the 'order of things.' Matters were hardly helped moreover by an assumption among some players that ventures into Wales were a lost cause, so why even bother to go there; a perverse attitude, not least in view of the fact that for many years Bath at home could beat some of the very best that Welsh rugby could throw at them. That being said however, it was at the Devon home of Torquay Athletic that Bath would find themselves embroiled in an incident that would lead to totally unexpected ramifications.

Now, regular fixtures between these two clubs had commenced only one season previously and Bath's heavy 21-6 defeat at Torquay's beautiful ground in April 1936 warned of the difficulties when facing this particular side; although it was re-assuring for Bath when wining 8-3 at home in the following September. So far…so good, but any supposed *entente* would change on Bath's visit to Devon on 20th March 1937. On this occasion Torquay, with some 1500-2000 spectators present, did not have things their own way, and in the closing minutes Bath's Peter Moon scored another try to virtually settle matters beyond Torquay's reach at 4-14. Moon however was clearly off-side, as Bath openly acknowledged later. Nonetheless, a small section of the home crowd now took matters a 'little further,' and the Chronicle & Herald (22nd March 1937) reported thus: *"As the teams left the field a crowd congregated in front of the main stand, booing and hurling derisive comments at the referee. One or two adopted a threatening attitude and to avoid any possibility of a serious incident, the players closed round Mr Newcombe, forming an escort to the dressing room." "It is to be hoped,"* added the Chronicle, *"that the matter will be speedily forgotten."* Unfortunately it was not!

In fact the Bath committee met on the following Monday and within a week it was announced that future fixtures with Torquay Athletic would be cancelled. The decision seemed draconian to say the least, one as regrettable as it was unexpected, and it would be easy to condemn the committee for the scale of its reaction. The Devonians after all were a much respected club and could boast an impressive record in West Country rugby. But it is near certain that uppermost in the minds of Bath would have been the need to avoid any risk of further trouble, either home or away. Moreover, the incident had raised some awkward questions. First, the next visit of Torquay to the Rec would undoubtedly arouse wide interest and almost certainly a large crowd. Secondly, there was the sensitive issue occurring two seasons previously against Blackheath, when a small Bath post-match demonstration had occurred on the Rec for reasons similar to that at Torquay. Nor was an 'event' from season 1907-8 likely to have been entirely forgotten, when following a violent home Somerset Cup match against Weston super Mare trouble had spread to the terraces itself, resulting with a temporary ban imposed upon Bath. Hence some or all of these factors may have influenced this drastic reaction. What is certain however is that their decision to discontinue fixtures was made quickly and decisively.

It is near certain that Weston super Mare would have followed this situation with more than just a passing interest. Indeed in recent seasons broad hints had been made concerning their desire that the past be forgotten and for a restoration of their regular fixtures with Bath. Rotarian T.B.Butter from the seaside town had expressed just this desire when visiting Bath Rotarians in January 1936. Emphasising to the Chronicle that *"the seaside town were somewhat peeved that Bath would not give them a match,"* he added humbly that *"Weston did not expect any of the best dates, but were nonetheless anxious to have the opportunity of renewing a sporting occasion."*

Naturally with the cessation of the Torquay dates, Bath suddenly found themselves with blank days to fill owing to events that long ago had caused formal fixtures with Weston super Mare to be broken off. So, Bath chose to apply some 'realpolitik.' The hatchet was buried almost immediately and normal relations with the 'Seasiders' were resumed in due course, a team now rated by the Chronicle as *"a very fine side, worthy to rank with the best."*

Making further amends meanwhile to the regrettable 'matter' with Torquay was the letter from Sale following their tour match at Bath, when despite losing 11-3 they expressed their warmest gratitude for the hospitality shown to them. *"We [Sale] were splendidly entertained by the Bath club, and Mr Simpkins, their secretary, made every effort to see we had a wonderful time. Their hospitality did not cease on the Saturday. We had an invitation for every member of the side to accompany some the team and officials on a visit to the magnificent Cheddar Gorge and the noted Cheddar Caves;"* adding that on the final morning *"we left the city that had shown us such exceptional hospitality.*

'Those were the days' some might say. Yes, on many occasions they were. But that depended on the occasion, and one need look no further than Bath's own experiences in the mid-1930's (Blackheath and Torquay spring to mind) for yet further proof that passions could spill over in rugby union as elsewhere in sport.

Meanwhile notwithstanding such unfortunate events in the Union code, the anxieties of schoolmasters with appointments in the North whose remit included rugby league coaching were assured by the RFU that this would 'not' affect their amateur status; Engineer-Commander Cooper (Chronicle & Herald, 23rd January 1937) stating thus: *"Schoolmasters are not committing an act of professionalism if they assist in the instruction of any form of sport, even if it is rugby League Football."* Ironically, there was no reason to suppose that rugby League needed to be regarded as outcasts by anyone.

When Bath opened their account for the 1937-8 season with a 19-17 home win over Llanelli, hopes were raised that the modest revival of the previous year might be more permanent, for this was a victory with the 'Wow' factor and the perfect start to a new season. Further hopes were raised too by the sublime qualities of Roy Harris; around whom a new era of success could hopefully be created; and who some observers now

GOTCHA! ...just as well for Leicester. Even Prince Alex Obolensky (far left) looks back in alarm as jinking Bath outhalf Harris leaves three Tigers sprawling (result: Bath 17, Leicester 13, season 1936-37)

Acknowledgements to Bath Chronicle

believed was a future England out-half with The Bath Chronicle among those singing his praises: *"His darts, fast and unexpected, nonplussed the opposition. They got [Llanelly] on the wrong foot, hopelessly beaten."* And wing B.V. Robinson showed that Harris was not the only star on show. *"Astonishingly quick at the uptake and amazingly determined in his running. His four tries will be long remembered."* Four tries against Llanelly? A winger's dream.

But early hopes were soon replaced by unwelcome reality, and despite the renewed captaincy of Gerrard, it became increasingly clear that wishful thinking alone could not ensure that post-1935 teams would automatically continue the momentum of their predecessors. The questions surrounding their forward strength continued. *"Wanting in weight and height, [they] do not get the ascendancy in the tight and in the line-out one would wish to see...."* (Chronicle & Herald, 4th October 1937).

Even so, Bath continued to display their curious unpredictable character. The January 11-0 win over Northampton was in the words of "The Captain" (Chronicle & Herald) 'astonishing,' as Bath *"swept [the visitors] off their feet."* Foss got the first, and Lance Wardle and Jack Bartlett the others, *"the outcome of dashing passing and glorious running. Bartlett's was a splendid affair. He ran like a deer and with beautiful judgement. A hand-off, a swerve, and a change of direction and he completely hoodwinked the defence.* The 8-0 win over Bristol in early March again brought out the superlatives from the "The Captain" (7th March 1938). *"[Bath] wiped out the memory of indifferent performances this season, touched heights almost unsuspected, and made the opposition look very unimpressive."*

Yet a lowly tally of thirteen victories for the season was hardly cause for celebration, despite further wins over quality opponents Gloucester and Moseley that helped to lift the gloom. But the scale of the re-building task would be shown all too clearly in the season's woeful final three games against Headingly, Old Merchant Taylors and Leicester respectively; each a defeat and at home (Leicester winning 0-27) and in all three matches Bath failed to score so much as a single point.

However, there was most certainly off-field cheer provided by the marriage between the striking Molly Taylor and Bath and England centre Ron Gerrard. Molly, like her father, was already a qualified architect and the wedding (19th November) was described in the Chronicle as a *"brilliant affair."* Best man was H.G. Owen-Smith, Gerrard's England colleague, and some four hundred guests attended the service at St. Mary's church, Bathwick. Then following the reception at the Pump Room an ancient Bath Chair 'miraculously' appeared in the Abbey churchyard awaiting one R. A. Gerrard, who was thus *"conveyed through cheering crowds along Stall Street to the waiting honeymoon car."* It was indeed a wedding fit for a sporting hero whose abilities and example had won the hearts of countless rugby followers, nor forgetting the heart of a remarkable young woman.

Ken Foss was then handed the captaincy for season 1938-9 and with it a squad that again included a number of as yet lesser known players. Time would be needed therefore to blend the more recent arrivals with seniors such as Gerrard, still good enough to earn an England Trial, though at full-back, not centre. Time however would be a luxury that would not be forthcoming, as events elsewhere would shortly reveal. So the task facing Ken Foss would not be easy, and Bath's late September defeat at Devonport Services reported by "The Captain" (Chronicle & Herald, 26th September 1938) articulated both the possibilities and the difficulties that lay ahead. In the backs the only regulars were scrum-half Norman Halse, and centres Bud West (sometimes full-back) and G. Forster. Youngster Tom Hicks showed promise, so too winger Fred Hayman (all 15 years of him) who come the conclusion of World War Two would appear for Bath again still a youth of 22 years. Scrum-half Halse, schoolboy international Tom Hicks and wing Jack Arnold would likewise resume their own promising rugby careers some six years later, and like Hayman all still young men. At forward the front-row of Unwin, Brown and Ash, with Foss and Grundy at lock, and Weiss, Bill Gay and Phillips *[looked] a pack good enough for any opposition, but there is not the fire, the team-work – anyway not till too late.* One exception was Bill Gay (father of Bath and England No.8 David Gay). *"A great forward"* wrote "The Captain."

This therefore was a team with long term potential, but short on experience, and this partly explains why a mere nine victories were won, although to be fair there were six draws, and the victories gained did include the likes of Bristol and Northampton. Furthermore, Bath's 3-5 landmark success at Kingsholm on 19th November 1938 was the club's first ever away win at Gloucester, one elevated into an elusive Double when Bath fought out a 6-5 home victory on 18th February 1939. But such triumphs were fleeting, and genuine concerns returned with a losing run of seven consecutive defeats to conclude the season that commenced with a 7-3 upset at Weston-s-Mare (restored by now to the Bath fixture list) and culminating with a 20-3 defeat at Neath. There was pride it is true with the selections of three-quarter A.V. Rogers and forward Bill Gay for Somerset in the 1938-9 County Championship final at Weston-s-Mare against Warwickshire; albeit that with the score poised on a knife-edge at 3-3 the Midland side clinched the result literally with seconds to spare thanks to a Bruce-Lockhart try under the posts (Seventy years of Somerset rugby, 1875-1945, p. 44).

But during the season eyes were looking elsewhere, to the Continent to be precise, and the world was about to change again; so time once more for reflection on two decades of rugby that had promised so much, not least at Bath when from that eventful day in September 1919 and their 3-16 victory at Leicester they would thrive with more than fifteen years of success and record crowds, albeit followed by four less certain seasons of re-building. Usually they held out the hand of welcoming friendship. Occasionally (Blackheath, March 1935) they had by contrast shown a more questionable side of their nature. Curiously a club who always held their great rivals Bristol in the highest regard were nonetheless the same Bath who since Somerset Cup days had long shared a distinctly uneasy relationship with Weston super Mare. So it was that Bath continued with their contradictions.

Their strengths included their warmth, a sense of family and at home especially their capability to beat some of the best sides in England and Wales; while their weaknesses included a lack of confidence away from the Rec, a drawback especially evident in Wales. Their geography too was both a help and hindrance, because despite earlier hopes Bath found that they could not shake free from the continued domination of Bristol and Gloucester; and there were no illusions on the Rec about the difficulties this posed. For they must turn the status quo on its head, reach heights never even dreamed of (let alone achieved) and dominate Bristol and Gloucester....simultaneously! Even the top sides of England and Wales might shudder at the thought, let alone a Bath club now languishing back in the lower reaches of the first-class rugby game. Yet that remained the challenge. Again it seemed impossible.

Chapter 19. IN THE LAP OF THE GODS. (1939-45)

In the mid-summer of 1939 the everyday life of the city seemed normal….on the surface at least. On the Rec the training had commenced by early August; it was learned that Lt. H. Withers (Army, Blackheath and Ireland) and Bryan Wallis (R.A.F. and Irish Trialist) were set to join Bath; numbers of former players were now intending to join up with the coaching staff; and talented scrum-half J. Parsons (Leicester & Cambridge Blue) was a definite recruit whose presence promised a brilliant half-back partnership with Roy Harris. While high up on Lansdown (16th August) jockey-legend Gordon Richards ran home four winners at the Bath races. The bookies must have been thrilled!

So all seemed well, like any other normal August. But come the 24th the Chronicle & Herald headlined conclusive news that things were far from normal: *"Bath ready if the worst comes,"* it proclaimed. Then in words that would have prophetic significance for the city, the report added: *"Bath, in common with the rest of the country, has received its special instructions to be prepared to affect a black-out in the event of need."* The particular need in this case referred to the possibility of air-raids, and Bath with an Admiralty Headquarters in its midst was potentially a strategic target and one situated barely a stones-throw from the Rec.

Then with Britain's declaration of war with Germany on 3rd September the preparations for the Bath v Llanelli curtain-raiser of the 1939-40 season on 9th September were brought to an abrupt halt. Hence on the eve of this prestigious encounter those typical pre-match forecasts and team reports were absent from the Chronicle & Herald pages. Instead the front page showed a striking photograph, not of the Bath line-up, but of the Somerset Yeomanry parading in immaculate order prior to their departure for a destination as yet 'unknown.' So there would be no Bath v Llanelli clash in September 1939. Indeed, there would be no Bath v Llanelli clash for another six long years.

As with the outbreak of conflict in the 1914-18 war, this new emergency threatened the continuation of any official form of sporting activity. But remarkably, rugby did continue in those early Autumn days of 1939, though admittedly not on a nation-wide format. Instead, matches were initially arranged on an 'ad hoc' basis with fixtures planned regionally, and for Bath this reached as far out as Exeter in the South West and to Newport and later Cardiff in Wales. However, although Bath played their first war-time game on 7th October, winning 30-6 on the Rec against an Admiralty XV, it was soon obvious that owing to military call-ups there would be a shortage of available players. Acting promptly therefore, the club and that same Admiralty XV agreed to join forces, and as a result (and for the duration of the war) the Bath & Admiralty RFC played as a combined club-team.

Their baptism (14th October 1939) was a home 17-15 win over a Mr McNamara's XV. One week later they hosted Exeter with a reported two thousand crowd attending. On this occasion they lost 9-20 and commenced a losing trend that continued until the 18th December when at last Bath won at Cheltenham with a welcome 0-23 away win. But although winning is always pleasing, actually playing was the all-important priority in times so threatening as these; it was an act of defiance; a message for friend and (especially) foe: 'we'll play our rugby come hell or high water…so get used to it!'

However, in view of the emergency there were genuine doubts as to whether or not this hastily planned war-time rugby programme could continue into a second season. In fact, such were the omens by the New Year that it seems that there were doubts that rugby could get beyond half a season, let alone a full one. Indeed there was no rugby for Bath in January 1940, nor rugby for Bath (or for many other West Country clubs) for the first seven weeks of 1940; for such were the uncertainties caused by the on-going military preparations and not helped either by the sometimes severe blizzard-type weather conditions sweeping across parts of the Country. On the 24th February however Bath & Admiralty travelled to Stroud. Again they lost. But what the 'heck'….they played; and it was smiles all round in late March (1940) when not only did they actually win a game (6-4), but their change of fortune was at the expense of an Army XV led by, of all people, home favourite R. A. Gerrard.

Yet the task involved in continuing the game in war-time cannot be underestimated, and the decision of the RFU to grant a two week extension to season 1939-40 extended a life-line to many clubs struggling to keep the show on the road, not least the gate-taking clubs so dependent on attendances. Another difficulty during a major war lay in actually obtaining sufficient players to field a team, let alone a competent one; likewise the 'back-room' task of administering a club in times of constant change. For example the difficulties of obtaining transport, the uncertainty of players' availability and the often unreliable means of communication were all problems confronting any club operating in such a predicament. In addition there was the critical financial shortfall caused by loss of gate-money.

But it was the final game at Weston super Mare on 20th April that was perhaps the most poignant for the Bath & Admiralty in season 1939-40, not least because Jack Arnold, G.C. Foster and Roy Harris were all preparing to join the RAF, the Armoured Corps and the Royal Artillery respectively. That the Seasiders won that day mattered little, because for the Bath lads this was an occasion to bid farewell to their fellow team-mates, none knowing when (or if) they might ever meet again.

So ended the fraught and far from normal season of 1939-40, whose significance is perhaps easy to overlook, while in fact it was nigh on a miracle that it even started, let alone finished. After all, those now struggling to organise rugby during a full-scale war were frequently compelled to make things up as they went along. Yet, in defiance of all temptation to simply throw in the towel and await the outcome of the conflict, the organisers stuck to their guns, if one will pardon the pun.

Nonetheless so uncertain had been the situation in the final week of this opening season that the "The Captain" (Chronically & Herald, 15th April 1940) had ruefully commented that the *future of war-time rugby was in the lap of the gods."* And yet unlike 1914-18 when official rugby was abandoned completely, the Bath and Admiralty among a number of clubs would continue to function throughout the war, and once again the reason was partly one of geography. For the city was situated within a reasonable distance to several nearby RAF bases and furthermore to the large military garrisons now stationed on the Salisbury Plain. It was these centres in particular that provided eager and willing sources of opposition, and not forgetting players. Meanwhile at the national level of the game not only did the prestigious Barbarians play on occasions, but likewise a number of unofficial international games were held. Sevens too proved popular, not least at Bath, where both inter-club and Services 7's tournaments provided a highly successful feature of late season rugby. And remarkably in such critical circumstances, the Middlesex Sevens (then England's premier inter-club tournament) would continue throughout the entire War.

But other (not always obvious) difficulties arose in maintaining an effective rugby side, not least the captaincy factor; and for the first two war-time seasons the leadership of a Bath & Admiralty team was often dependent on who might be available at any given time. Fortunately come 1941-2 the amiable John Wass was able to skipper the team on a more regular basis, thanks partly to his role as a civil engineer based at the Admiralty. From 1943 onwards it was the equally affable Austin Higgins who then took hold of the reins, while John Wass dedicated his efforts to the considerable task of club secretary. Meanwhile another difficulty that sometimes required a 'quick fix' was obtaining a referee. They too were subject to the 'call of duty,' leading to a predicament typified on 12th December 1942 when Bath hosted an RAF XV. The opposition arrived, but the referee didn't. So Dick Chaddock, Bath's otherwise indispensable treasurer suddenly discovered that he was now an equally indispensable referee. By all accounts he didn't do too bad a job either!

Then there was the normally sensitive matter of the Rugby League factor, or to be precise, the 'removal' of the Rugby League factor. This after all was war-time, and in view of the exceptional circumstances now prevailing, the RFU withdrew all Union barriers to those League players involved in Services rugby. True, there wasn't much else they could do and such a barrier was virtually unenforceable in war-time anyway. Moreover clubs such as Bath sometimes faced Services teams literally packed with League players. But! Bath not only played against League players, on occasions they even played with them. S.Morgan (R.A.F.) for example, otherwise of Hull Kingston Rovers, earned considerable praise at scrum-half for Bath in their win at Bridgwater on 9th December 1944.

And his appearance raised several pertinent questions. First, while the Union-League truce permitted League players to represent Services teams, it was questionable whether or not the RFU intended this liberty to extend to the selection of League players to represent non-Service teams? Whatever the answer may have been, it appears that Bath were 'open' about the matter and, apart from the 1939-45 period, the club obediently followed 'to the letter' the standard RFU ban regarding professional League players.

The matter did not stop there however, because the Bath & Herald's report of Morgan's debut for Bath (11th December 1944) suggests that in addition to Morgan, other rugby League players may have represented the club: *"It is a rare occurrence for a Rugby League player to figure in the Bath side...."* the Chronicle wrote. A 'rare' occurrence yes …. but not it seems an entirely unknown one. We might never know for certain. But it seems reasonable to draw the following conclusions: namely that the war-time Union and League truce was in practice more far-reaching than has been realised; that on occasions some clubs (including Bath) fielded a League player, and that the RFU (assuming that they were aware of this fact) took no action to stop it. If this was the case, one can only wonder at the contrast with the RFU's refusal to compromise on this issue in later decades, a refusal that would cause such divisions within the Union game itself towards the end of the century.

The aftermath of the North Stand following night-time bombing raids on Bath
Acknowledgements to Bath Chronicle

Meanwhile that other far greater conflict of 1939-45 continued, and for much of the time the threat lurked high above, hence the air-raid warning (printed on Bath match programmes) as follows: *"In the event of an alert, spotters will go on duty. If danger becomes imminent they will blow 3 blasts on their whistles. Play will then immediately cease. Shelter guides wearing white armlets will be available to direct spectators to shelter."* The threat moreover was always there and on the nights of 25th/26th April 1942 it struck directly at the heart of the city. *"Three air raids over two nights took the lives of more than 400 people,"* headlined the Chronicle, while *"900 buildings were destroyed and some 12,000 more were damaged."* Among this destruction was the home of Eddie Simpkins (and alas the loss of a photo-history of the Bath club), while the Rec took several direct hits from bombs possibly intended for the Admiralty building, leaving the West and North stands nothing more than heaps of mangled wreckage.

Then…..there was the fate of those serving beyond these shores, not least the loss as reported in the Chronicle & Herald (10th February 1943). It duly announced the *"grievous news"* that had arrived in a War Office telegram on the previous night, one that was subsequently diverted to the club chairman Capt. Stanley Amor who undertook to break the news to a suddenly bereaved family. For 'Gerry' Gerrard (now Major, Royal Engineers) had been killed four days after his 31st birthday at Alamein in January 1943.

The Chronicle expressed its deepest and sincere sympathies, and those of all Bathonians, to Molly Gerrard and her baby son Duncan, whose godfathers were Wing Commander B.V. (Robbie) Robinson, D.S.O. and D.F.C., and Capt. Pottinger who saw action against the Graf Spee in the battle of the River Plate. For Ronald Anderson Gerrard was the classic schoolboys' hero. There was the outstanding all-round sportsman whose sporting prowess included county cricket for Somerset and rugby for England. In addition there was the fearless soldier who in his final days would lead his sappers out into hazardous night-time operations on vital mine-field clearance tasks and who 'for his bravery in the push from El Alamein received the immediate award of the D.S.O.' But now…..it was farewell to a rugby legend, one whose qualities had proved an inspiration to a generation of Bathonians, and it was the Chronicle again who would provide the near perfect yet heart-rending lament: *"Now he sleeps on the battlefield in a spot that will be forever England."*

Naturally in a conflict of six years duration there were other Bath players who selflessly gave their lives for their Country, among them Royal Air Force wingers J.S. Bartlett D.F.C. and the aforementioned B.V. Robinson. In addition the Roll of Honour included half-back John 'Freddie' Rhymes, forwards Peter Moon and Leslie Phillips, George Nudds (Royal Navy), and 1920's three-quarters H.C. Partridge and Lt. Colonel 'Dick' James (Somerset Light Infantry). Their loss too was great.

Rather more comforting however were the events unfolding on the Continent during 1944 indicating that the end of the conflict in Europe was within sight. Indeed, the 1944-5 rugby season would close just five weeks short of VE Day; while another highly promising outside-half had now arrived in the city, namely Edinburgh University medical graduate Ian Lumsden, a young Scot who had impressed from that moment of his Bath debut in December 1943. Of steady hands and composure and an excellent long range kicker, the young doctor was a half-back with the ability to tactically dominate a game. He was destined to be Bath's first Scottish international. Austin Higgins continued as skipper, although if one anecdote is to be believed, it was only Lady Luck who ensured that he was. Because according to Jack Simpkins (son of Eddie) 'the redoubtable Austin managed to sleep peacefully through an entire night of the Bath Blitz only to awake the following morning to discover that half his home no longer existed.' Thus Austin, neither 'shaken or stirred' from the visit of the Luftwaffe, was obviously the perfect man to lead the club through their final war-time season; one that in early September would include a 5-24 upset against the **R.A.A.F.** (Royal Australian Air Force) whom Bath 'rated the best team of the War played on the Rec,' and then culminate first with a 0-3 upset at Nuneaton who (Chronicle & Herald 27th March 1945) claimed to be the only Midland club to continue throughout the war without a break, and Leicester (Bath winning 5-3) known during the conflict as Leicester Barbarians.

Five weeks later on 8th May it would be VE Day, and the official rugby game would resume in the Autumn. At Bath however the game had never stopped for the six years of conflict, an era when players from here, there and just about everywhere had carried the colours of the Bath & Admiralty. As for the Rec, bombs had been dropped right on top of it. As for the club treasury, the coffers were all but empty. But it was home! Bath had played on this green meadow since 1894 and no one (not even the Luftwaffe) was going to drive them away. It was, apart from anything else, a show of defiance. The Ritz had never closed. Bath had never stopped playing!

Chapter 20.   BATH (1945-50)……RUGBY YEOMEN.

It was during the late 1770's (Georgian Summer, by David Gadd, p.124) that the architectural genius that was Thomas Baldwin 'redesigned the Cross Bath with its curved frontage one hundred yards west of the pump room.' Fast-track to the rugby season of 1945-6 and that same Cross Bath (fully operational) provided changing facilities for Bath RFC as they embarked upon their first season of post-war rugby, one that would begin with their encounter against Welsh legends Llanelli. So far, so good; but the Rec was another matter altogether, because the ground that in those in pre-war days had sometimes hosted crowds of thousands now possessed not so much as a single enclosure and furthermore the club were seriously short of revenue. However a temporary West stand would soon be open for business, and a rugby family that had played the game throughout the war, sometimes with bombs falling onto their heads, would allow nothing to spoil the party for the Scarlet's visit.

Yet while a temporary enclosure was one thing, something to actually wear was quite another, with government issued 'clothing coupons' required before the club could purchase so much as a single shirt; and it was a grateful and doubtless much relieved Bath when a further 36 coupons landed on the secretary's desk prior to the start of the 1945 season. Unfortunately (Chronicle & H, 3rd September 1945) the club colours of blue, white and black were not immediately available, and for the following three seasons it was to be white shirts only, blue shorts and red socks….actually, not a bad substitute. And yet even at this most austere of times the club decided to donate the proceeds of the first game (versus Llanelli) to the Alkmaar Fund, established to provide much needed aid to this war-stricken Dutch city. Somehow it was a gesture such as this (Chronicle & H, 4th September 1945) that said so much about Bath.

But as the Llanelli clash loomed ever closer, it was difficult to predict how a re-formed Bath (or indeed any club) would perform after a lapse of six years. Indeed, while it is sometimes said that a team is as good as its 'last' game, in Bath's case (and of course the Welshmen) this last game happened six years ago, though it could be said with no little certainty that Llanelli were again likely to be 'one hell of a side.' As for Bath, this much was known: Austin Higgins (yes, he who reportedly had slept peacefully through a night-bombing raid) was both a robust forward and a morale boosting skipper. The admired 'Bud' West of pre-war days was yet again to prove a steadying hand of experience at fullback. Furthermore centre Joe Bailey (who had played for Somerset in their County championship final in 1935) could still live in top-class rugby despite his thirty six years of age, and out-half Lumsden, when available, was a master of his craft! Alas, the flying Scotsman was regrettably not available for that long awaited post-war opener on 8th September 1945, hence his absence from the following Bath line-up that ran out onto the Rec on that emotional day: *B. Capon, F.W. Thomas, J. Bailey, Les*

Moores, Pat Leahy, Tom Cuff, J. Parkin, C.P. Hosking, L. James, W. Barrow, J. Owen, C. J. Stewart, Tom Smith, Kenneth Weiss, Austin Higgins (Capt.).

But the fact that official rugby had commenced after six long years ensured that this was a day to remember. Hurriedly (where once a gleaming West Stand had stood) a temporary enclosure 'had' been constructed with steel scaffolding and corrugated sheeting at the then considerable cost of one hundred pounds. An estimated two thousand crowd attended, most of whom would have relished a home victory, although the 0-16 result to the visitors ensured that the Llanelli boys would be singing their hearts out all the way back to the Welsh heartlands; and so too Llanelli loyalist Gareth Hughes (see: 'One hundred years of Scarlet') who wrote thus:

"....I know exactly what I was doing. I was glued to the wireless, waiting impatiently for the result of Llanelli's first rugby match after the war. And I still recall the pride and exhilaration when the news was broadcast to an expectant nation-or at least the part of it which I, as a third former at Llanelly County School, represented. "Bath nil, Llanelly 16 points." My joy was boundless: and my pride was confirmed a few days later when a headline in a local newspaper proclaimed, "Impressive Start to Rugby Season." No addicted supporter at Stradey will be surprised to know that the Scarlets' margin of victory would have been greater "but for the inconsistent decisions of the referee, who twice disallowed spectacular, and what appeared to be legitimate, scores by Gerwyn Rees." The newspaper files of more than a century provide staunch evidence that every referee who ever set foot at Stradey should properly have been consigned to the nearest lunatic asylum. "Bath nil, Llanelly 16 points." A simple statistic, in my case never to be forgotten. Yet, in general terms, I have never been much interested in the general statistics which attach to the game. It has always seemed to me that the sociological aspects of rugby are very much more interesting than the arithmetical ones. That man of steel went straight from a hard shift in the heat and glare of the furnaces to play against a major touring team at Stradey seems to me to be the real stuff of rugby history...."

But after their opening season defeat it would be a case of wait-and-see as to whether or not a new post-war Bath era would repeat the pattern of their revival that followed the Great War of 1914-18. But six years (not four) had lapsed since Bath last played as a team, while a new West Stand was now an absolute 'must' if the club was to continue attracting gate-paying attendances sufficient to support the running-costs of a fully-fledged first-class rugby gate-taking club. But money was tight in those post-war days of limited means and rationing, where the price of Bath season tickets of £2 and 2 shillings (men) and £1 and 1 shilling (ladies) was actually serious money during this belt-tightening era. Saving transport costs too was another top priority for the hard pressed club treasurer. Yet the ship steadied, morale remained high and there were signs of genuine promise from a mid-season run that included a commendable draw at Llanelli, followed by wins over London Scottish, Northampton, Moseley (a double),

Wasps and....away at Gloucester! Indeed this 11-13 victory at Kingsholm (16th February 1946) was undoubtedly a much prized triumph and was furthermore Gloucester's first defeat inflicted by an English team that season. Yet this achievement came at a fearful cost. For Roy Harris, he of sublime skills and who but for the war would have likely been in contention for England honours, was seriously injured, and the effect on the club was palpable. Harris would never play rugby again, and despite a follow-up win over Moseley one week later, a despondent Bath would slide into an alarming losing run of nine defeats on the trot, save for victory over the O.M.T's, before a further home 5-17 upset against Leicester would finish off the season.

One reason in particular for this slump was the loss of Roy Harris. It was a serious blow, so too the fact that Lumsden was not always available either. Yet that being said, some wins were achieved against top opposition, even if a mere 16 victories was hardly something to 'boast about.' It was premature anyway to pass judgement so soon after the return to full-time rugby and re-building in such circumstances was to say the least a challenging prospect. But the swiftly re-formed Supporters Club who since their formation in 1920-1 had always 'knuckled down' and assisted in just about anything they could lay their eager hands on were again 'up and running;' while the award for the war-time's 'most dedicated follower' was won undoubtedly by Bristol (yes Bristol!) domiciled Mr A.E. Ley. His round journey to the Rec covered no less than 26 miles of travel. But 'have wheels-will travel,' and as the Chronicle (10th September 1945) admiringly reported, he had for many years regularly biked some 300 to 500 miles each season to support his beloved Bath. What a star!

Come the following 1946-7 campaign under new captain Ian Lumsden a confidence would hopefully return, plus signs of a further recovery from the worst effects of the War. The club fortunately was not short of invaluable support from behind the scenes, assistance that would extend to those precious clothing coupons, which were literally like gold-dust for sports clubs in these times of strict rationing. As the Chronicle & Herald reported (6th September 1946) 'Mr R. Bennett of Poole, who, bemoaning the Board of Trade for limiting Bath to a mere 18 coupons for 50 players, donated 18 coupons himself; Mr C. Willis of Shaftesbury Avenue, Bath, gave another 26; and not forgetting Mr A. Bruton from far west Plymouth who possessed no coupons, but kindly sent his vintage Bath jersey (but still usable) to the club.'

On the field meanwhile a 3-3 home draw against Llanelli in early September with a near five thousand crowd raised hopes of a 'new dawn.' Joe Bailey (only days from his 37th birthday) and deputising with distinction as both captain and out-half for the injured Lumsden, not unnaturally inspired a *"confidence in the newcomers"* upon whose shoulders so much would now depend. But a draw, however commendable, is not a victory, and when Bath fell albeit narrowly at Leicester and Swansea, then (though seven 1st teamers short) were literally crushed 45-3 by a rampant Devonport Services in late September, all bets were off!

Nonetheless in that by now typical Bath way….there would be a recovery. Bristol were appropriately the turning point thanks to a close mid-October 8-6 win and the Chronicle, not for the first time either, enthused over the abilities of skipper Ian Lumsden: *"He often saved his defence by his positional play, tackling and kicking, and*

IAN LUMSDEN ..... from Watsonian to Bathonian.

often his pack by use of the touchline. He was not spectacular, but he was amazingly sound and a 'tower of strength' at many critical points of the afternoon." The victory was followed later with an all-round team performance that clinched a mid-January 8-5 win over Cardiff. Even better was to follow when in the latter part of the season Bath arguably hit their best form since the early 1930's. Harlequins were defeated (3-0), then London Scottish (6-3) and Leicester (12-8); while Newport were held 13-13 away, Northampton fell (16-13) and Moseley (11-0). Finally Bath concluded their season with an 8-3 success against Gloucester. Only Bristol's 9-3 revenge win and a not totally unexpected 6-8 defeat by the irrepressible O.M.T.s over a partly rested Bath side interrupted the seemingly unstoppable late run of success.

Yet while Lumsden was undoubtedly the key individual of this team, the key factor in a season's total of 18 wins and 4 draws (though not forgetting ten defeats) was the pack. This was a new generation of forwards, and what forwards! *"No pack in England could have excelled Bath's in their match with Harlequins...."* enthused 'The Captain,' in his Chronicle report (3rd April 1947) of the one try to nil win over Quins (see above). *"Austin Higgins – could you find his master anywhere; – D.S Beard who is worth a place in any first-class side; W.G. Jenkins, a top-top aggressive wing forward; Dr [Allan] Todd, medico, like Lumsden at the Royal United Hospital, who appearing in his first game of the season was magnificent in the middle of the back row....and Farmer Bland from his broad acres on the Wiltshire Downs."* Nor were they the only ones, because chasing 1st team places were powerful Arthur Burcombe (later to captain Somerset), Len Harter and Bill Barrow. While with the home 8-3 victory over Gloucester that brought closure to Lumsden's one year captaincy the Chronicle (5th May 1947) was moved to comment thus: *"If [Bath] can keep the present players together and introduce some new blood in the United to fill the future vacancies in the Firsts [then] the record of this season, magnificent as it has been, will be beaten."*

It was no surprise therefore that the club would choose to play safe and continue with a similar forward-based strategy until such time as a new generation of backs might arrive; though that is not to deny that with the likes of three-quarters Kevin O'Shaughnessy and Stan Ascott the club now possessed a pair of fast, determined runners, and Jack Arnold was a totally safe 'pair of hands' at fullback. Yet the emphasis was based around a strong pack, tactics that may not win too many admirers, but can yield impressive results as season 1946-7 clearly showed; and for better or worse Bath's post-war reputation as a no-nonsense and forward-dominated side would remain for the next two decades at least.

Newport and Wales wing legend (Ken Jones) heads for Bath line. Bath in white shirts (l to R), A. Higgins, F. Hayman, S. Spence-Meighan, I. Lumsden.

Acknowledgments Bath Chronicle

Meanwhile the Chronicle & Herald's report (11th October 1946) of the Somerset v Middlesex county match answered a query that no one on the Rec had seemed to know for considerably longer than just two decades: 'why (one frequently asked) did Bath number their team shirts from 1 to 16 (not 1-15) and omit shirt 13?' Suspicion, as is often the case with this unjustly maligned number, was indeed the cause, but one that resulted from this same county rugby match played on 10th October 1946. On the face of it the drawn result had seemed hardly reason for concern, with the match concluding at 13-13, and the equalising third Middlesex try that levelled the score was run home by centre A.Venniker (St. Mary's Hospital) who by coincidence just happened to be wearing shirt number 13. Nothing out of the ordinary surely, except for the suspiciously minded Bath committee that was watching this game on the Rec. Somerset to the core, this coincidence could be not brushed off quite so lightly. And their problem was that 'damned' No.13 shirt. It was deemed to be an ill-omen, and it 'had' to go. Loyal Cidermen, their feelings were expressed the following day in the Chronicle with the following statement: the "Bath *club are excluding No.13 from the numbering of their players.*" Nor were they joking; and although the change was not in fact immediate, not least for administrative reasons, the fact is that during season 1951-2 the switch was completed, with Bath teams now numbered from 1-16 and so omitting number 13 altogether. Thus laid to rest was at least one long-held assumption, namely that the number had long been rejected in the belief that shirt 13 was worn by centre Clifford Walwin on the day of his fatal injury in 1920, an era anyway when a different shirt-numbering system applied.

The No.13 shirt query notwithstanding, the task of forming a back-division without the guarantee of Lumsden's presence was a setback for new skipper and centre Tom Hicks in season 1947-8, since the ever-reliable Scot had now commenced National Service with training at RAF Cranwell among the broad open spaces of Lincolnshire, and his presence on the Rec could not always be guaranteed. Nonetheless as the Chronicle had observed in the final days of the previous season: *"The fact remains that the better the opposition the better the Bath performance and the more uphill the struggle the more they seem to be able to pull out."* There was some truth in this assessment, and there would be no shortage of uphill struggle awaiting skipper Tommy Hicks to test its accuracy. In particular there were several performances that turned the proverbial form-book on its head. In early December for instance the highly rated London Scottish, who could field at least five internationals including 15 stone winger T. Jackson, fell 7-3 on the Rec when hitting the wall of a Bath pack inspired by leader George Reid. In early March Bath then overcame Bristol 10-8, again inspired by Reid's pack that included among others Jim Messer, Len Harter and Oxford Blue Michael Sutton. Come late April there would be hints that the following season might be very 'interesting' indeed, because during an 18-8 win over Moseley it was the Bath backs who proved to be something of a revelation; and outside-half Bryan Henson looked a genuine prospect in the absence of Lumsden with a performance that led to tries from centre Kevin O'Shaughnessy, wing speed merchant A. Wenyon and the brilliant Glyn John, nor forgetting a fourth from forward Len Harter.

Yet it would be at best a season of mixed fortunes with a lowly 15 wins and 2 draws from 37 matches played. But gutsy skipper Tommy Hicks (awarded the Military Cross in the War) never of course lost his nerve, and as the slowly improving results in the second half of the 1947-8 campaign hinted, his team were beginning to gel. There was a poignancy too when prior to the Boxing Day 9-8 win against Old Blues the club flag was flown at half-mast and the players quietly lined up for a short silence in memory of James Timmins, Bath's England Trialist centre (late 1890's to 1910) who had recently passed away. He had not been forgotten.

The club, still unsure of its place among the first-class ranks of English rugby, commenced the following season of 1948-9 with a September record of three defeats and a draw, hardly a cause for optimism. But, such early season disappointment would evaporate with an Autumn landmark victory whose impact would be expressed by the joyous reception awaiting the team's return at the Western Station from Wales on the night of 2nd October. The welcome was led by club president Capt. Stanley Amor, accompanied by chairman B.C. Barber, the committee and a large and very happy crowd of supporters. Cyril Bailey (heart and soul of any gathering) became impromptu Town Crier. Former secretary Victor Smith played a portable harmonium, and all around was music (well Victor Smith reckoned it was music) and much vociferous song. Oh, and crates of beer were available in 'healthy'quantity. Small wonder....Bath at long last had achieved their first ever win in Wales. Not only that, they had won it at Llanelli!! And things didn't stop there either, because Bath once again were wearing their traditional club shirts of blue, white and black. It could hardly get better than that, save for the knowledge that Lumsden was back in town and would soon be in action once more on the Rec.

The Rag Doll ....has never backed a loser.

Acknowledgements: Reg. Monk

Meanwhile amid the home-coming celebrations there stood skipper Dr Allan Todd, now proudly holding aloft a curious but much prized doll. It was not the prettiest of objects and hence was aptly known as the Rag Doll. But the obscure history surrounding its origins was later explained in the Llanelli v Bath match programme of 29th November, 1978: a '*Mrs Rosina Rothery of Bath had made the original soon after the First World War to be presented to the winners between Bath and Llanelli,*' and since then it has been hung from a cross-bar in the current victors colours whenever the two rivals meet. There was one further piece of information to add to this story, one explained on the eve of the post-war Bath v Llanelli match of September 1945 by the Chronicle & Herald (7th September 1945) that referred to the "*celebrated trophy, the 20 year old doll, given by Bath for annual competition by the two clubs.*" Assuming this to be correct (and why not), this indicates that the Rag Doll was first contested circa 1925, another fact perhaps not widely known.

Among the lessons of this landmark win at Stradey was that since the early days of Anglo-Welsh rivalry, victories in fortress Wales for an English side resulted from nothing less than an 80 minute spell of total discipline and total concentration; because in the Principality it was (and is) not merely physical strength, but also mental strength that is essential. There was at this time no harder rugby arena in rugby. Yet individualism has a part to play too, and this success would be remembered not least for a superb solo try more typical of Welsh three-quarter wizardry when Cornishman Michael Terry shot away, *"beating three opponents before searing down the middle to score beneath the bar,"* albeit Northam's goal-kick was (rather unusually) disallowed. New arrival Terry, who had recently commenced Physio' training at the RUH, was a centre of exciting potential, so hardly surprising that soon he would be an England Trialist. Meanwhile another Bath discovery was noticed that same day, namely a centre-cum-wing-forward by the name of Alec Lewis. He too would soon arouse the interest of the England selectors.

Another dazzling high profile win, this time against Harlequins (18-13) in late October on the Rec and achieved by a drop goal and no less than five tries as against two goals and one unconverted try by Quins, strengthened claims that Bath once again held a place among the ranks of first-class rugby. Their pack was probably as strong in the tight and as good in the loose as any in the Country. While outside the scrum Bath were further strengthened by the acquisition of 'utility' backs such as Michael Hanna; and so reliable was Graham Hawkes proving to be at out-half that against Harlequins it was Ian Lumsden who was paired at centre with Terry. This was a clever selection and Oh! what a threesome this proved to be. The Quins (Chronicle & H, 1st November 1948) *"muffed their passes under the devastating tackling of the Bath centres. Though Lumsden did not score himself, he played the role of opening-maker to perfection....his beautiful cross-kicks to the open side - these contributed handsomely to Bath's victory."* And, the *"match was a personal triumph for Terry, his fleet-footed resourceful running - once covering three-quarters the length of the field brought him three glorious tries."* The excellent Hawkes sent home a drop-goal, while skipper Todd notched a brace of tries himself to complete a near perfect Bath performance.

Such results looked excellent, as indeed they were; but upstaging the likes of Bristol was a different matter altogether. Yes, Bath would first hold them 3-3 at home, then later defeat them 0-3 away; while Gloucester's Autumn win at Kingsholm was conclusively avenged 13-3 in February on the Rec. Christmas came, Llanelli soon followed and Bath (with tries from Wilfred Williams and K. O'Shaughnessy) joyously sealed the Double over the Scarlets with a 6-0 home win on 28th December. Boyo, was that some Christmas! Not without significance either was Bath's 13-8 victory over Wasps in late February, not least as the Londoners (a recent addition to the Bath fixtures) were now described by the Chronicle 'as the fastest improving side in the capital, who in the previous season had won the Middlesex 7's for the first time in their history.' Equally encouraging was the 3-5 February victory at unglamorous but dangerous Newbridge, a side virtually unbeatable on their home territory. It was another win in Wales! Had Bath overcome their lack of self-belief when travelling into Celtic territory? It was too early to say.

More certain however was that this season of much achievement would expose the handicap of playing at this level of rugby without a reliable goal kicker. Bath gained a highly commendable 19 victories and drew 5 from 40 matches played. But they would arguably have won more but for the lack of a reliable goal-kicker. Yet Allan Todd's team (he gained a Scottish Trial during the season) was only badly defeated on one occasion with Newport's emphatic 34-8 win in April, a clear warning from the Valleys that Wales was only too capable of exacting heavy retribution upon any English side that had the temerity to trample on Welsh pride, as had Bath that season over Llanelli. Furthermore both London Welsh and Richmond took the winners honours, while London Scottish went one better and achieved the Double, and Exeter and Leicester overcame Bath on the Rec in late season. Yet such upsets notwithstanding, Bath had once again shown their ability to 'hold their own' among the elite, overcoming some of the very best teams in the Country. Any other club achieving such results would almost certainly have received no little credit for such achievements. But this was Bath; a club who lived within the shadow of that great rival 15 miles down the road….Bristol. And still there was no escape from that same shadow.

So the final season of the decade now beckoned, notable not least for the visit of Hylton Cleaver's International XV (15TH September 1949), a team literally packed with internationals, Trialists, Blues and Barbarians; and in an era when televised rugby was a rare treat, this was an occasion for the rugby follower to actually see the stars for 'real.' No surprises then that the stars won (6-21), but that did not dampen the enjoyment of the occasion nor overwhelm the steadfastness of two young props supporting Bath hooker Jack Francis, namely Tom Smith and John Roberts, a duo who would later forge a front-row partnership that would become a part of Bath rugby folklore.

Meanwhile it would have been fitting indeed if the momentum of the previous year had continued into the final season of five years of fluctuating fortunes. But a return of a mere fifteen wins and three draws from 39 matches was somewhat disappointing. There were some useful 'outsides,' including scrum-half Norman Halse and some quite superb performers in Michael Terry, and when available Scottish international Ian Lumsden. Yet overall club strategy remained somewhat 'orthodox and predictable,' and when faced with an expansive running side (and there were plenty of those around, not least in Wales) Bath were sometimes vulnerable. This weakness was exposed for example in defeats at Harlequins (24-6) and Swansea (26-8), and Bath could not rely on the strength of their forwards indefinitely, hugely impressive though they often were. Yet it should not be overlooked that under Len Harter's captaincy there were wins to savour, not least the forward inspired 6-3 December success against highly rated London Scottish and the late season home 8-3 victory over Newbridge. But there was no escape from the fact that there were 21 defeats during the season; a total that included the 11-5 humiliation at Stroud, a bitter pill to swallow. This was not the best way to bring the curtain down on the 1940's.

So one could hardly complain that rivals Bristol and Gloucester (usually deservedly) attracted the attention and the accolades; both known for their consistency and Bristol especially known for their expansive approach. Bath by contrast remained something of a puzzle, both difficult to analyse and difficult to predict. In the Chronicle's own words (Ch. 17) they *"played the yeoman way."* This in fact was as accurate a description as any, and it raises an interesting thought: because it is the yeoman who learns his trade and skills from the bottom upwards, and so learns them thoroughly. He becomes 'long' on experience, but remains in the background, often barely noticed. And though on rare occasions yeomen climb up the high ladder to the top, they are never expected to do so. Neither for that matter were Bath.

Footnote: Photo on page 114 is from the Bath v Newport match of 9th March, 1946 (result: Bath: 5 Newport; 20).

Chapter 21. GREAT DAYS! (1950-55)

Since the end of World War 2 five years of rugby had provided time for a return of stability to the club. Yet despite periods of intermittent success, it seemed that both Bristol and Gloucester could still sleep easily in the knowledge that Bath would not be disturbing their peace any time soon. Because the supposed poor relation of this West Country triangle badly needed a season that would grab headlines, produce the 'wow' factor and send a clear message to Bristol and Gloucester that this was now a three-horse race; similar in fact to the glamour days that surrounded the club throughout much of the 1920's and early 1930's.

But something was needed to provide the necessary stimulus to turn dreams into reality; and that stimulus was about to be provided with the appointment of the lion-hearted Alec Lewis as skipper and the likes of hooker Fred Hill (two post-war Victory internationals under his belt) around him. Hard as nails, Hill would now link up with John Roberts and Tom Smith to form a front row in one of the most powerful Bath packs ever; a pack that few would equal and even fewer would surpass.

The 1950-51 season for a Bath club saddened by the untimely loss of S.G.U. Considine (a war-time squadron-leader) who had unexpectedly passed away in late August,

Alex Lewis steams away from Bristolians Woodward and Bain (white shirts) Robin Hambly (far right)
Acknowledgements: Jack Simkins

opened with a defeat (though narrowly) at Leicester, followed by a half-expected home 0-16 upset against Hylton Cleaver's International XV on their second visit to the Rec; and although not yet by any means clear of their own financial difficulties Bath shared the gate-profits with the National Playing Fields Association and the club's own Memorial Fund dedicated in part to the families of Bath and District players who had lost their lives in the War.

There then followed an 8-8 home draw against Llanelli (18th September), a result that would have satisfied many senior clubs against opponents of such ability, and a game where the Bath pack did not merely look good, it looked potentially awesome, a fact emphatically demonstrated when their second try resulted from a full-blooded push-over try! A push-over try against the men of steel? Any side in England would be talking about 'that' for seasons to come. An Autumn 13-6 home win against Bristol was then as good a win as it gets against the best, with the exception that is from victories away from home against the best; and the January success at London Welsh who already that season had defeated both Coventry and Llanelli really did suggest that Bath might be closing in on Bristol and Gloucester.

Then as the season progressed the leadership of Alec Lewis (not to be confused with Trevor Lewis, another excellent back-row forward) became ever more evident. The Bath Chronicle, at first cautiously optimistic, now sensed something was 'really happening' down on the Rec, showering the team with praise. Thus the January victory at London Welsh had resulted by way of a pack that *shone in the line-out and was devastating in the loose;"* while ex-Bristol full-back Pat Sullivan won the unofficial 'Man of the Match' nomination for the Chronicle & Herald (15th February 1951) in the 8-3 victory against Gloucester. *"No one shone better than Sullivan. His catching and kicking and his positional play were immaculate;"* and not forgetting winger Donnelly's try *"that really won the game. It was typical of this flaxen haired speed merchant....taking advantage of a mistake by the other side and that race for the line."*

A cherished Double (plus bragging rights) was then achieved with Bath's 6-9 win at Bristol in early March, where the Bath pack *"under Alec Lewis worked like a machine."* While a potential problem owing to injury to scrum-half Mike Hanna was solved by the simplest of solutions within the club's own resources by recalling 'A' team skipper Halse (by now both a war and a rugby veteran), who it was duly discovered could still rough it with the toughest. Facing England's Pat Sykes in Bath's 8-3 victory over Wasps *"Halse's experience at the base of the scrum was invaluable."*

So began a seven-win surge that included the away triumph at Bristol, another at Saracens, while the 8-6 victory over Swansea (a Welsh great and not beaten by Bath since 1930) drew an ovation at the final whistle, where the performance of Bath's other Lewis (namely fellow wing-forward Trevor) *"was exceptional."* The all-time club record meanwhile stood at 25 victories as first achieved by the Philip Hope side of 1921-2, and surpassed by the 26 wins if (but only 'if') one accepts as valid an exhibition game at Blundell's School by the Vowle's side in the following season. Whatever one's judgement in this matter, Bath's form in season 1950-1 was now so hot that not merely 26, but an even higher win-total looked attainable; and on their final offensive there would be one defeat, two draws, and crucially three victories. First the home 23-5 success over Moseley brought the win tally to twenty five, while a Thursday evening 6-11 win at Taunton raised the total to twenty six. Then two days later the matter was put beyond any doubt whatsoever when in the return at Moseley an undisputed new club record of 27 wins was achieved on 21st April 1951.

This 3-9 victory (away!) was gained in the perfect way, with the Midlanders' lone drop-goal bettered by Bath's three tries, the last from highly promising back Alec Poulson. True, other West Country clubs had attained thirty or more wins in a season. But Bath were playing at the highest level of the first-class game, and there being no rugby union 'league' tables at this stage, standardised or otherwise, it was not possible for the rugby fraternity to accurately judge and compare the respective strengths of a rugby team. The absence of such a league table notwithstanding, the Chronicle calculated that the 1950-1 performance would have placed Bath not only in the top half, but in the top quarter of an unofficial first-class Table.

So ended an epic season, where not only was a new record set, but one accomplished in the heat of competition from a fixture list as strong as any in the club's history. The pack undeniably had been the key strength, and which in the record winning game at Moseley had bludgeoned over for yet another of their now almost predictable push-over tries, scored on this occasion by 6ft 4inch lock John Dingle. Five years earlier in December 1945 his first-class baptism had been delivered in blood (no exaggeration) when Bath, a forward short, plucked the talented line-out jumper from the King Edwards School XV and pitched him straight into the arena at Llanelli… of all places! He then stepped on to Stradey Park as a young 17 years old Boy. Eighty minutes later of a pulsating 3-3 rugby draw young Dingle strode off the park a Man!

As for the individual appearances made in season 1950-1 the Chronicle named the most regular Bath team as: *P. Sullivan, R. Hambly, G. Addenbrooke, R. Todd, W. Donnelly, K. Wilcox, M. Hanna, T. Smith, F. Hill, J. Roberts, J.Dingle, G.Brown, Trevor Lewis, Allan Todd, Alec Lewis (capt.).* Others too had played a prominent role, among them the brilliant young Welsh back Glyn John prior to his departure for National Service, and to the welcoming arms of London Welsh, but who when with Bath had *"set the Thames on fire when he ran from halfway right through the heart of the London Scottish side at Richmond to score."* Talent (especially at forward) just seemed to be everywhere, so too experience and it proved to be a highly potent combination. A return of 27 wins (an impressive 13 away from home) and 4 draws from 41 matches was proof enough of an exceptional season.

But while one could only praise their impressive total of victories, a question mark remained concerning the club's style of play. Yes, the back-line were frequently lethal in the tackle, but as early as the October 8-8 draw with Llanelli the Chronicle had expressed one reservation: *"....back play is not yet Bath's strong point. If only the three-quarters were equal to the pack, well, Bath could beat any opposition they are likely to meet."* It was this one deficiency that on occasions would leave the team short of options, as was the case in defeats at Gloucester (27-3), likewise 11-25 at home to Cardiff, followed later by a fearful 39-9 drubbing at Newport!

Yet just to complicate matters, there was no lack of 'individual ability' among that same back-line. Pat Sullivan, wings Guy Addenbrooke, Robin Hambly and Brian French, centres Bob Todd and Alec Polson, halfbacks Hanna and Kenneth Wilcox, and especially the brilliant Glyn John, would challenge for places in many first-class sides. However, missing on a permanent basis were play-makers outside the scrum such as Roy Harris and Lumsden, international standard outside-halves who would have thrived outside a pack so powerful and galvanised the back-division accordingly.

Nothing however could detract from the achievements of a side such as this, that feared no one, and who for another twenty years would provide a benchmark for future Bath teams to emulate. It never claimed to be among the more attractive teams to watch and maybe it lacked the glamour that surrounded the Vowles team of 1922-3 with the accompanying Somerset County Championship triumph of that same season. But criticising the Bath team was one thing; beating them quite another!

It was during the close season that the 'Bath Old Players' was founded (renamed 'Bath Past Players' in June 2005) and Alec Lewis accepted the captaincy for a second campaign; leading Bath (a reported 7,000 watching) to face H.B. Toft's International XV among his early season tasks. And what a fight Bath put up, albeit losing 9-17; but playing with 14 men after a broken shoulder injury to centre Robert Todd after 28 minutes. Yet utility back Guy Addenbrooke was seen at his best with the game's opening try: *"clever interceptor, vigorous and determined in his bursts for the line, a danger point at all times. He survived two tackles before he forced his way doggedly over the line;"* (Chronicle & H, 21st September 1951).

John Kendall-Carpenter
Bath and England

It was in January meanwhile that Alec Lewis was selected for his first cap, where he would be paired alongside Kendall - Carpenter (a try scorer for H.B. Toft's international XV and destined to join Bath) in England's back-row against South Africa at Twickenham. First there would be the small matter of a home encounter against Gloucester (a perfect warm-up for so demanding an international) and Lewis, after 'glancing through another batch of congratulatory messages in the dressing room,' inspired Bath to a 3-0 victory over one of the toughest opponents in England. Against South Africa, one of the toughest opponents in the world, things ended a little differently. England lost 3-8. But Lewis had impressed. He would gain another nine caps for his Country.

Back to the club scene and Bristol, earlier winners over Bath, were later avenged 6-3 on the Rec, likewise Newbridge (8-6), while Wasps, now very much a leading club in the capital, were held 8-8 in London. It was a narrow home 0-5 defeat against Cardiff in late January however that demonstrated again both the great strength and the one shortfall in the Bath team when opposing teams that could 'spread it wide.' Again the Chronicle & Herald (21st January 1952) emphasised that the *"Bath pack was as good as any in the Country."* But *"while the backs tackled extremely well.....little constructive play emerged from the backs as a whole and Bath badly need an opening-maker, which they now lack."* That opening-maker was of course another Roy Harris or Lumsden.

John Roberts, part of an immovable front row

Nonetheless one could hardly begrudge a total of 21 victories and 3 draws that concluded the season. No, but one could understand the deep regrets throughout the club at the decision of Alec Lewis to resign the captaincy, brought about by his ever increasing business commitments. Who could replace such a man, described by one of the leading judges as *"the greatest skipper in the history of the club"* (Football Herald & Chronicle 5th May 1951)? Who indeed? The answer was prop forward John Roberts; and encouraged by wins that included a 3-11 away victory at the sometimes excellent Devonport Services, the Roberts side prepared for the visit of Llanelli in early October 1952, along with an advanced warning from the Valleys: *"Expect fireworks from Lewis Jones."* Ah Lewis Jones, destined for greatness in a Welsh shirt and later Rugby League stardom at Leeds.

So Guy Addenbrooke, ex Swansea and Welsh Trialist, was brought into the centre to stiffen Bath in mid-field, although switched again to out-half on the day. John Kendall-Carpenter, now in the process of joining Bath, was rushed immediately into the side for his club debut. Yet nothing could stop Lewis Jones from casting that same spell over the Rec that he was in the habit of doing wherever he played; kicking (from all angles) two conversions, two penalties and running home a try to bring his tally to a remarkable 19 points from Llanelli's 25 points total. In reply Bath salvaged a lone Sullivan penalty, and the Chronicle again pin-pointed their long-standing weakness: *"Bath had as much of the play as [Llanelli], but the backs were uninspiring."* This shortfall furthermore was a factor when losing 3-16 at home against a Cardiff team complete with out-half genius Cliff Morgan in its ranks; evident too when Harlequins visited the Rec in early April with England centres W.P.C. Davies and A.E.Agar in their line-up for their 3-14 victory. And why did these opponents win?....*"because they were just too good outside the scrum."*

But just to confuse the doubters (of whom there were many), occasions arose when the Bath back-division 'did' hit form, and not just against the minnows. Bristol, exponents of open rugby, would have testified to this fact in their 9-3 Autumn defeat on the Rec. Admittedly all scores came from the boot (one a 40 yarder from Sullivan). But the Bath backs in the words of the Chronicle *"were brilliant."* Mick Hanna and Clifford Weston shone at half-back, while Addenbrooke, O'Shaughnessy, Hambly and impressive new arrival Peter Fearis looked top class. Again, Bath were at their 15-man best with a sparkling four-try total in their early April 16-3 win over the highly rated London Scottish, having previously struck perhaps their finest form of the season with ironically a defeat, not a win, at Neath in mid-March. Admittedly they fell 15-14, but Eddie Simpkins, who had followed Bath for some forty years rated their performance as simply *"the best display ever given by Bath in Wales."* A reported 4,000 crowd doubtless agreed and on the final whistle there was a loudspeaker request for *"three cheers for Bath for a wonderful exhibition of rugby football;"* proof that Bath could play the open, running game and.... play it in Wales! Furthermore a new scrumhalf discovery had arrived on the scene, namely ex-Bristol player Gio Sidoli!

In truth the 19 wins (and 6 draws) of 1952-3 could not equal the 27 victories of the record season, though the final home game (an 11-0 win over Gloucester) was headlined as a *"Real Thriller."* But it was abundantly clear that John Roberts was already stamping his own character upon Bath as the Chronicle had noted at Neath, where the *"result was a tribute to John Roberts's spirited and inspiring leadership."* And, even the supremacy of the Lewis record was in due course to be threatened.

On paper at least, the 20 wins (and 4 draws) from forty games of the following 1953-4 campaign and summarized by the Chronicle as *"one of outstanding wins mingled with defeats"* typified so many a Bath season. Of 40 matches played a mere handful were sufficient to reflect both the strengths and weaknesses of this so unpredictable club. The principal strength was at forward with a pack perhaps the finest in their history so far. The supposed weakness remained outside in the backs, although there were exceptions to this supposition. One such exception was at Rosslyn Park in late November, whom Bath had last played in 1924, then previously in 1905 and 1894, moreover winning narrowly on each occasion. They now won a fourth time, and P.J.M. (Chronicle & H, 30th November 1953) reported thus: *"though they failed to score, it was the Bath backs who impressed;"* adding that it was the re-appearance of England Trialist centre Mike Terry that proved crucial to his fellow outsides, among them fellow centre Len Hughes who *"put in some powerful dashes,"* and winger Hudson Adams, who *"played his best game since joining the club"* and *"stuck grimly to his [exceedingly difficult] task of marking English international Chris Winn."*

So just one player, in this case Terry, proved capable of making a crucial difference in the backs, while the 3-3 home draw against Leicester in early January was headlined as follows: *"Bath backs superb in defence."* Defence was another Bath strength. In the

January away encounter against London Welsh, already victors over Coventry, Neath and London Scottish, P.J.M. again spoke glowingly of the Bath 'outsides.' Of special note in their 6-8 win was 18 years old Welsh outside-half Royston Collins, taking ball *"brilliantly"* from scrum-half Mick Hanna. The pack too were outstanding; they 'had' to be at London Welsh, and Dennis Mattingley and Eric Hopton were *"so prominent....that Alec Lewis and Kendall-Carpenter were hardly missed."* But as P.J.M. so fittingly wrote: *"When two strong packs....get the ball back as often as possible, it is at outside-half that the match is won or lost. Collins hardly wasted a ball."*

Yet such victories were, as the Chronicle frankly admitted: 'mingled with defeats,' and one of those defeats was a mid-January 0-29 and seven try defeat against Cardiff on the Rec. No excuses for that, and though Bath's England Trialist back-row forward David Naylor missed most of the second half with an eye injury, the Welshmen fielded four reserves in their backs. So, if Bath supporters would (understandably) wish to forget such a debacle as quickly as possible, then their next home match (6th March) was a performance that they would wish to remember for as long as possible. The opposition just happened to be Bristol, a club poised on the verge of another great era of open rugby; but who doubtless to the surprise of many, had not won on the Rec since 1937! Neither did they win in March 1954. Oh no! Their *"all-star back division,"* wrote P.J.M. (Chronicle & H, 8th March 1954) *"was completely over-shadowed. It was a tonic to see two home-bred centres in [Cliff] Weston and [Tony] Guest playing like world-beaters."* World beaters....and against Bristol!

How fitting therefore (as reported alongside the match details) that on so successful a day several hundred spectators remained to witness the opening of the club's first permanent club-house at the North end of the Rec. Former player and then current committee member Mr Bert Anderson cut the ribbons, expressing thanks, among others, to the Recreation Ground Company for their co-operation. Now it seemed that the Rec (Bath's portion at least) was truly their permanent home; and surely no one would wish it otherwise. At least, that is how it seemed.

The season now entered its final phase with wins on the Rec over Newbridge and Harlequins; while the warm gratitude expressed in Bedford chairman Peter Perkins's letter to Eddie Simpkins spoke much for the ethos and warmth that underpinned the game during this era. He wrote thus: Bedford *"very much enjoyed the renewal of our fixture with Bath, and thank you all for your generous hospitality....;"* humbling words indeed in view of Bedford's 21-5 defeat in Bath's final (and successful) home game of the 1953-4 season.

Yet one more objective remained.....the club's first ever overseas tour. The destination was South West France, the opposition a trio of first-class French sides, the schedule consisting of three games in three days with departure from Bath at 4.25am on Friday, 30th April, and the first match scheduled to commence the following afternoon

126

(Saturday) against St. Claude. Ah! But this was France, a Land full of surprises, and after their Channel-crossing arrival from Southampton and two hours spent lying 'flat out' on their beds at the *'hotel de ville,* Bath awoke to learn that the opposition had mysteriously transformed from St. Claude into a full Jura-Lyonnais combined side (and surprise-surprise) were to be boosted by five guest French 'B' internationals for good measure. Sacré bleu!

It was fortunate therefore that Bath had travelled with a near full-strength squad, including big-guns in the pack such as lock George Brown, Frank Thomas, the increasingly impressive Eric Hopton and the now irrepressible Bryan Peasley, a recent Bath wing-forward acquisition from Maestag. The pack as usual performed impressively, but so too the backs, who unrecognisable from the outsides who had struggled against the likes of Cardiff, threw caution to the wind, and enjoying the time of their lives threw passes here, there and just about everywhere. The haul that day was six tries with Weston, Naylor, Guest, and Jim Vaissiere each scoring one apiece and wing Richard Bassett (exceptionally fast, barely 18 years) running home a brace. Meanwhile full-back Phil Hardy duly banged home three conversions to complete Bath's 3-24 rout, a victory duly described by the Chronicle as the *"near-perfect text-book style of the Bath XV."*

Against Givors on Sunday, and with French hooker Dupinay in their ranks, things were somewhat different. This French side were tough, and in French rugby terms that means 'really' tough. Meanwhile the news of the sheer scale of the tourists' win the previous day had put the home side on full alert. In fact Bath were the first English club to visit the town and the fixture duly attracted a record 4000 crowd to their impressive Olympic stadium. Mr Landsdown, British Consul at Lyons (and related to a Bath family) honoured the encounter with his presence and he was doubtless as relieved as Bath that the John Roberts side just managed to squeeze home for a 6-9 victory in what would prove to be their hardest game on the tour.

On Monday the tourists moved on to play Tour du Pin led by French international L. Junquas. But any hopes among the hosts that Bath might now be nursing too many knocks and bruises to repeat their opening performance at St. Claude were to be rudely dismissed. Emotion too was 'written' on Bath faces that day, as Alec Lewis, having recently announced his retirement from senior rugby, now led out his beloved club on to the field for one last time. It was to be an apt occasion for a Bath and England great, for his team played like men inspired, winning 0-17 with non-stop attacking rugby literally set ablaze by the flamboyance of Gio Sidoli at scrum-half. Alec Lewis appropriately was among the scorers, so too Peasley, Vaissiere (2) and Roy Collins, with Phil Hardy slotting home a conversion.

At the conclusion Bath were both happily exhilarated and happily exhausted. They had been greeted by warmth, champagne receptions and post-match celebrations in the unmatched tradition of French hospitality. In return Bath, under skipper John Roberts, had produced displays of vintage attacking rugby that raised an important question: 'why, since Bath could play open running rugby, did they not do so more often?' One answer was certainly the close proximity to Bristol, whose style and reputation attracted backs like a magnet. Other reasons were less obvious to pin-point; though Bath's undoubted forward strength brought its own considerable rewards.

Unfortunately the home Bath v Cardiff fixture in the following 1954-5 campaign was cancelled owing to serious weather conditions, an occasion that otherwise would have filled to capacity the new 1,100 seated West stand officially opened on 2nd October. But since Bath would complete this season only two victories short of the 27 club record, there would be much for the Bath Chronicle's new rugby correspondent, namely John Stevens (W.J.S.), to talk about.

As expected, Bath continued with a forward-based strategy, and by early February following wins over London Welsh (13-11 at home) and then 0-3 at Newbridge (only the third Bath win in Wales since the War), John Stevens gave his 'guarded' praise for the overall 'teamwork' of a side, now *"settling down into a solid – if not – brilliant team;"* and if anyone doubted the difficulties of winning in Wales then they need only ponder Bristol's 38-3 crash at Cardiff earlier that season. One week following Bath's success at Newbridge there would follow a more unusual game to report. The Rec (12th February) was covered in a blanket of snow; visitors Gloucester arrived; but two players had travelled separately by car, and alas the car broke-down. So Bath kindly offered to loan them two players (lock Angus Meek, and winger Brian French from Old Sulians). Gloucester expressed their deep gratitude and then proceeded to thump Bath 21-0! (Thanks Glos….and we love you too).

It was a different story however with Bath's inches-close 9-8 defeat at Llanelli in early April, very different in fact, and summed up by an admiring John Stevens thus: *"if the pack played such a large part in Bath's fine showing, so did the outsides. Shuttleworth* [brother of England scrumhalf Dennis Shuttleworth] *and Weston formed a fine combination at half-back, both using the touchline to great advantage. The threes, Guest, Curtis, Trenchard and Leonard all threw everything into the game and Hardy must be congratulated on his five points."* Such a performance at daunting Stradey Park, invincible to all that season save Cardiff, proved not least to Bath themselves that they could play expansive rugby if choosing to do so. Hence 'the 64 thousand dollar question' remained: 'what was it that stopped them from doing so?'

Other 'big' performances included home wins over Swansea, Harlequins, Northampton and *"in one of their finest performances of the season"* (W.J.S.) their 11-0 victory against Neath in late April; further proof that this was a season to remember; not least for the twenty five victories (and two draws) that culminated with a second unbeaten tour of France that saw wins over Dijon (0-14), St Claude (8-13) and Macon (3-8). Thus ended a five year era that had seen Bath not merely maintain, but improve upon their place in the tough arena of first-class rugby. Some critics mocked them for their

BATH AWAY! ....scrumhalf Gio Sidoli spins out the 'leather' as Bath attack St Claude. Colleagues (left to right) B, Peasley and D. Beard.

frequent reliance on a tight forward game and often their lack of enterprise outside the scrum. But as many of the strongest sides in England and Wales would discover during this period, Bath could be one hell of a hurdle to clear. And John Roberts, when years later recalling this same era, spontaneously repeated but two words: *"Great days!"* he said, *"Great days."*

Chapter 22.   ERA OF UNCERTAINTY. (1955-60)

As Bath stepped into the second half of the 1950's it was undoubtedly hoped that the results of the five previous years had laid a foundation for continued success. But much of the achievement during those same years were thanks to an exceptionally powerful pack; and though some of those experienced forwards remained, the superb John Kendall-Carpenter (captain, 1955-56) among them, a considerable responsibility would now depend upon newcomers. Indeed the *"team must to some extent be experimental, for the backs in particular,"* commented the Chronicle & H (9th September 1955) cautiously. In short, it was going to be a case of 'wait and see,' and weaknesses were to appear soon enough that alerted opponents to a vulnerability in Bath ranks with results falling dramatically during a four year slump between 1956-60. So, pushed aside once too often by a Bath forward battering-ram, opponents would now make preparations to settle old scores. It was going to be pay-back time.

Nor would the fault-lines in the team be solved quickly, and were not immediately noticeable. In fact the 17 wins and 18 defeats of 1955-6 produced a near equal balance of success and disappointment. Furthermore this was Bath, a club who could turn the unpredictable into an art form. No surprises then that Bath's inaugural game against Ebbw Vale that culminated with a mid-October 6-3 home win over the unofficial Welsh Championship winners two years previously had followed an earlier 14-0 defeat that same month at somewhat less glamourous Taunton. Another surprise, a big one too, had been revealed in the September 20-nil home win over Devonport Services who in these National Service days could sometimes field a team packed to the gunnels with star players. But on this occasion Bath's strength proved 'not' to be their pack, *"who have been the mainstay of the club in post-war years,"* but the backs, not least with Ron Shuttleworth and Cornwall out-half John L.Thomas who, wrote W.J.S: *"showed some of the best half-back play by Bath for years."* That was more like it. But there some pretty uncomfortable defeats during the season too.

One such upset was the 6-11 upset at the hands of US Portsmouth in early November, the visitor's first success at Bath since the War. Even worse was (is) to be at the wrong end of a Double, Bath's unfortunate fate against both Llanelli and Bristol. Oh dear! Young Second Lieutenant Robin Hambly however, a former winger with the club whose National Service with the Somerset Light Infantry was deferred to allow for the completion of his law studies, did not come off second best during emergency operations in Malaya (Chronicle, 21st October 1955). Noticing a communist dissident preparing to open fire on his unit the young officer *"got in the first shot,"* and that as they say 'was the end of the matter.' Amazing what rugby does to a man!

As for further results, the defeats were sometimes heavy, as was the case against the likes of Swansea (away), Harlequins at home and finally the 8-23 loss to Moseley on the Rec whose forwards *"showed the skill and speed of their three-quarters."* Yet the successes of this Kendall-Carpenter side included some absolute gems, not least the January 11-0 win over Leicester, and there are few results that give morale a lift as does a win over the Tigers. As for backs Wyn Holmes, Malcolm Smith (very fast) and Mike McCarthy, and likewise lock John Ramsay (former Watsonians) and prop Bill Law, all more recent 'faces' in the side, this triumph over Leicester was one of those days to remember. Yet if one performance might possibly have surpassed even the home success against Leicester, then that was the 3-15 away victory at London Welsh one week later. Bath (wrote W.J.S.) *"served up champagne rugby;"* and banged home two penalties and three tries to prove it, as against one try in return. 'Champagne rugby' served up there in the big city? Now that was the form that the club needed to produce more frequently if it was to silence those critics who still maintained that Bath were no more than the poor relations of Bristol and Gloucester.

Stealing a march on such prestigious rivals however was more simply said than done, as the following three seasons in particular would reveal. Yet despite the gloom (and there was plenty of that) there would be performances to admire, and season 1956-7 with a mere 15 wins, 5 draws and 19 defeats was no exception to this curious Bath trait. Devonport Services certainly enjoyed their trip to the Rec in mid-September, taking home a 6-14 win, their first success at Bath since 1949. Meanwhile John Roberts (again club captain) and his side enjoyed their own 3-13 victory at US Portsmouth in early November, and furthermore their discovery of a new sensation in their backs. The name was Ken Miners, and (wrote I.J.T.) it was *"after 15 minutes that the Services first saw his great potentiality. An orthodox movement developed swiftly. Miners raced past his opposite number with a deceptive swerve, and as he drew Bell, the full-back sent out a scoring pass to [6ft, 4in] John Dolman on the right wing."* Try! Oh if only his work commitments in Rhodesia were not to hasten his departure come the end of the season.

Talking of wingers, the giant Dolman was not the only danger-man whom Bath could field in the attack, because another was John Rees! Very fast and elusive, he looked real class, even if his team were having a bad day, as was the case when London Scottish ran home 22-8 winners in early December. Alas no champagne rugby that day in the big city. Nor was there much encouragement from a season's total of 15 wins only, five draws and no less than 19 defeats that included an overwhelming 27-6 success for a Gloucester side at Kingsholm partly inspired by Booth, their brilliant 18 years old scrum-half playing in only his second game for the Cherry and Whites. If it was any comfort to Bath, Gloucester would later wallop Bristol 21-3.

Yet just to confuse matters it was in early February that Bath met Gloucester in the return match, and winning 11-nil at Lambridge. It was wrote I.J.T. (Chronicle & H, 11th February) *"Bath's finest hour of the season,"* a day when formidable Gloucester appeared *"strangely subdued against the furious but calculating and efficient home eight;"* and where the performances of prop Fred Book, lock Frank Thomas and flanker

David Naylor among others stood out. True, the conditions were mud and rain, hence the game was moved from the Rec where conditions were even worse. But Bath seemed quite happy to spread the ball wide. Surprisingly they did not ignore their backs, and if scrum-half Paul Dart had yet to earn a reputation among Bath followers, he did now; while David Curtis, the recalled Addenbrooke and recent arrival Dennis Silk (Cambridge Blue) *"on the day were far more convincing than their opposite numbers."* There was another player *"whose positioning....handling, economical touch kicking and occasional enterprise warmed the heart."* He was a Marlborough College schoolboy, already a Dorset & Wiltshire County player, a National Hunt jockey and later a Cambridge Blue full-back; and if he too had yet to earn a reputation then he would now. His name was Ian Balding.

Dennis Silk

Yes, sunshine did break through the clouds during this otherwise disappointing season, though there was little point in denying the weaknesses shown on the field. Bath however were not in denial; far from it in fact, and they would have been the first to admit to their weaknesses and where at least one potential solution lay. It was pin-pointed moreover in their one try and 3-0 victory over powerful Wasps (Chronicle, 25th February). *"Take a Cambridge Blue named Silk, (wrote I.J.T.) place him alongside three-quarters of average ability, and you have a back division capable of holding the best sides in the Country. Add another Cambridge Blue and England player named Beer, place him in the back row, and you have a set of forwards which will rank among the best in the Home Counties."* Thus two outstanding players, one able to inspire the backs, the other the pack, could be sufficient to change the entire complexion of a team. 'But was it really that simple? And the answer, as events would later show, was 'yes.'

However there was little indication of such an answer just yet, as the depressing results of season 1957-8 showed, and neither the all too short presence of Barnstaple's young Devon (and later England Trialist) wing Mike Blackmore, nor the leadership of John Roberts could arrest the decline. For decline it was, with a tally of 11 wins only, 4 draws and a horrendous 27 defeats. Yes, the figures looked bleak indeed. How could they not! But only very rarely were Bath humiliated, though this was hardly an excuse. They were admittedly taken apart 26-3 at Leicester in September, and then 34-5 at Stradey Park in early October by a Llanelli side that *"had the hallmark of 'brilliant' on all it did."* But more typical were narrow upsets such as the 12-9 match at Bristol in late October and the 8-8 home draw against Leicester in early January. There were even performances to gladden the hearts of long suffering Bath supporters, pining for the days of not so long ago when a Bath pack steam-rolled its way through the ranks of the best that England and Wales could throw at them. Such a day was Saturday 15th

February 1958 when with the superb Dennis Silk injured and schoolboy Ian Balding required by his brother's racing stable to ride National Hunt at Lingfield Park, Bath

Ian Balding

hosted the Welsh emerging star that was Bridgend. Surely there was little chance of a home victory here. Well actually there was, not least thanks to the composure of outside-half Treleven Thomas, and winger David Ogden who (I.J.T.) *"scored two of the finest tries seen on the Recreation Ground in this or any other season."* That secured a 6-3 victory. It furthermore ignited the previously *"jaded look"* of the home pack. In short, Ogden's performance on that day was the spark that Bath needed and therein lay an important lesson! For if a good run of wins such as this could be achieved, then confidence and self-belief would rise accordingly; in other words 'two for the price of one.'

But a yet more profound retort to those who were tempted to write Bath off completely was the 10-6 victory over Llanelli in mid-March, the same Welsh wizards no less who had so humbled Bath in early Autumn. The Scarlets it is true were not at full strength, but their ranks were filled with plenty of Celtic class nonetheless. A try from wing Roberts and *"an amazing cork-screwing drop-goal from centre David Evans were proof of that."* But home tries from Peasley, and then lock Tony Jacob who completed a *"brilliant run by Trelevan Thomas,"* both converted by skipper John Roberts, brought the Rag Doll back to its original home.

Two other names figured in a season that did not deserve to be dismissed as lightly as its poor results suggested, of whom the first stamped his signature during the Boxing Day encounter against the Old Blues on the Rec before some 2000 spectators. Few at the club had probably heard of the 18 years old outside-half playing for Bath that day, nor realised that this talented Prior Park schoolboy was already a Dorset & Wilts county player. Well it did not take too long for those watching to realise that young Scotsman Ian Reid was star material. *"His 'foxy' breaks, his canny turns and his great burst of speed when it was most required, were all painful thorns in the Old Blues side;"* and Bath ran home 15-6 winners. The youngster was one to watch.

Eddie Simpkins. Devoted his life as secretary to Bath RFC.

The second name was that of Eddie Simpkins who passed away on 1st February (Chronicle, 3rd February 1958). 'E.F.S.' as he was affectionately called, was true 'blue, white and black.' Born in the city, he trained at St. Luke's College Exeter before returning to devote his entire teaching career in Bath, initially at Bathforum School, and then some 40 years at Oldfield Boys School. A promising centre at both St. Luke's and Bath, injury curtailed his active playing at 24 years. He then turned to administration matters, and became joint secretary in 1911 with Mr J.T. Piper until 1939, and later from 1948 - 1957. He had witnessed Bath play on no less than 66 grounds in England and Wales, and it is said that he never missed a single committee meeting. Much admired, much loved, what more can one say.

On paper at least the outcome of the following 1958-9 season under Gordon Drewett suggested that Bath really were drifting aimlessly in the doldrums. Worse still it appeared that there was little hope of escape. After all, 12 lone wins from 39 played was almost as depressing as the eleven victories in the previous season. But no less than eight matches were drawn, and defeats were reduced from a numbing 27 to 19, still too many, but an improvement nonetheless.

Yet one characteristic had not changed since Bath first stepped into the distant 1900's, their unpredictability; and it certainly wasn't going to change when Llanelli kicked off the 1958-9 season with their 25-11 win over Bath at Stradey Park, followed by Leicester's 25-6 victory one week later; and when Bath succumbed 9-19 at home to St. Mary's Hospital in late September things, putting it mildly, were not looking particularly promising. But a narrow mid-week 6-6 draw at Clifton in early October would reveal a remarkable talent now at Bath's disposal. *"Remember the name, Ray Gazard, because I can assure you that more will be heard of this blond, crew-cut winger with the velvet smooth running style"* (wrote R.N.M., Chronicle 2nd October 1958) of this former Welsh Empire (now Commonwealth) Games long jumper, and considered *"one of the Army's crack sprinters."* Few at Bath had ever heard of him. After seeing him in action against Llanelli three days since the Clifton match they not only knew about him; they couldn't stop talking about him.

He scorched over for a try double on his home debut within the opening 20 minutes *"that knocked much of the wind and confidence out of the visitors and gave Bath an initial advantage which they fought like Titans to maintain."* Indeed it 'lifted' the whole team to a higher level. Coaches call it self-belief, a sense that 'we too can reach for the stars.' Well Bath didn't quite get that far, but they defeated the Scarlets 8-6 nonetheless. Yet this was not merely a one-man show. Indeed how could it be, and others rose to the occasion. *"Gordon Drewett was brilliantly efficient and Joe Colford at stand-off made the utmost of the first-class service which the skipper threw out;"* while *"Barry Richards at full-back had another great game."* Of course although the home backs were displaying the form that their patient supporters had longed for, the Welsh giants could not be allowed to dominate the vital forward exchanges, and locks Frank Thomas and Tony Jacob, and back-row men John Jacobsen, Brian Peasley were among those who helped to ensure they didn't. Because above all this was a team triumph, and as R.N.M. concluded: *"This was their finest hour."*

But any hopes that such an achievement as this would signal a breakthrough were to be short-lived, because one week later Bath were overcome 21- nil at Bridgend, while in early December they fell 30-nil at London Scottish. With results so erratic, it was hard to predict what Bath would do from one week to the next. Well in February in the second drawn game that season against Gloucester (3-3) *"Pat Hill's hooking was perfect"* and in *"Beer, Phil Winchcombe and Malcolm Martin selectors have definitely found the best available back row."* But wrote R.N.M. *"if there is any man who has played a harder game on the 'Rec' this season than did Peter Parfitt, I should be pleased to meet him."* Ah Pete Parfitt….a local legend in the making.

In fact drawn results littered the season, with Neath, London Irish, Swansea and Bedford among the high profile names that could not better Bath on the day, nor Bath them. But there was no escaping the question mark hanging over a team that suffered no less than 19 defeats, yet could in late February raise their game to beat the likes of Wasps by 19-nil, opponents who significantly had been the first side that season to defeat Bristol. Equally significant was that such was the quality of the Bath outsides in this compelling match that this (wrote R.N.M) *"was the finest exhibition of constructive and class back play that a home side has produced on the Recreation Ground for possibly two of three seasons."* One literally prayed for such days to be the norm at Bath, rather than the exception.

In early April the club took a gamble on youth, selecting Paul Masters (18), Brendan O'Mara (17), Terry Hopson (19) and Peter Robinson and Gyn Robins (both 21) for the encounter at Torquay Athletic, the Devonians having already won an impressive 23 games from 28 played. All Bath rugby yearlings at the first team level, with Robinson and O'Mara actually making their 1st team debuts, the game itself *"ebbed and flowed like the spring tides and the largest crowd of the season must have wondered why the two teams hadn't played each other for 30 years."* Well….it was not actually 30 years, but rather 22 years (see Ch. 18) when on 20th March 1937 a late controversial try by Bath led to a post-match demo' by a small group of home supporters, resulting in a long cessation of fixtures. Now thankfully the past was forgotten, with no one in either club seemingly even aware of the fracas down near the sea-side long ago. Moreover when literally in the final 30 seconds of the match Paul Masters hurtled over for his first try for his club that would clinch a 11-12 win for Bath, there was no demonstration. There was applause instead.

The 1950's would now enter its final phase. It was to be a decade of contradictions. For five exciting years thanks not least to a pack rarely if ever equalled at Bath, there would be success sufficient to raise hopes that the club could perhaps reach the highest levels of the English game; only for disappointment to follow as results fell, at times alarmingly, during the following five seasons. The causes for such a decline were in part the need to find a new generation of forwards, though not forgetting backs, to replace the 'older guard.' Another hurdle was to rebuild a confidence shaken by the number of defeats during the second half of the decade. Yet even in the bleakest season of all, namely 1957-8, there were victories of which any leading club would be proud.

There was another conundrum for the club, now under the captaincy of pack leader John Jacobsen, to ponder. Should Bath attempt to follow the expansive tactics of nearby Bristol, whose 15-man running rugby in this same 1959-60 season had led to a remarkable 36 victories? Or should they perhaps adopt those of Gloucester, whose strength in their 8-28 win over Bath in December was (W.J.S.) built around their *"steamroller forward tactics backed up by clever half-back play and an adequate three-quarter line."* No guesses in view of their own style during the 1950's as to which option most suited Bath. Nonetheless there was a third option, one that five seasons later would be introduced by an unexpected arrival from London rugby, and whose influence would change the course of Bath rugby forever!

There would be signs of a turnaround with Jacobsen's team furthermore, with the club ending the season with 16 wins under its belt, and 5 draws. But no one could deny that the 20 defeats were again far too many for comfort. But when Bath defeated Llanelli 3-11 in mid-September, and in Wales moreover, many would have been forgiven for hoping that this inspiring victory might signal a return to those glory days of the earlier 1950's. And on occasions they did return, not least with the home win over London Scottish in early December, the later December 3-3 draw at London Irish, and finally a 6-10 victory against a London Welsh side (now playing at Richmond) literally crammed with internationals and trialists, and all three exile clubs now hitting scintillating form during this period.

But despite the highs, the too frequent lows in Bath's own form would continue, and heavy defeats at the hands of Bristol for example, who ran home 13-27 victors in October on the Rec, a 26-0 defeat at Wasps in late February, and a home 14-34 horror story in April at the hands of Harlequins explained why Bath could not make a breakthrough into the higher ranks of the game that in the early 1950's had seemed a tantalizing possibility.

Chapter 23. THE ULTIMATE CHALLENGE. (1960-66)

At the dawn of a new decade the comparison between two West Country rivals could hardly have been greater. In one corner stood Bristol, who in the previous 1959-60 season had attained a new club record of a remarkable 36 victories; while in the other stood Bath, lagging far behind their neighbour for much of the previous five years, akin to an isolated distant moon trapped by the gravitational pull of some vast planet. The disparity was enough to make strong men weep, because unless dramatic improvement was seen on the Rec, then the possibility of life as the permanent underdog awaited Bath for ever and a day. Yes, there were periods of success (and hope) for five seasons or more. But as sure as the tide of fortune came in, it then went out again.

This predicament was demonstrated in season 1960-1, when Bath under the captaincy of prop Angus Meek recorded 21 victories, a respectable total at the senior level of rugby in any normal circumstances, but one that raised barely a ripple against the near impregnable hull of local rivals Bristol. Bath's impressive mid-season 11-3 success over a high-flying London Welsh was another example of their capability, a performance notable too for a stunning 50 yard try by wing John Cousins, a towering 6ft. 4in newcomer and likewise a Gloucestershire County sprint champion. Next there followed a prestigious 15-3 win over Llanelli (captained by brilliant Welsh scrum-half Onllwyn Brace), followed later by Bath's 13-3 defeat of Swansea (wing Alan Howard-Baker hitting form). Yet even wins of this calibre made little impact on the generally held view that Bath trailed far behind Bristol in the ratings.

Laurie Rimmer: exceptionally fast wing-forward

That aside, the January 1961 selection of flanker Laurie Rimmer for England against South Africa at Twickenham, the tourists winning 0-5, and prop Pete Parfitt's nomination as an England reserve (non-travelling) for the February 1961 international against Ireland in Dublin, did help project the club's image more widely. But to be fair, and not discounting Bath accomplishments, critics could justifiably point to the other side of the coin, not least to the season's total of twenty-one defeats; some a cause for sleepless nights that included the January 32-5 drubbing at Northampton, the 22-9 upset at Rosslyn Park, the later 29-11 defeat at Bristol and the Easter collapse by 12-62 against Harlequins, Bath's biggest defeat in their history. Did Bristol suffer such defeats? No!

Other factors contributing to such fluctuations of form included the continual player turn-over and even now the occasional interest from Rugby League scouts, as happened to Bath with the arrival of RAF and Orrell full-back Bob Randall in Autumn 1960. Physically strong, tactically assured and an excellent goal-kicker, he impressed from day one. But after a mere eight games prior to Christmas, the talented Randall switched codes to join Widnes, the first Bath player to 'go North' since three-quarter Peter Fearis joined Blackpool Borough in 1950 and then onwards to St. Helens.

Yet while talented players departed, others arrived, and few better than young Brendan Perry. A gifted athlete who was already the 100 and 220 yards England Schools sprint champion, this St. Brendan's (Keynsham) Schoolboy was not entirely unknown to Bath, having appeared as a guest player in the previous 1959-60 season. Making matters yet more interesting was the fact that young Perry, a natural born outside-half, had been selected for the England rugby team (over 15's) against France. But it was hardly surprising that interest came from another direction too....Bristol! And since their inspirational captain John Blake just happened to teach at St. Brendan's it seemed that young Perry was destined for the Memorial Ground. Bath could but pray therefore that Perry might just have a change of mind and move to the Rec; and 'lo and behold' their prayers were answered. Perry chose a Bath shirt, and proceeded to gain just about every representative honour in the book save a full England cap.

Brendan Perry: an often brilliant outside– half.

Nonetheless this opening season of the 1960's witnessed no noticeable change to the status quo of West Country rugby, where proud Bristol would maintain their deserved pole position among the elite. Elsewhere an ever improving London Welsh would soon be stamping their own Celtic brilliance upon every rugby field they trod to become the 'darlings' of London rugby. Floodlight rugby, first experienced by Bath in their 16-3 defeat at Llanelli on Friday, 19th January 1962, became increasingly commonplace, likewise televised rugby, especially at the international level. But there appeared to be few reasons for predicting any dramatic transformation at Bath during the first half of the decade, although the club's mysterious knack of striking form at the most unexpected moments remained as always.... mysterious.

Indeed when new skipper Roy Farnham's team opened the 1961-2 campaign with a run of seven straight victories that included wins over Leicester, Llanelli and Bridgend, one could have been forgiven for believing that a breakthrough into the higher ranks of first-class rugby was possible. That 11-12 win at Welford Road for example, where the Bath pack "*gained such a stranglehold that Leicester's undoubted talent at the back of the scrum could do nothing to open up the game*" was Bath's first away win against the Tigers since that historic victory of 1919. Admittedly it was Gordon Drewett's reliable (very reliable) boot that put the points on the board, eclipsing the Tigers' two tries. But

Bath, pondering if they would ever win at Leicester again, travelled up to the Midlands to win, and not necessarily to entertain.

The return 13-6 home win over Llanelli was different, since it was Bath who ran into the open spaces, clinching two tries (both converted) and revealing the hopeful signs of genuine class developing among their younger backs. Frankcom swept home for one try, while O'Mara (by now a Somerset centre) and Brendan Perry showed that they had the ability and self-belief to threaten a side even of Llanelli's quality. In addition the experienced John Hawgood proved himself to be a player of composure and skill, as one would expect of a former Northampton full-back, and hopes were further lifted with the arrival of excellent former Rosslyn Park winger Nick Bruford and Irish Trialist back John Keepe. The 'Heavies' looked a promising bunch too, with Pete Parfitt and hooker Pat Hill now reinforced with further back-row cover from Cornishman Paddy Mulligan and Lance Clark, nor forgetting the youthful North Midland's lock Kevin Andrews.

Geoff Frankom :
electric speed

Indeed the 20 wins and three draws (as against 20 losses) of this Roy Farnham side suggested that the situation had hopefully stabilised since the second-half of the 1950's, and it was significant too that Bath ran home one hundred tries for the first time since the War. Meanwhile young flanker Phil Hall, a former England Schools International from Chipping Sodbury Secondary Modern, commenced an illustrious career on the Rec; and the 19 years old Geoff Frankcom (the lone freshman on the day) won his Cambridge Blue at Twickenham and scored the crucial winning try from a lightening dash and pounce upon an Oxford defensive handling error. Nor was Frankcom the only Bath player at Twickenham that day. For at fullback with the Light Blues was another Bath player, namely Ian Balding,

A further touch of the feel-good factor was added when post-Christmas (6th January 1962) Bath would complete their first Double over Leicester since season 1919-20 with an 8-5 home victory. It was hardly surprising therefore that the Chronicle went into over-drive with its plaudits, and not least for the laser-fast service of Bath's young Dorset & Wilts scrum-half Jamie Spencer! An enigma both on and off the field, for Spencer was an accomplished avant-garde artist, he would later return to Harlequins post his National Service days in Wiltshire and in 1966 win a cap for England against Wales.

To the casual observer the following 1962-3 season under the captaincy of Laurie Rimmer would have appeared to be one best forgotten. After all a mere 14 games were won, one drawn and 24 games lost, yet a record partly explained by the fact that for the 39 matches played no less than fifty nine players were called upon for first team duty.

So small wonder that the Chronicle concluded that the team *"never really had a chance to settle down."* Injuries, admittedly unavoidable in rugby football, added to the drawbacks, and it was no fault of the captain that problems were exposed soon enough against Harlequins at Twickenham. First, to Bath's acute embarrassment, their scrum-half failed to arrive, Laurie Rimmer nobly taking over this key role. In addition Bath's young linesman Bill Sykes was pressed-ganged into the back-row, never having played anything approaching first-class rugby in his life. As if this was not a handicap enough, within minutes Bath prop John Lacey retired hurt. So Quins, packed to the rafters with stars (among them wing John Young and scrum-half Johnny Williams, both England internationals) coasted to 29-3 win. This was just the start, as further set-backs then followed, including defeats to Taunton (at home), Devonport Services whom Bath had overwhelmed in the previous season, and a Gloucester team fielding seven reserves.

Yet despite the understandable concerns at such performances, Rimmer did lead from the front, while prop Dave Robson and hooker Chris Smith, captains respectively of the United and 'A' sides, ensured that the development of promising players was a number one priority. Individual ability was already available in the ranks moreover with winger John Edwards (a student teacher at St. Luke's College, Exeter), hooker Colwyn Owens, prop John West, nor forgetting the recent arrival of Warwickshire lock Phil Hall. Furthermore a handful of unexpected victories then forced critics to 'think again' before labelling the season as a complete write-off. Because in early March following an Arctic freeze-up that wiped eight games off the Bath fixture list, a mini-revival commenced with a 13-6 home win over powerful Neath, followed by a sparkling 17-12 victory over Richmond. And, when centre Tony Endall (formerly of Birkenhead Park) was paired with Geoff Frankcom for the Cambridge Blue's first club appearance of the season, Bath completed this three win spell of success with their 24-0 home victory over Nuneaton, a club not to be taken lightly during this period.

Thus for a few games at least, Bath played like a team, with full-back Hawgood, wings John Edwards and O'Mara, an effective half-back combination of young Julian Darling (son of Lord Darling) and the charismatic Brendan Perry among those demonstrating that the club did not lack for individual ability. Indeed the trio of wins was as encouraging as the quartet of defeats that followed was depressing, with not only Harlequins, but Stroud, London Hospital and Old Merchant Taylors all celebrating their Easter visits to the Rec with wins under their belts. But then? Then Rimmer's side produced another turn-around with a late season run that was pure Bath in its transformation. First Llanelli fell 6-3, then bogey side Exeter (19-3), and finally a 3-3 draw at Coventry, a team nigh on unbeatable on home soil, thus concluding a season that like so many before showed the yawning gap between Bath at their best and Bath at their worse, a gap seemingly as wide as the Grand Canyon itself.

Come season 1963-4 new captain Kevin Andrews's first game in command saw Bath race to a 30-0 win over the touring West German Representative XV, the biggest defeat of a tour in which the visitors had already fallen to Llanelli and Coventry. But this curtain-raiser notwithstanding, Bath would continue to produce their similar form since the mid-1950's, with embarrassing defeats followed by sometimes exceptional victories, and vice-versa. Indeed amongst the hardest humiliations to take, for humiliations they were, included drubbings at Leicester (22-3), Llanelli (32-3), Aberavon (23-6), Swansea (36-3) and a 6-21 defeat by a superb Rosslyn Park at home.

But this was Bath, perhaps the most unpredictable rugby family in England, where day usually followed night (and vice-versa), and where those who knew this club could have predicted that victories (notable ones too) would likely follow the downfalls. Sure enough they did. Powerful Pontypool (3-0), then away at Wasps (9-14), would each feel the full force of a winning Bath side whose unexpected resurgence could sometimes make mockery of the critic's scorn. There was even competition for 1st team places (always a healthy sign), and it was during Bath's encounter with Pontypool that an immaculate display by newcomer Chris Harvey was a foretaste of an ability that would see him supersede even the outstanding Hawgood as first choice fullback. Meanwhile in early season the swift-running wing Richard Andrew celebrated a two year lay-off from rugby with a show of form so impressive that he was immediately called-up for Somerset duties.

Another bonus was added with the arrival via Orrell, Sheffield University and Loughborough College of wing-forward Tom Martland, whose qualities were clearly evident in Bath's 9-3 success over Northampton in late December with *"Leighton Jenkins [former Welsh international] as ever utilising his experience, Tom Martland a bundle of non-stop energy and Phil Hall hunting tigerishly after the ball"* The following 11-0 win over Leicester was equally impressive, with a Bath pack ensuring that Leicester *"were continually held in a vice-like grip and had the life slowly squeezed out of them."* Here Peter Heindorff at No.8 accompanied Martland and Hall, and the fact that Heindorff in the early 1960's was both a lean and fast back-row forward would surprise many who later remembered him as a mighty 2nd row giant of a man. Meanwhile owing to injury to Brendan Perry it was Laurie Rimmer who played at outside-half against both Northampton and Leicester. But then Rimmer was a flanker of genuine pace (on occasions playing centre when backs were in short supply), and his competent half-back display was proof of a genuine forward/back all-rounder, an unusual combination.

In the New Year John Millman would be establishing himself as a first-choice scrum-half, and in early April prop Bill Carling, (a strongly built subaltern in the Welch Regiment) made his Bath debut in their narrow home 5-6 defeat by Llanelli. The name 'Carling' may ring a bell, as his son Will (a gifted centre) later made his England debut in 1988 and progressed to the captaincy of his Country. But it was the final game of this 20 win season that would inspire John Stevens (Chronicle) to reach for the superlatives thus:

"if ever Bath, in all their long history, have scored three more brilliant tries in one match than those which helped them to a sensational [14-9] victory over Bedford, no-one on the Recreation Ground can remember them." And from John Stevens compliments like that did not come easily. In particular Stevens spoke of Brendan Perry, whose *"amazing acceleration left England wing-forward Budge Rogers standing and staring and provided the launching pad from which Bath rocketed into unbelievable heights."* He spoke of another Perry burst that *"enabled Frankcom to dart through, as only he can, for the try which made him the leading try-scorer in the country this season."* Perry it was who then scored another gem from a Leighton Jenkins pass on half-way. It was Perry once more in the final minutes who broke from his own line to the half-way, there to feed Frankcom to race another 50 yards to score the winning try. As if this was not enough adrenalin, Bedford too had *"began like rampant lions,"* gaining two penalties, plus one drop goal and ensuring that this was a game of two teams producing vintage rugby; a fact confirmed by a spontaneous standing ovation accorded both teams on the final whistle.

Yet this was a day that spelled out an almost frightening message. For Bath had indeed reached the heights on this occasion….this one, lone occasion. But if they were ever to overcome their reputation as mere underdogs to both Bristol and Gloucester, then this one day of rugby splendour must (and here one repeats 'must') be repeated each and every week throughout each and every season. Only then would they be spoken of in the same tones of reverence accorded their rivals. This then, on the very day of their Bedford triumph, was that moment when Bath came face to face with the sheer scale of their ultimate challenge. It was a daunting and almost frightening prospect.

Notwithstanding the optimism resulting from the dazzling Grand finale to season 1963-4, the following 1964-5 campaign had barely begun before the club landed back to earth with as serious a bump as it could possibly get. It was not simply the fact that Bath fell 35-5 in early season at Llanelli, followed by utter humiliation by Leicester (8-31) and Aberavon (3-28) on the Rec that would set alarm bells ringing. Because rubbing salt into wounds were further Autumn defeats to normally less demanding opponents at Devonport Services (25-6) and a 22-14 fall at Bridgwater, setbacks that frankly would leave the club reeling and with precious few excuses for a humble season's tally of a mere 15 wins, 3 draws and no fewer than 28 defeats. Of course all clubs experience some dip in form from time to time. But Bath seemed to make a habit of it; superb one moment yet looking outclassed the next, thus remaining a club searching still for the elusive remedy to a problem that as yet they could not solve.

The business re-location of Kevin Andrews to the Midlands in January hardly helped, his regrettable departure necessitating a change of captaincy to a comparative (albeit excellent) newcomer, namely Gordon Margretts. He in turn faced a problem created by continual team changes (fifty three players called up for first team duty), and not forgetting many poorly attended training nights. Furthermore, until a reliable replacement for Millman at scrum-half was found, even Brendan Perry suffered a temporary loss of form. 'Could things get worse?' one asks. Indeed they could, because until the arrival of lock Clive Armstrong, Bath were bereft of that vital role in rugby, namely a consistently competent goal kicker. Finally, the sudden departure of Leighton Jenkins unbalanced the highly effective back-row. Small wonder therefore that John Stevens (Bath Chronicle) concluded that the Bath side of 1964-5 were *"a collection of individuals rather than a team,"* an opinion all too evident when in their final game of the season they literally collapsed 33-0 at Coventry.

Yet in a season of such disappointment there were glimpses of that resilience that had for long enabled the club to absorb the most severe of setbacks, and the guidance during the season provided by Roger Whyte, a much respected former Harlequin, assisted Margretts with the coaching responsibilities. Meanwhile hooker Clive Buckle, in the absence of Pat Hill, would prove to be valuable cover for both Bath and Somerset, while props Roger Smerdon and Peter Jenkins would show that they too could handle the rough stuff up front. In addition, the return of the fearless Ian Balding (who at one stage was even preferred at out-side half to an off-form Brendan Perry) added steadiness to a sometimes confidence-lacking back-division.

Even the high turnover of players yielded occasional dividends. John Monahan for instance, a young schoolboy wing at Kingswood School proved to be one discovery, so too Fettes School captain and three-quarter Alexander Russell whose stay at Bath was alas too short-lived. There were signs too of promise with recently arrived scrum-half Jim Galley, and once again there was the now almost predictable recovery. It commenced with a commendable 6-6 away draw at Newbridge, a power-house of a typical Welsh side unbeaten at home for 18 months and where full-back Allan Gay on his debut proved himself commendably steady at a venue known for 'not' taking prisoners . Next, Bristol's ten year reign of near total supremacy was halted in early April by Bath's 17-12 victory on the Rec, where even the presence of former England fly-half Richard Sharp could not prevent Bath's four-try winning performance. And for those detractors who dismissed such a victory as just a fluke, there followed Bath's 19-6 win against a Llanelli side fielding out-half genius Barry John (later Wales and British Lions), a victory that included three tries and two drop-goals, one a superb 45 yard effort from Brendan Perry.

Meanwhile there was the selection of Geoff Frankcom for that season's Home internationals, and although England would subsequently lose to both Wales and Ireland and draw with Scotland, their convincing 9-6 victory at Twickenham over France saw Frankcom at his superb best, where his smooth and effortlessly gliding speed was one highlight of a triumphant day.

Ironically, come the final stage of the season Frankcom would find himself in a most curious situation, resulting quite innocently from his new teaching appointment that necessitated a move to the Bedford club while simultaneously remaining a Bath player.

143

Hence he played in Bedford's late season 17-12 home win against Bath. Yet one week later (and quite legitimately under the amateur rules of that era) Frankcom ran out at Twickenham for Bath in their first ever attendance at the now hugely popular Middlesex 'Sevens.' In fact, and as half expected, Bath fell 13-0 to Rosslyn Park in the opening round, the 'Park' themselves then losing to the eventual London Scottish winners in the semi-finals. But in truth 'Sevens' was not yet a perfected art in the West Country, where even the likes of Bristol had returned empty handed from a previous foray into this now classic event. Nonetheless for the following Bath team of *'Frankcom, Brendon O'Mara, Brendon Perry, Tom Martland, and forwards Phil Hall, Clive Buckle and John Parsons,'* and not forgetting several coach-loads of Bath followers, it was an occasion to savour.

Naturally, Bath nurtured hopes that their following Centenary Season of 1965-6 could be celebrated with perhaps a revival of fortunes. For during their first one hundred years much water had flowed under the proverbial bridge. Those early years (the most difficult for any new club) had been their pioneer days. They had ventured from ground to ground, finally adopting their unique home on their beloved Rec. Slowly they had developed an increasingly demanding fixture list and by 1900 they had produced three international forwards, namely F. D'Aguila, H. Fuller and F. Soane. Joyful revival then followed a desperate slump during the early years of the 20th century, and either side of World War 1 Bath had produced two generations of outstanding backs. A further slump occurred from the mid-1930's prior to World War 2, during which time the Bath club (like the Ritz) refused to close, notwithstanding that their stands and facilities were literally bombed out of existence.

Revival again followed, before one of the mightiest packs in Bath history stormed relentlessly onwards during the first half of the 1950's. Then….there followed a decade of trial and error, of teams seemingly unable to settle into any standard pattern of play, yet occasionally hinting at revival with remarkable victories and displays of unexpected class. But no sustained revival ever came. And when at the outset of their Centenary Season the news broke that Brendan Perry had now switched to Bristol (temporally as it turned out), a disconsolate Bath Chronicle commented thus: *"his decision will come as a great shock and bitter disappointment to Bath members who have often been delighted by his brilliant attacking play."*

Not surprisingly it seemed that the future again looked uncertain. True, 19 victories (Margretts continuing as captain) in this Centenary year would be gained, though by including their post-season 3-15 win against Chateau Renard in France, Bath (then losing 17-9 at Nice) would depart from normal precedent that previously had excluded wins gained on tour. Nonetheless among the modest total of their 18 'domestic' victories there were a handful that 'caught the eye,' not least those against Oxford University, Wasps, Gloucester and Harlequins. Furthermore, there was pride with the selection of Bath three-quarter Alexander Russell for a Scotland Trial, and further

England Trials for Geoff Frankcom and former Bath players Kevin Andrews and Jamie Spencer (Spencer winning an England cap).

Yet there appeared to be no escape from the shadow cast by a supremely confident Bristol, while Bath by contrast seemed to tread a lonely path towards a direction as yet unknown. Moreover, as their Centenary neared its conclusion, the club could only reflect on another campaign so typical of the last decade. The same difficulties were evident. The club lacked a specialist goal-kicker, no fewer than 55 players were called up for first-team duty (nine at out-side half alone), and it proved near impossible to build anything approaching a regular side. Furthermore despite 19 wins, this season of one draw and 28 defeats suggested a continuation of 'more of the same.' That is, until the very last game of this same Centenary Season and the visit of the then formidable Bedford. Yet, by the end of a rugby extravaganza an irresistible and almost unrecognisable Bath had swept to a stunning 51-3 victory by way of eleven tries to a single score against an admittedly below-par Bedford.

The inspiration for this triumph had sprung not least from the mesmeric performance of a young Millfield schoolboy blessed with a precocious talent, namely out-half Vaughan Williams. Already a Somerset cap and a half-back partner to his fellow Millfield School colleague Gareth Edwards (later a Wales and British Lions legend), Williams ran home two outstanding tries and landed no fewer than nine conversions. Then partly thanks to a highly effective combination at centre of Gordon Margretts and Combined Services player Bob Stevenson (RAF) a seriously fast John Monahan shot over for four more tries. Thus by the second half (wrote John Stevens) Bath *were tormenting Bedford.....and their forwards began to frolic around like extra three-quarters."* Meanwhile other recent newcomers suddenly emerged on the scene to stamp their own signatures on the game, James Monahan (brother of John) for instance, No.8 David Gay (brother of Allen) and Bob Orledge, all members of *"Bath's ruthlessly efficient eight."*

It was an intoxicating brew producing a tonic of a win, and even though years of dashed hopes had taken their toll on the loyalties of even the most hardened of followers, this time the doubters need not have worried. For as the curtain came down on one hundred years of Bath rugby, all those present on that sun-drenched day were witness to the future. And the timing was positively exquisite. Uncertainties would be swept aside, confidence would be renewed, and 15-man rugby would now be the order (and practice) of the day! Indeed, a second 'coming of age' beckoned. And come one distant day Bath would meet head-on that awesome and ultimate challenge......and overcome it.

Chapter 24. THE ENLIGHTENMENT. (1966-69)

For Bath, the season of 1966-7 was the dawn of a new century of rugby football. 'If' at this pivotal moment it was possible to blend into one team all that was best in their first one hundred years, then such a XV would possess the attacking flair evident from the days of Alby Hatherill's captaincy (1910-11), if not before, and continue into the early 1930's under the captaincy of Mervyn Shaw. Added too would be the forward prowess of the early 1950's, and not forgetting those flamboyant attacking qualities evident on fleeting occasions, not least the runaway win over Bedford that brought one hundred years of Bath rugby to a thunderous conclusion. If!

How, therefore, would such a combined Bath team look in action? And quite possibly it would have looked similar (very similar in fact) to that side destined to commence Bath's second one hundred years of rugby, one that in the words of the Chronicle's John Stevens built the foundations for a *"revolutionary era of Bath rugby."* Profound words these may have been, but they did not exaggerate one iota the sheer scale of the transformation that would sweep through the club from those early September days of 1966-7.

Key factors lay behind the achievements that would now unfold, not least the fortunate coincidence of a number of highly talented young players arriving on the Rec, of whom at least six (Brian Collins, David Gay, Ian Duckworth, Bob Orledge, Mike Hannell and Mike Beese) would soon prove to be of international potential. Secondly, and crucially, Bath now possessed an actual surplus of class half-backs, an almost sublime luxury for a club who had often struggled in this key department of the game. Third....there was Peter Sibley! This thoughtful and quietly spoken winger from Blackheath, a recently arrived Monkton Combe schoolmaster who had only joined the club in the previous Centenary season, was fast-tracked into the captaincy one season after his arrival. So what were the qualities that led to such swift promotion? After all it was rumoured that he never relished marking an opponent who was both big and fast; and it was said jokingly that without his contact lenses there was a danger he might run off in the wrong direction and score for the opposition. Yet, there was just something about Sibbo' that impressed all who came to know him, and whose natural-born qualities of leadership would now galvanise a 'rough and ready' bunch of footballers into a fully functioning fifteen-man attacking team that would change the Bath image for ever!

Sibley the scholar, whose rugby CV included some forty games for Oxford University (though agonisingly never gaining a Blue) quietly promised all those who were prepared to listen (and initially many didn't) that his Bath team would forthwith adopt a strategy of 15-man running rugby, a claim that some dismissed as pure Home Counties fantasy. But a mere four matches into Sibley's reign an emphatic 14-8 home win against Leicester would cause the doubters to think again.

Among those taking note of the 'message' in this commanding victory was the Chronicle's perceptive John Stevens, who described the half-back pairing of Jim Galley and Vaughan Williams as a *"highly explosive mixture who proved lethal."* He wrote of the back-row of Fred Hicks, England Trialist Geoff Hines and Phil Hall who *"were in the midst of every facet of play, constructive or destructive;"* and he approvingly described a Bath side that by the interval had stamped their dominance with *"three spectacular tries."* Yet this was to be no 'one-off.'

Soon Bath would have the luxury of further additions to their resources with the arrival of scrum-half Malcolm Lloyd and at outside-half the acquisitions of Jack Thomas, Bryn Jenkins (Birmingham University) and later the return of Terry Hopson from Gloucester. Equally fortunate was the healthy competition for back-row places, with a strong list of candidates that included Keith Richardson, Ian Holmes and the ever improving teenager David Gay. In December the promise of 20 years old Bath winger John Monahan, now an undergraduate at Cambridge, was emphasised with his selection for the Southern Counties against the touring Australians. Of utmost significance too was the fact that the 15-man strategy that had achieved the emphatic win over Leicester would set a long-term blueprint, and with Sibley's influence writ large all over it. Within barely two months Bath were applying the rugby philosophy of their 'rookie' Home Counties skipper. Within one season commentators were re-appraising a Bath team they had tended to regard as solely forward-oriented. Within three seasons the 15-man running game was expected of Bath wherever they played.

Not everything was plain sailing of course in Sibley's first season of captaincy, after all Bath conceded 20 defeats. But among the many positives was the achievement of their 27 domestic victories (29 if including two wins on their German tour) that equalled the club's all-time record. Not bad for a new captain with only one season of experience on the Rec prior to his call-up to lead his adopted club. The general quality moreover of the 27 victories (not least away successes) was hard evidence of a club with a renewed self-belief, wins that included Bath's 0-3 away win at powerful Pontypool, thanks not least to faultless performances at full-back by David Dolman, and also Brian Collins who was selected that season as a reserve hooker for England Trials. The transformation was further emphasised by a post-Christmas run of four consecutive away victories at St. Mary's Hospital (0-20), Rosslyn Park (6-8), Gloucester (14-19) and Cheltenham 6-9 respectively, followed later by an impressive 3-16 triumph at Sale that sent news of a Bath revival to the North. Even the genius of Barry John could not prevent Llanelli falling 11-3 to a thoroughly professional Bath home performance in early April in a season that would prove to be a life-changer in the club's history.

However the best of the best was perhaps the aforementioned 14-19 away win against Gloucester in February, Bath's first victory at Kingsholm since 1948, and where *"Bath held [Gloucester] magnificently in the set pieces where Heindorff injected great fighting spirit and outplayed them in the loose where Gay, Hall and Martland latched* on to the ball in a flash." At centre Gloucester were repulsed by the cover of Paddy Hillyard and John Donovan, while Bath ran home *"three cracking tries"* from Ian Duckworth (2) and Hillyard. At full-back Gordon Mobley was a revelation. The modest Kingswood School-master had previously played only a handful of first-team games since first putting a Bath shirt over his shoulders in 1963 and was effectively third choice full-back. Yet his immaculate performance within the Gloucester cauldron included two conversions and two precision penalties from the touchline. Thus with reserve back-up so reliable there were no weak Bath links at Kingsholm, and the resulting Chronicle verdict was emphatic: *"Bath took their biggest step yet towards re-establishing themselves in the top flight of English clubs....and the mere fact that they did win was less important than the way in which they won....by persevering with that positive and imaginative football which Sibley has been emphasising all season."* Bath in other words really did possess, as Sibley insisted, the necessary pedigree to play 15-man rugby of real class, notwithstanding the many doubters who had assumed that forward play comprised the major part of Bath's DNA.

Sibley's Men (1967-68) L. to R standing: J. Messer (official), A. Gay, J. Monohan, P. Parfitt, R. Orledge, J. Parsons, D. Gay, J. Thomas, J. Galley, R. Ludlow (physio) sitting: W. Lye, G. Frankcom, P. Hall, P. Sibley (Capt.), P. Peindorff, J. Donavon, B. Hartley.

Acknowledgements: Bath Chronicle

148

Yet it was opportune indeed that the Sibley's inspirational captaincy coincided with far-sighted changes at the national level, among them the first of the R.F.U.'s ten pamphlets on coaching, an aspect, suggested John Stevens, *"believed to have been a dirty word at Twickenham"* (Chronicle, 21ˢᵗ December 1966); and who added that while some clubs had already appointed coaches, others had not, and that when one former international of a senior club was asked if they had a coach replied (apparently in all seriousness): *"of course not, we all have cars."* This was an opportune time therefore for Bath to enjoy resurgence, and although the following 1967-8 results were marginally less successful than those of 1966-7, as regards representative call-ups the club banner had rarely fluttered so prominently. First, County Championship rugby would retain its status for many seasons yet, with selection often a useful barometer in gauging a club's player strength. In fact during the season no fewer than six Bath players were called-up for Somerset's 9-3 win over Cornwall, namely backs G. Francom, Ian Duckworth, Vaughan Williams and forwards Peter Parfitt, Bob Orledge and David Gay. Dorset & Wilts (whose County division played mid-week) meanwhile called upon seven Bath players, including former Somerset backs Sibley and Galley, and forwards John Parsons, Dave Robson, Pete Heindorff, Bill Lye and Phil Hall. Significantly England selectors were now taking a much closer look at the club, and brilliantly fast winger Ian Duckworth, lock Bob Orledge (an outstanding line-out jumper) and No. 8 David Gay were selected for full England Trials.

Adding further publicity was the televising of the Bath v Devonport Services match on Saturday, 18th November 1967 for the BBC 2 Rugby Special programme, the first Bath game to be so televised. Five tries crossed the line in a fast and open game, one scored by Services wing Bardwell and four from Bath (Duckworth and Martland) and two from newcomer Leigh Robinson (RAF), who ran home for a brace on his debut.

Individual honours now materialised, although there was disappointment that Bath winger John Monahan 'missed' a Blue when at final selection John Spencer (later England and Lions centre) won the wing spot for Cambridge. Bath prop Jamie Monahan (brother of John) meanwhile won the first of his two Blues for Cambridge in the 1967 Varsity match; while the selection of nineteen years old No. 8 David Gay for England against Wales (20ᵗʰ January 1968) put the club's imprint yet more clearly upon the National rugby conscience.

There was drama too involving Bath winger Ian Duckworth. Rated by many as the club's finest (and fastest) winger since the War, he had shown impressive form in England's final Trial. Now, with fitness doubts concerning Rod Webb (Coventry), selectors had placed Duckworth on stand-by for the England v Wales encounter. Conveniently, on the eve of the international, Bath were booked over-night at a Teddington hotel, so enabling a Saturday morning fixture with Metropolitan Police prior to Bath watching the international at nearby Twickenham. Webb in fact failed his late fitness test and Duckworth was duly requested to step into the England side. But the winger, literally on the verge of an England cap and in the view of many commentators good enough to hold his place in the National side, had cried-off from the trip to London with flu.

Nonetheless club-mate David Gay did play in all four Home internationals that season,

David Gay ...."England's veritable young Lion" (Jean Prat, French rugby supremo).

Acknowledgments: Bath RFC

and duly confirmed the selectors' faith with his performance on his debut in the 11-11 draw against Wales. His four caps included England's always tricky encounter in Paris, and though the hosts won 14-9, certain French observers spoke admiringly of two English back-row teenagers: *"This David Gay; this Bryan West [Northampton].....how will we cope with them during the next three or four years?"* commented French rugby supremoes Jean Prat and Guy Basquet, adding: *"They are veritable young lions;"* praise indeed from across the Channel. Yet, to the bewilderment of Bath, and no doubt to Jean Prat and Guy Basquet, Bath's young lion would gain no further caps for his Country.

Meanwhile starting in late December, Bath would embark on a nineteen match phase that involved as daunting a set of fixtures as it gets in first-class rugby. The first opponents to fall were Northampton (8-3), followed by a string of top-grade victories that seemed to run off a conveyor-belt, including: Rosslyn Park (22-15), all conquering Moseley (12-11), Harlequins (21-8) and Llanelli (17-9). Commendable away draws were achieved too at Aberavon (6-6), Wasps (0-0) and Swansea (6-6). While those most notable (and noticed!) of achievements, namely actual 'away' victories, included wins at Liverpool (0-9), London Irish (8-12), Bristol (6-8) and Gloucester (6-18); and it was success at on-form Richmond (3-8) in late March, that inspired the Chronicle to comment thus: *"if further evidence was needed of what an improved side Bath are these days, it came on Saturday at the Athletic Ground where they effectively destroyed Richmond, one of London's most successful clubs."*

That same season the touring New Zealand All Blacks had stamped their authority over the rugby fields of the British Isles. Awesome as ever (and 11-23 victors over England), their precision of inter-passing and off-loading at forward was like a machine. With increased televised rugby moreover, such developments could now be studied more widely; and assisted further by the new emphasis on coaching, the game was now rapidly moving up a gear. The positive approach was replacing the negative approach, and the successful sides would prove to be those (as Sibley would predict) who *"sustained continuity through on-going phases."* In other words stop-start rugby was on the way out, continuity was on the way in, and there it would stay.

Neither would Bath be left behind, as Sibley's influence would set in stone a long-term ethos for attacking rugby, one from which the club would now never depart. Here of course it was essential that the reserve players would feel a vital part of the overall plan, able therefore to fill any gaps whenever needed, as is always the case at this level of rugby; and such was the confidence now present among the players and the high attendance at training, that the Rec became a second home for many, if not all, at the club. Thus John Parsons stepped effortlessly into the prop vacancy caused by Weston-super-Mare bound Peter Jenkins. At hooker not only Harvey Hill, but young Alan Parfitt proved more than merely adequate back-up to Brian Collins, and with David Lewis (in addition to Orledge and Heindorff) Bath could rely upon a trio of top-class locks. Meanwhile selectors could hardly believe their luck when post-Christmas former England scrum-half Simon Clarke arrived on their doorstep for the remainder of the season; a period when Bath possessed no fewer than three pairings of top-class half-backs. It was no longer a case therefore of who to select, but who not to select.

The season concluded with 24 Bath wins, 5 draws, and 14 games lost. But in view of the sheer quality of many of the victories, and they included the Double over Bristol, there was little doubt that Bath now possessed the capability to play at the top flight of first-class rugby. Even so Peter Sibley was under no illusions. Elected unopposed to skipper the club for a third successive season, he spelt out 'in plain English' the scale of the task now facing any senior club. Yes, he was confident that Bath *"have the right basis to play the sort of game that will be needed, but we shall need to improve our continuity of moves,"* he emphasised, and fortuitously a rule-change was to be introduced for season 1968-9 that would assist a Sibley inspired side to do just that!

The law would dramatically limit the scope to kick directly into touch beyond one's own 25 yard (22 metre) line, because to do so would now lead to a throw-in at right angles to that position from where the player kicked the ball into touch. It could prove a costly error, and basically consigned negative kicking tactics into the history books. But for attacking teams this law-change was a gift from Heaven, and effectively a 5th gear was available to those clubs willing to capitalise on this new rule. One such club was Bath.

The need for a specialist goal kicker for season 1968-9 appeared to be solved with the arrival of Redruth marksman Mike James. But on the centre's sudden departure in mid-season this vital role (often the difference between victory and defeat) was handed once more to the ever versatile Tom Martland, and not without some success either. But goal-kicking uncertainties aside, Brendon Perry (he of the electrifying bursts of speed and the lightning breaks) was coming home! The prospect therefore of Vaughan Williams, Jack Thomas and now Perry at outside-half, and not forgetting further cover at scrum-half post-Christmas with the arrival of the RAF's Tim Keane, strengthened yet further the club's extraordinary strength at half-back.

With Brendan Perry at out-half and Vaughan Williams at centre Bath opened their 1968-9 season with a promising 13-9 victory against Italian side Roma, the visitors travelling with twelve internationals in their squad. But after a month of mixed fortunes that included a two win and one defeat tour of Ireland, Bath's season did not really hit full throttle until the visit of then powerful Aberavon on 5th October. It was here that Bath expressed every quality that Sibley had instilled into the team, and among those reporting on the encounter was the Sunday Telegraph's Eric Hill who commented thus: *"a match to stir, almost fatally, even the most sluggish pulse, was magnificently won by a goal, two tries and a penalty, to a try and two penalties...,"* Observing too was an enthralled John Stevens. He described a team who won with *"a glittering, bubbling display of best champagne vintage, outplayed Aberavon in the finer arts of handling, passing and backing up;"* and adding that *"one lost count of the number of times that the ball was moved first one way and then brought back the other, passing through seven, eight and even nine pairs of hands with ease and assurance."* He continued: *"At times one might almost have mistaken them for the Bristol of three or four years ago and their endeavours were rewarded with three cracking tries."* An exaggeration? No, Sibley had simply unlocked a talent at Bath that he, perhaps alone, had recognised on his arrival at the club. His qualities of leadership would then add that one vital extra ingredient....inspiration!

Two weeks later Bristol were beaten 9-14 at the Memorial Ground, with a commanding Bath running in three tries as against one in reply. Neath then fell 10-8 on the Rec, before Pontypool (early season 25-15 winners in Wales) suffered a similar fate, losing 21-6 by a Bath team *"who dominated proceedings to a degree which would never have seemed possible a few years back."*

Admittedly defeats that included upsets at Bridgend (17-3) and then Swansea (8-24) at home showed that Bath were not unbeatable. But, one club now looking virtually invincible were the brilliant London Welsh, who arrived on the Rec in January with their 'turbo-charged' team of Welsh internationals and British Lions. They had already humiliated some of the biggest names in British rugby that season, including taking 30 points off Newport and another 23 off Northampton, and now all eyes were on Bath. In a titanic struggle London Welsh would triumph 14-23 in a contest that produced three Bath tries (one by newcomer centre Mike Beese) and four by the Welsh, a team so skilled in *"repeatedly switching the direction of attack,"* a team *"so adept at turning defence into devastating counter-attack...*and not forgetting *"their quick second phase possession."* In short, it was London Welsh who at this stage were the supreme masters of the new modern game.

A similar spectacle, though not a similar outcome, was later witnessed at Easter (Good Friday) when Harlequins, beaten that season only four times prior to their visit to the

Rec, arrived with six internationals in their line-up. But on a glorious Spring evening, as the Chronicle noted, it was now to be *"Bath's superb second phase football, backing up and switches of direction"* that inspired a three to one try count and a 15-5 home victory. Noticeable too was the performance of centre David Wilce, yet another gifted student teacher from St. Luke's College, Exeter, whose strong, straight running added real mid-field punch as he and his colleagues put a stranglehold on the game *"by outplaying their star-studded visitors at their own open game."* And if any among an estimated 4000 crowd had initially questioned Bath's ability to beat some of the very best teams in the Land by the use of positive, creative rugby, then any doubts would almost certainly have vanished by the final whistle.

It was fortunate indeed that the Sibley era coincided with an age of rugby innovation, where new lessons in forward-disciplines arrived with the 1967 New Zealand tourists, where long-needed limitations on direct kicking into touch were introduced, and where the RFU's positive encouragement of coaching would all yield a faster and more scientific form of rugby. For Bath it was therefore a case of the right captain at the right time, a leader who instinctively understood the implications of these highly positive changes now taking place.

There was however one administrative item of news that seemingly raised little attention during the season concerning the question of Sponsorship, though duly reported (Chronicle, 18th February 1969) thus: *"The committee of the home unions wish to make it clear that in accordance with the international rugby football board resolution on this subject, no club or other body under their jurisdiction may accept any commercial sponsorship and that the strict principles of amateurism which are fundamental to the game of rugby union must be upheld."* The Chronicle added that 'the International Board had already ruled against any form of sponsorship in 1966.' But, those wide-ranging developments in the late 1960's that would increase the popularity of the club-game (and its running-costs) would in time lead to an inevitable challenge to those same administrators who would not countenance any flexibility to their rigid interpretation of 'amateurism.'

Bath too were adapting rapidly to those developments, albeit that their otherwise creditable 24 wins of season 1968-9 were perhaps rather modest by Sibley standards. Yet their 645 points-total was a new club record, resulting furthermore from six fewer games than the previous record of 628 achieved by Sibley's side of 1966-7; and though 17 games were lost, the quality of the victories confirmed again that this was a Bath team capable of playing top rugby at the top level. John Stevens (like Gloucester, a strong advocate of the then novel idea of a 'squad system,') openly suggested that *"whatever the diehards may think, [rugby union] is becoming more professional in outlook."* Moreover, regarding Sibley's captaincy, John Stevens (Chronicle, 3rd May 1969) continued thus:

"His three years in command have been among the happiest and most successful Bath have known in recent years. More than that.....Sibley, bred on the firmer fields of Oxford and Blackheath and coming West late in his career, revitalised Bath rugby, lifting it out of depression, sweeping away old negative attitudes and restoring players' faith in their own ability."

Now, the reference to Sibley's previous experience at Blackheath (while not forgetting Oxford) is a reminder regarding a generally unrecognised aspect of his days at Bath. For Sibley's rugby philosophy and influence was partly of London origin, whereas in the West Country there was a tendency to regard London rugby (rightly or wrongly) as physically less demanding and so vulnerable to a more aggressive brand of the game. Indeed, with the exception of Bristol players, West Country internationals had tended to be forwards rather than backs and West Country clubs (again with the exception of Bristol) as forward orientated. The effect of Sibley's London influence on Bath however was sudden, dramatic....and certainly unexpected. Yes, the hardness at forward remained. But virtually overnight Bath discovered a latent ability and desire to play open, expansive rugby, and to do so against all-comers. And thought-provokingly, this same open policy that steered Bath on course towards a remarkable future, had London rugby's signature written right across it.

There was no going back now!

Chapter 25.   MIXED SIGNALS. (1969-75)

In his Chronicle summary of Bath's 1968-9 season, John Stevens had stressed that a squad system as is now understood in rugby (until this point a more generalised term that referred to a collective group of players) was now an absolute 'must' for Bath. The strategy effectively removed (inter alia) *"the concept of first team and reserves."* It would be adopted soon enough throughout the first-class game, and it would prove a godsend to Bath when they commenced the critical task of continuing the remarkable legacy set by their previous captain.

Tom Martland: injury curtailed his captaincy.
Acknowledgements: Bath Past Players

For season 1969-70 Tom Martland was elected captain. An inspirational wing-forward (he could play full-back at senior level if required), he was an ideal choice with a talented pool (a squad in fact) in support. It needed to be, because a succession of injuries, some serious, would afflict the club from the earliest stages of the season, and later described as the *"worst injury list experienced in 105 years of rugby at Bath"* (John Stevens, Chronicle 2nd May, 1970). As luck would have it, one such casualty was Martland himself, a knee injury causing his absence from early October to March and hence a set-back that required an emergency captaincy-change to former West German international Peter Heindorff. Then matters got progressively worse. Orledge required a cartilage operation, followed in due course by Chris Perry (broken ankle), wings Peter Glover and Harry Barstow (broken legs), vice-captain Brian Collins, Brian Fear and David Wilce (all cartilage injuries), and Ian Duckworth (fractured cheekbone).

Yet, despite this toll a new club record would be achieved, so hardly surprising that John Stevens would further conclude in his end of season summary (2nd May, 1970) that: *"much of the credit must go to Heindorff who, with a mixture of determination, encouragement and almost bullying, made a fine side out of what remained."* Ah yes, and included in 'what remained' was wing forward Roger Walkey, a quite outstanding acquisition from London Welsh, not forgetting the revised squad system that streamlined team organisation during an epic injury crisis, and in addition an indispensable source of local players from the Bath Combination.

But the season had commenced with something of a surprise, namely the unexpected announcement by Ian Duckworth at the club's first trial (Thursday, 28th August) that he and the former Miss Sandra Wood had married at noon that very same day. Matrimony however did not deter the happy couple from delaying their honeymoon for two days until completion of the second trial on Saturday, nor to Duckworth's willingness to play in Bath's 12-5 victory against the touring La Rochelle on the following Wednesday (3rd September). Now that's dedication for you! Meanwhile not for the first time in their long history Bath would be repeating their well-known habit of gaining both outstanding victories and inexcusable defeats, nor forgetting some inches-close near misses. The September 14-13 knife-edge defeat at Newport for instance, where despite a try count of three against two in Bath's favour, it was not enough to clinch victory in the first fixture between the two clubs in seventeen years. Then there were the defeats, usually close encounters, but not always. The December 39-13 crash at Gloucester for example, next the late January 11-30 upset against Northampton on the Rec, and not forgetting the earlier January 27-5 loss at London Welsh. Indeed how could one forget, as the awesome Welsh in the words of John Stevens *"are a most brilliant and gifted side, capable of weaving spells to confound even the best opposition."*

Among the 'highs' however there was a legion of individual stories to tell. There was Walkey's stunning performance in Bath's remarkable October 10-17 victory at powerful Aberavon, when notwithstanding injuries to Barstow (leg fracture) and Martland (knee injury), Bath produced *"wonders of determination and team spirit."* And amid the turmoil, Walkey then proceeded to kick two penalties (one from 45 yards), a further touchline conversion, and as an emergency wing later ran home two superb 70 yard tries.

Then in early November, with Bath less five players on Somerset duty, young colts player Alistair Watson (son of actor Jack Watson) was thrust into first team action at Saracens who had not lost at home since February 1968. No matter, with Watson playing *"his part in a pack it was difficult to fault,"* a determined Bath triumphed 6-11. Then there were the performances of sheer class of supposedly reserve players in Bath's numbing 14-35 win at Pontypool in mid-November, the biggest win in Wales in the club's 'previous' 104 year history. First there was former Cheltenham full-back Walt Casey, whose *"strength and attacking ability.....brought him two most splendid tries which Waterman could not have bettered."* While Brendan Perry excelled on the wing with another two 'lightning' tries; and Ian Holmes showed that he (like David Lewis) could handle impressively the No.8 role vacated by David Gay's departure to Harlequins. Indeed, as John Stevens commented, with Bath it was now *"difficult to assess exactly what is the strongest line-up,"* another vindication of the New Model Squad system.

It was a near certainty moreover that after Bath's 24-16 victory in late December against Newbridge (Bath's final game of the 1960's) these most hardened of Welshmen were haunted at the mere mention of one Roger Elliott. For albeit Newbridge won the try count by three to one, Bath (or rather three-quarter Roger Elliot) won the penalty count with seven penalties sent flying through the sticks, and all thanks to the boot of the former Oldfield Old Boys 'wunderkind.' And just to add salt into wounds was the fact that Elliott only took on kicking duties because of an injury to Bath's own maestro with the boot.....their brilliant Welshman Roger Walkey!

Not surprisingly representative honours resulted during a season that included the visit to the British Isles of the sixth South African Springboks, notwithstanding certain spontaneous political opposition throughout their tour. Both Jim Waterman and Geoff Frankcom played in the Western Counties 3-3 draw with the Tourists at Bristol (31st December). While in January it was the Southern Counties who faced the South Africans at Kingsholm with three Bath players in their ranks, namely John Donovan, Mike Hannell and Phil Hall. Against such demanding opponents few gave the Counties any hope whatsoever, drawn as they were from this less fashionable division of Dorset & Wilts, Berkshire, Hertfordshire, Buckinghamshire, and Oxfordshire. Yet the narrowness of their 0-13 defeat (many feared they might be trounced) indicated that within the ranks of this less fancied grouping were players of genuine class. Bath's own contingent (as John Stevens reported) did not disappoint either: *"Phil Hall, a blend of patient watchfulness and natural improvisation,"* and *"Mike Hannell augmented his sound scrummaging with some enterprising contributions to the loose exchanges,"* and *"none of the backs were out of their depth....but rising above them all was centre John Donovan. His attacking flair as he occasionally swirled away with phlegmatic poise was a source of comfort to the Counties."*

It is quite possible that at least one (perhaps two) other Bath players might have played for the Southern Counties at Kingsholm that day, but for the terrible misfortune that struck on 1st December when Bath's Irish Trialist prop James Monahan, following a strenuous training session, died at his parents' North Wiltshire home. Both James and his brother John had played for Bath, London Irish and Cambridge (although only James gained a Blue), and it is understood that each player was on the shortlist for selection against the tourists. Save for the earlier tragedy, these highly talented brothers might have stepped out against the Springboks too.

Meanwhile as Bath embarked on the second half of the season the hopes of achieving a new record post-Sibley would depend on whether or not they could continue to plug the gaps arising from unforgiving injury problems; hence an unusually heavy reliance was made on the player-resources of the Combination, and not forgetting the elegant staff-room at Marlborough College. Indeed in the narrow but creditable 19-21 victory at Metropolitan Police in mid-January no fewer than three Marlborough schoolmasters represented Bath, namely prop Mike Hannell and colleagues Alan Conn (also prop), and No.8 Ian Murphy. One week later and Walcot's Brian Fear (lock) and Oldfield Old Boys Brian Eames (wing) answered the S.O.S. when making their debuts in Bath's late January 9-20 win at St. Mary's Hospital. A further newcomer was scrum-half Robbie Lye from Walcot Old Boys, yet another Combination discovery. With Heindorff believing however that Robbie (younger brother of club flanker Billy) was back-row potential, he was selected at No.8 with United, and then one week later promoted to the 1st team against Rosslyn Park. Bath lost 9-19 at home. But they had struck gold. For Lye would be the stuff of local legend.

So the show was kept on the road in a season that despite all the odds proved to be inspiring. Those most coveted of victories, namely away from home, where a team really can export its reputation, were exceptional, and would have credited any club in England and Wales. Aberavon (10-17), London Irish (9-11), Pontypool (14-35), Saracens (6-11), and not forgetting Bath's first ever win at Swansea (9-11), all exported the Bath trademark into the far corners of the rugby domain. The home wins too were sometimes outstanding. A fine London Scottish team who fell 32-11 was to be at this juncture Bath's biggest-ever win over the Exiles; while Leicester (13-9), a totally dominated Harlequins with 5000 watching ((27-6) and Llanelli (16-8), were among major victories that emphasised Bath's capability of overcoming the best opposition in the Land.

In addition one could only admire the dignity of Tom Martland, who in his captaincy season was denied by injury from the front-line action for which he so craved and thrived. But regaining fitness, he was recalled in early April to play at full-back against Sale, where both his composure and a superb 35 yard drop-goal was a feature of Bath's 16-6 victory against opponents consistently rated among the best teams in the North. Bath thus moved onwards and ever closer to a new record, and when Bedford (already crowned as unofficial club Champions of England & Wales) were emphatically overcome 20-6 in late April, Bath had indeed achieved a new club record of 28 victories, a tally that would have placed them in the top quarter of any standardised England & Wales league table. In fact they promptly created another new record of 29 wins when beating Exeter in the following week, prior to travelling to friendly Holland for a two match and two victory tour. This then was Bath's emphatic answer to those who questioned whether the club really did possess the 'depth' to continue the Sibley doctrine.

Elsewhere another decision that aroused little immediate impact, although reported in the Chronicle (3rd March, 1970) concerned former Scottish international scrum-half Tremayne Rodd, who was now *"declared a professional by the Scottish rugby Union after covering the 1966 British Lions tour as a journalist."* This it was argued *"transgressed the rules as to professionalism as laid down by any union."* 'But did it,' one asks? Well that depended on the times one was living in, because not everyone would continue indefinitely to accept such strictness of interpretation. Indeed the day would come when the ranks would 'make' for Twickenham, and the Game's authorities would find themselves compelled to meet the players' demands for reform on their terms.

Peter Heindorff not surprisingly was elected to continue the captaincy in the following 1970-1 season, a campaign that led to 26 victories (of which some were outstanding), two draws and again only 13, defeats. Encouragingly, much credit for this continued success was thanks to the quality of more recent arrivals, including an impressive quartet from Clifton, namely lock Ken Plummer, hooker Mark Robinson, and centres Graham Steer and Mario Polledri, all proof 'writ large' that those clubs on the outer edge of the first-class sphere could produce players capable of 'living' at the highest level of the game if supported by experienced colleagues around them. In fact Polledri (likewise Steer on his debut in Bath's victory over Llanelli in the previous season) was thrust straight into first team action in Bath's home 11-9 victory over Leicester. Equally impressive was the remarkably mature performance of young Combination scrum-half Bob Ascott (Stotherts), perfectly at home throughout Bath's April 12-8 victory against Newport, their first against the Welsh giants since 1933.

Ironically, the scrum-half slot could have been a nightmare of a problem, a position so constantly disrupted during the season that no fewer than seven players were called up for duty in this pivotal role. Yet following the hamstring injury to Malcolm Lloyd, replacements John Deverell and Tim Lerwill (both Army), Chris Perry, Bob Ascott, Millfield schoolboy Richard Harding (later Bristol & England) and on one occasion Robbie Lye, all filled the breach with a competence so assured that Bath barely noticed the constant disruption. In fact so well did these and other newcomers fit into life with the club, that notwithstanding the absence of nine regulars for Somerset against Gloucestershire in November, a Bath side filling the gaps with reserves overcame Saracens 9-6 on the Rec. Even when the excellent John Donovan departed for Torquay Athletic in December to leave a gaping hole in the back-line, Simon Burcher (the previous season's Welsh Secondary Schools captain) and medical student Peter Burrowes (formerly Rosslyn Park) suddenly appeared 'out of the proverbial blue' to stabilise the situation. Furthermore John Tredwell (Cambridge Blue) and John Ashcroft (Army) were outstanding cover in the back-row; so too wing Neil Mathias-Williams (down from Oxford) and former Newport and Rosslyn Park three-quarter Geoff Phillips in the backs.

For a back division there is understandably no better feeling than playing behind a dominant pack, as was the case during this period on the Rec. Indeed Bath possessed a set of forwards that in the words of John Stevens, was *unbeatable in a season in which the club's power was recognised and opposition tended to spoil and cover accordingly.* Moreover when the backs did their bit for the club and hit form, as occurred for example in their late Autumn 14-11 victory against Neath, Bath showed (as John Stevens described) *what a devastating side they can be, with right-wing Glover once more the outstanding try-grabber.* No surprise then that in February the same 'outstanding' Glover was recalled by England in their 14-14 drawn encounter against France at Twickenham.

Peter Glover: Effortless speed

Acknowledgements: Bath RFC.

Another encounter of a somewhat different kind had previously occurred at Kingsholm, involving the Western Counties (Somerset & Gloucestershire) versus the touring Fijians. The tourists had already demonstrated on their tour that they were capable of playing dazzling open rugby; and now they would demonstrate something a little different. Bath's Jim Waterman and Mike Beese both played on this occasion (in fact 10th October, Fiji's Independence Day) and as the Chronicle reported it was a certainty that neither they nor their colleagues *"will ever wish to take part in anything remotely resembling such a holocaust again."* Strong words indeed (nonetheless justified); and despite frequent injuries the Western Counties did win (25-13), while Mike Beese (now at Liverpool RFC), played an eye-catching stormer of a game; a performance that did not go unnoticed by watching England selectors.

In fact it was during the 1970's that the senior game was increasing its demands upon players in terms of both the quality and quantity of opposition, and the wisdom or otherwise of the 'end of season tour' now came under scrutiny at Bath following their late campaign trip to the French strongholds of Angouleme (losing 33-12) and La Rochelle (losing 17-6). 'Lightweight-games' these were not. On the contrary! Furthermore, the club still faced a Somerset Cup final to play on their return. Little wonder therefore that some commentators would argue that a pre-season tour with players keen as mustard for some early action (nor forgetting warm-up team practice) was a better option; and as it happened, would become the preferred choice anyway for many first-class clubs in the future.

On the evening of 8th May the club concluded its season when facing the 'Somerset & Bath Police' in the final of the newly restored Somerset Knock-Out Cup, not played since pre-World War One days. The task may have looked easy, except it wasn't, although as expected Bath did win a dour struggle 13-8 on the Rec. The close result however was a timely warning that in K.O. Cup competition there is no second chance, no opportunity to play exhibition rugby, nor must one ever under-estimate the opposition, nor fall into the trap of fielding a weakened side.

The 'mental attitude' and fitness levels could often be the deciding factor too, and it was in this context that the arrival of Tom Hudson as director of physical education at Bath University in January 1971 could not have been more perfectly timed. A British pentathlon champion who had represented Britain in the 1956 Olympics, Hudson arrived with an impressive CV. A former physical education lecturer at Sheffield and

160

Swansea universities, a rugby coach at Llanelli and who had served with the Guards Independent Airborne Company, his experience was potentially invaluable to any side participating in the hard knocks of cup rugby. Initially, Hudson made clear that his first priority would be devoted to his new role at the university. But come the mid-1970's when this initial task had been accomplished, Hudson would be forming one part of a remarkable coaching triumvirate.

By season 1971-2 an era had passed, or to be precise the Sibley era, and the responsibility of preserving his legacy into the future remained, as it had with Heindorff, priority number One. A number of players with invaluable experience remained, but there was the need to blend the 'old' hands with newer 'faces,' not always the easiest of tasks. Yet there was one certainty: 'there would be no return to negative tactics.' Bath after all had discovered that they too could play among kings, and that is the company that they now intended to keep.

So, leading the club at the culmination of five seasons of unrivalled success was 'not' straightforward, although at least two excellent candidates, namely Phil Hall and Roger Walkey, remained in 'the final frame' for the captaincy nomination. But the question was: 'which player should step into the captaincy shoes first?' With Hall's longer experience at the club some believed that he should get the 'nod,' with Walkey likely to follow. The committee nonetheless chose Walkey, his already demanding role made yet more difficult with the early departure of Bob Orledge to Bristol and a temporary move by Jim Waterman to Clifton. However, early season home wins against Pontypool (12-6) and an emphatic 23-13 success over Moseley suggested it could be 'business as usual.' But defeats soon followed, some heavy. Cheltenham (they clinched the 'Double' over Bath) and a string of upsets that included defeats by St. Mary's Hospital,

Roger Walkey: showed huge promise since arriving from London Welsh.

Acknowledgements: Bath Chronicle

Exeter and U.S. Portsmouth would all dent Bath's reputation in the first half of the season; so too did the away 30-7 drubbing at Saracens and an ominous 0-34 loss to Llanelli at home.

Yet quite suddenly Bath's perhaps forgotten powers of recovery would lift the gloom following an uplifting New Year 17-15 win over Leicester, and a subsequent haul of wins that included Ebbw Vale (19-6), Harlequins (27-13), Sale (20-8) and a notable 15-6 home triumph against Northampton in late April, victories that called for a reappraisal of Walkey's team. Another morale-boost had resulted from an away 9-12 victory in late February at Wasps, albeit a club who like their West Country victors had now found themselves in a similar stage of transition with a mere five wins under their belts so far that season, as against a dozen already chalked up by Bath. Furthermore the departure of Waterman to Clifton was cushioned by the quality of former Bristol full-back Bruce Thompson, whose performances were so impressive as to gain him selection for both Somerset and as a reserve England Trialist that season. Impressive too was former Walcot wing Terry Norris, a classic example of the ability to be found in the Combination, and whose 20 tries topped Bath's points scoring-list in this, his debut season in first-class rugby; and the season that saw the introduction of the four-point try.

Invaluable too during this period was the presence of those now elder statesmen, including hooker Alan Parfitt, the versatile Brendan Perry, and not forgetting winger David Taylor (ever steady and ever reliable), who like Perry could boast a decade-long service to Bath. Reassuringly locks Radley Wheeler and Brian Jenkins matured noticeably as support for Heindorff, and further recognition of the qualities within Walkey's team was the selection of prop Mike Hannell and wing Peter Glover for England's three-match early season tour to Japan. Nor, despite the 'pull' of nearby Bristol did the arrival of new talent at Bath dry up; and Oxford Blue Peter Binham at centre, and for a short period former Moseley and England wing Martin Hale, lost little time in showing off their own qualities in Bath colours.

Season 1971-2 was therefore a rugby journey of highs and lows, of bumps and bruises, of a salutary 27 defeats and yet 23 sometimes inspiring victories. In short, it was a season of mixed signals and in fact the first of a trio of uncertain years. Yet Walkey it was who had held Bath's head above water through the first of these problematic seasons, and not without considerable credit. But two more years of inconsistency would follow, and it would be Phil Hall's turn to take over at the 'helm,' with the assistance of former club full-back David Dolman (cousin of former wing John Dolman), who during Walkey's captaincy was nominated as Bath's first officially appointed coach.

Among the first responsibilities for the new skipper was to lead his side against the visiting President's XV that bore the name of Molly Gerrard (widow of pre-war great Ron Gerrard). President of Bath from 1971-3, and believed to be the first Madame president of a rugby union club in England, her guest team captained by Bristol and England hooker John Pullin included 13 internationals, and (watched by a reported 4000 attendance on the Rec), won 15-30 in a game that proved worthy of an inspirational pre-war Bath legend.

But Hall could not avoid that same unavoidable hurdle that had confronted Walkey, namely those expectations that had risen as a result of the previous Sibley era. Indeed Hall's 1972-3 campaign, one achieving a creditable 24 victories, was summarised by the Chronicle simply as a *"season with little more than an average record."* Well, an 'average record' may have been one way of summarising the campaign, but until the mid-1960's such a total would have been hailed as a minor triumph. But no longer, as Roger Walkey had already discovered.

Again as with Walkey's team, there would be at least one early departure of a key player, when in mid-October Mike Hannell moved across to Bristol; though sadly within two years this most likeable of sportsmen would not recover from a sudden and serious illness. Again there was a mix of the newcomers and the Old Guard whose experience often proved invaluable. Former England No.8 David Gay for example performed outstandingly at lock when necessity required, while his 14 touch-downs topped the season's individual try list from a Bath total of 133. Alan Parfitt at hooker (Martyn Gould providing excellent cover when needed) never had a poor game, likewise scrum-half Malcolm Lloyd.

But for reasons of sheer necessity there were occasions when Bath took a real gamble with selection, as occurred for instance in early February when young King Edward's schoolboy Andy Sparkes was thrust into action at Gloucester for his senior debut. Now Kingsholm is no place for a boy, especially one wearing a Bath shirt over his back; yet alongside the hard tackling Nick Hudson at centre, Sparkes showed real grit as Bath closed in on Gloucester to within two points in a narrow 18-16 defeat. Meanwhile the departure of brilliant runners Peter Glover and Ian Duckworth had left Bath seemingly vulnerable on the flanks. However David Flower proved a useful recruit, while Tony Hicks (son of Tommy) was recruited from Walcot Old Boys in mid-season. His selection was yet another astute piece of Bath scouting within the Combination ranks, and his 12 tries at wing placed him second only to David Gay in Bath's try-list that season.

It was in 1971-2 that the Rugby Union had introduced the National Knock Out Cup, with Twickenham chosen to stage the final. Thus at long last the green light was granted for R.F.U. competition at the club level, one that soon enough would have an electrifying effect upon the English game. But, those long acquainted with Bath's yeoman character would have been forgiven for questioning whether this particular club could ever take themselves seriously enough to succeed in such a competition. After all, when all was said and done, Bath enjoyed their rugby, and as this competition would soon reveal, cup rugby is first and foremost about winning and little if anything about enjoyment. In short it was a 'take no prisoners attitude and let the devil take the hindmost,' or something very similar. Thus would Bath, one wondered, be prepared to abandon their natural good nature and adopt a touch of the Machiavelli? If not, then they were unlikely (very unlikely in fact) to ever reach the dizzy heights of Twickenham. And the early indications were hardly encouraging, since in their initial forays into this new competition the club appeared not unlike a somewhat perplexed group of innocents abroad, and their visit to supposedly lowly Matson (Gloucestershire) in the preliminary round for the 1972-3 K.O. Cup revealed some of the pitfalls of this new competition. Yes, Bath made it home by 6-18 at Matson. But an overwhelming victory this was not! Instead this was another warning that getting anywhere near the gates of Twickenham, let alone actually getting through them, was not going to be easy.

Fortunately Phil Hall was hardened by years of rugby at the 'sharp' end, who knew only too well that for donkeys years Bath had been a club mocked one week, yet praised the next, and few encounters in season 1972-3 would more vividly show these two sides of their character than their mid-October visit to the Memorial Ground. Prior to the start of this flood-lit encounter the Bristolians (losing only at Cardiff so far that season) were proud recipients of the twin pennants for winning both the English and the Anglo-Welsh unofficial championships of the previous season. Yet by the end of the evening Bath had inflicted (in the words of John Stevens) a *"superb demolition job against a side which began almost arrogantly, but by the end were reduced to fumbling ineptitude."* And encouragingly for a club in the throes of re-building, it was two newcomers who shot home for the clinching converted tries in Bath's 7-12 win. First winger Geoff Hughes (previously Pontypool) scored, later followed by tough-tackling centre Edward Holly (previously Esher) who climaxed a 70 yard Bath surge *"to score another try of classic simplicity."* This victory of such quality suggested that Bath might be capable of overcoming 1971-2 National Cup holders Gloucester nine days later in the 1st round proper of the competition. But Gloucester, alerted by the performance at the Memorial Ground, had prepared their defences accordingly. Primed and ready, they repelled all that Bath could throw at the castle walls of Kingsholm to earn a 16-0 home victory.

Phil Hall ....led a dramatic 42-0 revival against Leicester.

Acknowledgements: Bath Chronicle

Yet this was not a season confined solely to learning painful lessons about National cup rugby, because there were times (as at Bristol) when it was Bath who, far from being the pupils, were instead the masters, and rarely was this more devastatingly shown than in their remarkable home victory over Leicester in early January. The encounter followed a dismal December month that included a 40-10 downfall at Llanelli, a 23-14 upset at Northampton and a Boxing Day 18-22 humiliation against Clifton. It was of little surprise therefore that barely a handful of spectators braved the atrocious elements that descended over the Rec for the visit of the Tigers. But what a treat awaited those who did. Because a seemingly over-confident Leicester (34-4 victors at Welford Road in September) and possibly confused by the

164

presence of identical twins David and Peter Jenkins in the Bath backs (their brother Brian was playing at lock) were now to be put to the proverbial sword. For at the culmination of eighty minutes of pulsating rugby that witnessed eight Bath tries (yes eight!) that included a hat-trick from an inspirational Phil Hall, it was Leicester who were subjected to one of the biggest defeats in their proud history by 42-0! Ah Bath….the masters of the 'Big'surprise!

It was the surge of form that commenced with a 25-3 win over Wasps in late February that gave further notice that under Phil Hall and Walkey the club had not abandoned (nor would it) the Sibley philosophy of attacking rugby. It was not merely that Bath would win impressively (assisted by the immaculate goal-kicking of Bruce Thompson) against the likes of Richmond (31-12) and the Harlequins (37-10). Rather it was a trio of March victories over Welsh opponents Swansea (15-9), Ebbw Vale away (21-22) and Bridgend (21-0) that provided the vital clues, results that would doubtless have brought out the flags in the capital if achieved by a London club. For it was this experience against Welsh opponents, then consistently the toughest opponents in the British Isles, that was showing signs of producing long-term dividends. Because since Sibley days especially Bath looked upon such competition as a perfect opportunity to learn everything that this rugby Principality had to teach, while simultaneously overcoming the psychological barrier that not infrequently affected many, if not most, English clubs when visiting Welsh territory.

The victory over Bridgend, who had beaten Cardiff only three days previously, was but one example; and albeit that this hard-fought encounter was marred by a fractured jaw injury to Bath Prop Bill Mottram ("*a sad episode for which neither side was blameless,*") John Stevens concluded that this powerful Welsh club were overcome "*in a superb display of modern rucking….by a Bath pack which is now an awesome force.*" Stevens in fact had now seen Bath's future, if not before. It was informative too that in their penultimate match of the season Bath not only defeated National K.O. Cup holders Gloucester by 16-7 on the Rec, but did so fielding an entire reserve front-row of R. J.Elliott, Martyn Gould and Frank Carter, and this against opponents whom Bath had not beaten since 1968.

So, the 1972-3 campaign concluded with 2 draws and 24 victories, with some wins so impressive as to suggest that Bath fully justified a place among rugby's own Ivy League, but for the fact that it was a season also of 23 defeats, none more severe than a 59-4 humiliation at Moseley in early September. And not for the first time this pointed the spotlight on that difference between Bath at their inspiring best and Bath at their inexplicable worst? It raised too another important question in this new age of increasingly competitive rugby union: could Bath ever have the confidence to match away performances with those at home, and could they ever adopt a more 'professional' and frankly downright 'bloody-minded' approach to their rugby? Because unless the club could improve its consistency and furthermore carry its Rec form into the most hostile arenas in the game, then they would never get even close to winning the National K.O. Cup.

Rarely have Bath experienced so chequered a rugby year as that of the following season of 1973-4. It had literally everything the script-writer could wish for: despair, elation, low farce and high drama. Defeats?....there were 28. Wins?....there were 26. A popular captain was suspended by his own club. A sickening injury ended a promising rugby career. A National Cup match was literally thrown (and blown) away. A charismatic full-back re-established himself from days spent mainly in the rugby-wilderness. A brilliant English half-back arrived. It was the stuff for the writer of fiction. Yet fiction it was not, and with the aid of hindsight it would have alerted pundits to the helter-skelter season that lay ahead. Two early defeats against Pontypool (0-7) and at Leicester (16-3) were compensated with a startling 43-7 home win over Moseley, adversaries who only one season previously had humbled Bath with a 59-4 thrashing at the Reddings. Here some new faces shone, including centre Vince Gaiger (formerly Devizes) and back-row man Andy Mills; older faces were prominent too, including prop Peter Jenkins, returning after six years in rugby 'exile' at Weston-super-Mare and Midsomer Norton; and back again at his best was that mercurial talent that was Jim Waterman. Against Moseley he kicked superbly for nineteen points and ran home a scintillating try, and as the Chronicle enthused: *"it all added to another of those remarkable displays which Bath manages to produce periodically over the past few seasons."* Periodically yes! But displays produced 'periodically' wouldn't get Bath or Jim Waterman anywhere near a Twickenham Cup final. Only consistency at the highest level would do that.

Anyway, celebrations post the Moseley victory were to be short-lived, as one week onwards Bath all too typically fell 22-4 at old foes Exeter. Worse still, after a 'robust retaliation' on an opponent who had *"perpetrated on him* a *particularly painful foul,"* skipper Hall got his marching orders! *"Hall is no angel,"* rued the Chronicle (24 September, 1973) *"but this time he was more sinned against than sinning."* Unfortunately for the ever-popular skipper, the committee did not see things quite so sympathetically, and with a decision unprecedented in Bath's then 108 years of rugby history they suspended their own captain for two matches. Hall, whose *"first reaction was to resign,"* then decided otherwise (to the huge relief of both players and supporters) and accepted the judgement gracefully, as he did the one-week ban later imposed by the Somerset R.U. for the same incident. Meanwhile in late September a sickening injury to the young three-quarter hopeful David Jenkins occurred during the United XV's encounter with Harlequins Wanderers. As sometimes happens in sport, the cause resulted from a seemingly innocuous collision with an opponent. But almost immediately onlookers feared that something was amiss from the manner that Jenkins collapsed in agony. Neither were they mistaken, for the youngster had suffered a seriously damaged knee injury, and fatefully he would never play serious rugby again, a shattering blow for one so young and of such glowing promise.

Four weeks later (27th October 1973) the club for whom David Jenkins had promised so much hosted the South & South Western Counties against the touring Australians, the first international tourists to visit the Rec since the South Africans in 1912. This mercifully was a happier occasion, no less than a 15-14 prestigious win over the Australian tourists. While in early January there followed another triumph, this time at club level when Bath struck form again, and inspired by sparkling performances from their new Lancashire and England Under-23 outside-half John Horton and centre Mike Beese (now a full England international) they overcame Leicester 20-3 at home. That was a 'Big' win. Another encouraging result followed, namely a convincing 19-3 success over Rosslyn Park, both positive victories that augured well for the National K.O. Cup where R.M.C.S. Shrivenham were overcome 27-6 in the preliminary round.

Next, Bath were drawn at home against Cheshire side Wilmslow. But....incessant mid-week rainfall was turning the Rec into a quagmire, and by Saturday it was effectively unplayable. Therefore, notwithstanding that Wilmslow had stayed nearby overnight on Friday, Bath would have been perfectly justified to demand a postponement. Instead, on the morning of the match club officials made frantic overtures to secure another venue, and in so doing committed the team to play a crucial first-round National Cup game at a totally unprepared Kingswood School. Situated high up on the Lansdown Hill, the pitch was admittedly firmer than the Rec, but totally exposed to gale force winds and rainfall now sweeping across Lansdown heights. Thus the committee, in the words of the Chronicle (11th February, 1974) had *"merely exchanged one set of farcical conditions for another."* Moreover there were no enclosures whatsoever for spectators, assuming that any would brave the elements in view of such atrocious conditions. While any hope of benefiting from an otherwise lucrative Cup tie was to be one more item on a long list of self-inflicted damage.

Making matters even worse was the fact that the captain was not even consulted about the matter, while a number of the Bath team (none of whom were even remotely familiar with the Kingswood pitch) only learned of the transfer to Kingswood when arriving for the game on the Rec. Small wonder that to everyone, apart from the committee, this decision to literally throw away home advantage was simply inexplicable. The effect furthermore on the morale of the Bath team, now effectively condemned to an away fixture, was frankly unprintable. Confidence gave way to sudden doubts, and before a mere handful of spectators the storm-lashed game subsided into a chaotic version of a rugby match. Bath meanwhile, notwithstanding their potentially match-winning backs, subsequently lost 6-17 in a game summed up by the Chronicle as nothing less than a *"morale shattering defeat."* Credit naturally could not be denied to a victorious Wilmslow team. But the fact was that it was 'off' the field where this vital game was really lost.

The experience was a profound jolt for a club who, sometimes quite outstanding in senior club football, appeared to be mere novices when faced with the harsh realities of the National Cup. For in this recently launched competition there was but one over-riding priority, namely 'winning!' Indeed, in all probability Wilmslow could hardly have believed their luck when the Bath committee literally exhausted themselves on the morning of the cup encounter frantically searching for another venue (any venue), so throwing away their vital home advantage. Adding yet more discomfort was the painful fact that if Bath wanted to learn how to win in Cup football, then two nearby rivals were exceptionally well qualified to teach them......Gloucester (winning finalists in 1972) and Bristol (finalists, albeit losing, in 1973)!

Fortunately Phil Hall was a strong leader, qualities rarely more needed than in the aftermath of the Wilmslow debacle. Nonetheless, among the immediate consequences of the cup defeat was a shake-up of the Bath front-row. Geoff Pudney (formerly Saracens) and ex Welsh schoolboy international Bob Hawkesley were preferred at prop and young Devizes recruit Steve Horton was given an extended run at lock; and in their first ever Sunday home club game a still shell-shocked Bath somewhat cautiously overcame Cheltenham 6-4, scant reward for a committee blunder that bordered on the inexcusable.

Sterner tests meanwhile lay ahead, not least the next challenge at Wasps. But fielding young Downside schoolboy centre John Bramall and John Horton oozing class at outside-half, an inspiring Phil Hall crashed over for a winning try and Bath had secured a confidence restoring 15-16 away win. Yes, they would sometimes continue to suffer in Wales. But their 21-18 home victory over Neath in March, followed by an impressive five-try 26-6 win over Sale, and furthermore a 20-6 success against Harlequins were clear evidence that Bath had the capacity to recover quickly from the most severe of setbacks.

It was undeniable that Bath had indeed taken some knocks in those three seasons of rugby since Sibley and then Heindorff had reigned with such commanding authority, though that perhaps was to be expected. Nonetheless the foundations that they had laid remained intact under the leadership of Walkey and Hall, both handed a truly challenging task when following in the footsteps of their two recent predecessors, yet who nonetheless succeeded in keeping the club heading in the right direction. This then was to be 'their' legacy. Because though maybe somewhat tarnished, the 'family silver' had indeed been preserved, thanks again to Walkey and Hall.

Chris Perry, formerly of Oldfield Old Boys and a player of an impressive versatility, whose sporting skills had been fine-tuned during a two-year sports-scholarship at Millfield School, was handed the captaincy for 1974-5. He had already played first team rugby for Bath at full-back, centre, scrum-half and wing-forward, not bad for a sportsman who was also a Somerset (2nd X1) County cricketer. Such all-round prowess furthermore seemed barely possible with one so mild of manner and of such youthful appearance. Yet he was not elected captain for nothing. *"Spoil and hit 'em hard,"* demanded Perry of his Bath 'infantry' prior to their October clash at Bristol, and that is exactly what they did, winning a 9-10 nail-biter. They did it again in early March, their 13-4 victory achieving their first Double over Bristol since 1967-8.

But things would not always run quite so smoothly for the new skipper, albeit that Bath had stormed off the starting blocks with victory in the Cheltenham Sevens (beating favourites Bridgend 18-16 in the final); and concluding the season with a 41-3 success over Old Redcliffians to win the Somerset Cup….again. But these two trophies notwithstanding, Bath would continue to send out those same mixed signals, not least in terms of the National K.O. Cup. Here, Bath were drawn to play their first-round encounter at Falmouth in mid-November, only too well aware that they had only narrowly squeaked home 13-11 on the Rec against the Cornishmen in September. Now they would be playing far from home, and if they were honest still haunted somewhat by the Wilmslow experience, nor forgetting that Kernow is a lonely corner of the Land for outsiders threatening their fierce rugby pride.

To anyone conversant therefore with the intense rivalry of West Country rugby it would come as no surprise to learn that the game itself was most certainly NOT a 'vicar's tea party.' Indeed by the closing stages the clash (for 'clash' it was) ended *"on a thoroughly bad-tempered note with some ugly brawling in the packs."* Fortunately from a Bath perspective it was Radley Wheeler and Robbie Lye who steadied matters with their domination of line-out play, while a re-called Heindorff set about *"generating a massive shove…..that helped push the Cornishmen yards back in the scrums."* But it was uncomfortably close, finishing at 9-9 by way of three penalties apiece; and by sole virtue of the 'away side rule' Bath now advanced into the next round.

Now Liverpool RFC beckoned as opponents for the 2nd round in early February, and as Mike Beese could have told anyone: 'Pool were not to be taken lightly, especially on their home territory,' and as a result Bath were taking absolutely no chances. They forsook any thoughts of open rugby and adopted instead the same tactics they had applied against Bristol in mid-October, namely to *"smother Liverpool into mistakes, coupled with some good cover and hard tackling."* It was not attractive; nor was it intended to be. It was designed only to achieve a cup victory, which it did with a 6-12 win. Coincidentally it was Bath's first away success since winning at Bristol in October, and Liverpool's first defeat since that same date. So with this change of attitude, namely that National Cup rugby is first and foremost about winning, the signs looked promising when Bath gained valuable home-ground advantage for their quarter-final tie against supposedly lowly Morpeth from distant Northumberland. That is until approximately one hour prior to the match itself on 8th March. Then suddenly a recent haunting memory stirred when literally *"the heavens opened….producing mud, the great leveller."* And of course such conditions are a godsend to any would-be giant-killers. So it was that on a rain-soaked Rec the weather once again fatefully intervened, so too the spectre of Wilmslow, and the Northern invaders thus captured the only thing that matters in Cup rugby....a 9-13 win!

For Chris Perry this defeat would remain the one great regret of his captaincy. A leader from the front, he could only reminisce from the side-lines as his Morpeth opponents strode onwards into the semi-finals. Here, they too would lose at home to Rosslyn Park, who themselves would fall at the final hurdle against Bedford (28-12) at Twickenham, while Bath could only ponder what might have been.

The club scene is however a different 'world,' though the contrast between Bath at home and Bath away was sometimes glaring. In early December for instance there was a 49-4 humiliation in the capital at the hands of London Scottish (losing 1974 Cup finalists). Two weeks later such woes went very public indeed when, by way of the BBC's Rugby Special, Bath were seen to slide and slither upon a rain-soaked Llanelli pitch and endure a 30-0 drubbing. While in early February London rugby would doubtless have taken another critical note of Bath's 21-0 defeat at Rosslyn Park.

Yet such upsets 'abroad' often obscured a quite different 'picture' at home. Leicester, London Irish and Gloucester were among Bath's home victims in the first part of the season. While post-Christmas Bath's victory toll included victories over a still superb London Welsh (13-8), the Saracens, Wasps and Harlequins. And almost certainly Bath's finest performance of the entire season was their 12-6 victory over Newport in early February. The Welshmen had lost only once previously that season, few English clubs could get anywhere near them and yet: *"Bath not only outplayed them up front but produced far more enterprise outside."* And doing the outplaying up front were Bath props Pudney, Meddick, and hooker Alan Parfitt, a trio ably supported by locks Brian Jenkins and Mike Plummer, plus a back-row of Robbie Lye, Clive Harry and Phil Hall. As for enterprise outside, there was John Horton and: *"the artistry of Bath's Lancashire-born fly-half was there for all to see."*

It was performances such as this, not the away upsets that sometimes occurred, that help to explain the reasons behind the highly commendable 28 wins that season; albeit that John Stevens by including the Somerset Cup quarter-final win over Keynsham in February refers to a record equalling 29 victories (Chronicle, 3rd May, 1975), while official club records had not included the Somerset Cup results until the semi-final stage when Bath defeated Weston-super-Mare in mid-March. Whatever view one takes on this particular matter, and Bath were sometimes reluctant to claim wins against Junior opposition as official victories, this was a season more significant than anyone at the time would have likely realised. First, the club's capital-base was strengthened considerably with the introduction of floodlights, a facility initially launched for the Boxing Day win against Clifton, and soon followed in January when successfully hosting the Royal Navy. Secondly, in addition to the return of class players such as

Roger Walkey and his priceless experience, Bath welcomed a number of 'interesting' new faces to the Rec, including Peter Fryatt from Hampshire club Tottonians, teenager Mike Richardson, and John Davies from St. Brendan's Old Boys.

All three backs arrived from Junior football, and reflected Bath's willingness to recruit and experiment with players from outside the boundaries of the first-class game. All three were 'terrific' goal kickers. All three topped over 100 points that season and ironically all three occupied one third each of the season as Bath's designated goal kicker. Fryatt (full-back or wing) arrived on the recommendation of Hampshire County and dominated the opening third of the season. Richardson followed until ruled out by injury. Then Davies fulfilled the kicking role. Their impact was profound. Indeed, Bath's final tally of 647 points included a huge contribution of 347 from goal kicks alone; while the 74 penalty goals attained was a hit-rate unprecedented in the club's entire previous history. And the fact was that in first-class rugby the 'boot' was now vying to be king.

Others would now come knocking on the door of the club, including Bristol centre Dave Alred (a future international kick-specialist coach), and two young backs who in early April were given their senior baptism in Bath's losing 15-3 encounter at powerful Northampton. One was St. Luke's student Steve Donovan (brother of John); the other was Prior Park College all-round back John Palmer. Steve Donovan's stay at Bath (likewise that of Fryatt) was to be all too short-lived. But Palmer's stay was to be longer, and come the next season of 1975-6 Bath would be fielding a back division of a lethal potential. Horton, Beese and Palmer were players any first-class side would give their proverbial right arm for. In addition the compulsive genius that was Jim Waterman (now an Oxford Blue) would be lining up alongside them....as captain! And from distant Falmouth a strong-running young winger by the name of Barry Trevaskis had not forgotten that Cup game with Bath..... nor Bath him. He too would soon make the long journey from Cornwall to the Rec.

And although no one could possibly have guessed it at the time, the foundations for another remarkable era of Bath rugby were quietly being laid.

Chapter 26. AGE of PROMISE. (1975-80)

It was fitting indeed that Bath's season of 1975-6 would prove to be as colourful as new captain Jim Waterman's equally colourful nature. Lessons would be learned, some painfully. Records would be achieved, some startling. It seemed too that all the hard graft of Roger Walkey, Phil Hall and Chris Perry had helped to pave the way for a new era of confidence that might now take-off under the adventurous personality of Waterman.

Jim Waterman ....brilliant attacking player

Acknowledgements: Reg Monk

But this was still Bath, a club whose characteristic inconsistencies had always made the task of future predictions unusually difficult. Nor was season 1975-6 to be entirely exempt from this general rule, one launched like a rocket with 3-35 win at Taunton (their Centenary year), followed by a 30-15 free-flowing gallop over Pontypool. This typified one side of the Bath personality. Another side was then duly exposed with a 30-12 trouncing from Newport, next a 37-7 salutary lesson at Leicester and a 40-18 crash at the hands of a *"superbly drilled Moseley."* Would Bath ever change their ways, one wondered? Frankly, the Sibley reforms notwithstanding, it was at the time anyone's guess.

Soon enough thoughts turned to the National RFU Cup in mid-October, now sponsored, and thus to be known as the John Player Cup; and thankfully from a Bath point of view they had been awarded a home-tie for their initial encounter. So far so good, except that they were drawn against Bristol. For Bath, this was the ultimate dream tie if winning, but the ultimate nightmare if losing. Bath lost! Likewise did rugby's reputation, as Waterman's men fell 15-24 in a contest remembered especially for *"some ruthless tackling.....and sadly some fearsome displays of temper."*

Yet with this avenue once more closed for another season, they set about concentrating on non-cup games....and in the process Bath bagged some very big fish indeed to achieve a new official club record of 32 victories. By early February London Irish and London Scottish had returned homewards empty-handed. Likewise a high-flying Rosslyn Park, defeated 24-0, yet perplexingly for Bath good enough to reach their second successive cup final at Twickenham, albeit losing 23-14 to Gosforth.

Meanwhile the Rec remained nigh on impregnable against Welsh opposition, with in addition to Pontypool, wins over Bridgend (10-9), Neath (15-9), South Wales Police (22-15), Cardiff (9-4), Ebbw Vale (15-6) and sweet revenge over Newport (9-4). The successes against Cardiff and Newport not surprisingly rate a special mention.

Cardiff were hosted first, their mid-February visit drawing an estimated 4000 attendance to the Rec, not least to witness 'for real' the Wales scrum-half genius that was Gareth Edwards. But on this day, in the words of John Stevens: *"even the legendary Edwards was over-shadowed as Horton....first toyed with Cardiff, then destroyed them with his superb kicking and running...."* Against Newport in April an early second half injury to Phil Hall thus depleted Bath to thirteen fit players. But *"in a bruising, sometimes brutal affair"* the defiant Waterman inspired a never-say-die defence that subsequently thwarted (just!) everything that Newport could hurl at them.

It was a hard task playing against the Welsh, and there was only one way to do it....their way! They were tough as teak, fearless, hugely talented and justifiably confident. Yet this tally of seven wins was evidence that Bath could indeed 'do it the Welsh way,' and that during this season at least the Rec had become a graveyard of Welsh rugby aspirations. Few English clubs had ever been in a position to make such a claim, and in truth this was only half a claim. For Bath's own six forays into Wales that season had led to six defeats and Llanelli (victors at Stradey Park) did win at Bath. But, if the psychological barrier that thwarted so many English teams when venturing into the Valleys could be surmounted, then there might be no pinnacle that Bath could not reach one distant day. It was a tantalizing thought, one that would have occurred to few if any at the time. But it was not without a substance of truth nonetheless.

It is always good timing to join a club that, like Bath, were heading for a new record, and fortunately a fund of talent was available for the gruelling fifty match season of 1975-6. From the outset Bath called-up both Oxford Blue wing Ian Dunbar and Army prop Rod Campbell for the opening victories against Taunton and Pontypool. Soon youngsters Chris Thomas from Wales (wing) and out-half Mark Sutton would be thrust into the deep end; and later invaluable contributions were provided by, among others, centre Robin Hone, winger Rob Wyatt (RAF & Combined Services), scrum-half Tim Lane (ex Bristol), and locks Hugh Leman and former Sale forward Peter Boyle. Another unforgettable discovery was 24 years old, 18 ½ stone and 6ft 5in lock giant Adam Litowczyk. Having earlier impressed in United ranks, he made his debut under floodlights in Bath's November revenge 12-6 victory over Bristol, a senior baptism to remember and this from a supposed 'rookie' who in the previous season was playing for Cirencester RFC.

Yet among the least expected selections was Bath's sudden call-up in early November of Avonvale hooker Tony Edwards. There was nothing unusual of course in Bath fielding players from the Combination. But to draft them immediately into first-team duty was not only unusual, it was almost unheard of. However, one week previously

Bath had fallen 22-13 at St. Mary's Hospital (admittedly on a County day) and the selectors were in no mood to listen to excuses from anyone. Allan Parfitt anyway was still injured and Bath (by-passing better known candidates) thrust Edwards straight into the senior side that narrowly overcame Bridgend. That the 30 years old Avonvale hooker would then demonstrate that he could 'live' amongst opponents that would later include the likes of Bristol, Gloucester and Cardiff was proof of his ability. That Bath possessed the intuitive judgement to make so bold a selection was proof of their long-standing knowledge and faith of the strengths within Combination rugby.

Despite the increasing success as the season progressed there were no immediate international demands on Bath, although Horton was believed to be on the verge of an England cap and John Palmer was attracting interest from national selectors. Nonetheless the likes of Nick Hudson, Mike Beese and Horton in the backs, and forwards Bert Meddick and Ken Plummer all appeared for Somerset. David Gay too remained a class player. Furthermore Phil Hall, Robbie Lye and Geoff Pillinger were now as street-wise and experienced a trio of back-row men as most clubs could ever muster. They needed to be, because since losing narrowly at Richmond ten matches from the end of the season, Bath knew they simply must win at least seven of their remaining nine matches to beat the club record of 29 wins. They knew too that standing in their path were the likes of Newport, Llanelli, Harlequins and bogey sides Bedford and Exeter. Notwithstanding this daunting challenge they won not seven, but eight more matches, and in doing so they literally crushed Harlequins (35-9), Bedford (35-7) and Exeter (37-6). The Rec was literally buzzing!

On the final day of the season Bath had to honour not one, but two important engagements. There was the visit of a fast-rising Nottingham, while simultaneously Bath would be a guest side in their first-ever participation in the prestigious Snelling Sevens at Cardiff. By coincidence this final day of a truly eventful season was in fact May Day, and Oh.... what an emotional day it would prove to be. In beating Weston-s-Mare 22-7 four weeks previously Bath had already won the Somerset Cup for the 5th time, while their victory over Exeter had 'guaranteed' their entry into the following season's John Player Cup. Master-kicker John Davies (recruited from St. Brendan's Old Boys by previous skipper Chris Perry) would complete the season with a remarkable club record of 425 points that consisted of 7 tries, 53 conversions and 97 penalties; and the now legendary Phil Hall would be retiring with a new official record of 580 first-team Bath appearances under his belt.

Moreover, despite key players on Sevens duty at Cardiff, Bath won their final game of the season by 10-6 against Nottingham, so establishing the aforementioned record of 32 victories. It was an outstanding achievement, on the glorious first of May, and one that climaxed Phil Hall's remarkable rugby career. While in Cardiff a 7000 crowd attended the Snelling Sevens; and Bath, travelling with a team of J. Palmer, M. Beese, J. Horton, T.Lane, D. Gay, A. Parfitt and R. Love (with reserves J. Roberts and M. Richardson)

174

won warm applause when initially overcoming Welsh Merit Table champions Pontypridd 16-6, next defeating fellow guest side Moseley 30-16, before losing 24-12 to a Newport team who fell 18-8 to hosts Cardiff in the final.

It was only two weeks after Bath had attained their new 32 win record that readers of the Bath Chronicle (15th May) were treated to an eye-catching headline. It stated thus:

"*Can Bath become the best rugby club in England.....?*" And (though it seemed somewhat fanciful at the time), the answer according to former Great Britain pentathlon champion Tom Hudson was 'YES.' Domiciled in the city since early 1971 and director of sport at Bath University, Hudson had recently joined the Bath training staff; and his message to the club included a bold challenge to "*win the John Player Cup.*"

Tom Hudson ....knows how to train a rugby team
Acknowledgements: Reg. Monk

'Who exactly is this Tom Hudson?' was the response from not a few Bath followers and.... 'was this Mr Hudson not aware of Bath's almost embarrassing track-record so far in National Cup rugby?' But criticism was not going to frighten this former member of the Guards Independent Airborne Company, and anyway Mr Hudson was not trying to kid anyone. In fact he was being perfectly serious. Indeed he was not only a man of infectious enthusiasm, but one with an impressive record among the giants of Welsh rugby. As The Chronicle added, he had helped lift Llanelli "*to probably the best club side in the world.*" Furthermore, this was the same Tom Hudson who was now to bring his invaluable experience to the Rec, and bringing too the most demanding training schedule that Bath had ever seen, let alone put into practice. Furthermore John Horton, the new captain for season 1976-7 was impressed, though whether the club under the Lancastrian, or anyone else, would ever rise to be regarded as the 'best rugby club in England' was an entirely different matter.

But undaunted, Hudson spoke thus: "*You have a good club – one of the oldest in England – but you can make it a better one if you make use of the facilities available.*" So in affect this Northern arrival in the city was telling his new West Country charges to forget any self-congratulations for their previous season's record and instead aim for the supreme goals in rugby football, and that of course included the National K.O. Cup. But to do so Bath would first need to step across that crucial threshold that divides mere first-class clubs from a small elite of truly top-class clubs. But this did not deter Tom Hudson from proclaiming that Bath could not merely join this elite, but effectively lead it! In which case during Hudson's first season on the Rec there would be a number of clubs in England and Wales only too willing to put his claim to the test, and do so where it hurts most....on the rugby field.

Pontypool's home 46-6 victory in Bath's 1976-7 season opener followed by a 22-3 defeat at Newport emphasised that fine statements off the field do not necessarily guarantee success on it. The same message echoed loud and clear with later upsets (nay crashes) at Neath (35-19), Llanelli (36-0) and late-season lessons from Newport at home (7-32) and at Bedford (44-15). Making matters worse was Bath's October fall at Bristol (35-10) and a late March 51-7 nightmare defeat at Gloucester.

So, what exactly was the missing ingredient in Bath's DNA? Well, their immediate response to the Gloucester disaster partly helps to answer this query, because they proceeded to trounce Richmond 25-4 on the Rec. But, away from home Bath remained too often a team lacking that 'something of the devil' in their psyche. Indeed, they remained in many ways the club that they always had been, and one that could be summed up in a few words: 'an unpredictable enigma.' But such teams do not win National K.O. Cup finals, and many knew it. But Hudson not only knew it. He was determined to change it.

Yet the continuing potential at the club was there for all to see, as proved with a creditable 27 victories during Horton's first year of captaincy, a total including some top notch scalps that included Leicester (19-10), Harlequins (10-4), Wasps (24-18) and Welsh opponents Aberavon (12-9), Newbridge (6-3) and a 7-9 away success at Bridgend. New faces arrived too, among them prop Dougal Spaven, former Gloucester scrum-half Richard Nichols, Old Whitgiftians hooker Tony Mason, ex Newbridge wing-forward Roger Hill and powerful centre Chris Bird. Further talent meanwhile travelled along the well-trodden Combination 'corridor' to the Rec, notably young winger Gary Townsend (Trowbridge), centre Andrew Smith (Chippenham) and scrum-half Paul Smith (Combe Down).

Naturally, while this bountiful supply of talent bode well for the club's future, almost predictably there was to be yet another chapter to the on-going saga of Bath and the Cup, now fast becoming either a farce or a nightmare, depending upon one's sense of humour. Horton's men had been drawn away to play a demanding (but highly attractive) first-round tie at London Welsh in early December, and on the morning of the 'big' day both Bath and some two hundred expectant supporters headed for the capital. Nonetheless, although no warnings had been received by Bath, there were to be certain reservations about the supposedly hard surface of the pitch at Old Deer Park. But the first that Bath knew anything about it did not occur until both teams were actually on the field of play waiting for the kick-off whistle to sound. It was then that host captain Jim Shanklin *"indicated he considered the pitch was too hard to play."* Horton begged to differ. But Shanklin, having first led his team on to the field, then promptly led them off again. The home captain *"was roundly booed by his own supporters,"* while Bath were absolutely livid. As club secretary Jack Simpkins said: *"if we had known we might have at least have been able to stop supporters travelling up for nothing."* Not until the 8th January was the matter finally resolved when, with the original sense of cup expectancy by now long gone, London Welsh won 18-3 in a *"scrappy, rather niggly match."* But nothing could diminish the aura of the Cup itself however, not for Bath or anyone else. Indeed the 1977 competition, won 27-11 by Gosforth against Waterloo, was by now the most important event in the rugby calendar. But once again, things just didn't seem to go right for Bath.

Yet that season's decision by the RFU to accept sponsorship of the National Cup by John Player naturally opened the gates for clubs do likewise.

Indeed, such welcome largesse came Bath's way in early March 1977 by courtesy of local stockbrokers Godfrey, Derby and Co. of George Street, who (for the first time in the club's history) sponsored Bath's 3-3 home game with Bristol and in addition purchased a new set of jerseys (costing some £300) for the same game. Small this sum may have been, but its effect was anything but. For sponsorship into Rugby Union had come to stay and would prove a welcome source of revenue. Just a few words of caution however might have occurred to some followers of the game, for 'he who pays the piper sooner or later calls the tune,' and certain unintended (and doubtless unexpected) consequences now lay ahead.

Less unexpected perhaps was the outcome of Bath's post-domestic season tour to France. A strenuous campaign had only just finished, and making matters worse was a shortage of available players. Notwithstanding these drawbacks Bath, despite a second-half injury to prop John Cunningham, did win 19-10 against Libourne, with the names of John Horton, Gary Townsend, Mike Beese and Dave Alred on the score sheet. In their second match however Bath struggled to even raise a team of 15 fit men, hardly the way to beat a side such as Begles who, despite a Beese try converted by Alred, strode onwards to an overwhelming 52-6 victory. Such an outcome as this was a reminder of those crucial lessons learned from the inaugural 1954 French tour of the John Roberts team: first and foremost ensure that a full-strength side will be available, with proficient reserves in support. Secondly, ensure that the tour must rank as a 'not to be missed event,' because nothing less than a club's reputation will be at stake; hardly the case for Bath at Begles.

The appointment of Jim Waterman for a second term of captaincy in season 1977-8 promised one thing if nothing else.....action! What kind of action was another matter altogether. But the fact was that the mere name 'Waterman' was sufficient to ignite excitement and expectation among the Bath faithful, because his erratic genius had ensured that he never, ever disappointed his many admirers. He had always lived life in rugby's fast lane, and though but an injured spectator for Bath's 27-9 season-opener victory against Pontypool, the style of play had the name and spirit of their skipper written all over it. But another long season lay ahead to judge if Bath really were capable of matching the predictions of Tom Hudson. In fact not for the first time their 1977-8 campaign was a mix of outstanding victories interrupted by some truly embarrassing defeats.

Coventry was one example of this inconsistency, where Bath were hounded to a November 42-4 submission, an awful trouncing and an upset partly resulting from *"Bath's powder-puff pack which was shoved back yards in the set scrums."* Though not unknown, it was unusual for Bath to have such a weakness at forward, and it was fortunate that during this era the backs were not infrequently able to compensate for such a drawback, as occurred in the return against Coventry in March. Then with *"thrilling attacks which often started deep in their own 25"* Bath avenged earlier defeat with a 21-13 victory. But they were not as yet 'a team for all seasons,' and although defeating Exeter 16-25 away on a balmy September day, in the club's 1st round John Player encounter, coincidentally at Exeter again, the hosts applied *"a commonsense display suitable to the trying conditions,"* applying tactics that led to a 20-6 victory on a quagmire January pitch that left Bath to ponder if their fortunes in cup rugby would ever change.

For a chastened Bath however it was important to assess the possible reasons for yet another cup defeat. First, in knock-out rugby the supposedly weaker teams will rarely be so naive as to attempt to out-play a supposedly superior attacking team. For that would be rugby suicide. Instead they confront strong attack with stout defence and pounce on any errors that present themselves. Hence the better footballing sides are sometimes beaten as does the tortoise sometimes beat the hare; and an especially good street-wise club for Bath to study was based not that far away either. Fancy stuff was not their priority, while winning was, hence no surprise regarding Gloucester's triumph in the 1978 John Player Cup Final.

Meanwhile the first-class careers of Brian Jenkins, Radley Wheeler, David Gay, Bert Meddick and others were now drawing to a close. Their example nonetheless would be invaluable to a younger generation of forwards who would now be arriving on the Rec in the coming months and seasons. Among these was young Gareth Chilcott from Gordano (Bristol), hooker Chris Legg and lock Neil Spencer, who all shone at forward in Bath's inspired October 25-9 victory against Neath. It was encouraging too that a front-row of comparative newcomers, namely Peter Ford (ex. Salisbury), hooker Chris Legg and Phil Davies (ex. Penarth and Llanelli) showed promise not only in Bath's home 28-16 victory over Leicester in early January, but furthermore in Bath's outstanding 11-17 away win at Bristol in March where David Gay, playing at lock, ran home the winning try.

Later former Bristol prop Rod Speed, lock Colin Chappell and flanker Gerry Parsons (another trio of newcomers) stamped their own impressive mark in Bath's brilliant seven try and 9-39 victory at Richmond in early April; a performance of Waterman's team at its fluent-playing best, performed in London's own rugby heartland and partly inspired by one John Horton, now a full England international since his February debut at Twickenham, albeit in a narrow 6-9 defeat by Wales. Another achievement was the earlier debut of Alan Jenkins at centre in Bath's 0-26 win at U.S. Portsmouth in late November. Albeit this was to be a rare first-team appearance, Alan was the fourth and youngest of the Jenkins rugby family to play at senior level for Bath, a record believed to be unique in the club's entire history.

But sentiment apart, the fact was that by the late 1970's rugby football was taking itself more seriously than ever before. Something would be lost as a result; yet something would be gained. Coaching was developing more 'professionally,' so too the administration, and not just among the senior clubs either. In addition, the commercial and business world was now taking a closer interest in the rugby game, and attendances at club matches were increasing significantly. Already in the mid-1970's the RFU had agreed a sponsorship deal with John Player for the National K.O. Cup, an arrangement that benefited not only the RFU but furthermore those clubs participating in the competition. Later, certain leading Welsh clubs commenced their own separate sponsorship deals with Adidas, although *"officially deplored by the Welsh Rugby Union."* Several English clubs then made similar agreements, among them Bath, who at the start of the 1977-8 season negotiated a sponsorship deal with Adidas worth approximately £3,000 over the following three seasons. To be precise (Chronicle, 6th September, 1977) this involved the annual supply to Bath of no less than *"40 complete sets of kit-shorts, jerseys and socks – 12 [rugby footballs] and, to start with, 40 hold-alls."* Such a deal in more recent times may appear 'small fry.' But it was merely the beginning and later much, much larger sums would flow into the game. Of interest too was that despite the initial disapproval of the Welsh RFU to shirt sponsorship, Bath had nonetheless faced no opposition whatsoever from the Rugby Union for their own similar arrangement.

Another professionalism-issue arose (Chronicle, 20th April, 1978) when Bath full-back Dave Alred revealed that he had signed a three year contract with Minnesota Vikings to play in American grid-iron football. It was Alred's kicking style, and crucially his ability to kick goals quickly that had first attracted the attention of his intended employers. Indeed such was the value attached to a reliable kicker in US football that Alred revealed he would *"earn more in four months there than I would get in eight years as a teacher here."* But there was a simple reason for the interest of US football in this reliable English goal-kicker. As the Bath full-back said: his role was *"just to kick-off and kick the goals,"* adding that in grid-iron you *"have about 1.3 seconds to kick at goal before the opposition gets to you. That means two steps and bang."* There were only two hurdles now facing Alred before embarking on a new and exciting experience across the Pond. First there was the need to obtain a US government work permit. That proved no difficulty. Secondly, he would require clearance from the RFU that playing professional grid-iron in the USA would not prevent his return to rugby union football at a later date. That, as Alred would later discover, would be another matter altogether.

For his club however the season would end with a trio of sparkling victories, prior to Bath's second appearance in the Middlesex Sevens at Twickenham. First Newport were overcome 15-9 on the Rec, a win over Welsh opponents making some amends for Bath's overwhelming 45-7 setback at Swansea in March. Next Taunton fell 0-56, with Bath's Jonathon Roberts (son of former skipper John), Robbie Lye and Geoff Pillinger literally causing havoc among the opposition. Finally against a highly entertaining Bedford side on the Rec, Bath concluded their season of 28 victories with a 45-28 win and *"another marvellous feast of open rugby and a glut of spectacular tries."* Of these, the first was run home by young wing prospect Paul Simmons. But of further significance was the fact that two of Bedford's tries were scored by their England winger Derek Wyatt, set to join Bath for the following season, and demonstrating to an admiring Rec crowd that he was indeed a player of pure class.

The annual Twickenham Sevens would now be the final stage of Bath's 1977-8 season, and having already won the earlier Oxford tournament with an emphatic 32-6 win over Oxford University in the final, Waterman's men headed for rugby HQ with high hopes for another good day in the Spring sunshine. Before a packed 'house' Bath reached the last eight with their 18-12 win over London Scottish. But, their progress would stop with a 14-6 defeat at the hands of Rosslyn Park, while Harlequins proved themselves to be the stars of the show with their victory in the final.

Derek Wyatt: Oxford Blue and England, later MP for Sittingbourne.

Acknowledgements: Bath RFC

'Sevens' rugby however is a side-show, albeit a joyful one. But the serious business takes place in the 15-man game and Mike Beese, the new skipper for 1978-9, now faced the challenge to maintain Bath's position at the top level of the game. The former England centre, both thoughtful of mind and likeable of character, was a determined leader and his one year of captaincy would prove to be among the most exciting in the club's history. Despite four matches cancelled, there would be a total of 31 victories, three draws and a mere 10 games lost; and again specialist kicker John Davies, albeit playing in barely a third of the fixtures, would be the leading points-scorer for the fourth year in succession with his tally of 133 goals sent flying through the woodwork. It was a season too when a new coach from the North East (Jack Rowell, all 6ft 6in of him) would arrive to add his already considerable knowledge and experience to developments down on the Rec. But above all it was a season when Bath would prove beyond any doubt that they could 'handle' the very best that even Wales could throw at them (usually!).

But yet again fortunes in the Cup would disappoint, this time on a grim February day at the London Welsh, whose 28-18 win brought Bath's cup hopes to a shuddering halt. Adding to the disappointment was the intended departure of Bath's England Trialist scrum-half Steve Lewis, soon to return homewards to Ebbw Vale, and no club likes to lose players of his abilities. Yet the season had begun with a cracking 10-26 victory at Pontypool, and when in late September Bath triumphed 8-12 to gain their first-ever away victory at Neath, things had looked genuinely promising for the inevitable pressures that lay ahead in the John Player Cup. The London Welsh 'put paid' to those aspirations however, and no one was complaining that they did not deserve their victory. But when Bath later hosted Cross-Keys in early March, somewhat different emotions surfaced. These two clubs had not played regularly since pre-First World War days, and this match (or rather dual) was anything but a meeting of Old Friends. Indeed it was an encounter that *"flared fitfully into open warfare,"* albeit that Bath won convincingly 22-0.

But to be fair matters could get equally non-friendly in England, as they most certainly did during Bath's visit to Plymouth Albion (10th October, 1978). First, there was the 'small' matter of West Country prestige. Secondly, this meeting was a South West Merit Table encounter, and clubs in the top four grouping at the end of season would be guaranteed an automatic place in the first-round proper of the John Player Cup the following year. But this, as the Chronicle explained, hardly justified the events that followed. For while there was precious little rugby, there were numerous *"late tackles, flying boots, flurries of fists and blatant trampling. Neither side was blameless."* Indeed the Chronicle described the match as nothing less than *"reminiscent of the bloodbath West Country derbies of old,"* and that was just about the worst advert that rugby could possibly earn for itself.

Bath, fortunately perfectly capable of looking after themselves, did squeeze home by 12-13. But this was certainly not a night to remember, nor was it surprising when two players after an 'exchange of pleasantries' received their marching orders. But there was to be a twist to the tale. For the players involved were flankers Simon Jones of Bath and Roger Spurrell of Albion, and despite the latter's dismissal, the flaxen haired Spurrell would not only decide to join Bath in the near future, he would later rise to captain them.

Meanwhile Bath were becoming mentally tougher and more confident when away from home, not least because of experience gained inside the 'take no prisoners' zone of Celtic rugby; and this hardening of attitude was increasingly evident in a number of highly significant results during the season. Twickenham for instance, where for the first time in their history Bath triumphed 4-15 over Harlequins, no longer overawed the West Countrymen. Indeed they half expected to win, such was their growing self-belief. There was another reason to remember this particular encounter however, for with only five minutes remaining Bath touch-judge David Jenkins managed to get himself sent off! In actual fact he had made a *"light-hearted remark to someone in the crowd,"* but one that the referee Mr Williams *"thought was aimed at him."* Thus former Bath player David Jenkins, who had never been dismissed as a player, now received his marching orders as a touch-judge instead, a 'feat' that has remained an all-time club record, and likely to remain so….forever.

Mike Beese ....one of the most successful post-war captains.

Acknowledgements: Reg Monk

Humour aside, there were further results of significance in the run-up to Christmas. Coventry were overcome 23-3 on the Rec, so too at home both Gloucester (20-10) and the return against Harlequins (21-10). But among the most notable features of the season was that Bath now ranked among a small group of English clubs capable of holding their own against Welsh teams. There were in fact glimpses of this potential in the past, but now this was becoming reality. It was unfortunate that the encounters against Cardiff and Ebbw Vale fell foul of the weather. Yet of the 13 matches against Celtic opposition only two, namely Newbridge on a County day and at Bridgend, were lost. In addition Bath drew at Newport and Llanelli, defeated both Pontypool and Neath away, and likewise overcame Aberavon, Cross-Keys, Swansea, Newport, Pontypridd, South Wales Police, and Llanelli at home. Few if any English clubs could match such a record as this.

Entirely in keeping with his generous nature, Mike Beese ignored his own huge contribution to the team and instead heaped praise not least on the younger players in his ranks, among them out-half prospect Neil Hopkins (soon to be capped for England colts), and who as a Millfield schoolboy in the previous season had helped Bath defeat the RAF on his debut that included a superb 45 yard penalty goal. Wing Simon Jarvis, himself ex-Millfield, impressed on his Bath debut in the 25-10 Autumn win against U.S.Portsmouth. In addition prop Gareth Chilcott and backs Mark Sutton and John Palmer all received the call-up to the England U.23 squad, and the line-out ability of Derrick Barry was proving invaluable.

Beese furthermore described winger Paul Simmons *"as the most improved young wing in the country,"* praise indeed when considering two other wingers now carving out reputations throughout the game. Of these the first was 18 years old Bryanston schoolboy David Trick. Already an England U.19-group international of stunning speed, he 'screamed' over for a hat-trick on his senior debut in Bath's 36-16 defeat of South Wales Police in mid-April. Another winger was former St. Luke's College Exeter, Bedford, Oxford Blue and England international Derek Wyatt. Now a master at Dauntseys, he was a highly deceptive winger, a quality so forthrightly demonstrated in Bath's superb late season 23-6 win against Llanelli. Watched by the club's biggest crowd of the season, Bath *"produced some quite glorious running and handling,"* and the admired Wyatt ran over for a superb hat-trick that took his season's total to no fewer than 29 tries. This tally was not merely impressive, it equalled the club record set by Bath utility forward George Haydon 48 years previously.

Though not immediately recognised for its effect upon the club, a coaching-trio consisting of former Bath forward Dave Robson, Tom Hudson and Jack Rowell was now emerging into a triumvirate so successful that during the following decade it would attract not only domestic, but international recognition. And, it was this coaching input that partly explained Bath's outstanding 1978-9 campaign, where having started the season *"like greyhounds in the slips,"* they continued the rugby year like the US Cavalry in full charge-mode. Indeed the pace never ceased, and only after a nine-win blitz commencing in early March and concluding with a 13-21 away win at Bedford in late April did Bath even pause for breath.

Yet success did not change, nor it seemed would it change, the sense of family at the club; and two players expressed such sentiments with John Stevens (Chronicle, 23rd April, 1979). First,Welsh-born England Trialist flank-forward Gerry Parsons commented that he had seriously considered retiring at the end of the season as now *"the demands of first-class rugby were a bit too much,"* and yet *"I think I would miss it terribly, especially at Bath, which is just about the most friendly club one could imagine."* Likewise Mark Sutton, now returned from studies in France and who had played superbly in Bath's early season 18-6 victory over Romanian side Bucharest, duly concurred. Notwithstanding that in the following season this highly promising England U.23 squad member was not guaranteed a regular place, Sutton announced that his future was on the Rec: *"It's simply that it's such fun being involved in the sort of rugby Bath are playing at the moment that I wouldn't dream of going anywhere else."*

The 'professionalism' saga meanwhile would not disappear off the radar, and as mentioned former Bath and Bristol full-back Dave Alred had (April 1978) requested a judgement from the RFU regarding a professional contract in American grid-iron football with Minnesota Vikings. In April 1979 Alred, having actually completed a season in grid-iron, did receive the reply, stating that he 'would be suspended indefinitely from the game.' It appeared that he had infringed the Union bye-law that banned anyone who received money for specialist skills such as place-kicking. But as there was no hindrance to professional cricketers for example playing rugby union it was debatable whether or not the drafters of this presumed law of rugby (assuming it was a law) intended its affect to extend to a totally different form of football such as American grid-iron? Whatever the answer to that question, the Alred judgement clearly showed that a rigid interpretation of the rules would not be relaxed one iota.

Ironically the RFU's verdict turned out to be, in American jargon, 'a great career move.' But the time for Dave Alred to dispatch his letter of gratitude to Twickenham for their decision to ban him would come later.

Now it was the task of John Horton to lead Bath into the final season of the decade, fittingly achieving a new record of 37 victories, one draw and a mere 10 defeats; and it was hardly surprising that the Rec was attracting yet more highly promising players, including the aforementioned flanker Roger Spurrell and wing Barry Trevaskis, both making their first team debuts in Bath's 58-0 win over Seahawks, the early season tourists from California. Alongside these two Cornishmen was former London Scottish prop David Butcher, soon to catch the eye of England selectors, and England Schools star Brian Kenny at hooker. Meanwhile young prop Richard Lee from Wellington RFC proved his own considerable worth against the might of Bristol, and strengthening the pack yet further were lock giants Michel van der Loos from Holland and former Loughborough Colleges Welshman Howard Thomas. Never, but never, had the club been so blessed with such an abundance of ability and creativity.

Naturally, possessing a surplus of class players is the one headache that selectors and coaches just love to experience. But it calls for leadership at the highest level, and a willingness among players to accept that literally no one is guaranteed a first team place as of right. The players understood this, and morale remained extraordinarily high. In addition the old adage that 'to be great then one should live among greatness' now rang true, and the Rec was an exciting place to be. Waterman at 35 years of age was still regarded by John Stevens as a player of an *"undying genius,* "and Derek Wyatt as a *"try-scorer extraordinaire;"* while skipper John Horton after a year in the wilderness *"finally came of age internationally"* when marshalling his England backs to a 24-9 win over Ireland at Twickenham in January. No fewer than five Bath players had been called-up for the South and South West team to play the New Zealand tourists in November (though losing 0-16), namely Mike Beese (captain), John Palmer, John Horton, Damien Murphy and Simon Jones. Four Bath players were called-up for the England U.23 squad, namely: John Palmer, David Butcher (prop), Mark Sutton and Bryanston schoolboy David Trick. While wing-forwards Simon Jones and Gerry Parsons featured in the final full England Trial at Twickenham.

As for results, some victories were simply dazzling both in their scale and the manner of their application. Indeed, one wondered if any side would be safe from a potential Bath onslaught. Certainly not Pontypool, beaten 16-9 in the season's opener, nor current JP Cup holders Leicester beaten 9-10 away, nor Moseley beaten 22-11 on the

Rec, and not forgetting Bath's first ever Double over Newport (3-6 away and 17-7 at home).

For Bath devotees it was like walking on air. Budge Rogers, chairman of the England selectors, watching the 22-11 victory over Moseley, pin-pointed the sheer energy that Bath now brought onto the field of play. Bath he said *"just don't know when to stop attacking....even when things aren't going right for them....and they're a very exciting side to watch."* Soon it would be Bristol's fate to experience not only this same non-stop wave of attacking football, but also the electrifying speed of 18 years old schoolboy David Trick. As he surged to a try hat-trick in Bath's 38-17 win, John Stevens (Chronicle, 22nd October, 1979) wrote in awe of his *"remarkable pace and attacking skill."*

Yet even this triumph did not better the November visit to Twickenham and the subsequent 17-41 win against the Harlequins. For this, as John Stevens reported (Chronicle, 5th November 1979) was undoubtedly among the most brilliant and significant Bath victories of the decade: *"[Bath] produced the sort of rugby which the London public has often read about but so seldom seen in a devastating period at the end when they scored five of their seven tries."*

Wyatt and Trick bagged a brace of tries apiece, and the schoolboy's second was *"a superb 60-yard run outside his opposing wing and back inside the full-back"* and was simply *"the score of the match."* Though as Stevens cheekily added, prop Bert Meddick would disagree. He after all completed the rout with his score in the closing minute *"with a try he will cherish above any other."* And, at long last London had seen Bath at their best. Indeed, by clinching the double over Harlequins with a home 27-10 win in mid-December, Bath looked unstoppable; and when in early December the London Scottish were duly humbled 36-7, former Bath international Alec Lewis was moved to acclaim Horton's side as the 'the best ever in the club's history.'

Not surprisingly, such performances were arousing increasing interest from another direction, in this case the Rugby League, and their attention was focused on two players in particular. The first was England B international John Palmer, and the second was David Trick. As the Bath Chronicle reported in mid-December, the offers made to both these outstanding backs were not in fact accepted, but it is not difficult to understand the reasons that led some Union players to switch codes. Young Trick after all was but an 18 years old schoolboy when first invited to go North with a seven thousand pounds offer from Widnes in cash, and literally placed before his eyes. Then one year out of school, Oldham offered the young wing a then mouth-watering offer of twenty thousand pounds; and such a sum in the later 1970's was very serious money indeed!

On a somewhat different level of the game this same period would include some heartfelt regrets, and among these was the occasion of Bath's Autumn 6-28 win at St. Mary's Hospital. The victory apart, this was to be the last time that these two clubs would ever meet again on a rugby field, and among those who came to bid farewell to this remarkable Hospital side was Arnold Ridley. He would feel the poignancy as keenly as any, not least as it was Arnold himself who as a former Bath fixtures secretary had initiated this annual meeting half a century previously in the late 1920's. Nonetheless there was an inescapable reason for this parting of the ways, namely the growing gulf between the upper echelon of first-class clubs and those now finding the pace a little too hot. These included the London Hospital sides and the leading London Old Boys clubs that until the 1970's had played with such distinction at the highest levels of the first-class game.

Horton's Bath however continued onwards and upwards, and this was another season when it was advisable to whisper softly any mention of Bath when in Wales. True, they did not win everything when confronting the Dragon, and they fell by the wayside at Llanelli and at Aberavon. But they overcame both Newport and the South Wales Police away, and apart from a 22-22 draw at home against Neath, Bath proved that the Rec was not a comfortable place for a Welsh team. Here they lowered the colours of most of the best in the Principality, and it was some hit-list! For Pontypool, Newbridge (Bath less ten players on County duty), Bridgend and Ebbw Vale all returned homewards empty-handed.

But another old foe, but this one barely fifteen miles down the Avon, would cause Bath to be very wary of the dangers of over-confidence. For having suffered an Autumn 38-17 drubbing on the Rec, Bristol then planned a 'stop-Trick-at-all costs' strategy in early Spring, and in so doing trumped Bath by employing a cross-field drift tactic that isolated the Bath flyer. It succeeded. Bristol won 44-6!

Sobering too was the uncertainty that lingered still within the Bath psyche when it came to the John Player Cup. For in March, Bath at home, fell 3-6 in the quarter-finals to London Irish who then strode onwards to a Twickenham final, though losing 21-9 to Leicester. Thus a Cup run that had commenced with a sweeping 30-6 away win at Marlow, followed by an impressive 12-19 away victory at Liverpool, now ended once more in bewildered dejection in the quarter-finals at the hands of London Irish on home territory. Fortunately, entry into the 1st round proper for the following season was assured when it was confirmed in late March that Bath were already in an unassailable position in the top four of the South West Merit Table; and by this stage the club was closing in on a remarkable new record of 37 victories, clinched in late April with their home 22-16 success over Bedford.

How the late Eddie Simpkins, the National Cup defeats apart, would have loved such times as these, and not least when on 14th February 1980 his son Jack Simpkins (Bath's general secretary) was honoured, alongside Coventry secretary Alf Wyman and former Bristol and England forward David Rollitt, at the annual dinner of the Rugby Writers Club at the Press Centre in London; all duly praised by the Writers Club chairman

Tony Bodley (Chronicle, 15th February, 1980) for *"the stalwart service of the trio to the game over many years."*

But after a season of such dazzling rugby, could the momentum continue? Or would Bath fade under the sheer pressure of maintaining the exacting standards that they had now set themselves. 'Could something once again go wrong?' After all, it did against London Irish! Well, this much one could say: since the mid-1960's Bath had undergone a slow, and until recently, little-recognised transformation. But now the whole rugby community was judging this enigmatic club from the West far more seriously. Just one tantalizing question remained however: 'could happy-go-lucky Bath actually take themselves more seriously?' It was ironically the same question that Tom Hudson five years previously had 'dared' the club to confront. The following decade, a tumultuous one as it happened, would reveal the answer to this most crucial of questions.

Chapter 27. COUNTDOWN TO THE SEASON THAT CHANGED EVERYTHING. (1980-3)

The season of 1980-81 arrived, a stepping stone into another decade; while behind lay the 1970's where successive captains had preserved the Enlightenment of the Sibley years that had laid the foundations for a once unglamorous, albeit happy, West Country club to hopefully hold a place among the higher ranks of first-class rugby. Robbie Lye was the new skipper, with coaches Jack Rowell, Dave Robson and Tom Hudson in support. As for the squad, they had by now proved that they could reach near perfection as a team, and it was much credit to the committee that Bath now offered players participation in one of the strongest fixture-lists in British rugby. England Trialist full-back Charles Ralston (ex Rosslyn Park) had been drawn to the Rec, so too lock Andy Marriott (ex Swansea) and prop Kevin Neale (ex London Irish); while hooker Simon Luxmore and lock Nick Williams (both Somerset players) joined from Clifton. All five, soon to be joined by other recruits including Penryn full-back Chris Martin, would subsequently prove their undoubted qualities.

Prestigious wins continued, away at Moseley and Neath for instance, and home against the calibre of Leicester, Aberavon, Maesteg (their first ever visit to Bath), Coventry, Harlequins and London Welsh. Then come late season there followed a trio of brilliant victories over Wales's finest. First Newport fell 9-3, where Phil Turner (ex Bristol) showed the sheer strength in depth at Bath's disposal with a rampant back-row performance alongside Gerry Parsons. Then followed wins over Llanelli (16-3) and Cardiff (18-11), adding to the season's total of 30, again exceptional by any standards

There were setbacks too however, not least concerning injuries, with half-backs Damien Murphy and John Horton among the early season casualties. Horton's fractured cheekbone seemed to be the more serious. John Palmer too was side-lined for a considerable period and Derek Wyatt was now devoting more time to his career. Hence the dazzling back-play of recent years was not always in evidence; and by now opponents had wisely adopted more defensive-based tactics whenever facing Bath. So defeat at Pontypool (23-13), then on the Rec against Wasps (12-27) and home and away falls to Gloucester were among salutary lessons that nothing could be taken for granted.

But there just 'had' to be something that 'was' taken for granted....the John Player KO Cup of all things! But surely, one asks, lessons had been learned the hard way by now? It would seem not however; because on 30th March 1981 the committee decided against re-entry into the Somerset Cup for season 1981-2, which if successful would have provided Bath with an alternative route into the National Cup for 1982-3. Admittedly there were other issues to consider, not least the ever increasing representative demands for players from the leading clubs, and anyway, a top-four place in the South West

Merit Table would instead guarantee a place in the following 1981-2 National Cup….wouldn't it? Well yes, and it did. But then Bath had best keep their fingers crossed that they would gain a top-four Merit Table place come season 1981-2, so as to ensure entry to the 1982-3 National Cup; because if they didn't there would be no Somerset Cup to rescue them since they had chosen not to enter it, even though they could probably have won it with a reserve team.

As for the current 1980-1 JP Cup campaign, Bath carried their hopes with them to Nottingham, having previously overcome Richmond in a Horton-inspired 6-12 away victory in January. But the Nottingham game was played on a quagmire of a pitch that had lain completely under water only hours prior to kick-off. Even so *"Bath dominated most of the match."* With half-backs Steve Lewis (now returned from Welsh club rugby) and Horton controlling tactics with their *"sound kicking for position"* they led from a Charlie Ralston penalty. But, with ten minutes remaining the referee, according to Bath, *"indicated he was awarding them a penalty when Nottingham strayed offside at a ruck and hounded Horton into error."* However, the referee then *"deferred his decision for advantage."* But since *"Horton's clearance went straight to an opponent"* Bath claimed that there was 'no' advantage. Worse immediately followed when Nottingham's Baron Bedford collected Horton's clearance and countered with a speculative kick himself from which home winger Clive Pitts ran on to score an unconverted try for a 4-3 cup victory. Oh, it was grim being Bath at times such as these.

Yet if Robbie Lye's side had reached those longed-for gates at Twickenham, such a day would have provided the perfect send-off for three Bath and Somerset players due to retire. The first to announce his departure was lock Brian Jenkins, whose senior baptism in 1970 launched a career that would extend to 282 first team outings. Leaving too was prop John (Bert) Meddick, veteran of near 350 senior games. While the third bidding farewell was England centre Mike Beese, he of the long stride and clamp-like tackle with some 316 senior Bath games to his credit.

Dreams of cup glory however would have to wait yet again, with Bath pondering how it was that their cup fortunes were so often at odds with their often superb club performances. Season 1981-2 moreover was not to buck the trend, either on or off the field. An England Trial (Chronicle, 10th December, 1981) was re-located to the Rec, only for this prestigious event to be re-directed back to Twickenham for the following week. While on the playing side new captain Damien Murphy would suffer an early Autumn cartilage problem that took him out of action for much of the season.

This not only proved especially regrettable for Damien Murphy personally, but unsettling for a club whose pre-season preparations had included a carefully planned rugby tour of Florida. Yet before the home season had barely started, Murphy's injury had saddled the club with a major captaincy headache and the loss of an excellent scrum-half. As for leadership of the team, a somewhat ad hoc arrangement would be

189

applied, with vice-captain Spurrell taking over at the helm. But complicating matters yet further he too suffered a fractured jaw, and Horton stepped into the breach on a temporary care-taker basis until Spurrell's return. As expected, such captaincy-changes combined with injury problems disrupted on-field performances, though by no means always. Indeed, despite heavy defeats that included a 41-0 drubbing at Swansea and a 57-15 shocker at Llanelli, wins against Moseley, Neath, Harlequins, Coventry and Newport for example showed that Bath had not lost their touch. While it was during this same period that the committee in its wisdom handed the coaching triumvirate of Rowell, Robson and Hudson the unqualified freedom to decide upon team tactics, strategy and training for the foreseeable future.

The task of combining the best of an English club (in this case Bath) with a strong Welsh influence would shortly come to magnificent fruition, and would be helped not least by the arrival of Scotland B hooker Rob Cunningham from Gosforth, highly promising England Colts back-row forward Jon Hall, and not forgetting lock Nigel Gaymond from Bristol; although it would be some three months (Chronicle, 1st March, 1982) before Gaymond sensed that he was now fully fledged 'blue, white and black,' and so in a position to make comparisons: Bath *are a different club with different attitudes.....perhaps even friendlier though not always quite as competitive. They have their own ways of doing things here and it takes time to acclimatise. Now I'm beginning to enjoy it."*

It is likely that Gaymond's words would have resonated with many newcomers, and his decision to switch from the Memorial Ground soon rewarded him with an established place in the Bath 'engine room' alongside another recent arrival, namely Irish international and line-out specialist Ronnie Hakin. A vital new second-row partnership had thus been discovered at a critical time, so adding strength to the front-five of a pack upon whom huge demands would be made as the club in due course challenged for the highest honours in the game.

The timely addition of forwards Cunningham, Gaymond and Hakin was then matched outside the scrum with the arrival in December of Oxford Blue centre Simon Halliday. Another talent from Downside School, the young three-quarter from Shaftesbury was the target of at least two leading London clubs, and the reason for their interest would soon become apparent. For Halliday was fast, a superbly balanced runner, and possessed a natural ability to wrong-foot opponents at speed. Thus having recently lost Mike Beese, Bath now found Simon Halliday, and if this was not good fortune enough, Halliday's Dark Blue colleague and back-row forward Tony Brooks now joined Bath ranks too.

Bath's open-house recruitment policy attracted others from less orthodox rugby backgrounds however. Indeed ex St. Luke's student Mitch Patching arrived as an established soccer player good enough to have run-out for Eastbourne (Borough), a club that at times had competed in the ranks of the National Conference League. Yet

Patching could play equally well at both codes, as he demonstrated when leading the Bath pack in their January 27-0 rout of Northampton. Joining too was Berkshire county utility forward Roy Matthews, formerly of Maidenhead RFC, who albeit not a regular senior player, performed like a seasoned veteran in Bath's November 18-22 victory at Coventry, an encounter that Matthews stated was *"a memory he will always treasure."*

Yet those now moving to 'pastures new' included England wing Derek Wyatt and the seemingly ageless Jim Waterman who in September at Newport had played his 415th senior game for Bath at a remarkable 36 years of age. True Corinthians, both these athletes combined intellect with rugby individualism. Both teachers, Waterman was by now a rugby playing deputy-headmaster at 950-pupil Stockwell Hill comprehensive school, Bristol; and Derek Wyatt was now combining an MSc degree in education at Oxford along with journalism for two national newspapers. Waterman spoke warmly of his days at Bath, remarking that *"Bath's rugby has certainly changed over the last 14 years, and mainly for the better."* But as forceful off the field as on it, he added this one caveat: the game is now *"....more competitive, winning is more important than it used to be, and no club can afford to stand still or they could be left behind."*

Equally forthright was the outspoken Derek Wyatt. Aiming his comments at Rugby Union's hierarchy, the future MP for Sittingbourne (Kent) suggested that the game should adopt 'professional administrators, club officials with relatively recent playing experience, fewer games and smaller committees.' And he concluded (Chronicle, 8th April, 1982) with these challenging words: *"Professionalism is coming, like it or not. Rugby is lagging behind and changes may not arrive until the 1990's....but there is no doubt that they are on the way."* His predictions would prove to be uncannily accurate. Furthermore the perceptive winger had already raised an issue that would now hit the club for six during the same current 1981-2 season: *"We still, amazingly, do not have all our merit table matches on a Saturday,"* he queried, *"and thereby put at risk our considerable reputation, not to mention endangering our bank balance."*

And, as sure as night follows day, Bath not only dropped out of the JP Cup by way of their opening round 9-11 defeat at home to Rosslyn Park, they then failed to qualify for the following season's competition owing to a failure to reach the top four of the South West Merit Table. Yes, Bath had comfortably defeated both Plymouth Albion and Camborne, who ironically both qualified for the following season JP Cup action along with Bristol and Gloucester. But unlike Bath, Camborne did not play Gloucester. Moreover Albion's request (owing to four players on County duty) for their game with Gloucester to be excluded from the table was granted; notwithstanding that Gloucester (with ten regulars absent) chose from the outset to accept the result and duly won. It was beyond parody. Yet if Bath had won the Somerset Cup in season 1981-2 (an outcome that was highly likely), there would have been an alternative route into the National Cup in season 1982-3. Just one problem: the committee had not entered the club for the 1981-2 Somerset Cup.

191

Therefore, despite their highly commendable 29 wins, Bath could only feel a sense of under-achievement; and it hardly helped matters that rivals Gloucester would now reach Twickenham for their third final, there to share the spoils from a 12-12 drawn game with Moseley. But at long last, Bath had indeed learned from yet another salutary lesson. They promptly took out the insurance-policy offered by the Somerset Cup for the following 1982-3 season, and significantly in view of previous miscalculations, they would rarely, if ever, put a foot wrong again.

Nonetheless, by the conclusion of the following 1982-3 season Bath were probably the best club-side in England, though it seemed unlikely at the outset when skipper Spurrell's team were *"crushed 37-16 by [the] Pontypool pack"* in early September. But if such a defeat caused alarm, then it was to be a false one. For within a week calm was restored with a 24-15 home win over Leicester, followed by a 3-12 success at Newport; and aside from the fact that this was only Bath's second win at Rodney Parade in their history, it was the sheer quality of this performance that gave hint of the events that would follow in the second half of an epic season.

Trick too had returned from a gap-year in the U.S.A., ominous news for opponents, and John Stevens (Chronicle, 23rd September, 1982) duly described the impact of the winger's return at Newport. Within seven minutes Trick's *"smouldering pace burst into flame when he was launched into flight almost from his own line by the combined skills of John Horton and Alun Watkins. Horton played a miss-ball move to Alun Watkins who drew the opposing wing brilliantly before setting Trick away on a blistering 60 yards run deep into the home half. He wriggled out of one cover tackle and then outwitted the defence before his inside pass sent centre Alun Rees away for a crucial try score."* Yes, Trick was back! Moreover when in October at Twickenham his searing pace led to a try-treble for an England XV against the touring Fijians he duly confirmed the faith of then England skipper Steve Smith, who previously had proclaimed that Trick was *"the fastest man I have seen on a rugby pitch for ten years."*

Somehow one began to think that everything was 'coming right.' Team spirit was high and perhaps not surprisingly yet more talent would make a pilgrimage to the Rec, not least back-row forward Paul Simpson (Gosforth's 'player of the Year' the previous season), Young England Colts lock John Morrison, and later hooker Kevin Adams (Avon & Somerset Police), plus brilliant scrum-half prospect Richard Hill from St. Luke's College, Exeter. However, notwithstanding ever mounting pressures on the senior clubs, the Rugby Union announced that all County Championship games must in future be played on pre-set Saturday dates. In theory this was not an unfair ruling. In practice it was anything but! Thus Bath, from whom Somerset now relied for most of their County side, found themselves depleted of no fewer than 21 players on certain County weekends, supplying thirteen for Somerset, five for Dorset & Wilts, two for Cornwall and one to Northumberland. It was a heavy responsibility to carry for one club from whom so much was now expected.

Come November and with County duties now receding, two notable away victories against Harlequins (7-21), and at still formidable London Scottish (9-21), suggested that Bath, now able to field a team of their choosing, might enjoy a successful second half of the 1982-3 campaign. But in early December one mighty test for supremacy remained in their path.....Gloucester! That Bath possessed the better backs was not in dispute. But that was no guarantee of success against such formidable masters of the forward game, not least since in recent years doubts remained concerning Bath's own strength in the pack.

Another question remained as yet unanswered, and this concerned the leadership-style of ex-paratrooper and Bath skipper Roger Spurrell. Indeed but for injury, Damien Murphy would likely have remained club captain, and the flaxen-haired Spurrell himself admitted in early season that *"the responsibility of captaincy got to me and perhaps I was thinking about it too much....I was more worried about what people were doing around me than what I was doing myself. I forgot to play my own game."* In which case against Gloucester he remembered how to play his own game again, because instead of relying on the backs, Spurrell's Bath went straight for the jugular and chose instead to battle it out at forward. In previous years such a strategy would likely have been suicidal. But not this time, not with this headstrong Cornishman in charge, and on a cold winter's day two packs proceeded to 'slug it out' with no prisoners taken. As John Stevens reported, the *"game wasn't so much full-blooded, but rather full of blood, with punches being thrown with abandon, boots used for anything but the purpose intended and ugly brawls reviving memories of the bad old days."* In addition Bath prop Richard Lee and Gloucester flanker Mike Teague got marching orders for fighting *"in a bruising encounter in which no quarter was asked or given."*

This was as hard as one could get 'it' in the West Country, and that's hard! For not since the 1950's and the teams of Alec Lewis and John Roberts had a Bath captain so much as contemplated the idea of challenging Gloucester in a trial of strength at forward. Yet this was the strategy that Spurrell chose to adopt without a second thought, and the resultant psychological effect from a 21-12 victory was to be profound. Thus a front row of Gareth Chilcott, Rob Cunningham, Richard Lee, supported by locks Nigel Gaymond and Ron Hakin, and the back-row of Roger Spurrell, Phil Turner and Paul Simpson had given notice of Bath's ability to match head-on arguably the most feared pack in England. And on that same dank December day a unique Cornish captain had been born.

December passed and on New Year's Day 1983 Leicester succeeded where Gloucester had failed, avenging their earlier setback on the Rec with their own 21-9 win at Welford Road. Yet Spurrell's team would never look back from this moment of defeat. Instead they were now set to add a new chapter to the story of not merely Bath, but English rugby too, and arguably it was to be among the most remarkable (and certainly the most unexpected) chapters ever written. It commenced with a 16-11 home win over still impressive London Welsh, and would then lead to a 26 match unbeaten run that apart from two draws would scatter all opposition to the four corners of England and Wales. Northampton (16-19), Ebbw Vale (3-7) Plymouth Albion (3-30) and the final 15-30 success at Bedford ranked among the away wins; while Rosslyn Park (35-12), Swansea (30-14), Llanelli (31-28) and Maesteg (45-10) were included among a galaxy of home victories. Indeed even at fortress Kingsholm the hard men of Gloucester could get no closer than a 7-7 draw; while Bristol, destined for a 28-22 JP Cup Final triumph against Leicester, were defeated 21-16 in their early April run-in to Twickenham.

However it was John Mason's report for the Daily Telegraph following Bath's emphatic 28-9 win over Cardiff in late April that typified the reaction of the National Press to a West Country revival that could no longer be ignored. "***Mighty Bath bring back the smiles***" was the banner headline, and John Mason wrote thus:

"Bath are proud of impressive statistics that reflect a successful season. But the figures alone convey only part of the commitment and little of the enjoyment a well-drilled side have created for all concerned since early January. On Saturday Bath demolished Cardiff, which few English clubs ever do....."

"So even before Jack Simpkins, Bath's secretary whose family have been associated with the club for generations, says simply: 'this is the best side we've ever had in my time,' there is a temptation to sit up and take notice.

The manner of the dissection of Cardiff bore out practically every expectation. Bath's players have confidence in themselves and in each other. There is a warming team spirit readily obvious and, dare I say it, they have re-learned to play with a smile.

That the match also had explosive moments of temper told a story too. To assert a waning authority Peter Hughes - at his best one of England's better referees – had to lecture the captains, neither, presumably, entirely used to the role of gamekeeper.

Martin, Bath's fullback, Halliday, maturing splendidly, and the canny Horton, cleverly pulling the strings, headed the better attacks, while opposite them, Ring showed plainly why the Welsh selectors promoted him for the match against England.

Then there was Trick, full of running and the searing speed to go on the outside. Nor did Lakin and Golding cease in their efforts in Cardiff's back row. Yet of all the medals I would cast, the most handsome would go to Hakin and Simpson, sterling Bath forwards."

Trevaskis, Halliday, Trick and Martin scored Bath's tries, Palmer converting three and landing two penalty goals. Cordle got across for Cardiff on the right, a forward pass having been permitted on the left, and Ring kicked the conversion and a penalty goal."

Barry Trevaskis: The Cornish flyer became a record try scorer.

Acknowledgements: Bath Past Players

Thus Bath were near to completing the most successful season in their history, a season too when David Trick in March would win the first of his two full England caps at Lansdown Road, Dublin, albeit Ireland winning 25-15. And irony of ironies, Bath's exit from the JP Cup had allowed the club to concentrate solely on blending a squad of talented individuals into a near unstoppable winning team. In fact Bath walked away with both the South West Merit Table and the Somerset Cup; a new club record of 38 victories was attained with 3 draws and a mere 9 defeats; no fewer than 205 tries were run home; a new record of 1,278 points was amassed and the 32 try total of wing Barry Trevaskis broke the previous 29-try record held jointly by George Haydon (1930-1) and Derek Wyatt (1978-9). Indeed as John Steven's concluded, this was a *"rugby season to savour for years to come."* Yet it would prove to be even more than that: because it was the season that literally changed everything!

Chapter 28.   THE YEAR of DESTINY. (1983-4)

As Bath launched their campaign for 1983-4, it seemed that this was a club with everything. There was their beautiful ground, their devoted supporters, their astute coaching panel and in addition a team that had won respect the length and breadth of the Land. But one yawning gap remained....the National K.O. Cup! True it was that Bath's often flamboyant rugby could brighten even the darkest of winter days. But if they could not now win the Cup with the superb squad that had swept all before it during the previous unforgettable season, would they ever win it!? This was the question that hung over the Rec at the outset of 1983-4, and the doubts and the uncertainties even now remained.

Nor were ambitions helped by the as yet unpredictable effects upon Bath of the re-organised County Championship, a competition that would compel the club once again to provide at least a dozen or more players for the Somerset side. Would such call-ups exhaust Bath resources to breaking- point; or might the County Championship provide yet more invaluable knock-out cup experience that could enhance their quest for JP Cup glory?

Other pressures (and opportunities) were now apparent at the wider level of the game, not least an increasing interest from the commercial world, one reflected in the Autumn announcement that England, following the Welsh example, would in due course adopt sponsored rugby boots for their international games. Nike in England's case were the chosen suppliers, the RFU receiving as a result £90,000 over the following three years, 'with the money directed exclusively towards youth rugby' (John Stevens, Chronicle, 15th October, 1983).

Such contractual arrangements however invited the potentially awkward question as to who exactly was attracting this level of funding into the game, and the simple answer was....'the players!' But while these same players gained nothing financially from such deals, there were rumours already circulating that a professional rugby union 'circus' was soon to be launched; and such were the concerns raised by this possible threat that at the commencement of the 1983-4 season no fewer than 120 leading English players received a letter demanding a 'loyalty pledge' to the Rugby Union. Among those contacted (Chronicle, 9th September, 1983) were eight members from the Bath squad (one was Roger Spurrell), all of whom reportedly had no objection to signing, albeit that it was understood that the pledge *"would certainly have no legal obligation, only a moral one."* But while there was precisely nothing that the governing body could do if a player did decide to pursue his trade elsewhere, the request did reveal the concerns of the RFU as regards the possible ramifications of player-involvement in lucrative commercial deals, and furthermore the unpredictable consequences that might one day result from such activity.

Bath meanwhile concentrated upon two other priorities in particular, none more so than their unfulfilled hopes for JP Cup success, and in addition Somerset's own quest for glory in the re-vamped (Thorn EMI) County Championship, one that now placed Dorset & Wilts in the 4th Division group of counties, but Somerset among the demanding standards of the First Division grouping. Fascinatingly, Somerset's County progress was to run virtually parallel to the advances of Bath in the JP Cup; and the first real evidence that possible triumph in both tournaments might be within reach came with Somerset's 15-12 win over Lancashire in early October on the Rec. It was mighty close, but it was achieved against one of 'the' best county sides in England, and the post-match assessment of Red Rose skipper James Syddall was pertinent: *they (Somerset) were superbly disciplined and deserved to win."* Furthermore Somerset coach Jack Rowell, who rarely wasted words, was moved to add that *"We've finally learned how to play cup rugby...."* And since 13 players in Somerset ranks that day hailed from Bath, Rowell was effectively referring to the merits of both county and club.

So Somerset, their reputation now enhanced by victory over Lancashire, travelled to Exeter in late October and proved sufficiently strong to return homewards with an 18-27 win under their belts. There was yet further success when Somerset narrowly defeated Middlesex 10-9 at Bridgwater in November. But this encounter came at a sickening price, one instantly evident from the moment that the brilliant Simon Halliday literally dropped like a stone with *"a horrendous dislocation and double fracture of the left ankle after 32 minutes."* It was a freakish injury, but side-lined Halliday for the remainder of the season, delayed his already predicted international career and left his Somerset colleagues visibly shaken by the event. Neil Hopkins, now with Weston-super-Mare, deputised commendably, but the serious injury had cast a shadow of gloom over the Somerset post-match dressing room.

The subsequent semi-final against Yorkshire in late November on the Rec was to be another narrow win, as the 15-12 margin denotes. This encounter however did not come at a price, but rather a controversy, when a drop-goal attempt from John Horton failed to carry over the bar, albeit allowed by the referee. So, 'what's to do' in such a situation? True, one could tell the referee that 'he's got it wrong!' Yet how many tries for example are claimed and awarded that are not tries? Or how many tries are fairly grounded but are disallowed? Who really knows? All one can do, and in this case the press, the media and many in a four thousand crowd indeed 'did do,' was to point out the error. But for hapless Yorkshire, who played so gallantly and sportingly, there was at least to be honour in defeat. For Somerset by contrast, openly admitting that luck was on their side, there would be their first county final since 1939.

By now, with Bath's probable first-choice team already battled-hardened thanks to experience where they least expected to find it, namely the re-vamped County Championship, thoughts turned to the JP Cup; and two brilliant victories in late

October and early November respectively had already demonstrated that Bath had not lost their dazzling touches of the previous season. First Neath were overcome 67-0 (then Bath's biggest-ever win over Welsh opponents), and a total so remarkable that BBC Wales phoned back to the Rec to have the score verified before announcing the result. Eleven tries were grounded, John Palmer converting ten, and the Bath Chronicle's John Stevens was left near speechless, although sufficiently composed to report that it was simply a *"day when the superlatives ran out."* One week later and Bath headed for Newbridge, unfashionable maybe but a highly dangerous outfit. Indeed, having dispatched the proposed South and South West team (now preparing for action against the touring All Blacks) with a 21-6 win only days previously, Newbridge looked good enough to avenge Bath for daring to inflict such humiliation upon Welsh reputations. But eighty minutes later Bath had proved to a large home crowd exactly why they had overcome Neath, and with supposedly reserve back-row forward Phil Turner playing as if he was an international regular, Bath put a stranglehold on the game to secure a highly impressive 12-22 away victory.

There was one team nonetheless during this period, perhaps the only team, who were capable of 80 minutes of rugby power such that no team could hold them. This team were Pontypool, the pride of Monmouthshire and a side formed around men who crafted steel in the mills and hacked coal deep down in the mines; and only days before Christmas they departed from those same mills and mines to avenge these 'English upstarts' who had ran amok against Neath and then on sacred Welsh soil had overran Newbridge! Furthermore 'Pool' had come prepared with a strategy, one brilliant in its simplicity. So it was that these visitors from the Valleys duly controlled the entire match around the might of their forwards, an eight so dominant it had to be seen to be believed. Welsh international forwards Graham Price, Eddie Butler and Jeff Squire looked world class, while the tactical kicking of halfbacks Dave Bishop and Mike Galsworthy was simply copybook precision. Their grip was vice-like. They dominated the line-out for their half-backs to boot kicks 40-45 yards upfield. Then when near the Bath 25 they suddenly sent the ball out wide and four 'Pool' tries resulted that included a hat-trick for young debut winger Pat Hayes. It was stunning. It was thought-provoking, and Bath were left to ponder a 6-23 defeat on home soil. And....when the final whistle echoed into the dark night sky the Rec fell strangely quiet.

Many teams would have been psychologically shattered by so comprehensive a defeat, and with Bath less than four weeks away from their opening (third round) JP Cup clash with Headingley such an upset could hardly have come at a worse time. Or so it seemed. But soon enough Bath would themselves employ these self-same ruthless tactics when deemed necessary. In fact barely one week later powerful Northampton were overcome 16-6 on the Rec, with forwards Chris Folland, Gregg Bess, Nick Maslen and Oxford Blue Tony Brooks prominent in a pack that, with Horton's astute kicking, adopted a game plan not dissimilar to that so forcefully employed by

Pontypool. While come January Bath gained another tonic of a win thanks to a highly impressive 9-40 victory at London Welsh, significantly their first success at The Welsh for twenty four years.

Two weeks later however Headingley were due to arrive, and this time Bath were taking absolutely no chances whatsoever. The Yorkshiremen were a highly regarded club, yet had not been seen in Bath for over thirty years. Moreover if Northern sides Wilmslow and Morpeth had proved capable of overcoming Bath in Cup football, then a major club such as Headingley posed a very real danger. So former Rec favourite Brendan Perry, now a selector, had already been assigned to travel into Devon, there to attend an Exeter v Headingley match and prepare a thorough dossier on the merits of these Northern visitors.

The assessment made for sober reading. First, Headingley were coached by former Scotland three-quarter star Ian McGeechen and the experienced Peter Nash. Secondly a rich seam of county experience ran through the club that included England back-row forward Peter Winterbottom. Third, three of their number (members of the Yorkshire semi-final team against Somerset) were now familiar with the Rec. It was hardly surprising therefore that Perry reported thus: *"Don't underestimate them. They are nobody's fools."* He then added a further warning: *"if we decide to mix it with them, I think we could be in for a tough time....I feel we will do better if we run the ball wide."* Running it wide!? Then Bath, haunted still by memories of rain-soaked Cup encounters in years gone by, could only pray that the conditions would now remain dry. If not, then Bath knew only too well that sodden pitches can be a great leveller!

The preparations nonetheless paid off on the day, a thoroughly workmanlike Headingley eventually worn down and subjected to a 17-0 defeat. It did look close for fully 40 minutes of a non-scoring first half. But then on a damp surface that nonetheless still allowed for a running game, Bath tightened their grip post the interval. Barry Trevaskis ran home an opening try. Richard Hill (already close to an England cap) then struck for home with a 40 yard burst to launch Horton for a second try, Ralston converting. Finally Bath stamped their overall superiority with a perfectly executed try by Chris Martin and Spurrell's men were (excuse the unintended pun) home and dry!

The men from the North were no push-overs however, a side moreover *"whose pack, under the tireless Winterbottom, did a great disruptive job in the scoreless first half."* But winning can become something of a habit (as can losing) and significantly the Somerset cup experience that season had simultaneously helped to develop Bath into a potentially winning JP Cup side too. Indeed as Jack Rowell commented in his post-Headingley appraisal: *"it was perhaps our best-ever cup performance."*

Another performance, this time an individual one, had been watched by a TV audience of millions when in November England had faced the might of New Zealand at Twickenham. It was 'touch and go' from start to finish. It was total tension throughout.

It concluded with an England 15-9 victory and it produced a performance that would earn national acclaim from Bath's unstoppable flanker Paul Simpson. Come February and Simpson was picked for England again, this time against Scotland in Edinburgh, and joining him (although on the bench) were Bath colleagues Richard Hill and Jon Hall. Hall, 21 years old, would duly win his first cap as replacement during the match for the injured Winterbottom, while Hill would soon follow, capped by England during their summer tour of South Africa. Three internationals in one season! Never before had Bath achieved such an honour.

Likewise never before at Bath had yearning for Cup success been so intense. Indeed preparations for their next Cup encounter against Blackheath literally consumed the entire energies of the Club, and Blackheath (long known as 'The Club') were no push-overs. But if one game had further emphasised Bath's impressive form then this was their commanding 13-6 home victory against Gloucester in early February. A massive psychological 'lift,' this was a victory achieved by first containing their opponents at forward and then only later unleashing their backs, tactics so clinically employed by Pontypool and tactics that Bath would now apply as and when needed for the remainder of the season's Cup campaign. Notable too was a superb performance from second row forward Nigel Redman. Deputising for the injured Hakin and a mere 19 years of age, the young recruit from Weston-super-Mare appeared quite undaunted by the reputation of the opposition. Indeed he *repeatedly stole the ball off the mighty Fiddler,"* a highly regarded England lock forward. Thus had another star been born and as a result, a selection headache in the not-too-distant future.

So in late February Bath headed for the capital with ten straight wins behind them, and The Club were about to be the eleventh; albeit a biting east wind swept across the Rectory Field, only a modest crowd of 1500 was present, and the hosts closed the first half with a 12-7 lead. Come the restart however Spurrell's men decided that it was high time to demonstrate more forcefully the reasons for their formidable reputation. Six tries in total were run home, John Palmer kicking conversions and penalties galore, and Bath duly swept to a 12-41 victory. Another mission accomplished.

In the post-match review Blackheath chairman of selectors John Williams, formerly of Bath combination club Old Sulians, held few doubts from so thorough a victory: "*I just can't see anyone touching Bath on this sort of showing. What a back row they've got and what pace in the back division."* True, a senior London club had been overcome away. But Bath would learn of their next Cup opponents with a certain degree of caution. It was to be the ever-improving Wasps, but thankfully on the Rec.

Thus for a brief period Bath could relax (well sort of) from the growing pressures that a Cup campaign will inevitably bring, and it was therefore a happy crew that travelled westwards in late February to play an evening floodlit game at Exeter. Charlie Gabittas, a recent recruit from Plymouth Albion, was awarded his debut for Bath and the Devonian county out-half promptly returned the compliment with his own converted try, a second conversion and a 40 yard penalty gem from wide out. Meanwhile at both forward and outside Bath dictated events throughout, and until late into the game it seemed that an equally happy Bath crew would be travelling back home again that same evening. But, minutes from the final whistle all this was to change. Something (or possible nothing) caused a flurry of fists between the two packs involving at least a dozen players. But it was out of character with a mostly sporting game, and it appeared to be an incident that almost certainly could have been settled by a stern lecture to both sides from the referee. However to the dismay of Bath someone got their 'marching orders,' and that someone was none other than prop Gareth Chilcott. At the very least an automatic 30-day suspension was an absolute certainty!

Now despite the fact that twice during his six previous seasons at Bath this courageous prop had been lifted from the base of a collapsed scrum with knee injuries so severe that his entire rugby career had seemed threatened, Chilcott had what is commonly termed as 'reputation' in the annals of front-row play. In particular this opinion was based upon a near one year suspension in season 1981-2 for 'dangerous use of the boot' during a Bath v Bristol derby on the Rec. That was not all, because the Somerset disciplinary committee had emphasised that if Chilcott was sent off again then he 'could expect a very long sentence indeed, and much longer than the previous one imposed.' This caveat in particular filled Bath supporters with trepidation, because if applied literally then Chilcott, assuming that Bath reached Twickenham, would be side-lined.

So it was hardly surprising that the normal happy atmosphere that characterises the homeward journey from an away victory was overshadowed by fears of a long suspension, and despite his colleagues' best efforts there were simply no words in the entire English language that could comfort a totally disconsolate Chilcott. There was just one hope however, namely that the Bath prop was by no means the only sinner in the rumpus that night, so providing at least one mitigating factor that might just influence the decision of the disciplinary committee. Fortunately all the circumstances at Exeter were indeed taken into consideration, although Chilcott did not escape unscathed. Indeed his otherwise certain selection for the county final was barred by the additional two weeks added to the 30-day suspension. But crucially, should Bath reach Twickenham then Chilcott would be available.

Two weeks later in the second weekend of March a tense crowd of 6,000 witnessed two of the best currently performing sides in England step out on to the Rec to contest the JP Cup quarter-final. The atmosphere was electric; the Wasps pack in the words of coach Rowell was *"one of the biggest collection of opponents I have ever seen;"* and the two sides were 'on paper' so evenly matched that it was nigh on impossible to have made any meaningful pre-match forecast. Or so it seemed. But there was one strategic decision that was to prove decisive, namely Rowell's insistence that in the event of

Bath requiring replacements during the game, then specialist cover must be available at both scrum-half and at hooker.

Sure enough, within 30 minutes Bath replacements Chris Stanley and Greg Bess (scrum-half and hooker respectively) were required to fill the key gaps left by the dual injury loss of scrum-half Richard Hill and hooker Rob Cunningham. This as it happened was to prove critical as Wasps, on losing scrum-half John Cullen in the first half were now dependent on replacement Mike Boyd, a natural fly half. The change to the balance of the two sides was noticeable almost immediately, as Boyd for all his efforts was ill at ease in the scrum-half role. No such difficulties hindered Bath however. Instead they now looked the more stable team, comfortable in the knowledge that both the experienced Stanley and Bess knew their respective trades well.

Even so Wasps proved mighty opponents. Out-half Mark Williams sent home a smart drop-goal, likewise Nick Stringer a conversion and penalty, while their immense pack steamrolled over for a push-over try by Andy Dun (and not many sides did that to Bath). Yet Spurrell's men maintained their composure despite huge Wasps pressure throughout. Horton, (diagonal kicks here and sudden breaks there) was a master tactician as always. Nigel Gaymond crashed over from a tap penalty (and not many players did that to Wasps). Then with tensions mounting in the final period and the result still wide open, Horton suddenly created space on the right flank 'box' for David Trick to race home for his first try. Then with a crucial victory within their sights, but not as yet certain, the excellent Stanley chipped over a perfectly placed drop-kick into the same box for Trick to pounce for Bath's third try. Meanwhile John Palmer, a picture of calmness throughout, accounted for four penalties and a conversion.

Then that final whistle blew to bring the curtain down on a day that brought credit to the game itself, though utter dejection in the Wasps dressing-room, contrasting with sheer elation (and relief) felt among a winning Bath team. The semi-final lay ahead, and quite suddenly one dared to hope that Twickenham could be reached.....at last! Nottingham away would now be the final obstacle (a formidable one) between Bath and their hopes of cup final triumph. But again the weather intervened, and this time so intense was the storm that swept over their Beeston ground that the Midland club were compelled to postpone the tie.

So priorities immediately switched from club matters to the County Championship, and a spate of late injuries within the Somerset camp led to a county debut for Bath prop Chris Lilley and further late call-ups for Chris Stanley (scrum-half) and hooker Greg Bess on the eve of the Twickenham final. Furthermore Bristol wing Gareth Williams was side-lined by injury and so Bath winger Paul Simpson was rushed into the Somerset line-up. Hence on the day, with Twickenham blessed with warm Spring sunshine, fourteen Bath players strode on to the field for **Somerset**: *C. Ralston, D. Trick, (R. Hopkins, W.s.Mare, 75 mins), J.Palmer, A. Rees, P. Simmons, J. Horton* *(capt.), C. Stanley, C. Lilley, G. Bess, R. Lee, P. Stiff (Bristol), R. Hakin, J. Hall, R. Spurrell (P. Turner, 55 mins), P. Simmons.*

The encounter was watched by an estimated 20,000 West Country crowd, and it was to be a day that would undoubtedly belong to Gloucestershire. Somerset by contrast did perhaps carry too many reserves, and their revised front-row was confronted by the massive power of a Gloucestershire eight that included the awesome front-three of Phil Blakeway, Steve Mills and Malcolm Preedy. It proved too much, and thanks partly to six tries from backs Ralph Knibbs, Stuart Barnes, Alan Morley (2), Richard Harding and forward Simon Hogg, as against a lone late try (and a good one) from Alun Rees, the honours were Gloucestershire's as they literally coasted home for an impressive 36-18 victory. Somerset nonetheless were humble in defeat, acknowledging the strength of their triumphant opponents and as John Horton commented post-match: *"We were beaten by a far better all-round side on the day."*

Attention now returned to the forthcoming semi-final at Nottingham, and although the Midlanders did not quite equal the Wasps outside the scrum, this rapidly improving club were a strong 15-man side without a single weakness. Forwards Neil Mantle (England) and Gary Rees (later England cap) and not least future England full-back Simon Hodgkinson were players worthy of the utmost respect. In addition not only did Nottingham enjoy a home advantage, their Beeston ground was a place of painful past memories.

But on 7th April there would be no deluge, Beeston was firm and suitable for open rugby and albeit scrum-half Richard Hill and hooker Rob Cunningham were to be side-lined by injury, their respective deputies Chris Stanley and Gregg Bess had already proved against Wasps that they could 'handle' the demands of the big occasion. This was the case too regarding young lock Nigel Redman, already an England U.23 international and drafted late into the Bath pack owing to Ronnie Hakin's withdrawal with flu.

To the surprise of most pre-match forecasters however Bath's strategy was not based upon the 15-man running game. Instead the plan was more orthodox, with a front-five containment of Nottingham's formidable forwards, supported by the back-row mobility of Spurrell, Jon Hall and Simpson, and not forgetting the tactical kicking of the peerless Horton. Nonetheless the encounter was to prove a grim struggle of attrition and it was specialist kicker Hodgkinson whose penalty put the home side in front after 30 minutes. The score-line then remained a nail-biting 3-0 to Nottingham until the final 15 minutes. Furthermore second-half injuries led to the retirement of key players John Palmer at centre and Nigel Gaymond at lock, albeit that their respective replacements Charlie Ralston and Jon Morrison proved outstanding despite the ever mounting tensions on the field.

Yet although chasing a 3-0 deficit for much of the game, Bath crucially maintained their composure, and come the last quarter Rowell's strategy was taking effect! By now the Nottingham pack had been neutralised and their backs worn down by non-stop tackling as *"Bath took a firmer grip with pressure rugby which forced Nottingham into error...."* Replacement Ralston then slotted home two penalties, his second from 40 yards; and finally as *"Nottingham became increasingly desperate"* Bath prop Chris Lilley to his great surprise (and everyone else's) found himself in the unlikely position of outside-half.

But that was not all! Because Lilley (this time to his team-mates' astonishment) then calmly flighted a perfect diagonal kick that was vintage Horton over the Nottingham defence and into the box, and who should be there to gleefully seize the ball but David Trick. He shot for the line, snatching the try that settled matters once and for all and Charlie Ralston, calmness personified, strode up to stroke the ball over the bar for the conversion and a 3-12 victory. Oh what joy! Bath had made it to Twickenham, where by extraordinary coincidence they would face Bristol.

It was now that the club entered the final countdown, inhaling every drop of the intoxicating atmosphere that had enveloped the Rec from the moment of the semi-final victory. Yet other obligations remained and players, noticeably wary of injury, cautiously won 22-19 against Llanelli, but in a game nonetheless where Chilcott ran out for his first game since suspension. He had trained hard during his absence; looked in fine fettle; and everyone at the club was just happy and relieved to see him back on the field.

But injury-doubts could not be avoided entirely, and concerns remained over the availability of (among others) the dynamic Richard Hill, still not fully recovered from the hamstring problem incurred in the quarter-final against Wasps. Indeed team secretary David Lamb could only inform the media and concerned Bath followers that Hill *"is now much happier and hopes to be playing over Easter."* Fortunately the club's increasingly 'professional' medical and physio' team (then currently led by chartered physiotherapist Gareth George) was working flat-out to get the 'A' team on the field for the final; though fingers for some players were tightly crossed. As Gareth George stated: *"the games are much more competitive, and also simply because at this time of year the ground tends to be rather hard and unyielding if you hit it heavily."*

Less of a distraction was the clash of shirt colours between Bath and Bristol, a matter that was resolved by the simple toss of a coin at the Rugby Union. Bath won the call, hence were classed as the home side and therefore would wear their 'away' strip on the day! *"Say that again,"* many would have asked, doubtless bemused that a home team would be compelled to wear their 'away' colours. But rules are rules as they say, and according to the laws of rugby union it was the home side who were required to change their normal strip should a colour clash occur. In practice however it was protocol rather than a 'must do.' Nonetheless Bath were happy to oblige and equally happy to learn that they would be allocated use of the England home dressing room on the day, a privilege arousing no Bathonian objections whatsoever.

Nor were there objections raised regarding the sum of £3,375 guaranteed to both clubs from John Player as the finalists' share of the sponsor's £95,000 total for that season's cup competition. True, such figures might seem rather paltry from today's standpoint; yet in the mid-1980's such a contribution was more than sufficient to bring a pre-Twickenham smile to the faces of the respective club treasurers. Meanwhile there was general satisfaction with the appointment of international referee Roger Quittenton to officiate the final. True, few referees are favourites with every team, and make no mistake Quittenton (of the London & Sussex society) was firm, indeed a little too firm for some peoples' liking. But he was unstintingly fair, and his eve-of-match comments to the Bath Chronicle were an insight into the character of the titanic encounter that lay ahead: *"I know what Bath-Bristol derbies can be like, but having controlled both clubs and knowing so many of their top players so well, I don't think there will be any problems."* Significant words, as events would shortly reveal.

There only remained last-minute fitness tests, and thanks not least to physio' Gareth George and fitness-chief Tom Hudson (Bath University) Bath announced that they would be fielding their first-choice fifteen. Sadly this determined that there would be no place for admired Irish international Ronnie Hakin in the starting line-up, as the scrummaging power of Nigel Redmond was deemed critical in the expected set-scrum battle against the street-wise Bristol pack. They were an entirely different proposition to Nottingham and moreover they knew Bath from A to Z. There was one 'but' however, one not picked up by the press prior to Twickenham, and one ironically with its roots in the dominating 36-18 County Championship triumph inflicted by Gloucestershire with a large contingent of Bristol players against a Somerset team fielding a virtual Bath team. Might Bristol be lulled into over- confidence? Some predicted that it might!

It was John Stevens however whose prophetic pre-match analysis in the Bath Chronicle would be as close as any clue to where and how the game would be won when suggesting that the *"battle with Spurrell, Jon Hall and Paul Simpson in the loose probably holds the key."* Thus on the cup-final day of 28th April all the euphoria of reaching Twickenham was tempered with the realities of the mammoth task facing Bath. Bristol were current cup holders, a team for the big occasion, a club who for generations ranked among the elite of English rugby, and whose long shadow still hung over Bath. Could Bath at long last free themselves from this self-same shadow? Because make no mistake this crucial question was indeed that same 'ultimate challenge' asked of the club at the conclusion of their Centenary year; and the only men who could provide the answer as they stepped out onto Twickenham (in their 'away' white shirts) were captain Roger Spurrell and the yeoman of Bath.

Bristol: *P. Cue, A, Morley, R. Knibbs, S. Hogg, J.F. Carr, S. Barnes, R. Harding, R. Doubleday, D.J. Palmer, A. Sheppard, N. Pomphrey, P. Stiff, P. Polledri, D. Chidgey, M.Rafter (capt.).Replacements: I. Duggan, J.Watson, L.Yandell, D. Hickey, K.Bogita.*

Bath: *C.R.Martin, D. Trick, J.A. Palmer, A. Rees, B. Trevaskis, J. Horton, R.Hill, G. Chilcott, R. Cunningham, M.R. Lee, N. Gaymond, N. Redman, R. Spurrrell (Capt.), J.P. Hall, P. Simpson. Replacements: A. Watkins, C. Stanley, C. Lilley, G. Bess, R. Hakin, P. Turner.* **Referee:** R. Quittenton (London/Sussex Societies).

Roger Spurrell and Bath's 1984 Cup Final team.... L to R (**top**) D. Robson (coach), G. George (Physio), C. Stanley, R. Cunnigham, G.Bess, A. Watkins, P. Turner, N. Redman, N. Gaymond, J. Hall, R. Lee, C. Martin, C. Liley, A. Rees,
R. Hakin, P. Simpson, J. Rowell (Coach). (**Front**) P. Pothecray (Medical), B. Trevaskis, J. Palmer, J. Horton, R. Spurrell (Capt.), R. Hill, D. Trick, G. Chilcott. (Twickenham 1984)

Acknowledgements: Bath Chronicle

Exactly as John Stevens had predicted a key influence of this do-or-die battle was Bath's back-row of Spurrell, Jon Hall and Paul Simpson; another was the tactical mastery of out-half John Horton whose drop-goal within the opening five minutes would steady Bath nerves and show Bristol that this was going to be a long, hard day. Both back divisions oozed class, and Trick's speed was a potential match-winner upon the firm, open Twickenham spaces. But risk-taking was for another day. For this game was above all about forward supremacy, and the dynamic first-half performance of that supreme Bath back-row dominated both ruck and maul, leading to Simpson's unstoppable charge for the line and the game's first try. The swirling Twickenham wind played its mischievous part too, seemingly unsettling John Palmer who failed with his first four opening-half penalty attempts, but who landed a touchline gem just

206

prior to the interval. But with danger man Stuart Barnes notching an earlier penalty for Bristol it was obvious that the 10-3 half-time score was too close for comfort, and too close for Bath as yet to risk running the ball wide.

Redman (5) charges into Bath's pack against Bristol, inches from try-line. Rees (12) awaits.

Acknowledgments Derek Carter

Yet there was one second-half certainty, because sooner or later Bristol would be compelled to fight back. The question was how? Pressure mounted. Bristol's back-division was fed the ball more frequently. The Bath defence was now to be seriously tested. For the 21,000 crowd who could 'but stand and stare,' the unfolding drama was almost frightening in its intensity. But the Bath defence held firm save but once, when within 15 minutes of the re-start scrum-half Richard Harding darted through from close range for a try, Barnes converting.

With the score poised on a knife-edge at 10-9 some 25 minutes of play remained, and during this period the entire nature of the Bath and Bristol rivalry hung in the balance.

"Not an inch was asked or given," wrote John Stevens, and although at times it seemed that Bristol might yet break through the Bath defence, *"they were ruthlessly scythed down by Bath's devasting tackling."* But, in the final minute Bath's Barry Trevaskis, who had defended like Horatio on the bridge throughout the match, felled England wing Alan Morley with a late tackle. It was a penalty, wide out on the right, and young Stuart Barnes would take it. The master kicker, whose five penalties and a conversion had proved decisive in Bristol's 21-18 semi-final win over Harlequins, steadied himself for the crucial kick. Twickenham fell silent.

Barnes struck the ball. It went high, it had the range but....maybe that curious Twickenham wind intervened as the kick veered away from its target. Quittenton's whistle blew. It would not be heard again that day.

John Carter (and his assistant Nick Johnson),commentating live to the city on the Bath Hospital Broadcast Society radio was momentarily lost for words, before breathlessly announcing the news of the triumph along the air-waves. Thousands of joyous Bath followers swarmed over the wide Twickenham spaces, glowing in pride as Roger Spurrell led his team wearily up the steep Twickenham steps to receive the Holy Grail of English rugby.....the John Player Special Cup. Oh, and how the much-loved Arnold Ridley (7th January 1896-12th March 1984) would have loved such a day!

Jack Rowell described the victory as *"the greatest day in our history."* Referee Roger Quittenton spoke of *"one of the hardest matches I have ever had to referee, but there wasn't a boot or fist out of place. It could have gone either way, but I also thought Bath just had an edge and deserved to win."* So, after all these long years of toil, struggle and effort to achieve a place among the elite of rugby, a once lowly Bath had reached the zenith of the English game. They had journeyed to Twickenham from a sleepy West Country city as yeoman. But they would depart as gladiators! It was indeed their day of destiny, the day when Bath had confronted and finally overcome that once fearful 'ultimate challenge.'

Chapter 29. EXCALIBUR! (1984-6)

Bath, having now achieved the prize that they cherished above all others, could thus relax for a few summer months, enjoy their Canadian tour and bask in the glow of their supreme triumph. At long last it seemed that a shadow had been lifted after endless years of Bristol domination, though even now one obstacle remained....Gloucester! Ah Gloucester, how the mere mention of that name still rankled down on the Rec. For sure Bristol had fallen on that glorious Twickenham day. But Gloucester remained defiant still. There was one certainty however, namely that as Bath prepared themselves for season 1984-5 it was beyond all reasonable doubt that the club now possessed one of the best sides (perhaps 'the' best) in England, having attained a top four place in the Anglo-Welsh Merit table for the previous seven seasons and winning 29 from 39 games in their recent glorious cup winning year. They were 'the' team to beat now, and rivals couldn't wait to haul them off their pedestal. Such was the price of fame.

Yet in truth it was a price worth paying. Because with all the attention (be it warm or hostile) and with all the new-found glamour status it just felt 'great' to be Bath. What is more, they were and would remain very much a 'family' club, albeit blissfully unaware of the tumultuous years that lay ahead. Everyone seemed to know everyone else, be they players or followers, and the Combination continued to play a vital role. On the eve of Bath's September 1984 visit to Moseley for example, when Rob Cunningham, Greg Bess and Jimmy Deane were all side-lined through injury, only one viable possibility remained, namely Avonvale hooker David Russell. His experience with Bath amounted to a mere one game in the Spartans. That one match was enough however. Indeed it 'had' to be enough, as anxious Bath selectors virtually dragged Russell out of bed (he was still recovering from flu) in order that he attend the 1st XV pre-match Thursday evening training session. And sure enough the Avonvale boy did himself and the Combination's reputation proud. Bath won 6-19 at the Reddings, adding to their 44-9 home win over Moseley in the previous season when another Combination player, namely Dean Padfield from Old Culverhaysians, proved yet again that despite the rapid changes in rugby in recent years, ability could be found right on Bath's own doorstep.

It was fortunate too that the senior side were further augmented by the ever-improving United XV. Devon wing Peter Drewitt for example, formerly of Exeter, was but one of a number of players of genuine class who could be relied upon for first team action whenever needed. It often was. A further acquisition was wing Martin Sparkes (younger brother of mid-1970's Bath back Andy), who admitted that when he played his first senior game on the wing he *"was paralysed with fear because everyone seemed to be running around at about a hundred miles an hour."* But this strong-running three-quarter, along with for example fellow backs Pete Blackett and not forgetting powerhouse Tony Gunner, proved ever-reliable reserves. Meanwhile a further insight into Bath's player-resources was demonstrated on 22nd December when 'thanks' to fixture congestion the club was called upon to play first team fixtures against Pontypool and Sale simultaneously on the same Saturday. In fact Bath were entitled to withdraw from one of the two encounters, but instead basically said *"Oh what the hell"* and just got on with it! The First XV thus travelled into Wales under Roger Spurrell, falling to an 18-10 defeat; while United (written off completely by some forecasters) admittedly lost 7-25 at home to a full strength Sale, but by no means a disgrace against one of the top-rated sides in England.

As for recent arrivals, perhaps none compared to a discovery brought to the club's attention on a County day earlier in the season when the Spartans were required to step up a level and play United's away fixture against the Swindon 1st XV. Spartans won! Not only that, the hugely experienced Robbie Lye, now the Spartans skipper, could not stop singing the praises of a certain young back who, he claimed, possessed a quite remarkable potential. He could have added (perhaps he did) that the youngster was maybe a 'mite too pleased with himself for some tastes.' Indeed on one notable occasion in the following season the young protégé received some plain-talking advice from an established Bath and England winger, who warned the 'yearling' in plain English of the pitfalls of youthful over-confidence, advice incidentally from which the 'youngster' would be forever grateful. Thus was boyhood transformed into manhood, and thus began the rugby story of one Jeremy Guscott.

It was at Bath's Ralph Allen School where Jeremy first held a rugby ball in his hands, although not the only rugby-playing 'nursery' within the boundaries of the city. For at the foot of the southern valley slopes below Ralph Allen there is Monkton Combe where Vincent Coates learned his rugby skills; and down the northern slopes stands King Edward's school where Geoff Frankcom's abilities were honed. Prior Park, alma mater of John Palmer is another such 'academy' and across the city on Lansdown Hill sits Kingswood, almost certainly in 1868 the first rugby playing school in Bath. In addition the game has been played for decades at Beechen Cliff, Culverhay, St. Gregory's and Oldfield, each school a priceless source of talent that has helped forge a rugby city with rugby a key part of its sporting identity.

Meanwhile in early season Simon Halliday had resumed training following a specialist course at the RAF sports rehabilitation centre in Surrey, and so successful was his recovery that he had regained a first team place by late October; and bolstering the club yet further was former Exeter University and Scotland B prop David Sole and England U.23 No. 8 forward David Egerton. Previously, Bath would have been fortunate to have been the choice of just one such player; now both, despite the proximity of Bristol, chose Bath.

Understandably this recently-acquired super-power status brought with it selection problems, few more sensitive than the issue at half-back in December when John

Palmer (now an international since England's summer tour of South Africa) was selected to play at outside-half for Bath at the express request of the England selectors. He duly was selected in Bath's victories over Exeter at home and away at Harlequins. Established out-half John Horton not unnaturally saw things somewhat differently. Indignant at a selection decision that he claimed had resulted from outside interference in domestic club policies, the 13-cap international announced his immediate retirement from both Bath and rugby football. Supporters were horrified by this unexpected upheaval, albeit that the club insisted (Chronicle, 14th December, 1984) that Horton was merely rested and remained *"a very important part of our squad for our defence of the John Player Cup."* Not everyone, though sympathetic to the selectors' dilemma, were entirely convinced by this explanation.

To the relief of Bath, with whom in his own words Horton had experienced *"eleven wonderful years,"* the admired Lancastrian retracted his threat to retire. Not so Ronnie Hakin who in late March announced his departure from the Rec. A six-cap Ireland international lock, the much-liked 34 year old schoolmaster, understandably deeply disappointed not to have made the JP Cup line-up at Twickenham in the previous season, sensed that Gaymond and Redman would remain the first choice second-row. His loss was keenly felt; but so too an increasing acceptance within the club that such difficulties were sometimes unavoidable. For Bath were by now moving in the proverbial 'fast-lane,' and attracting attention from even the government itself when on 17th November the Sports Minister Neil Macfarlane chose to attend the Bath v Coventry encounter. He duly witnessed a home 23-6 victory, concluding thus: *"I think I have been watching the best side in England."* But though very difficult to beat, Bath were not unbeatable, albeit their results were indicating that they might just be one of those teams capable of winning those key games that 'must' be won; and as they prepared for their automatic entry into the third round stage in late January, a back-to-back Cup triumph seemed not beyond their capabilities.

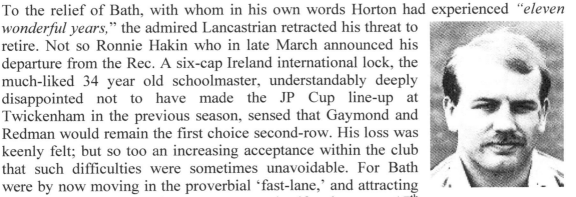

Nigel Redman: hugely versatile lock for Bath and England.

Acknowledgements: Bath Past Players

Their cup opener was a home tie against the battlers from the Forest of Dean....Berry Hill; and though not everyone beyond the confines of Gloucestershire knew too much about this club, Bath did know. Hence no attempts were made to elaborate, but instead to adopt a pragmatic approach designed to hold the 'Foresters' at forward and then to take chances when (hopefully) they arose. The tactics could not be faulted and duly earned a 24-3 victory, with Bath running home 4 tries to add to a typically smart Horton drop goal and one Palmer penalty. For Berry Hill meanwhile, inspired throughout by flanker and skipper Ian Seymour, there was a lone penalty success from fullback Jeff Powell to savour. But these hardy 'foresters' 'were true to their reputation, and as John Stevens reported, the Gloucestershire Cup holders were never overawed, and produced a *"thoroughly disciplined and fiery display which denied Bath the chance of asserting complete command."*

The next cup opponents were Blackheath in February at home, a quite different proposition to the dour, yet dangerous, Berry Hill. Unfortunately severe weather now intervened to interrupt the rugby programme, and with January literally 'written off,' the only game Bath could arrange between their home win over Rosslyn Park in late January, and their cup date, was a Sunday friendly at distant Brixham on 16th February. For Bath this match was to be a desperately needed opportunity for match practice, and the result was therefore largely immaterial. But it was just as well that it was, because Brixham were now to produce 'the' surprise of the season. They won! It is difficult to say how they won, because *"in every department of play, Bath were in another class to their gutsy Devon opponents...."* However within ten minutes home wing Sean Irvine flighted home a huge drop goal from wide out, soon followed with his straightforward penalty bang in front of the posts. Late in the game, by which time Bath had exhausted virtually every tactic in the coaching manual, Irvine sent home another simple penalty prior to Bath's John Palmer scoring a perfectionist try and conversion. But it was a little too late to prevent a now joyous and previously unfancied Brixham from clinching a win that was greeted with near disbelief across the rugby heartlands of England.

Fortunately this was not a cup game, but a warm-up for Bath's encounter against Blackheath, and as Bath's priority in Devon had been to practice running tactics after a depressingly long period of non-action, their main strategic purpose was achieved. So it was hardly surprising that against Blackheath a more conservative approach was adopted. Admittedly Blackheath's giant lock Doug Hursey was impressive throughout, likewise half-backs Crispin Read and Nick Colyer. But Bath held too many aces, and in reply to a lone Colyer penalty, Spurrell's men ran home 6 tries (2 converted) with Trevaskis scoring a hat-trick and John Palmer stroking home 3 penalties. An impressive 37-3 win was thus achieved, a success duly described by John Stevens (Bath Chronicle) as *"another thoroughly professional display...."* It was precisely this professionalism that Bath duly 'carried' to Sale in the quarter-finals. Their back-row of Spurrell, Hall and Simpson were simply too hot to handle, and their defence in the backs could not be breached, despite Halliday's 30th minute injury (thankfully not serious) that necessitated all-rounder Chris Stanley to deputise. But their pack produced *"a fearsome display of rucking and mauling....."* Moreover, although Sale full-back Graham Jennion slotted over 5 penalties, Bath superiority was emphasised with their two tries (Simpson and Trick), a drop-goal gem from Horton and four penalties, of which three were coolly executed by David Trick, much to the surprise of Bath followers, previously unaware of his considerable kicking prowess.

Four clubs now remained in the Cup, each sharing a dream, each aware that they stood tantalizingly close to the chance (and for many players their one and only chance) of treading the sacred turf of Twickenham. They read as follows: London Welsh, Coventry, Bath and.....Gloucester! And, if there was one team in all England whom Bath wished to avoid at this stage then that team 'was' Gloucester. Furthermore if there was one venue that Bath wished to avoid then that ground was Kingsholm. Yet, if Bath were in all truth the best side in England then they would now have the opportunity to prove it, because they were to learn soon enough that they had indeed been drawn against Gloucester.....away! This therefore was nothing less than the semi-final the equal of all semi-finals, one certain to entail a forward battle that John Stevens predicted *"would not be for the faint hearted."* And you could say that again! For this would be a collision between two age-long rivalries, where one would now witness rugby's version of a 'fight to the death.'

On the eve of the game Gloucester's acting captain Paul Taylor (in the absence of their England and RAF captain John Orwin) vowed that Gloucester would *"explode the myth that Bath are the best side in England,"* and with his side playing on home territory not many would have bet against his prediction. But Bath held aces in their line-up, not least John Horton , who would not only send over a vital drop goal, but proved himself yet again a master-general able to control a game with his astute tactical kicking into space and his ability to break out from danger and so turn defence into sudden counter-attack.

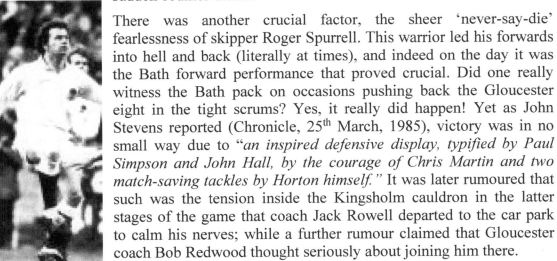

John Horton:
Inspirational
outside–half.

There was another crucial factor, the sheer 'never-say-die' fearlessness of skipper Roger Spurrell. This warrior led his forwards into hell and back (literally at times), and indeed on the day it was the Bath forward performance that proved crucial. Did one really witness the Bath pack on occasions pushing back the Gloucester eight in the tight scrums? Yes, it really did happen! Yet as John Stevens reported (Chronicle, 25th March, 1985), victory was in no small way due to *"an inspired defensive display, typified by Paul Simpson and John Hall, by the courage of Chris Martin and two match-saving tackles by Horton himself."* It was later rumoured that such was the tension inside the Kingsholm cauldron in the latter stages of the game that coach Jack Rowell departed to the car park to calm his nerves; while a further rumour claimed that Gloucester coach Bob Redwood thought seriously about joining him there.

Gloucester's Tim Smith meanwhile had run through for two tries and a penalty. Likewise Bath's Richard Hill had plunged over for a try converted by John Palmer, thus adding to his vital penalty and Horton's drop goal. Yet not until the third minute of injury time when Gloucester full-back Tim Smith's last gasp penalty attempt swung wide did Bath

213

raise their tired arms in triumph, with the cheers of some hundreds of their travelling supporters in a 12,000 crowd saluting their supreme triumph. Yes it was close ('boy was this one close') with Bath on the right side, just, of the 11-12 result. But once again a single point (as at Twickenham one year previously) separated defeat from triumph. Once again it would prove to be a case of winner takes all.

Thus a second cup campaign had led to the imposing portals of Twickenham to face the London Welsh whose 10-10 draw at Coventry had (under the 'away rule') ensured their own place in the final. True it was that the Welsh were no longer the equals of their glittering predecessors who had so captivated British rugby of previous years; yet equally true that Bath even now admired the potential dangers from this outpost of Welsh rugby-flair. Nonetheless since their past 'amateurish' forays in the competition Bath were a cup side transformed. What however had brought about this transformation? One answer was the coaching triumvirate of Rowell, Robson and Hudson. Another was Roger Spurrell, whose leadership at Twickenham against London Welsh would be his last game as captain. Often brilliant, always tenacious, he was not interested in coming second, only in winning; and he didn't mind too much what opponents thought about his lack of diplomacy either. It has been reported (though never officially) that the Cornishman had been sought by the national selectors on the eve of England's January 1985 encounter against Romania. But contact alas could not be made in time. It is however certain that the flaxen haired Spurrell, already an England Trialist, would have served his Country as he had always served Bath, namely with an unflinching and almost reckless bravery.

Meanwhile at Twickenham (27th April) accents both West Country and Welsh among a 32,000 crowd echoed around the sun-drenched stadium; while a superstitious Bath, sensing that those white shirts against Bristol might just be their lucky colour chose to wear white shirts again; and as captains Roger Spurrell (Bath) and Clive Rees (London Welsh) led their respective teams on to Twickenham's immaculate surface as follows one wondered: 'could Bath win a back-to-back cup Double?

Bath: C. *Martin, D.Trick J. Palmer, S.Halliday, B. Trevaskis (J. Guscott 40 mins), J.Horton, R.Hill, G.Chilcott, G.Bess, R.Lee, N. Gaymond, N. Redman, R. Spurrell (capt.), J. Hall, J. Simpson.*

London Welsh: *M. Ebsworth, J. Hughes, R. Ackerman, D. Fouhy, C. Rees (Capt.), C. Price, M. Douglas, T. Jones, B. Light, B. Bradley, E. Lewis, J. Collins, S. Russell, M. Watkins, K. Bowring.* **Referee:** *R. Quittenton (London/Sussex Societies).*

Almost from the outset the superb back-row of Spurrell, Jon Hall and Simpson stamped its authority across the wide Twickenham acres, as *"Bath swarmed forward, bristling with menace and purpose, and struck the vital psychological blows within 15 minutes...."* John Palmer (partnering Halliday at centre) sent home the first of his four successful penalties despite a mischievous Twickenham wind. Trick then sped around his man for a try converted by Palmer, before scrum-half Hill surged for the line to feed Chilcott, whose subsequent try aroused a crescendo so loud that ear defenders should have been compulsory as a safety precaution. Thus within 30 minutes Bath were already 18 points clear.

The Welsh, with potential match-winners in their Wales international trio of winger Clive Rees, centre Robert Ackerman and scrum-half Mark Douglas, and in addition giant 6ft 7in lock John Collins (Wales 'B' squad) never gave up. Yet their five successful penalties from Lydney born out-half Colyn Price were not sufficient to threaten Bath's overall superiority, whose domination thus secured a 24-15 victory. It was, wrote John Stevens, *"another highly-professional Bath job...."*And it was exactly this professionalism that few commentators previously had ever associated with 'happy-go-lucky' Bath.

Jack Simpkins…. His two-year presidency witnessed two John Player triumphs.

Acknowledgements: Reg. Monk

On Sunday evening the team toured the city centre again in an open-top bus, acclaimed to the rafters by jubilant citizens. *"Cheers, clapping and car horns made a cacophony of sounds and amateur cameramen used all kinds of vantage points, from balconies in the Circus to trees, to get a good snap of their heroes;"*(Chronicle, Ian Abbott, 29th April, 1985). In Chapel Row even the good clergy of Holy Trinity Church stepped outside to add their congratulations, while en route girls were seen to jump aboard the team bus (cheeky so-and-so's) to get an adoring close-up of their favourites. Then at the Pump Room the players were met by the Mayor and Mayoress of Bath, namely Mr Tony and Mrs Muriel Rhymes, thence to a civil reception for the team, their wives and girlfriends. It was a joyous weekend, one that celebrated both a season of 30 victories (one draw and only 8 defeats), in addition to a coveted back-to-back cup final triumph. Such was this achievement moreover that it was no longer fanciful to suggest that Bath might be forging a quite new rugby kingdom, one ironically barely a stone's throw from the Abbey where in AD 973 King Edgar was crowned as the first king of all England.

But if such a kingdom was to be founded then the three successive cup winning triumphs of Leicester from 1979-81 must at the very least be equalled. Could any other club reach such heights? Could Bath sustain their onwards march? Bath loyalists may have nurtured such dreams…. but dreams are one thing; reality quite another. So might the views of others beyond the Rec help to answer such questions? John Mason (rugby correspondent, Daily Telegraph) who had talked often to Jack Simpkins and others at Bath, had commented (the 1985 Bath v London Welsh cup final programme) that he had *"been struck that the club's relatively recent run of success nationwide has not altered any of them one scrap. There is an air of deprecating modesty, bordering on pessimism at times, running through the club."* By contrast the equally renowned Alan Gibson, from a somewhat different perspective, wrote thus: *"The present Bath side has enjoyed its temporary role of being the best in the land, but I think it is not one to which they instinctively respond;"* adding thus: *"Yes, it has been very agreeable, Bath's run at the top, and it will be very pleasant to look back on: but a relief when it is over. It is not their natural style."*

Not every Bath follower would have agreed (or perhaps wished to agree) with Alan Gibson's viewpoint; but it was possible that Bath's extraordinary rise to prominence might be a short term 'one-off,' an occurrence by no means unknown in sport? On the other hand maybe a new future was already taking shape, born perhaps at that moment when exhausted yet triumphant, Bath had departed the muddied field of Kingsholm in that epic 1985 cup semi-final clash. Because it was on that day a crucial psychological hurdle had been cleared and one sensed that almost any obstacle, anywhere, could now be cleared.

Success however (and possibly this was Alan Gibson's point) is not always the easiest companion to live with and can place enormous pressures on a club. Indeed it is one thing to reach the top, but quite another to stay there; and Bath who for so long had been the hunter were now the hunted, and the following 1985-6 season would therefore prove to be an ever-more-demanding campaign. It was partly for this reason that the coaching triumvirate, so as to be 'ahead of the game,' visited Hull Kingston Rovers in late November to make a first-hand study of rugby league training techniques and match preparations. Reportedly they were deeply impressed by what they saw. It was significant too, and that is putting it mildly, that the RFU gave its (admittedly) guarded approval towards this unexpected perestroika with the League code; while John Stephens added a further observation (Chronicle, 25th November 1985), namely that rugby *"has changed more in the past five years than in its entire history. It will probably never be quite the same again even when present evolution of the game is completed, which it isn't yet."* There would prove to be much truth in this statement, not least because this was no longer the past, but the inevitable arrival of the future; and to the amazement of English rugby it was a once lowly Bath, often ignored and once known for slogging it out in the lower reaches of the first-class game, that now stood at the apex of the changes that the Union game was undergoing.

But time stops for no one, and with the arrival on the Rec of young Bristol and England outside-half Stuart Barnes, John Horton, whose brilliance had galvanised Bath into a team that could match any in the Land, would now switch to Bristol for one final season of senior rugby. There was no denying however that Barnes was a player of a maturity beyond his years, a player capable of upholding the standards set by his illustrious predecessor. And what a honeymoon he experienced from his debut over Plymouth Albion (40-0) that launched a Bath Autumn offensive that included an astonishing 15-40 victory at Leicester away, home successes against Pontypridd (45-19), Moseley (50-10), Llanelli away (15-18) and home triumphs over Bristol (26-7), and finally a dazzling 16-13 floodlit classic against Cardiff in late October watched by an estimated 10,000 attendance, a crowd so large the gates were locked for reasons of crowd safety.

Phil Cue, another Bristolian, moved across to the Rec during this same season, bringing with him a justifiable reputation as a classy full-back, although it was not until Bath's late-season 19-10 home win over Llanelli that it was realised that Cue was furthermore a first-rate outside-half. At the same time England's Lancastrian winger Tony Swift arrived from the Swansea club, likewise fellow Welsh club player Malcolm Roberts, the former Pontypridd hooker; while during the season Cornish farmer Graham Dawe decided that he too would test his potential at the higher level, a potential that would lead to his rapid rise to prominence with his newly adopted club and later with England, so reiterating the view of Charles Gabbitass and others that it was now almost essential for players such as Dawe (travelling from Launceston no less) to join clubs outside the far South West if regular first-class rugby was to be gained.

Notwithstanding so many hopeful signs for another successful season, doubts understandably remained as to whether Bath could match Leicester and achieve 'the Treble,' though that did not discourage the club from trying. Prior to the start of the season the squad had commenced a rigorous (Hudson-prepared) programme of 'conditioning with an emphasis on 'endurance, muscular development and heart-lung efficiency.' In addition the squad was dispatched on a pre-season SAS-type training weekend in Wales, emphasising that the club was taking things very seriously indeed. So it was hardly surprising in view of Bath's explosive launch into the season that some 75% of their points were coming in the final 20 minutes. "*It's their fitness,*" many were suggesting, although fitness coach Tom Hudson explained that there was more to fitness than people realised. "*Any athletics coach can get rugby players physically fit but that won't win them matches. It's about conditioning, psychologically and physiologically,*" he forcefully added.

Thus in theory all seemed set fair. But if only rugby, particularly cup rugby, was so simple! Indeed with little more than a month prior to Bath's J.P. Cup opener at Orrell, an exasperated Jim Galley (speaking on behalf of himself and fellow selectors Brian Jenkins and Geoff Pillinger) bemoaned the increasing pressures upon the rugby game. No longer was the County Championship the only distraction, because now call-ups for players came from other directions, including the new Inter-Divisional championship and a newly-established (albeit welcomed) John Smith sponsored National Merit Table.

By late Autumn therefore it was difficult to field anything approaching a first choice side, a crucial period explained Jim Galley when the *"first-class club season should be reaching a climax before the start of the John Player Cup in January,"* while exactly at that moment when Bath hoped that they would have a settled side at their disposal there were bound to be international calls-ups.

It was this predicament that quite possibly explained Bath's decidedly shaky performance in their J.P. Cup match at Orrell, when thanks only to the safety net of the 'away' rule they escaped back to the West Country still free to compete in the next round. But things had simply not gone right against the Lancastrians. Although the Bath forwards duly dominated one of the heaviest packs in England, the dangerous Bath back division inexplicably seemed unable to capitalise on such a golden opportunity. The end result was a 16-16 draw, with both teams running home two tries (one converted) and two penalties apiece. But thankfully there was that 'away' ruling, and it was with a sigh of relief that Bath departed Lancashire-country with their passport into the next round still intact.

The following round at Moseley presented no such problems, despite the need to cover the frost-hardened pitch with 1,300 straw bales as protection against overnight frost, so allowing a 6,000 crowd to watch an eagerly awaited game that otherwise might well have been postponed. The Bath pack was awesome, laying the foundations for a 4-22 victory; and while skipper John Palmer's side drew huge satisfaction for so competent a win, not least *"founded on another superb demonstration by Nigel Redman,"* there was nonetheless seething anger within the Bath camp regarding a facial injury to loose-head David Sole, now a full Scotland cap. In the 17th minute he was assisted from the field groggy, in genuine pain and with the ugliest fractured nose injury that many had ever witnessed, one resulting from an opposition forward's elbow (a recent recruit to the Reddings) clashing into his face. The referee merely issued a mild rebuke to the player responsible, yet awarded a penalty to Bath, one that Barnes duly banged through the posts. Come professional rugby however with its pro' referees, linesmen and the watching TMO, perhaps far harsher disciplinary action might have resulted regarding an incident that was in fact totally out of character with usual Bath/Moseley matches.

Next it was London Welsh, another away tie; a fact that did not concern John Stevens as much as the forward-orientated methods that Bath had been employing in both their previous cup rounds against Orrell and Moseley. *"What has happened to that almost entirely international back division...?"* asked the Chronicle rugby correspondent, aware of a growing frustration among supporters at tactics that some regarded as negative and who questioned the reluctance to open up the game to one of the best back divisions in the game. However John Stevens duly provided the answer, namely that sheer pressure was now taking its toll, not least because every opponent now regarded a cup game against Bath as a virtual cup final in its own right. Dare Bath take risks with a bit of fun-rugby thrown in to please the masses? The answer was an emphatic 'Non!' Risks were out. Pragmatism was in! It was as simple as that.

Nor was there any noticeable change in the quarter-final at London Welsh. Once more it was a case of safety-first; and if it was any comfort to those criticising Bath's cautious approach, cup rugby encounters elsewhere, especially in the later rounds, tended to be played no differently. Bath duly won 10-18, and on away territory moreover where wins always come that much harder. And who knows, if drawn at home in the semi-final, Bath might just choose to cut loose and bring those potentially outstanding backs into action. Talking of backs, the selection of Simon Halliday for his England debut in their 21-18 victory against Wales at Twickenham (January 1986) led to delight among the Bath faithful, all only too aware of the arduous (and inspirational) fight-back the brilliant centre had made since his serious injury two seasons previously. Delight too was expressed with the re-call of Gareth Chilcott (first capped against Australia in November, 1984) for England's later victory over Ireland at Twickenham (March 1986), and John Palmer adding to his caps as a replacement during the same match.

Meanwhile the semi-final pool of London Scottish, Wasps, Leicester and Bath again included one team and one ground that Bath had fervently hoped to avoid. But it was to be a forlorn hope, because as with the semi-final against Gloucester in the previous season it literally couldn't get worse than this.....Leicester away! Yes Leicester, the team who had already won 'the cup treble,' but whom Bath in early season had swept aside 15-40 at Welford Road, but who ominously had struck form again, only too clearly demonstrated by their 8-15 away quarter-final victory over Harlequins. So in order to rest the team for the monumental task that awaited them at Welford Road, one week prior to the semi-final a near reserve Bath XV were handed the baton against Lancashire club Vale of Lune and duly demonstrated that most, if not all, could have secured a regular first-team place virtually anywhere elsewhere in senior rugby. Typical of such players was prop Ian 'Taff' Davies, now returned from Gosforth; while wing Ian Abbott and scrum-half Steve Knight ran home tries in Bath's 16-4 home victory, and the back-row of Nick Riou, Kevin Withey and Nick Maslen was further evidence of Bath's remarkable wealth of back-row forwards. This was significant, because in the forthcoming semi-final, it would be the rested back-row of Spurrell, Simpson and the ever-improving David Egerton who would prove so dominant a threat throughout a truly enthralling encounter.

So it was that the penultimate game on the road to Twickenham was played on a calm Spring day. The calmness was deceptive however, for tensions around Welford Road were at barometer-high levels as arguably the two best sides in England locked horns for another fight to the finish. Home advantage notwithstanding, it was Leicester's misfortune to meet a Bath team who no longer seemed over-awed by any opposition, nor daunted by any occasion. For that is the only conclusion that one could draw from

Bath's eventual 6-10 victory by way of one try and two Stuart Barnes penalties against two Leicester penalties from Dusty Hare. The narrowness of the margin of victory concealed nonetheless the true scale of Bath's domination, a superiority described by John Stevens thus: Bath *"taught Leicester such a lesson in the art of pressure rugby in this pulsating semi-final that a final margin of the only try by centre Simon Halliday could be regarded as scant reward on the run of play."* While England international and Leicester skipper Les Cusworth humbly remarked thus: *"That pack of theirs is a fearful proposition and John Palmer has got his backs so well organised.....it's difficult to see who's going to beat them."* Wasps however, with their own 11-3 semi-final success against London Scottish, might just be the right candidates for such a task.

Nor were Bath taking any chances against their rejuvenated London adversaries. Coached by former All Black Derek Arnold, they boasted a string of class players that included (assuming fitness) brilliant utility back Huw Davies, centre Richard Cardus, wings Mark Bailey and Simon Smith, full-back Nick Stringer and prop Paul Rendall, all (yes 'all') England players. Hence every available recent video-film of games involving Wasps were carefully scrutinised and a thorough report prepared on remaining pre-final Wasps matches; while Bath's final form-guide included home wins over Newport (24-18), followed by victory over Llanelli (19-10). But, despite superb performances during the season, not least against Leicester, a start place could not be found for David Egerton in the final, as two equally-matched sides took the field under the watchful gaze of a 24,500 crowd at Twickenham (26ᵗʰ April, 1986) as follows:

Bath: *C. Martin, D. Trick, J. Palmer (capt.), S. Halliday, A. Swift, S. Barnes, R. Hill, G. Chilcott, G. Dawe, R. Lee, J. Morrison, N. Redman, R. Spurrell, J. Hall, P. Simpson.*

Wasps: *N. Stringer, S. Smith, R .Cardus (capt.), R. Pellow, M. Bailey, G. Rees, S. Bates (P. Balcombe repl.), G. Holmes, A. Simmons, J. Probyn, J. Bonner. M. Pinnegar, K. Moss, M. Rigby. M. Rose.* **Referee:** *F. Howard (Liverpool Society).*

It was ill-luck that had robbed Wasps of the services of England prop Paul Rendall, side-lined on the eve of the final with measles. But there were casualties among Bath ranks too, although the fact that Barnes had incurred a broken toe, and that a John Palmer groin injury would limit both his running and kicking were handicaps carefully concealed from Wasps, the media and the public generally. This was just as well, because within 25 minutes of play Bath trailed by 13-0 against their rampant opponents, whose 18 years old Harrow Schoolboy Gary Rees (outside-half) launched his backs into a spate of masterful handling. It was a joy to watch, unless you were Bath, as the Londoners demonstrated the arts of running into space, assured passing and faultless off-loading. It was hardly surprising therefore when backs Nick Stringer and Roger Pellow finished precision moves with stunning tries apiece (one converted), with Stringer then coolly slotting home a straightforward penalty.

Indeed such was the Wasps domination that many teams might have raised the white flag by half-time. But not so Bath, the team for all occasions! Furthermore, it was at that stage when the Londoners surged into a 13-0 lead that a Wasps player (it is reliably reported) looked Spurrell in the eyes and said: 'now you'll learn what it's like to lose.' Of all the players to provoke, Spurrell is the last one on planet Earth to select for ridicule. Moreover other Bath players were in earshot too. And coincidentally or not, it was at this point that the Bath fight-back commenced. Swift shot over for a blind-side try, followed by a successful penalty. Whether or not Wasps then sensed something was amiss when Trick, not Barnes or Palmer, strode up to take the kick, or whether anyone realised at this crucial moment that Trick was literally a bag of nerves was anyone's guess. Nonetheless Trick's penalty attempt did skim over the bar....just! And Bath did indeed turn on the power-play in the second half.

Gradually the Wasps pack was subdued, although not without a dire struggle; and as Bath tightened their grip and by now a vengeful Spurrell had stormed over for another try, scrum-half Hill flashed over for a third and war-horse Simpson crashed over for the fourth. But lest it be forgotten, winger Trick proceeded to play a vital role as deputy kicker, who with a penalty already under his belt then added three superbly struck conversions. And it was the last of these from near the touchline that would be boosted (literally boosted) by the assistance of a Twickenham steward known already to the England winger on his previous visits to Rugby HQ. Trick, gasping for a drink of water in the stadium's heat-trap was offered a flask by the kind-hearted steward, and the thankful recipient thus took a sip from that same flask. But....water it was not! It was sherry, and there was no better way to revive 'one' David Trick on a hot early summer's day. He duly sent the ball flying through the posts and Bath were on their way to a 17-25 victory and a third successive Cup Final triumph.

So, for another of those joyous Sunday evening open-bus tours through the streets of an adoring home city, and not forgetting the gathering in Chapel Row of the Holy Trinity congregation whose earnest prayers had again been answered; then onwards to the Pump Room reception by the Mayoress (Mrs Jan Hole). It was here that Bath captain John Palmer now candidly explained to the good lady that *"for the past two years, the Mayor has come into the changing room and seen us in all our glory after the game. It was disappointing that it could not happen this year."* Now John Palmer.....it was a bit late to inform the Mayoress of that now!

So it was that yet another, even higher, mountain had been conquered, namely a third consecutive National Cup triumph that equalled the achievement of Leicester, a triumph that many believed could never be matched by another team, let alone Bath. After all, even five years ago, let alone ten, they were regarded at best as a one-off success story, a club whose star would shine but briefly; yet contrary to many a prediction, still shone brightly. Indeed Welsh recruit Mark Roberts remarked at the conclusion of his short yet notable Rec days (1985-6) that *"nothing in [his] rugby career before or after compared to the intensity of the experience I had while playing for Bath;"* and it was an intoxicating experience for those devoted to this club and city to be a part of it all. But for how long could that star still shine? That was the question now.

How long indeed; the tensions, the preparations, the need to get the timings just right as regards the fitness of a squad able to battle through the 1986-7 season into a fourth successive Twickenham final. So the loneliness that sometimes befalls those leading the pack, a world where friends are few, where opponents are many, would continue; while those who knew only the fearsome side of Bath on the field would hardly have recognised those stalwarts who worked tirelessly for the club off the field. Only occasionally would they share the lime-light, but their contribution was immense.

Clive Howard (whose wing-three-quarter son Chris later captained Bath Youth) could not have guessed that when accepting the role of general secretary in 1982 he was not only stepping into the shoes of the now legendary Jack Simpkins, but about to take over the reins of a club destined for national, even international, acclaim. Yet calm of nature and deeply likeable, this former Staffordshire county sprinter and a wing for his local side Newcastle-under-Lyme personified the ideal club official. With Bath now very much high-profile there was for this Building Society manager sometimes a near avalanche of letters filling his in-tray, be they from the RFU Twickenham, from other clubs and from an ever-widening fan base, some of it international. In addition there was the increasing interest of the media. *"Sometimes I almost forget what my wife [Ann] and children look like,"* he was heard to reflect. But always calm despite the responsibilities heaped upon him, Clive Howard was that ideal club official, who as the saying goes: 'was never in the way, yet never out of the way.'

A contribution of another kind was to be clearly demonstrated during Bath's 6-3 victory over Leicester in September when John Palmer collapsed at the feet of a Tigers surge near the Bath goal line. Lying motionless, his injury was initially thought to be genuinely serious, and among the reporters that day was the Guardian's David Frost, a witness to the resulting 17 minutes emergency action commendably marshalled by referee Laurie Prideaux. David Frost wrote thus: the *"care, skill and efficiency with which the Bath club dealt with this nasty accident was a lesson for all 1,500 clubs in the country. Bath had two GPs and an orthopaedic surgeon on the spot, and a stretcher was immediately available."* Meanwhile *"Palmer was fitted with a surgical collar. An ambulance was sent for and driven across the pitch to where Palmer was lying."* The Bath and England centre was then duly rushed to the RUH hospital.

To relief throughout the club it was learned on the following day that John Palmer's injury was not serious. But the incident demonstrated the advances that Bath (and indeed many clubs) had made in the provision of expert support; and here Bath were indebted to their own Honorary Medical team led during this period by Dr Kevin Gruffydd Jones and fellow physicians, namely Doctors Simon Burrell, Robin While,

Ian Grandison and Mess'rs Philip Bliss and Cledwyn Jones; while further invaluable assistance was provided by an honorary Physio team of Fiona Phillips, Rebecca Williams, Heather McKibbon, and now led by senior Physio Julie Bardner who had taken over this crucial role from Gareth George. And as injuries were unavoidable (not least at this level of rugby), 'crucial' is not an exaggeration.

Fortunately apart from the brief Palmer scare the opening weeks of the new season were largely injury free, a period during which recent arrival Andy Robinson (former Loughborough Colleges) positively thrived during Bath's opening September blitzkrieg that included away wins at Pontypool (10-23), Plymouth Albion (10-41), Moseley (0-36) and then Newport (6-33); and within a month observers were comparing Robinson with his dynamic predecessor Roger Spurrell. Meanwhile with Bath's aforementioned 6-33 victory at Newport, new captain Richard Hill's side ran home no fewer than six tries (one by former England schoolboy international centre Ben Cundy) to record their biggest victory so far 'on' Welsh soil, and among a six thousand home crowd that witnessed the events was the Guardian's Clem Thomas (25th September, 1986). He wrote admiringly of the West Countrymen's *"sheer strength of purpose and superb-balanced 15 man attacking rugby,"* adding significantly that no longer *"do Welsh teams hold any fears for them."*

This last comment acknowledged the fact that Bath had now overcome the presumption widespread among English clubs that Welsh near invincibility could not be broken, especially on Celtic soil. But now with a fixture list and an approach that was Anglo-Welsh in all but name, Bath had overcome this psychological barrier. Come late September yet further recognition was emphasised with the appointment of Richard Hill as the new captain of England, an honour never previously accorded a Bath player; while in the New Year Graham Dawe won the first of his five England caps, notwithstanding that in the drama of England's 19-12 upset in Cardiff that season a free-for-all at forward (with sinners on both sides) did lead to a one match suspension for England lock Wade Dooley and Bath trio Richard Hill, Gareth Chilcott and the recently capped Dawe. This did look bad on Bath, but if there was any excuse it was that years of campaigning in Wales had arguably produced players hardened to give as good as they got.

Bath's first cup opponents were Plymouth Albion on the Rec in late January. Significantly despite the comfortable-looking result of 32-10, it remained 'game on' until the final quarter when Bath's extra fitness and experience proved decisive. Yet there were occasions when the Devonians displayed sufficient all-round ability to not only send their excellent wingers Steve Walklin and Ray Westlake racing home for one try apiece, but indicated that if only clubs in the far South West could strengthen their fixtures with more top-grade opposition, then the Albions of this world could be serious contenders for honours themselves. There next followed the visit of the London Welsh, whom Bath had overcome 53-16 merely one month previously, yet whose once dazzling brilliance even now stirred the imagination and drew a 6,000 crowd to the Rec. But 'the master and pupil role' was now reversed, and after eighty minutes of action Bath strode off the Rec as 30-4 victors over the legends of yesteryear.

Moseley were next on the agenda as Bath's quarter-final opponents, though not before the Rec played host to the England B team's 22-9 victory over France B on 20th February; an ideal opportunity for watching England selectors to see Bath's Nigel Redman and in addition their non-stop human dynamo of a flanker Andy Robinson, two players who Rec followers had already correctly predicted were near certainties for future full-international call-ups. The following weekend visitors Moseley arrived to be greeted with a heavy pitch ill-suited to open, running rugby, so hardly surprising that they adopted the dour forward game at which Midland sides are adept. Furthermore Bath were grateful indeed that visiting captain Ian Metcalfe could only succeed with one lone penalty from seven attempts, not sufficient to overhaul a drop-goal and penalty from Barnes and a Barnes converted penalty try. But it was close, and Bath needed to draw upon every ounce of strength from their own hugely experienced pack to finally subdue a formidable Midland challenge with a 12-3 win.

With opponents from the South West, West London, the Midlands all overcome, it was northern challengers Orrell who would seek to block Bath's path to another Twickenham final and dare one even think it, let alone say it: 'achieve a triumph without equal in English rugby.' It was late March, a swirling Pennine gale had discouraged any serious attempts to attack outside the scrum and Richard Hill's team would instead concentrate their prime efforts through their pack, a tactic that would subsequently 'spell doom' to the luckless Lancastrians. With a front-row wall of David Sole, Graham Dawe and Gareth Chilcott, the opposition were pitilessly broken apart at set scrums. With the might of Jon Hall (*"world class"* in the words of John Stevens) and fellow back-row colleagues David Egerton and Andy Robinson, a total of six tries then followed, three of them push-overs. With total domination up-front Bath (who had struggled to get a 16-16 draw one season previously) now literally hammered Orrell into the turf as they steamrollered towards a landslide 7-31 victory.

It was *"almost slaughter of the innocents,"* concluded John Stevens. It was more than that, nothing less in fact than conclusive proof that Bath could now export their most awesome 'home' form into the arena of any side in England and Wales. For not only had this once unglamorous rugby family reached the gates of Twickenham for a fourth successive time, on each occasion they were compelled to overcome the semi-final encounters on their opponents' territory. Twickenham of course was neutral, a citadel both uplifting yet frightening in its towering magnificence; a venue where Bath on the 2nd May would once again face the Wasps, semi-final victors at home over Leicester.

These two clubs, who had fought out a tenacious final the previous year, not surprisingly shared a healthy respect for each other; and Bath again studied their 'brief' very thoroughly indeed, aware that with the exception of the as yet uncapped scrum-half Stephen Bates the Londoners could field an all international back-division. Meanwhile Wasps captain and flanker David Pegler (Chronicle, 1st May, 1987) spoke thus of Bath: *"They are England's team of the 1980's and the prototype of what the next generation of successful clubs must be."* So, on a sun-drenched day the scene was set for two of England's finest as they stepped out onto Twickenham's sacred turf as follows:

Bath: *C. Martin, A. Swift (J. Guscott, 55 mins), S.Halliday, J. Palmer, B. Trevaskis, S. Barnes, R. Hill (capt.), D. Sole, G. Dawe (G. Bess, 23 Mins), G. Chilcott, J. Morrison, N. Redman, J. Hall, A. Robinson, D. Egerton.*

Wasps: *H. Davies, S. Smith, K. Simms, R. Lozowski, M. Bailey, R. Andrew, S. Bates, P. Rendall, S. Simmons, J. Probyn, C. Pinnegar, J. Bonner, M. Rigby, M. Rose, D. Pegler (Capt.).* **Referee:** F. Howard (Liverpool Society).

It was this attempt for a fourth successive cup triumph that would test Bath both mentally and physically like never before, and with barely ten minutes remaining it was rampant Wasps who led by a thoroughly deserved margin of 12-4, with doubtless many in the 35,500 crowd now predicting that this top London side were set to clinch it! For near 70 minutes it was their pack, with the back-row of Mark Rose, Mark Rigby and David Pegler hunting and spoiling like rampant hounds, who were masters of the field. By contrast Bath, uncharacteristically tense and unsure, seemed overburdened by the magnitude of their task. Save for a Nigel Redman try (a good one), Wasps had tightened their grip with a Rob Andrew drop-goal and Huw Davies penalty, followed by a smartly taken try, again by the outstanding Huw Davies and Andrew converting.

Indeed, with the clock fast approaching 70 minutes of play it seemed that Bath might at last have reached 'a bridge too far.' However an opportunity was suddenly presented to Stuart Barnes with a penalty chance from a difficult angle and with the wind a potential hazard. But the kick from 40 yards out was bang on target and suddenly Bath were ignited into the fearsome force that all opponents dreaded. Ten minutes remained. Ten minutes that belonged to a Bath team that now extracted every ounce of physical and mental strength it possessed. First a Hill-Barnes dummy and then swift pass to Halliday saw the England centre storm to the line for a try, Barnes converting. Now scenting victory, the real Bath swung once more into action. Barnes received good ball and headed for the line. A ruck followed, Hill collected, fed Redman and the lock stormed over for his second try, Barnes converting. It was barely ten minutes of clinical destruction, but enough to put Bath 19-12 ahead. Referee Fred Howard's whistle was heard again. Game over! Game won! A fourth successive JP Cup triumph and Bath had achieved the near impossible!? Well, not quite!

True, the whistle blew to signal the Stuart Barnes conversion. But hundreds of fans (mistakenly believing that Fred Howard had signalled the end of the game) spilled on to the field in celebration. In fact there had been a brief pitch invasion five minutes earlier when Halliday's converted try sent Bath into a lead. But this second incursion was so large that referee Howard, who had intended to continue the game to ensure a full 40 minutes of play-time, was reportedly communicated by RFU secretary Dudley Wood to conclude the match 'there and then,' believing that it would be impossible to re-start the game. Although purely celebratory, the temporary chaotic scene (albeit calm soon followed) was hardly how Bath would ever have wished this momentous triumph to reach its dramatic climax; and the post-match party at the Rec later that evening was noticeably subdued; likewise the Sunday celebrations around the city culminating as usual with the civic Pump Room reception hosted by the Mayor of Bath, Mr Sam Jane. 'Would the club,' one asked, 'be banned from the competition for the following year?' Would the media, until now so supportive, now turn their ire upon Bath? A worrying few days thus followed.

The issue however was perhaps best put into perspective by Sunday Times rugby correspondent Stephen Jones (10th May, 1987) who reminded readers that the second invasion occurred when the 'clock already showed seven minutes of injury time had passed.' Moreover, considering that the crowd on this occasion was a new record of 35,000 (at least two thirds thought to be Bath supporters) Stephen Jones added: *" How on earth is the game going to increase its following if it turns its nose at new followers? Every year, Bath's success attracts more people to the final and more people to rugby."* Indeed his only criticism of Bath was that following their cup triumph they had put *"as much sweat and energy into apologising for themselves as they put in the cup run."*

To the comments of Stephen Jones one could simply add that in cricket, for example, it is quite normal for crowds to literally storm across the field in joyous acclaim at the climax of crucial County competitions and Test matches…. The Ashes!? And this fact perhaps influenced the RFU governing body. Indeed save for the suggestion from some quarters that the Rugby League method of concluding a match with a klaxon signal might be adopted, Bath were not reprimanded for the events in the closing stages at Twickenham. Indeed it was known that the incident had caused deep anguish throughout the club and overshadowed that otherwise triumphant moment when these one-time journeymen from the West Country raised Rugby's own sword of Excalibur to achieve a feat unequalled in English rugby.

Chapter 30. A BOLT OF LIGHTNING. (1987-90)

As English rugby prepared itself for season 1987-8, a now familiar question reverberated around the clubs of the Land: 'could Bath's cup run be extended for a 5ᵗʰ year?' It no longer seemed impossible; albeit increasingly impatient rivals for the English crown were closing in, circling the Rec like vultures, searching for the merest sign of weakness in fortress Bath's seemingly impregnable defences.

To add to the JP Cup, the season now offered a newly-launched and fully-standardized League competition (the Courage League) with twelve clubs per division, each contesting one game a season and Bath (not surprisingly) included in Division One, and promotion and relegation included in the structure. The first effect was to make non-standardized Leagues obsolete; the second was to add a more competitive element into rugby union. Indirectly there would be a further factor for Bath, who after four unbeaten years in non-stop cup campaigns might find the added 'weight' of the Courage League especially difficult to shoulder. Indeed their opening Courage encounter at Leicester in September suggested that this might be the case. The Tigers, fine-tuned during their tour in New Zealand and Australia, were razor-sharp throughout, fully deserving a 24-13 win in front of an 8,000 home crowd and *"holding Bath with surprising ease in tight forward exchanges and outplaying them in the loose...."* Leicester it seemed could again be a major threat in the JP cup. One week later and Bath faced old foes Moseley, and blocking everything that the Midlanders could hurl at them, won 14-0 comfortably on the Rec. Moseley (ironically in view of later events) appeared to be the lesser threat.

Meanwhile along with welcoming highly-rated St Ives lock/No.8 Martin Haag to the Rec, Damien Cronin (ex Prior Park) would win his first Scotland cap during a season of mixed fortunes that included a warning delivered in early December with Bath's superb 9-16 Courage League win at Gloucester. Yet the realisation that the new Courage League format was heading for success would come (in the opinion of some followers) at a cost, namely the inevitable downgrading and decline of the once-revered County Championship. Hence when John Horton (36 years young and now player-coach of Combe Down) agreed to lead Somerset into their 1987-8 encounter against Gloucestershire, one could only reminisce how merely four years previously these two rivals had contested the final at Twickenham in front of thousands. Yet almost immediately interest in the County game had waned, and senior clubs would only release their reserve players (if that), and junior clubs would now make up the short-fall.

Another alteration would allow (within reason) the game to continue while an injured player was being treated on the pitch, a law-change that virtually killed off overnight the not unknown practice of the 'tactical injury' so as to slow down a game at crucial periods. Crucial too (though not without its 'lighter' moments) was Bath's opening cup campaign at Lichfield, a club who had in recent seasons belied their supposed junior status with cup encounters that had seriously tested the reputations of both London Welsh and Harlequins. But it was Bath's reputation that had alas suffered from the post-match Twickenham pitch-invasion of the previous season that (to the club's mild astonishment), so concerned the local chief of police, that a large contingent of constabulary had been drafted in to first escort the visiting Bath supporters to the home ground, and secondly to remain in the background, but keep a watchful eye on events should trouble suddenly unfold. It is true to relate however that the Staffordshire police need not have worried. Trouble there was none! It is furthermore true to record that with a five thousand crowd watching, Richard Hill's side ran home nine tries, winning by 3-43 against their plucky opponents, and in the words of at least one admiring home supporter proved they were simply *"the best team in Britain."* They would need to be. Their next cup opponents were to be Leicester.....away!

Leicester, who by this stage in early February were looking odds-on to win the newly introduced Courage League in its inaugural season and subsequently doing precisely that; whose domination in early September had subjected an ill-tempered Bath into an emphatic 24-13 defeat; who again held home advantage in front of some 11,000 thousand passionate supporters in the 13,000 crowd, and not surprisingly looked favourites to bring Bath's epic cup-run to an end. But.....after 80 minutes of compulsive action, where Bath's John Palmer had produced *"a near perfect display of tactical kicking,"* and the Bath pack had produced *"a display of awesome power and efficiency,"* and where full-back Phil Cue had struck two penalties, Palmer a drop-goal and David Egerton a crucial try in answer to a Nick Youngs try converted by Dusty Hare, it was the West Countrymen who had clinched a dramatic 6-13 fourth round cup triumph.

An equally dramatic quarter-final encounter would shortly follow at Moseley, a fine side, yet one by now almost weary of the seemingly endless defeats at the hands of the West Countrymen; and following Bath's mighty achievement at Leicester it seemed that another defeat was likely when within 40 seconds Bath were awarded a penalty from 50 yards out. Phil Cue struck cleanly and true. Bath were 3 nil up!

But quite suddenly Moseley, fielding a pack huge in stature, chose this exact moment to show that it could hold, even dominate, the most feared opponents in English rugby. Their front row of Mark Linnett, Chris Barbor and Graham Smith, their locks Al Recardo and Richard Denhardt, their tireless back-row of England's Nick Jeavons, S. Masters and Peter Shillingford would not bow nor give an inch to the Bath eight. Some 15 minutes of huge pressure followed and a shove deep inside Moseley's own hell-fire corner saw Shillingford crash over for a push-over try. It was a roar of Midland defiance, one that now appeared to cast a spell over their opponents. Normally when Bath fell behind in cup encounters there came that almost predictable moment when they decided that the niceties would end and the serious stuff begin. But on this day it never did begin. Kicking duties switched from Cue, to Guscott and finally to David Trick, but to no avail, albeit some attempts missed the target by barely an inch. Confusion then appeared to grip every Bath attempt to rectify an increasingly desperate situation. But nothing worked! Moseley meanwhile tackled and harried everything that moved. It wasn't pretty, as if they cared. It was however the perfect strategy on the day. For the Midlanders sensed, correctly so, that they had caught Bath at that key moment when four years of cup rugby had left them tired, jaded, and crucially no longer hungry. They were literally 'running on empty.'

Minutes passed by, until only seconds remained. Then, with the score on 4-3 the final whistle echoed over the Reddings and throngs of Moseley's faithful erupted into ecstatic joy. For on that day a rugby giant had fallen, for how long one could not say; and Bath supporters, some two thousand in number, did not stay long. Instead they drove off into the night, deep, deep in their own thoughts.

For Bath the Moseley defeat had potentially inflicted a deep psychological wound, one painfully suffered in the full glare of national publicity and no little 'schadenfreude;' and as a consequence the club now stood at a cross-roads that pointed towards two quite different destinations. One road led to the past; the other to the future. Or to borrow an iconic phrase: *"it would either be the beginning of the end.....or the end of the beginning."* Would the remarkable Bath triumphs of recent seasons simply be a freakish accident of rugby history, as suggested by Alan Gibson's pre-match comment (match programme, 1985, Bath v London Welsh final): something *"very pleasant to look back on: but a relief when it is all over?"* Or, could Bath recover and prove that their rugby dynasty was here to stay? For make no mistake, a West Country rugby city felt this defeat to its very bones, mourned too the loss of the cherished crown and dreaded the thought of a future in the shadows, a future of memories only, the glamour and acclaim that had proved so intoxicating all gone.

The task therefore was to sweep bitter disappointment aside, accept the realities and move onwards. Furthermore, the realities were not difficult to pin-point. First, Bath's unprecedented achievement in winning four successive Cup triumphs had taken its inevitable toll upon the players, the club and its resources. Indeed so huge were the demands of the previous four seasons that sooner or later the club would need a fuel-stop; hence the shattering and unexpected crash at Moseley. Yet still the club held trump cards, including their youthful and richly talented squad, plus a coaching triumvirate now revived since the return of Tom Hudson from a two years absence and....a devoted legion of followers!

True it was that the remainder of the 1987-8 season would now lack the glamour of recent years, and some voices were unwisely calling for wholesale changes. But over-reaction was the last thing the club needed. Instead for the first time in four years there was a golden opportunity to relax; and save for one ill-tempered 21-9 League victory

229

against Harlequins, who ironically would later defeat Bristol to win that season's JP Cup final, relaxation is what they were able to enjoy. Meanwhile David Egerton, Bath's 6ft 5in back-row forward won his first of five caps against Ireland in that season's Dublin Millennium match, while on the same day (23rd April) out-half general John Horton was invited to play one final match for Bath (his 379th for the club) prior to his retirement from a game that he had graced for much of his now 37 years. The opponents were Bedford, the result was 35-7 to Bath, and not only did the maestro stroke home the conversion of former Plymouth Albion winger Steve Walklin's try, but in the closing minutes sent over his 125th Bath drop-goal to arouse a rapturous applause from a 3,000 strong worshipping home crowd.

Finally Bath completed the season with Courage League action at Sale. Safe in fourth place in the new League competition, Bath travelled north without a care in the world. It was jokes and banter all the way, and less seven of their internationals rested for the forthcoming England tour to Australia, much on this day would depend upon a number of Bath's less experienced personnel. Watching the game unfold however, one could have been forgiven for thinking that the club were at full strength, so care-free and yet so assured was their play. Skipper Hill's side notched 8 tries (seven converted) and five ran home by the brilliant Guscott alone. Wings Barry Whitehead and Mark Westcott proved a revelation, out-half Jon Bamsay looked an outstanding half-back prospect and prop Steve Kipling not only scrummaged down powerfully, but crunched over for his maiden senior try for Bath. Sale, sadly already relegated (though not for long) played their not insignificant part too, with three Graham Jenion penalties and a two try burst from former Bath winger George Stanton. Yet it was the carnival atmosphere on the field that suggested that perhaps the psychological blows following the Moseley defeat hopefully belonged to the past. Moreover one thing seemed near certain, simply that Bath appeared to be the happy-go-lucky family of not so long ago, and that their spirits had recovered more quickly than their rivals would have hoped.

By season 1988-9 many enthusiasts might have known of the respect for two English clubs as expressed by former Cardiff and Wales scrum-half Terry Holmes, now playing in Rugby League. His then recently launched book 'My Life in Rugby' included his views on the respective strengths of Welsh and English rugby. While arguing that little differed in the quality of players, he suggested that generally the Welsh teams benefited from the more competitive aspect of their inter-club rivalry, as was frequently evident whenever English sides faced their Welsh counterparts. However, he argued that there were two exceptions to this general rule, adding that *some of the hardest games I've played in have been against Leicester and Bath.* How appropriate therefore that come the end of the season it would be these same two rugby families who would meet at Twickenham to contest a truly epic challenge for English rugby supremacy.

For Bath the season under their new captain Stuart Barnes could hardly have started better. Fresh from a relaxing-style tour of Thailand, Malaysia and finally Holland, a journey that notched five straight wins including victory over French champions Toulon in Leiden, Bath now proceeded to run riot at Pontypool with a 9-50 domestic campaign-opener that registered their 'now' biggest-ever win on Welsh soil. Shown live on BBC Wales, Peter Bills (The Times 5th September) wrote thus: " *Bath played such breathtaking rugby that many of the basic skills captured by the television cameras covering a club match live for the first time ought to become mandatory viewing for youngsters.*" Indeed rampant Bath would remain unbeaten for 30 matches until mid-February, by which time the 4th round of the cup (now sponsored by Pilkington) had already been completed. Yet it was not merely the quantity of victories that impressed, but the quality also, for some of British rugby's finest were listed among the vanquished. Llanelli for instance were defeated initially 12-25 and 4-20 respectively in Wales before their 43-25 fall at Bath in mid-April. In fact it barely mattered whether or not Bath played 'home or foreign,' as Courage League away opponents Harlequins (9-26), Rosslyn Park (6-19) and Moseley (0-38) would all doubtless have testified; and likewise defeated home Courage League opponents Gloucester (19-9) and Bristol (16-9). Even the two drawn games were exhilarating to witness, namely the October 24-24 sublime spectacle with visitors Stade Toulousain and the December 21-21 result at Newport with a virtual reserve side during a Divisional match weekend.

But cup rugby is different, as Bath could testify when one season previously, bemused and shell-shocked, they had succumbed at Moseley to cup humiliation; and now as the 3rd round loomed (that stage of the competition when the senior clubs entered the fray) it was to be visitors Oxford RFC who in late January would be the first to test Bath's cup resolve. The match looked straightforward on paper (as once it did at Brixham!), and though cup rugby is where giants are known to fall, Bath were too hot to handle on the day. "*Their support work is absolutely superb,*" Oxford skipper and flanker Roy Davies (formerly of Sale) later concluded after a cavalier home performance had yielded 16 tries (9 converted by Stuart Barnes) of which full-back Audley Lumsden and wing Tony Swift had touched down four apiece, and fellow back Freddie Sagoe had claimed a hat-trick. Nonetheless much to the delight of both Oxford and a generous 5,000 home crowd the visitors did get on the score-board too, thanks to Andy Tiplady's penalty and a further Tiplady conversion of a full-back Steve Lazenby try. But the final result of 82-9 spelled out a warning, voiced by Oxford skipper Davies: "*I can't see anyone to touch them.*"

Now it would be Hereford's turn to test this prediction, and sensibly Bath would be taking no chances, not least as their opponents had reached the 4th round thanks to a highly creditable 10-6 home win over Tyndale, a club little known in the West Country but rightly respected in the North as a tough no-nonsense Northumberland outfit. For the Herefordians therefore this was a dream tie; the chance of a life-time to play a top side and with the additional financial bonus provided by their guaranteed half-share of the attendance receipts, a standard practice in the National K.O. Cup, albeit the combined attendance receipts from the semi-finals and the final were directed to the RFU for general distribution throughout English rugby.

So with some £2,000 gate revenue already assured (Chronicle, 10th February, 1989), plus another £1,800 from sponsors Pilkington for all 4th round losers (should Hereford lose!), this team built upon men of the Forest of Dean, mid-Wales and local Herefordians now prepared for cup action against four-times winners Bath; and with the early February conditions in fact suitable for running rugby, running rugby it seemed would be the order of the day. But in a first half where Hereford had *"played with such passionate commitment and tackled so well that they limited Bath to just one score,"* Bath's finest backs did not enjoy the freedom of the park. In addition the visitors, led by flanker Alan Hill, revealed two impressively good defensive kickers in out-half Nick Morgan and full-back Stuart Dovey. So effective moreover were these tactics of containment that Bath were now compelled to adopt a totally different strategy for the second half. Out went any ideas of an easy afternoon. Instead Bath concentrated on grinding down Hereford in a no-nonsense game of attrition, while superior fitness would also take its toll. Thus nine further tries were added to Freddie Sagoe's first half opener and the score-board closed at 48-0. Nonetheless, through their first-half endeavours Hereford had stamped their mark upon the Rec; had earned the respect of a 5,000 strong crowd and departed homewards with Bath captain Stuart Barnes singing their praises.

So far, so good; as not only were the previous ties played on home soil, but Bath had avoided the 'heavyweights.' Now that was about to change. Yes, they were cruising through the Courage League like a demolition squad; and yes, they had overcome two courageous cup opponents. But in drawing Bristol (last season's finalists) for the quarter-finals, Bath were now facing one of the biggest beasts of all. Again on home territory, the match was an 8,500 sell-out; and significantly only recently the RFU had introduced an instruction that from the quarter-finals onwards all touch-judges must forthwith be chosen from a pool of neutral qualified referees now ordained with the authority to 'draw the referee's attention to any incidents of foul play.'

It was a logical and broadly welcomed change. It was furthermore a quarter-final that the recently empowered touch-judges Matt Bayliss (Gloucestershire) and Keith Hosking (Devon) would likely never forget, and not merely because it was played on a mud-bath to beat all mud-baths. Rain, sleet and snow just emptied onto the already saturated Rec. Not merely pools, but ponds of water accumulated virtually everywhere, and yet somehow two teams not only played on it, they played open running rugby on it. They passed and they held passes. They went for try scores and they got try scores. They tackled like men possessed, ran themselves to near exhaustion, and at the final whistle they virtually collapsed from their endeavours in a ferocious struggle played at an equally ferocious pace. It was furthermore the game that initially Bristol had wished to play and Bath had not; but after 80 minutes of knife-edged drama it was the game that Bristol wished had not been played and Bath were delighted that it had.

How referee Andrew Mason kept the game going was a miracle, yet witnessed that day was one of the greatest cup-ties many observers claimed they had ever seen. First it was Bristol who shook the hosts with a performance so commanding that by the time of their 4-12 half-time lead it seemed questionable whether or not Bath could close the gap in conditions so atrocious. Bristolian and England full-back Jonathan Webb was in peerless form, coolly sending two penalties over the posts and gliding home for a try he duly converted from a perfectly executed Paul Collings and Simon Hogg switch pass movement. Bath's reply was a superbly executed passing move between John Hall, skipper Barnes and Halliday that culminated in a Guscott try.

The second half however saw a home side fight-back that would have broken through virtually any opposition in England, save the seemingly un-breakable defence-wall that was Bristol. Moreover the two Stuart Barnes early second-half penalties reducing the score to 10-12 were not sufficient to steal a lead with the clock only three minutes from full-time. Then despite a final desperate Bath surge at forward for victory, one that reached the Bristol line, it was opposing skipper Andy Dun's pack who were awarded a life-saving put-in. A Bristol victory now seemed assured as Harding fed the set scrum. But those treacherous conditions played one final trick. The slippery ball spat out of the scrum at an awkward angle, and Bath scrum-half Richard Hill, a tiger as ever, snatched at the ball, somehow held it, and shot over the line. Barnes could not add the conversion. But it did not matter. It was now 14-12 to Bath, and too late for a Bristol reply. Thus ended a magnificent trial of strength played between two giants, but with only one winner. Yet if there was one message above all from this titanic quarter-final, it would be the return of Bath's grim determination to fight back from a losing position, just about the last bit of news that English rugby wanted to hear.

However, winning trophies was not the sole objective at Bath, and there were reasons enough to celebrate other accomplishments, not least the rise and rise of Gareth Chilcott. Long known as a maverick with one too many dismissals from one too many battles on his rugby CV, the Rec favourite who could handle both sides of the front-row war zone had by now undergone a transformation. Yet few knew of his other battles fought against the ravages of near-crippling injuries sustained in earlier days, some so severe that this tree-feller from Compton Dando was twice told that he might never play rugby again. Arguably the greatest threat to his sporting future had been a congenital malformation of his knee joints, an injury that in a previous era would have finished his sporting career. But thanks to the masterful skills of specialists at the RUH a recovery gradually followed. Hence Chilcott, known affectionately as 'Coochie' (or 'Oddjob,' as in James Bond's Goldfinger) was by now both role-model and hero. Indeed in the aftermath of his international performance during his Country's 11- nil home win over France in early March (1989) he was hailed as 'the iron man of

England!' Selection for the British Lions summer tour would soon follow; and the former bad-boy of English rugby now found himself elevated to cult-figure status.

But now for Chilcott and his Bath colleagues another steep slope suddenly loomed ahead, the spectre again of Gloucester in another semi-final.....at Kingsholm! A sell-out crowd of 10,500 watched. Full-back Tim Smith's penalty gave Gloucester an early lead. The forward onslaught and tackling was as ferocious as that witnessed in the Bath v Bristol quarter-final. Referee Roger Quittenton kept matters under tight control nonetheless. The Bath back-row of Jon Hall, Dave Egerton and the tireless Andy Robinson were possibly the stars among stars on the day, while the mature tactical kicking of Barnes and the darting breaks of Hill at half-back rattled Gloucester sufficiently to ensure that they could not dominate events. Even the fearful shower of 'bombs' falling out of the sky from the boots of Gloucester backs Mike Hamlin and Damien Cummins failed to un-nerve full-back Audley Lumsden, Bath's superb young utility-back discovery. He proved unshakeable, so too skipper Barnes whose two penalties put Bath into a fragile three point lead. But although no side will fight harder than Gloucester when only one score down, Bath's re-born ability to absorb even the most tenacious of pressure held off the final furious attacks to secure a 3-6 thriller.

It was learned soon enough that with their 7-16 victory over Harlequins, Leicester would be faced in the final; and coincidentally would meet Bath twice within seven days with the mutual concluding Courage League match fixed one week prior to the Twickenham date.

These then were interesting days, not only in rugby matters on the field, but in financial matters off it. Because the reality was that if the game was to expand then clubs would need money! It was therefore heartening for Bath that in the New Year (Chronicle, 9th January 1989) they had finalised a £150,000 sponsorship agreement with the South Western Electricity Board (SWEB), 'the biggest-ever such deal so far in club rugby.' Even Leicester's then current £100,000 brewery sponsorship was now eclipsed. It was significant too that RFU secretary Dudley Wood congratulated Bath *on the outstanding comprehensive nature of the whole scheme...."* essential moreover if the club, in the words of secretary Clive Howard, was to realise plans to not only improve their facilities, but furthermore to assist Bath to widen horizons into European rugby and hopefully to tour into the Southern hemisphere. In other words Bath were not only thinking big, they were now thinking global.

Something else (or to be precise 'someone' else) was also set to go global in the not-too-distant future. As yet he was a member of the Bath squad busily preparing for both League and Cup Final action. But cometh the hour....cometh the man! And that man would be the charismatic Jeremy Guscott; and that hour would be England's clash on 13th May against Romania, who six months previously had overwhelmed Wales. Once told by David Trick to let his rugby (not his mouth) do the talking, the boy wonder would proceed to do precisely that. Will Carling was injured, so the selectors gambled on Guscott. Three dazzling tries on his debut in his Country's 58-3 win in Bucharest and the selectors had seen enough. The boy (sorry...the young man) was promptly selected to join Chilcott for the British Lions in Australia. There it was confirmed what some had long predicted....Guscott was world class! It was as simple as that.

But prior to Guscott stepping on to the international stage, he and his colleagues on 29th April were set to confront Leicester, whose 15-12 home win of the previous week had holed Bath's unbeaten League record, though not as it happened their crowning as Courage League champions. Twickenham however is 'another country,' a pageantry of rosettes, of teeming throngs, of champagne picnics in nearby car-parks, of smiles and electrifying excitement among the fans. Meanwhile the Bath team and officials had stayed overnight at a West End hotel; so hardly surprising that such expense left little change, if any, of the £3,750 Pilkington sponsorship guaranteed to both finalists. But Bath were adamant that such an outlay was money well spent. Furthermore, although the huge gate receipts for the final (likewise the semi-final) were distributed by the RFU amongst the entire English rugby game, the success at Bath had already led directly to their considerable SWEB sponsorship deal.

Sadly a serious neck injury had thwarted the near-certain selection at full-back of England B international Audley Lumsden, although the hugely experienced John Palmer would prove invaluable on the day. And what a day! A world rugby club record of 59,300 and two of the best teams in England to fight for the crown:

Bath: J. *Palmer, A. Swift, S. Halliday, J. Guscott, F. Sagoe, S. Barnes (capt), R. Hill, G. Chilcott, G. Dawe, R. Lee, J. Morrison, D. Cronin, J. Hall, A.Robinson, D. Egerton (P. Simpson 53 mins)*.

Leicester: *W. Hare, B.Evans, P. Dodge (capt), I. Bates, R. Underwood, L.Cusworth, A. Kardooni, S. Redfern, T. Thacker, W. Richardson, M. Foulkes-Arnold, T.Smith, J. Wells, I. Smith, D. Richards.* **Referee:** F.Howard (Liverpool Society).

Again, this was to be a contest between equals. Yet someone had to win. Each team could play it tight or open, each possessed match-winners, each fielded internationals, each had won a hat-trick of successive cup victories, and it was the toss of a coin as to who would triumph. In first-half action Leicester lock Tim Smith contained the line-out threat of Bath's Morrison and Cronin. The Tigers' back-row of John Wells, Ian Smith and the mighty Dean Richards held Bath's renowned back-row in check. On fifteen minutes Halliday (perhaps the best centre in England) intercepted a Leicester pass into empty space near half-way, a lethal threat nonetheless saved by Underwood, perhaps the one back in England then able to catch the Bath centre from behind. Leicester pressure was enough however to provide an opportunity for England full-back Dusty Hare (playing his final senior game) to send over two successful penalties and secure for Leicester a 6-0 breathing space at half-time.

But this tenuous lead was not wide enough to dent the self-belief so evident in Bath's second-half performance. Not disheartened by Leicester's opening half resilience, their own back-row of Jon Hall, Dave Egerton and the tearaway Andy Robinson (Whitbread Rugby World player of the year) now prowled the field like famished wolves. Meanwhile it was The Guardian's Robert Armstrong who perhaps best described the stunning performance of Scotland lock Damien Cronin who *"drove with the kind of awesome momentum that scatters defenders like pigeons."* Thus gradually the Bath eight took a second half command, and as John Stevens wrote: *"the physical strength and scrummaging techniques of the Bath pack was decisive."* Never more so in fact than a titanic surge on 78 minutes that created a ruck 25 yards out from the Leicester line on the left flank. Again the still hungry back-row (Paul Simpson having replaced the injured Egerton) shielded the ball to Hill who fed danger-man Barnes. The Bath skipper, having coolly slotted home two second-half penalties (neither easy) sensed instinctively that he could go for the 'kill,' and feinting a pass to power-wing Fred Sagoe instead cut inside two despairing defenders to literally crash-dive over the line. It was 10-6. The conversion failed. But it didn't matter. Barely two minutes remained.....too late for gallant Leicester!

Once more for the fifth time in six seasons Bath had triumphed in the Cup. Actually they had won the cup (now Pilkington Cup) and Courage League Double. Once more it was the Sunday evening joyous open bus journey around the streets and houses to acknowledge the adulation of a rugby-proud city. Onwards to the Pump Room, the mayor no less than Commander John Malloy awaiting to entertain the team to a civic reception, and an evening amid the splendour of the Abbey and the Roman Baths. Unforgettable!

It was 1989-90, a season that would conclude an epic decade for Bath, and it seemed that nothing could surpass the sheer scale of the achievements since that first Twickenham triumph of 1984. Well, something in fact did! But first things first, and Bath would launch their new season in typically flamboyant style, ending a September carnival with a 13-17 victory at Neath in a month's rugby that had included home wins over Pontypool, Harlequins and an emphatic 32-12 success over Romanian champions Steaua Bucharest.

An excellent start, although the request by the England selectors that in the interests of international preparations the national squad players should restrict their pre-Christmas schedule solely to Courage League and Divisional matches placed restrictions on virtually half the current Bath first team. Yet come 3rd February 1990 the brilliant 7-26 England victory against France in Paris (Richard Hill and Guscott both playing), and described by coach Geoff Cooke as *"one of England's finest performances in our rugby history,"* did support the national selectors' argument.

Furthermore, two factors softened this England squad requirement on Bath resources. First, the quality of the United side was now so high, (their own home gates on occasions were topping 1,000 spectators) that quality back-up for first team matches was readily available. Secondly, Bath's new five-year plan had widened the net to encourage the arrival of new talent that included a trio of Nigerian-born, but West Country educated players, namely Oxford Blue prop Victor Ubogu, 'Dayo' Adebayo and Steve Ojomoh. Furthermore a number of these newcomers were pitched in at Aberavon in early October, among them former England schools internationals Adebayo and Alistair Saverimutto (backs) and flanker Steve Ojomoh. Playing too were Jon Callard (ex Newport) at full-back and prop Chris Folland, as Bath *"then proceeded to destroy Aberavon with a blistering display of finishing power"* to secure a 6-32 away win, their biggest ever at Port Talbot.

The winning trail would then continue until early March, bar defeats at the hands of French visitors Toulon (whose 14-26 victory in mid-October avenged their previous season's defeat by Bath in Holland), and Swansea's 17-9 success in late December. The Cup remained Bath's chief target though, the senior clubs joining at the third round stage, and Harlequins drawn 'out of the hat' on the Rec, thus a home tie providing some compensation for facing opposition so potentially strong as Quins. Not for the first time however the elements would now intervene, and with conditions reminiscent of the epic Bath v Bristol quarter-final of the previous season Harlequins wisely selected a wet weather side for the encounter.

Predictably the game developed into a hard slog where two packs contested a game of raw attrition, and it was fortunate too that Bath were far from inexperienced in such conditions. The Quins fielded England's Paul Ackford and Richard Langhorn at lock, plus an all-international back-row of Mickey Skinner, Peter Winterbottom and Chris Butcher; and only the best could equal such power and class. Happily for Bath they possessed some of the best, including locks Redman, and try-scorer Cronin who crashed over for the game's lone try converted by Barnes. In the second half (referee Ian Bullerwell having ordered a shirt-change for both teams at half-time) Barnes made a touchline penalty kick look easy. That gave Bath a 9-0 margin, one they never increased nor needed to, as for all their efforts the Quins could not gain the desperately needed catch-up points.

Next Headingley would be arriving from the North, on paper at least a kinder draw. But heavy (mid-February) rainfall offered the tough Yorkshire side their best chance of getting even. They too could normally handle such conditions, although not Bath's reaction to the early successful penalty by Headingley's Matthew Johnson, when almost immediately the home pack took matters into their own hands, *"driving forward with awesome thoroughness."* Four tries then followed, with Hall powering over for a brace. Barnes struck home with a further three conversions and a penalty, and Bath were clear at 25-3 within five minutes of the re-start. Thus with the job effectively completed Barnes and his mud-covered team were content to simply preserve their comfortable lead. Tempers flared on occasions as the conditions deteriorated yet further, but it was another workmanxclike victory and a place in the quarter-finals was now assured.

Richmond, with former Bath hooker Rob Cunningham on their coaching panel, would provide the opposition, so enabling Bath to avoid potentially greater threats lurking in a dangerously strong quarter-final pool that included among others Leicester and Gloucester. But Bath were taking no chances, not least as one week previously observers dispatched from the Rec had witnessed the West Londoners hold visitors Bristol to an impressive 21-21 draw. In the quarter-final however it was evident that a gutsy Richmond, *"whose tackling and covering was of the highest order,"* had peaked one week too soon. For despite an early lead from out-half Martin Livesey's penalty, their undoubted courage could not constrain indefinitely Bath's mastery at forward, a domination that proceeded to establish a platform for a six try haul and 3-35 victory.

Richmond clearly did not lack for individual ability, as wing Jim Fallon (soon to join Bath) among others showed. But their geography denied them the easy access to the rugby strong-hold of Wales and thus the opportunity of regular action against the likes of Llanelli, Swansea, Pontypool and Cardiff. In this quarter-final against a Bath club battle-hardened against Celtic opposition this drawback showed. But whether something similar would show in the semi-final was less certain, because Bath were drawn away at.....Moseley!! Now, in the Autumn the Midlanders had already fallen 27-9 in Courage League action on the Rec. But the Reddings was not the Rec, but a venue of recent painful memories. It was hardly surprising therefore that Moseley skipper Bob Barr could not resist injecting a touch of mischievous psychology into the pre-match preparations. His words were few, but none missed the intended target: *"we are well aware that they [Bath] still remember vividly what happened the last time they came up here in the cup,"* and he wasn't wrong either.

For Bath did indeed remember, and true it was that a psychological hurdle must first be overcome before anyone in the city would even dare think of a cup win at Moseley. Nor did it calm the anxieties of Bath followers when it was learned that the brilliant Guscott was inexplicably excluded from the Bath line-up. Furthermore, although Moseley were by now languishing in the lower reaches of the Courage League, in Edinburgh only one week previously Scotland, led by former Bath prop David Sole, had defeated clear favourites England by 7-13 to win the Grand Slam. Was this an ill-omen?

The answer was an emphatic 'Nein!' and watched by an estimated 9,000 crowd Moseley's *"heavyweight pack was systematically dismantled by the ruthless efficiency of the Bath' eight,"* namely a front-row block of Chilcott, Dawe and Victor Ubogu, the line-out domination from Redman and Cronin, and the incessant marauding of back-row lions Andy Robinson, Simpson and Egerton. Thus three tries resulted, the first a 30 yard sprint home by wing Tony Swift followed by a Chilcott charge-down score, and finally Callard (so assured at full-back) swerved effortlessly home for a third. Barnes

238

nailed all three conversions and added a penalty; while for the hosts there was little to savour apart from a Carl Arntzen penalty and a Chris Allen try. But the score-board read 7-21 on the final whistle. It had been an afternoon of cold, clinical destruction, and for Bath a release from the memory of humiliating defeat. Now at ease with themselves once again, the club was in the right frame of mind for another final, and it was just as well that they were.....because their opponents this time at Twickenham would be Gloucester!

Gloucester, 12-17 semi-final victors away at Northampton, a team hard as iron, defeating Bath 13-6 at Kingsholm in early season but falling 12-9 at Bath in February....this was going to be 'some' final. Furthermore there were places still to be won, so tight was the competition. Just how tight in fact was demonstrated in Bath's early April 6-25 win at Newport less ten regulars; with Haag prominent at lock, likewise Steve Knight and Keith Plummer proving themselves excellent half-back partners, and wing Peter Blackett staking his own Twickenham claim during his best season yet. Trick then rekindled memories of past glories with a 40 yard streak towards another score. Hooker Jimmy Deane (all high-octane energy) snatched a third, while recent arrival Jonathan Webb, who had departed from Bristol both disillusioned and seemingly out of favour with England, sealed an impressive debut at full-back with three conversions, a penalty and a gem of a try. Thus possessing strength in depth, even the club's finest could not rest for fear of losing a coveted place against Gloucester.

Yet Gloucester somehow have always been different to any other club in England, unique in fact. Defiance personified, they can put the fear of God into some opponents, and one slip-up by Bath at Twickenham could spell disaster. But although Gloucester were no novices outside the scrum, their great strength lay in the 10-man game; while Bath (if winning sufficient ball) could play expansive 15-man rugby and run riot. But when on the 5th May the following combatants stepped out of the tunnel at Twickenham few would have realised that never once in their history had Bath ever really opened-up against Gloucester, and it was conjecture only that they would do so now in the stifling tensions of a cup final:

Bath: *J. Callard, A. Swift, S. Halliday, J. Guscott, A. Adebayo, S. Barnes (capt.), R.Hill (S. Knight, 71 mins), V. Ugogu, G. Dawe, G. Chilcott, N. Redman, D. Cronin, A. Robinson, K. Withey, D.Egerton.*

Gloucester: *T. Smith, D. Morgan, D. Caskie, R. Mogg, J. Breeze, M. Hamlin (capt.), M. Hannaford, M. Preedy, K. Dunn, R. Pascall, N. Scrivens, J. Brain, J. Gadd, I. Smith, M. Teague.* **Referee:** F. Howard (Liverpool Society).

Bath it was who ran out from the tunnel. Gloucester by contrast walked, as had victorious Scotland in Edinburgh against England in March. Some therefore among the capacity 52,000 throng (attendance limited by stadium expansion) may have perceived that Gloucester tactics would mirror those of Scotland. If so, they perceived correctly, and so commenced a final described by the Sunday Times as *"probably the most remarkable club match ever played."* Two fearsome packs initially locked horns in a struggle for forward domination, and two full-backs were tested to a barrage of 'bombs' booted high into the sky by half-backs Hill and Barnes (Bath) and Hamlin and Hannaford (Gloucester). Stalemate at first, but then fireworks after barely ten minutes when Bath flanker Kevin Withey seized loose line-out ball and ran blind-side, weaving and breaking grasping tackles for fully 50 yards to score in the left corner, Barnes calmly converting as if kicking a 'sitter' in front of the posts. Soon Barnes kicked home a long-range penalty with the same nonchalance, and Bath, with a 9 point gap, suddenly looked a side liberated.

Their pack proved the equals of the Gloucester front five, and thriving on the magnificent contributions of Cronin and Egerton in line-outs and loose, an increasing supply of clean ball was dispatched, via Hill, into the hands of a back division thriving on ball fed in perfect conditions. And now, Bath really 'cut loose!' Guscott (fed by Halliday) then broke diagonally clean through, fed Swift whose return pass saw the British Lion streak inwards for try number two, Barnes coolly converting again. Next it was the turn of the assured Callard, who seizing ball some 30 yards out kicked ahead once, then twice and amid utter confusion in Gloucester ranks tore home for try number three.

Soon Bath's lead would extend to 25 points when on the verge of half-time, a wayward Gloucester pass dangerously near the Bath line was dramatically intercepted by Tony Swift. With an instinctive swerve and jink wrong-footing two opponents the Lancastrian bullet suddenly saw virtually an entire field of open space in front of him, and with two of Gloucester's fastest trailing in his slip-stream the winger struck.....like a bolt of lightning! Try!

It was simply stunning and stunningly simple, and cometh the lightning, cometh the storm! While Bath were now in complete command, Gloucester were now enduring the worst 80 minutes in their otherwise glorious history. Within two minutes into the second half the superb Stuart Barnes (ironically not enjoying one of his best kicking days) nonetheless extended the lead with another penalty. A temporary Bath 'breather' then followed that allowed Gloucester a well-executed Kevin Dunn try converted by Tim Smith. But Bath did not relax for long, and from the moment that Gloucester flanker John Gadd got marching orders it was carnival rugby all the way to the final whistle. Heat beat down upon a sun-drenched Twickenham, so hot it reached a reported 90 degrees out in the middle. Wisely in such conditions when injuries interrupted play, Bath, as ordered by their coaches, sheltered within the cooling shadows of the West stand. Not so Gloucester. Again, Bath played all the right cards.

Next Callard and Swift demonstrated their inter-passing skills to send the Lancastrian shooting over for his second try. Graham Dawe then waltzed through for another try, Barnes converting. It mattered not that in the final ten minutes Steve Knight effortlessly replaced scrum-half Richard Hill. Everything was working like clockwork. So the deluge continued and the superb Withey, with another break, fed the charging Redman who crashed over for try number seven; while prop Victor Ubogu, not one who likes to be upstaged, then poached loose ball from careless Gloucester handling to charge home for number eight behind the posts. How fitting that the peerless Halliday (soon to leave Bath) was invited to administer the 'coup de grâce' with the conversion attempt. Simon's kick duly sailed between the posts, and at last Gloucester's agony was over.....48-6!!

The interception! The Bolt of Lightning ! In short Tony Swift,
Bath 48 v Gloucester 6, 1989-90, Twickenham Cup Final

Acknowledgements: Bath Chronicle

So ended the 1980's, unquestionably the most remarkable decade for Bath since their formation in 1865, and arguably for English club rugby too; a decade whose final enthralling act was aptly staged upon the green field of Twickenham. The national press, not surprisingly, heaped undiluted praise upon the performance, with both The Independent and The Sunday Express proclaiming that "*It was slaughter in the sun.*" The Observer wrote of "*a thunderous occasion and a thunderous match played at breathtaking speed.*" The Mail on Sunday described the event as "*one of the most complete displays of 15-man rugby you could ever wish to see.*" For those lost for words, as many were, perhaps it was necessary to rely upon the abstract to explain a result so dazzling, so extravagant, as simply 'surreal.' Or in the words of the Sunday Mirror, Bath were now *"the uncrowned kings of club rugby."*

Uncrowned kings? Well no longer! For the total victory at Twickenham had enthroned Bath as the undisputed ruling dynasty of an entire English rugby domain.

Chapter 31. TO PLAY WITH ONE HEARTBEAT. (1990-94)

It was during the summer months of 1990 (Chronicle, 28ᵗʰ August 1990) that John Stevens, the 'voice of rugby,' chose to retire from a profession (and in his case a vocation) that he had served for 37 years. During more than three decades with the Bath Chronicle he had established himself as friend to more than a generation of Bath players, and moreover to countless readers, who followed his perceptive reports on the everyday life, setbacks and successes of a club that he loved. He spoke always from the heart, and his 'word' would earn a respect and an authority for which any sports writer would crave. But do not be lulled into assuming that JS (affectionately known as **'scoop'**) *ever 'pulled his punches.' For he could (and not infrequently did) say things as he saw them. He was no home-side flatterer therefore. But all who knew him, and it seemed that most of the city did, always respected his thoughtful honesty, and over the years his word became almost gospel.*

In his place The Bath Chronicle appointed the young Alan Pearey, the son of the then current president of the RFU, namely Mike Pearey, former Royal Navy and Barbarians centre three-quarter. Alan too would soon enough be adopted into the Bath rugby family, and in his inaugural season on the Rec he would have much to tell.

It was summer 1990, a new decade beckoned, and Bath busily prepared for their departure to Australia in early August for the most ambitious tour in their history so far. But in the background to this otherwise joyful time there lurked a shadow of discontent among a certain section of the club; for to the startled dismay of everyone (both players and countless followers) coaches Dave Robson and Tom Hudson had unexpectedly resigned! The issue, so one was led to believe (Chronicle, 3ʳᵈ August, 1990), concerned their dissatisfaction with the management committee, not merely regarding the chaotic fixture congestion at the outset of the forthcoming domestic season, but furthermore widely conflicting opinions as how to plan for the club's long-term future. Alarm, not surprisingly, was the immediate reaction throughout the club, a close-knit rugby family now fearful of the possible consequences of this break-up of arguably the most revered coaching team in English rugby.

Only three months previously the world seemed a different place, as Bath basked in the glory of their dazzling Twickenham triumph. Yet already it was obvious that an ever-improving cadre of elite clubs were now aware of a breach in Bath's otherwise impregnable armour, a breach not inflicted from without, but from within. *"I think that Bath will go down-hill,"* Dave Robson (Chronicle, 3ʳᵈ September, 1990) further stated, words that would have sounded like music to a cluster of rivals, each hungry for the prestigious silverware now stacked up in Bath's ever bulging trophy cupboard.

Yet if this was not enough uncomfortable news for Bath to ponder, on the day of their departure to Australia eight Bath players (all with first-team experience) announced a mass exodus from the club, among them the outstanding Phil Cue, Barry Trevaskis and Ben Cundy; and soon to be followed by forward stalwarts Jon Morrison to Bristol and Twickenham hero Kevin Withey to Newport.

In fairness to those departing elsewhere, their best days were either over and/or better opportunities for regular first team rugby were available elsewhere. And Clifton, newly promoted to the National League Three and who over the years had provided a number of outstanding players to Bath, would now be the chief beneficiaries of this exodus. Meanwhile four seriously difficult matches between the 9th to 22nd August awaited Bath Down Under. While on their return a ludicrous total of four top flight games were scheduled to be played within a mere eight days in the first week of September, a schedule that comprised just one of a number of reasons for the Robson/Hudson resignation.

But Australia is, well Australia! The opposition was top-ranking, the rugby was hard, and yet Bath (less those on tour with England in Argentina) proved marginally stronger at forward throughout. Enjoyment was another aim (and why not?), and as Stuart Barnes explained *"although winning was high on the agenda....developing fitness and team spirit for next month's domestic season [was] equally important."* The opener at Cairns (Northern Queensland) against a star-studded international Barbarians team, and a game hailed *"as one of the best ever seen on the ground"* climaxed with 24-27 Bath victory. The second against a Darling Downs Invitation XV was a 19-19 draw. Next were Queensland fielding some of Australia's finest talent, and a narrow 21-19 defeat for the tourists. Finally Bath faced Australian club champions Randwick and Aussie legend Mark Ella. True to form, the out-half wizard duly climaxed a 60 yard handling movement with a try gem, and Bath less nine of their 1990 cup finalists fell 20-3, notwithstanding refereeing described (rightly or wrongly) as 'atrocious' by Bath team manager Richard Seaman. However, in terms of sheer enjoyment, of new friendships, of levels of fitness attained and rugby experience gained, the tour was deemed a success.

And on return any lingering doubts would soon be dispelled, notwithstanding that an ad hoc team was tasked with opening the season at Pontypool (not the nicest experience for an under-strength side), and suffering a 34-17 drubbing as a result. The following day would be the real test however, when touring Romania (victors over France four months previously and ironically mentored by Dave Robson) were over-run 38-9 by a rampant Bath team that was superior in every department, not least at centre where an on-form Jon Bamsey blended impressively with Oxford student Phil de Glanville. Three days later, the third match in five days, top French side Toulouse were over-run 44-6 in a win described by The Chronicle as *"an awesome performance."*

Ten days onwards and Cardiff arrived on the Rec, only to return to Wales the worse for a 45-23 defeat; and if any more doubts remained as to whether or not Bath possessed the capacity to recover from those internal pre-season shocks, then such misgivings would be dispelled by their stunning Autumn Courage League form that returned six straight victories over some of England's best and climaxed with a 3-9 victory at Leicester! Heady stuff, and inspiring results that suggested that Bath had solved the morale-sapping coaching dilemma more successfully than anyone would have dared predict. But solved it was, and moreover by keeping things simple. Thus an internal problem was made good by an internal solution, and relying on instinct Bath lost little time in recruiting from their own home-produced resources. Thus the hugely experienced Simon Jones and John Palmer were appointed to join Jack Rowell's coaching panel, with Gareth Chilcott as player-coach. As for the effect, it was as dramatic as it was swift, and proof that Bath did not need to 'sweep' the Country in order to recruit other high profile coaches to the Rec.

Jack Rowell ....a very great coach.

Acknowledgements: Reg. Monk

But soon enough another shock occurred when, having mastered and overcome Leicester 3-9 at Welford Road in the Courage League, they subsequently fell 0-12 one week later to the Midlanders on the Rec in the 3rd round of the Pilkington Cup, a venue where no opponent had succeeded against Bath in the competition since Rosslyn Park in January 1982. This was to some degree another Moseley 'moment.' But there were differences, because the team were not suffering from fatigue, their injury list was no more severe than Leicester's, and unlike at Moseley they lost on home territory. Quite possibly over-confidence was a factor for this set-back. However, another undeniable cause was the commanding performance of Leicester's England No.8 Dean Richards and the eye-catching debut of a then little known youthful lock by the name of Martin Johnson. A dozen years later he would captain England to World Cup glory in Sydney.

Yet interestingly, in sharp contrast to the soul searching that followed the aftermath at Moseley, this latest cup defeat drew a quite different response. Certainly there was deep disappointment at so early an exit from a competition of such electrifying excitement. Yet no excuses were given, instead an acknowledgement that the better side won on the day. Moreover Bath had 'moved on,' accepting that upsets were inevitable and that it was fanciful to believe that a team could win everything. Anyhow, pride could be restored in other fields, not least the Courage League, and here Bath's response was to be little short of inspirational.

Inspiring too was the performance of the back-row trio of Andy Robinson, David Egerton and blindside flanker Jon Hall. Indeed Hall, after a partly self-imposed three year international absence, not least through injuries, was again recalled for England against Argentina in November. Alas, the curse of injury would strike again while training in Lanzarote, ruling out Hall from the 1990-1 Home Championship and the opportunity to shine in the window of opportunity for a coveted England place in the Rugby World Cup of the following season.

Mercifully injuries did not impact too much on the progress of a new cadre of Bath players, and whose abilities were demonstrated (and not for the first time either) in Bath's 42-6 December home win over London Welsh. Cornwall lock forward recruit Andy Reed (Plymouth Albion), front-row new boys Chris Atkins and John Mallett, utility forwards Gareth Adams and Julian Olds would all prove themselves 'up to the mark' at this level; so too a string of potentially exciting backs, among them young Cornish scrum-half Ian Sanders, powerful wing Jim Fallon (formerly Richmond) and Laurie Heatherley, a typically tough New Zealand centre and probably the first Kiwi to play in a Bath first-team shirt.

One week later (19th December) guest side Bath played Toulouse in their own Centenary rugby celebrations, and as Heatherley would find out, French teams do not relish losing to an English club, and certainly not on Gallic soil. So it was that Toulouse (much chastened by early season defeat at Bath) would ensure that Heatherley and his team-mates were to experience a game that none would ever likely forget. Entente Cordiale it wasn't! Instead as Bath Chronicle correspondent Alan Pearey described events, it was *"a dreadful advertisement of rugby union."* John Bamsey, playing centre, added that the match was *"like something out of the Mexican soccer League,"* while coach Jack Rowell needed only one word to summarise the encounter: *"scandalous!"* For the record an improvised Bath team (Christmas week not being the wisest time for the committee to dispatch a team across the Channel) would lose 23-6 to their hosts on a night best forgotten. However, as a gesture of seasonal goodwill skipper Nick Maslen and his Bath team did diplomatically attend the post-match dinner (reportedly much to the surprise of Toulouse), albeit that this visit was not to rank among the club's most cherished of memories.

Yet bar one or two exceptions the 1990-1 season would prove to be another rugby year to remember, and mainly for the right reasons. Not least of these was a Bath v Wasps encounter in early November, a contest that in the words of columnist Alan Pearey produced *"a fabulous rugby spectacle,"* and not forgetting a memorable finish. With the score poised on 26-26 club favourite David Trick (still scoring tries whenever called up for first team duty) was presented with a conversion attempt that if successful would have won the game for Bath. The winger (no mean goal kicker it should not be forgotten) missed! He not only missed, his kick ended up in the West stand. Furthermore, following the wing maestro's woeful attempt that would have clinched the result, the appreciative roar from a 3,000 home crowd echoed across the wide expanses of the Rec. One asks: 'Had the world gone mad?' Well actually 'no.' Because this otherwise illogical reaction was nothing less than the perfect climax to a Charity match, held to raise trust funds for the family of 20 years old winger Raphael Tsagane (tragically killed in a road accident during Wasps 1990 Easter tour) and for the courageous young Stephen Roberts, who in the same previous season suffered a serious neck injury merely days prior to his 18th birthday while playing at forward for Bath Youth. Thus the final result never mattered. The purpose did. And Trick understood instinctively the manner in which the game should be concluded.

At the competitive level however some serious business lay ahead when from March onwards Bath faced a final tranche of five Courage League clashes, and few tougher than the aforementioned Wasps. Indeed as with Pilkington Cup defeat at home against Leicester in November, so now Bath suffered a 15-16 Courage League defeat at home against Wasps in March. But as with no loss of self-belief from an earlier Cup upset, there now followed no loss of self-belief from a League upset. Instead Bath just got on with things, and in the final run-in got four from four when successes at Nottingham away (9-22), Gloucester away (15-17), Rosslyn Park home (45-21) and Saracens away (6-49) brought the Courage League Championship to Bath.

So again Stuart Barnes had proved himself both inspirational player and leader, while exciting new arrivals had quickly filled the gaps caused by the early loss of experienced players. A hastily reorganised coaching panel had successfully stepped into the 'shoes' of two of the best coaches in the club's history, and a temporarily unsettled Bath club predicted 'to go downhill' were now League champions of England. And if this was not encouragement enough, another trophy would follow when a hastily-recruited Bath side (with a mere two coaching sessions under Simon Jones and Andy Robinson) duly won the Worthington Best Bitter National 7's tournament. Held on the Rec (previously at Richmond) and now in only its third year, a near 5,000 home crowd roared home Jon Callard's side to the final. London Irish were overcome first (28-6), then Bath squeezed home against a superb Rosslyn Park side (16-8). Later they overhauled Sevens supremo's Harlequins by 10-0 in the semi-finals prior to sealing a 24-10 final win over a star-studded Leicester.

Commenting upon the season's achievements of 29 victories (one draw and a mere 4 defeats), plus a major Sevens title and especially the Courage Championship, head coach Jack Rowell spoke thus: *"Each year we try to improve the quality of the basics and move our game on,"* a straightforward explanation for a far from straightforward story of unparalleled success. Yet the simple fact was that for fully a dozen years or more Bath had navigated their way through the labyrinth of an ever- changing rugby world, with its intensity, its increasing challenges, the ever rising standards and the new opportunities (and temptations) that the game now offered. *"It's all about evolution,"* added Rowell. Quite so, and Bath had adapted to that evolution to a degree once thought to be near impossible for a club deemed too set in its ways and too unfashionable to keep the pace of rugby's transformation.

Andy Robinson was to be handed the reins of captaincy in season 1991-2, while Brian Ashton, former Orrell and England B scrum-half who recently had commenced teaching at Kings Bruton was now recruited to the coaching panel, and among the new intake of players Ben Clarke (No.8 from Saracens) ranked among the most interesting. Other arrivals too would waste little time in making their own mark, as out-half Duncan Willet (England Students XV) demonstrated in the opening season 28-12 win over Pontypool. Likewise Autumn wins over Richmond (10-9) and Plymouth Albion (34-3) revealed the exciting potential of, among others, prop John Mallett and backs Iestyn Lewis, Andrew Webber and Ian Palmer. A further indication of the sheer depth of talent in the Robinson camp was the selection of scrum-half Steve Knight, utility forward Mark Crane and flanker Nick Maslen (United skipper) for the South West Divisional side that season. No one doubted the need furthermore for at least two, if not three, players for each position at this hugely demanding level of rugby, nor doubted the abilities of such supposed reserves, typified when the likes of Colin Atkins (hooker) and Pat McCoy (lock) were drafted in as late replacements for their Courage League debuts against Bristol in December on the Rec; and where both draftees never once looked out of their depth in a winning forward team-effort described by the Chronicle as 'staggering.'

Meanwhile the second Rugby World Cup (RWC) commenced with England versus New Zealand at Twickenham on 3rd October, with Bath's Nigel Redman, Richard Hill, Jeremy Guscott and Jonathan Webb each playing a role during the course of England's progress. Alas Jon Hall had not as yet fully recovered from injury, while the previous self-imposed international exile of the brilliant (but maverick) Stuart Barnes was judged by rugby commentators generally (and much to the regret of many) to have caused his exclusion from the final World Cup squad.

England could not overcome the Kiwis in their opening game, losing 12-18. But they recovered commendably to reach the final via wins over Italy (Bath's Webb and Guscott capturing 32 of the points in England's 36-6 victory), USA (37-9), France (a brilliant 10-19 away triumph in Paris) and a tenacious 6-9 win over Scotland in Edinburgh. So far so good, until the final at Twickenham, where Australia would seal World Cup victory by their 6-12 defeat of Will Carling's England, with Bath's Jon Webb, Guscott and Richard Hill alongside him. *"You never forget the pain,"* Jeremy Guscott later reminisced, and he spoke for millions of his own Countrymen. Fortunately for Bath the ever more lucrative post World Cup offers for the brilliant Guscott to move across to Rugby League (not least those from Leeds and St. Helens) could not tempt him away, not even a League bid from Australia rumoured to reach the millionaire level. Instead this most coveted of players chose a long-term career option with his then current employers (British Gas), and so his parent rugby city breathed a sigh of relief, likewise England.

But away from the international scene some fearsome challenges now lay ahead, and when in early December Bath fell 10-9 at Orrell in the Courage League, rivals smelled blood. That was not all, because (Chronicle, 13th December, 1991) a one point deduction had hit the club for fielding a non-registered player in a previous League game, namely Bath's hard earned 21-26 away win at London Irish. Skipper Robinson was fuming at the administrative lapse, only too aware that so closely matched were the top teams that a single point could cost Bath the League title if, as was highly likely, the championship race produced a tight finish.

The team secretary honourably accepted responsibility for the error (namely the failure to register Laurie Heatherley), but Bath appealed nonetheless, submitting that the 'said' rule was designed to prevent players already League-tied to one club from switching to another club in the same season. But Heatherley (now a much valued utility back) had arrived at the club directly from New Zealand in the previous season. Moreover as he was not already League-tied, Bath argued that his case fell outside the aim and intention of the rule. In fairness the RFU duly accepted *that the omission to register was inadvertent....*" But, the unfortunate reality was that point reductions had already been levied against other clubs in the lower Courage Leagues, so setting a precedent; and with the necessity to ensure a uniformity of judgement, Bath's appeal failed.

There was nonetheless one man who was not entirely reconciled with a decision that he regarded as both excessive and made in haste. And that man was Andy Robinson. In his first year of captaincy he was (always had been) a ferocious competitor, and his indignation at a penalty imposed for an unintended error that he regarded as outside the remit of the said rule led the new captain to apply his considerable energies at winning if not the League, then the Pilkington Cup, currently held by Harlequins. Here, in late November Bath had already disposed of Nottingham with a 52-0 home victory, thanks not least to a ten try bonanza and a *"fusion of pace, power and sheer variety of moves....that would have destroyed any opposition."*

Post-Christmas Bath would be tested against four opponents who at their best could block their path to at least one trophy (if not two), although not if Bath produced their early January League form that overwhelmed Leicester 37-6 in front of a crowd so threateningly large that gates were shut prior to the kick-off; while in late February it was Gloucester who suffered a similar League fate, falling 29-9 on the Rec to a Bath club now recording their sixth win from seven games against their former near-unbeatable rivals. But Courage League results, however convincing, did not guarantee success in the Cup, and Bath could not relax for a single moment in their following 4th and 5th round Pilkington cup games. Both were on away territory against Northampton and Bristol respectively, and each tie was strength-sapping in its intensity. At Franklins

Gardens Bath held their nerve to win 9-13, thanks to a Jim Fallon try, two Barnes's penalties and another from Jon Webb against three penalties from Northampton's Jon Steele.

Then it was onwards to a 5th round clash at Bristol, another local rivalry often imposing a tension almost unbearable upon those who carry the hopes (and fears) of two proud West Country cities. True to form it was eighty minutes of attrition, but thankfully for Bath a clash where they wrestled a 6-15 win through a Phil de Glanville try converted by Jon Webb, two Barnes's penalties and one from Webb, as against Mark Tainton's two penalties for Bristol.

Thus once again as so often in recent years Bath had shattered Bristol hopes, and once again the tide of fortune seemed to flow with them. But, if Bath departed from the Memorial ground with a sense of relief, then such feelings were to be short-lived. For soon enough the semi-final draw was announced ….Gloucester versus Bath at Kingsholm! And although the season had provided more than its fair share of challenge already, the real drama was about to begin, and not just in the cup, but in the League also! So for a third time Bath would journey to Gloucester for a cup semi-final, with skipper Robinson predicting that so unlikely was the chance that Orrell or Northampton could at this stage be overhauled in the League, then Kingsholm would be win or bust!

Tension? You could cut it with a knife; and if you had wanted to escape, forget it, because there was no escape as some 3,000 plus Bath supporters had motored up the M5 to join an estimated sell-out 12,000 crowd for this 'do or die' encounter. The gates were closed, the spectators so closely packed that a bolt to a safe haven away from so fearful an atmosphere was near impossible; and two of the greatest cup-fighting teams strode upon the most intimidating arena in rugby football, there to do battle until they dropped.

Barnes, who else, kicked Bath into an early lead, and Tim Smith levelled things ten minutes later, merely the opening exchanges that would move Alan Pearey (The Chronicle, 6th April, 1992) to report that *"never can the passion and fury of West Country cup rugby have been more in evidence than it was at Kingsholm on Saturday."* Nerves were seen even amongst these hardest of men, Bath alone conceding no fewer than 26 penalties and Tim Smith duly sending four through the posts, plus a drop goal to add to that from Gloucester colleague Neil Matthews. But, Bath possessed the class in the backs that Gloucester did not, not least wings Jim Fallon (whose training schedule included one thousand press-ups a night) and the ageless Tony Swift.

Ah Swift! Don't mention that name in Gloucester, because once again he would strike to deadly effect when the Cherry and Whites, defending a precious 18-15 lead into injury time, failed to stop Hill from feeding Barnes when in close range of the Gloucester line. A double miss move followed, the ball then reaching Fallon now surging for the line. Pulling the cover seeking to block his path, Fallon fed the ball to

Swift who silently and dangerously had slipped into the Bath line from his opposite wing. Try! Barnes converted from wide out. Suddenly it was 18-21. Game On!

With Bath the away team and three tries clear, only a try could now save Gloucester, a situation that could allow Robinson's team to close the game down with the clock fast reaching end-time. Surprisingly they counter-attacked from the kick-off and advanced rapidly into Gloucester's 22. Here a huge cross-field pass by Webb to Guscott was fed on to the accelerating Fallon. Now rated the most powerful runner in English rugby, he casually brushed aside two tackles for his second score and Barnes sweetly converted from wide. An 18-27 triumph; Twickenham beckoned again; and Bath scarves fluttered in their hundreds as their joyous supporters drove homewards down the M5 in celebration.

One week later at Rosslyn Park there would be yet more celebration, and for reasons that would be as unexpected as they were welcome. It was the penultimate weekend of the Courage League, a competition that Bath had feared they had lost any realistic chance of winning owing to the early season point reduction. But with a trip to Twickenham assured, a relaxed Bath enjoyed a comfortable 13-21 afternoon win at Roehampton; and on the final whistle it was handshakes all round, into the bath for a soak and yet, even before a pint had been swallowed by thirsty players, a roar arose among Bath supporters in and around the clubhouse. But why? Drama elsewhere, that's why, as sports results flashed across TV screens and radio, reporting that 'League front runners Orrell and Northampton had both fallen at the hands of Wasps and Nottingham respectively.' The news spread around the Roehampton ground like wild-fire. Bath's final League match was just one week away against 4th placed Saracens, at home! Win this one and the League was Robinson's. Game on!

The North Londoners were all aggression (not that this worried Bath) and in skipper and England centre John Buckton they gained a late consolation try to add to Ben Rudlings conversion and two long range penalties. But Bath at full strength save for the promising Iestyn Lewis at centre in place of the resting Guscott, *"sent them packing with such contemptuous ease that there was almost a sense of bathos about the proceedings."* Four tries were run home thanks to former Saracens No. 8 Ben Clarke (already a Rec favourite), then Fallon and two from 'the Master' himself….Stuart Barnes. While the second half dismissal of Justyn Cassell was but one sign of Sarries' frustration during an afternoon of clinical destruction; whereupon the ever more prestigious Courage League was won for a third time, and one week onwards an upbeat Bath would face Harlequins (15-9 semi-final victors over Leicester) in the Pilkington Cup final with the satisfaction of one 'Major' already under their belts.

So it was handshakes all round again, a long soak in the bath, the beers, and the champagne? Well, not before another message had reached the Rec, one further twist in the 'tale' of season 1991-2 and news that aroused gasps when first heard in the West stand Press box: 'on-field trouble at Quins v Gloucester….double dismissal….

251

Harlequins forwards Richard Langhorn and World cup hero Micky Skinner sent off!' And that meant only one thing: both players would miss Twickenham. There was no *schadenfreude* at Bath. If anything there was sympathy regarding the dismissals of two players who in effect would now face a double punishment owing to the automatic period of suspension that operates from the moment of dismissal. Yet whatever the outcome at Twickenham, Bath had already won the Courage Championship with their ten from twelve wins, one draw (intriguingly 18-18 at Harlequins), and the one defeat at Orrell, a venue reached by Dr Jon Webb after a four hour rush up the motorway, having already performed surgery throughout the night.

In early season meanwhile Bath had won away at Cardiff (9-10) for the first time in their history (only their eleventh win over the Welsh giants in 41 games) and won it the hard way. Ben Clark got marching orders before half-time; the refereeing was in Bath's view positively perverse (and that is putting it very diplomatically indeed); and early on a seemingly perfectly good try by the hapless Clarke was 'curiously'disallowed. But the forthcoming Bath v Harlequins clash at rugby HQ would not merely eclipse the late season carnival events of the Worthington National sevens and the Middlesex sevens (Bath reaching the semi-finals and quarter-finals respectively), it would surpass in drama even the exhilarating Courage League. Indeed not for the first time in recent years the media would struggle to find the required superlatives as two outstanding teams fought for rugby supremacy in a rugby duel described by Peter Jackson (Daily Mail) as *"the most momentous cup final of all."* It was to be furthermore the last occasion that the majestic Halliday (now with Quins) would be seen prior to his retirement, and the farewell appearance of England 'B' battering-ram Jim Fallon prior to his departure to Rugby League.

Neither player could have better chosen a more memorable game to bid their farewell, a cup final witnessed by a capacity 53,000 crowd packed into a Twickenham still undergoing enlargement, where a classic would unfold, one duly described by Alan Pearey (Chronicle, 4th May, 1992) as *"rugby from another planet:"*

Bath: *J. Webb, T. Swift, P. de Glanville, J. Guscott, J. Fallon, S. Barnes, R. Hill, G. Chilcott, G. Dawe, V. Ubogu, M. Haag, N. Redman, A. Robinson (capt.), S. Ojomoh, B. Clarke.*

Harlequins: *D.Pears, D. Wedderburn, S. Halliday, W. Carling, E. Davis, P.Challinor, C. Luxton, M. Hobley, B. Moore, A. Mullins, N. Edwards, P. Ackford, P. Winterbottom (capt.), M. Russell, C. Sheasby.***Referee:** F. Howard, Liverpool Society,

The sheer pace, the determination, the bravery and the tackling produced a spectacle that was a privilege to witness, and somehow Bath clung on in the early stages against a relentless tide of attacks. At times it seemed like a replay of Waterloo. It was that 'darn' close. And in the thick of the 'smoke' *"Will Carling was a colossus."* The encounter equalled anything Bath had experienced at Kingsholm, against whom that same season Brian Ashton had remarked: *"We've proved time and again that our mid-field is as good in defence as it is in attack."* And on this day it is just as well that it was!

At the interval Harlequins were deservedly 12-3 ahead, thanks to two penalties from David Pears and a Peter Winterbottom try that completed a thundering forward onslaught (Pears converting). The line-out efforts of England lock Paul Ackford were majestic, and so assured was the Harlequins play that many a pundit would have placed a substantial bet on their leaving Twickenham clasping a shiny silver cup. But, their opponents were Bath, the club that possessed a plain 'bloody-minded' refusal to admit defeat and the wherewithal to turn reality on its head. And sure enough within minutes of the re-start Webb sent home his second penalty that duly signalled a phase of massive Bath counter-pressure that would otherwise have broken a brick wall, but not the body-shuddering Harlequins tackling. So the tenacious struggle continued, until ten minutes from end-time when Ben Clarke, Dawe and Ojomoh at last blasted a hole through the Quins defence. A pass to Guscott, a feed on to de Glanville and a try! Webb coolly converted. 12-12. Game On!

Extra time and Twickenham was now a cauldron. Guscott goes for a drop….just wide. Pears attempts another, then two more, so does Paul Challinor, each wide of target. Barely sixty seconds remain, and after near 100 minutes of pulsating brilliance it seemed that the rugby gods had decided that justice demanded (who could disagree) a drawn outcome and thus a shared trophy.

But upon that arena stood an impulsive genius who would dare to defy even the watching gods. A line-call for Bath. They shortened it. Redman jumps and feeds ball to that same rebellious talent known to one and all as Stuart Barnes. There, surrounded by exhausted cup heroes to a man, he calmly took aim, then sent a drop-kick of near 45 yards skimming (just) over the cross-bar. There was not even one second left of play, let alone sixty. And gallant Harlequins, so noble in defeat yet magnificent throughout, were thus in the words of Alan Pearey denied a successive cup triumph by *"a flash of unforgettable brilliance."* But then that is genius for you, or putting it another way: 'that was Stuart Barnes.'

Stuart Barnes: sheer brilliance!
The Drop-goal!!

So Andy Robinson proved that he too was a leader among men, whose tenacious qualities had inspired his troops to win the League and Cup double, thus gaining 28 wins, one draw and a mere 4 defeats. Not a bad start for a new young skipper.

Bath thus stepped into season 1992-3 having achieved no fewer than six Cup and three League Championships in a mere nine years; and not surprisingly attracting the continued interest from their peers as to reasons for such remarkable success. Notwithstanding that London Irish had fallen 21-26 to visitors Bath (November 1991), their coach Gorge Hook had spoken thus: it *"was a great thrill to shake hands with Jack Rowell....I've looked at tapes which he has produced on fitness training, I've read the Bath manual for the 90's about European rugby and where they're going....I would hope that London Irish could incorporate many of the things I've learned from Jack Rowell."* Coach Allen Foster offered similar praise in the aftermath of his Rugby RFC side, overcome 32-0 to League defeat at home later that same 1991-2 season. Bath, he said, were *"the most complete footballing side in English rugby."* While (Chronicle, 5th October, 1992) Blackheath coach Kevin Short, having filmed for training purposes Bath's home 51-0 win against The Club, spoke thus: *"We've come to the rugby university today."*

Dave Robson: Former player turned long-serving coach.

Acknowledgements : Reg. Monk

Bath's reputation nonetheless had extended far beyond home shores, not least through the influence of former coach Dave Robson, whose five year corporate rugby-plan for Namibia was already yielding benefits within this emerging rugby nation. In addition Robson was further involved with rugby development in Romania, USA, Holland and Belgium.

So perhaps it was not surprising that by this stage the media sometimes spoke metaphorically of the 'Bath rugby Empire.' Their ability to transform unknown players into high-level performers for example, their family-club warmth that could revive the careers of the likes of Jon Webb, these were among the characteristics that partly explained the fascination that Bath aroused in others, among them (perhaps not surprisingly) the Services, some of whom had by now identified with a rugby family that had risen from a small West Country city to the very pinnacle of the rugby game. The 45 strong crew of minehunter HMS Brecon for instance had not only honoured the club on occasions with their support on the Rec, but had hosted the Bath club during shore visits at Newport and Gloucester. The somewhat larger warship, namely the

254

aircraft carrier HMS Ark Royal no less, paid a further huge compliment by adopting the club as their own.

But it had to be admitted that if the much-admired Bath could win when others might have given up all hope, they could also lose when other high profile sides would probably have won, and the 1992-3 season would reveal the return of this unwelcome trait. A pre-season tour of Italy would first be undertaken, a two match itinerary where another recruit would reveal exciting potential, namely Llanelli born out-half Craig Raymond. Victories over Record Cucine Casale (15-62), whose President Vanni Maggiore had earlier exclaimed: "*All the town is dreaming of playing against English players*," and then 15-18 against Benetton Treviso would result, and although few lessons would be learned on the field, others would be learned off it (Chronicle, 8th September, 1992). Among these was the fact that both Italian Division One teams were sponsored clubs (in Treviso's case by the high profile Benetton firm); and both clubs imported prominent overseas players such as All Black Zinzan Brooke and Treviso's Australian wing David Campese. Thus awash with money (Chronicle, 16th September, 1992) both clubs could (and reportedly did) pay top international players some pretty hefty top salaries; whether for coaching or playing it was hard to say. Furthermore by the 1990's the issue of money was fast becoming a hot topic of debate in the supposedly amateur world of rugby union in the British Isles; and to put it bluntly it was increasingly obvious that the definition of amateurism appeared to differ, depending upon whose language one was speaking and upon whose territory one was playing.

Debate at the commencement of the new 1992-3 domestic season however was initially dominated by a set of new law changes, over 40 in number, and introduced with the aim of creating a yet more open game. These included the raising of a try to five points, limiting a Mark to within the defendant's 22 line, banning the scrum-half from dummying to coax opponent's off-side and blood injuries to be treated immediately. There was general approval too for the allowance of a 'quick throw-in' anywhere between where the ball crossed into touch and the goal-line of that team throwing in but…only with the use of that same ball kicked into touch.

As Bath 'shot off' the starting blocks for the early season Courage League campaign, clinching a haul of five wins out of six games, it appeared that such changes suited their type of game, revealed not least by the sheer class of their Autumn victory at Bristol (31st October). Notably this was the 200th game between these two ancient rivals. But unlike the 3-3 drawn encounters in both the original derby in 1888 and later the 100th in 1936, the 200th game would be an 8-31 Bath rout, a score and performance that would have astonished their predecessors and a result that dwarfed their previous 'best' at Bristol, namely a 0-12 win in distant 1912. By season 1992-3 however the balance had dramatically changed, and as Alan Pearey wrote: "*….there can rarely have been a backs performance quite so devastating as that dished up by the reigning League* *champions."* Albeit the hosts succeeded in securing a Jamie Johnston try and a Mark Tainton penalty, Bath's flowing 15-man rugby led to tries from Tony Swift (2), Ben Clarke and the immaculate Jon Webb. The England full-back furthermore converted all four tries, plus struck home a penalty, while calmly demonstrating every aspect of modern full-back play with his precision interventions into the backs and his perfect lines of running. Unlike two seasons previously when cat-calls greeted the ex-Bristolian, now he was acclaimed by an admiring crowd for each and every touch of a majestic performance.

The next League encounter, a 3-13 win at Leicester, proved equally impressive and no doubt equally ominous for second division side Waterloo, due to host Bath one week later in the 3rd round Pilkington Cup. But, if there are many reasons (not to mention excuses) for giant-killing upsets, the sensational defeat that the Lancastrians duly inflicted upon Bath on that bleak November day is easily explained: 'Bath were quite awful.' In actual fact the hosts were little better. But they succeeded in dragging Bath down a level, a tactic that sometimes works and certainly worked on this occasion. Half-back Paul Grayson proved to be the local hero, kicking home three penalties, his nine points sufficient to cancel out a Tony Swift try (and a good one) plus a Jon Webb penalty. Yet that still made it 9-8 to the Northerners, a result arousing near disbelief throughout the game and temporary horror when the news reached Bath.

So what explanation was there for so inexplicable an outcome? One possible answer was the psychological factor that 'favourites' carry upon their shoulders when facing an 'underdog;' and Bath, for many decades a David amongst Goliaths, did not always feel comfortable when this position was reversed. Bob Jenkins (sports commentator, Bath Chronicle) later described such a phenomenon as the 'minnow syndrome.' There was perhaps some truth in this. But life as they say must go on, as indeed it did. Yes, the cup venture had hit the 'buffers' before it had barely started in a Pilkington campaign that would see Leicester the eventual winners. But a Bath club kicking itself for a largely self-inflicted failure at Waterloo now set about restoring its self-respect with renewed ambitions in the Courage League. Moreover with the Divisional Championship now underway and heavily reliant upon first-choice Bath players, it was an opportune time again for so-called reserves to show off their own prowess. And show it they most certainly did with a triple run of December victories at Nottingham (17-24), Richmond (22-38) and home to London Welsh (37-7).

Not for the first time either newcomers caught the eye, namely props Darren Crompton and Bristol recruit Dave Hilton, plus the discovery of 21 years old South African Mike Catt, whose home senior debut in Bath's January 47-5 non-League win over London Irish revealed a remarkable maturity. With a British passport now in his hands (his mother was English) and recently domiciled in the city since leaving Stroud, selectors and supporters alike soon predicted that a special talent was now in their midst. He could play literally anywhere in the backs (save perhaps scrum-half) and one decade later the young man from Eastern Province would play a critical role in England's triumphant World Cup winning side. And irony of ironies, save for a delay in responding to Catt's initial enquiries to Gloucester, he might never have joined the Rec. By contrast Bath offered the newcomer a trial run-out in a floodlit reserve game, and within eighty minutes of rugby the Bath selectors and spectators realised his potential. Soon enough England selectors would realise it too!

National selectors had meanwhile taken note of other Bath players, and it was with much pride on the Rec when in mid-October prop Victor Ubogu won his first England cap in their 26-13 win against Canada (held as it happened at Wembley); while at Twickenham (14 November 1992) Ben Clarke made his debut in England's 33-16 victory in South Africa's return from the international political wilderness, with Phil de Glanville winning his first cap too as replacement. Further delight was expressed from all corners of the Rec when in December the hugely talented (but injury-prone) Audley Lumsden won his Oxford Blue at Twickenham.

But representative calls did not end there, because both flanker Julian Olds and hooker Hugh Butler (now playing for the British Club of Bangkok) experienced 'their' first taste of international rugby....for Thailand! How, one asks, did such things happen? Well, Thailand bless 'em were (pardon the pun) a bit short of tall players. So as Major Anan Boonsupa (TRU) explained (Chronicle, 10th November, 1992): Thailand decided to select *"from an excellent batch of ex-pat ruggerites in the country"* for the forthcoming Asia championships. And make no mistake, it was sure some debut for the two ex-pats from Bath, with their adopted Thailand falling 97-6 to South Korea. But, fighters that these Thai fellows are, much was redeemed with a convincing 55-10 win over Malaysia, although a 32-15 defeat to Hong Kong meant that Thailand (despite 'gallant' Bath support) could only manage third place in their championship group, with powerful Japan the eventual champions.

Not only on the field, but off the field, this still basically amateur sport was expanding fast. Attendances were increasing, while the recent Rugby World Cup had attracted a wider national audience and an ever-increasing commercial interest. For example (one of many) SWEB's already considerable sponsorship of Bath had recently been increased by a not insignificant 20%. In other words rugby was good for business, and business was good for rugby.

Not surprisingly a number of supporters (among them Bath businessman Malcolm Pearce) were increasingly aware of the necessity to update the infrastructure of the club; and the committee decision in the previous season to oppose the appointment of a full-time club administrator was, in the opinion of many members, an opportunity missed. *"I think the club should be managed professionally,"* stated Malcolm Pearce (Chronicle, 28th September, 1992), and while he sought no change to rugby union's amateur status, other changes were now vital, he argued. Such views were widely supported by the membership, some of whom pointed to the revival of a previously-struggling Northampton. Staring down at the abyss, a near mutiny by their supporters had led to a complete re-organisation of the management, plus the appointment of a full-time paid coach and a Birmingham firm assigned to organise the commercial aspects of the club.

Concerns, though not so dramatic, culminated (Chronicle, 25th November 1992) with an extraordinary general meeting (EGM) at the Rec. Conducted under the chairmanship of professor Cyril Tomkins, the agenda included (inter alia) the issue of plans to widen and improve both the commercial management at the club and the proposal for an increased role for players at the committee level. But in contrast to the aforementioned events at Northampton, this meeting did not produce the drama that many supporters (and not least the media) were expecting, due partly to certain positive decisions already taken. First, a business group at Bath University was currently making a full study of the club's management structure, with a report and recommendations to follow in due course. Secondly, in addition to the cumbersome 30 strong management committee, an executive committee of seven members was now established, one designed to meet on a fortnightly basis, and on a daily basis if circumstances demanded. Third, the construction of a futuristic stand on the Rec had now received the 'go-ahead.'

Significantly an item on the EGM agenda calling for the resignation of the present committee was blocked anyway by rule 7.3 of the club constitution, a rule that 'only' permitted such drastic an action if taken at a full AGM. So with the leading item on the agenda now side-lined, there followed in the concluding words of club chairman John Gaynor *"a full and frank exchange of views.* But it was hardly an outcome for headlines, not least because not so much as a single vote was taken throughout the entire proceedings. The meeting however drew an impressive five hundred members, so many that closed circuit TV was installed to ensure the overspill could watch the events from adjoining rooms in the clubhouse. But while many opinions addressed to the committee on the need for management improvements were 'heated' to say the least, it was quite obvious that the membership, although advocating changes, desired no de-stabilising 'shock and awe' tactics; and that while they wished for improvements, these they sought from within the established structure of the club. That then was the message of the night!

A message of a different kind was delivered loud and clear with three startling New Year results. First in early February England 'A' led by Jon Hall and including the human dynamo Steve Ojomoh swept aside Italy 'A' to the tune of 59-0 on the Rec in front of an 8,000 crowd. Later and undoubtedly one of 'the' results of the entire English season, Bath strode quietly on to Kingsholm seemingly oblivious to the fact that this was supposedly the most daunting rugby arena in the British Isles. 'Daunting?...you must be kidding,' Bath's calm demeanour appeared to say. And barely reaching 4th gear let alone 5th, they strode off a silenced Kingsholm ground with a 0-20 Courage League victory under their belts.

There then followed a result so extraordinary that one would have been forgiven for thinking that it was a hoax, except that it wasn't. Nor was the identity of the opposition a mis-print. Instead Bath really did inflict a 79-3 points win over Swansea who indeed were the then current reigning Welsh champions. True it was that the visitors were not at absolute full-strength, but then neither were Bath. True too that Bath ran home 13 tries (Callard converting 7) against a lone Aled Williams penalty, so inflicting upon Swansea the biggest defeat in their proud history. And with young scrum-half Jamie Knight (brother of Steve) making a remarkable full 1st team debut since his serious injury incurred when playing for England Colts against France in 1989, and lock Sean O'Leary (ex Wasps) prominent in a highly mobile home pack, Bath's night of total rugby produced a result that belonged to the realms of fantasy. Except it wasn't fantasy.

Missing from the Bath line-up on that night of nights was a certain Stuart Barnes. But this gifted tactical master would not be absent from England's encounter against Scotland in early March. With the media and a number of 1st Division coaches losing patience with a back-division under-performing through lack of a half-back 'play-maker,' and all pleading for a Stuart Barnes recall, the 'Prodigal' son duly re-energised the England attack, resulting with a 26-12 victory that denied Scotland both the Calcutta Cup and the Triple Crown. Yet as if to emphasise again the sheer extent of Bath's rugby influence, Damien Cronin (now with London Scottish) and Bath's Andy Reed (qualified through his Edinburgh-born mother) packed down together in the Scotland second row.

Casting an anxious eye over Barnes on that eventful day was Wasps captain (and England reserve scrum-half) Steve Bates. Jokingly (or maybe not) he said of Barnes: *"Perhaps we could poison his food."* One week later (13th March, 1993) and Wasps would 'engage' (for want of a better word) in Courage League action on the Rec, and this time no one was joking. First, not only did the game draw a capacity crowd, but many tried to gate-crash and many arrived too close to kick-off. Forget scrummages on the field, there was more than one scrummage off it (with two persons fainting in the scramble to get into the ground). Wisely the game was delayed for five minutes. But this caused yet more dressing-room tension; and when finally unleashed at kick-off, two totally hyped-up teams went into (literally 'into') each other like 'bats out of hell.'

Within ten minutes so 'hot' did things get among the two packs that referee David Matthews (Liverpool Soc.y) was compelled to read the Riot Act: *"next bit of trouble and someone goes off!"* It made not a blind bit of difference, and then…Guscott tackled Fran Clough hard but fair, and then…he tapped Clough with his boot stupidly but light-footed, and then….Clough (not without reason) rushed at Guscott who ducked to avoid 'malicious contact.' The crowd in the West stand, under whose noses the episode occurred and whose Bath-partisanship by now could have given Kingsholm a run for its money, only added to the pressure as first the referee consulted with his touch-judge and then dismissed…. a despairing Clough. To the Wasps (again not without reason) it was an utter injustice pure and simple. Yet the referee's action may well have saved the game from descending into chaos. Mercifully things calmed down somewhat, but mistakes (there were 36 penalties) littered the next 65 minutes of rugby with Bath finally winning 22-11. Though Wasps would have doubtless disagreed, there may have been some truth in the Bath post-match verdict that *"Wasps set out to intimidate and got their just desserts."* Be that as it may, for the record books Rob Andrew sent home two penalties (one from inside his own half) and Phil Hopley ran home a try. While for Bath Guscott scored his 90th try for the club (Webb converting), Webb kicked 4 penalties, and Barnes a drop goal.

Lessons forgotten however must sometimes be re-learned, and the ever growing intensity of rugby competition since the inauguration of the National Cup in 1972 was proof that high profile sporting events excite a high octane competitive spirit among both crowd and participant. The standardised Leagues would be no exception to this rule, as the passions so evident in this Bath v Wasps encounter vividly showed. But let no one think that such all-consuming intensity was new to rugby union. It was not! Long forgotten the problems may have been, but pre-First World War days of the Somerset cup were but one example of passions breaking through the safety barrier. And there were others! Yet although since 1888 the ultimate sanction of a dismissal had been available, referees had often been understandably reluctant to use so total a punishment. For decades past however a simple rule-change could surely have solved this dilemma, namely a short, sharp ten minute shock into the sin-bin, whose availability in seasons past and in the Bath v Wasps clash could have proved invaluable; a highly effective form of summary justice moreover whose time had surely come. And come it did, although not fully implemented at the senior club level until season 1998-9.

Soon, the 30-man squad for the British Lions tour of New Zealand was announced. Rob Andrew of Wasps was among the names. Included too was Damian Cronin (formerly Bath, now London Scottish) and Bath's Stuart Barnes, Jeremy Guscott, Andy Reed and Ben Clarke. Bath and Wasps meanwhile were 'neck and neck' in the closing stages for the Courage League title. However the 1992-3 season was not only about winners; it was also about losers, because Division One was to be reduced to a mere ten clubs for the following season, and as a result an unprecedented four teams would be relegated. It was at this juncture therefore, if not before, that the top flight clubs were understandably drifting away from a culture of camaraderie and instead facing a struggle for their survival at the highest level. It was a frightening thought in an ever-changing rugby game.

Despite such harsh realities, a game of a quite different character between a Bath International XV and a President's XV would be held on 4th April on the Rec in memory of former Welsh lock Mark Jones. Mark, a 6ft 5in and 17 stone solicitor was never a first choice forward at Bath. But 'boy' could he not play a 'mean' game when his 22 senior call-ups did come his way. A gentle giant, he typified the ability of that reserve pool within the club who never, ever let Bath down when the 'call to arms' came their way. After four seasons from 1984-88 Mark departed first to Swansea, then Clifton, to seek more regular senior rugby. But it was later in Autumn 1992 that the Rec learned that this endearing young player of 29 years had lost an eleven month fight against serious illness, news that brought sadness to all who knew him. So his former club remembered Mark Jones, and did so in a manner befitting so pleasing a person to know.

With the 1992-3 League campaign now reaching a climax at both ends of Division One, Bath, much to their regret, were preparing for life without the retiring Jonathan Webb. His last game on the Rec was a non-league 'friendly' against Gloucester, neither side at full strength owing to League priorities, and the visitors winning 16-17 on the day. But Webb, calm as ever, produced his full repertoire of skills, namely *"the torpedoed touch-line kicks, the sure hands, the penetrative running;"* nor forgetting a brace of typical Webb tries to the acclaim of his legion of admirers, who on the final whistle swept on to the Rec to wish their hero well for the future.

With only one League match remaining, the Courage title hinged upon the respective fortunes of Wasps at home to Bristol and Bath away to Saracens. It was here that Webb would play his final game. Fittingly a significant role would be played by Jon Callard (on this occasion selected on the wing), Webb's designated full-back successor. With challengers Wasps winning narrowly 7-6 at home to Bristol, Bath were given one hell of a fight by the already relegated Saracens. But in the closing minutes Robinson's men squeezed home by 13-19, thanks not least to Callard's two tries on the day. As events would shortly show, it was the perfectly scripted handover from the current England full-back to his younger successor at both club and international level. It was likewise the perfect climax to a season of 27 wins and 5 defeats where Bath, albeit humiliated by early Pilkington cup defeat at Waterloo, dug themselves out of a hole to win their fourth League title.

Neither would the following 1993-4 campaign under the captaincy of the lion-hearted Jon Hall lack for challenges, albeit commencing at friendly Garryowen, where, watched by a 4,000 Irish crowd bitterly disappointed by Jeremy Guscott's late withdrawal through injury, six tries (four converted) ensured a comfortable 8-38 away victory. Somewhat sterner obstacles lay ahead, though with an early season return of five from five over Bristol, Northampton, Orrell, Gloucester and Wasps respectively it seemed likely that Bath would be among the chase for honours in the Courage League. But despite form so 'hot,' one could not ignore the impact of the ever-increasing toll of injuries at this higher level of rugby, a problem only too evident during Bath's ferocious 10-18 win at Bristol in September. Often thirty one persons (not thirty) were seen on the field owing to the almost constant necessity for Bath's assistant physio Heather McKibbin to treat an endless stream of casualties on the pitch. And that was just the Bath list of walking wounded.

Furthermore with the club's four recent British Lions (Barnes, Andy Reed, Guscott and Ben Clarke) all nursing troubling injuries originating from the recent New Zealand tour, head physio Julie Bardner (Chronicle, 23rd October, 1993) now entered the fray with some no-nonsense comments. It was the Lions she was most concerned about, players whom she argued *"had about a ten month playing season with not enough time to recover at the end of it"* and *"the human body is just not designed to cope with the punishment these players are expected to go through."* Referring then to the rigours of training and the demands of League, divisional, cup ties and internationals she emphasised: *"Ideally it would be great if they did not have to play every week."* Ideally it would. But so keen were players to resume action on the field, especially if a first team place was at stake, that all too often they would risk their chances of a full recovery just to get back into action as quickly as possible. So it was a tribute to the fortitude of both players and medics alike that on 30th October (1993) no fewer than eleven fit Bath players ran out at Redruth in the colours of the South West to do 'battle' with the touring New Zealand All Blacks; and lined up alongside team colleagues Paul Hull, Nick Beal, Kieren Bracken and Andy Blackmore were Bath's Jon Callard, Phil de Glanville, Audley Lumsden, Mike Catt, and at forward Chris Clark, Graham Dawe, Victor Ubogu, Nigel Redman, Andy Robinson, Jon Hall (captain) and Ben Clarke.

Knowing only too well the value of home support, Graham Dawe was requested on the eve of the encounter to appear on Cornwall TV so as to implore the faithful to fill Redruth to capacity, notwithstanding that eleven starters were Bath men and Dawe alone wore the Cornish 'Black and Gold' on County days. His rallying call worked. Fifteen thousand crammed the terraces. The game was such as will always stir Cornish hearts: passion and sheer guts! Above all there rose the mighty presence of skipper Jon Hall; and he would regain his England place against Scotland in February. His fellow forwards were not far behind, among them Chris Clark, recent loose-head arrival at Bath; who not surprisingly would win his Oxford Blue in December.

But the attrition took its toll: Ojomoh (Bath's 12th player on the day) replacing Andy Robinson, D.Sims for Andy Blackmore and Paul Holford for de Glanville. De Glanville's eye injury, one requiring fifteen stitches, was a shocker and allegedly not acquired purely by accident; but he would shortly avenge the tourists at Twickenham. The Kiwis however won the day by way of a Jamie Joseph try and five Matthew Cooper penalties against Paul Hull's drop goal and Callard's four penalties. But the narrow 15-19 margin over a virtual Bath XV was proof of a mighty struggle fought out against a near Test strength New Zealand side.

So with mission almost accomplished it was back to the Rec (fitness matters now in the hands of Ged Roddy, Director of Sports Development, Bath University) and from whose treatment room five starters (Callard, de Glanville, Ubogu, Redman and Ben Clarke) and three replacements (Barnes, Dawe and Jon Hall) were selected for England against New Zealand in late November. Alas the brilliant Guscott, who during the summer had declined a half million pound offer to switch to Rugby League (believed to be Leeds) remained side-lined with injury sustained with the Lions. But de Glanville's faultless defensive qualities were to prove invaluable, likewise the maturity of Redman ('man of the match' claimed All Blacks coach Laurie Mains), and so too the four debut international penalties of Jon Callard that bettered J. Wilson's trio for the tourists, and earned the new Rec favourite instant Twickenham adulation. These, added to the Rob Andrews drop goal won for England a famous (and rare) 15-9 victory over the might of New Zealand, who only one week previously had overcome Scotland 51-15.

The Bath international contingent then stepped straight back into December club action that commenced with a League victory at Harlequins (12-14), where local and national hero Gareth Chilcott would alas bid farewell to senior rugby. Success at home to London Irish (28-8) then followed and furthermore an opening round 24-11 Pilkington Cup victory over Wasps. So far, so good, likewise the perfectly cordial after-match atmosphere that had followed the Quins match; a curious fact in view of allegations (first by Harlequins, then London Irish) that would follow, accusing Bath (inter alia) of eye-gauging and biting.

But rightfully granted the freedom to put their side of the story (Chronicle, 13th December 1993), Bath secretary John Quin, skipper Jon Hall and chairman John Gaynor scrutinised the match video sent down from the Harlequins. Their opinion concluded as follows, as *"a result of our investigation....no evidence of any misbehaviour by a Bath player which can be adjudged a deliberate act was observed."* With that response the matter was subsequently laid to rest by both parties.

No sooner had this issue subsided however than another appeared to take its place (Chronicle, 20th December, 1993) when Bath found themselves facing allegations by Bristol of attempting to lure players (two in particular) to the Rec. True or otherwise, it was a fact well known for decades that Bath and Bristol (and not forgetting Clifton) had operated an open-door policy regarding the movement of players between clubs, and doing so without anyone batting an eye-lid. Moreover when Simon Jones (Bath chairman of selectors) responded by stating that *"if someone tells us a player is interested we check..."* he was merely stating the obvious. Or as Steve Bale had put it equally bluntly (The Independent, 10th Jan. 1989) *"nobody much loves a winner, as Bath have found in their long years of success."* Indeed so, and perhaps significantly no use was made by Harlequins or London Irish of the 'citing' procedure (already introduced) that permitted watching officials to raise a foul-play issue within the following twelve hours.

One thing however was certain: the days of playing rugby solely for the fun of it were alas disappearing. It was not surprising therefore that the senior clubs especially grew increasingly unsure about their long-term chances of survival at the top level. The dreaded 'drop' meant falling gates and loss of sponsorship, and allegations of foul play (true or otherwise) were one possible symptom of the jitters now affecting the game.

As if these trials and tribulations were not enough, criticism now came from sources much closer to home with a plea from Combe Down requesting that Bath scrap their U.21 team, launched only in the previous season. With former player and still ardent Bath supporter Chris Lilley (now coaching Combe Down) acting as spokesman for other Combination clubs, it was claimed that talent was being diverted to the Rec at too young an age, and leaving junior sides bereft of youthful newcomers. It was a powerful argument, and one that threatened the long-established bond between Bath and the Combination. Gloucester too had recently introduced an U.21 side, raising similar concerns among their own Combination.

But despite the rationale of such objections, when in late season the touring Netherland's U.21's were overcome 46-3, the result suggested that Bath U.21's were here to stay; though ironically they would play no further part in the club's future beyond November of the following season, when to the surprise of many the team was disbanded. Thus Chris Lilley was to be vindicated by a reappraisal of Bath's future recruitment policies and their decision to instead channel players from 18 years onwards directly into the Spartans (or higher), and simultaneously to develop the potential of the newly-formed Bath Emerging Players squad.

It was no surprise of course that there were two schools of thought concerning the increasingly competitive element in rugby football. Indeed many clubs rated the Leagues quite the best thing that had ever happened, an innovation that had introduced further excitement and purpose into rugby union. Yet the new developments came at a cost, not least as regards the gradual loosening of ties with the Welsh rugby heartlands. Once it would have been unthinkable that the electrifying Anglo-Welsh encounters could be another casualty of a changing rugby world. But with clubs now frequently selecting half-strength teams for such non-League fixtures and with attendances falling as a result, the magic of yesteryear was lost seemingly overnight with the onwards march of supposed progress.

If the clubs fielded full strength sides *"we could fill any ground in the country,"* Neath team manager John Williams had remarked on witnessing his side fall 13-27 at home to Bath (both teams under-strength) in Autumn 1990. Bath's Jack Rowell concurred, adding that *"there should be an Anglo-Welsh League and after that you've got to bring the French in as well because that's how big the game is."* But there was no Anglo-Welsh League; and while many on both sides of Offa's *Dyke* mourned this sudden decline, it was too late. The onwards momentum towards a new order was now unstoppable.

Exactly where this new order would take the game was as yet far from clear. But during 1993-4 Bath appeared to be heading for a possible League and Cup double, and the young talent that continued to be attracted to the Rec included the RAF's utility back Ed Rayner, winning his Blue for Oxford in December. Then in mid-February the human powerhouse that was Steve Ojomoh would earn his first England cap against Ireland at Twickenham.

Many years now of producing this glittering gallery of stars had nonetheless led some followers to expect (even demand) a five-star exhibition on each and every occasion. But life in the fast lane was not an exhibition, but a near ten month long marathon. True it was that Bath could on occasions produce almost fantasy 15-man running rugby, for example their September home 46-17 win over Gloucester. But injuries, representative calls and loss of form hamper all teams at some time or other, and it is a mature side that learns best how to overcome these inevitable handicaps. This maturity was to be tested in the 5th round cup tie in January against Bristol, where Bath created just enough space to run home tries from Ojomoh and Catt, with Barnes converting both, and a highly disciplined defence that limited Bristol to Mark Tainton's three penalties, sufficient to ensure a home 14-9 victory. Touchingly on this same occasion there was to be a respectful one minute's silence by the 7,500 spectators in memory of former player, club official and Bath devotee Jack Arnold, who had sadly passed away soon after the Bath v Bristol League match two weeks previously.

Meanwhile the quarter-final at Saracens watched by Andrew Baldock (Chronicle, 28th February, 1994) revealed the same discipline as applied against Bristol, and Bath, *"largely efficient, if rarely flamboyant....briskly went about their business."* There were no frills at Southgate, just the ability to control the agenda throughout, leading to tries from de Glanville, and a scorcher from Adebayo that showed *"what wonderful magic Bath can conjure when it all clicks."* And despite Andy Tuningly's two conversions for Sarries, Callard's two conversions and three penalties put clear water between the teams and a 6-23 win for Bath.

But, the semi-final opponents just happened to be the Harlequins away, a far different proposition. A televised game, it was to be the stuff of nervous breakdowns for both sets of supporters. First, it was the Quins who were literally swept aside in a 25 minute Bath storm that left the hosts trailing 0-19 as first Swift, then Barnes and next Callard all sped over for searing tries. Bath looked unstoppable. But there were two sides on the Stoop, and Harlequins duly stepped forward to display some of their own tricks. They had plenty of them. First came a Paul Challinor penalty, then a Martin Pepper try and next a penalty try. But that was not all, because further massive 'Quin's pressure led to a Justyn Cassell try followed by Challinor adding a drop-goal to his two conversions. And as the clock ticked away towards no-time that meant only one thing: Harlequins were now heading homewards with a remarkable 25-19 semi-final victory seemingly in their grasp.

Just one problem….a team called Bath with several minutes remaining on the clock; and as if taunting a battling Harlequins in the final seconds of the 1992 cup final was not torture enough, mischievous Fate returned to play one more trick upon 8,000 by now emotionally drained spectators. So it just 'had' to happen: Catt broke through to pass on to Callard to pass on to Swift and ominously for Harlequins, the try line was already within his sights and range. Two broken tackles en route and the Lancastrian was now over the line and touching down near the posts. Callard steps forward and calmly sends over conversion number three. That made it 25-26 to Bath. Touché.

*"We never lie down and die…"*said Jon Hall, and perhaps never truer words spoken as Bath performed yet another of their Houdini escapes from the jaws of defeat; and with news that Leicester would be co-finalists at Twickenham it was the Midlanders who remained the one club capable of disproving Hall's prophetic words. Three weeks onwards the Harlequins would again be faced in the League, and Jon Hall's side needed only a draw to win their 5th Courage championship outright with the luxury of a game to spare. It was hardly surprising therefore that a totally confident Bath scorned playing it safe, instead unleashing all their fire-power from the 'off.' Four tries resulted; a 32-13 victory followed; and cause for spontaneous celebration that continued as inspirational skipper Jon Hall received the Courage trophy from RFU president Ian Beer, formerly of England and appropriately Harlequins and Bath.

There was now a two-week respite until Twickenham, and with the League silverware now safely on their trophy board the selectors chose to rest the probable Twickenham team, handing the last Courage match (against London Irish) to experienced utility forward Nick Maslen, who took another bone fide United team to Sunbury for the aforementioned full Division One League game, with Kevin Yates, Tim Beddow, Darren Crompton and Eric Peters among the forwards. Irish, admittedly demoralised since losing their struggle against relegation, were nonetheless powerful opponents. However an inches close 31-32 win was achieved, thanks to three tries (one from wing Mark Woodman) and assisted by a 17 points contribution from the boot of out-half Ed Rayner. It was no mean achievement from the club's supposedly 2nd string.

Rayner and hooker Tim Beddow were duly selected among the replacements for the Pilkington cup final (7th May) in preparation for the formidable threat of a Dean Richards-led Leicester; and Twickenham, filled to its recently enlarged 68,000 all-seater capacity (a new world club record) echoed with the chants of passionate support as the two adversaries stepped on to that hallowed green turf:

Bath: *J. Callard, A. Swift, P. de Glanville, M. Catt, A. Adebayo, S. Barnes, R. Hill, D. Hilton, G. Dawe, V. Ubogu, N. Redman, A. Reed, A. Robinson (S. Ojomoh 48), J.Hall (capt.), B.* Clarke.

Leicester: W. Kilford, T. Underwood, S. Potter, L. Boyle, R. Underwood, J. Harris, A Kardooni, G. Rowntree, R. Cockerill, D. Garforth, M. Johnson, M. Poole, J. Wells, N. Back, D. Richards (capt.). **Referee:** E. Morrison (Bristol/RFU).

Two of England's finest? Well yes…. but Leicester's tactics were puzzling to say the least, and Andrew Baldock (Chronicle, 9th May, 1994) spoke for many when commenting that the *"Tigers seemed hell-bent on intimidation, and it was to everybody's detriment."* True, and it was to everybody's surprise as well, especially with the array of attacking potential that Leicester brought with them to Twickenham. 'Negative tactics?' ….about the last strategy in the coaching manual to beat a street-wise team like Bath in a cup final.

Two great packs confronted each other; likewise two high quality back divisions; and this promised to be the making of something special. But for some obscure reason an air of caution was evident throughout. There was no passion to be seen…no drama! Former Harlequins and England lock Paul Ackford, reporting for the Sunday Telegraph (8th May) wrote: *"Passes were dropped, tackles missed and there was an undercurrent of tension, but the match never exploded into life."* It was hardly surprising therefore that Twickenham remained a try-free zone until ten minutes after the break. But when the tries did come it was Bath who ran them home. First it was Barnes launching de Glanville who, suddenly aware that Swift was drifting into clear space far out on the right, kicked over the Leicester cover and into the Lancastrian's path. Rory Underwood slipped and Swift shot for the line…his 152nd try for Bath. With five minutes remaining scrum-half Hill fed Callard who reached deep into Tigers territory. Then short of space he floated a pass that reached the hands of Mike Catt…try number two with Callard converting beautifully to add to his three penalties. By contrast Leicester were simply not themselves, and although packed to the gunwales with class, they kept their powder dry, save for three Jez Harris penalties. It was such a waste of their undoubted talents.

However, the 21-9 result reflected the superiority of a Bath side who, for the first time in their cup final history, had abandoned their previous 'lucky' white shirts for the standard colours of blue, white and black. They had now won their eighth knock-out cup trophy and their third League and Cup Double, and whatever it was that was thrown at them, be it criticism off the field or fearful challenges on it, they just kept on winning when it mattered. Again Paul Ackford wrote: *"It is impossible to do justice to their achievements."* And then with the mind of the soothsayer he pondered thus: perhaps Bath *"should turn professional and take on Wigan at rugby League. Now that would be a real contest."* Indeed it would!!

Bath thus wore the crown of English rugby once again. They had played 37 games, lost a mere seven and…won the Double; and naturally in the real world a club would be delighted to win one Major, let alone two. But to win three Majors would be deemed the stuff of dreamland. Well, Bath did win three! Because following their Pilkington cup Triumph a 7's team under Jon Callard embarked for Twickenham one week later, this time to have a go at the Middlesex (Save & Prosper) Sevens, the top 7's competition in Britain and one that Bath had never won.

Neither did their chances look too promising, with one hour (and only 'one 'hour) of pre-tournament training to prepare the side. Indeed in their first round opener against London Scottish when 21-0 up at the interval, a startling Exiles recovery left Bath clinging on for dear life to scrape through on 28-26. But they recovered sufficiently to deal with Loughborough Students (24-0), and then left Saracens trailing 19-0. In the final Eric Peters, Gareth Adams, Martin Haag, Audley Lumsden, Ian Sanders, Jon Callard (capt.) and Ed Rayner found Orrell sterner stuff to deal with. But notwithstanding tries from Naylor and another from Wynn converted by Paul Johnson, Bath as so often held one card too many. Tries from Rayner, Lumsden and Callard, plus Callard's two conversions were sufficient to seal a 19-12 triumph. The Double for season 1993-4 therefore? No…the Treble!

But, on the news of his appointment as the new England rugby manager, there would now be a future without Jack Rowell. Hartlepool born, educated at Hartlepool Grammar School, later Oxford, a John Player winning coach at Gosforth (later Newcastle Falcons) and an executive company director, his leadership at Bath had proved simply inspirational. A 'player's coach,' or as one says in the Services 'a soldier's officer,' he instilled a self-belief throughout his squad that proved to be dramatic; while the hopes and responsibilities that he carried upon his shoulders were sometimes enormous. His departure would be keenly felt. But such were the benefits of his influence that the 'good ship' from which he would soon bid farewell was destined to sail onwards as if he was still on the bridge.

Shortly before his farewell following the Courage League decider against Harlequins he had spoken thus (Chronicle, 25th April, 1994): " *We have built a Rolls Royce, one that is a lot easier to drive than it is to build. I have sought to make the players strong…mentally, physically and technically…and to play with one heartbeat.*" 'To play with one heartbeat?' Ah yes, just five words of pure rugby poetry that would inspire any team, anytime, anywhere.

Chapter 32. THE BURIAL OF THE HATCHET. (1994-96)

On the surface all seemed perfectly normal throughout much of the 1994-5 rugby season. Bath remained 'the' team to beat; and not a single side did beat them until mid-March at Cardiff. Their futuristic South Stand, breath-taking to look at, was open for business. Talent continued to head to the Rec from all parts of the British Isles, including Scotland scrum-half Andy Nicol, and Ireland winger Simon Geoghegan, whose *"dashing 70-yard solo try brought the loudest, longest ovation"* and earned him the instant devotion of the Rec crowd in Bath's October 22-11 League victory over Harlequins. *"Pure box office material"* added the Chronicle's Andrew Baldock of the Irish flyer.

Not surprisingly the national media went into a 'hyper-active frenzy' on learning of Jeremy Guscott's return from long-term injury and his selection for League action at West Hartlepool on the 15th October. That put paid to any previous press priorities at Quins, Leicester (et al). Even the Sun sent a reporter, and by all accounts West Hartlepool couldn't remember when, or if, such a response had ever happened before. They would remember however the mad rush for tickets (their press officer receiving *"more ticket demands in one day than he normally does in a season"*) and they could hardly forget the outcome either, because West Hartlepool narrowly missed creating another national headline, just failing (18-22) to topple Bath from their lofty perch.

Meanwhile young ex Clifton College flanker Ed Pearce stole half the show and former Harlequin Richard Butland (backs) stole the other half in Bath's Autumn 33-26 win over Oxford University; with both players joined in late November by fullback Phil Belgian, wing David Timmington, scrum-half Phil Harvey and locks Craig Gillies and Tim Maguire in Bath's 65-7 win over Loughborough Students, a non-League encounter that allowed both teams to put aside the result and produce a non-stop galaxy of handling. Another young talent then grabbed the accolades during Bath's knife-edged 9-10 League win at Bristol in mid-January, a derby-clash where the result did matter come hell or high water. Trailing 9-0, Bath then struck back, not least thanks to the sparkling Welsh flair of Llandovery scrum-half Marcus Olsen.

Days later there was an important announcement. It concerned (hold your breath) Bath players Ed Pearce, centre Ben Stafford, scrum-half Phil Harvey, full-back Phil Belgian, lock Craig Gillies and Andrew Blyth, George Truelove, Fraser Waters, Roy Winters and Trevor Woodman, all ten players selected for the season's England Colts squad preparing for internationals against Italy, Scotland, Wales and France. Later prop Kevin Yates, Martin Haag, Gareth Adams, Darren Crompton and Jon Sleightholme were chosen for the England A tour to Australia and Fiji; while in late March further news arrived for yet more seniors, namely the selection of Jon Callard, Mike Catt, Ben Clarke, Graham Dawe, Phil de Glanville, Jeremy Guscott, John Mallet, Steve Ojomoh and Victor Ubogu, all nine selected for England's 1995 World Cup party to South Africa. Selectors beyond the borders then called up Glasgow born Eric Peters (back-row) and prop David Hilton for their January debuts against Canada. Phew!

Yet despite all this excitement there remained the serious business of Cup rugby, and having already disposed of 4th round opponents London Scottish by 31-6 at home in December, Bath now headed northwards for 5th round action at Orrell in January. A dangerously unpredictable place is Orrell, and Bath knew it. They knew it when 16-6 down at half-time, and but for a masterful line-out display by Martin Haag they might still have known it 40 minutes later. But despite the howling winds and rains that commonly sweep down from the nearby Pennines, Bath held their nerve, and fought back to earn an admittedly narrow 19-25 win. But a win is a win and Bath went through to face quarter-final opponents Northampton, an historic club, though not in fact enjoying one of their better seasons. This fact was obvious to a 7,500 Rec crowd virtually from the kick-off and with two tries (worth five points since season 1992-3), both converted by the immaculate Callard, plus his four penalties, Bath cruised to a 26-6 victory and onwards to the semi-finals on 1st April.

Bath (you guessed it) were drawn away for the penultimate stage, and not for the first time pitched against glamour side Harlequins, traditionally strong in Cup rugby. Actually Bath made things look surprisingly simple, or in the words of Andrew Baldock (the Chronicle): *"Saturday was one of those wonderful Bath occasions-great rugby in great weather with great supporters roaring their heads off."* Or to be precise it was a 13-31 away triumph with tries by de Glanville and two from Swift, two Callard conversions plus his three penalties, and a Catt drop goal, as against tries from Staples and Challinor and a Staples penalty.

It was dreams of Cup glory again, though only if fellow finalists Wasps could be overcome, and for the first time in years there was an unexpected feeling of uncertainty regarding Bath's prospects at Twickenham. Indeed so inept was the Bath performance when losing13-18 at home to Sale on the final Saturday of Courage League action, that not only were Leicester duly crowned as League champions ahead of second placed Bath, but suddenly it seemed perfectly feasible that Wasps might at long last overcome Bath in the Cup. As Andrew Baldock wrote of the Sale encounter: *"On this evidence, Wasps can sleep easily and afford to let Bath have the nightmares."* Further doubts arose by the late injury-withdrawal of the brilliant Jon Hall, due (like Swift) to retire after the Twickenham date. Thus a back-row forward described by Jeremy Guscott 'as quite simply the finest rugby player he'd ever known,' would not alas be leading out his team at Twickenham for a last and perhaps glorious farewell.

More drama however, this time on a national scale, would now unfold. Because below the surface of the rugby game tensions were stirring, as they had been for some considerable time. When therefore feelings erupted into 'open space,' as they shortly would, the previously unchallenged control imposed by the RFU since its formation in

1871 would evaporate virtually over-night. The cause of the unrest was the RFU's stringent policy regarding amateurism, and since the mid to late 1980's voices had been increasingly raised from sections of the game (and media) asking for at least some flexibility on this matter. Admittedly the governing body didn't actually shoot the messenger. They just ignored him instead. But the simple fact was that considerable sums of money were now pouring into a rugby success story, and as a direct result commercial interests, the media, administrators and the advertising industry were among those benefiting financially, and that is with one notable exception….the players!

But the refusal to at least consider the possibility that an advertising deal, for example, between a sports kit producer and players might simply be a normal business transaction, was deemed off-limits. Off-limits or not, in 1982 the Welsh RFU (Bath Chronicle, 14th December 1982) had stated that *"it was saddening to learn"* that certain former Welsh internationals had on occasions received payment for wearing sponsored rugby boots. It was further reported *"that there are other companies involved;"* and rumour during this era (it is stressed 'rumour only') suggested that such arrangements extended to other Home international players, and to at least one entire international team. Ironically such a ban was arguably a restraint of trade and thus *prima facie* illegal. Heaven help the player however if known to have broken the rigid interpretation of amateurism as still imposed by the RFU! Those attitudes for example that had led to the ban on Tremayne Rodd for freelance rugby journalism, Dave Alred for playing US pro' Grid Iron football and would ban 1994 Cambridge Blue out-half Adrian Spencer for previous appearances in Rugby League (as an amateur!) were attitudes that had not changed.

Beyond the confines of Twickenham however something had changed….and many senior players (not lacking wider support either) had just about 'had' enough. It was their efforts after all that had led rugby union to new heights of popularity, and not forgetting either that international games could by this stage generate some £1.5 million a match. Le Monde for instance featured an article about the Bath club prior to the England v France match in February, and the Chronicle, (9th February 1995) reported that 'Bath rugby shirts were among the top sellers in Japan, Africa and the US.' Indeed at an 'emergency meeting of the Courage League first division clubs' (20th April) Bath chairman Richard Mawditt spoke for many when stating: *"We, as first division clubs, are fed up being dictated to, even ignored. We want to have a clear place in the structure and a better form of communication within the RFU."* Moreover the governing body were facing open defiance from certain sections of the game, and since sporting prowess has never hindered employment prospects, it was significant that at least one major London club made no apologies for admitting that jobs could be arranged without difficulty for leading players if so required. Nor was such a practice confined to London clubs, it should be added.

Meanwhile Leicester had established a trust fund in 1993, with the purpose of 'generating cash for their players;' and (Chronicle, 7th April, 1995) Bath, under the guidance of businessman Malcolm Pearce, launched a similar project, namely their own limited company (Bath Players Initiative) geared to 'market off-field activities' both for the benefit of the players and a chosen charity. In effect the two clubs were introducing a format for a part-time professional rugby game, and if only the RFU had at least considered the advantages of such a scheme , then huge difficulties in the not-too-distant future might well have been avoided.

But it seemed that the gloves were 'off!' The RFU would not compromise, it was too late, and comments by England captain Will Carling broadcast on a channel 4 documentary ('The State of the Union') two days before the Cup final would see to that. His views seemed perfectly rational, among them the comment that "....*everybody seems to do very well out of rugby except the players."* Few, it seemed, would disagree!

Carling's comments however included a somewhat personal reference to the senior members of the RFU, whom he described (in West Country vernacular at least) as a 'bunch of 57 old faggots;' though 'faggots' was not the exact word that Carling used. It was spoken in jest, a 'leg pull' really that anyone with even a modicum of humour would normally brush aside with a shrug and even a smile…but not the RFU! Thus at the East India Club, St James's Square, a statement was hurriedly drafted by the RFU president Dennis Easby and his executive committee, and duly announced to the Nation on the morning of the Twickenham showpiece. The statement said: "*it has been decided with regret that Will Carling's captaincy of the England team will be terminated forthwith and an announcement concerning his replacement will be made shortly. In the light of the views Will Carling has recently expressed regarding administrators, it is considered inappropriate for him to continue to represent as the England captain, the Rugby Football Union and, indeed, English sport.*" Significantly, not all members of the wider RFU committee agreed with the statement, among them the Army representative Lt. Colonel Graham Lilley, a former Bedford, Army and Barbarians flanker. "*Way over the top,"* he remarked. Others too shared his views.

The timing however of the statement (let alone its tone) that coincided with the rugby Cup Final that same afternoon and with England earnestly preparing for the World Cup two weeks hence was calamitous; and if intended to have been a suicide note then it could hardly have served its purpose better, a fact that the administrators would realise at the exact moment that the two finalists stepped out of the tunnel and on to the sacred Twickenham turf as follows:

Bath: *J. Callard, A. Swift, P. de Glanville, J. Guscott, A. Adebayo, R. Butland, I. Sanders, K. Yates, G. Adams, V. Ubogu (J. Mallet 73min), M. Haag, N. Redman, A. Robinson, S. Ojomoh, B. Clarke.*

Wasps: *J. Ufton, P. Hopley, D. Hopley, G. Childs, N. Greenstock, R. Andrew, S. Bates, D. Molloy, K. Dunn, I. Dunstan, M. Greenwood, N. Hadley, L. Dallaglio, M. White, D. Ryan.* **Referee**: *J. Pearson (Durham/RFU).*

It was customary on such occasions for the finalists to be introduced to an invited dignitary who, at perhaps this most dramatic few days of rugby union history just happened to be Dennis Easby. It genuinely was one of those moments when one didn't know whether to laugh or cry. Suffice to say that the introduction-formalities were a strained affair, and the chants of *"Carling, Carling"* that had echoed around a packed Twickenham suddenly ceased. Instead booing now greeted the RFU president. The message was unmistakable, and Bob Jenkins (sports editor, Bath Chronicle, 11th May 1995) subsequently hit the nail on the head when writing that the trouble with the 'blazers' is *"that they think English rugby belongs to them."* Well at Twickenham on 6th May the RFU was to learn a painful lesson....they now owned precisely nothing!

But what a final! Seven tries (five from Bath), non-stop attack, bone-shaking tackling....it was two of England's best showing English rugby at its best; and the off-field drama swirling around the rugby globe was forgotten for the next eighty minutes of blistering action in blistering heat. Wasps were deemed by most forecasters to be pre-match favourites, as TV match-commentator (and former Bath captain) Stuart Barnes concurred in this, his first major broadcasting assignment since commencing a new media career. Bath after all had appeared jaded in that late-season home defeat by Sale, and the masterful Mike Catt (like Hall) had since withdrawn. But as Paul Ackford (Sunday Telegraph, 7th May) later commented: *"the professional critics must learn never to write off the West Country champions;"* appropriate advice as events would show. During the opening 40 minutes half-backs Sanders and Butland, both known to be class players on their day, grew steadily in confidence and the whole Bath team responded accordingly. There was furthermore the majestic presence of lock forward Martin Haag. Perfectly capable of playing No.8 or lock at the highest level, his colleagues had long predicted that he would play for England one day. Indeed he would, and on this sunny afternoon he demonstrated exactly why. He was everywhere. His two tries (the first within five minutes) were confirmation of that. Ben Clarke then galloped over for a third before Sanders and Callard set up Tony Swift for the fourth.

Ah Swift, the perfect name for a perfect winger. The maestro turns inside. Then he accelerates round three defenders trying to catch him. No chance. He's over....try number 161 for his Bath collection, alas his last for the club. Engulfed by his team-mates, you could almost feel the emotion that swept through the ranks of his adoring followers. 'Farewell Swifty, Bath won't forget you my son!'

When on 65 minutes Callard rounded off a Butland-Guscott created overlap for a try to add to his four conversions it seemed that it was all over; well not quite. Wasps, although losing 16-36 on the day were a class act themselves. Rob Andrew's four penalties (Callard notched a brace for Bath) warned of gifting him goal opportunities anywhere within his huge kicking range, which if the wind was behind him started at the half-way line. Meanwhile prop Paddy Dunstan and Damien Hopley at centre finished off tenacious pressure with individual tries to emphasise that no team can ever drop its guard against these London guys. There was furthermore the menacing threat of the Wasps back-row of England international Dean Ryan, White, and a certain Laurence Dallaglio destined for World Cup greatness in 2003.

But this was Twickenham, almost a second home now for Bath, and if proof was needed of such a claim, this was their ninth Cup triumph in twelve seasons. Nor could one overlook the performance of Phil de Glanville, shouldered with the leadership just days prior to a vital Twickenham encounter. The captaincy for the following season was thus his for the taking; and the club he was now destined to lead had triumphed again at Twickenham, had achieved the runners-up slot in the League to Leicester and had completed 34 games, winning 25 with 4 draws and a mere 5 defeats. Now at the culmination of arguably the most dramatic year in rugby history, Bath and coach Brian Ashton during the short close-season could hopefully 'take a breather.' They deserved one.

Before the season closed down completely however one engagement remained on the Bath calendar, namely the annual club dinner at the Pavilion on 10th May. Always a jolly affair, the guest of honour on this occasion had aroused more than the normal level of interest, because by yet another quirk of fate it just happened to be the president of the RFU himself, Dennis Easby. By now Carling had been reinstated as England captain, not least because all other contenders to replace him (notably Rob Andrew and Dean Richards) had announced that they would refuse to accept the captaincy in such circumstances. Moreover the England squad had politely requested that the RFU re-think its actions, while the national press and the rugby fraternity had almost unanimously come out in support of Carling.

Not surprisingly there was a somewhat uneasy atmosphere prior to the after-dinner speeches, and a subdued groan was audible as the RFU president rose to speak. If however some had come to mock, soon enough they had reason not to. Dennis Easby, who by his own admission to the press was *"resigned to the fact that I will be the most unpopular man in British sport,"* was nonetheless a man of charm, grace, no little contrition and....humour. He sat down to warm, prolonged applause. As Stephen Jones (Sunday Times, 7th January 1996) later reported: *"He and his wife were also brave enough to travel everywhere with the team during the world cup. Even the hardened professionals in the team paid tribute to him for not hiding."*

There was irony in all this. For since changes regarding amateurism in rugby union were now inevitable, Dennis Easby suddenly seemed an ideal candidate to lead the game through the stormy waters that lay ahead. How come therefore that the hierarchy at Twickenham had remained so remote from the changing mood within the sport, and so reluctant to contemplate at least some form of compromise on the issue of amateurism? We may never know for sure. But that same evening at Bath in the presence of the RFU president himself, one was acutely aware that recent events had changed the Union game forever.

An omnipotent dynasty no longer ruled by Divine Right. Yet, as so often following revolutions (and make no mistake a revolution this was) no one had the slightest idea who now would lead the new Order. Yes….the King is dead! Long live the King! But which King? No one knew.

The action on (and off!) the field would continue into the following 1995-6 season, not least for a Bath club that in Autumn League action not only routed Bristol 52-19 at home to secure the biggest winning margin since these rivals first met in 1888, but then effectively surpassed this feat in March with their stunning 5-43 victory….away! And such was the value attached to 1st team representation in Bath colours that young prop Neil McCarthy gained selection for England U.21's against Ireland in November after only three senior outings. Another one to watch was 18 years old William Gay (son of former Bath and England No.8 David Gay), winning selection that season for England Schoolboys at lock against Japan. Meanwhile the stupendous form of Andy Robinson led to his international recall for England against South Africa at Twickenham in November, albeit England fell 14-24; and come January the former Wakefield wing Jon Sleightholme received the news of his call-up for England, this time against France in Paris.

But it would be impossible to ignore the ramifications that commenced from September 1995 when the International Rugby Board (IRB) had suddenly announced that the union game was now professional. Soon enough this decision would dominate an otherwise stupendous season at Bath and lead directly towards two hugely significant events for the club. First there would be the occasion of a life-changer of a club meeting. Secondly, Bath would be called upon to uphold the prestige of the entire rugby union game against arguably the most formidable rugby League force in the world….Wigan.

For this was to step into the kingdom of the Unknown, where hard-earned freedoms brought with them far from easy responsibilities, nor forgetting endless headaches. True, professionalism had been accepted in principle, but its application was a different matter altogether. Indeed apart from the fact that players could now be contracted for international matches (likewise a fee paid to international referees and touch judges) there was no recognised blue-print for the wider club professional game.

Meanwhile two recently formed groups, namely the EFDR (English First Division Rugby) and EPRUC Ltd (English Professional Rugby Union Clubs) were fast losing patience with the new chairman of the RFU executive, Cliff Brittle, who they argued was stalling efforts to establish a professional format. Indeed there would be suggestions of a 'breakaway' by a group of senior clubs if their own plans were to be shelved by the RFU. The counties furthermore, who formed a powerful voting group, did not always see eye to eye with the senior clubs, and according to Bath secretary John Quin, *"....their actions may ultimately force the first division clubs to go their own way."*

Among the first shocks to the system would result from the Autumn announcement that England international Rob Andrew had accepted an appointment as rugby director at renamed Newcastle Gosforth (later 'Falcons'), and this for a reported signing-on fee (Chronicle, 20th October 1995) of £750,000! This staggering figure dwarfed the £40,000 annual fee recently offered to the 21 members of England's elite international squad, and the rumour that other top players would soon follow to Newcastle (some did) quickly aroused fears among rivals that their star players might depart in a new regime of cheque-book rugby. Such fears were justified. First, any chances of establishing a part-time professional game, one which a number of first-class clubs could probably have financed, were thrown out of the proverbial window. Secondly, despite the admirable achievements of Gosforth in the 1970's, they were hardly a club that attracted the gates that could sustain such a massive financial outlay. But they didn't have to! Their financial clout was provided from elsewhere, in Newcastle Gosforth's case thanks to the backing of North East businessman Sir John Hall, Newcastle United F.C. chairman and multi-millionaire. Thus it was immediately realised that money alone could literally buy a whole team of rugby stars, akin in fact to cheque-book soccer at clubs such as Sir John Hall's Newcastle United, and so introduce a new 'culture' that could change rugby union out of all recognition. And when Sir John Hall was quoted as saying: *"I am not investing in a professional sport to have it run by amateurs,"* he wasn't joking. This was a pity, because the game would realise soon enough that the professionals weren't always that much good at running it either.

Fortunately Bath chairman (Professor) Richard Mawditt, Secretary and Registrar of Bath University, was adamant that the club must not be left stranded and defenceless by cheque-book raiders now strongly rumoured to be hovering over the Rec. Nor would he countenance any thoughts of a 'professional club breakaway' from the RFU. But he insisted *"Bath have to maintain our place into the 21st century;"* in other words there was no alternative but to swim with the tide and adopt professionalism. This proposal was duly placed before the members for approval, or otherwise, on the evening of 11th March 1996 at the Pavilion.

The membership (they were present in their hundreds) were requested to vote on the proposals accordingly, and arguments both for and against the motion were invited from the 'floor' during the course of the meeting. It was soon apparent from the reaction of the gathering that the proposals would meet with overall approval, and the crucial vote was taken: 806 in favour, six against and eight abstentions. It was an emphatic vote of confidence for Richard Mawditt and the committee, and an acceptance by the membership that Bath simply had to bite the bullet of professionalism, even if they didn't like the taste. In short it was realism versus romanticism, and realism won. The decision not only made media headlines, it even attracted interest across the Atlantic, so widespread in fact that club PR officer Ken Johnstone received an 'approach from a Wall Street agency concerning the possibility of a share issue.' Thus the technicalities of the vote (Chronicle, Neville Smith, 12th March 1996) would lead to the establishment (and transfer of assets) to a trust company; for the existing trustees to be members of the council of the trust company; and for the dissolving of the Club and forming a limited company, namely Bath Football Club Ltd. Painful though such changes were to many members, they were absolutely necessary in the circumstances. The predators meanwhile (no doubt drooling at the prospects of a dawn raid on a Bath squad that included 17 full internationals) would have to look elsewhere for spoils.

Notwithstanding the scale of the off-field drama that was dominating so much of the season, matters on-field were reaching a climax too and Bath, lest it be forgotten, were not only among the front-runners in the League, by this stage they had already reached the semi-finals of the Pilkington Cup. Getting there however had been far from plain sailing. The pre-Christmas 4th round challenge of Northampton on the Rec had required overcoming opponents who were leading the charge in Division Two and looking dead-certs for promotion, while atrocious conditions unearthed memories of Wilmslow and other cup disasters of earlier years. But a full house of 8,500 nonetheless witnessed a hard-earned 12-3 victory, with Callard's lethal boot winning the kicking dual with his four penalties against Paul Grayson's lone reply for the Saints.

Meanwhile the next stop was away at lowly Division Two Wakefield. Lowly!? This hard team of Yorkshiremen came within 60 seconds of causing the biggest cup upset in English rugby since, well…. Bath's 9-8 defeat at Waterloo in season 1992-3. It was home skipper Mike Jackson who Bath could blame for the damage, his four penalties keeping his gutsy side ahead (if only by a hairs-breadth) from Callard's two penalties and a Guscott try. But just when it seemed that Wakefield were home, recycled ball was spun out by Sanders to half-back partner Richard Butland and close enough for a 'go' at the line. The pair chose to attack on the narrow side, with less defensive cover and just enough space for Butland to do the damage. Try! Wakefield's faithful, cheering themselves hoarse throughout, were silenced. One minute ago it was 12-11 to the Yorkshiremen. Now it was 12-16 to those pesky southerners. Bath….they sure knew how to make themselves unpopular.

One week later, a Bath team angry with itself for its shortcomings in the North, let rip against Wasps with a sparkling 36-12 home League victory, followed by their 12-19 quarter-final Cup win at Bristol. That left four teams in a final pool that included Bath and Gloucester. Naturally it just 'had' to be the Kingsholm boys who were drawn against Bath.

But this time there was one consolation….at least it was to be a home tie! Or was this a consolation? For let it not be forgotten that Bath sometimes seemed more comfortable in the role of under-dog when playing Cup rugby. On home territory however they would be expected to win, and if not, then Heaven help them from the derision of jubilant Glos' supporters who would be singing their hearts out all the way back to Kingsholm.   That the respective coaches moreover were Bath's Jon Hall and Gloucester's ex Bath legend Richard Hill (who knew all the secrets of the Rec) added spice to the impending challenge.   Home advantage however did help, so too the immaculate kicking of Callard. He would coolly (Oh, so coolly) send five penalties sailing through the posts, the first within two minutes of the start. He would then convert from wide out the spectacular solo try of wing Ade Adebayo that sent Bath 19-3 ahead minutes into the second half, at which point it seemed that Gloucester could be heading for a thoroughly unpleasant afternoon.

But never take your eyes off the Cherry and Whites. They also know a thing or two about fighting back. A Martin Kimber drop goal had already given Gloucester at least a fighting chance. While a real gem of a try from scrum-half Scott Benton converted by Mark Mapletoft suggested that the visitors were getting a little too close for comfort. The fact that they did not was due to Bath's defensive capabilities, and when required they were considerable. It was 19-10, and despite a typical and threatening Gloucester fight-back 19-10 it remained. Bath it seemed were by now virtually impregnable against all-comers, save for the possible challenge of Leicester. Ah the Tigers, aristocrats of English rugby and not for the first time Bath's cup final opponents.

The Courage League meanwhile would be settled in late April with a draw on the Rec against Sale. But this was hardly your average drawn game. On the contrary it concluded on 38-38, with Bath (totally dominant in the first half, yet run ragged in the second) fighting for their very lives to earn a shared result; just enough to squeeze home for a League Championship triumph by a single point over Leicester. And Leicester it would be once again on 4th May at Twickenham, where the two contestants would step out from the tunnel into glorious sunshine to the roar of a Twickenham filled to capacity with an expectant 75,000 crowd (another new world club record):

Bath: *J. Callard, A. Lumsden, P. de Glanville (capt.), A.Adebayo, J.Sleightholme, M. Catt, A. Nicol, D. Hilton, G. Dawe, J. Mallett, M. Haag, N. Redman, S. Ojomoh, A. Robinson, W. Peters.*

Leicester: *J. Liley, S. Hackney, S. Potter, R. Robinson, R. Underwood, R.Malone, A. Kardooni, G. Rowntree, R. Cockerill, D. Garforth, M.Johnson, M. Poole, J. Wells, N. Back, D. Richards (capt.).* **Referee**: S. *Lander (Liverpool).*

Such teams as this were/are supposed to produce an afternoon of vintage open rugby…. 'supposed to' that is. In fact the Tigers (winning the lion's share of possession) instead *"chose to grind Bath into the Twickenham turf."* Indeed for much of the match that is precisely what they did. And, they seemed to have it in the bag when barely five minutes remaining lock Matt Poole stole Bath line-out ball and crashed over for a second try, adding to that of out-half Niall Malone in the opening minutes (John Liley converting), plus a Liley penalty.

Bath, replying with two Callard penalties and a Mike Catt drop goal were trailing 15-9, and if Liley's normal pin-point accuracy had converted the second Tigers try then Leicester would surely have put the result beyond reach. But a converted try for Bath, however unlikely at this stage of the match, could still steal it from Leicester's grasp, and in a tight finish Bath's fighting powers were legendary. Now with Leicester's hands all but on the trophy it was Bath who suddenly went on the rampage. "*Throwing themselves at Leicester in a concerted charge,* (Dick Tugwell, Bath Chronicle) *they swarmed into the Tiger's 22 following a determined run by centre Adebayo Adebayo and proceeded to run a series of penalties, before referee Lander became weary of Leicester's persistent offending and blew for that crucial penalty try.*" Law 26, clause 2(d) had thus kicked in, so allowing for either a penalty or penalty try for persistent infringement of the laws. That gifted Callard a sitter bang in front of the posts and the seven priceless points that would wrench that cup out of Leicester's hands. He couldn't miss surely? And neither did he miss. Thus Bath, masters of the great escape, had triumphed again for a 16-15 victory! Leicester meanwhile, completely lost for words, looked utterly devastated.

It was Bath's tenth Cup triumph. Not only that, it was their fifth Cup and League double, and as John Mason (D. Telegraph) exclaimed: "*Given different reasons, the record beggars belief.*" Leicester too found it hard to believe. But sport, like Nature, can be cruel, and so anguished was their young (and brilliant) flanker Neil Back that on the final whistle his youthful emotions got the better of him. He pushed aside referee Steve Lander, a potentially dreadful lapse from which he apologised in person, and would later regain his good name with quite stunning displays for England.

For Bath, for whom winning in the last stride was now the norm (some opponents might call it sadism), one further test remained. Because in early December the gauntlet had been thrown down that challenged this West Country club to play Wigan, one game under League rules in the North and one under Union rules at Twickenham. And Bath accepted without a second thought. It was an awesome and potentially high risk undertaking, and nothing less than the reputation of the Union code was at stake. As for the opposition, well, Wigan were generally regarded as the best Rugby League club on the planet.

Fortunately, some 'inside' information was available in the person of Gary French, who hailing from the North had previous rugby League experience to call upon. In fact apart from the World War Two period, he was the first League recruit to play union for Bath. A hooker, he had gained his Bath 1st team baptism in the final Courage match against Sale and he was willing to bet that Bath would win under the Union code rules. But under League rules against Wigan (Chronicle, 4th May, 1996) it was a different matter. *"They are the best there is,"* he said. *"It will be very difficult to hold them in a game where it is much easier to score tries."* And he warned: *"You simply must not miss a tackle...."*

Gary French knew what he was talking about, and on the evening of 8th May Wigan, full-time professionals, would unleash a stunning 82-6 display of non-stop handling at Maine Road, Manchester, running home 16 tries as against one by Bath. *"They were just fabulous...."* said Jon Callard, the scorer of Bath's lone try on the night. *"One minute we thought we had them going nowhere and the next they just took off again."* But the masters from the North were not finished yet. They next swept down to London at the weekend, running off with the Middlesex Sevens thanks to their 38-15 victory over Wasps in the final. Wasps captain Laurence Dallaglio (Chronicle, 13 May, 1996) marvelled at what he saw. *"Their sheer power, fitness, lines of running and support play were awesome,"* he said. He then added: *"For the sake of all of rugby union Bath must beat Wigan."*

So with the pride of Rugby Union at stake the two contestants stepped out upon a sun-drenched Twickenham on 25th May as follows:

Bath: *J. Callard, A. Lumsden, P. de Glanville (capt.), Adebayo (J. Ewens 57m), J. Sleightholme (R. Butland 73), Catt, I. Sanders, K.Yates, G. Dawe (G.French 74), V. Ubogu (N. McCarthy 46) M. Haag, N. Redman, A. Robinson, E. Pearce. S. Ojomoh.*

Wigan: *K.Radlinski (Smyth 75m), J. Robinson, H. Paul, G.Connelly, M.Offiah, J.Lydon (Cassidy 41), C.Murdock, T.O'Connor, M. Hall, N.Cowie, G. West (Tallec 50), A.Farrell (capt.), S.Tatupu, V.Tugamala, S.Quinnell.* **Referee:** *B. Campsall (Yorks/RFU panel).*

The likes of Jason Robinson, Henry Paul (both later in Bath colours), Martin Offiah, Joe Lydon, Andy Farrell (later Union player and coach of Saracens and England), Scott Quinnell and Va'iga Tugamala were enough to set the nerves on edge just by reading their names on the team-sheet. Add that kind of pressure to the fact that Wigan had already inflicted an 82-6 onslaught at Maine Road and one would have some idea of the atmosphere down in the Bath dressing room as they prepared to face their recent tormentors once again.

However while Wigan had exposed the gulf between Union and League at Manchester, Bath would now expose the gap between League and Union at Twickenham. Indeed come the 50th minute, by which time Bath had surged into a 39-0 lead, and their front row of Yates, Dawe and Ubogu had lifted the Wigan front trio out of the scrum so often that it seemed time to throw in the towel, some among the 40,000 crowd were seriously wondering if Bath could put 80 points on the board. But in the last quarter the Bath 'tank' was virtually empty and Wigan's professional level of fitness began to make its mark. It led to three tries, all gems, that would narrow the gap; but not enough to overtake Bath's seven (six of them real scorchers), plus their deserved penalty try when Wigan had killed the ball while being steam-rolled backwards at a five yard scrum. That seven try tally and a Callard penalty ensured a 44-19 victory at the final whistle and…. the restoration of Union pride and self-belief.

Sleightholme hands off Jason Robinson. Bath 44 v Wigan 19 at Twickenham 1996
Acknowledgements: Bob Ascott.

It proved to be an historic day, not least for Bath's former League hooker Gary French who replaced Graham Dawe late on, and for 18 years old Colston schoolboy Joe Ewens (England U.19 captain) who stepped into the fray as replacement wing on 57 minutes. Ian Sanders too was in confident mode, appearing totally underwhelmed (as did the entire Bath team) by the occasion; hence the push-over try and the six touch-downs from Ade Adebayo (a double), Sleightholme, Catt, de Glanville and the dynamic Sanders. What an occasion! Majestic Wigan, humble in victory then noble in defeat, proved themselves the supreme ambassadors of their code. Scrum-half Craig Murdock, scorer of two superb tries (the fearsome Tuigamala crashed through for their third) spoke thus (Chronicle, 27 May, 1996): *"The pace of the game was phenomenal. All credit to Bath for winning and for the way they played."*

So on a glorious May day at rugby HQ the two codes had at long last 'drawn a line' under the disputes of the past. The game really could move forwards. Watching from the stands was Wigan's injured half-back legend Shaun Edwards. His post-match verdict somehow said it all: *"That was the finest game of rugby union I have ever seen."* And so it was that Bath and Wigan had closed the book on one hundred years of divide since the Great Schism, and simultaneously had opened the first pages of a new chapter in harmony between the two codes.

Chapter 33. The MAELSTROM (1996-2000)

The summer months of 1996 would see British rugby preparing to 'sail into deep, unchartered waters.' Oh yes, those ideas of professionalism had seemed so simple in theory. In practice they were to prove anything but; and if there was one abiding fear among the first-class clubs it was the dread of relegation from the top level and dropping out of senior rugby altogether. Yet there were interesting exceptions to such anxieties, among them Newcastle Gosforth, who thanks to Sir John Hall's millions seemed safe, for the time being anyway, from such dangers. Yet whichever side of the fence one stood, the situation was summarised by Mick Cleary and Norman Harris (Observer, 16th February 1997) thus: "*when the green light was given 18 months ago, clubs were forced to go from quaint, parochial amateur outfits to lean, vigorous and slick businesses in a matter of a few weeks....*" Well some were not exactly parochial amateurs, but few if any were prepared for the shock-waves that now followed.

On the Rec there was urgency to ring-fence if possible the talented players at the club, some "*understandably tempted by a flood of staggering contract offers from other clubs*" (Dick Tugwell, Chronicle, 29th August 1996). Ben Clarke accepted a reported £500,000 to join Richmond, and who could blame him, with club-mates Darren Crompton, Chris Clark and Adam Vander joining him at Old Deer Park. That the club did not lose other star players however was due to several factors, not least the efforts of their Director of Rugby Jon Hall. Another blessing was the crucial close-season intervention of businessman Andrew Brownsword who, recognising the huge importance of the rugby club to the city, provided a £2.5 million financial safety-net that would ensure the stability so necessary during this period of rugby upheaval. Thus not only could Hall now hold on to the majority of his galaxy of stars, he could actually strengthen his squad. Nor did he concentrate solely on union talent. Hence by early September not only were lock Brian Cusock (Leinster) and young wing prospect Mike Horne playing on the Rec, but so too rugby League arrivals Christian Tyrer (Widnes), former Wales and British Lions flanker Richard Webster (Salford) and brilliant backs Henry Paul and Jason Robinson (Wigan).

A glimpse furthermore of the exciting possibilities of the new Union and League alliance was revealed in Bath's 87-15 win over Swansea in early September. Henry Paul impressed, "*scoring two magical tries,*" and Jason Robinson's first of two was typically finished off with "*a jink inside, a flash of instant acceleration and he was in the clear, ghosting in by the posts to a huge roar of acclaim.*" O Brave New World! Well not exactly.

In truth the game was in a state of semi-chaos. England had initially been threatened with exclusion from the Home Five-Nations owing to a pre-season separate TV deal with Sky; an early September England training session was abandoned owing to a boycott by the entire squad; and a continued threat by the English Professional Rugby Union Clubs (EPRUC) to breakaway was not resolved until late Autumn, a schism (Chronicle, 4th October, 1996) that would have excluded every player in Divisions 1 and 2 from England selection. Meanwhile financial difficulties were already afflicting a number of clubs, not least in Wales, where Llanelli were already reported to be facing bankruptcy, and Neath and Swansea were among other major clubs struggling to come to terms with the hurried introduction (indeed 'imposition') of professionalism. So serious was the situation in fact that the Welsh Rugby Union felt it necessary to send in accountants Price Waterhouse to examine the books of their leading clubs; a predicament that threatened any hopes of founding an Anglo-Welsh League that had seemed (to some people at least) a natural progression in the new professional age.

Bath's opening Courage League match at Orrell meanwhile was encouraging. Richard Webster instantly proved what a loss he would be to Rugby League with his power and debut try. The exciting Mike Horne on the wing ran home another try from his first touch of the ball. While young utility back Matt Perry, son of former Bath favourite Brendan Perry, duly displayed a remarkable potential. Further encouragement included an Autumn League run that included a 29-45 success at Gloucester, and later a staggering 76-7 home win against Bristol that saw Charlie Harrison at scrum-half and Jason Robinson at full-back in a Bath performance that was to "leave a Rec crowd spellbound."

Furthermore the season would see Bath (de Glanville in his second year of captaincy) take their first steps into European competition (the Heineken European Cup) with an emphatic 55-26 Pool A victory over Edinburgh. But this recently launched-competition would throw up obstacles all over the place, one soon provided by courtesy of Pontypridd and their thoroughly deserved 19-6 win in Wales. This left Bath with the essential task of beating not only Treviso, but French aces Dax if they were to have any chance of venturing beyond Pool A of the tournament. The Frenchmen duly arrived with five internationals in their ranks, a daunting array that included giant lock Olivier Roumat. Not surprisingly Bath were on their guard, effectively (and wisely) closing down the threatening French flair at source. The result? 25-16 to Bath. With Treviso then overcome 27-50 in Italy it was a quarter-final date at Cardiff in mid-November, by which time not only had England thankfully been re-instated into the Five-Nations, but Phil de Glanville was nominated as the next England captain.

The de Glanville appointment aside, it was Cardiff who won 22-19 in an absolute thriller,

when to the puzzlement of many at Bath, kicking-ace Jon Callard languished on the bench during an encounter that was not without at least three kickable penalty opportunities. What 'might have been' was clearly witnessed two weeks later when Callard notched five flawless penalties and three conversions in Bath's 36-17 win over touring Western Samoa; a match furthermore that saw the debut of new Rec international arrival Federico Mendez (Argentina), a raging bull of a front-row forward, and a further appearance of US Eagles captain Dan Lyle at lock. In January another Argentinian giant would arrive (commencing a notable Rec career) in the form of 6ft 6 ins and 19 stone lock forward German Llanes.

Despite exit from European competition, there remained plenty of action with the League, the National Cup, and the 5th round December 33-0 rout over London Irish that opened up other opportunities. But the last thing the club needed at times of rapid change were internal difficulties; and although it was known that such problems were already happening elsewhere, it was now reported that they were happening at Bath regarding head coach Brian Ashton's deep concerns as to his exact role within the club re-organisation. To the shock of many, he resigned in January, and issued (7th January, 1997) the following statement: *"I leave Bath taking some wonderful memories with me. It was a privilege working alongside so many talented players."* Significantly Ireland, not going to miss an opportunity like this, nominated Ashton as advisory coach to the Irish national squad within a week of his departure.

Another announcement followed two weeks later with Andrew Brownsword's decision to appoint himself as chairman, and so take direct command of the club. It seemed a logical step in the circumstances, not least with Bath's exit from Europe and the departure of the highly-rated Ashton. Tony Swift meanwhile, as articulate a businessman as he was a superb player, was nominated as chief executive. This strengthening of the 'boardroom' was to prove timely. Because Bath, out of Europe, would very soon be out of the Pilkington Cup when in 6th round action against Leicester in February they slumped 39-28 at home.

The off-field reaction was almost immediate. Andy Robinson was confirmed as head coach. Nigel Redman was accorded responsibility for the forwards. Dave Robson would shortly re-join in a youth development and recruitment capacity. In addition the task of overall manager was handed to former Leicester and England centre Clive Woodward, recent coach at London Irish. No one realised it at the time, but the Woodward-Robinson duo at Bath would later prove to be one of a profound importance. But, there would be no place on the staff for Jon Hall ….another shock!

When speaking of Hall, one speaks in awe of a player who ranks among the finest forwards in Bath history, yet whose fate (and likewise that of others) was to step into a pivotal role as Director of Rugby at the most difficult and dangerous time in rugby history. In less-demanding days there would have been time to 'grow' into such a role. No longer….time was now of the essence. Indeed between April 1996 and May 1997 the departures of Tony Russ (Leicester), Paul Turner (Sale), Barrie Corless (Moseley), Peter Williams (Orrell), Mark Ring (West Hartlepool), Dick Best (Harlequins) and Jon

Hall (Bath) were testament to that. As Peter Jackson stated (D. Mail, 14th May, 1997): when it comes to the sacking business *"the game has taken less than one season of full-blown professionalism to become every bit as ruthless as soccer...."*

The disruption notwithstanding, the team produced their most deadly home form with later demolition-jobs on the likes of Orrell (40-14), Sale (84-7), Gloucester (71-21) and Leicester....whom Bath crushed 47-9 with the help of six tries. That was enough to secure the runners-up slot in the Courage League, qualification for Europe, plus the selection of eight current Bath players, namely Adebayo, Catt, de Glanville, Sleightholme, Ojomoh, Mallett and the uncapped Martin Haag and Kevin Yates for the forthcoming England tour of Argentina, where both Haag and Yates won their debut caps in England's 20-46 victory over the hosts in May 1997.

So, Bath had survived the first full year of professional rugby union amid an oncoming maelstrom that had yet to reach its full destructive power. When it did come however it would be taking no prisoners....as events frighteningly close to Bath's own doorstep would shortly reveal.

In pre-season (Chronicle, 21st August, 1997) an announcement flashed across the rugby landscape....Jack Rowell had resigned as coach of the National team, and a deeply disappointed Phil de Glanville, speaking for many including England (and now Bath) hooker Mark Regan had this to say: *"He has had a wonderful career as England coach....."* Days later Bath, who could field three international captains in de Glanville (England), Dan Lyle (USA), and Andy Nicol (Scotland) fell 13-20 at home to Rob Andrew's multi-million pound Newcastle Falcons in the now Allied Dunbar Premiership, prior to action at Harlequins one week later. There England 'A' out-half Richard Butland's superb performance of five penalties, a conversion and a try masterminded a 20-27 victory under new skipper Andy Nicol, whose team were heading for an absolute roller-coaster of a season. Three key trophies were in the melting pot, namely the League, the National Cup, and....the Heineken European Cup. In one contest Bath would go hot and cold; they would crash out from another; and in the third they would triumph in a manner that would test the nerves of the strongest souls on earth. Enriching the playing-pool meanwhile was Ieuan Evans, a former Llanelli and Wales wing in the classic elusive Welsh mould, who in Autumn League action on the Rec *"conjured up two brilliant tries....as Bath clinched a decisive 47-31 victory over Allied Dunbar Premiership One rivals Richmond..."* Not to be left out, fellow countryman Nathan Thomas at flanker soon displayed the form that would lead to his recall to the Wales squad for their future summer tour of South Africa. Furthermore in November two outstanding 20-year olds, namely hooker Andy Long (formerly Bournemouth RFC) and Matt Perry at full-back, made their debuts for England against Australia at Twickenham (result: 15-15).

In United's earlier home 71-17 rout of Moseley, recently signed Zimbabwe international out-half Kennedy Tsimba's try hat-trick had revealed the exciting rugby potential of the African Nations, while teenage back Iain Balshaw contributed 26 points from two tries and eight conversions, and Mike Tindall at centre demonstrated a power sufficient to break through a brick wall. Then in March tight-head prop Chris Horsman, recovering from an illness so serious it had threatened his entire rugby career, would be honoured within weeks of his recovery with a call-up for the England U.21's against Scotland at Murrayfield.

Meanwhile European action had commenced in early Autumn with Bath taking their reputation (and their bodies) to fortress Pontypridd. This rugby stronghold, as near to a Welsh version of Gloucester as you could get, was a daunting rugby battleground. As Victor Ubogu remarked: "....*they don't lose that many games here....*" Well on this occasion they did, and with the help of tries from Ubogu, another from Butland, and a conversion and three penalties from Callard (who else), Bath clinched a critical 15-21 away victory.

Confronting Borders at Hawick proved a rather simpler task one week onwards, Bath winning 31-17 with a 5-1 try count in their favour to show for it, thanks to touch-downs from flanker Russell Earnshaw (2), Perry, Ojomoh and Chris Horsman, as against a single try from Borders' Tony Stanger. But the next challengers were reigning Heineken champions Brive in the following week on the Rec, hardly the easiest of guests to deal with. But 'dealt with' they were (just!), not least because of the response of the pack to coach Andy Robinson's exhortations that to win they simply must "....*dominate the French side up front.*" Hence with Nigel Redman omnipotent throughout, his colleagues held out against the Gallic masters with "*superb tries from Matt Perry and Mike Catt;*" and 17 priceless points from the boot of Callard that contributed towards an inches-close 27-25 victory.

After so bruising a struggle against one of Europe's finest, the return visit of Borders looked to be a nice easy afternoon. But we should have known all along that Bath are sometimes vulnerable, curiously so, when expected to win comfortably. Well, they did win, but it was worryingly close. Possibly the departure of Clive Woodward (appointed as England coach) had temporally unsettled the team. Nonetheless the 27-23 result against a battling Borders side was more of an escape than a victory. Again Callard's boot proved crucial with his five penalties and a conversion adding to his own try and another from Eric Peters. But Borders had not come to admire the city of Bath in all its Autumn glory. Oh no, they had come to put 'one' on the Sassenachs, and they very nearly did, with tries from Bryan Redpath, Michael Dodds and Tony Stanger, plus two penalties and conversion from Craig Chalmers that came uncomfortably close to spoiling the party.

In the return at Brive and a fervently passionate 12,000 home crowd the party was indeed spoiled, the cup holders gaining La Revanche with a 29-12 victory in the splendid Parc Municipal des Sports. Yet if Bath could clinch their following home leg against Pontypridd in Pool C and the other results went right for them, a quarter-final was theirs. And so it proved when in October the boot of Callard (now Woodward's replacement as club player-coach) notched another five penalties to add to a Mike Catt drop goal and a Dan Lyle try, as against a Neil Jenkins penalty and a conversion of Gareth Wyatt's try. The route to the quarter-final in early November was now assured. It would be against Cardiff, thankfully at home, yet still tough as hell.

And tough it would prove to be. But thanks to some outstanding individual performances, Bath's reward was a 32-21 win of massive importance. Callard as per usual contributed hugely with five penalties and a conversion, his accuracy punishing a Cardiff side frequently pulled up by French referee Didier Mene for offside. Cardiff however, unhappy with numerous penalties against them and the disallowing of a possible Craig Morgan try, saw things differently. The angst moreover spread to the Cardiff followers (Chronicle, 10th November, 1997), and not only did the referee at the final whistle find *himself surrounded by a group of visiting supporters as he tried to leave the field....,"* (Bath's Richard Webster, Callard and Ieuan Evans quickly intervening to calm the situation), he was later provided with a police escort to his car. It was fortunate that the incident did not escalate, as matters of crowd control fall (within reason) to the host club, in this case Bath.

Elsewhere the English contingent were falling like flies, with Harlequins, Wasps and Leicester all succumbing to French opposition; and that left Toulouse (the inaugural Heineken winners in 1996), Brive, Pau and Bath in the final draw. The dice fell in Bath's favour. They got Pau, and crucially another home tie.

Then in the space of one week in mid-December Bath lurched from one extreme to the other. First in League action they crashed 50-23 to their biggest ever defeat at Saracens. Next they survived virtually everything that the potentially brilliant Pau could throw at them. The try count was equal with one apiece from Ubogu and French international Philipp Barnat-Salles. But the penalty count fortunately went in Bath's favour with Callard's five and David Aucagne's three. The pattern of play was attacking French flair versus Bath's stone-wall defence, not forgetting some piercing running from the superb Matt Perry. Defence triumphed, just, with a 20-14 Bath victory that concluded with skipper Andy Nicol leading his exhausted but elated team on a joyous lap of honour. The final beckoned in late January. The opponents would again be Brive at neutral Bordeaux.

Vive Brive! It certainly looked that way. Victors by 29-12 against Bath in their earlier Heineken tie in France, they were doubtless further heartened by the news that a week prior to the final their opponents had suffered another crash, this time with their exit from the English National (now Tetley's Bitter) Cup against Richmond by 17-29....at home! That put the Frenchmen, playing on French territory, as favourites. Just one Bath characteristic of which they may have been unaware however: Bath's defiance when thrust into the role of David versus Goliath! Whatever the case, all questions would be answered when on 31st January 1998 the two opposing sides stepped out onto the magnificent Stade Lescure as follows:

Bath: *J.Callard, I.Evans, P.de Glanville, J. Guscott, A. Adebayo, M. Catt, A.Nicol, D.Hilton, M.Regan (F.Mendez 77), V.Ubogu, N. Redman, M. Haag, N. Thomas (R. Earnshaw 71), R. Webster, D. Lyle.*

Brive: *Penaud, J.Carrat, Lamaison, Venditti, S.Carrat (Viars), Arbizu, Carbonneau, Casadei, Travers, Crespy (Laperne 49), Alegret, Manhes, van der Linden, Magne, Duboisset (Sonnes 70).* **Referee:** *J. Fleming, (Scotland) .*

Heineken Cup Final 1998. Richard Webster blocks Brive forward drive. Other Bath players (L to R) Ubogu, Hilton, Lyle, Nicol.

Acknowledgements: Bob Ascott.

Watching were a reported 35 million on TV and an estimated 6,500 Bath supporters amongst a packed stadium that could have been sold out twice over; and for much of this exhausting encounter Brive led. As Steve Hill wrote (Chronicle, 2nd February, 1998): Brive (ahead 15-6 at the interval) *"....dominated the first half to such an extent that victory for the French side seemed a formality."* Indeed it did, especially during a ten minute spell in the second half when Bath's defence faced seven successive scrums from five metres out, yet somehow survived to ensure that Brive could not cross for a score that would surely have sealed the result. And it was Bath who then struck home with a crucial game-changer when 22 metres out from the Brive line Dan Lyle fed Nicol, who launched the deadly Guscott into open space. Unselfishly he lined up Callard for the run home....and a try and conversion to the fullback closed Bath to within two points of the Frenchmen at 15-13. This was countered however by an Alain Penaud drop goal to put Brive back in front on 18-13, only for Callard to flight home two penalties in reply, leaving Bath tenuously 18-19 ahead at normal full-time.

Home and dry? Not on your life! Near five minutes of extra-time remained and Brive went into full counter-attack mode. First Lamaison (seeking to add to his five successful penalties) spliced a penalty chance. Bath breathed once more. But then came the golden chance for out-half Lissandro Arbizu to settle matters with a straightforward drop-goal opportunity directly in front of the posts. Nerves got to him. The kick veered wide; and just when tensions reached breaking point the final whistle sounded. Jubilation!

On Sunday evening the team bus slowly chauffeured skipper Andy Nicol and his returning heroes through the streets in scenes *"hardly ever seen before in the city."* In Victoria Park alone an estimated two thousand crowd had braved a cold winter's night to acclaim the victors with rapturous cheers and applause. Thus in a season that included early exit from the National K.O. Cup, but a creditable 3rd place in the Allied Dunbar Premiership (nor forgetting a £2 million sponsorship deal with Blackthorn Cider for three years) Bath were now crowned as 1997-8 Kings of all Europe.

But make no mistake, storm clouds were approaching ever closer to the Rec, a reality that could no longer be ignored when Bristol, who with a meagre two League wins all season, dropped out of the top flight after a two leg play-off with Division Two leaders London Scottish. Such an outcome would until recently have been unthinkable. But as their relegation showed, no one was safe now. The uncontrolled rush to professionalism was taking its toll. It was every man for himself.

But though Bath 'appeared' to be relatively safe, confusion abounded elsewhere; and nowhere was this more evident than in Wales. Wales?! That Land of rugby artistry that had so inspired Bath? Yes, 'that' Wales. A rescue package of a reported £1.2 million had already been loaned by the Welsh RFU to save seven leading clubs from financial collapse within eighteen months of the launch of professionalism. While Llanelli, slayer of rugby nations, let alone rugby clubs, found themselves in the words of chairman Ron Jones (D. Mail, 11th December 1997) struggling in a *"rugby environment which is so uncertain that nothing surprises us any more;"* and that included the need to balance the books with Wigan Kiwi half-back import Frano Botica on £10,000 a match!

'Brave new world' this was not. But then revolutions rarely follow the path intended. (Ciaran Byrne, Sunday Telegraph, 8th February 1998) spoke of a 'once formidable Moseley, who by 1998 had applied for voluntary administration and sold the

Reddings;' adding that *"many [clubs] are on the verge of bankruptcy [and] the traditional rugby esprit seems to be dying out."* Furthermore Coventry, a giant of the recent past, had simply disappeared 'off the radar.' Yet, if professionalism had been introduced in organised stages of, for example, three to five years each, then that priceless asset of time could have allowed the game to adapt accordingly to those new demands thrust upon it. Or as Blackheath chairman Frank McCarthy commented ruefully (D. Mail, 12th April 1998): *"We should have taken two years over professionalism and done it properly. Instead, we tried to do the whole thing in about two weeks and made a mess."* And Bath, under new skipper Richard Webster (his captaincy interrupted in mid-December by an eye injury in the home defeat by Northampton) would be denied the chance to defend their Heineken crown, because 'English First Division Rugby' had, wisely or otherwise, withdrawn their members from the 1998-9 competition due to a dispute over both the commercial income and the control of the European tournament.

On the Home front, de Glanville would be the first Bath player to wear a No. 13 shirt since the early 1950's, following a League decision to harmonise numbers, and it proved to be lucky-13 with Bath winning 36-27 against visitors Wasps (5th September, 1998). But tensions soon came loud and clear, hardly surprising with the club enduring six straight League defeats commencing in late Autumn 1998, and with jeers and cat-calls breaking out during Bath's 11-19 home upset by Saracens, not the ideal reaction one week prior to Christmas. Fears of relegation were certainly one cause, and hardly helped either when hopes in the National (Tetley's Bitter) Cup ended abruptly with a 25-22 defeat at Newcastle Falcons. Thus Bath, so recently on top of the world, were now struggling mid-table and no more certain of their future than anyone else amid the rapid changes engulfing rugby football.

Relegated Bristol meanwhile, fighting for their financial life during summer 1998, were nonetheless rescued by Bath businessman Malcolm Pearce, and with the club leading the field for promotion duly announced (Chronicle, 18th January, 1999) to a startled world that they planned to buy out London Scottish and thus take over their Premiership fixtures for the remainder of the season. Pure fantasy this may have seemed. But since in all the confusion there was no actual guarantee that Bristol would gain promotion at the season's conclusion, a buy-out could in theory circumnavigate this hurdle. Was this legal? Probably yes. But was this feasible? Again probably yes if….money was available to finance such ambitions. And Malcolm Pearce, a high profile activist in West Country rugby circles was adamant that the necessary money 'was' available. Whether the threat of so unorthodox a take-over as this led directly to the subsequent RFU guarantee of promotion between the Divisions that would in fact ensure Bristol's return to the top-flight is unclear. What was clear however was that professionalism had opened the gates to completely unexpected business forces that answered to their own interests first and foremost; and if the game's governing body didn't like it, then bad luck mate!

Despite their inconsistent form in 1998-9, Bath had welcomed the arrival of All Black half-back Jon Preston and current Irish international centre Kevin Maggs, two high-profile faces among a recently-arrived group that included Lee Mears (hooker), Steve Borthwick (lock), and in addition scrum-half Steve Hatley and lock Ben Sturnham. But there was no doubting that the absence of European competition during the season did leave a void, not least as Bath were the reigning champions. And neither was this issue helped by the necessity to achieve a top six League place in order to gain Euro' entry for the following year, a task that during much of the 1998-9 season looked far from certain.

But any problems on the Rec were frequently dwarfed by those elsewhere and nowhere more so than at Richmond. The full extent of their plight was not widely known until the announcement in early March 1999 that benefactor Ashley Levett could no longer finance a professional club that already had cost him a staggering £8 million. The loss of his support meant that the club fell into the hands of administrators; a nightmarish predicament. For what it was worth, Bath could offer their sympathy for Richmond's plight. But they could not possibly prevent the fate that now awaited this famous rugby family, then playing (but not for much longer) at the Madejski stadium of Reading FC.

That fate was to see Richmond ejected from the Premiership as a direct result of the rule of English First Division Rugby Ltd, namely that a club in administration 'automatically forfeits its right to membership of the elite.' Since the Premiership (Peter Jackson, D. Mail, 13th May, 1999) was already a reported £30 million in debt, the finances of top flight English club rugby itself could not sustain any further losses without the possible collapse of the entire pro' game in England. It was somewhat ironic therefore that former Oxford Blue, Cardiff and Richmond scrum-half Andy Moore (David Kent, D. Mail, 30th November 1999), by now thoroughly enjoying life with a Benetton-sponsored Treviso, had some advice to offer: *"I prefer the whole ambience of rugby in Italy....Most players have jobs and that's clearly the way to go for the future."* His was another voice supporting a part-time professional format upon which a more stable professional game might have been successfully founded.

But even worse was to follow for Richmond. They would be allowed neither the time nor the leeway to play and negotiate their way out of administration, notwithstanding that Association Football allows such a possibility. Instead, one of the oldest and most respected clubs in England was forced to drop down to the very basement of the entire English League system; while of their fellow kindred Exiles only the more viable London Irish would keep their identity intact at the top level. It was brutal treatment. But Bath (like others) could not stop to help a fallen friend. Instead harsh reality demanded that they must fight for priority number one, namely to hold on to their position in a Premiership now fraught with increasing danger. If qualification for the following season's European Cup could be attained then that would be a bonus; though such hopes had appeared remote, that is until the late March clash at Saracens, the same 'Sarries' whose 11-19 win in December had aroused such unsettling derision from a disenchanted Rec crowd.

Now on a Spring day those previous jeers turned to rousing cheers as Bath turned the form-book upside down and, helped by sparkling performances from young Welsh scrum-half Gareth Cooper and lock Steve Borthwick, they returned homewards 14-33 winners. Suddenly there was an outside chance of clinching a Heineken Cup place if other results went 'right,' although at the conclusion of the season there would be the 'small' matter of overcoming London Scottish by a minimum 36 points, yet an obstacle cleared with a staggering 76-13 victory. Thus Bath had secured a 6th (Allied Dunbar) League position and the last remaining seat on the train for Europe, not a bad 'return' for season 1998-9.

Notwithstanding the struggles and the internecine conflicts so much in evidence during these early years of professionalism, there were undeniable positives on the field of play, not least improved levels of fitness. Fitness usually means points on the board, and although top amateur sides were by no means slouches in this department, the sight of anything less than a 100% fit player at the pro' level was now a rarity. Coaching too, for long a strong point at Bath, was becoming professionalised and thus more scientific (and it was heartening that former coach Jon Hall in his role at Garryowen had guided his Irish charges to the 1998-9 All Ireland Final, albeit losing 14-11 to Cork Constitution). In addition the overall skill level was higher, while goal-kicking with some top level 'spot-kickers' was now becoming almost an art form.

Another feature (apart from the sending-off option) was the introduction of the ten minute 'sin-bin' rule now available to Allied Dunbar Premiership referees as from season 1998-9; an innovation (Neville Smith, Chronicle, 7th December 1998) experimented during the previous season and welcomed by young top-flight referee Chris Reeks from nearby Norton St. Philip: the *"ultimate thing is that the players, coaches and referees all wanted it,"* he insisted. And, he emphasised a crucial benefit resulting from the change, namely that *"the sides are certainly more disciplined now and there is less foul play than there was last season."*

In any normal period the season of 1999-2000 would have been an occasion to celebrate an often glorious century of rugby union. But this time not everyone would be attending the centenary banquet. Historic names who merely a few years back would have been automatic invitees on any top table guest list (Richmond and Blackheath, London Welsh and Scottish, Moseley and Coventry for example) would be among the absentees. While in the northern heartlands of rugby League even the best of union clubs (Waterloo, Orrell and Wakefield among them) were finding it financially unbearable to compete professionally. If not Rugby League, then soccer was the threat, and West Hartlepool RFC, with Sunderland and Newcastle United in one direction and

293

Middlesborough in the other, were compelled prior to season 1999-2000 to throw in the towel and withdraw from the ever-depleting ranks of the pro' rugby union game.

Fortunately there was no immediate threat from either soccer or Rugby League at Bath, and despite the departure of Rec favourites Jim Fallon (who had briefly returned from Leeds R.L.) and former Welsh and British Lions wing Ieuan Evans, nor forgetting the absence of Guscott, Matt Perry and de Glanville on Autumn World Cup duty for England, Bath would re-discover their winning touch, though for how long in times so uncertain one could not (indeed dare not) say. Yet by the second half of the season the club was producing some displays under new captain Jon Callard that were positively inspired. Nor had they started too badly either with a sparkling September 10-30 win at Harlequins, a success that included eye-catching performances from Welsh newcomer Gavin Thomas at flanker, Irish prop Clem Boyd and the incisive running of Aussie centre Shaun Berne.

But if there was to be one blot on the landscape then it would be the agonisingly-close exit from the Heineken European Cup, where a one point upset in Wales would prove to be decisive in that season's 'Group from Hell.' The chief danger were pre-tournament favourites Toulouse, though Swansea were not far behind; and Padova being Italian and therefore unpredictable posed another threat. The mathematics furthermore indicated that at least one away win must be clinched, nor forgetting that unless something unexpected happened, opponents literally 'must' be beaten at home.

Well something unexpected did happen. First, Bath lost 25-32 against Toulouse at home in their opening tie, but won magnificently 14-19 in France, an encounter that included five from five successful kicks from All Black Jon Preston and prop Jon Mallett producing a mighty performance against one the strongest front-rows in France. This put Bath and Toulouse neck and neck; while emphatic victories away (15-56) and then home (41-0) against Padova, plus a 20-9 home win over Swansea produced further results that would probably have assured Bath a place into the last eight, save for an earlier 10-9 injury time defeat at Swansea. That upset 'killed' it for Bath. And if this was not disappointment enough they suffered again with a 13-6 defeat at Kingsholm in their opening National (Tetley's Bitter) Cup tie.

Nonetheless the superb January away win at Toulouse had helped to galvanise Jon Callard's men into a Bath side perhaps not seen since the game had turned professional four seasons ago. Indeed barely a foot was put wrong in the second half of a season that produced a string of victories both home and away. Nothing gets the message across better than winning away, in this case forcefully delivered at the respective doorsteps of Newcastle Falcons (16-20), Gloucester (16-36) and Northampton (13-17). Even more impressive was the nine-try and 16-64 victory at London Irish, a win partly inspired by the sheer power of Ben Clarke (now returned from Richmond). It was a performance of such quality that Stuart Collier (Chronicle, 13th March, 2000) was 'moved' to comment thus: *"....rarely in the professional era had the team appeared to believe so firmly in their collective ability."*

At home meanwhile, wins over Bristol, Sale, Saracens and a crushing 77-19 victory against Harlequins suggested that Bath (to the relief of their followers) were adapting successfully to the new professional era; so too Leicester, who with their huge natural resources were seemingly unsinkable, and whose 43-25 League victory over Bath at Welford Road on the last day of the season determined that the Tigers took the title for a second year, with Bath as runners-up.

No one was bemoaning second place however; and it was encouraging too that the younger generation on the Rec were now repaying the faith placed upon their youthful shoulders, among them backs Mike Tindall and Iain Balshaw, both commencing England international careers in the inaugural 'Six Nations' Championship encounter against Ireland at Twickenham on 5th February 2000. Tindall scored on his debut, Balshaw replaced Matt Perry late on, and Kevin Maggs played wing for Ireland. Further promise too was revealed by Bath flankers Angus Gardiner and Gavin Thomas who ran out for England and Wales respectively in the England v Wales 'A' international on the Rec in early March, England winning 14-9.

So ended a sometimes epic and yet turbulent rugby decade, one that would end with a tinge of sadness for Bath at the news of Victor Ubogu's impending retirement from a club he had served for so long and with such distinction. Ever a favourite, he led out the team to the sound of an emotional farewell in Bath's final home game against Saracens; while his own regrets at leaving a club and a city that meant much to him were shared furthermore by another player soon to depart the Rec, namely 6ft 10in former Wallaby lock Warwick Waugh. His appearances for Bath (with Kiwi Jon Preston, Aussie Shaun Berne and American Dan Lyle currently in their ranks) had been limited by the rule then applying that two overseas players only could play simultaneously in League games. Hence the departure of Waugh from a city that he had in his own words *"fallen in love with,"* emotions (expressed in this case by an Australian) that provided another clue to Bath's remarkable achievements and equally their fortitude in the face of adversity. That clue was (and is) simple to define: *"a shared love of both the club and its parent city."*

Chapter 34. THE FATEFUL HOUR. (2000-03)

Come the opening season of the 21ˢᵗ century Bath had reason to hope that they had escaped from the upheavals of the past five years. It had been a bumpy ride at times, but others had fared considerably worse. The much respected Ben Clarke was now captain, and Jon Callard (safe hands personified) had stepped into the role vacated by Andy Robinson's call-up to the full England coaching staff. Meanwhile backs Tom Voyce, Stuart Bellinger and prop forward David Barnes were numbered among the new arrivals.

But 'bets were off' for much of the first half of the now Zurich sponsored Premiership of season 2000-001, despite an early season trio of wins that included a 38-22 victory over Harlequins. But defeats from the likes of Northampton away and a 21-33 home upset against Saracens were reasons for caution. Heineken Cup hopes were likewise somewhat mixed, with an opening 26-13 home win over Castres in October, followed by defeats at Newport and Munster. Castres were later overcome 19-32 in France and Munster were convincingly defeated 38-10 on the Rec (two excellent results); but second chances don't come often in the Heineken, and the ground lost by those earlier defeats could not be recovered.

Jerry Guscott England v Tonga 15/10/1999
Jeremy Guscott scores and Mike Catt supports

Acknowledgements: Bob Ascott

The National Cup ('Tetley's Bitter') was proving no more successful, with Bath crashing out of the competition at their first attempt with an 18-24 home defeat against, wait for it....Gloucester! While rubbing salt into wounded pride was the 16-9 upset at the Memorial Ground in December, Bristol's first victory against their arch rivals for thirteen fruitless years; and where Bath's promising Sam Cox (19 years old) was presented with arguably the hardest task in rugby, namely stepping into the shoes of the retiring Jeremy Guscott.

But the season would not pass without drama at the highest level of the game when Bath's international contingent had found themselves in the heat of a dispute described by England manager Clive Woodward as *"one the saddest days in the history of English rugby union."* The issue involved a disagreement with the RFU over players' match fees, and only days after Bath's Matt Perry, Mike Tindall and Mike Catt had featured in England's uplifting November 22-19 victory over then current World champions Australia, the entire England squad simply withdrew their services until their demand was met. They sought (Chronicle, 22nd November, 2000) a match guarantee fee-ratio of 70 per cent up front and a win bonus of 30 per cent, as opposed to the RFU's offer of an alternative 60/40 per cent ratio. The RFU, perhaps still chastened by the experience of the mid-1990's schism, duly agreed with the demands of the players. Two days later, with Bath's Mark Regan recalled as hooker alongside club team-mates Balshaw, Tindall and Mike Catt, England achieved a 19-0 victory against the Argentinians.

It was another victory however, namely Bath's pre-Christmas 56-20 home win over London Irish that would restore the necessary self-belief that led directly to a sparkling second half of the season, revealing again Bath's capacity to leap from darkness into the light in the space of a single week. Defeats became rare, victories the norm, with a later Mike Catt-inspired 13-58 victory (this time at London Irish) that led their captain and Ireland international Conor O'Shea to generously speak thus of Bath: *"They were class."*

The surge duly put the club among the pack chasing Leicester in the Zurich Premiership, where the Tigers looked to be favourites for the title. Or so it seemed, save for a totally unexpected announcement in early February and reported by the Chronicle's Owen Houlihan (8th February 2001) as follows:*"....the winners of the Zurich play-offs will be crowned English champions, rather than the side that tops the Premiership table."* Making matters not merely confusing, but nigh on ridiculous was that it was planned that the League's top 'eight' finishers would be involved in the play-offs. This raised the outside possibility (but not in theory impossible) that Leicester then currently nine points clear of the field could lose an entire season's efforts by way of one slip-up in the play-off pool, while the side in 8th position could come through on the 'inside lane' and win the League Championship, plus a Heineken place thrown in for good measure. Thankfully one month later the Premiership Rugby's marketing arm relented, and sanity returned with their decision whereby whoever finally topped the League table would indeed be crowned League champions.

Yet not everyone dismissed outright some form of play-offs for the Premiership title, among them Bath's Bob Calleja, who explained (Chronicle, 3rd March 2001): "....*there is a need for the clubs to raise revenue because we are not getting any from the RFU, and the play-offs do make the end of the season more exciting, particularly for the clubs qualifying in the top eight.*" In other words the urgent need for more finance was now well and truly setting the agenda, whether this was healthy for the game or not, as the case may be. In fact the play-offs for season 2000-1 commenced as originally stated, although as a competition separate from the Premiership itself. Furthermore Bath, assisted by former Wigan 'great' Ellery Hanley as temporary defensive coach, would reach the final after a tantalizing 31-36 semi-final victory at Wasps, so leading to the following side stepping out at Twickenham against Leicester on Sunday 13th May as follows: *Matt Perry, Iain Balshaw, Kevin Maggs, Shaun Berne Tom Voyce, Mike Catt, Gareth Cooper, Simon Emms, Andy Long, John Mallett, Mark Gabey, Steve Borthwick, Angus Gardiner, Ben Clarke (capt.), Dan Lyle; and including substitutions during match of backs Sam Cox and Rob Thirlby, and forwards Mark Regan, David Barnes, Gavin Thomas and Andy Lloyd.*

Steve Borthwick. Bath v Sale 13/10/2001
Borthwick jumps, Lyle lifts

Acknowledgements: Bob Ascott

With the Tigers already crowned League champions there was a sense of anti-climax, hence no surprise then for a rather modest 33,500 attendance. But both teams wanted to win and Tigers, wary of the Bath backs, arrived with a simple strategy to dominate the game at forward. As their giant captain Martin Johnson said: "....*if we had given Bath an inch, they would have run in the tries as they showed against Wasps last weekend.*" And so it proved from the moment that the Tigers declined a penalty chance bang in front of the Bath posts, instead launching Johnson onwards and over for a try, Tim Stimpson obliging with a conversion. Tries from Austin Healey and Winston Stanley followed later, with Stimpson's second conversion and a penalty lifting the final total to 22-10.

For Bath, lacking a reliable supply of good ball, it was not a happy afternoon; and apart from a first-half Matt Perry penalty and a late handling-move that sent replacement wing Rob Thirlby over in the right corner, Perry converting, it was generally defensive duties all afternoon. Even a glorious 50 yard run that saw Shaun Berne sweep past seven opponents was to end with a sickening leg fracture injury and his replacement by Sam Cox. So Leicester's day it was to be, and when one week later in Paris they defeated Stade Francais to win the Heineken European Cup it would be their day again.

Yet gaining 3rd place in the Zurich (hence qualification for next season's Heineken) was evidence of another good season for Bath, while in April scrum-half Gareth Cooper won his debut cap for Wales against Italy and likewise lock Steve Borthwick his own debut cap in a record England 48-19 triumph over France at Twickenham. By late April Mike Catt, Iain Balshaw and Matt Perry received their call-ups for the Lions tour of Australia; Tom Voyce, Mark Regan and Andy Long gained selection for the England 2001 summer tour of Canada and USA; likewise the as yet barely known Bath back Ollie Barkley (19 years), recently of Colston's School (Bristol) and selected for the same tour, and who would win his first England cap against the USA, notwithstanding that he had yet to play a single full game in senior club rugby. In addition the respective international debuts of Andy Lloyd (lock/back row) and Gavin Thomas (back-row) for Wales on the Welsh summer tour of 2001 to Japan clearly provided evidence of the quality within the squad.

So all appeared to bode well for the following 2001-2 season; and albeit Bath would fall 10-6 in their season-opener at newly promoted Leeds, this did not prevent Tykes coach Phil Davies (ex Wales) from generously predicting that *"Bath will, without a doubt, be challenging for the title;"* and added that *"they are a quality side who have got a lot of world class players."* True, they did. But by the end of September three further League defeats, the last a horrendous 48-9 drubbing at Leicester, left some serious questions to be answered, though an Autumn run of Heineken success at Biarritz (6-14), then at home to Swansea (38-9), followed by a competent home and away double over Edinburgh offered hope for new captain Dan Lyle and coach Jon Callard ….for the time-being at least.

Furthermore there was reason to praise the speed of reaction by the European Rugby authorities to general manager Bob Calleja's call that they urgently revise their official policy regarding player-access to fluids during Heineken matches. Alarmed by the real possibilities of dehydration, not least during Bath's late September win at Biarritz in temperatures reaching 27 degrees, Calleja (Chronicle, 5th October, 2001) sought a relaxation of the strict ruling whereby players seeking fluids were compelled to move off-field to do so. Merely days later Calleja was notified by European Rugby of a rule-change with immediate effect that allowed water-carriers (under less-restrictive conditions) to bring liquid on to the field.

There was to be no change to the club name however, despite a suggestion from some quarters that the club should follow the then current trend of, for example, Sale 'Sharks' and Newcastle 'Falcons.' In fact such ideas had once been 'in vogue' at Bath during their 19th century days; and here it was making an appearance once again. This time the idea was put to the popular vote, and some imaginations ran wild. But despite (or perhaps 'because of') nominations that included Bath Dragons, the Bullets, and not forgetting the Wreckers, the response was somewhat muted. Even the Romans, the smart-money favourite, failed to gain sufficient support. So once again the idea bit the dust. 'Bath' it was and 'Bath' it would stay!

Nor would there be a change of venue either, Bob Calleja announcing in December that Bath would stay on the Rec, and not as rumoured seek greater crowd capacity by moving home games to, for example, Swindon FC on a ground-share basis. Yet, while a large majority of supporters, local businesses and indeed the city could not bear the thought of departure from so beautiful a ground as the Rec, increased capacity with its additional revenue was now a priority; and here there would be an unexpected hurdle to jump!

Yet of the events (on and off the field) during the first half of the season, none were to be more poignant than the heart-felt respect shown prior to the Bath v Saracens match on Saturday 15th September following the 'nightmare' of New York, 9/11. A hushed silence had fallen over the Rec during the one minute's silence, an especially painful experience for Bath and US Eagles captain Dan Lyle, whose father (fortunately not among the twin tower victims) nonetheless headed the New York Military Academy.

Perhaps with thoughts elsewhere, Bath didn't win on that day, and by the half-way stage of the season it was painfully obvious that the lack of League form was beginning to raise deep concerns; and matters were hardly helped by constant demands on the Bath squad by England (and Wales!) for international players. True, no excuses were offered when despite fielding ten full internationals Bath fell 12-20 at home to London Irish (fielding three) in their opening shot at the National Cup (now Powergen-sponsored) in mid-December. But it is undeniable that club preparations will be affected if contending simultaneously with heavy demands upon players at the international level. Such was the case at Bath.

Just how demanding such pressures can be was duly emphasised in late January when Bath, preparing for a crucial Heineken quarter-final against Llanelli (losing furthermore 10-27) were handed a £5,000 fine (suspended) for retaining six players otherwise required for an England training session prior to Calcutta Cup action in Edinburgh. Coach Jon Callard was adamant that 'England Rugby Ltd' (the club/RFU organ administering England's international affairs) had granted permission for the player-retention. But whoever 'waved through' the request could not (or would not) be identified when requested by Bath to do so, leaving one to reflect on the salutary lesson that misunderstandings do sometimes occur in matters of verbal communication, as seemed to have been the case here.

But it was the League performances that were to arouse genuine fears of the dire (indeed appalling) consequences of possible relegation, and the fact that once a team falls into the spiral of defeats, the dread of the 'big drop' can become self-fulfilling. One might have assumed that Bath, until recently kings of all they surveyed, were immune from such a fate. But one would be wrong; and not making matters any easier was the departure of head coach Jon Callard in early March, handing over the reins to assistant coach (and former Wallaby hooker) Michael Foley. Arriving mid-season to oversee the forwards and now accepting the role of team director, Foley immediately appointed former Bath and England centre John Palmer as backs coach. But, time was fast running out!

And….it seemed that time already had ran out by late April when Bath crashed to a five try 36-9 defeat at Newcastle Falcons with just two must-win matches remaining, one at Gloucester followed by a rejuvenated Wasps at home. Plagued by injuries prior to their do-or-die mission at Kingsholm, Michael Foley could only pray as his make-do side prepared for so crucial an encounter, perhaps mindful of the sympathetic words of England's Matt Dawson following Northampton's recent 11-29 win at Bath. Aware of Bath's predicament, the Saints scrum-half commiserated thus (Chronicle, 28th March, 2002): *"No team in the country apart from Leicester perhaps can really afford to lose players of the calibre of Mike Catt, Matt Perry, Kevin Maggs, Gareth Cooper and Andy Williams to long-term injuries in a league as competitive as the Premiership."*

It is deeds and not words however that win matches, and it was to be the task of former US Eagles scrum-half Kevin Dalzell to lead a young Bath back-line (including Spencer Davey on his Premiership debut) into the cauldron that is Kingsholm. Another Rec youngster, Wales U.21 flanker Gareth Delve, celebrated his own debut with a late try. But there were no other celebrations that day for Bath; only a 68-12 humiliation and the haunting realisation that season 2001-2 might possibly be their last in Premiership rugby. Yet there remained nonetheless one chance of escape. For at the base of the table were Leeds, recently and crucially overcome 23-12 on the Rec. Nonetheless if Leeds won their final game (at home to Gloucester) and Bath lost at home to Wasps, the Tykes would survive.

'Out of the blue' however and for reasons of the RFU's stringent conditions of accreditation into the Premiership, both Bath and Leeds were granted their 'get out of gaol card.' For Rotherham, National League Division One champions had failed to complete the '85 stringent criteria' required for promotion. The club protested vehemently, and understandably so. But the RFU and English Rugby Ltd refused to budge an inch. It was as clinically simple as that! So the clouds lifted and Bath and Leeds lived to fight another day, notwithstanding that both clubs lost their respective final games, and Bath anyway would have survived....just! Yet now it was obvious that no Premiership club was fully safe from relegation, any more than the Titanic was unsinkable; and despite the aforementioned words of Leeds coach Phil Davies that Bath *"are a quality side who have got a lot of world-class players,"* the club had endured a frightening experience. Soon, things would be downright terrifying!

Indeed no sooner had Bath stepped out of the quagmire of season 2001-2 than come season 2002-3 they stepped right back into it again. True, the arrivals of French prop Alessio Galasso, Welsh international hooker Jonathan Humphries, back row men Adam Vander and Andy Beattie, plus backs Alex Crocket (England U.21), ex Bristol scrum-half Ross Blake and Australian U.21 half-back Chris Malone from Exeter Chiefs, would boost morale, while the opening season 22-24 victory at London Irish, was a bright start to the new campaign.

Nor for the first time would Bath excel in at least one competition, in this case the Parker Pen Challenge Cup, a home and away cup event for those clubs in the top European Leagues failing to qualify for the Heineken. Yet progress (or rather lack of it) in the Zurich was to be a different matter, very different in fact; so too the 8,250 crowd capacity limit of the Rec. Ticket demands frequently exceeded ticket availability, while Premier Rugby had now stipulated that a minimum capacity of 10,000 must be reached by the end of season 2003-4. Meanwhile a Court action resulting from an as yet little known group's opposition to further Rec development had recently ruled that 'supervision of the Rec should now pass to a charitable trust.' It was now impossible to predict when this hugely important issue might be resolved.

Yet the season was not without its brighter moments, although few and far between, and there was much pride when in February alongside club-mate Gareth Cooper, Jon Humphreys of Bath captained Wales against England in Cardiff, albeit a win for Clive Woodward's ever-improving English side; and the League debut in March of Samoan international back Elvis (yes, 'Elvis') Seveali'i, when against Saracens the former Wellington Lions winger sure had 'em all kinda shook up' (as the Chronicle's Mike Tremlett put it) with a chip-and-chaser for an 80 metre try that aroused rapturous applause around the Rec. Flanker Adam Vander too hit form that day, demonstrating the reasons for his England A re-call in a desperately needed 30-9 win that lifted the club off the bottom of the League table.

Rare brighter moments apart however, coaches Michael Foley, Brian Smith and Richard Graham found themselves wrestling with a further quandary: because while the pack under captain Danny Grewcock was seen to *"match or better Northampton, Leicester and Gloucester,"* the outsides were often under-performing. In the 29-16 defeat at Kingsholm in February for example, Bath fielded an entire international back-line, yet never once did they cross the Gloucester line, a shortfall that led Brian Smith to comment ruefully (Chronicle, 11th February, 2003) that Bath have *"got a star-studded international back division on paper. The trouble is the game isn't played on paper, it's played on grass."*

Here one reflects upon the often dazzling performances of the Bath backs from the mid-1970's to the later 1990's, a period where the outsides were led by the undisputed generalship of two half-backs, namely John Horton and Stuart Barnes. Their tactical nous, mastery of tactics and their ability to change strategy during a game as and when required were masterful. True, Bath were now blessed with the talents, among others, of Mike Catt. But like John Palmer before him, Catt was an outstanding all-rounder, and as with all utility backs he was selected when and where his talents were most needed. He was generally used as a commando-back therefore, rather than as a one-position specialist, and this lack of a more permanent half-back playmaker perhaps explains the lack of cohesion now sometimes evident with the Bath outsides.

Meanwhile the admirable progress in the European Challenge Cup (sponsored by Parker Pen) would have generated considerable excitement in any normal season. But this was not just any normal season. Indeed when by mid-January Grewcock's team had got past opponents Gran Parma (Italy), Bridgend and then Montauban (France) to reach a semi-final slot against Saracens, Bath's League form was literally about to nose-dive. Thus come late April when Bath reached the Challenge Cup final itself, they were nonetheless two League games away from possible oblivion. So too was another rugby family....Bristol!

Fate is never kind to both parties in a dual, and when in the penultimate weekend of the Zurich League programme of 2002-3 Bristol ironically faced Bath (winning 30-20) in front of some 21,000 at Bristol City's Ashton Gate, it seemed that the dice had already fallen in their favour; and even if Bath then won by a landslide against Newcastle Falcons, it would come to nought if Bristol likewise won at London Irish. Seven days remained, seven days of preparation for two crucial results that would decide the respective futures of two clubs whose rivalry was perhaps unique in English rugby. For Bath, their destiny no longer in their own hands, all else was now irrelevant. Their Powergen Cup venture (the Premiership clubs entering in the 6th round) had ended in a disappointing 29-30 quarter-final defeat at home to Northampton. Irrelevant! Their endeavours had led them to the European Challenge Cup final itself. Irrelevant! Survival in the Premiership....that it is what mattered now. Nothing else!

Only recently a joint Bath and Bristol statement suggesting a possible merger would only intensify further those pressures during the countdown to the fateful hour when one of these two rivals would drop out of the top division. Mergers after all do not always succeed, especially when in the case of Bath and Bristol the identities of the respective clubs so closely reflect the identities of their parent cities. Indeed, Mike Tindall later added (Chronicle, 9th May, 2003) that *"if the only thing which saves Bath from relegation is a merger with Bristol, it will be tantamount to survival by default;"* adding *"....and I love this club too much to want the merger with Bristol to go ahead."* Thousands of Bathonians and Bristolians would likely concur.

But come the 10th May there came the fateful hour, a moment in Bath history duly summarised by the Chronicle's Mike Tremlett as *"the most important game in the club's entire 138-year old history."* That was no exaggeration, and Jack Rowell (club director of rugby) had already warned (Chronicle, 9th December, 2002) that *"the team which goes down, unless it keeps its players, could go into oblivion."* Such therefore were the awesome responsibilities thrust upon the shoulders of the Bath team that saw action that day: *Ian Balshaw, Elvis Seveali'i, Kevin Maggs, Mike Tindall (Mike Catt, 72mins.), Tom Voyce, Olly Barkley, Gareth Cooper, David Barnes, Jon Humphreys (Lee Mears, 64), Jon Mallett (Matt Stevens, 52), Andy Beattie, Danny Grewcock (capt.), James Scaysbrook, Nathan Thomas, Dan Lyle (Gareth Delve, 62).*

Mike Tindall. Wasps v Bath 07/02/1999
Powerful running Bath and England centre

Acknowledgements: Bob Ascott

The match, under the watchful eye of Cheltenham referee Chris White, did not start well for Bath, soon trailing 0-6 from two Jonny Wilkinson penalties and facing a Falcons side full of confidence thanks to five wins in their last seven outings. But nerves settled noticeably when later Cooper fed Balshaw from the base of a ruck. A powerful burst of speed and the full-back was under the posts for Barkley to convert. Wilkinson then replied with a 40 metre penalty wide out to reclaim a 7-9 Falcons lead, only for Bath to respond with the perfect answer when hooker Jon Humphries fired the starting pistol on a handling move that reached Tindall, then Balshaw and then Voyce. Again wide out and with the line firmly in his range, there was no stopping this boy. Try number two and....anything Wilkinson could do, so too the ever-improving Barkley, his conversion from the touchline sailing serenely through the posts to put Bath 14-9 ahead.

Half-time and news came from Reading: 'Irish were leading 24-13! It was a critical psychological boost for Bath and suddenly the pressure shifted onto Bristol.

But within the opening minutes of the re-start a bullet-like 40 metre drop-goal by Wilkinson reduced the Bath lead to 14-12, far too close for comfort. Bath however had shown that it was they, not Falcons, who were best equipped to score tries, and on 50 minutes they struck again. Falcons 'messed-up' in their 22. Tindall pounced on a stray ball and Bath, a side angry with themselves for underperforming too often during the season, were in no mood to miss a chance like this one. The pack stormed forward and a fired-up Nathan Thomas made it try number three. The conversion attempt was wide out. No problem….Barkley just made it look easy, and doing a Wilkinson sent the ball gliding through the posts. Grewcock and his pack were now in full command down in the engine room. The outsides, supremely led by Barkley, were now in command of the open spaces. Ten minutes from time the bench sent Catt on to the park to replace Tindall at centre. It was a further sign of confidence. No way were Bath going to let this game slip through their fingers, not now. Falcon attacks became increasingly less threatening, while further Bath pressure led to the inevitable penalty award. Barkley duly collected the three points and Bath were now 24-12 ahead going into the home straight.

Job done? Far from it! For Bath's Premiership survival (and quite possibly their entire future in senior rugby) depended upon another encounter. Apprehensively, and fully aware of its implications, the Rec crowd held its collective breath. Then….a voice on the tannoy interrupted the stillness and the sound of sheer relief could have lifted the roof off the West stand. Irish had won 41-21! Bath 'had' survived. Countless prayers answered.

If Bath had lost that day then perhaps the defeat would have formed the epilogue of their otherwise remarkable story. Their early struggles, their almost innocent early attempts to emulate their mighty neighbours at Bristol, their tentative steps towards first-class rugby status, and finally their stunning domination of English (nay British) club rugby in the latter two decades of the 20th century….an extraordinary tale that would perhaps have passed into memory. Yet it was to be Bristol who might now face such a fate, a rugby family from whom Bath had learned so much that was so good.

On Sunday 25th May 2003 there remained one more engagement for a tired yet highly relieved Bath, namely the Parker Pen Challenge Cup final against Wasps at the Madejsk stadium, Reading; and it would be the following two line-ups watched by an 18,000 attendance, that took the field that day: **Bath:** *Matt Perry, Ian Balshaw,Elvis Seveali'i (Mike Catt, 56mins), Kevin Maggs, Mike Tindall, Olly Barkley, Gareth Cooper, David Barnes, Jonathon Humphries (Lee Mears, 52), John Mallett (Matt*

Stevens, 54), Andy Beattie, Danny Grewcock (capt.), Gavin Thomas (James Scaysbrook, 43), Nathan Thomas, Dan Lyle (Gareth Delve, 61).

Wasps: *Mark Van Guisbergen, Josh Lewsey, Fraser Waters, Stuart Abbott (Ayoola Erinle, 64), John Rudd (Kenny Logan, 31), Alex King, Martyn Wood, Craig Dowd, Phil Greening (Trevor Leota, 61), Will Green, Simon Shaw, Richard Birkett, Joe Worsley, Paul Volley (Peter Schrivenor 64), Lawrence Dallaglio (capt., Mark Lock 64).*
Referee: *Nigel Williams (Wales).*

If already relegated, this day would have been almost unbearable for the Rec faithful, since a rampantWasps ran home six tries as against Bath's four. The Londoners, in confident mode from the start, sent Josh Lewsey, Fraser Waters and Phil Greening over the whitewash for first-half tries; followed by another three for Martyn Wood (soon to join Bath), Kenny Logan and finally Trevor Leota, all six scores converted by No.10 Alex King, who, adding a further brace of penalties enjoyed an absolute field-day with the boot. Things were less happy for Bath, though one could only gasp at the two huge 50 metre plus penalties from out-half Olly Barkley, whose own try and conversion were followed by further tries from Scaysbrook; and rather ironically after skipper Grewcock's dismissal in the final 15 minutes there followed two more, first from Tindall and then Balshaw's own try and conversion to end the day with Bath the worse for a 48-30 defeat.

Yet while there would be no Parker Pen Challenge Cup (and with it entry to the following season's Heineken Cup) to proudly place on the sideboard, Bath knew that by holding on to their place in the Premiership (if only by their finger-tips) they had overcome the terrifying pressures of the one challenge that really mattered.

Chapter 35. WALKING A TIGHT-ROPE (2003-10)

Having survived the nightmare test of the previous season, no one would have dared predict the *transformation* at Bath that followed merely one season later, despite the demands upon the club equalling anything faced in the previous two years; demands now including the 2003 World Cup call-ups for Ireland's Kevin Maggs, Scotland's Simon Danielle, and the selections of club captain Danny Grewcock, Iain Balshaw and Mike Tindall for England; not forgetting Mike Catt either, who only recently had been coaxed back to match fitness by the skills of Bath's young Queensland physio' Chris Malloc.

With six key players absent for near a third of the 2003-4 season, coaches John Connelly, Michael Foley and director of rugby Jack Rowell were landed with an almighty headache, namely a partial re-think of the season's strategy and an urgent need to sign up short-term replacements as cover. Hence half-back Chris Malone was hastily recalled from Bristol, while Robbie Kidd (Otago Highlanders) and Springbok Wylie Human (Blue Bulls) were among those recruited at short notice. Joining them too was Springbok Robbie Fleck (Western Province), who not only shone on his debut in Bath's decisive November 31-17 home win over Leicester, but (Chronicle, 3rd November, 2003) spoke thus of his new rugby home: *"I've been very impressed with the set-up here at Bath….the whole professionalism of the club, the managers, the coaches and the players, has been unbelievable."* This was praise indeed, especially so by a player from the thoroughbred rugby stronghold that was South Africa. And as if to prove his point, Bath, led by acting skipper Jon Humphreys in Danny Grewcock's World Cup absence, were a team transformed; so much so that by late October, with six straight wins from six, they sat on top of the Premiership by a clear eight points. Barely five months previously they were literally fighting for their lives.

By mid-October meanwhile eyes were directed towards Australia and the unfolding drama of the World Cup. Almost immediately an SOS call had sent Bath scrum-half Martyn Wood (ex Wasps and England) flying out as emergency half-back cover, only to learn on arrival that the problem in the England camp was resolved, hence his prompt return homewards to fill the emergency his absence had created at Bath. Next came news that Danielle had already made his mark with a brace of tries in Scotland's victory against the USA (Dan Lyle playing for the States); and a Martin Johnson-led England were slowly (and on occasions narrowly) moving ever closer to achieving their own dreams. Jonny Wilkinson (assisted by the previously exiled Bath goal-kick specialist Dave Alred) was busily causing exasperation among opponents, and the always fearless Danny Grewcock (though later injured) featured in the initial rounds. Later in Sydney (22nd November 2003) his Bath colleagues would all play their part during England's classic 17-20 World Cup final triumph over Australia; while in

January a grateful West Country city would duly honour Messrs Catt, Balshaw, Tindall and Grewcock (England's World Cup squad all now MBEs) and England's assistant coach Andy Robinson (now an OBE), the freedom of Bath.

Yet it was perhaps not surprising in view of Bath's desperate struggles during the previous two seasons that some rivals sought excuses for the suddenness of Bath's unexpected recovery. Must be a fluke or something, some sources seemed to suggest. But no, it wasn't. It was genuine, and as Alex Crockett commented in mid-season: "*Most observers outside the club seem happy to suggest that we are where we are because all the Premiership clubs were playing without their World Cup stars.*" So too in fact were Bath, six players no less, and apart from the occasional hiccups they would carry on upwards and onwards….just like old times.

Well not quite like old times, and there were no excuses when sent packing 21-10 in their quarter-final Powergen quarter-final National K.O. defeat at the otherwise struggling Tykes. Progress in the Parker Pen (European) Challenge Cup however was a different matter, as Bath swept through virtually unscathed until the semi-final stage. Then came Montferrand, and a Bath home 29-15 win raised genuine hopes of a successive Challenge Cup final appearance; only for those same hopes to be dashed by the Frenchmen's home 38-22 win (assuring them a 53-51 overall points advantage) that sent Montferrand to the final instead, but where they too would be narrowly overcome 28-27 by the Harlequins.

Although Bath's minimum objective was to gain a top six Zurich League position and hence a place in the following season's Heineken Cup, their priority was to top the League table, and come their last game and a 42-13 home triumph against Gloucester that is exactly where they stood. It was not however time for the champagne just yet, as Gloucester ironically could ruefully testify. Because in the previous 2002-3 season 'play-offs' had been formerly introduced, whereby the team topping the table at the completion of the regular season would play the winner of a play-off between teams two and three in the table for the Premiership title; and Wasps, although trailing a full 15 points behind Gloucester in the final League table, nonetheless won the play-off final at Twickenham. Now, albeit trailing six points in second place behind Bath at the conclusion of the 2003-4 regular season, the Londoners were again heading back to HQ to confront the West Countrymen in the play-off final.

Yet notwithstanding the old adage that 'knock-out competition winners can be lucky, but league champions never are,' any discussion of the morality or otherwise of the play-offs was now purely academic, because they had arrived on the calendar, probably to remain there indefinitely. That being said, it was during Bath's three week spell of non-activity until the play-off final that Wasps had won the Heineken Cup 27-20 over Toulouse at Twickenham, and this suggested that the Londoners were peaking at the right time. Furthermore if Bath thought that they had at least escaped the danger of pre-final injuries through their three weeks of non-activity then irony of ironies and literally minutes prior to kick-off, Matt Perry, his brilliant rugby career saved by 'ground-breaking surgery,' twisted his ankle in the team warm-up. An emergency team change was required immediately and Catt, passed fit only that same morning, was rushed into the fullback vacancy by head coach John Connelly to join the teams now stepping onto the field as follows:

Bath Rugby: *M. Catt, A. Higgins, R. Fleck, K. Tindall (Ollie Barkley 76min), A. Crockett, C. Malone, M.Wood (H.Marten 80m), D. Barnes, J. Humphreys (capt. Lee Mears 55m), D. Bell (M. Stevens 48m), S.Borthwick, D. Grewcock (R. Fidler 80m), A. Beattie, M. Lipman (J. Scaysbrook 80m), Zak Fiaunati.*

Wasps: *M.Van Gisbergen, Josh Lewsey, F. Waters (M. Denny 79m), S. Abbott, T. Voyce, Alex King, R. Howley, T. Payne, T.Leota (B.Gotting 53m), Will Green, S. Shaw. R. Birkett, J. Worsley, P. Volley, L. Dallalio (capt.).* **Referee:** *Chris White.*

One will never know whether or not Perry's injury affected the result, although it could not possibly have occurred at a worse moment. Yet not least due to Bath's superb pack (little changed throughout the season) they led 3-0 at the interval thanks to Chris Malone's penalty on seven minutes. Within a minute of the re-start however a 35 yard drop-goal by Wasps out-half Alex King levelled matters, and in a game described by Mike Tremlett (Bath Chronicle) as an *"an 80-minute pitched battle played at Test match levels of intensity"* it seemed that just one more score could be sufficient to settle matters. Indeed it appeared that Bath might have done just enough when Borthwick's line-out domination again fed Malone, allowing the half-back time and space to flight a 30 yard drop-goal beauty over for a 6-3 Bath lead. But, on 65 minutes former Rec favourite Tom Voyce held on to a loose pass within the danger zone, immediately sending Abbot away for a try, fullback Mark Van Gisbergen converting. That put Wasps 10-6 ahead, adding further pressure on Bath, whose massive late rally could not quite breach a 15-man defensive wall. So once again the play-offs concluded with the team placed second in the regular season winning the Premiership Championship title.

Yet in a league of such quality, Bath (their 18 victories two more than nearest rivals Wasps) had regained their self-belief. In addition their six players called-up for World Cup duty emphasised the quality within the squad. While prop Matt Stevens (South African born of English parentage) and flanker Michael Lipman would win their first caps against New Zealand on England's summer tour of Australasia. Only twelve months previously the club had been staring into the abyss.

It was the sumptuous beauty of South Africa that Bath chose for their 2004-5 pre-season training venue, and although losing 29-23 against Natal Sharks in a warm-up game, it was former Springbok half-back and Sharks coach Kevin Putt who had seen enough to predict 'that Bath would again emerge as one of the top teams in the Zurich Premiership in the forthcoming season.' And although in early season the club endured a 18-33 utter humiliation from Newcastle Falcons at home (unfortunately right in front of a then record 10,400 Rec crowd who probably deserved a refund), by early March under the captaincy of Jon Humphreys and coaches John Connelly and Michael Foley they had already made it into a top-four League position and furthermore would be odds-on favourites to win the National (Powergen) Cup.

But whether among the front-runners or struggling in the danger zone, there was little escape from the ceaseless pressures facing all clubs in the Premiership. *"The demands on squads these days are incredibly tough but the play still keeps getting better and better"* commented Falcons director of rugby Rob Andrew (Chronicle, 23rd September 2004). Indeed when on 23rd August 1997 the Premiership had first opened for business the reported cumulative attendance for that weekend totalled 28,370. For the first weekend of season 2004-5 that figure had jumped to a reported 82,358. It was hardly surprising therefore that the game was now stipulating that grounds must plan for a minimum capacity of at least ten thousand as another condition of the Premiership.

It was furthermore a near certainty that the strides that had been made had enabled England to capture the coveted World Cup in the previous season; and replying to suggestions from some among the game's hierarchy that certain clubs 'were being obstructive and doing nothing to help England's cause' (Chronicle, 11th September 2004), it was Australian John Connelly who duly responded thus: *"There is no England without the clubs."* Precisely so!

Meanwhile second choice players were as vital as first choice (not infrequently their equal in ability), and Bath's excellent Autumn run of wins for example was dependent upon this vital pool of reserve strength. Mindful of this, skipper Jon Humphreys sang out the praises for the likes of locks James Hudson and Rob Fidler, flanker James Scaysbrook and utility back Alex Crockett, all deputising so ably during the absence of players either injured or on international duties.

The development of young academy talent was another priority, and it was hugely encouraging when the likes of back Kieran Lewitt for instance played an absolute 'blinder' and scored a try-stunner in Bath's late September 10-18 win at Harlequins. While in early March, 19 years old centres Tom Cheeseman (already attracting attention from Welsh selectors) and Ryan Davis (captain of the England U.21side) were thrown in at the deep end due to an injury crisis and played like veterans in the 18-10 victory over Worcester. Meanwhile another young back laying the foundations of a highly successful Rec career was Nick Abendanon, who along with club teammates Chris Brooker and Mike Myerscough featured in late season for England in the inaugural U.19 World Cup, hosted by the eventual winners South Africa.

Yet another talent was England U.19's wing Ian Davey, who not for the first time would *"show his electric pace out wide when he was given the opportunity in Bath's home EDF Cup match against Ospreys"* (Chronicle, 9 Oct. 2006). Later the speed-merchant (he could run a 10.9 seconds 100 metres) left three defenders for 'dead' when scorching over the white-wash for one of five Bath tries in their superb 20-33 league win at Newcastle Falcons in October 2007. A desire for regular 'starts' however would lead Davey to Bedford in 2008, where his exceptional pace would not surprisingly soon place him among the top try-scorers in the Championship. There was surely a lesson here, simply that there was too much talent for a Premiership of a mere 12 clubs.

By now the entire Premiership was reaching out across the rugby globe, and reflected at Bath with the arrival of backs Joe Maddock from New Zealand, and South African Frickkie Welsh (Blue Bulls) who instantly impressed with a try-double on his debut in Bath's 30-37 November win at Saracens (Chronicle, 8th November, 2004). He had this to say of his first impressions of English rugby: *"The pace was very quick at times, but not that much quicker than back at home...."* 'Not that much quicker than back at home'....in South Africa!? Time was when one would have been flattered to have been rated 'not that much slower than in that fearsome stronghold.'

Meanwhile although Bath were making steady progress during the season in the Powergen all-English Cup, Heineken hopes against a far wider spread of opponents that included challenges from France and the Pro 12 clubs from Italy, Ireland, Scotland and Wales were hopes that would vanish in January with Leinster's 23-27 win on the Rec, a defeat that halted ambitions of reaching the quarter-final stage and emphasised again the intensity of competition now faced in European-wide club competition.

By good fortune however the National Powergen Cup was still 'on' and with Premiership clubs joining the competition at the 6th round stage, Bath surged to a home 33-7 win over Harlequins with hooker Lee Mears displaying the class that led coach Connolly to conclude that *"England might start taking a serious look at him."* Soon they would. But by the quarter-finals there were no easy games left, a factor proved only too clearly with the desperately close 23-24 win at Sale; and when Bath were drawn out of the hat to meet Gloucester at Kingsholm in the semi-final it would be time for a real test of nerves, a test nonetheless that Bath would win (19-24) in the dying minutes of extra-time with an electric sprint and corner try by Andy Williams, who had returned to the Rec as a fully-fledged Welsh scrum-half cap and now proving himself to be a first-rater of a wing.

With so impressive a success, it was vital that Bath did not fall into the trap of over-confidence, albeit their Cup-final opponents Leeds Tykes were struggling deep down in the Premiership danger zone. On the other hand one can over-do caution, and with a possible League and Cup double now a possibility, the Rec was undoubtedly a happy place to be. Adding to the cheer was the full international debut of prop Duncan Bell when sent on as replacement in England's 39-7 win over Italy one week following the Kingsholm drama. Danny Grewcock, Matt Stevens and Mike Tindall were furthermore selected for the forthcoming British & Irish Lions tour of New Zealand, although injury and fitness problems would later force the unfortunate Tindall to withdraw.

311

Things regarding Tindall would then get worse, because not only would this great player be departing from the Rec come the following season, but after eight years at Bath he would be joining Gloucester; and that did not go down too well on the Rec. Mike Tremlett (Bath Chronicle 4th February 2005) was in no mood to pull his own journalistic punches either. Deploring Tindall's departure, he suggested (inter alia) that allowing a world class player to leave the club "*was based on a fallacy....that anybody out there gives a tuppeny damn [as to] whether or not Bath conform to a Premiership salary cap [that was] rendered laughable because nobody else pays it any heed.*" And Bath (who had already released Iain Balshaw to Leeds at the conclusion of season 2003-4) again seemed reluctant, according to Tremlett, to agree an annual £150,000 to keep the world-class Tindall on the Rec, notwithstanding that some Premiership salaries were reputably as high as £200,000. So arch-rivals Gloucester seized their chance. Who could blame them?

Meanwhile there was a major Cup final to prepare for, and although reportedly 1/4 favourites to win (Chronicle, 15th April 2005) John Connolly warned that the Leeds "*record in the last month has been outstanding.*" You could say that again, for since the semi-finals the Tykes had not only defeated Leicester and Gloucester, but followed this by victory over the Harlequins in a crucial relegation battle that had not only lifted Leeds off the bottom of the table, but of equal importance, had lifted their spirits by several notches too. There were further factors to ponder, namely the narrowness of Bath' 28-30 November win at Leeds in the one clash between the two finalists so far that season, and the potentially serious absence from the Bath line-up of skipper Jon Humphries, Steve Borthwick and Mike Tindall.

Nor could one ignore the experience of the Leeds coaches Phil Davies and former Bath and England international Jon Callard. Callard furthermore, soon to join the English National Academy coaching team, knew Bath inside out. So with 'all to play for' the two contestants stepped out at Twickenham on 16th April before 57,000 spectators as follows, **Bath:** *Matt Perry, Frikkie Welsh, Andrew Higgins, Olly Barkley, Joe Maddock (Brendan Daniel, 59 mins), Chris Malone, Nick Walshe (Martyn Wood, 66), Matt Stevens, Lee Mears, Duncan Bell, Rob Fidler, Danny Grewcock (capt.) Geraint Lewis, James Scaysbrook, Zak Feaunati.*

Leeds Tykes: *Ian Balshaw (capt, Diego Albanese, 3 mins), Andre Snyman, Phil Christophers (Craig McMullen, 26 mins), Chris Bell, Tom Biggs, Gordon Ross, Alan Dickens, Mike Shelley, Mark Regan (Rob Rawlinson,73), Gavin Kerr (Matt Holt, 60), Stuart Hooper, Tom Palmer, Scott Morgan, Richard Parks (Dan Hyde 60), Alix Popham (Jon Dunbar, 69 mins). Referee: David Pearson (RFU).*

One is never quite sure of the tactics opponents will employ. But against a Bath club positioned eight places and 18 points clear of Leeds, the Yorkshire side seemed likely to adopt a stonewall defence, and then seek to capitalise from any possible mistakes by their opponents. They assumed correctly; their tactics worked a treat; and from the moment in the first half when Tykes and Scottish international out-half Gordon Ross (replying to a Malone penalty for Bath) sent over two Leeds penalties to gain a 6-3 lead, it was Bath who would be playing 'catch-up.' The narrow 6-3 margin would then increase thanks to a touch of sheer class, again by courtesy of Ross, when his astute chip ahead presented a gift of an opportunity for Chris Bell to score bang under the posts. That put the un-fancied underdogs 13-3 ahead.

Two further Malone penalties narrowed the margin, suggesting that Bath could yet re-take control. But if the Tykes were waiting to pounce on further mistakes then they were about to be gifted one on a plate when with Bath on the offensive, the normally immaculate Malone risked a 50:50 pass that dropped straight into the hands of Tykes South African wing Andre Snyman. He was suddenly staring into 70 metres plus of clear space and a try under the posts was his for the taking. He took it! And this score was to prove the turning point both numerically and psychologically. The Leeds defensive tactics did not change one iota throughout the second half, and frankly nor did they need to, despite Bath securing some '85% of the possession and over 65% of territorial advantage.' Meanwhile an increasingly anxious Bath discovered that their repeated attacks were far too predictable and far too orthodox. It would be 12-20 with Malone's fourth penalty, but 12-20 it would stay. There was no change of game-plan, and the simple option of the high kick over the Tykes defence, a tactic that might just have yielded dividends, was ignored.

There were no complaints. It was a match won fair and square by a brave team of underdogs from a Rugby League stronghold where union clubs rarely capture the big headlines; and this despite losing skipper Balshaw on three minutes to injury (lock Hooper taking command). Just to rub salt into wounds Leeds visited the Rec for the final League game of the season, returning home having secured a safe 8th Premiership position from their 6-10 victory against a Bath club reaching fourth. But, for another rugby family the immediate future looked less bright, and that family were Harlequins, or to be precise a now relegated Harlequins. That a club of this stature could not avoid such a fate was another indication of the pressures in the Premiership, although Bristol's promotion back to the Premiership provided reassurance that Quins too might quickly return. Yet merely one off-season could condemn a club to rugby's version of La Guillotine. True, cups and trophies added excitement, and looked just great on the sideboard. But these were now simply 'extras.' Relegation was the number one fear; avoiding it the number one priority.

Come the new 2005-6 season that would introduce a change to the play-off format, concerns regarding an opening run of three League defeats were eased somewhat thanks to an emphatic 16-27 win at Falcons, one that included four tries by courtesy of Matt Stevens, Martyn Wood, Zak Feaunati and James Scaysbrook under new captain Steve Borthwick.

But there would be a few more of those tricky off-field issues for the top clubs to think about, of which one was fortunately resolved soon after the new season began, and involved an attempt by the RFU to 'central-contract' England's elite players, thus making them subject first and foremost to the requests of Twickenham as opposed to their parent Premiership clubs. This attempt failed owing to strong objections of both Premier Rugby and the Premiership clubs, and the alliance proved to be unbreakable. The Chronicle's Mike Tremlett moreover (14th October 2005) did not doubt the outcome if such a policy was implemented. Central contracts he wrote would: *"end the most competitive club League in world rugby."*

Competitive it certainly was, and throughout season 2005-6 Bath found it a struggle to escape from the lower half of the now Guinness-sponsored Premiership. However a handful of vital victories would prove sufficient to ensure safety from relegation, and these included a treasured double over Gloucester, the second win (15-18 at Kingsholm) highlighted by a superlative 50 yard chase and try-saving tackle by wing Andrew Higgins. Another success was achieved against an in-form Wasps in January. Inspired by French international wing David Bory, and a debut try from centre Eliota Fuimaono (recently signed as short-term cover during the 6 Nations alongside fellow Samoan international forward Jonny Faamatuainu), Bath turned the form book upside-down with an emphatic 28-16 home victory. A fortnight later, minus Matt Stevens, Borthwick, Grewcock, Lee Mears (all on England duty) and flanker Gareth Delve winning his debut cap for Wales against Scotland, a much changed Bath XV headed for the capital and a date against Saracens, a club it should be added that had grown hugely during the previous twenty years. Yet with Zimbabwean hooker Pieter Dixon (formerly Western Stormers), lock Peter Short, and Joe Maddock at fullback among its ranks, Bath's makeshift side calmed relegation jitters with a 29-34 away win that ensured a very happy homewards journey along the M4 corridor.

There would be a further happy homewards journey with the return in early January of Brian Ashton, so solving (it was hoped) the club's nation-wide search for a head coach replacement due to John Connolly's return to Australia in December. Top coaches do not just grow on trees, and not only would Connolly shortly be appointed as Australia's national coach, it was then learned that Michael Foley, having accepted the post as assistant coach, would be joining him at the end of the season too. Thus would another coaching trio move onwards, a Connolly-Foley-Rowell triumvirate who from Connolly's arrival in July 2003 had engineered, in the words of Mike Tremlett, *"one of the most remarkable turnarounds in Premiership history,"* (Chronicle, 25th November, 2005).

The availability of Ashton (coincidentally managing the National Junior Academy at Bath University at the time) was therefore a godsend; and among the Lancastrian's priorities was to secure the retention of a number of key players whose contracts were shortly due for renewal. Borthwick was reportedly high on Leicester's most-wanted

314

list, and Saracens it was rumoured could hardly wait to get their hands on Olly Barkley's signature. While regarding inwards recruitment, an impressive list of arrivals heading to the Rec included Samoans Faamatuainu and Fuimaono, Auckland scrum-half Billy Fulton, likewise Tongan international prop Taufa'ao Filise, all 6ft 4in and 19st 5lbs of his Pacific power ready to be unleashed. Michael Foley, who had emphasised that *"continuity and recruitment were vital to the club's long-term future."* would surely have approved.

On-field, a disappointing season in League competition was partially compensated with progress in the Heineken and Powergen Cups. The latter, formerly accommodating every club in English club rugby (wonderful days!) was now reformed as an Anglo-Welsh competition, limited to the twelve Premiership clubs, plus the four Welsh regional teams of Newport Gwent Dragons, Cardiff Blues, Llanelli and Ospreys (Swansea-Neath). Potentially exciting with the welcome renewal of Anglo-Welsh rugby, the triumphant finalist (if an English club) qualified for a Heineken place for the following season. With three English and one Welsh club placed in four separate pools, Bath swept through to the semi-finals against Llanelli thanks to previous wins over Bristol at home, then (and not least owing to Chris Goodman's outstanding back-row performance) the Ospreys away, followed by Gloucester at home. With home advantage again raising hopes for a passport to the final, visitors Llanelli spoiled the party with their 26-27 victory, reason enough for singing their hearts out back to West Wales; although the singing would doubtless have stopped with 'their' defeat in the final against Wasps, now fast taking over the mantle from Bath as the masters of Cup winning rugby.

Heineken progress however reached the quarter-final stage thanks to sufficient points gained in the first stages against opponents Leinster, Bourgoin and Glasgow Warriors. Bath's reward (for want of a better word) was then a quarter-final date at Leicester, a tie so electrifying that it was switched to Leicester City's Walker Stadium, where a capacity 32,500 crowd witnessed a magnificent 12-15 Bath triumph. A semi-final at Biarritz beckoned. One step away from the glamour of a European final! Even so there remained a yet greater objective; and despite the seemingly comfortable margin of eleven points in mid-April separating Bath from a Leeds side struggling at the base of the Premiership, Brian Ashton was taking no chances. Thus prior to a Bath v Bristol league game one week prior to the Heineken semi-final in France, he stressed the absolute priority of survival in the top-flight: *"this is more important in the long term than next week [at Biarritz]....we want to be here in the Premiership next season. It's fantastic to be in a Heineken Cup semi-final but that's next week not this week."* And, it was Ashton's words that put things into perspective. Because it was the subsequent 31-16 victory over Bristol that would not only lift Bath to near certain Premiership safety, but would soften the blow in the following week when losing 18-9 in France.

At the conclusion of the Guinness Premiership campaign Bath finished in a disappointing (but crucially safe) 9th position. Higher up the table meanwhile there had been a veritable scramble for a top four play-off slot, with Sale in top position, followed by Leicester, London Irish and Wasps respectively; and under the revised format the 1st placed side played at home against the 4th, and the 2nd placed side played at home against the 3rd. It was fair (whether or not one agreed with such a play-off system) and teams one and two (Sale and Leicester) went through to the final, where for the first time since the play-offs were introduced in 2002-3 the team topping the regular League table, namely Sale, defeated Leicester to win the Championship title. Justice it could be said was thus seen to be done….at last!

But the 2005-6 season could not pass without acknowledging a statement from former international Rob Andrew, one that spoke of *"the suffocating fear of Premiership relegation,"* a fear he argued that 'could have a major effect on England's preparations for the 2007 World Cup' (Chronicle, 30th January 2006). His timely warning expressed that feeling of dread felt by any club fighting for its survival down in the depths of the relegation zone, and as early as January no fewer than five clubs were already struggling in that fateful place, separated by a mere nine points. *"The implications of relegation for any club are staggering,"* and Andrew added: *"People don't understand the problem though, and I don't know who is going to sort it out because I don't think there is anyone who is capable."*

He continued, *"We can't get out of this cycle unless they sort relegation out. The more the conflict between England and the clubs continues, the worse it is going to get because there is too much pressure on sides. There is not a poor team in this League, but somebody is going to go through the trap door in May."* That somebody in fact would be Leeds, and the exit of this gutsy Yorkshire club sounded another warning. Because with their departure from the top tier there now remained only two Premiership standard-bearers north of the Trent, namely Sale and Newcastle Falcons. If one club, or Heaven forbid both, should drop out of the top echelon then Rugby Union's writ would effectively cease at Leicester, and likewise reduce considerably the code's influence in the rival northern Rugby League heartlands. It was increasingly obvious therefore that the spectre of the drop was overshadowing all else in the Premiership, and Rob Andrew had now taken it upon himself to step up to the rostrum and challenge someone, somewhere, 'to sort it out.' That *"suffocating fear"* of which he spoke, the huge outlay in effort and cost required to climb back into the Premiership if relegated (assuming that one survives the maze of the promotional play-offs)….these were just some of the realities that contributed to that constant fear. Quite simply, the clubs were walking a tight-rope.

2006-7 would prove to be another of those roller-coaster seasons of which Bath were now well acquainted. Results both good and bad poured in during the early stages with a 24-19 defeat at Gloucester, then a 43-25 home win thriller over Leicester, a 33-18 upset at Northampton, and finally a 17-11 home victory over a gutsy Worcester still 'finding their feet' in the Premiership. Hopes for stability received a set-back however with the unsettlingly quick (though understandable) departure of Brian Ashton with his call-up to the England coaching staff during the close-season, a loss that put Bath in a vulnerable situation. Rated by Mike Tremlett as *"the northern hemisphere's top attacking coach"* the club were left frantically searching for a replacement who 'just might' be out of contract. 'Out of the blue' two newcomers (virtually unknown on the Rec) were recruited to assist forwards coach Mark Bakewell, of whom the first was former Castleford rugby League star Brad Davis as defence coach, and fellow Australian Steve Meehan, whose experience as backs-coach at Stade Francais had attracted the attention of the Bath management.

There was no underestimating the huge responsibility that was now heaped upon their relatively young shoulders as the new pair stepped into a Premiership described by fellow Australian Shaun Berne (back in Bath colours after a five year absence) thus: there *"isn't a domestic League in world rugby which makes the comparable demands on players or, for that matter coaches,"* (Chronicle, 2nd September, 2006). In fact the pair had barely enough time to unpack their bags before Bath demonstrated the full repertoire of their numerous contradictions. First, with defeats at Bristol, then at home to Ospreys and finally a 30-12 fall at Gloucester, the club would soon wave goodbye to any further participation in the now EDF Energy-sponsored Anglo-Welsh Cup by early December. But, by mid-April this same Bath club, having scattered aside opponents with (in most cases) nonchalant ease, would storm into the final itself of the European Challenge Cup. Likewise among the highlights of the club's Premiership campaign was the arrival of former Leeds Rhinos and Great Britain back Chev Walker. His baptism in Bath's November 20-14 win against Newcastle Falcons, only a month since switching codes, revealed the 24 years old Walker looking equally comfortable in the 15-a-side game. Albeit selected on the left wing (he preferred centre), his presence was felt across the park. His defence was sound, and when the ball got into his hands it was a case of 'watch-out, sparks could fly.' Furthermore, Walker's summary of his first afternoon in Union was humbling from one so gifted: *"I felt vulnerable at times but it was a great comfort to have somebody like Matt Perry out there to keep me right."*

But head coach Meehan was far too experienced to underestimate the task of creating a confident championship-chasing Premiership rugby team. He stressed the need for consistency, and not making things easier for him was the fact that Bath were regrettably earning a reputation for gifting penalties. Injuries too were a headache (admittedly not only for Bath), and especially frustrating when considering the sudden transformation when Matt Stevens (side-lined for eleven months) re-joined the front-row in Bath's January League match against Quins on the Rec. The 24 year old tight-head *"lifted Bath's forward play on to a different plane;"* a domination that produced four tries from skipper Borthwick, Joe Maddock, Chris Malone and Samoan Eliota

317

Fuimaono in a 31-23 victory that ranked among Bath's best performances of the season.

Yet even better was seen with Bath's performances in the 2006-7 European Challenge Cup. First it was 14-21 at Montpellier, followed by a 42-17 win on the Rec. Next Connacht fell 21-19 in Bath, and then 24-36 in Ireland, followed later by a Harlequins side overcome 18-24 at the Stoop, then 20-14 at Bath. And then…. there was to be one of those glorious days when Bath 'go slightly barmy.' It was the Challenge Cup quarter-final against Bristol and at half-time Bath walked off the park the wrong side of a 10-12 score-line. Forty minutes of pulsating action later they strode off that same park with a 51-12 victory under their belts, and an 8 to 2 try count in their favour that included a trio from rising star Nick Abendanon, soon to be a full international on England's summer tour of South Africa. Saracens, now on full alert in the semi-finals and playing on home soil, provided an especially tough challenge; but not tough enough to prevent Bath inching home in a 30-31 nail-biter that opened the gateway to a final between Bath and French side Clermont on 19th May at the Stoop.

The financial reward from a successful campaign in, for example, the European Challenge Cup (formerly Parker Pen Challenge Cup), partly assists in financing a Premiership club, and the Bath figures for the previous season of 2005-6 (Chronicle, 30th January 2007) that referred to profits of £283,000 suggested that fiscally all was well. But figures can be deceptive, and as chief executive Bob Calleja remarked, they were only *"superficially encouraging."* Indeed the total was partly *"achieved because [of] a good run in the Heineken Cup and [because of] compensation from the RFU for releasing Brian Ashton from his coaching contract."* Furthermore "the *total wage bill amounted to £2,2 million,"* and 'player contracts, coaches, physiotherapists and other staff totalled 62% of over-all costs.' Concluding the financial report with a reference to a possible European Challenge Cup success that would additionally provide the winner with a financially beneficial Heineken place for season 2007-8, it was emphasised that the club were *"still very much relying on the decision over the development of the Rec."*

Ah, the Rec, (Chronicle 9th November, 2006) whose much-discussed future during this period was subject to a covenant made in April 1922 between the trustees of the estate and the Bath and County Recreation Ground Trust. That the *"Corporation will not use The Recreation Ground otherwise than as an open space and will not show preference to or in favour of any particular game or sport, club, body or organisation"* was among the conditions of this original 1922 conveyance; and as it happened Bath RFC had never departed from this principal, having over the decades shared this large expanse with cricket, hockey, lacrosse, tennis and indeed other sporting activities.

A more contested issue however was the fact that the 1922 document also *"excludes all building of any kind;"* and it was this condition that opponents argued would block any plans for an enlarged three-sided horse-shoe-style development proposed by the club.

318

However, years before the 1922 document had been drafted and signed, there existed two buildings (constructions) that had already been built, namely the original West stand (since replaced) and the cricket club pavilion. Significantly no one associated with the 1922 document (be it drafters or signatories) had raised any objections to these building projects. But then why should they? Because neither of the buildings, nor those that followed, were built 'on' the Rec, but around its perimeter, and hence it could be forcefully claimed that they were not infringing upon either the wording or the intentions of the conveyance.

Meanwhile the campaign to 'Keep Bath Rugby at the Rec' had been launched 'big time' by the Bath Chronicle in its editorial column of 16th September 2006, emphasising that *"forcing Bath Rugby off the Rec would be akin to pebble-dashing the Royal Crescent,"* and adding that the *"club is responsible for bringing a huge amount of money into the local economy and is at the heart of the community of Bath."* The arguments, both for and against, then went into overdrive. It was 'touching' therefore that in addition to the huge wall of local support, it was the views of many from way beyond the city who also felt something 'special' about this unique ground. Joanne Owers from Hertfordshire for example, who despite her proximity to the big London clubs, was a regular visitor and spoke thus: *"It is 130 miles each way and I come to every home game....I don't miss one."* Supporter Tony Strudwick from Surrey wrote that *"he believed there was a symbolic relationship between the city and the club."* Fran Eddolls who travelled regularly from Southampton concurred.

The media big-names likewise joined the chorus. The Rec *"is a beautiful and historic location and is in such a unique setting....it personifies Bath,"* commented former England hooker and by now TV/Radio rugby pundit Brian Moore. Broadcaster John Inverdale (the Daily Telegraph 8th November, 2006) described the Rec as *"one of the most beautiful in the country."* While by mid-November the Penny Brinton-led Supporters Club petition (assisted by Helen Grace) had already reached the 20,000 signature mark for the 'Keep' campaign.

Local businessmen and tourist chiefs lost no time to voice their own support, Robin Bischert of Bath Tourism Plus declaring that *"The Rec is iconic. Very few cities have such an accessible stadium – it attracts people to the city rather like The Coliseum."* While former city tourism chief Peter Rollins spoke of a previous survey revealing that *"besides the Roman Baths and the wonderful Georgian architecture, Bath Rugby came up time and time again."* Mark Jackson of Helphire, a major club sponsor, spoke of *"a great opportunity to develop a major resource to the city."*

And....Bath Rugby chairman Andrew Brownsword (Chronicle, 12th January 2007) articulated to perfection the emotions felt by so many, so deeply, as follows: *"keeping rugby at the Rec was vital,"* he said, *"not just for the club but for the community as a whole. It is my city, the city I love, and I think Bath rugby is the beating heart of this fantastic city."* Of relevance too had been the quarterly Burgess Salmon index (2005-

6), reporting for the regional group 'Business West,' indicating (inter alia) that the then current lack of sporting success in the south west was adversely affecting the regional economy, but that Bath Rugby were bucking this trend. This was no surprise to Chief executive Bob Calleja who, stressing the importance of regular Rec attendances of some 10,500, emphasised (Bath Chronicle, 4th April 2006) that a recent survey had revealed that *"retail outlets improve turnover by 20 per cent on match days."*

The Chronicle (17th March 2007) then reported that two independent surveys had indicated the overwhelming support for the club to remain on this historic ground. Of these the official Strategic Review revealed that 83.1% backed the rugby club option for Rec development, 8.9% backed the somewhat similar Bathsport group plan for a new arena complex, while 6.6% backed the motion to remove all sporting activity from the Rec entirely. The decision was now principally a matter for the Charity Commission, permission which come June 2013 would be granted, although even then hurdles remained.

On the pitch Bath would reach a humble yet safe 8th position, and it was not until their 12-20 success at Newcastle Falcons in their final League game that they would notch an away win; by which time the admired Matt Perry had retired and cover for his departure fulfilled by the promising (former) Falcons utility back Michael Stephenson. But.... a victory in the European Challenge Cup final against Clermont Auvergne would certainly change the complexion of an otherwise unspectacular 2006-7 Premiership campaign; and come 19th May at the Stoop it was left to the following **Bath** side to provide that change: *Nick Abendanon, Joe Maddock, Eliota Fuimaono, Olly Barkley, David Bory (Tom Cheeseman, 50min), Shaun Berne (Chris Malone, 60min), Nick Walshe (Andy Williams, 61min), David Barnes, Lee Mears (Pieter Dixon 72min), Matt Stevens, Steve Borthwick (capt.), Danny Grewcock, Andy Beattie (Peter Short, 62min), Michael Lipman, Zak Feaunati (James Scaysbrook 61min).*

Opposing Borthwick's team were **Clermont Auvergne:** *Anthony Floch, Aurelien Rougerie, Grant Esterhuizen (Seremaia Baikenuku, 59min), Tony Marsh, Julien Malzieu, Brock James, Pierre Mignoni, Laurent Emmanuelli, Mario Ledesma (Brice Miguel, 64min), Martin Szelco (Goderzi Shvelidze, 62min), Jamie Cudmore, Thibaud Privat (Loic Jacquet, 44min), Michel Dieude (Gonzalo Longo, 45min), Sam Broomhall, Elvis Vermuelen.* **Referee:** *Nigel Owen (Wales).*

This would be another Cup day when there could be no complaints about the outcome, Clermont's three tries to one in their 16-22 victory was hard evidence of that; and the fact is that when French sides get the wind in their sails one is left to sit back and simply admire their deftness of touch and their Gallic flair. Making things worse, Clermont would prove themselves generally excellent in defence. Indeed despite leading 6-3 at the interval through two Olly Barkley penalties to one by Clermont's Australian half-back Brock James, Bath had not seemed entirely comfortable. Clermont by contrast had looked a team with something extra up their sleeves just waiting to be unleashed.

And, come the second half unleashed it was. First Clermont wing Julien Malsieu's pace took him over the line, James converting. Next, clean ball was quickly recycled for the backs to launch Tony Marsh into the corner. Then there came what seemed to be the killer-blow when the ever dangerous James chipped over the Bath defence and with the bounce going kindly scored under the posts. Clermont were now in command, and Clermont knew it! Trailing 6-23, Bath to their credit threw caution aside and staged a fight-back that led to Joe Maddock crashing through four tackles to land a try beneath the posts, Barkley converting. Later a driving maul led Bath to believe that Peter Short had touched down for a second try, only for 'television match official' (TMO) Gareth Simmonds to decide otherwise. A long range 40 metres penalty by Barkley then sent pulses racing amongst the 10,134 mostly Bath supporting crowd. But again 'Non,' as Clermont's lead proved to be out of range, sending the French side homeward bound with the European Challenge Cup safely in their possession.

It was now four attempts in five years that a trophy had eluded Bath at the final hurdle of a major competition, and much soul-searching resulted among players and supporters alike. Prop David Barnes and skipper Borthwick expressed concerns about

Butch James: Bath's Springbok outside half: none better at unlocking defences.

Acknowledgments Bob Ascott

an expected exodus of players, a worrying list that included Andy Williams, Chris Malone, and David Bory. Gareth Delve in addition seemed to be heading to a high-flying Gloucester. Moreover with the lack of consistency in their League performances there was little to suggest that the club could achieve a high Premiership position come the following season. Even so things could have been worse, and with the relegation of Northampton, another club many would have assumed was nigh-on impregnable, Bath (and not only Bath) could count their blessings that they had at least secured their first and foremost objective, namely survival in the Premiership.

Come 2007-8 Alex Crockett would be acting captain during the World Cup absence of Steve Borthwick, Matt Stevens, Lee Mears, Olly Barkley (all England) and Samoan Eliota Fuimaono, and Bath launched their own season with warm-up friendlies (all won) against Llanelli away, Edinburgh and Leinster; and it was at Llanelli that the less widely known names of Matt Banahan, lock Mike Myerscough and back-rower Chris Goodman were seen on the Bath score-sheet with tries apiece in an 17-21 away win. Another arrival would soon attract favourable attention, namely Michael Claassens from Free State Cheetahs, one part of a world-class Springboks half-back pairing that would include out-half Butch James from Natal Sharks.

In addition the acquisitions of New Zealand back-rower Daniel Browne from Northampton, lock Martin Purdy from Wasps, Lorne Ward from Harlequins, Neil Clarke (Launceston), Wootton Bassett-born scrum-half Mike Baxter (from less-known Pertemps Bees) and powerhouse prop Paulica Ion from Steaua Bucuresti of Romania, would hopefully answer satisfactorily those who had openly questioned the club's resolve to remain among the front-runners of English rugby. Or as Bath's Bob Calleja had remarked: *"If the criticism was about the club's ambitions, what has happened here over the summer has underlined the real ambition there is here to succeed."*

The Rugby League influence of defence coach Brad Davis would prove to be of considerable value, and the former Wakefield Trinity and Castleford Tiger had been immediately impressed by the 'response of the squad and their eagerness to learn' from that moment of his arrival. The key Rugby League lessons to impart, he explained, included the importance of 'discipline in the defence line, the ability to double up in the tackle, and gang-tackle ball-carriers so as to limit the ground they make and the danger they pose.' While some teams apply a drift, rush or scramble defence, Davis emphasised that 'the smart team can play all three as and when required.' He concluded (Chronicle, 3rd September, 2007): *"The target is always to defend high as a team, to win the ball back in your opponents half and harness the most dangerous form of possession – turnover ball – to launch attacks from the shortest range possible."*

So as to hit the ground running a 'leadership & team-building' training camp in Wales had been included during the summer recess, and come the starting pistol for Guinness Premiership action coach Meehan (Chronicle, 3rd September 2007) put his 'neck on the line' and backed his team to gain a Heineken place and a top four play-off position in the Guinness Premiership. Soon it seemed that he had made a thoughtful prediction, and by late October's 20-14 victory over Leicester it was a joy to witness a rejuvenated Bath that oozed confidence, had notched six wins from seven, and were neck-and-neck with Gloucester at the top of the Guinness Premiership. Everyone, including Samoan flanker Jonny Faamatuaine, twice 'man-of-the-match' in wins over Harlequins and London Irish, was hitting their own personal targets; and it appeared that Meehan and his fellow coaches knew something that certain doubters did not.

By contrast to Bath's highflying form at home, England's initial defence of the Webb Ellis trophy barely reached third gear at the start, with a modest 28-10 opening win against the USA thanks partly to 18 points from Barkley; then slumping to 0-36 defeat against South Africa, prior to restoring confidence with wins over Samoa and Tonga. Brian Ashton's side then struck the form of which it was capable when defeating quarter-finalists Australia, followed by a superb semi-final victory over hosts France, before facing (again) South Africa in the mid-October final. Happily this was no repeat humiliation; instead a contest between near equals that concluded at 15-6 to the South Africans. Pride, albeit not the World Cup, was restored.

Among those triumphant Springboks however was someone of considerable interest to Bath, namely outside-half Butch James, set to join his new club colleagues on the Rec in a campaign for the Guinness Championship, the EDF Energy Anglo-Welsh Cup and the European Challenge Cup. But with opening round defeats at home to Sale and then away at Cardiff, Bath would end their EDF Cup campaign almost as soon as they had started it.

The European Challenge Cup by contrast was a different matter altogether from that moment when hapless French side Auch were overcome 6-28 in early November, and so perfectly did Claassens blend with James as to inspire the watching Mike Tremlett to report that the one hundred-odd travelling Bath supporters had perhaps witnessed *"the birth of a midfield partnership which provides the creativity that Bath supporters have yearned for since the glory days...."* From that moment onwards Bath did indeed sweep past (home and away) opponents Auch, Italian side Overmach Parma, then French opponents Albi, prior to overwhelming Leeds (by now Leeds Carnegie) 57-5 in the quarter-finals. That would lead to a semi-final against on-form Sale; but not until late April. Meanwhile Bath would blaze a trail through the season with such confidence that it seemed that even a Premiership and European Challenge Cup double might just be a possibility.

But preparing players for nine-months of gruelling action in the Premiership is partly dependent upon an off-field task-force that must work non-stop throughout the year, a responsibility in the hands not just of the coaching team, but with those involved with conditioning and likewise team management. Another branch of the club was (and is) the academy, managed at this time by former Camborne player Frank Butler and guided by recommendations from, among others, junior rugby coaches, teachers and other contacts throughout the South West. A carefully prepared short-list of nominated players is then watched in action by members of the academy coaching staff, and if judged to possess the necessary potential, they are then invited to spend a number of weeks involved in full-time summer training at the club. When this phase is completed, the players (parents are consulted too) decide whether or not to join the academy, including those opting to continue academic studies alongside their rugby development; and the value of this source of recruitment can be judged by the fact that in some seasons as many as 45% of the Bath senior squad has consisted of (past or current) academy-produced players.

Meehan's prophecy meanwhile of a top four League position 'was' achieved with Bath gaining 3rd place in the regular season and thus drawn at 2nd placed Wasps in a play-off pool that saw 4th placed Leicester drawn away at top-table side Gloucester. It is here that the endeavours of a nine month hard slog of a League campaign can be turned upside down in the space of eighty minutes, as would be the case once again. Third placed Bath's progress was halted at 2nd placed Wasps, about which there could be no complaints. But 4th placed Leicester would defeat 1st placed Gloucester to earn a final date at Twickenham against Wasps. And Wasps won.... their 4th Premiership title in the last seven seasons, though yet to top the regular season table.

But as one gate closed for Bath, another had already opened, their convincing 36-14 semi-final home victory securing a place in the final of the European Challenge Cup. Ironically Steve Borthwick and Olly Barkley (at such a time as this) would shortly head for pastures new, namely to Saracens and Gloucester respectively.

Another departure at the top level of the game was that of local boy Tony Spreadbury, a para-medic by profession and until season 2007-8 an international referee on no fewer than 41 occasions, whose wide experience furthermore had included both amateur and professional eras of the game. Described by Phil Winstanley (Premier rugby's manager) as *"one of the most charismatic referees in world rugby,"* Spreadbury now announced his retirement from the international arena, though not from rugby entirely. Friendly and smiling by nature, many were the times in amateur days when Tony gathered on the terraces among the faithful to watch the mid-week games and exchange rugby banter. But, on the field it was always 'Mr Spreadbury Sir', and with eyes like a hawk it was only rarely that a misdemeanour would ever escape the shrill sound of Mr Spreadbury's whistle.

Meanwhile Bath knew that a test of nerves awaited them on Sunday (25th May, 2008) at Kingsholm in the final of the European Challenge Cup. Admittedly their opponents Worcester had finished a lowly 10th in the regular League season to that of 3rd placed Bath. But during the last five seasons Bath had suffered failure in four major finals, and if nagging doubts overshadowed their confidence, then Worcester (an official attendance figure of 16,106 watching) would likely expose them:

Bath Rugby: *N. Abendanon (T. Cheeseman 78m), J. Maddock, Alex Crockett, Olly Barkley (S. Berne 70m), M. Banahan, Butch James, M. Claassens (N. Walsh 78m), D. Flatman (D. Bell 61m), Lee Mears (Pieter Dixon 70m), M. Stevens, S. Borthwick (capt.), D. Grewcock, J. Faamatuainu, M.Lipman (Peter Short) 68m, D. Browne (Zak Feaunati 70m).*

Worcester Warriors: *T. Deport, M. Garvey. D.Rasmussen (Rico Gear 71m), S. Tuitupou, M. Benjamin, Shane Drahm (J. Carlisle 78m), Matt Powell (Ryan Powell 65m), Tony Windo (Matt Mullan 52m), Aleki Lutui, Tevita Taumoepeau (C.Horsman 56m), G.Rawlinson, C.Gillies (W. Bowley 68m), Drew Hickey (Netani Talei 44m), P. Sanderson (capt.), Kai Horstmann.* **Referee:** *Christophe Berdos (France).*

Wisely, Bath did not make the potentially fatal error of under-rating their opponents. Alex Crocket, among others, was outstanding in defence, containing the threat of Worcester backs Dale Rasmussen and Sam Tuitupou. Skipper Steve Borthwick (five steals against) de-fused the potential danger of the Worcester jumpers, and step by step the Bath pack (including a brave Michael Lipman with 17 stitches in his mouth) gradually established an overall mastery at forward. So, despite two Shane Drahm penalties for Warriors, Bath struck a critical psychological blow with tries from flanker Jonny Faamatuainu and fullback Nick Abendanon for a 15-6 interval lead.

This pressure was maintained throughout the second period, and despite Drahm's dependable boot sending over a third Worcester penalty and their No. 15 Thinus Delport darting over for a last gasp try converted by replacement out-half Joe Carlisle, Bath were just that bit too strong. Nor was Barkley's name off the score-sheet (it rarely ever was) and he duly stamped his own authority in the kicking stakes with two penalties, plus a conversion, with Butch James adding another. That made it 24-16 on the final whistle, bringing to an end to a ten year drought since a major trophy was brought back to the Rec. Admittedly it was not 'the' top European trophy. It was the 2nd tier. But it felt great to win 'silver' again.

Bath Front Row 2006: Duncan Bell, Lee Mears, David Flatman.

Acknowledgments Bob Ascott

As for Steve Meehan, his success would have come as no surprise to Juan Martin Hernandez (*El Magico*) of Stade Francais. Universally acclaimed as inspirational in Argentina's outstanding 3rd place in the recent World Cup, he had during the competition spoken briefly to the Chronicle's Mike Tremlett. Meehan, he said, was *"a coach with the golden touch."* El Magico had spoken!

It was perhaps not surprising that a Michael Lipman-led Bath stormed into season 2008-9, all guns blazing, with a scorching run of Guinness Premiership victories (briefly interrupted by Gloucester and Harlequins) in an otherwise unbeaten surge that reached the far end of December; this with a squad further strengthened with the acquisitions of Australian lock Justin Harrison from Ulster, former Leicester scrum-half Scott Bemand, and lock Stuart Hooper from Leeds (and England Saxons) whom many Rec followers remembered only too well from his outstanding performance for the Tykes in their 2005 Powergen Cup final triumph against Bath.

But it was in the October early days of the Heineken Cup that some 1,500 travelling Rec supporters experienced one of those heart-stop moments when with barely two minutes remaining at Toulouse the brilliant Abendanon added a second try to that of Claassens, putting Bath 15-16 ahead; and if possession had then been secured from the kick-off, Bath probably needed only to boot the ball into the streets to win a remarkable away victory. Instead a ruck ensued, followed by a penalty (wide out) to the French side. Ominously however No. 10 David Skrela had already kicked five penalties, and the marksman (agonisingly for Bath) did not fail with his sixth. Toulouse? They had snatched an 18-16 victory in the last seconds.

Even so, with victories home and away against Newport Gwent Dragons, Glasgow and a 3-3 home draw with Toulouse in late January, Bath had clocked sufficient points to reach the quarter-final and an early April date at Leicester. Watched by near 27,000 at the Walker Stadium, Bath again trumped the try count by 2 to 1 thanks to Shaun Berne and Joe Maddock. But this time it was Sam Vesty banging home five penalties as against Bath's two that would put the score at 15 points apiece. And then....with a minute left on the clock Julien Dupuy dummied through from close range for a try-gem and a 20-15 Leicester victory. Agony again!

So another day 'of almost there....but not quite,' and bitter disappointment for Bath supporters, nor forgetting the club treasurer. For the big competitions attract the sponsors, bigger attendances and TV revenue; with revenue so vital in the task of financing a Premiership club. Indeed the Chronicle further revealed (4th September 2008) that the club expected a trading shortfall of £375,000 for the then current year; while recent discussions over the possibility of raising the Premiership's salary cap raised another issue, since it was one thing to increase the cap, but quite another thing for clubs to finance it. Thus Wasps, a flagship club whose Buckinghamshire home at Adams Park was not the biggest in the Premiership, nor their gates the largest, could only watch as soon some of their finest would sign more lucrative contracts in French rugby.

Yet there was movement within the Premiership this side of the Channel, and this included Bath's signature of Saracens and England No.8 Ben Skirving in April 2009, and the earlier arrival (August 2008) of New Zealander Shontayne Hape from Bradford Bulls. Hape, fourteen rugby League internationals to his credit, nonetheless modestly

Abendanon with ball, others (L to R) Dave Wilson, Hape, Claassens, and Carraro. Bath v. Newcastle Falcons.

Acknowledgments Bob Ascott

insisted during the season that he remained merely a student of the union game, stating: *"I'm having to learn a lot of new things here….things like releasing the ball after the tackle, clearing out at the break-down and the way we have to line up much deeper in the back-line in attack and defence are all new to me."* He further added*: "I'm having to work to improve my catch and pass game as well because League is played very flat."* But if Hape reckoned he had much to learn, he would soon prove that he was a very good learner, as revealed (not the first time either) during Bath's early March 45-8 win over Bristol. The Chronicle was impressed: *"[Hape] convinced the Rec that he is the real deal in union,"* adding that *"the rapturous applause he received when substituted with a quarter of the game to go said it all."*

In Bath's 36-25 win over the Falcons later that month it was the turn of Rob Hawkins (appropriately on his 50th club appearance and a hooker of unusual speed and handling skills) to win the plaudits as the Chronicle's Star Man, and whose *"athleticism and power in the loose has been magnificent, not only against Newcastle but ever since he stepped up into the starting XV following Pieter Dixon's knee injury."* Finally, not least thanks to the seven spot-on goals from out-half Ryan Davis, Bath's 33-18 win over Saracens would lift them to a highly commendable 4th position, thus the play-offs. But between them and the final stood the small matter of Leicester away; and on the day the best team won 24-10. The Tigers would be celebrating again when winning the Championship final.

So ended Bath's season, one that in sharp contrast to a Bristol club relegated again, provided sufficient reason for genuine optimism for the following 2009-10 campaign; save that on the day following the semi-final the club would be 'rocked' by a reported incident in London. It was then that a group of players had headed off to the capital to 'wind down' from a gruelling nine month-long season, and where their first stop would be 'The Church at Kentish Town.' Here all was well, the proprietor later stating (Chronicle, 21st May 2009) that *"as far as Bath Rugby were concerned, they were absolutely not a problem."* So far, so good, and the group later reached a Fulham venue where players from another rugby club had gathered. Here there was not merely a problem, but an alleged drugs problem, and the incident quickly attracted the attention of the press (both local and national) with reports of excessive drinking and rumours (it is stressed rumours) of drug-taking.

To their great credit (Chronicle, 21st May, 2009) the club's reaction was swift. With the blessing of the RFU they immediately activated their own powers of summary justice and demanded that a small group of players undergo a drugs test. Two did so, and were found 'clean.' Another player had already resigned and left the club, while three more (known to be devastated by the events) refused to participate on a point of principle. As a result the matter was placed before an RFU disciplinary panel led by His Honour Judge Jeff Blackett in early August. Here a charge of taking prohibited substances was dropped at the outset, but: 'the trio refusing on principle to fully co-operate were banned for nine months for failing to submit to doping tests.'

Admittedly another Premier club (the unfortunates who got caught) came under the spotlight during this period for their involvement in a 'fake blood-injury' substitution, but this only partly diverted from Bath some wounding press comments.

Yet, although such condemnation was fully justified, the media overlooked one crucially important aspect, namely that Bath Rugby did not (indeed had not) run away from their responsibilities from the outset. On the contrary, for without any prompting the club instigated an immediate and 'open' investigation into the incident. Indeed, one need only ponder the reaction to drug-use in the ranks of certain other major sports to realise how differently Bath Rugby reacted. Because by their unconditional response to this dire situation there is some justification to suggest that the club had set a zero-tolerance standard, and thus a clearly defined precedent for others to follow should matters of drug-use ever land on their own doorstep. And, it is for other Sports (some rather more lenient in such matters) to follow Bath's example if they so wish.

There were no illusions however about the difficulties ahead as season 2009-10 commenced, and Bath knew that they must now face the music, not least from their own deeply worried supporters. A shadow hung over the club, and there was no denying that some awkward weeks, and possibly months, lay ahead. It was a time therefore for leadership, a time for positive rugby on the field, and then hopefully there would come a time to forgive and forget.

The re-build of an undeniably damaged reputation (one that had taken years to forge) would commence with the appointment of Michael Claassens with a captaincy as difficult as it is possible to imagine; while assisting him would be a group of carefully chosen 'elders', namely Danny Grewcock, Joe Maddock, David Flatman and Stuart Hooper, and not forgetting the highly experienced David Barnes, then chairman of the Professional Rugby Players Association (PRA) and who had recently accepted an invitation to join the RFU's 'Image of The Game Task Group' (alongside, among others, Lawrence Dallaglio).

Another acquisition was Nick Blofeld, recruited as chief executive and whose experience included his management of Epsom, the subsequent modernisation of its facilities and not forgetting his service with the Gurkhas and previous captaincy of the Combined Services rugby team. Coaching remained in the capable hands of Steve Meehan, Brad Davies, kicking coach Rowley Williams, and recent arrival and former Bath player Martin Haag as forwards coach. In addition to Ben Skirving in the playing-squad there would be recently-capped prop David Wilson (England & Newcastle Falcons), Fiji half-back Nicky Little, and fellow Australians Matt Carraro (backs) and loose-forward Julian Salvi. They comprised another promising intake, although not for the first time there would be lengthy injuries to Butch James and Olly Barkley, both world class players.

Any hopes however that Bath would avoid one of those dreaded relegation battles would be short-lived, and it didn't help that Bath's Guinness Premiership began at fortress Kingsholm, where the 24-5 defeat by Gloucester was sufficiently severe to dent any early pre-season optimism. By December, by which stage Bath had won merely one League game in ten outings, alarms bells were ringing loud and clear, not least after a home nil-16 rain soaked horror-show at the hands of London Irish in late November. Basic errors, plus penalties handed on a plate to Irish, and seemingly an absence of any inspiration whatsoever led hordes of despairing Bath supporters to head off early to their home-fires in near despair, a sight virtually unknown on the Rec.

But, what a difference even a single victory can make; especially one gained at the expense of Gloucester who in late December were decisively beaten 28-8 on the Rec, an emphatic win notable not least for Nicky Little's four penalties and conversion. This win proved invaluable, both for the points gained and the uplifting psychological boost during such an unsettling period. Prominent too was the collective home back-row performance of Julian Salvi, recently arrived Springbok No.8 Luke Watson and Andy Beattie, their drive *"emasculating Gloucester's attacking ambitions,"* as opposing skipper Gareth Delve generously conceded post-match. And though the surge of confidence resulting from the scale of this single victory against the 'auld' enemy would not necessarily be understood by those not acquainted with the nature of this ancient rivalry, the home supporters instinctively understood the force of its almost spiritual effect. Because this proud yet currently much troubled Bath family were experiencing one the most damaging periods it had ever faced. But suddenly the clouds lifted, and there was a sense throughout the entire club that the worst might be over.

Soon there followed confirmation that Butch James and Olly Barkley were close to full recovery from injury; while waiting in the wings was a batch of 'young guns' only recently tested (and found good) at first team level, namely centre Ben Williams, lock Scott Hobson, flankers Guy Mercer and Josh Ovens, and props Nathan Catt and Mark Lilley (son of former Bath favourite Graham Lilley). Nor was coach Brad Davis kidding when warning his starters: 'watch out you guys, these youngsters are after your places.'

Confidence now returned almost overnight, and a Bath team who had notched merely one League win pre-Christmas, would lose merely one League game post-Christmas; and in a near unstoppable surge towards the play-offs the realisation that Bath had re-discovered their true selves was never more emphatically shown than in their 22-35 revenge win at London Irish in early February. Next Barkley, back to his brilliant best on his return in Bath's 37-13 win over Worcester one week later, demonstrated what straight running down the middle can do to a back division; while Butch James (in conjunction with coach Meehan) showed again their 'uncanny ability to unlock defences.' More encouraging news then followed with confirmation during the latter weeks of the season that Leicester's fearless England flanker Lewis Moody and their highly versatile back Sam Vesty would both arrive for the following season, so too Scotland No.8 Simon Taylor from Stade Francais.

Such was the post-Christmas recovery in fact that the 19-35 televised victory on St. George's Day against nearest rivals Wasps at Twickenham not only drew a 60,208 attendance but saw Bath closing in on a play-off place in the Guinness Premiership. Here, once forward superiority had been secured by the interval, the lethal half-back partnership of Claassens and Butch James took over. That sent the backs into overdrive with a try hat-trick from Joe Maddock, another try from Barkley who duly added three conversions and three penalties to the score-sheet.

Prior to kick-off British troops had abseiled into Twickenham complete with flags of St. George swirling alongside them; Land of Hope and Glory was played (and sang!); and there was one further gesture shown, one reaching back to January when a young girl of 12 years had stepped on to the Rec alongside skipper Michael Claassens as the Bath team mascot. Later the squad, who alongside the club were frequently involved in community work, had arranged a chauffeur-driven car to drive her and her family to Twickenham for the 6-Nations match against Wales. There, it was VIP treatment and a meeting no less with Jonny Wilkinson and Steve Borthwick. But the lovely young girl (Chronicle, 6th May, 2010) was far from well, and but days prior to the game against Wasps she lost her brave struggle against leukaemia. So it was that as Bath strode onto the sacred turf of Twickenham, skipper Michael Claassens and his entire team wore white armbands in her memory. Yes, it was 'that' kind of day.

Two games remained for Bath in this season of contrasts, one that would reach its climax with the club's final League game against Leeds Carnegie amid a carnival atmosphere on a Rec bathed in warm May sunshine; and roared onwards by an ecstatic home crowd, a vintage Bath swept home to a 39-3 victory in a near peerless display of often sublime attacking rugby. The win anchored Bath securely into 4th place in the Premiership; albeit the play-off at Leicester would prove a hurdle that could not be cleared, the Tigers winning 15-6 and next the final itself at Twickenham. But that apart, the season had seen despair turn to joy!

Michael Claassens. Bath v Saracens 10/09/2011 (L to R) Ryan Caldwell, Simon Taylor, Ben Skirving , Michael Claassens at scrum-half

Acknowledgements: Rob Ascott

In April meanwhile the city had already learned that a new owner, Bruce Craig, had taken over the reins at Bath. *"For me [he said] buying Bath wasn't a monetary thing – it was about a passion,"* and the former half-back with Racing Metro (who later turned businessman while founding a near one billion pound pharmaceutical distribution company in France), was now setting his sights on plans to establish (inter alia) a rugby centre of excellence. Based at nearby Farleigh Hungerford in a magnificent mansion straight out of the pages of Downton Abbey, it would shortly be equipped with state of the art training facilities to match anything, anywhere, in rugby.

Andrew Brownsword, who loved the city with rare devotion, was certain that he had found the right man for so demanding a role. And let there be no doubt that in the still revolving stage of Premiership rugby a sense of vocation for such a challenge was (is) essential. The member clubs live at times on a financial knife-edge, and the club owners/chairmen are a special people who know that they will sometimes face intensely difficult times. To Andrew Brownsword the club thus owed an enormous sense of gratitude for his 14 years as trusted guardian of Bath Rugby; likewise to Bruce Craig for accepting so great (and so important) a mission.

So in this season of contrasts Bath had come through another tortuous test of their nerve, and during a period of soul searching that at one stage had struck at the very heart of this West Country rugby family, they were now the stronger for it. Penance had been served by a club that accepted from the outset its collective responsibilities over a post-season revelry that alas had gone too far. However, the leadership to its credit had acted decisively (and openly) in dealing with an incident deeply regretted. And now there was genuine optimism that *"the winter of Bath's discontent"* was transformed by the sheer scale and suddenness of that transformation.

Andrew Brownsword (right) hands over to Bruce Craig (left) in front of Farleigh House, Bath Rugby's unique Headquarters.

Acknowledgments: Bath Chronicle
15th April 2010   332

Chapter 36. THE ENIGMA. (2010-2015)

Come season 2010-11 Bath stood within 'touching distance' of their 150th anniversary, by which time a half-century will have passed since the Enlightenment that immediately followed their Centenary year. What an extraordinary coincidence! What an extraordinary club! Unable for a hundred years to escape the shadow of Bristol (and not forgetting Gloucester), the Sibley years would revolutionise the club's belief in itself and literally transform its style into 15-man attacking rugby and pave the way for the likes of future international outside-half John Horton to weave magic across the fields of England. True, there were times during the 1970's when form was sufficiently unpredictable as to raise doubts as to whether or not the club really could continue the momentum and, the initial forays into the National K.O. Cup were so farcical that thoughts of ever reaching a Twickenham final seemed the stuff of dreamland. Fantasy!? By the late 1980's Bath were sitting upon the throne of English rugby.

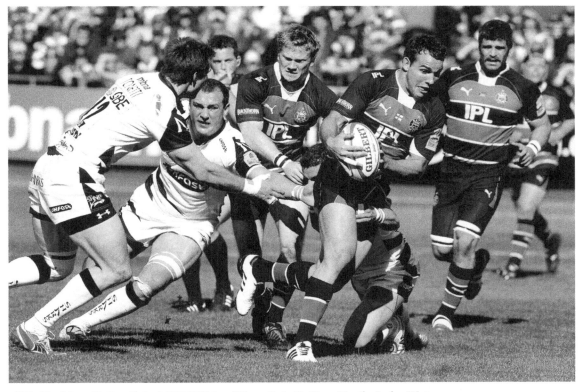

Olly Barkley Bath v Sale 25/09/2010. Others L to R Sam Vesti, Luke Watson

Acknowledgements: Bob Ascott

The professional era then followed in the mid-1990's, changing the entire rugby landscape. In the resulting confusion some of the greatest clubs were brought to their knees, though Bath survived, despite their nightmare season of 2002-3 that brought them standing over the very edge of the precipice. One season onwards and they topped the regular-season table (though losing the League play-off final against Wasps). 'How,' one asks, 'do such things happen at Bath, the one-time underdogs of the West Country Triangle?' Coincidence perhaps, or is it simply one of those questions that will remain unanswerable?

There was another question as the club commenced their 2010-2011 season under the captaincy of Luke Watson: could Bath win a 'Major' in the count-down to their anniversary? It would be perfect timing. The Rec was now increased to a 12,300 capacity, a number of new players had arrived on the scene, bringing with them quality and experience. There was winger Jacques Boussuge (French 7's international), John van der Giessen, Argentinian power-house lock Ignacio Fernandez Lobbe, and not forgetting Scotland 'A' scrum-half Mark McMillan from Glasgow Warriors. Hooker Ross Batty arrived too, with former Scottish and British Lion Simon Taylor from Stade Francais adding support (and competition) to young back-row prospects Josh Ovens and Guy Mercer; while Lewis Moody, more bruises on his body than you could possibly count without a computer, duly captained England (with Hape in the backs) to a 35-18 home triumph over Australia.

So it was hardly surprising that Bath, when hitting form, showed they could pack a real punch, as demonstrated by a September 31-16 win over Sale, with two more newcomers, namely wing Tom Biggs and Australian centre Matt Carraro, looking highly promising. Encouraging too was a 20-13 success against London Irish. Yet the Premiership is full of traps for the unwary, and defeats at Northampton (31-10) and Leicester 21-15) showed just how tough life can be at this level. In fact by early January Bath lurked worryingly close to the foot of the table, the last place one wants to be, and found themselves in a hopeless position in the Heineken. Moreover despite some encouraging performances they fell one win short of a semi-final place in the LV Cup.

Admittedly the LV Cup is not as challenging as the Heineken, but its merits are many and include generous sponsorship funds and, an excellent opportunity to give 'starts' to the likes (in Bath's case) of promising scrum-half Chris Cook, utility back Jack Cuthbert who played a 'blinder' in Bath's 29-18 November win over Cardiff, and likewise full-back Nick Scott in Bath's splendid 12-26 victory at Leicester in February.

Olly Barkley however, a first-team starter naturally, was playing at peak form, with his telescopic kicking accuracy causing nightmares to opponents. The marksman bagged six penalties and a conversion in the post-Christmas 24-25 win at London Irish, while prior to the early March visit to Kingsholm he had reached an 81% success rate with the boot. Yet, it was at Gloucester (16,500 watching) that grim misfortune struck during a 34-22 away defeat. Promising centre Ben Williams would score one of three Bath tries. But a freak injury resulting from a collision with Butch James saw Barkley collapse with a double leg-fracture. Medics from both teams rushed to his side. A mask was placed over his head and nitrous oxide administered. A splint was applied to his leg and throughout this period Kingsholm watched in hushed silence. Respectful and sympathetic applause then accompanied the player when stretchered from the field, and the televised encounter revealed an admirable generosity of spirit among the Kingsholm faithful.

One could only speculate as to when Barkley might return, though it was known already that two players, namely Luke Watson and Butch James, would not be seen in Bath colours again. Both, at the season's conclusion, were South Africa bound to join Eastern Province Kings (Port Elizabeth) and Golden Lions respectively. Both would depart with treasured memories, expressed by Luke Watson thus: leaving Bath is *"the most difficult decision I've ever had to make,"* and Butch James: *"I have made great friends....and have been amazed by the Bath supporters...."* Another surprise followed, though one not entirely unexpected in some quarters from the moment that former British Lions coach Sir Ian McGeechen (a former Scotland international) had arrived as performance-director at the commencement of the season, and who within ten weeks was appointed 'director of rugby and Number One in the chain of command.' *"Would it be a dream team, or would it be a recipe for friction,"* Tom Bradshaw had previously surmised (Chronicle, 31st March 2011); and the end of season departure of Steve Meehan suggested the latter.

Few however would forget the excitement that Meehan had injected into Bath's style of play during his four previous seasons at the club, nor the lethal back-division that he had helped to shape and one that expressed the Queenslander's own rugby philosophy; and albeit that only once during his tenure was a major trophy (namely the European Challenge Cup, May 2008) brought home to a city longing for silverware once again, the Meehan era would be one to remember. However there was more than a ripple of excitement with the announcement that Gloucester's England lock Dave Attwood (6ft 7in) would arrive for the following season and likewise Springbok flanker Francois Louw from Cape Town club Stormers. In the backs meanwhile former Leicester and England centre Dan Hipkiss signed on the dotted line; and one should not forget the significance of his visit to Farleigh House that influenced the deal: *"it's an exceptional set-up,"* he said.

On the field it would be one of those seasons of confusing contrasts, but where Luke Watson's side saved arguably their season's finest performance for another St. George's Day televised epic at Twickenham. Bath produced a virtuoso performance, winning 10-43 against Wasps (38,000 watching), with Tom Biggs over for a try hat-trick, a Banahan double and another from Carraro, all master-minded by outside-half Sam Vesty's immaculate performance and his five conversions and a penalty.

So it was a year of disappointing defeats and sparkling victories, nothing new then for a club erratic one moment, then superb the next. Indeed in early January Bath had dropped to 4th from the base of the Premiership. At the conclusion of the season however they had reached to within one victory short of a top four play-off place. That was no surprise however to those who knew Bath, and it didn't take long for utility back Sam Vesty to work out the strengths from the weaknesses at his new club either (Chronicle, 12th May 2011): *"when things go well we're an awesome side and we're so difficult to defend. We just need to be a bit more consistent and win those tight games...."*

In other words, if Bath could recapture their consistency of 'earlier days,' then Twickenham might be within reach again, exactly as the departing and admired Steve Meehan suggested (Chronicle, 12th May) following the club's 42-12 win against Falcons that concluded the season. Speaking of *"a lot of great memories to take away,"* he added that he *"expects [Bath] to lift the Premiership trophy soon.*

Soon or otherwise, new skipper Stuart Hooper was to be handicapped at the outset of season 2011-12 with the unenviable task of leading his troops over the top minus six players on World Cup call-ups, namely England captain Moody, Banahan, Lee Mears, Davy Wilson, plus Francois Louw (S.A.) and newcomers Anthony Perenise (Samoa), and not forgetting Kiwi half-back Stephen Donald, rushed late into the Kiwi World Cup side and whose critical penalty ensured their 8-7 final triumph over France. But Premiership clubs are often able to cast their net wide, and World Cup notwithstanding, there would now be another tranche of newcomers, including Ryan Caldwell (lock, Ulster), Carl Fearns (back-row, Sale) and props Charlie Beech (Wasps); nor forgetting the thrilling potential of St. Helens utility back Kyle Eastmond set to join later. Talk about a wealth of competition for places, not least in the back-row with Simon Taylor, Ben Skirving, Guy Mercer, Andy Beattie and Fearns among some scintillating candidates for starts.

But proof (as if it was needed) that rugby players lived between the proverbial 'rock and a hard place' was confirmed later with the news in March that Lewis Moody (the man without fear) whose reckless courage had led him into hell and back once too often, would be forced into retirement from active rugby. Was an admiring Tom Bradshaw speaking in jest when saluting this warrior thus? [The] *"tale of his injuries, operations and comebacks will doubtless form a textbook for first year medical students;"* or was he being serious? Nonetheless, it was a sobering thought that highly promising academy lock Scott Hobson, with eight 1st team credits to his name, would be unable to return to senior-level rugby (and perhaps any rugby) owing to injury sustained against Pays d' Aix, and that was in a 2010 pre-season friendly!

But there were problems for some at the club level too. Newcastle would endure another exhausting relegation battle, this time to no avail; and there would be a further piece of news that would shatter any complacency left in Premiership ranks when it was learned in early April that 'Wasps' needed a buyer to save the club from administration. The harsh reality was that their ground-share with a soccer club out in High Wycombe attracted too few supporters (barely 7,000 on average) and lay too distant from their traditional support-base. Two years previously this proud London club and Bath had attracted 60,000 through the turn-styles of Twickenham and near 38,000 in the previous season. If such a club as Wasps however now faced possible oblivion, who might be left standing?

Bath meanwhile would have to be content with a disappointing 8th place at the culmination of the Premiership regular season; while only a home 16-13 win over Montpellier (where newcomer Stephen Donald's exquisite 'over-arm-miss-pass' opened the Red Sea for Olly Woodburn to glide through for a gem of a try) would light up an otherwise depressing Heineken campaign that included a 52-27 hammering at Leinster. But at least the club were safe from the drop.

Spirits were partially lifted moreover thanks to an LV Cup campaign that reached the semi-final stage, and one that revealed a new seam of promising academy talent that included Will Skuse (back-row), Will Tanner (hooker), Will Spencer (lock) and backs Richard Lane and outside-half Heathcote. But it was defeats, and two in particular, that would impact on the club like few other upsets for years past. The first was the home LV Cup semi-final defeat to Leicester in March that followed Bath's otherwise impressive form against previous opponents, including recent cup wins over Northampton (46-16) and Exeter (3-31) respectively. But for the semi-final against Leicester (not at full strength), home advantage was squandered, the line-out at times was a scramble, and scrums, free kicks and penalties (plus a 16-17 victory) were gifted to Leicester as if it was a Christmas party. The second defeat, again at home, occurred in late March with a 6-26 league crash to Northampton. As Tom Bradshaw reported (Chronicle): 'against Tigers, Bath fumbled a crucial line-out from their own throw-in near their own line that led to the Leicester try; while the line-out against Northampton was in disarray.' Despair is not too strong a word to describe feelings felt around the terraces, emotions furthermore expressed forcefully with the vitriol and online messages (not forgetting alarm) that followed these two setbacks.

The ramifications were by no means finished yet. Sir Ian McGeechan was set to depart anyway, while forwards-coach Martin Haag, graciously accepting that he should accept some responsibility, would be departing too. If Bath had won the LV Cup things may well have ended differently, helped no doubt by their 17-12 final home match of the season against brave but struggling Wasps in late April. But perhaps the departure of Meehan may have unsettled matters somewhat, though one cannot be certain. What was certain however was that the club 'did' act quickly? Former Springboks assistant-coach Gary Gold, who almost performed the impossible by saving Falcons from relegation, was appointed head coach, along with former England defence coach Mike

Ford, and furthermore Toby Booth and Neal Hatley from London Irish, with Brad Davis remaining as the lynchpin.

There was a need to 'tighten-up' on Bath errors in set-piece play, to improve overall line-out performance and win the close-result games, and as former England international hooker Brian Moore had earlier stated (Chronicle, 15th December 2011): *"the Bath team he played against used to strike terror into opposition hearts. That fear factor* (as he sees it) *is no longer there."* Nor was it there when at Welford Road a 24,000 crowd witnessed Bath's 28-3 defeat at Leicester in their final league game of the season. Yes, the revised Bath coaching-staff found themselves with much to think about if trophies of any description were to be brought back to the Rec.

To regain 'self-belief'....this surely numbered among the key objectives for season 2012-13. Bath did not lack for class however, but it did seem that they had lacked the confidence to fulfil their potential, and not surprisingly the hunt continued for yet more experience to add to the squad. Some interesting names now appeared at Farleigh House, including England hooker Rob Webber (Wasps), Wales prop Paul James (Ospreys) and lock Dominic Day (Scarlets,). Less known were flanker Nick Koster (Western Province), Argentinian international wing Horacio Agulla and Army Fijian back Samesa Rokoduguni, though that would shortly change with Roko's storming try-double against LV Cup opponents Newport Gwent Dragons, Agulla's five in Bath's two leg Amlin Cup wins over Calvisano and likewise Koster's 60 yard break for another in the home 67-11 leg against the outclassed Italians. Talent? It seemed to be everywhere. The problem was it was just about everywhere one looked throughout the Premiership; and the key challenges came in the shape and formidable form of the likes of Leicester, Northampton, Saracens and a revitalised Harlequins. Could Bath raise their team-game to equal these likely top four candidates? That was a question that only the team could answer.

At the individual level some queries were soon answered, among them the awesome potential of Kyle Eastmond, whose brilliance was shown in Bath's early season 30-23 win over Wasps with his mesmerising 25 yards run through a human barrier of five (some say six) defenders for a try that was the nearest thing to poetry in rugby. And the march to the Amlin Cup (now European Challenge Cup) quarter-finals and especially the LV Cup semi-finals provided exciting rugby, though still no silver for the trophy cupboard. Furthermore, while it was truly an emotional day when in late September Olly Barkley (thankfully returned to fitness) banged 16 points over the cross-bar in the 31-10 win over Sale prior to his departure to Racing Metro, a long-striding utility back by the name of Ollie Devoto, one year out of Bryanston School, would thankfully step right up to 1st team action during the same season.

Two other players would be stepping down however, namely hooker Lee Mears with 42 England caps during his 16 devoted years at Bath, and the more recent arrival Dan

Hipkiss, both wisely heeding medical advice to retire from the game or risk possible further consequences as a result.

The pro' game meanwhile continued its unstoppable evolution into the New Age with Bath Rugby owner Bruce Craig and head coach Gary Gold arguing (Chronicle, 15th November, 2012) that the *"rugby world must wake up and realise [the] need for a global season."* And who could 'not' understand their reasoning with so many key rugby competitions in the Southern hemisphere clashing simultaneously with those in the Northern hemisphere, yet with players in the Premiership for instance (eg: Bath's Louw and Agulla) required for international commitments in their respective Countries; nor forgetting the Autumn and the Home international-tournament's impact on those clubs providing the largest number of players. So, in bringing their concerns into the open Bruce Craig and Garry Gold were making no secret of their desire for change.

Further interest was aroused with Saracens' announcement in December that play on their recently laid artificial synthetic surface at their new Allianz Park home in Barnet would commence in the New Year. 'Plastic fantastic' claimed Chris Roy (D. Mail), with a prediction that others would likely follow; though apart from Falcons there has been no stampede, and to be honest not everyone is supportive of such a change, perhaps concerned 'that artificial surface equals artificial game.'

Another concern for every club occurs when a player in a specialist position is side-lined, as happened mid-season with injury to scrum-half Claassens; and notwithstanding the availability of excellent scrum-halves Mark McMillan and Chris Cook, Munster No.9 Peter Stringer was rushed down to Farleigh House as cover ('just in case'). Few supporters remembered this Irish international from the distant past. Indeed he was in his mid-thirties. But when sent into LV debut action in late January against Exeter (Bath winning 16-6) he became Bath's 'instant hero.' A week later Gloucester fell 5-32 at Kingsholm and with hopes justifiably high it was off to the Harlequins for the semi-finals in early March. But the Quins proved too high a hurdle to clear, winning 31-23, and likewise Bath's Amlin Challenge Cup quarter-final opponents Stade Francais on the Rec in April.The Gallic challengers, winning 20-36, were simply too good, albeit they too would fall 34-13 to Leinster in the final.

Hooper's team furthermore could not get beyond 7th position in the final League table, notwithstanding Bath's undeniable potential so clearly shown by the inclusion for England's summer tour to Uruguay and Argentina of Dave Attwood, Dave Wilson, Rob Webber, and with Kyle Edmonds celebrating his first cap (against Argentina) with a breath-taking try. Moreover, 7th position should be placed in its correct context, so 'hot' was competition in the Premiership. The standards were constantly rising; the gap between the top six and the lower six clubs was inches close; and as Rob Andrew had previously stated, there was 'not' a weak team in the entire league. True!

Bath v. Stade Français. Jonny Fa'amatuainu with ball. Dave Wilson, (left) Stuart Hooper (right).

Acknowledgements: Bob Ascott

But Bath's dreams would not go away. They longed to reach a top-four place and tread the green turf of Twickenham again. Mid-summer preparations included a week-long visit to the Spala Olympic Training Centre in Poland, and their 2013-14 League campaign got off the starting blocks with an encouraging 0-21 win at Newcastle Falcons and next a very clear statement with a 27-20 victory over Leicester on the Rec. At Farleigh House there was another draft of talent to strengthen the squad. George Ford, Micky Young (both Leicester), Matt Garvey, England three-quarter Jonathan Joseph, David Sisi, Anthony Watson (all London Irish), Alafoti Fa'osilia (Bristol), Gavin Henson (L.Welsh), Leroy Houston (Colomiers) and Juan Pablo Orlandi (Racing Metro) all numbered among the 'new boys on the block,' and teaming-up with an exciting looking Bath holding a top-four Premiership slot by January. Only the unexpected mid-season departure of popular coach Gary Gold would now cloud the horizon.

His farewell notwithstanding, Bath were cutting a swathe through competing LV and Amlin Cup opponents like a dreadnought; and in a season of outstanding individual performances, perhaps one player in particular stood out, namely out-half George Ford. Released from reserve (bit-part) duties at Leicester and now a guaranteed starter at Bath, the 20 year old duly enchanted the Rec with sublime running, astute kicking, glorious tries and the mark of a genuine play-maker. He was an England cap (off the bench against Wales and Italy) come the Six Nations. Included among some outstanding league encounters meanwhile was the knife-edged winning double over Gloucester; albeit a 15-13 home win was later tarnished by a violent 17-18 confrontation in April where Gloucester (having two men sent-off, another two sin-binned) finished with eleven men, and Bath (no angels themselves on the day) having had three of their own sin-binned during a match described by Lee Nolan, Mail on Sunday, as "*a day of shame at Kingsholm.*"

Yet the game is not necessarily more violent than in amateur days. On the contrary, a new generation of professional referees were (are) stricter, possessing both the yellow and red cards (a significant advantage), and even the most ill-disciplined players on earth would think twice before arguing with their decisions. Rugby, it is submitted, is the better for such changes.

Furthermore, one match alone (as at Kingsholm) does not define a season that hinted at better days ahead, and a season that saw Bath closing in on a top-four Premiership place and two possible cup finals. Indeed it was a highly polished LV Cup quarter-final performance at Leicester, one that included three conversions and three penalties from Chronicle Star Man Gavin Henson, that would clinch a 17-35 passport into the LV semi-finals at home against Exeter in March. Since Bath had already defeated the Chiefs three times that season, it seemed likely that they would triumph a fourth time and even more likely when within the first minute an interception and pass to Agulla and a final off-load to Leroy Houston for a try saw Bath off to a flyer. But….what is this curse that overshadows Bath in LV Cup semi-finals? Over-confidence….who knows? All one can say is that Bath, equipped to win this match on paper, lost it on the field. Exeter just played things sensibly, while Bath at times played as if it was a 7's tournament. The unfancied visitors, who had never beaten Bath since the introduction of professionalism, duly won 19-22 and triumphed again 15-8 in the final against Northampton. Foolhardy Bath could hardly complain.

But in an unstoppable run in the Amlin Challenge Cup where, among others, lock Will Spencer and again winger Richard Lane excelled, Bath faced semi-final action away to Wasps. A tough hurdle this one, but one that Bath cleared with an 18-24 win, having survived a nerve-racking final five minutes without a sin-binned Eastmond. Meanwhile, a cherished top four Premiership place now hinged on a minimum of at least one victory against either Harlequins or Northampton, with the Saints confronted first in early May. It was soon evident that the two teams were evenly matched with a try apiece from Ford (a beauty) and Elliott, and likewise a conversion and four penalties apiece from Ford and Myler. But the possible (nay probable) difference was the early injury to hooker Rob Webber, and then 'as luck would have it' another injury to sub' hooker Ross Batty. With Hooper's plea for uncontested scrums rejected, prop Nathan Catt nobly volunteered to accept the role on 55 minutes. But the advantage now swung Northampton's way. Even so, Bath held out for a 19-19 draw, but a situation that now necessitated an 'absolute' victory at Harlequins if a top-four slot was to be clinched. That too proved out-of-reach....just, with Bath falling 19-16 at the Stoop and leaving Hooper's men one place outside the loop in fifth position.

Yet the Amlin Challenge Cup final against Northampton at Cardiff Arms Park (Friday, 23rd May) offered one last chance of glory, and a matter that would be decided by the following two teams: **Bath:** *N. Abendanon, Semesa Rokoduguni, J. Joseph, O. Devoto, A. Watson, G. Ford, M. Young, P. James, T. Dunn. D. Wilson, S. Hooper (capt.), D. Attwood, C. Fearns, F. Louw, L. Housten, Replacements: P. Stringer, G.Mercer, N. Catt, A. Perenise, G. Henson, H.Agulla, E.Guinazu, D.Day.*

Northampton: *B. Foden, K. Pisi, G, Pisi (Wilson), L.Burrell (Stephenson), G. North, S. Myler, L. Dickson (Fotuali'l), Corbisiero (Waller), Haywood, Mercey (Denman), Manoa (Day), Lawes, Clark (Dowson), Wood (capt.), Dickinson.*

Although Bath's local-born young hooker Tom Dunn would produce a 'massive' performance in the absence of Webber and Batty, George Ford was awaiting surgery on a damaged shoulder, and this may have explained his three critical penalties that strayed off target during the game. But he sent home a conversion for Anthony Watson's glorious try from 60 yards out, and a further trio of penalties. Yet Saints won the try count through Dowson and Foden, and the precision-kicking of Myler split the posts with a conversion and six penalties for a 30-16 Amlin Cup final victory. Again there would be no trophy for Bath to bring home. But this time there was a difference. For this was a Bath team that suggested it could go one better come the following season.

There are however basically three sections in the Premiership during a season. First, there is the group fighting for a top-four place. Then there is the middle-territory, usually safe but out of the race for the top. Third is the relegation zone, a place of constant fear, and despite a brave fight-back Worcester would drop out of the Premiership in 2013-14. The consequences of such a fate had already been given prominent voice by Rob Andrew (Chronicle: 30th January 2006) when warning that *"the implications of relegation, for any club, are staggering,"* albeit Worcester regained a Premiership place at the culmination of 2014-15. Well, no less an authority than Sir Ian McGeechan (S.Telegraph, 4th May 2014) would now add his own thoughts to this on-going dilemma. He was not opposed to relegation per se, but objected strongly to the current format and believed that the Premiership be increased to 14 clubs, with Bristol and Leeds Carnegie added to the current twelve-strong grouping. Such a system, Sir Ian argued, would allow *"coaches and players the opportunity for competition....but also to develop the game and tactically push it forwards, because there could be that openness in the play that the fear of relegation often shuts out."* Only after periods of five years, Sir Ian continued, should relegation apply; though others might argue that the 'annual' promotion and relegation factor forms the very essence of a thriving league competition.

A suggestion that the Championship be merged into the Premiership, but with teams playing opponents once only each season, not twice, could possibly be another item for the agenda in this crucial debate; although notwithstanding one's opinions, Sir Ian had now stood upon the rostrum and added urgency and significance to this all-important issue. It is to be hoped (it is submitted) that others add their voices too.

Matt Banahan with ball (L to R) Faosilva, To Dunn, Devoto (on ground), Hanson, Wacokecoke, Chris Cook.
Bath v. Scarlets, September 2014

Acknowledgements: Bob Ascott

In the Chronicle meanwhile (21st August, 2014) Super League champions Wigan (Warriors) honoured Bath with their presence at Farleigh House for two days of cross-code training and an exchange of ideas. They came, they saw, and they were much impressed. Shane Wane (Warriors head-coach) stated that *"it's been a great benefit coming down here, so if [Wigan] can return the favour and do anything for Bath in the North West we'd gladly do it. Bath's a fantastic club and the facilities are second to none."* Praise indeed!

Two weeks later Bath head coach Mike Ford spoke thus of his squad: 'they are chomping at the bit to get the new Aviva Premiership season under way.'

On 6th September Bath opened their season with a 20-29 victory at Sale. On 20th September they went crazy (so did their fans), running home five tries to defeat Leicester 45-0! *"Quite stunning,"* wrote Steve James (S.Telegraph, 21st September). "V*ery rarely in the Aviva Premiership will you see a performance that screams a message as loudly as that issued by Bath here. They are the real deal. They will be contenders this season."* In early October skipper Hooper's side then beat those uncompromising Saracens 21-11, and it seemed already that the Telegraph's Steve James's prediction would likely be vindicated. On occasions Bath did in fact fall at some of the fences, but only to recover, sometimes to startling affect.

One such set-back commenced with the visit to the Glasgow Warriors (18th October, 2014) for Bath's opener in the European Rugby Champions Cup (successor of the Heineken), where the Pro 12 club delivered a salutary lesson in how 'to really move the point of contact' throughout a game that would subject Bath to a humbling 37-10 defeat. A week later and four-times European Champions Toulouse arrived with a star-studded XV, winning narrowly by 19-21. That was two defeats before Bath had even got started, and no club 'had ever qualified from a pool in Europe's top competition having lost their opening two matches.' Admittedly Bath's reputation was partly salvaged thanks to their win-double over Montpellier, first 5-30 away followed by 32-12 at home. But lying in wait were Toulouse….in France! So across the Channel, there surely to suffer humiliation? No….there to scatter all predictions to the four winds and on a dank winters day triumph 18-35! New skills-coach Darren Edwards must already have decided that Bath was his kind of club.

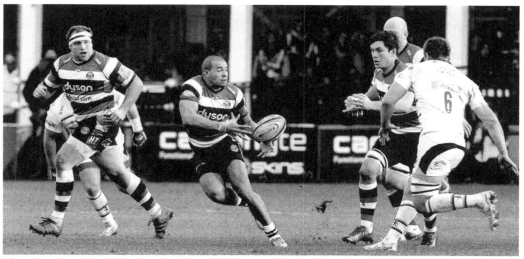

Jonathan Joseph with ball, other (L to R) Thomas, Louw, Garvey.
Bath v Wasps 10/01/2015

Acknowledgements: Bob Ascott

An admiring Chris Foy (D. Mail, 19th January 2015) duly wrote of the *"demolition of one of Europe's superpowers [as] a result to rank with the finest achieved by Premiership teams in Continental combat,"* and adding that *"this was a stand-alone performance of stunning quality and magnitude."* Daniel Evans (Chronicle, 22nd January 2015) spoke in awe of, among others, Jonathan Joseph's brilliance, and although George Ford would kick goals all afternoon, the victory was built around four dazzling tries. Banahan clinched the first. Chris Cook then casually took an interception (merci beaucoup) and with 80 metres of clear space ahead he shot away for number two. Joseph swept home for number three. So outstanding were Bath that with only 26 minutes on the clock they were already 7-22 ahead, with their travelling supporters probably in need of tranquillizers, so euphoric was the atmosphere becoming.

There was however the 'small' matter of the bonus point. Not a problem! On 71 minutes the magical Joseph ran on to his own grubber-kick and weaved his way through desperate defenders to switch-pass with sub-hooker Ross Batty. He found Francois Louw in support, this supreme flanker then literally swallow-diving over for try number four. C'est magnifique!

Albeit Toulouse were ever-dangerous, with lock Yoann Maestri and wing Huget clinching home tries, while Toby Flood was as ever spot-on with the boot, this only added to the impact of Bath's remarkable achievement; and if results now went in their favour and Glasgow could be subdued, then a path into the quarter-finals was now 'on the cards,' a prospect that at one stage had seemed an impossibility. However, someone 'up there' must have supported Bath too, because Montpellier, whom Bath had already trounced twice, would then beat Toulouse. That left one obstacle between Hooper's side and the quarter-finals….Glasgow Warriors.

And the Warriors were 'some' side, though it was just their luck to face a Bath pack in dominant form, and whose coaches for much of the season would utilize, during a match, two sets of front-row forwards during a game. Hence against the Warriors Paul James, Rob Webber and Dave Wilson were replaced post the break by Nick Auterac, Ross Batty and Henry Thomas; and with this strategy Bath (not for the first time), edged things up front. *"A rumbling maul and massive pack-effort prompted referee James Lacey to award two [converted] penalty tries"*(Daniel Evans, Chronicle, 29th January, 2015), and with two penalties from Ford, Bath got home 20-15 against an impressive Warriors side who ran home tries from Dunbar and Vernon, one converted, and a Russell penalty. It had been an exciting journey, one that now would continue into the quarter-finals across the Irish Sea.

It was in Dublin however (4th April) that the European rugby dream would end, and it did not help matters against opponents Leinster that Bath's poor discipline conceded no fewer than 18 turnovers, and in addition 12 penalties, six of which went flying through the posts thanks to Ian Madigan's deadly accuracy. Yet despite Leinster looking totally dominant throughout the first-half, notwithstanding a mesmeric try from Ford, the home side (D. Mail, 5th April) were later *"hanging on for dear life as wave after wave of Bath attacks threatened to deliver one of the great European comebacks."* In fact with Hooper's converted try bringing the score to 18-15, Bath closed to within 15 metres of the Leinster's line for one last attempt for possible victory. But *"Garvey was harshly penalised by [referee] Garcia with seconds on the clock"* (Sam Peter, D. Mail), and to the huge relief of most amongst a near 44,000 crowd the whistle was sounded for full-time. But Bath had proved, not for the first time this season, that they were a dangerous side once again.

Other possibilities remained however, and though Bath's pool 1 LV Cup hopes would eventually end with 10-13 defeat to Ospreys, the value (among others) of this competition was fulfilled with the opportunities given to the 'young guns,' as exemplified by the debuts of Rory Jennings (out-half), Will Homer (scrum-half) and prop Max Lahiff in a highly creditable late January 21-23 win at Harlequins. One week later and full-back Tom Homer (brother of Will) was given his club debut in league action at Saracens almost before he had time to unpack his bags at his new club. A proven goal-kicker (he had a 50 metre range) Homer banged home four from four; albeit Bath fell 34-24, a set-back as competition now intensified for a top four league place. Defeat or not, Saracens had graciously permitted a pre-match one minute's silence in memory of four lives lost (one a four year old girl) in a tragic recent accident in Bath.

There would be no set-backs for England's young lions however, who in March, led by Bath's Charlie Ewels, and with fellow club-mate Roy Jennings at out-half, had won the U-20's Six-Nations with their 24-11 victory over France at Brighton's Amex stadium in front of over 12,600 rugby followers. They almost went one better when reaching the final of the U-20's World championship, with Bath's Charlie Ewels (again capt.), Rory Jennings, centre Max Clark and Will Homer in the England side, but falling 21-16 against New Zealand in Cremona, Italy.

Another star would soon be seen, with the announcement (Chronicle, 9th October) of the imminent arrival of Sam Burgess, Rugby League's World Player of the Year, and creating a stir as dramatic as any recorded in the city's sporting history. True to his reputation he produced a man-of-the-match performance in early October for Sydney Rabbitohs in their NRL Grand Final 30-6 win over Canterbury Bulldogs, despite sustaining an eye socket injury and a broken cheekbone in the opening minute that would necessitate specialist surgery. Nonetheless on 28th November the cross-coder they all wanted to see came off the bench to rapturous applause on 63 minutes, filling the full-back berth during Bath's 25-6 victory over Harlequins. Burgess, 6ft 5in and 18 stone of speed and power, and whose tackle probably breaches the Geneva Convention, initially played as a three-quarter, scoring his maiden try in Bath's early January win over Wasps. He was then promoted to England Saxons in their 9-18 win against Irish Wolfhounds in Cork in late January and later switched to No.6 in the Bath back-row.

This, many critics believed, was his ideal position and his best chance for full England honours.

A very different 'event' had hit Wasps fans at the same time as the news of the arrival of Sam Burgess, when it was announced (Sam Peters, D. Mail, 8th October, 2014) that the London club had completed *"a multi-million pound purchase of Coventry City's [all seated 32,000] Ricoh Arena,"* with an expected sponsorship deal from a prominent car manufacturer, and home matches to commence in December. Many Wasps fans were reportedly furious; many commentators questioned the wisdom of stepping into the rugby boundaries of Leicester, Northampton and Worcester, and it was questionable whether or not Wasps could export their identity from the South East into the Midlands. But for Wasps, saved from bankruptcy two seasons previously by businessmen David Thorne and Derek Richardson and according to captain James Haskell losing £3million a year *"the move [was] a commercial necessity."* Few were aware that any Premiership club was facing losses such as this. They were now!

Sam Burgess with ball, others (L to R) Devoto, Eastmond, Watson, Cook.
Bath v. Gloucester May 2015

Acknowledgements: Bob Ascott

The stampede meanwhile for a top-four place was intensifying, and Bath had looked a probable, though not a definite, candidate from the moment of their electrifying performance against Leicester in mid-September. Yet it was not until a 26-27 win at Harlequins in early May that a play-off place was assured (their first since 2010), and it was anything 'but' easy. Bath had not won a league match at Quins since 2004, and one could see why. Indeed coach Mike Ford later stated (Chronicle, 14th May, 2015) that *"the Premiership's brutal and if you don't play well, or you don't prepare well, you can get beaten by anybody."* Well Bath, amid intense pressure, thankfully did play well. Tries came from Louw, Aguilla and Chronicle star man Leroy Houston. Banahan's second half 60 metre dash and try-saving tackle on centre George Lowe prevented an otherwise certain try. George Ford (showing nerves of steel) struck home a 40 metre penalty from a tricky angle to edge Bath one point in front inside the final six minutes, and Harlequins bade farewell to winger Ugo Monye who shot over for the hosts' two tries on an emotional night that commenced with a minute's silence to mark the 70th Anniversary of VE Day. It was a night to remember.

Thanks to other critical results over the same weekend, Bath would finish second in the regular season, thus their first-ever 'home' semi-final, and an advantage that might prove crucial against their opponents Leicester, one of England's danger sides. Whether or not Bath's 50-30 win over Gloucester one week prior to the Tigers' visit was any guide to the outcome of the semi-final was anyone's guess. But no one could have predicted the rugby carnival that would lead to a remarkable Bath victory on 23rd May before yet another capacity Rec crowd of 13,350.

Sam Peters (D. Mail, 24th May) wrote of a Bath team that *"turned scraps into five-star fare….that should not only excite their own fans, but all supporters of English rugby;"* adding that *"the way Bath are playing will surely fill [England coach Lancaster] with joy."* The stars were many, actually all those on the field with a Bath shirt on their backs.

As Daniel Evans (Chronicle, 28th May, 2015) wrote: Bath *"had less ball and less territory, but once they got a sniff of the line they were deadly, seven tries deadly."* Of these Banahan stormed over for the first-ever semi-final hat-trick, with Eastmond, Stringer, Ford and Watson weaving their way over for the other four. It was rugby pageantry, a 47-10 victory, and on the final whistle an outburst of sheer joy engulfed the Rec. The home players walked around this famous ground, milking the applause, many holding in strong arms their proud, adoring young children who smiled and laughed as only children can. Yes, Bath were heading to Twickenham for their first Premiership final since 2004. They would face Saracens.

A glorious sun-drenched day, a carnival atmosphere, an official 80,891 attendance….Oh, and a rugby cup-final thrown-in for good measure, that was the sporting-menu at Twickenham as the two following teams (primed for action) stepped onto the wide green acres of Rugby HQ on Saturday, 30th May 2015:

Bath: *Watson (Devoto 8), Rokoduguni, Joseph, Eastmond, Banahan, Ford, Stringer (Cook 67), James (Auterac 48), Batty (Webber 47), Wilson (Thomas 49), Hooper, capt. (Day 55), Attwood (Garvey 59) Burgess, Louw, Houston (Fearns 61).*

Saracens: *Goode, Strettle (Barritt 66/Hodgson 70), Taylor, Barritt (Ashton 61 blood), Wyles, Farrell, Wigglesworth (De Kock 56), M.Vunipola (Barrington 77), George (Brits 53), Du Plessis (Figallo 49), Hargreaves, capt, (Wray 32), Itoye (Hamiton 67), Burger, B.Vunipola.* **Referee**: Wayne Barnes.

In October Bath had beaten Saracens 21-11 on the Rec. In February Sarries had returned the 'compliment' by beating Bath 34-24 at the Allianz Park. On paper it looked 50:50, though on the field their strategies were different. Sarries were cool and calculating pragmatists. Bath, during this season especially, were cavaliers personified. One thing was a near certainty however: this would be a clash of styles. It would also prove to be a clash resulting from a high tackle from Owen Farrell on Antony Watson within two minutes.

Watson, a key strike-player in Bath's attack, would not return to front-line action again, with the excellent Ollie Devoto his replacement. Yet Devoto is not primarily a full-back, but a centre, and Bath's balance was clearly disrupted. Farrell meanwhile not only escaped a red card, probably correctly, but a yellow too. Some say he was lucky. So too were Saracens, as the out-half scored the opening try on seven minutes when some neutrals in the press-box said he should have been watching from the bench, and later won nomination as 'man of the match.'

But in perfect conditions Bath would not only lose too many turn-overs and come off worse in set-piece play, they began to compensate for this lapse by playing risk-rugby far too early, a dangerous ploy against this Saracens side. This gifted two further tries, one from hooker Jamie George, celebrating his call-up to the England squad, and another from winger Chris Wyles.

So far Bath had only a Ford penalty to offer some hope of catch-up, but even that was neutralised when Wilson (unjustly it is submitted) was penalised for an alleged late-tackle. Farrell couldn't miss in front of the posts, and on the break Saracens were already 3-25 ahead. It didn't look good for Bath.

As Daniel Evans wrote (Chronicle, 4th June 2015): *"Bath's attacking prowess - a mightily impressive sight this season - relies heavily on precision. The passing, handling and timing of their options need to be spot-on for what can be a majestic machine when it functions."* But street-wise Sarries had prepared their brief well. They predicted the tactics of their opponents, and the majestic machine didn't function; and though Bath would show glimpses of their attacking abilities in the second-half with a Kyle Eastmond run finished off with a try from Joseph, and Ford demonstrating his now immaculate kicking with his conversion and three penalties, this was not their day, though one will never be sure of the effect of Watson's injury on the course of the game.

The honours instead belonged to Saracens with their three-try tally, two conversions and three penalties that would lead them to a 16-28 Aviva Premiership final victory.

For Bath's huge and dejected following that numbered among the 80,000 plus crowd that day, let us ponder however the words of Daniel Evans (Chronicle): *"Sometimes, you have to lose to taste victory. Sometimes, you have to show chinks of weakness to strengthen your armour. Despite the heartbreak at Twickenham, Bath's exciting and talented squad have exceeded expectations this season and produced some memories that will last for years. Next season they will be shooting for the stars, both at home and in Europe."*

Yet disappointment aside, it was a glorious season, with attacking rugby produced by the most adventurous Bath squad for years. They took risks, as they did throughout the year. But that was part of the excitement of watching them. Their attacking flair was rewarded with some dazzling victories, and on occasions (as at Twickenham) some bitter defeats. But they were a breath of fresh air, their followers loved them for it, and very probably their opponents admired them for it. As Steve James wrote (S.Telegraph, 21st September, 2014) after the 45-0 defeat of Leicester; *"[Bath] are the real deal."*

Once the club played in the backwaters of the game, overshadowed by Bristol, and little noticed at the national level save for the occasional international player they produced. Some clubs might have resented this lack of recognition, considering the county players yielded up to Somerset, and not forgetting Dorset & Wilts. Resentment at Bath? Forget it….not in their nature. But a passion for the game in this small, tight, West Country community would on occasions attract four to five thousands (sometime more) to the Rec as far back as the 1920's and 30's. Therein lay one clue to the Enlightenment that Peter Sibley would inspire in the mid-1960's….this leader who tapped into this same passion within the club and its parent city, a city that throbs on match-days.

By the late 1970's there was a consistency to Bath's form, both at home and more importantly away. That is when others began to sit up and take notice of this somewhat unexpected arrival now causing 'mischief' among the top sides, and doing so on its own terms, not theirs.

There followed the twenty year reign from the early 1980's, an era when Bath's supremacy was unmatched anywhere in English (nay British) rugby. It was a domination that might never be equalled. Their rugby was a joy to watch. We wondered if we would ever see such glorious days again. Well, would even the soothsayer have made so bold a prediction: *"we have seen such days again, in 2014 – 15 to be precise, on the eve of Bath's 150th Year celebrations."*

Once more one asks: "How have Bath from their lowly beginnings reached such heights?" They were for so long the underdogs but, they liked it that way. They became the 'boy' king in Rugby's Camelot. That was 'their' style. Curiously when the position was reversed Bath have sometimes seemed bewildered and vulnerable. Totally unexpected Cup defeats (Moseley, Waterloo, Leeds Tykes) reveal this trait.

Even in the pressure-world of the Premiership however, Bath have never tried to be something that they are not. *"To thine own self be true,"* it is said, and the club has rarely departed from these wise words. Nonetheless, this only partly answers the question, because there is something different about them, a difference that is hard to define. Yet, though Bath are not necessarily unique, of one thing we can surely be certain:

"Bath are an Enigma. They always have been. History suggests.... they always will be!"

RUGBY BOOK – BATH CHRONOLOGY.

1823: at **Rugby School** a pupil (**William Webb Ellis**) reportedly runs with a football, contrary to the rules as played at that time. **In 1841** the practice of 'running with the ball' was formally adopted by Rugby School.

1843: Guys Hospital rugby club are founded, and are now generally recognised as the first ever rugby club to be formed.

1858: Blackheath (The Club) are founded and claim to be the first 'open' club ever formed. However **Liverpool RFC** (later Liverpool St. Helens) argue that their formation on 19th December 1857 establishes their claim as the first 'open' club in rugby football.

Marlborough v Clifton College on 20th November **1864** is probably first ever inter-schools match in England. Marlborough win by one drop goal.

*(**Note: Merchiston Castle** (Edinburgh) v **The High School**, 13th February **1858**, probably the first inter-school match in British Isles (see book: The Edinburgh Academical Football Club Centenary History). Meanwhile **Edinburgh Academy** v **Merchiston Castle**, 11th December **1858** commenced, probably the oldest continuously played inter-schools match anywhere in the British Isles.*

1865: Bath are founded (by a "few gentlemen of the city"). Their first venue was the spacious **North Parade ground,** home of the Bath Cricket Club, at rent of two shillings and sixpence (a half-crown) per game. As was the norm in this era, they were called Bath Football Club.

1868/9: 'a form of rugby' is played for first time at **Kingswood School,** almost certainly the first school in Bath to adopt rugby football.

1871: on 26th January 1871 the **Rugby Football Union (RFU) founded** at the Pall Mall Restaurant, No.1 Cockspur Street, London (near Trafalgar Square). A committee subsequently agrees a definite national set of 'laws' for the game of Rugby Football.

On 27 March 1871 the **first ever international match** is played at Raeburn Place, Edinburgh, Scotland winning against England by one goal and one try against one try, and teams consisting of 20 players each.

1871: Keene's Bath Journal reports on *"an interesting match that was played on the North Parade ground."* The result was Bath (4 rouges) versus Bedminster of Bristol (one goal, 7 rouges and one try). The Bedminster goal was kicked by **W.G. Grace** (Gloucester and England cricket legend).

1872: Francis D'Aguila, Royal Engineers and Bath player is capped at forward for England against Scotland, as Bath's first international. His brother **J.D'Aguila** was to captain both Bath (1882-84) and on occasions Somerset. **Clifton** are formed in same season during which time they beat Bath twice.

1873: Gloucester Football Club was founded. By the 1900's they had developed into one of the most formidable rugby teams in England.

1875/6: Somerset commence county matches; though the **Somerset** Rugby Football Union was not formed until 1882.

1877: England v Ireland (5th February at the Oval, London) are first international teams to play with sides **reduced to fifteen players** (England win by 2 goals and two tries to nil).

1878-80: Major **Francis D'Aguila** (Bath & England) is decorated for service in the **Afghan War** of 1878-80.

1879: first **Calcutta Cup** match played, then as always between England and Scotland (result was drawn). Cup donated by Calcutta Rugby Club, India (membership then mainly of 3rd Buffs regiment) who elected to gift a cup to the RFU (made from melted down rupees from club bank account).

1882: the **Somerset Rugby Union** is formed at a meeting held at the Clarence Hotel in Bridgwater. Somerset immediately became the parent county of the Bath club. In this first season Herbert Fuller of Bath is among those selected to play for the county.

1882: Bath's **Herbert Fuller** (he also played for Clifton) wins his first cap for England, against Scotland. A forward he wins 6 caps. He had already captained Bath from 1874-6.

1882: **Rule interpretation** still causing some difficulties in the rugby game. Bath's match at Devizes abandoned (when Bath, so it is reported, were ahead) owing to an outbreak of heated argument as to differing interpretations of the rules by the two teams. It was never concluded as to whose interpretation was actually correct.

1885: *referees now commenced the use of whistles and touch-judges the use of sticks (later flags).*

1888: Bristol Football Club was founded.

1888 (27th October): Bath played Bristol on the Kensington Meadows, Bath. It seems very likely from reliable records that this was the **first ever game** between the two clubs. The result was a draw (3 minors each). Bath played with **four threequarters** for the first time in their history in this inaugural match (according to the match programme for the 100th Bath v Bristol match, 29 Feb.1936).

The Bath Centenary 1865-1965 booklet records that the first Bath match played at Bristol witnessed **Francis White** of Bath scoring *"the winning try at Bristol **minus his shorts,** the remains of which were still in the hands of the Bristol fullback when White ran round to ground the ball behind the posts. The applause lasted until the goal kick* *was taken."*

1888/9 season saw the arrival of the **New Zealand Maoris**, the first ever Dominion side to tour England. Bath's **Frank Soane and C.J.B. Moneypenny** selected for Somerset side which loses 4-17 against the tourists.

1890-91: three sandwich men were now engaged to 'walk' the main streets on match-days to **advertise** Bath home matches.

1891-92: during this season Frank Soane and C.J.B. Moneypenny became the first Bath players to represent the **Barbarians** (founded in 1890).

1893: Frank **Soane** wins first cap for England, against Scotland. A forward, he wins total of 4 caps.

1894: in 1894 Bath make the crucial decision to move from nearby **Henrietta Park** to The Pulteney Meadows **(The Rec)**. The **Bath v Exeter** game (06.Oct.1894) which Bath won is reportedly Bath's first ever inter-club match on The Rec. After almost thirty 'nomadic' years, Bath now possessed a permanent rugby home. On 24th December 1894 **Bath played the Barbarians** for the first time, losing 0-14 (on The Rec). The clubs then faced each other in 1896, the result being a 13-13 draw (2 goals and 1 try apiece). They were to play again in 1897, the Barbarians winning 3-8.

1895-96: it was decided to award **Bath caps** to players who during a season had played at least 10 matches for the 1st team.

Insurance was now paid to injured players, on condition of a medical certificate being obtained. One case was awarded £5 (good money then) for a near six week absence through injury; while ten shillings was awarded to another case in which a player missed work for a week.

Various venues have been utilised as a club-house/HQ by Bath, including the adoption of the **Angel Hotel** in Westgate Street in 1895 (where 'smokers, get-togethers etc were also held), while a room at No. 4 Bath Street was likewise hired at a weekly two shillings and sixpence rent for the club secretary and treasurer. At the turn of the century the club had moved to the **Crown Hotel,** Old Orchard Street, where they remained until 1914. A move was then made to the **Old Red House** (New Bond Street), which would remain as favoured HQ until 1954 and the opening of **the Club House** on the Rec.

In November 1896 the club decided that teas would be paid for at the **club's expense** for away teams playing beyond a ten mile radius of Bath. This would apply to all three teams.

Training: the Riding School, Montpelier, Julian Road was **rented** for training nights on Tuesdays and Fridays.

The GWR, the Midland Railway and the Somerset & Dorset Railway declined to allow reduced **Cheap Return Tickets** for Bath's away games.

1896: Herbert Fuller (Bath & England) (2 Jan. 1896) died in Streatham by way of a cerebral tumour. Admired by many, his loss was deeply felt. A Cambridge Blue who would represent the university on the Rugby Union for many years, he was laid to rest at Lansdown Cemetery.

Frank D'Aguila, Bath's first international and later a major with the Royal Engineers, died in July 1896.

1897: it was decided to ensure that a bottle of **best brandy** was always available on the Rec, but for *"use in case of accident or illness, for players only."*

1899: after much negotiation, Bath and **Walcot RFC** agree that Walcot be permitted to play at the Kensington Meadows at rent of £3 p.a., plus the release to Bath of two Walcot players if so requested on a Friday night by Bath.

Devon win the **County Championship** (by a goal) against previous season holders Northumberland at Newcastle. The first Western County side to win the Championship, their victory set in motion a West Country domination of the Championship for the next twenty-three years.

1900: Portsmouth vice-captain **George Trerise** was **fatally injured** on The Rec (16th April). Bath were mortified, but Portsmouth captain Mr Edmonds wrote saying that the game had been *"more free from rough or unfair play than any game he had ever played."*

1901: J.B.S. D'Aguila died. One of two sons of Francis D'Aguila (Bath & England), J.B.S himself was a highly popular player for both Bath and Somerset.

1901-2: The **Bath & District Rugby Combination** is established.

1902: Flood-Lights on Bath training nights were introduced. This innovation was thanks to the support of Mr Hine (local ironmonger and committee man). He arranged a set of oil lamps to be positioned around the ground on training nights. No fee for their use was required. The first recorded floodlit rugby match was played in 1878 - **Broughton v Swinton** – far earlier than is often realised.

1904-05: the **Bath Schools Rugby Union** is founded. During this era (and beyond) clubs would sometimes request a **guarantee** so as to cover travel costs (etc.).

1904: J.G. Milton, while still a pupil at Bedford School, is selected as a forward for England against Wales on 9th January 1904 (venue: Leicester), match drawn at 14-14.

1905-06: on 21st October 1905 the Bath threequarters **James Timmins** (captain) and **R. Meister** play for Somerset against the New Zealand tourists, the visitors making their first ever visit to the British Isles (result: Somerset 0, New Zealand 23). Venue: Taunton, crowd estimated at near 9000.

1905-6: Bath win a **mere seven games**, leading some commentators to wonder if the club could survive in its present form. A slow, but steady recovery would follow however.

1906-07: Bath's threequarter **R.Meister** plays for Somerset against touring "South Africans" (result: Somerset 0, South Africans 14). Venue: Taunton.

1907- 08: Bath play their first ever game against **Harlequins,** losing 49-8 at The Quins (19th October 1907). Later that season (21st March 2008) Bath overcome Harlequins by 9-8 at home, following a **two week ban** against Bath for crowd trouble on the Rec during a Somerset Cup game against Weston-super-Mare.

Bath host Racing Club de France on the Rec **(1st Nov, 1907)**, their first overseas opponents. The result was a 6-6 draw.

1908-09: Bath threequarters **J. Timmins** and **R. Ascott** both play for Somerset against touring Australians (result: Somerset 0, Australians 8). Venue: Taunton.

1909: Bath's **Tom White** switches codes, joining professional club Oldham of the Northern Union (later **The Rugby League**). Joining him in the professional code by 1912 were **Tom West** (Rochdale Hornets), **R. Ascott** and **Riley West** (both Hull Kingston Rovers) and **J. Robinson.**

1910: previously, shirts of blue & black were the basic **club colours** until 1906-7 when white shirts were adopted. Then in 1910 the present colours of '**blue, white and black**' hoops were adopted, and duly described in that order. Also: *international matches commence at **Twickenham** from January 1910 with the England v Wales encounter (although Harlequins had played club matches on the pitch in the previous season).*

Bath Chronicle (13th Jan. 1912) confirms that a "***Bath Club cap** is given to a player who puts in ten 1ST XV matches in one season.*"

1912: on 3rd October in Bath, Somerset play the South African tourists on The Rec, (result: Somerset 3, South Africa 24). Included in Somerset team were Bath players **Vincent and Norman Coates** (backs), **F. Hill** (scrum-half) and **W.F. Warde** (forwards).

1912-13 season: Bath wing **Vincent Coates** played in all five England internationals, including match against South Africa. His six tries in one season was an England record, ironically surpassed in following season by fellow England wing C.N. Lowe (Blackheath) who scored eight.

1913-14: Taunton Albion (initially named Rowbarton Albion on their formation in 1901) would cease to play again after season 1913-14. The club merged into the **Taunton club** in the post 1914-18 era.

1914 (on 1st September) Bath (Britain now at war with Germany since 4th August) send telegram to Leicester, stating that the Bath club (with much reluctance) would have to withdraw from their forthcoming match at the Tigers in view of the worsening situation. Every club in the Country was doing likewise. Official club rugby would now effectively cease for the duration of the war. **Anzac Forces** use Rec at various stages of War as required.

Plymouth Albion are formed (circa 1915) with an amalgamation of Devonport Albion and Plymouth RFC. **Devonport Services** had commenced recorded matches in 1904. **1914-18:** at various stages during the 1914-18 conflict the Rec is **requisitioned by the Armed Forces.**

1919: in mid-February of 1919 the RAF (prior to April 1918 the Royal Flying Corps) vacated the Rec. It was now available for rugby again. Barely days later (22nd February 1919) Bath play their **first post-war club** game against a Bristol XV, **winning 8-3.**

1919: on 27th December Bath host opponents Cross-Keys. Bath back **Clifford Walwin** suffers **fatal injury** from accidental collision with an opponent.

1920-1 season: **Bath Rugby Supporters Club** formed. Dedicated work is given to (inter alia) helping Junior clubs by way of aid and players-insurance cover, and organising trips to International games which reportedly were so successful that **some tourist agencies copied them.**

1921 (September): **Bristol** depart from their County cricket ground venue and commence playing at the **Memorial ground**. Bath play their first game at the new venue on 28 Jan. 1922. It was a home win for Bristol by **8-3.** By coincidence, on the Rec (22 Feb. 1919) Bath had previously won the two clubs' first post-war game. Again this was a home win by **8-3** for Bath.

1922 (13 April): Bath play French club **Stade Bordelais** on the Rec (13 Apr.1922), Bath winning 11-3. In same year Bridgwater merged with Bridgwater Albion; the combined club choosing to retain the name of **Bridgwater Albion.** Also in season **1921-2** Bath attain **new club record of 25 victories.**

1922-3: Bath's **26 wins** is new club record, but only if an *'exhibition'* game at **Blundell's School** is accepted as an official 1st team match.

1925 (13 Apr): S.G.U. Considine plays wing for England against France (Paris), England winning 11-13. During the game the Bath genius was injured and would never play serious rugby again. (Circa 1925) a Bath supporter gifts the so called **Rag Doll** to all future winners of Bath v Llanelli rugby matches.

Season **1925-6**: Diamond Jubilee year, and the club's first **England Trial** (19th December 1925) held on Rec, 8,000 reportedly attending. In Autumn 1925 the club's new **North stand** (seated) was opened. Bath unexpectedly experience a loss of form, with **only seven wins gained**, exactly the same total attained twenty years previously in 1905-6. But a rapid recovery achieved in following season.

1931-2: George Haydon sets **new club try-record of 29 tries.**

1932 (2 Jan): Bath centre **R.A. Gerrard** wins his **first cap for England** in their encounter against South Africa at Twickenham. Rslt: England 0, South Africa 7. Bath's new **West Stand** (replacing the original) was opened at start of season **1932-3** (6 Sep 1932)).

1934: Bath's **R.A. Gerrard** played in the winning Barbarians team in the **Twickenham Sevens tournament.**

1934: in the close season of 1934 the **Bath Ex-schools XV** is established for young players between 14-16 years.

1935 (16 Mar): a controversial try awarded to visitors Blackheath (who won 8-13) leads to a post-match **demonstration** by small vociferous group of angered Bath supporters.

1935: The **Bath Colts XV** (16-18 years) is established. By 1980 it would be re-organised as the **Bath Youth XV.**

1936 (4. Jan): England defeat New Zealand by 13-0. Bath's **R.A. Gerrard** plays key defensive role in England backs.

1936 (29 Feb): the **100th official match** between Bath and Bristol. It resulted in a 3-3 draw on the Rec, the same score as that made in the inaugural game played in 1888 on the Kensington Meadows.

1937 (20 March): a controversial late try by Bath (who won 4-14) at Torquay Athletic led to a **post-match demonstration** by angry home supporters. Much to the regret of many, future fixtures between the clubs cancelled by Bath as a result, though later restored in post-World War Two era.

1938-39: Bath gain their **first ever away win at Gloucester** (3-5) on 19 Nov. 1938; Bath then clinch the Double with their return home win (6-5) on 18 Feb. 1939.

1939-40: as a result of the escalation of the war, Bath's opening match against Llanelli on 9th September 1939 is cancelled. Official rugby ceases. Nonetheless rugby (and professional soccer) continue on a regional format among many clubs in the British Isles. Bath now play as the **Bath & Admiralty RFC** (formed in Sep.1939) throughout duration of war.

1944: 9th December, Bath win at Bridgwater and field **rugby league** scrum-half **S. Morgan** of Hull Kinston Rovers.

1945 (08 Sep): post-war official rugby commences once more, and Bath host Llanelli (who win 0-16), six years less one day since their previous game cancelled at outset of World War Two. Owing to war effort, rugby kit now depended upon availability of government 'clothing coupons,' and Bath are restricted to white shirts only, blue shorts and red socks. Not until season 1948-9 would Bath return to wearing shirts of blue, white and black.

1946-7: Bath's **Ian Lumsden** now playing for **Scotland** at outside-half. With a club policy change announced in October 1946 Bath chose to **abandon shirt No.13.** Change not fully implemented until season 1951-2 with shirts numbered from 1-16 and omitting No. 13 (see too: **Ch. 20).**

1948: Bath gain their **first ever away win in Wales** against Llanelli (0-3) on 2 Oct.1948; Bath then clinch the Double against the 'Sospans' with their return home win (6-0) in late December1948. In opening week of February 1949 Bath win 3-5 at powerful Newbridge to record **their 2nd ever win in Wales.**

1951: Bath's 3-9 away win at Moseley on 21st April 1951 set **a new club record** of 27 wins in a seasons, beating the previous record of 26 wins gained by the Vowles 1922-3 side.

1951: the **Bath old Players Association** is formed, later re-named **Bath Past Players** in June 2005.

1952: against South Afrca at Twickenham in January 1952 **Alec Lewis** plays his **first international** for England at the age of 31 years. Result: England lose 3-8.

1952-3: famed Oxford Blue **John MacGregor Kendall-Carpenter** joined Bath and during season of 1952-3 both he and Alec Lewis were playing for England.

1954: a **new club house** was opened on 6th March 1954 following Bath's 16-6 win over great rivals Bristol. This was their first ever club house on the Rec.

1954: another **West Stand** (replacing the stand destroyed in the War) is officially opened on 2nd October 1954 seating 1100 plus spectators.

1954: in late April Bath head for France in their **first-ever overseas tour**. They return with a triumphant victory 'treble' under their belts.

1957: Bath's Old Sulian out-side half **Brian Weston** wins **Blue for Oxford.**

1959: fixtures between **Bath and Torquay,** withdrawn since March 1937 owing to post-match demonstration at Torquay, restored on 4th April 1959, Bath winning 11-12 away.

1961: in January Bath wing-forward **Laurie Rimmer** gains the first of 5 caps when **selected for England** against South Africa at Twickenham (England losing 0-5). In February Bath prop **Pete Parfitt** is chosen as a reserve for England against Ireland.

1961: at Twickenham (December) Bath centre **Geoff Frankcom** and Bath fullback **Ian Balding** simultaneously win **Blues for Cambridge** in the narrow win over Oxford, Frankcom clinching the winning try.

1962: Bath's first experience of playing under **floodlights** occurred at Stradey Park on Friday evening, 19th January 1962, Llanelli winning 16-3.

1965: in January 1965 Bath centre **Geoff Frankcom** gains the first of his 4 caps for England. Bath invited for their first-ever appearance in the Twickenham **Middlesex 'sevens' classic,** and are beaten 13-0 by Rosslyn Park in first round.

1965-6: Bath celebrate their **Centenary season.**

1967: on 18th November 1967 the Bath home win over Devonport Services is televised on BBC 2's Rugby Special, the clubs **first televised game.** At Twickenham (December 1967) Bath's **James (Jamie) Monahan** (former Kingswood School pupil) wins his Cambridge Blue at prop. The light Blues achieve a narrow victory.

1968: in January Bath's **David Gay** (19 years) wins his first England cap at No.8 against Wales at Twickenham (11-11 draw).

1968-9: Bath set a **new club record of 29 victories** in a season.

1971: Bath wing **Peter Glover** re-called for England in 1971 Home Championship, and in September both **Mike Hannell** (prop) and wing **Peter Glover** are selected for England's three match tour to Japan. In season **1971-2** ex Bath fullback **David Dolman** (cousin of former club wing John Dolman) was appointed the club's **first official coach**.

In season **1971-2** the RFU launch the **National Knock-out Cup** for English clubs, Gloucester winning inaugural final at Twickenham against Moseley 17-6. **Try** increased to **4 points**.

1972: in January Bath's **Mike Beese** (although with Liverpool at this time) wins his first cap for England at centre against Wales at Twickenham (England losing 3-12).

1974-5: at Twickenham (December) Bath's **Jim Waterman** wins his **Oxford Blue** playing full-back. Light Blues win a narrow victory. On Boxing Day Bath introduce **floodlights on the Rec** in their win over Clifton, soon followed when hosting the Royal Navy in early January.

1975-6: Bath set a **new club record of 32 wins** in a season.

1978: in February Bath's **John Horton** wins his first of 13 caps, playing at out-half **for England** at Twickenham in their narrow 6-9 defeat against Wales.

1979-80: Bath set a **new club record of 37 wins** in a season.

1981: at Twickenham (December) Bath's **Derek Wyatt** wins his **Oxford Blue**. **Simon Halliday** and **Tony Brooks**, two fellow Oxford Blues (playing alongside Wyatt) joined Bath one week later. Cambridge won.

1982-3: Bath set a **new club record of 38 wins** in a season. **Barry Trevaskis** sets new club record of **32 tries.**

1983: in Dublin (March) Bath wing **David Trick** wins the first of his two England caps (Ireland winning 25-15).

1983-4: in November 1983 Bath flanker **Paul Simpson** wins his first **England cap** in the 15-9 victory against New Zealand at Twickenham. In same season Bath flanker **Jon Hall** wins his first **England cap** against Scotland at Murrayfield (Feb. 1984).

1984: on 28th April Bath win the **John Player Special Knock-out Cup final** for the first time in their history, defeating Bristol by 10-9 at Twickenham. Bath scrum-half **Richard Hill** wins his first **cap on the England** summer tour of South Africa, likewise Bath utility back **John Palmer.**

1984-5: Bath's **Gareth Chilcott** (prop) and **Nigel Redman** (lock) win their first **England caps** against Australia at Twickenham (Nov.1984). Bath fullback **Chris Martin** wins his first **England cap** at Twickenham against France (Feb. 1985).

1985: on 27th April Bath (fielding 9 England internationals) again win the **John Player Special Cup final** for the second successive year, overcoming London Welsh 24-15 at Twickenham.

1986: Bath centre **Simon Halliday** wins his first **England cap** (January 1986) against Wales at Twickenham; **David Sole** wins his first **cap for Scotland** v France in same 5 Nations Home Championship; on 26th April 1986 Bath win a third successive **John Player Special Cup final**, overcoming Wasps 25-17 at Twickenham.

1986-7: **Richard Hill** is appointed **England captain** for the 1986-7 season's Home Championship, Bath's first international captain; **Graham Dawe** (hooker) wins his first **England cap v Ireland** (February 1987); meanwhile Bath win an unprecedented fourth successive **John Player Special Cup final**, winning 19-12 at Twickenham against Wasps.

1988: in January 1988 Bath lock **Damian Cronin** wins his first **cap for Scotland** against Ireland, while in April Bath back-row forward **David Egerton** wins his first **England cap** against Ireland in the Dublin Millenium match. Bath's unprecedented run of four successive cup final victories ends with 4-3 quarter-final **defeat at Moseley** (27th February 1988). Flanker **Andy Robinson** wins first **England cap** in victory against Australia at Twickenham (5th November 1988).

1987-8 would see the commencement of a **fully standardised English Rugby Union league** with **the inaugural season of the Courage League.**

1989: in May, **Jeremy Guscott** scores try hat-trick on his **England debut** in victory against Romania in Bucharest. Guscott, Andy Robinson and Gareth Chilcott all selected for **British Lions** on summer tour of Australia. Bath win their first league and cup **Double** by winning the **Courage League** for the first time and the **Pilkington Cup**

(previously John Player Special Cup) with their 10-6 win over Leicester at Twickenham.

1990: Bath win the **Pilkington Cup** by defeating Gloucester 48-6 at Twickenham.

1990-1: Bath win the **Courage League**, and complete their season by winning their first **Worthington Bitter National sevens** tournament.

1991-2: backs **Jon Webb, Jeremy Guscott, Richard Hill** and forward **Nigel Redman** all selected for England's **World Cup** squad, each playing during the tournament. Bath win **the Double**, winning the **Courage League**, and the **Pilkington Cup** with a 15-12 victory against Harlequins at Twickenham.

1992-3: The **200ᵗʰ game** between Bath and Bristol is won 8-31 by Bath at the Memorial Ground Ground (31ˢᵗ October 1992). Prop **Victor Ubogu** wins first **England cap** in win against Canada (October 1992); in November back-row forward **Ben Clarke** and centre **Phil de Glanville** win first **caps in England's** win against South Africa: in December utility back **Audley Lumsden** wins his **Oxford Blue**. In the Home Championships lock **Andy Reed** wins his first **Scotland cap** in their defeat by England at Twickenham (March 1993). Bath win the **Courage League**. **A try** increased to **5 points**.

1993-4: in November 1993 **Jon Callard** wins his first **England cap** at Twickenham, England winning 15-9 against New Zealand. In December at Twickenham, Bath's **Chris Clark** (prop) and utility back **Ed Rayner** win **Blues for Oxford.** In February 1994 **Steve Ojomoh** wins his first **cap for England** against Ireland. In March 1994 **Mike Catt** wins his first **England cap** against Wales at Twickenham.

By winning the **Courage League** Bath won **the League/Cup Double** for the third time, and the **National knock-out cup for the 8ᵗʰ time** with their 21-9 **Pilkington Cup** victory over Leicester. One week later Bath won the **Middlesex (Save & Prosper) Sevens** at Twickenham for the first time in their history, so winning three Majors in one season.

1994-5: nine Bath players are selected for the **1995 England World Cup** party to South Africa, namely Jon Callard, Mike Catt, Ben Clarke, Graham Dawe, Phil de Glanville, Jeremy Guscott, John Mallett, Steve Ojomoh and Victor Ubogu; prop **John Mallett** winning his first **England cap** against Western Samoa. Bath win the **Pilkington cup**, their **ninth Cup Final** success in 12 years (May 1995).

1995-6: in January 1996 wing **Jon Sleightholme** wins first **England cap** against France in Paris. On 4ᵗʰ May 1996 Bath, having already won the **Courage League**, win their **tenth Cup Final (Pilkington)** and their **fifth Cup and League Double.** Later in May 1996 Rugby League side **Wigan** win 82-6 against Bath under RL rules at Maine Road, Manchester. In late May **Bath** defeat Wigan 44-19 under Union rules at Twickenham, and a century of divide between the two codes ends.

Season **1996-7**: rugby union commences a **newly professionalised** Courage League.

In November 1996 **Ade Adebayo** wins his first **England cap** against Italy at Twickenham. In December 1996 **Nathan Thomas** (flanker) wins first **cap for Wales** against South Africa. In May 1997 **Martin Haag** and **Kevin Yates** win debut caps in England's victory in Argentina.

1997-8: in summer 1997 **Jeremy Guscott** (joined later by **Mike Catt**) played on the British & Irish Lions tour of S. Africa. In November 1997 Bath's **Matt Perry** (f.back) and **Andy Long** (hooker) make their **debuts for England** v Australia (15-15) at Twickenham. On 31st January 1998 Bath defeat Brive 18-19 at Bordeaux to win the **(Heineken) European Cup**, the first British club to do so. Season 1997-8 would see the **Allied Dunbar Premiership** succeed the Courage League.

The '**Sin-bin**' option was adopted for Allied Dunbar Premiership One and Two from season **1998-9**. Also in Bath's first league match of 1998-9 de Glanville wore **No 13 shirt,** the first time the club had worn this number since early 1950's. It proved lucky 13, Bath winning 36-27 over Wasps.

1999-2000: having fluctuated between 10 and 14 clubs at the top level since the advent of a standardised league in 1987, the **Premiership** is now set at 12 clubs. **Guscott, Matt Perry and de Glanville** play for England during the Autumn **World Cup** of 1999, England losing to S. Africa in the quarter-finals. In the **inaugural Six Nations** Championship at Twickenham (5th February 2000) **Mike Tyndall** at centre scores try on **debut for England** in 50-18 win against Ireland and **Iain Balshaw** makes **England debut** as sub for Bath fullback Matt Perry in same match.

2000-1: debut for Wales of Bath scrum-half **Gareth Cooper** against Italy in April 2001; later back row forwards **Andy Lloyd** and **Gavin Thomas** both **debut for Wales** on their summer tour to Japan, Lloyd scoring try in Welsh victory. In summer 2001 **Iain Balshaw, Matt Perry, Mike Catt** and Bath new-boy **Danny Grewcock** selected for Lions tour of Australia. Also in summer 2001 Bath backs **Tom Voyce** and **Ollie Barkley** win debut **caps for England** against USA in their Country's tour of North America, Barkley having yet to play a full game in senior club rugby. In Season 2000-1 the **Zurich Premiership** succeeded Allied Dunbar, and **bonus points** introduced to matches.

2002-3: hooker **Jon Humphreys,** already a Welsh cap when arriving at Bath, **captained Wales** against a winning England side in Cardiff (February 2003); scrum-half and Bath club colleague **Gareth Cooper** also playing. On 25th May 2003 Bath play Wasps in the **Parker Pen Challenge Cup final**, losing 48-30 at the Madejski stadium, Reading. Bath wing **Simon Danielli** wins **debut cap for Scotland** v **Italy** (Aug. 2003) in World Cup warm-up match. In season 2002-3 a **new PLAY- OFF system** was introduced **to decide the Premiership champions.**

2003-4: Kevin Maggs (Ireland), **Simon Danielle** (Scotland) **and Danny Grewcock, Iain Balshaw, Mike Tindall and Mike Catt** (all England) played for their respective Countries in the 2003 Autumn **World Cup** in Australia. Despite top side of the 2003-4 Zurich Premiership regular league table Bath would fall 10-6 to Wasps in the **Play-off final** at Twickenham. Meanwhile **Michael Lipman** and **Matt Stevens** win their **debut caps** on England's 2004 summer tour of Australasia.

2004-5: in March 2005 **Duncan Bell** wins debut full **England cap** in the 6 Nations win over Italy at Twickenham. **Danny Grewcock, Matt Stevens** and **Mike Tindall** win selection for the British & Irish Lions tour of New Zealand, although Tindall later withdraws for injury/fitness reasons. At Twickenham (April 2005) Bath lose 20-12 to Leeds Tykes in the **Powergen National Cup final.**

2005-6: in November 2005 **Lee Mears** (hooker) wins **debut cap** in England's win over Manu Samoa at Twickenham. In February 2006 **Gareth Delve** (back-row) wins debut **cap for Wales** against Scotland at Cardiff. Season 2005-6 would see the **Guinness Premiership** succeed the Zurich Premiership, with an **alteration** to the Premiership **play-off format. The RFU National Cup competition** (launched in 1972) was now limited to the 12 Premiership clubs, plus the four regional Welsh sides, in an **Anglo-Welsh Cup competition.** The **European (formerly Parker Pen) Challenge Cup** would next be known (for sponsorship reasons) as **the Amlin Challenge Cup.**

2006-7: In early season Leeds Rhinos and Great Britain centre **Chev Walker** switched codes to join Bath. In post-Christmas league encounter at Ashton Gate (Bristol City FC), Bristol defeat Bath 16-6 and **crowd of 21,203** attend. Bath unable to reach beyond the first Pool stage of the now re-named **EDF Energy Anglo-Welsh Cup**, but reach the final of the **European Challenge Cup**, losing 16-22 to Clermont Auvergne. Against South Africa (summer tour 2007) **Nick Abendanon** wins debut **cap for England**.

2008: The Bath foursome of **Lee Mears, Michael Lipman, Matt Stevens,** and **Steve Borthwick (**who led England against Italy in Rome) all feature for England in the Six Nations of 2008. All four players, plus **Olly Barkley,** selected for the summer England touring side to New Zealand, **Borthwick as captain**. In May Bath win the **2007-8 European Challenge Cup** 24-16 against Worcester Warriors.

In season **2008-9** the **Aviva Premiership** succeeds the Guinness Premiership.

2009-10: Matt Banahan wins first **cap for England** in victory against Argentina (in Manchester), June 2009. EDF Energy Cup is **re-named the LV Cup** (Liverpool & Victoria insurance group) owing to sponsorship change.

2010-11: in June 2010 **Shontayne Hape** (ex Kiwi Rugby League international) wins debut **England rugby Union cap** on tour match in Australia. The **National Division One is renamed as the Championship**; but a play-off format included to determine promotion to the Premiership. In April 2010 **Bath** announce move to new headquarters at **Farleigh House** (Farleigh Hungerford) with state of the art training facilities.

2011-12: Bath's season begins less four players picked by England for the **2011 World Cup** held by (and won by) New Zealand: **Lewis Moody** (capt.), **Matt Banahan, Lee Mears** and **Davey Wilson.**

2012-13: in January 2013 Bath out-half **Tom Heathcote** wins **debut cap for Scotland** against Tonga at Murrayfield. In second half of 2012-13 season Saracens commence Premiership rugby on their innovative '**synthetic surface**' at their new Allianz Park ground. Bath's **Rob Webber, Davey Wilson, Dave Attwood** and **Kyle Eastmond** selected for England's 2013 summer tour of Argentina and Uraguay, Eastmond scoring brilliant try on debut in England's win over Argentina.

2014: Bath out-side half **George Ford** wins debut cap for England (off bench) in post-Christmas Six Nations win over Wales (Twickenham).

In the **2014-15** season **Autumn internationals** Bath backs **Samesa Rokoduguni,** and also **Anthony Watson** (off bench) win their **debut caps** against New Zealand at Twickenham (NZ win 21-24). While Bath forwards **Dave Attwood, David Wilson, Henry Thomas, Rob Webber** and **backs Kyle Eastmond, George Ford, Jonathan Joseph and Anthony Watson,** also appear for England at various stages of the Autumn Internationals and the 2015 Six Nations Championship; likewise prop **Paul James for Wales.**

2015: Sam Burgess made his **England Saxons** debut in their 18-9 win over Ireland Wolfhounds in Cork in late January. Meanwhile under head coach **Jon Callard** (former Bath & England) Bath lock **Charlie Ewels** captained England to win **the U-20's Six Nations Championship** with a 24-11 win over France at Brighton's Amex stadium, 12,600 watching. Bath outside-half **Rory Jennings** scored 14 points with 'the boot.'

In Cremona, Italy, Bath's **Charlie Ewels (capt,) Rory Jennings (out-half), Max Clark (centre) and Will Homer (scrum-half)** all play in England's U-20.s **World Championship final** in June against New Zealand, the Kiwis winning 21-16.

Nick Abendanon (recently moved from Bath to Clermont Auvergne) voted '**European Player of the Year.**'

At conclusion of 2014-2015 regular-season Bath achieve 2nd place and so reach **semi-finals** at home against Leicester, winning 47-10.

30th May 2015 Bath lose 16-28 against Saracens in the **AVIVA Premiership Final** at Twickenham (over 80,000 attendance).

31st July 2015; It was announced that Bath's appeal at the Royal Courts of Justice had been upheld. This decision allows for expansion of the Rec and its facilities, so as to fulfill the aim of "providing a world-class sporting, community and cultural venue in the city."

Late August 2015; the following Bath players are chosen for the **England World Cup Squad**: Rob Webber (hooker), David Wilson (prop), and backs Anthony Watson, George Ford, Jonathan Joseph and Sam Burgess., **Also**: Dominic Day (lock, **Wales**), Paul James (prop, **Wales**), *now moved to Ospreys*, Alafoti Fa'osiliva (flanker, **Samoa**), Francois Louw (back-row, **S. Africa**), and Horacio Agulla (wing, **Argentina**).

- A Goodly Heritage. A History of Monkton Combe School, by A.F. Lace (printed for Monkton Combe School by Sir Isaac Pitman and Sons Ltd. Bath 1968).
- A History of Clifton College 1860-1934, by O.F. Christie, published by J. W .Arrowsmith, Quay St, Bristol.
- A History of Marlborough College (1843-1893), by A.G. Bradley, A.C. Champneys and J.W. Baines, printed by Hazell, Watson & Viney, Ltd, London and Aylesbury. Later revised and continued by J.R. Taylor, H.C. Brentnall and G.C. Turner (1923); ALSO first surviving Marlborough RFC logbook with report of 'first Marlborough v Clifton College match.'
- American Olympic R.F. Team v Blackheath, April 1924, match programme; USA win rugby football Olympic Gold, Paris, Minnesota Museum of Rugby.
- Barnstaple RFC, archives (see: the Michael Hughes profile of Mike Blackmore, 10 Jan. 2008).
- Bath Central Lending & Reference Library archives of Bath Chronicle (and related journals), The Podium, Northgate Street, Bath, BA1 5AN.
- Bath Chronicle (The) *incorporated with Bath Weekly Argus*, and sister papers Bath & Wilts Chronicle (& Herald), Bath Weekly Chronicle, Bath Football Herald: with reports from (inter alia) 'Football Talk,' 'Play up' and "The Mascot."
- Bath Football Club 1865-1965, Centenary booklet (printed by The Mendip Press Ltd), Bath.
- Bath Football club (R.F.U.), official Year Book Season 1993-1994 (Triple Triumph). Published and edited by Ken Johnstone; produced and printed by Francomb Printers Ltd.
- Bath RFC Minutes – Club committee meetings (1944-5, 1945-6).
- Bath RFC Past Players archives; archivist Geoff Pillinger.
- Bath Records Office (The), The Guildhall, Bath; for details of (inter alia): Bath College Register 1878-1908 (Richard Clay & Sons, Bread Street Hill, London and Bungay, Suffolk).
- Bath RFC club archives/records (various).
- Bath Competitive College & Hermitage School records.
- Bedford School magazine 'The Ousel' (1896-1904), Ref: J.G.Milton.
- Bristol RFC archives; Mark Hoskins (archivist).
- Boys Own (The), 1907-8 edition.
- Bystander (The) 15 February 1928.
- Cardiff Rugby Club, history and statistics 1876-1975, by D.E. Davies.
- Cheltenham College (archives).
- Clifton College (archives), and Sri Lanka 2004, Rugby & Netball tour (magazine).

- Complete who's who of England Rugby Union Internationals (The); Raymond Maule, Breedon Books Sport. I SBN: 1-873626.10X.
- Daily Mail (The), article by Robert Lacey (King George V), 29 July 2004.
- Edinburgh Academy (archives).
- Edinburgh Academicals Football Club Centenary History (The), printed by Pillans and Wilson Ltd, Edinburgh and Glasgow.
- Eton College (archives).
- For College, Club and Country' (A History of Clifton Rugby Football Club), by Patrick Casey & Richard I. Hale, MX Publishing Ltd, 335 Princes Park Manor, Royal Drive, London N11 3GX.
- Georgian Summer, by David Gadd, Moonraker Press, 26 St. Margarets street, Bradford-on-Avon, Wiltshire. SBN. 239.00167.2
- Gladiators of a Roman City, by Harry W. Barstow.
- Keene's Bath Journal. `
- Guys, King's & St. Thomas' Hospitals RFC, 'a brief history.'
- History of Kingswood School (The), by Three Old Boys (Charles H. Kelly, 2, Castle st., City Rd and 26 Paternoster Row, E.C. 1898.
- Kingswood School, Bath, archives.
- Langholm RFC, 1871- 1971 (Centenary book).
- Marlborough College (archives).
- Match programmes of: Bath, Bristol, Gloucester, Leicester, & (various).
- Matthew Bloxam's Letter, "The Meteor," Rugby at Bigside/William Webb Ellis.".
- 'Men of a Stout Countenance' (autobiography of R.A. Gerrard, by D. Crichton-Miller) – dp publications, Abertillery, Gwent, UK.
- Merchiston Castle School, see 'The Merchiston Register.'
- Minnesota Museum of rugby, USA.
- Monktonian (The), first issue, Lent term 1879, 1897-1904, and Monkton Combe School (archives).
- Official England Rugby Miscellany (The), by Stuart Farmer, Vision Sports Publishing, 2 Coombe Gardens, London, SW20 0QU.
- One Hundred Years at Raeburn Place 1854-1954 (A short history of the Edinburgh Academy's playing field), printed by T. and A. Constable Ltd., Hopetoun Street, Printers to the
- University of Edinburgh.
- One hundred years of Scarlet (Llanelli RFC history).
- Picture Post (magazine), 7 December 1946, 'the life of a rugby club,'
- Rugby Football at Cheltenham College 1844-1944; by E.Scott Skirving, 1945; (Cheltenham, Darters bookshop).
- Rugby School (archives).
- RULES of the Wiveliscombe Foot Ball Club, 1872.

- Seventy years of Somerset rugby 1875 – 1945 (HY. Bryant & Sons, printers, High Street, Wellington, Somerset).
- Sunday Times Magazine 7 January 1996; Will's tough ruck, Stephen Jones,
- Torquay Athletic RFC archives.
- Torquay press, 'Football Herald' (of Herald Express), see match report: Torquay v Bath (20th March 1937).
- Triple Triumph, Official Year Book, season 1993/4; produced and printed by Francomb Printers Ltd, England.
- Walcot Old Boys Centenary 1882-1982, ISBN 0950959206 (WOB 100 MFG 1983).
- World Rugby Museum, Twickenham: www.rfu.com/museum (Tel:020 8892 8877)

Tables of Results, Presidents and Captains

PRESIDENTS: The known role of Honour:

1882 - 1883	Major General C. Fitzroy Mundy
1883 - 1884	R. B. Bagnall-Wild
1884- 1885	
1885 - 1886	Col. Chandler
1886 - 1888	
1888 - 1898	Sir Robert Blaine
1900 - 1926	Captain F.W. Forester
1926 - 1927	A. J. Stuart Gould
1927 - 1938	J. H. Colmer
1938 - 1946	Dr R. Scott Reid
1946 - 1950	Captain S.L. Amor OBE
1950 - 1952	A. Ridley O.B. E.
1952 - 1954	Sir James Pitman
1954 - 1956	Major L. D. Wardle
1956 - 1958	B. C. Barber
1958 - 1960	Dr R. Scott Reid
1960 - 1962	W .S. Bascombe
1962 - 1964	C.H.G Beazer
1964 - 1966	B.C .Barber
1966 - 1967	H. J. Crane
1967 - 1969	J .F. Bevan-Jones
1969 - 1971	D.M. Smith
1971 - 1973	Mrs Molly Gerrard
1973 - 1975	G.S. Brown
1975 - 1977	H.L. Bradford
1977 - 1979	C.H.G. Beazer
1979 - 1981	W.J.F Arnold
1981 - 1983	G.S. Brown
1983 - 1985	H.J.F Simpkins
1985 - 1987	J.W.P. Roberts
1987 - 1989	N.P. Halse
1989 - 1991	A.O. Lewis
1991 - 1993	L.A. Hughes
1993 - 1995	G.W. Hancock
1995 - 1997	B. Perry
1997 - 1999	A.J. Meek
1999 - 2001	R. A. Berry
2001 - 2003	P.G. Hall
2003 - 2005	J. Barber
2005 - 2007	P. Bliss
2007 - 2009	J Rowell
2009 - 2011	A Gay
2011 - 2013	D Trick
2013 - 2015	M. C. Beese

Captains 1st XV

1874-1876	H. G. Fuller
1877-1878	J. Petgrave
1881-1882	E. Digby
1882-1883	H.S. Jacobs
1883-1884	A.K. Cunninghame
1887-1890	W.A. Walker
1890-1898	F. Soane
1898-1899	F. Derrick
1899-1900	Norman Biggs
1900-1902	G. Ruddick
1902-1903	F. J. Cashnella
1903-1906	T.B. Timmins
1906-1907	R. Meister
1907-1908	T. West
1908-1910	A. Ford
1910-1911	A. Hatherill
1911-1913	Norman Coates
1913-1915	P.P. Hope
	WAR YEARS
1918-1922	P.P. Hope
1922-1924	H. Vowles
1924-1925	S.G.U. Considine
1925-1927	W.J. Gibbs
1927-1928	I.J. Pitman
1928-1929	W.H. Sheppard
1929-1931	I.J.M. Spence
1931-1933	M.V. Shaw
1933-1934	B.C. Barber
1934-1936	R.A. Gerrard
1936-1937	N.W. Matthews
1937-1938	R.A. Gerrard
1938-1939	K.J. Foss
	WAR YEARS
1945-1946	A. Higgins
1946-1947	I.J.M. Lumsden
1947-1948	T.W. Hicks
1948-1949	A.W. Todd
1949-1950	L.S. Harter
1950-1952	A.O. Lewis
1952-1955	J.W.P. Roberts
1955-1956	J.McG. Kendall Carpenter
1956-1958	J.W.P. Roberts
1958-1959	G.F. Drewett
1959-1960	J. Jacobson
1960-1961	A.H. Meek
1961-1962	R. Farnham
1962-1963	L.I. Rimmer
1963-1965	K.P. Andrews
1965-1966	G.F. Margretts
1966-1969	P,Sibley
1969-1970	T.Martland/P. Heindorff
1970-1971	P.Heindorff
1971-1972	R. Walkey
1972-1974	Phil Hall
1974-1975	Chris Perry
1975-1976	J. Waterman
1976-1977	J. Horton
1977-1978	J. Waterman
1978-1979	M.Beese
1979-1980	J. Horton
1980-1981	R. Lye
1981-1982	Damien Murphy/R. Spurrell
1982-1985	R. Spurrell
1985-1986	J. Palmer
1986-1988	Richard Hill
1988-1991	S. Barnes
1091-1993	Andy Robinson
1993-1995	Jon Hall
1995-1996	P. de Glanville

Captains 1st XV since Club turned Professional

1996-1997	Philip de Glanville
1997-1998	Andy Nicol
1998-1999	Richard Webster
1999-2000	Jon Callard
2000-2001	Ben Clarke
2001-2002	Dan Lyle
2002-2004	Danny Grewcock
2004-2005	Jon Humphreys
2005-2008	Steve Borthwick
2008-2009	Michael Lipman
2009-2010	Michael Claassens
2910-2011	Luke Watson
2011-2012	Stuart Hooper
212-2013	Stuart Hooper
2013-2014	Stuart Hooper
2014-2015	Stuart Hooper

Bath Football Club 1st XV Records

Season	Played	Won	Lost	Drawn	Points For	Points Against
1895-1896	33	11	14	8	180	207
1896-1897	35	20	12	3	235	233
1897-1898	36	13	19	4	186	268
1898-1899	34	16	15	3	177	163
1899-1900	29	12	14	3	127	201
1900-1901	33	17	15	1	235	179
1901-1902	30	8	17	5	147	260
1902-1903	33	15	16	2	209	211
1903-1904	31	9	19	3	158	258
1904-1905	39	21	15	3	401	285
1905-1906	33	7	24	2	151	210
1906-1907	29	12	15	2	150	199
1907-1908	32	9	20	3	196	319
1908-1909	35	18	15	2	312	216
1909-1910	36	15	12	9	237	198
1910-1911	35	16	16	3	264	203
1911-1912	32	20	11	1	332	263
1912-1913	34	21	12	1	376	195
1913-1914	35	22	12	1	334	228
1914-1918				War Years		
1918-1919	11	6	5	0	111	64
1919-1920	39	20	15	4	458	273
1920-1921	38	21	14	3	462	220
1921-1922	40	25	9	6	413	157
1922-1923	45	26	16	3	380	233
1923-1924	40	18	18	4	310	283
1924-1925	37	22	13	2	389	321
1925-1926	35	7	27	1	167	246
1926-1927	35	21	13	1	330	296
1927-1928	39	22	14	3	325	309
1928-1929	41	17	22	2	396	359
1929-1930	37	19	15	3	388	265
1930-1931	37	22	12	3	452	250
1931-1932	38	25	12	1	418	280
1932-1933	38	24	13	1	356	247
1933-1934	36	20	16	0	330	353
1934-1935	40	20	19	1	330	302
1935-1936	34	13	18	3	239	288
1936-1937	34	18	13	3	314	242
1937-1938	34	13	20	1	173	312
1938-1939	35	9	20	6	161	315
1939-1945				War Years		
1945-1946	36	16	19	1	367	423
1946-1947	32	18	10	4	274	20
1947-1948	37	15	20	2	274	278
1948-1949	40	19	16	5	346	326
1949-1950	39	15	21	3	267	355
1950-1951	41	27	10	4	324	277
1951-1952	39	21	15	3	314	249

Bath Football Club 1st XV Records

Season	Played	Won	Lost	Drawn	Points For	Points Against
1952-1953	40	19	15	6	359	291
1953-1954	40	20	16	4	331	293
1954-1955	42	25	15	2	403	296
1955-1956	38	17	18	3	289	334
1956-1957	39	15	19	5	315	320
1957-1958	42	11	27	4	282	371
1958-1959	39	12	19	8	290	398
1959-1960	41	16	20	5	364	364
1960-1961	44	21	21	2	418	437
1961-1962	43	20	20	3	470	409
1962-1963	39	14	24	1	324	409
1963-1964	45	20	22	3	342	377
1964-1965	46	15	28	3	563	688
1965-1966	48	19	28	1	479	483
1966-1967	48	27	20	1	628	466
1967-1968	43	24	14	5	540	368
1968-1969	44	24	17	3	645	521
1969-1970	43	29	13	1	710	480
1970-1971	41	26	13	2	660	478
1971-1972	50	23	27	0	745	817
1972-1973	49	24	23	2	875	723
1973-1974	55	26	28	1	823	693
1974-1975	46	28	17	1	619	539
1975-1976	50	31	18	1	850	634
1976-1977	46	26	18	2	749	659
1977-1978	49	28	20	1	984	754
1978-1979	44	31	10	3	853	440
1979-1980	48	37	10	1	962	557
1980-1981	50	30	18	2	819	549
1981-1982	49	29	19	1	801	719
1982-1983	50	38	9	3	1278	555
1983-1984	39	29	10	0	870	468
1984-1985	39	30	8	1	923	400
1985-1986	43	33	7	3	1055	507
1986-1987	44	36	7	1	1167	519
1987-1988	44	28	12	4	1098	549
1988-1989	44	36	6	2	1262	521
1989-1990	41	35	5	1	1166	379
1990-1991	34	29	4	1	984	392
1991-1992	33	28	4	1	774	363
1992-1993	32	27	5	0	1112	321
1993-1994	37	30	7	0	891	499
1994-1995	34	25	5	4	839	474
1995-1996	34	26	7	1	1005	562

Bath 1ˢᵗ XV Professional Results 1996-97 onwards

Season	Played	Won	Drawn	Lost	Points for	Points against	Total Table points	Place
1996-97	22	15	1	6	863	411	31	2nd
1997-98	22	13	0	9	575	455	26	3rd
1998-99	26	15	0	11	698	574	30	6th
1999-2000	22	15	2	5	690	425	43	2nd
2000-01	22	14	0	8	680	430	70	3rd
2001-02	22	7	0	15	311	524	33	11th
2002-03	22	7	2	13	385	490	36	11th
2003-04	22	18	0	4	508	311	79	1st
2004-05	22	12	2	8	407	366	58	4th
2005-06	22	9	1	12	441	494	46	9th
2006-07	22	8	2	12	428	492	45	8th
2007-08	22	15	0	7	526	387	69	3rd
2008-09	22	13	2	7	530	441	65	4th
2009-20	22	12	2	8	450	366	61	4th
2010-11	22	13	1	8	427	367	62	5th
2011-12	22	9	0	13	365	412	44	8th
2012-13	22	10	1	11	452	434	53	7th
2013-14	22	14	2	6	495	388	67	5th
2014-15	22	16	0	6	625	414	75	2nd

ABOVE figures show END of REGULAR SEASON RESULTS AND POSITIONS SINCE SEASON 1996-7 WHEN PROFESSIONAL RUGBY UNION COMMENCED.

REVISED CURRENT POINTS SYSTEM: 4 pts for win, 2 pts for draw, 1 bonus pt for scoring 4 tries or more, and 1 bonus point for losing by 7 pts or less. MAX points permitted: 5 pts per game. Bonus points are sometimes critical in final PLACE position at end of regular season, though since season 2002-3 the Premiership winners will be decided by the play-offs between the top FOUR teams.

PLAY-OFF FINALS involving BATH:
2003-2004:   BATH lost 6-10 to WASPS.
2014-2015:   BATH lost 16-28 to SARACENS.

Tables of Results to show
Bath Rugby Club's progress through the decades

1900's to 1980's

Tables of results courtesy of Bath Past Players unless otherwise stated.

1905-06

Date	Opponents	Venue	Result	For	Against
23/9/1905	TAUNTON	H	W	12	0
30/9	PONTYPOOL	H	L	0	22
14/10	PENYLAN	H	L	0	5
28/10	PENARTH	H	W	9	4
4/11	CHELTENHAM	A	L	3	16
18/11	EXETER	H	L	3	8
25/11	LYDNEY	A	L	0	12
2/12	BRISTOL	A	L	6	20
9/12	GLOUCESTER	A	L	0	16
16/12	NEATH	H	L	3	6
23/12	WESTON-SUPER-MARE	A	L	0	11
26/12	MOUNTAIN ASH	H	L	13	16
27/12	OLD EDWARDIANS	H	D	3	3
30/12	CLIFTON	A	W	3	0
6/1/06	BRISTOL	H	L	8	9
13/1	CHELTENHAM	H	L	0	3
20/1	BRIDGWATER	A	L	3	14
27/1	CLIFTON	H	L	6	8
3/2	EXETER	A	L	0	19
10/2	WESTON-S-MARE	H	W	8	3
17/2	PENARTH	A	L	3	17
24/2	TAUNTON	A	D	0	0
3/3	NEATH	A	L	8	19
10/3	BRIDGWATER	H	W	12	0
17/3	PONTYPRIDD	A	L	3	14
24/3	PONTYPOOL	A	L	5	17
31/3	BRISTOL	H	L	3	6
7/4	MOUNTAIN ASH	A	L	8	20
14/4	LYDNEY	H	L	6	7
16/4	LENNOX	H	W	17	0
17/4	PONTYPRIDD	H	L	0	10
20/4	CLIFTON	H	W	6	0
21/4	GLOUCESTER	H	L	0	3
	T B Timmins (Capt.)			**151**	**308**
	Played 33 Won 7 Lost 24 Drawn 2				

1913-1914 Features:- Early Season Ruminations - Tedium of Railway Travel - Functions of a Trainer - Dangers of Rugby - Northern Union - Association Jealousy - v Llanelly - Spirit of the Game - Review.

Date	Opponents	Venue	Result	For	Against
13/9/1913	Leicester	A	L	5	19
20/9	Penylan	H	W	18	5
27/9	Bridgwater	H	W	29	3
4/10	Exeter	H	W	9	0
11/10	Devonport Albion	A	L	6	15
18/10	Bristol	A	L	0	5
25/10	Bridgwater	A	L	0	6
1/11	Wellington	H	W	33	0
8/11	Llanelly	A	L	8	15
22/11	Abertillery	H	W	10	5
29/11	Gloucester	A	L	0	19
6/12	Pontypool	A	L	0	11
13/12	Machen	H	W	15	7
20/12	Cheltenham	H	W	6	3
26/12	Crumlin	H	W	3	0
27/12	Penylan	H	W	6	3
3/1/1914	Clifton	H	W	16	3
10/1	Old Edwardians	A	W	11	6
17/1	Gloucester Regiment	H	W	22	13
31/1	Bristol	H	W	9	0
7/2	Penylan	H	W	6	3
14/2	Pontypool	H	L	0	5
21/2	Penarth	H	W	9	8
28/2	Coventry	A	L	3	14
5/3	Middlesex Hospital	H	W	9	3
7/3	Clifton	A	W	15	0
14/3	Devonport Albion	H	D	3	3
21/3	Exeter	A	L	6	9
28/3	Llanelly	H	W	5	0
4/4	Bridgwater Albion	H	W	6	3
11/4	Cheltenham	A	W	8	3
13/4	Coventry	H	W	41	10
14/4	Leicester	H	W	14	3
18/4	Gloucester	H	L	3	10
25/4	Penarth	A	L	0	16
				334	228
	Played 35 Won 22 Lost 12				
	Drawn 1				
	P.P.Hope (Capt)				

With a strong fixture list, Bath managed to preserve their home record for well nigh 6 months.

1922-1923 Features:- Rugger Night - County rift - Ground improvements - Supporters' Programme - Stoop's tips - Church Service - Lucky Programme - Down a Mine - A Bit of a Do - Makeshift side - County Champs - Honorarium.

Date	Opponents	Venue	Result	For	Against
2/9/1922	LEICESTER	A	L	8	16
9/9	NEWTON ABBOT	H	W	15	6
10/9	GLOUCESTER	A	L	5	17
23/9	UNITED SERVICES	H	W	9	4
30/9	PLYMOUTH ALBION	A	L	0	3
2/10	CAMBORNE	A	W	18	0
7/10	ABERAVON	H	W	18	0
11/10	BLUNDELL'S SCHOOL	A	W	17	0
14/10	MOSELEY	A	W	19	3
21/10	EXMOUTH	H	W	14	3
28/10	BRIDGWATER	A	L	0	3
4/11	STROUD	H	W	10	3
11/11	LLANELLY	A	L	9	10
18/11	LONDON WELSH	H	W	20	0
25/11	OLD EDWARDIANS	H	W	8	0
2/12	CROSS KEYS	H	W	4	3
9/12	LONDON WELSH	A	W	7	0
16/12	EXMOUTH	A	L	8	11
23/12	OLD BLUES	H	W	6	3
26/12	MOUNTAIN ASH	H	D	0	0
27/12	GLOUCESTER	H	W	9	6
30/12	PLYMOUTH ALBION	H	W	13	0
6/1/1923	STROUD	A	W	22	0
11/1	CLIFTON	A	L	3	9
13/1	DEVONPORT SERVICES	H	W	5	4
20/1	BRISTOL	H	L	8	10
27/1	MOUNTAIN ASH	A	L	3	13
3/2	BRIDGWATER	H	D	3	3
10/2	NEWPORT	H	L	0	4
17/2	BRISTOL	A	L	0	11
24/2	R.A.F.	H	W	6	0
28/2	OXFORD UNIVERSITY	A	W	9	0
3/3	NEWTON ABBOT	A	D	3	3
10/3	PONTYPOOL	H	W	4	0
15/3	BRISTOL UNIVERSITY	H	W	12	0
17/3	LLANELLY	H	L	3	7
19/3	ABERAVON	A	L	3	26
24/3	CROSSKEYS	A	L	3	19
31/3	ST. THOMAS HOSPITAL	H	W	22	0
2/4	PONTYMINSTER	H	W	13	0
4/4	LEICESTER	H	W	17	3
7/4	BLACKHEATH	H	W	13	10
11/4	BRISTOL	A	L	0	3
14/4	MOSELEY	H	W	8	0
21/4	PONTYPOOL	A	L	3	17
	Played 45 Won 26 Lost 16 Drawn 3			380	233
	H. Vowles (Captain)				

AGM 19/6/1922

T J Gandy and J T Piper elected as Life Members.

Proposed - that the Bath Football Club affiliate with Somerset County Rugby Union.

Amendment that it was not desirable. After much discussion the original motion was not carried and meeting agreed to hold another General Meeting to discuss affiliation and draw up rules.

1931-32 Features:- New Jerseys - New Law - Physical Training - Hot exchanges v Bridgend - Agreed Bath City on Rec 5/5/1931 - "Springbok" - Gerrard - Cashnella - A wonderful Day - v Leicester - F Soane Dcd.

Date	Opponents	Venue	Result	For	Against
5/9/1931	LEICESTER	A	L	0	6
12/9	SWANSEA	H	L	5	8
19/9	UNITED SERVICES	A	W	10	3
24/9	CLIFTON	A	W	21	5
3/10	ST. BARTS HOSPITAL	H	W	18	8
10/10	BRIDGEND	H	W	16	15
17/10	BRISTOL	A	W	13	11
24/10	LONDON WELSH	H	W	9	8
31/10	HARLEQUINS	A	L	0	19
7/11	OLD PAULINES	H	W	32	3
14/11	NEATH	H	L	3	4
21/11	LLANELLY	A	L	0	16
28/11	EXETER	H	W	10	3
12/12	RICHMOND	H	W	13	6
19/12	ST. MARY'S HOSPITAL	H	L	14	16
26/12	OLD BLUES	H	W	15	11
28/12	PONTYPOOL	H	W	5	3
2/1/1932	DEVONPORT SERVICES	H	W	16	0
9/1	NEATH	A	L	3	6
16/1	GLOUCESTER	A	L	3	8
23/1	CAMBORNE	H	W	14	0
30/1	PLYMOUTH ALBION	A	L	0	15
6/2	LLANELLY	H	W	5	3
13/2	LONDON WELSH	A	W	21	7
20/2	NORTHAMPTON	A	W	18	5
27/2	EXETER	A	D	6	6
5/3	BRISTOL	H	W	11	6
10/3	NEWPORT	A	L	0	16
12/3	PLYMOUTH ALBION	H	W	14	3
19/3	DEVONPORT SERVICES	A	W	16	8
26/3	NORTHAMPTON	H	W	14	6
28/3	OLD MERCHANT TAYLORS	H	W	9	3
29/3	LEICESTER	H	W	11	9
2/4	UNITED SERVICES	H	W	29	16
9/4	CAMBORNE	A	L	8	9
11/4	NEWTON ABBOT	A	L	0	6
16/4	LONDON IRISH	H	W	28	0
19/4	GLOUCESTER	H	W	8	3
	Played 38 Won 25 Lost 12 Drawn 1			418	280
	M V Shaw (Captain)				

1944-1945

Date	Opponents	Venue	Result	For	Against
7/10/44	R.A.F.	H	W	16	0
14/10 *	R.A.A.F.	H	L	5	24
21/10	BRISTOL	H	L	3	8
28/10	B.A.C.	H	W	8	0
4/11	R.A.F.	H	D	5	5
11/11 **	R.N.A.S.	H	W	20	0
25/11	PARACHUTE REGIMENT	H	L	6	8
2/12	R.A.F. LYNHAM	H	W	29	3
9/12 #	BRIDGWATER	A	L	16	6
16/12	ROTOL	H	W	9	8
23/12	CARDIFF	A	L	3	12
13/1/45	R.A.F. XV	H	W	38	0
20/1	R.A.F. XV	H	W	37	3
3/2	ST. MARY'S HOSPITAL	H	W	15	13
10/2	R.A.F. COLERNE	H	W	20	0
17/2	CARDIFF	H	L	0	13
24/2	OXFORD UNIVERSITY GREYHOUNDS	H	W	16	3
3/3	R.A.F. ST. ATHAN	H	W	6	3
10/3	R.A.F. MELKSHAM	H	W	33	0
17/3	BRIDGWATER	H	W	10	0
24/3	BRISTOL	A	L	6	9
31/3 +	NUNEATON	H	L	0	3
2/4 ***	LEICESTER BARBARIANS	H	W	5	3
				306	124
	Played 23 Won 15 Lost 7 Drawn 1				
	Flt. Lieut. D D Evans (Capt.)				

*Best team of the War at the Rec.

"Bath entertained to dinner afterwards. A rare courtesy in these austerity days."

** Royal Naval Air Service – side never had 15 men on field at any time!

+ Peter Brown (Pre war Bath hooker) home on leave from Middle East – left the field with a cut eye and went to surgery of Club President – Dr. Scott Reid for 4 stitches. He did not return to the field. In later life, P H Brown was to undertake intensive research, write and produce the 1865-1965 Club booklet.

***2000 spectators.

July 1945 Lance-Corporal L. Phillips reported missing in Normandy.

1950-51

Date	Opponents	Venue	Result	For	Against
9/9/50	LEICESTER	A	L	6	8
14/9	HYLTON CLEAVER'S INTERNATIONAL XV	H	L	0	16
16/9	LLANELLY	H	D	8	8
21/9	BATH & DISTRICT COMBINATION	H	W	6	3
23/9	DEVONPORT SERVICES	H	W	3	0
30/9	DEVONPORT SERVICES	A	W	11	3
2/10	PENZANCE & NEWLYN	A	L	0	14
3/10	FALMOUTH	A	W	13	11
7/10	WESTON-S-MARE	A	W	3	0
14/10	SOMERSET POLICE	H	W	6	5
21/10	BRISTOL	H	W	13	6
28/10	EXETER	H	L	12	14
4/11	UNITED SERVICES	A	W	15	3
11/11	LONDON IRISH	A	W	11	0
18/11	NEATH	H	L	3	6
25/11	ST. MARY'S HOSPITAL	H	D	5	5
2/12	LONDON SCOTTISH	A	W	16	9
9/12	CLIFTON	A	W	11	3
16/12	WESTON-S-MARE	H	W	11	0
23/12	GLOUCESTER	A	L	3	27
26/12	OLD BLUES	H	W	11	0
6/1/51	OLD CRANLEIGHANS	A	W	6	3
13/1	LONDON WELSH	A	W	8	0
20/1	CARDIFF	H	L	11	25
27/1	ST. MARY'S HOSPITAL	A	W	6	3
3/2	NEWPORT	A	L	9	39
10/2	GLOUCESTER	H	W	8	3
17/2	LEICESTER	H	L	3	15
24/2	WASPS	H	W	8	3
3/3	BRISTOL	A	W	9	6
10/3	SWANSEA	H	W	8	6
17/3	LONDON IRISH	H	W	5	0
24/3	HEADINGLEY	H	W	16	3
26/3	OLD MERCHANT TAYLORS	H	W	3	0
31/3	SARACENS	A	W	11	0
7/4	LONDON SCOTTISH	H	D	0	0
12/4	BRIDGWATER	A	D	0	0
14/4	MOSELEY	H	W	23	5
19/4	TAUNTON	A	W	11	6
21/4	MOSELEY	A	W	9	3
28/4	NEWBRIDGE	A	L	3	16
	Played 41 Won 27 Lost 10 Drawn 4			324	277
	A.O. Lewis (Captain)				

1966-67 Features:- Bill Carling - Players arranging own games - Jeremy Spencer - Centenary Book - The Sibley Touch - Two Sets of Brothers - A Ripping Time.

Date	Opponents	Venue	Result	For	Against
1/9/1966	ZUMMERZET BABAAS	H	W	25	8
3/9	LLANELLI	A	L	0	14
5/9	BROUGHTON PARK	H	L	3	6
10/9	LEICESTER	A	W	14	8
15/9	WESTON-SUPER-MARE	H	W	13	6
17/9	EBBW VALE	A	L	8	24
22/9	CLIFTON	A	W	19	3
24/9	ST. MARY'S HOSPITAL	H	W	15	13
29/9	BRIDGWATER	A	W	21	6
1/10	ABERAVON	H	L	11	18
8/10	NEWBRIDGE	A	D	16	16
15/10	BRISTOL	A	L	3	6
22/10	DEVONPORT SERVICES	H	W	24	8
29/10	BRIDGEND	A	L	0	21
5/11	NEATH	H	L	5	19
12/11	SARACENS	H	W	6	0
19/11	PONTYPOOL	A	W	3	0
26/11	UNITED SERVICES	H	W	14	0
3/12	LONDON SCOTTISH	A	L	9	10
10/12	GLOUCESTER	H	L	11	16
17/12	LONDON IRISH	H	W	14	6
24/12	RUGBY	H	W	17	6
26/12	OLD BLUES	H	W	30	3
31/12	NORTHAMPTON	A	L	6	11
14/1	LONDON WELSH	H	L	13	20
19/1	R.A.F.	H	W	6	5
21/1	METROPOLITAN POLICE	H	L	18	21
28/1	ST. MARY'S HOSPITAL	A	W	20	0
4/2	ROSSLYN PARK	A	W	8	6
11/2	GLOUCESTER	A	W	19	14
18/2	CHELTENHAM	A	W	9	6
25/2	WASPS	H	L	0	3
1/3	LEICESTER	A	L	3	11
4/3	BRISTOL	H	L	6	24
18/3	MOSELEY	A	L	9	19
23/3	HARLEQUINS	H	L	5	13
25/3	LIVERPOOL	H	W	11	6
27/3	OLD MERCHANT TAYLORS	H	W	25	0
28/3	SHEFFIELD	H	W	14	9
¼	SALE	A	W	16	3
4/4	LLANELLI	H	W	11	3
6/4	STROUD	H	W	24	3
8/4	EXETER	H	W	14	3
11/4	WESTON-SUPER-MARE	A	W	11	5
14/4	COMBINED SERVICES XV	A	W	52	3
15/4	WEST GERMANY	A	L	5	9
16/4	VICTORIA CL.	A	W	9	3
22/4	COVENTRY	A	L	3	32
27/4	TAUNTON	H	W	24	8
29/4	BEDFORD	A	L	6	9
	Played 50 Won 29 Lost 20 Drawn 1			**628**	**466**
	P Sibley (Captain) P.R Hall (Vice Captain)				

LAWS:- International Board proposed standard numbering of players.

1979-80 Features:- v Pontypool - California Tour -v Moseley - 'Tricky' -A Faultless Bastion – van der Loos - President's Room - v Quins - What a Shocker! - Exit Cup - Horton's Silky Skills - Trick at his Best - SW Sevens - Kendall-Carpenter honoured - Burgeoning talent.

Date	Opponents	Venue	Result	For	Against
1/9/1979	PONTYPOOL	H	W	16	9
5/9	NEWPORT	A	W	6	3
8/9	LEICESTER	A	W	10	9
15/9	MOSELEY	H	W	22	11
18/9	SEAHAWKS (SAN JOSE, CALIFORNIA)	H	W	58	0
22/9	LLANELLI	A	L	6	14
25/9	CLIFTON	A	W	33	13
29/9	NEATH	H	D	22	22
3/10	SOUTH WALES POLICE	A	W	13	4
5/10	ABERAVON	A	L	15	17
20/10	BRISTOL	H	W	38	17
27/10	ST. MARY'S HOSPITAL	A	W	28	6
31/10	CHELTENHAM	A	W	16	9
3/11	HARLEQUINS	A	W	41	17
10/11	NEWBRIDGE	H	W	21	16
17/11	COVENTRY	A	W	3	0
24/11	UNITED SERVICES (PORTSMOUTH)	A	W	29	12
1/12	LONDON SCOTTISH	H	W	36	7
10/12	GLOUCESTER	A	L	3	10
15/12	HARLEQUINS	H	W	27	10
22/12	PLYMOUTH ALBION	H	W	16	12
26/12	CLIFTON	H	W	15	4
1/1/1980	CARDIFF	A	L	4	16
5/1	LEICESTER	H	L	12	22
9/1	ROYAL NAVY	H	W	22	10
12/1	LONDON WELSH	A	L	7	37
19/1	METROPOLITAN POLICE	A	W	20	12
26/1	MARLOW	H	W	30	6
½	ROSSLYN PARK	H	L	9	10
6/2	R.A.F.	H	W	21	0
9/2	CHELTENHAM (On Civil Service Ground)	H	W	25	10
15/2	BRIDGEND	H	W	22	10
23/2	LIVERPOOL (2nd Round John Player Cup)	A	W	19	12
28/2	EXETER UNIVERSITY	H	W	27	0
8/3	LONDON IRISH (Quarter Final of John Player Cup)	H	L	3	6
14/3	NUNEATON	A	W	6	3
17/3	EBBW VALE	H	W	24	6
22/3	RICHMOND	A	W	27	15
26/3	GLOUCESTER	H	W	24	9
29/3	EXETER	A	W	19	4
¾	GLAMORGAN WANDERERS	H	W	28	15
5/4	BRISTOL	A	L	6	44
7/4	WILMSLOW	H	W	46	7
12/4	BIRKENHEAD PARK	A	W	22	3
16/4	NEWPORT	H	W	17	7
19/4	LLANELLI	H	W	13	6
26/4	BEDFORD	H	W	22	16
30/4	PONTYPRIDD	A	L	3	49
	Played 48 Won 37 Lost 10 Drawn 1			**962**	**557**
	J P Horton (Captain)				

MANCOM 19/7/1979
John Horton endorsed the acceptance of Roger Spurrell as a playing member of the Club.

1982-83

Date	Opponents	Venue	Result	For	Against
1/9/1982	CHELTENHAM	H	W	38	11
4/9	PONTYPOOL	A	L	16	37
11/9	LEICESTER	H	W	24	15
18/9	MOSELEY	A	L	11	13
22/9	NEWPORT	A	W	12	3
25/9	LLANELLI	A	L	10	15
29/9	HAVANT	H	W	21	9
2/10	ABERAVON	H	W	17	16
6/10	WYVERN 1st Round of Somerset K.O. Cup	A	W	76	3
9/10	LIVERPOOL	A	L	4	12
16/10	BRISTOL	A	L	4	6
23/10	UNITED SERVICES	A	L	16	18
30/10	NEATH	A	L	21	22
3/11	Bath XV v MARLOW (Not in statistics 16-10)	H	W		
6/11	HARLEQUINS	A	W	21	7
10/11	CLIFTON	A	W	20	6
15/11	NEWBRIDGE	H	L	3	12
20/11	COVENTRY	H	W	19	15
1/12	SOUTH WALES POLICE	H	W	28	0
4/12	LONDON SCOTTISH	A	W	21	9
11/12	GLOUCESTER	H	W	21	12
12/12	FROME Somerset Cup	H	W	46	6
18/12	HARLEQUINS	H	D	13	13
27/12	CLIFTON	H	W	53	4
1/1/1983	LEICESTER	A	L	9	21
8/1	LONDON WELSH	H	W	16	11
15/1	METROPOLITAN POLICE	A	W	34	15
19/1	ROYAL NAVY	H	W	27	13
22/1	EXETER	H	W	74	3
29/1	NORTHAMPTON	A	W	19	16
2/2	R.A.F.	H	W	43	4
5/2	ROSSLYN PARK	H	W	35	12
9/2	WESTON-S-MARE (Quarter Final Somerset Cup)	H	W	43	7
12/2	GLOUCESTER	A	D	7	7
26/2	FYLDE	H	W	31	12
2/3	CHELTENHAM	A	W	31	9
5/3	GORDANO (Semi Final Somerset Cup)	A	W	10	6
7/3	PONTYPRIDD	H	W	19	6
12/3	SWANSEA	H	W	30	14
15/3	EBBW VALE	A	W	7	3
23/3	EXETER UNIVERSITY	H	D	6	6
26/3	RICHMOND	H	W	32	18
2/4	BRISTOL	H	W	21	16
4/4	NEW BRIGHTON	H	W	53	10
9/4	NEWPORT	H	W	13	7
12/4	PLYMOUTH	A	W	30	3
16/4	LLANELLI	H	W	31	28
20/4	MAESTEG	H	W	45	10
23/4	CARDIFF	H	W	28	9
27/4	OLD REDCLIFFIANS **Somerset K.O. Cup Final**	W-SM	W	39	10
30/4	BEDFORD	A	W	30	15
	Played 50 Won 38 Lost 9 Drawn 3 R Spurrell Captain)			**1278**	**555**

Bath's title

FINALLY Bath have broken Pontypool's stranglehold by claiming The Sunday Telegraph's "original" English-Welsh merit table title for 1985-86.

The John Player Special Cup holders also retained the English title, leaving Pontypool with the consolation of topping the Welsh table once again.

Next season, under our promotion system first introduced last year, Saracens will replace Northampton and Glamorgan Wanderers take over from South Wales Police in the premier table.

Waterloo have retained the Northern title in the first season since it was split into two divisions and promotion-relegation introduced. Next season Durham City move up to replace Hull & East Riding. Plymouth Albion retained the South West clubs title after a season-long tussle with a rejuvenated Taunton.

English—Welsh

	P	W	D	L	F	A	Pts	%
Bath	22	16	1	5	436	302	33	75
Pontypool	18	13	0	5	350	250	26	72·22
Cardiff	25	17	1	7	493	362	35	70
Swansea	24	14	1	9	453	339	29	60·42
Coventry	19	11	0	8	322	325	22	57·89
Llanelli	26	14	2	10	573	385	30	57·69
Neath	21	12	0	9	349	257	24	57·14
Leicester	21	12	0	9	359	538	24	57·14
Newport	24	11	3	10	370	342	25	52·08
Gloucester	20	10	0	10	253	301	20	50
Nottingham	7	3	1	3	133	90	7	50
Moseley	22	10	0	12	316	321	20	45·45
Bristol	22	9	0	13	328	408	18	40·91
Wasps	11	4	1	6	167	188	9	40·91
Newbridge	18	6	2	11	246	350	14	38·89
Harlequins	13	5	0	8	218	259	10	38·46
Bridgend	20	6	1	13	254	370	13	32·5
L Welsh	18	3	1	14	243	420	7	19·44
S W Police	8	0	2	6	107	192	2	12·5
Northampton	11	1	0	10	129	300	2	9·09

English

	P	W	D	L	F	A	Pts	%
Bath	17	13	0	4	387	192	26	76·47
Leicester	23	16	0	7	493	304	32	69·57
Gloucester	18	12	0	6	307	220	24	66·67
Nottingham	13	8	1	4	323	155	17	65·38
Wasps	20	12	1	7	393	327	25	62·5
Moseley	18	11	0	7	285	256	22	61·11
Saracens	15	9	0	6	228	255	18	60
Coventry	17	10	0	7	293	251	20	58·82
Bristol	18	10	0	8	359	250	20	55·56
L Scottish	14	7	1	6	178	247	15	53·57
Harlequins	19	10	0	9	304	248	20	52·63
L Irish	16	7	0	9	223	253	14	43·75
Rosslyn P	16	7	0	9	231	296	14	43·75
Blackheath	13	5	1	7	154	194	11	42·31
Richmond	20	8	0	12	320	358	16	40
L Welsh	15	3	2	10	228	287	8	26·67
Northampton	18	4	0	14	208	339	8	22·22
Bedford	17	3	0	14	155	483	6	17·65
Met Police	13	2	0	11	181	364	4	15·38

ABOUT the AUTHOR:

Harry W. Barstow first witnessed the extraordinary landscape of Bath one Spring evening in the late 1960's. It was love at first sight. Shortly afterwards he joined Bath RFC and was soon aware that the city and Bath RFC (later Bath Rugby) are almost one and the same thing.

A winger, he played for the Army at Twickenham against the Royal Navy and the RAF, and played near twenty games in a first team shirt for Bath in the late 1960's and early 1970's. In the late 1970's he played for Hannover (Victoria) in North Germany. Rugby has always been part of his life. Indeed, he proposed to his future wife just before a storm-lashed Bath quarter-final Cup win against Bristol in February 1989 that virtually flooded the entire Rec.

With an early career in the Army (Infantry) from private to captain, followed by Teacher Training at St. Luke's College, Exeter, and then service with the Royal Army Educational Corps, he later read Law at the University of the West of England. Teaching Law (mainly at the City of Bath College of Further Education) would result.

'Bath the Enigma' has been a labour of love, both for the club and its unique parent city.

In accordance with the author's wishes, all profits from sales of this book are to be donated to a designated Bath Charity.

Also From MX Publishing

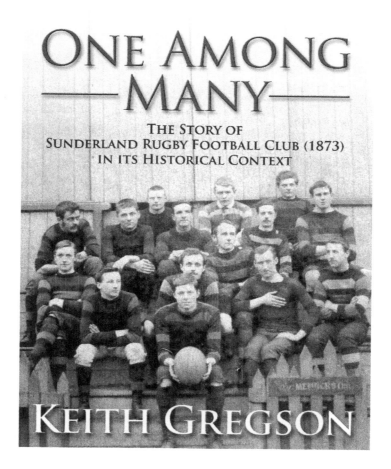

The story of a typical English rugby club set in its historical context linked to the tale of the rare survival of a multi-sport Victorian complex. This will be of interest and use to local people, sports enthusiasts and serious sports historians.

Also From MX Publishing

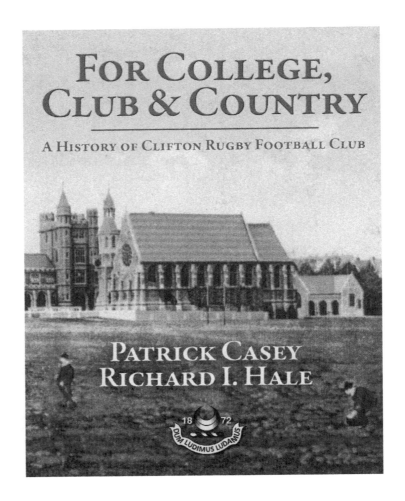

"Richly illustrated with team photographs over more than 100 years, this is a fascinating piece of social history based around one of the oldest rugby clubs in the country. Providing moving accounts of club members who lost their lives in the two World Wars, this is an important and fascinating history of a club that has retained a strong community focus." **The Bookbag**

Also From MX Publishing

Rugby Football During The Nineteenth Century

Reprint of the original by Bertram Fletcher Robinson in the 1880s, introduced by Patrick Casety and Hugh Cooke and compiled by Paul Spiring.

Argentina Rugby World Cup 2023

Argentina made history at Rugby World Cup 2007 by finishing third in the world. The South American nation finished the World Cup ahead of traditional powers including Australia, Ireland, New Zealand, Scotland, Wales and hosts France - all have previously hosted matches in multiple World Cup tournaments. In finishing third in 2007, Argentina became the only Rugby World Cup semi finalist who has not yet hosted a Rugby World Cup.Since then rugby has undergone significant changes to at last adjust to professionalism. Now a part of The Rugby Championship Argentina is a rugby nation in rapid transition and Argentina has officially been accepted as an elite team backed by a responsible union. With England hosting in 2015 and Japan in 2019, it will be time for a Southern Hemisphere country to host in 2023. By 2023 Oceania would have hosted three World Cup's, Africa one, Asia one and Europe four and the Americas zero. Rich in tradition and packed with talent Argentina 2023 is certain to be a roaring success.

Lightning Source UK Ltd.
Milton Keynes UK
UKOW07f0405151115

262723UK00001B/10/P